*NEW PERSPECTIVES*

# Computer Concepts 2012

**INTRODUCTORY**

U/20

CONTAINS A
BookOnCD

FOR A FULLY INTERACTIVE
LEARNING EXPERIENCE

Parsons :: Oja

# COURSE TECHNOLOGY
## CENGAGE Learning

**New Perspectives on Computer Concepts, 2012, Introductory**
**June Jamrich Parsons, Dan Oja**

Executive Editor: Marie Lee

Senior Product Manager: Kathy Finnegan

Product Managers: Katherine C. Russillo, Leigh Hefferon

Associate Acquisitions Editor: Amanda Lyons

Developmental Editor: Deb Kaufmann

Associate Product Manager: Julia Leroux-Lindsey

Editorial Assistant: Jacqueline Lacaire

Technology Project Manager: John Horn, Chris Conroy

Senior Marketing Manager: Ryan DeGrote

Senior Content Project Manager: Jennifer Goguen McGrail

Photo Researcher: Abby Reip

Art Director: GEX Publishing Services

Cover Designer: Roycroft Design

BookOnCD Technician: Keefe Crowley

BookOnCD Development: MediaTechnics Corp.

Prepress Production: GEX Publishing Services

For product information and technology assistance, contact us at
**Cengage Learning Customer & Sales Support, 1-800-354-9706**

For permission to use material from this text or product, submit all requests online at **www.cengage.com/permissions**
Further permissions questions can be emailed to
**permissionrequest@cengage.com**

Library of Congress Control Number: 2011920719

ISBN-13: 978-1-111-52908-6

ISBN-10: 1-111-52908-6

**Course Technology**
20 Channel Center Street
Boston, MA 02210
USA

Cengage Learning is a leading provider of customized learning solutions with office locations around the globe, including Singapore, the United Kingdom, Australia, Mexico, Brazil, and Japan. Locate your local office at:
**international.cengage.com/region**

Cengage Learning products are represented in Canada by Nelson Education, Ltd.

To learn more about Course Technology, visit **www.cengage.com/course technology**

To learn more about Cengage Learning, visit **www.cengage.com**

Purchase any of our products at your local college store or at our preferred online store **www.cengagebrain.com**

Printed in the United States of America
1 2 3 4 5 6 7 15 14 13 12 11

# TABLE OF CONTENTS

## ORIENTATION

O-4 **Section A: Getting Started**
O-4 Computer Equipment
O-5 How to Turn Your Computer On and Off
O-6 Windows Basics
O-7 Mac OS X Basics
O-8 Mouse Basics
O-9 Keyboard Basics
O-10 Working with Windows Software
O-12 Working with Mac Software
O-13 Help
O-13 QuickCheck A

O-14 **Section B: Documents, Browsers, and E-mail**
O-14 Creating Documents
O-16 Internet and Web Basics
O-16 How to Use a Web Browser and Search Engine
O-19 Working with E-mail
O-21 QuickCheck B

O-22 **Section C: Security and Privacy**
O-22 Securing Your Computer and Data
O-23 Avoiding Viruses
O-24 Preventing Intrusions
O-25 Blocking Spyware and Pop-up Ads
O-26 Protecting E-commerce Transactions
O-27 Avoiding E-mail Scams
O-29 Protecting Your Privacy
O-30 Safe Social Networking
O-31 Onlline Privacy and Safety Guidelines
O-31 QuickCheck C

O-32 **Section D: BookOnCD**
O-32 BookOnCD Basics
O-35 Multimedia and Computer-Scored Activities
O-36 New Perspectives Labs
O-37 Tracking Your Scores
O-39 QuickCheck D

O-40 **Section E: NP2012 CourseMate Web Site**
O-40 Web Site Resources
O-41 Web Site Access
O-42 CourseMate Web Site Tour
O-43 Student Edition Labs
O-43 QuickCheck E

## CHAPTER 1

## COMPUTERS AND DIGITAL BASICS

4 **Section A: All Things Digital**
4 The Digital Revolution
8 Convergence
10 Digital Society
13 QuickCheck A

14 **Section B: Digital Devices**
14 Computer Basics
16 Personal Computers, Servers, Mainframes, and Supercomputers
19 Handheld Devices
20 Microcontrollers
21 QuickCheck B

22 **Section C: Digital Data Representation**
22 Data Representation Basics
23 Representing Numbers, Text, Images, and Sound
26 Quantifying Bits and Bytes
27 Circuits and Chips
28 QuickCheck C

29 **Section D: Digital Processing**
29 Programs and Instruction Sets
31 Processor Logic
33 QuickCheck D

34 **Section E: Password Security**
34 Authentication Protocols
36 Password Hacks
38 Secure Passwords
41 QuickCheck E

42 **Issue: Are You Being Tracked?**

44 **Computers in Context: Marketing**

46 **New Perspectives Labs**

47 **Review Activities**
47 Key Terms
48 Interactive Summary
50 Interactive Situation Questions
50 Interactive Practice Tests
51 Learning Objectives Checkpoints and Concept Map
52 Projects

53 **On the Web**

**CHAPTER 2**

# COMPUTER HARDWARE

56  **Section A: Personal Computer Basics**
56  Personal Computer Systems
58  Desktop and Portable Computers
60  Home, Game, and Small Business Systems
62  Buying Computer System Components
66  QuickCheck A

67  **Section B: Microprocessors and Memory**
67  Microprocessor Basics
71  Today's Microprocessors
72  Random Access Memory
74  Read-Only Memory
74  EEPROM
75  QuickCheck B

76  **Section C: Storage Devices**
76  Storage Basics
78  Magnetic Disk and Tape Technology
81  CD, DVD, and Blu-ray Technology
84  Solid State Storage
86  Storage Wrapup
87  QuickCheck C

88  **Section D: Input and Output Devices**
88  Basic Input Devices
90  Display Devices
92  Printers
94  Installing Peripheral Devices
97  QuickCheck D

98  **Section E: Hardware Security**
98  Anti-Theft Devices
99  Surge Protection and Battery Backup
101 Basic Maintenance
103 Troubleshooting and Repair
105 QuickCheck E

106 **Issue: Where Does All the E-waste Go?**

108 **Computers in Context: Military**

110 **New Perspectives Labs**

111 **Review Activities**
111 Key Terms
112 Interactive Summary
114 Interactive Situation Questions
114 Interactive Practice Tests
115 Learning Objectives Checkpoints
    and Concept Map
116 Projects

117 **On the Web**

**CHAPTER 3**

# COMPUTER SOFTWARE

120 **Section A: Software Basics**
120 Software Categories
121 Application Software
122 Utility Software
124 Device Drivers
124 QuickCheck A

125 **Section B: Popular Applications**
125 Document Production Software
130 Spreadsheet Software
133 "Number Crunching" Software
134 Database Software
137 Graphics Software
139 Music Software
140 Video Editing and DVD Authoring Software
140 Educational Software
141 Entertainment Software
142 Business Software
142 QuickCheck B

143 **Section C: Buying Software**
143 Consumer Basics
146 Software Copyrights and Licenses
151 QuickCheck C

152 **Section D: Installing Software and Upgrades**
152 Installation Basics
154 Installing Local Applications
158 Installing Portable Software and Web Apps
159 Software Upgrades and Updates
161 Uninstalling Software
161 QuickCheck D

162 **Section E: Security Software**
162 Security Software Basics
166 Security Suites
167 Antivirus Modules
169 QuickCheck E

170 **Issue: How Serious Is Software Piracy?**

172 **Computers in Context: Journalism**

174 **New Perspectives Labs**

175 **Review Activities**
175 Key Terms
176 Interactive Summary
178 Software Key Terms
178 Interactive Situation Questions
178 Interactive Practice Tests
179 Learning Objectives Checkpoints
    and Concept Map
180 Projects

181 **On the Web**

## CHAPTER 4

# OPERATING SYSTEMS AND FILE MANAGEMENT

**184 Section A: Operating System Basics**
184 Operating System Activities
189 User Interfaces
192 The Boot Process
193 QuickCheck A

**194 Section B: Today's Operating Systems**
194 Microsoft Windows
197 Mac OS
200 UNIX and Linux
201 DOS
202 Handheld Operating Systems
203 QuickCheck B

**204 Section C: File Basics**
204 File Names and Extensions
205 File Directories and Folders
207 File Formats
211 QuickCheck C

**212 Section D: File Management**
212 Application-based File Management
214 File Management Utilities
215 File Management Metaphors
216 Windows Explorer
218 File Management Tips
218 Physical File Storage
221 QuickCheck D

**222 Section E: Backup Security**
222 Backup Basics
224 File Copies and Synchronization
226 System Synchronization
227 File and System Backup
230 Bare-Metal Restore and Virtual Machines
231 QuickCheck E

**232 Issue: Cyberterrorists or Pranksters?**

**234 Computers in Context: Law Enforcement**

**236 New Perspectives Labs**

**237 Review Activities**
237 Key Terms
238 Interactive Summary
240 Interactive Situation Questions
240 Interactive Practice Tests
241 Learning Objectives Checkpoints
and Concept Map
242 Projects

**243 On the Web**

## CHAPTER 5

# LANS AND WLANS

**246 Section A: Network Building Blocks**
246 Network Classifications
247 LAN Standards
248 Network Devices
249 Clients, Servers, and Peers
250 Physical Topology
251 Network Links
252 Communications Protocols
255 QuickCheck A

**256 Section B: Wired Networks**
256 Wired Network Basics
257 Ethernet
259 Ethernet Equipment
262 Ethernet Setup
264 QuickCheck B

**265 Section C: Wireless Networks**
265 Wireless Basics
267 Bluetooth
268 Wi-Fi
268 Wi-Fi Equipment
271 Wi-Fi Setup
273 QuickCheck C

**274 Section D: Using LANs**
274 LAN Advantages and Challenges
276 Sharing Files
278 Sharing Printers
280 Network Troubleshooting
281 QuickCheck D

**282 Section E: Security Through Encryption**
282 Wi-Fi Security
285 Encryption
287 QuickCheck E

**288 Issue: Who's Stealing My Signals?**

**290 Computers in Context: Education**

**292 New Perspectives Labs**

**293 Review Activities**
293 Key Terms
294 Interactive Summary
296 Interactive Situation Questions
296 Interactive Practice Tests
297 Learning Objectives Checkpoints
and Concept Map
298 Projects

**299 On the Web**

**CHAPTER 6**

## THE INTERNET

302 **Section A: Internet Technology**
302 Background
303 Internet Infrastructure
305 Internet Protocols, Addresses, and Domains
309 Connection Speed
311 QuickCheck A

312 **Section B: Fixed Internet Access**
312 Dial-up Connections
314 DSL, ISDN, and Dedicated Lines
316 Cable Internet Service
318 Satellite Internet Service
320 Fixed Wireless Service
321 Fixed Internet Connection Roundup
321 QuickCheck B

322 **Section C: Portable and Mobile Internet Access**
322 Internet to Go
323 Wi-Fi Hotspots
325 Portable and Mobile WiMAX
325 Portable Satellite Service
326 Cellular Data Services
329 QuickCheck C

330 **Section D: Internet Services**
330 Real-Time Messaging
331 Voice Over IP
332 Forums, Wikis, Blogs, and Tweets
333 Cloud Computing
334 Grid Computing
336 FTP
338 File Sharing Networks
339 QuickCheck D

340 **Section E: Internet Security**
340 Intrusion Attempts
342 Securing Ports
343 Routers and NAT
345 Virtual Private Networks
345 QuickCheck E

346 **Issue: What's Happening to Free Speech?**

348 **Computers in Context: Banking**

350 **New Perspectives Labs**

351 **Review Activities**
351 Key Terms
352 Interactive Summary
354 Interactive Situation Questions
354 Interactive Practice Tests
355 Learning Objectives Checkpoints and Concept Map
356 Projects

357 **On the Web**

**CHAPTER 7**

## THE WEB AND E-MAIL

360 **Section A: Web Technology**
360 Web Basics
362 HTML
364 HTTP
365 Web Browsers
367 Cookies
369 Web Page Authoring
371 HTML Scripts
373 QuickCheck A

374 **Section B: Search Engines**
374 Search Engine Basics
378 Formulating Searches
382 Citing Web-based Source Material
383 QuickCheck B

384 **Section C: E-commerce**
384 E-commerce Basics
386 E-commerce Site Technology
389 Online Payment
391 QuickCheck C

392 **Section D: E-mail**
392 E-mail Overview
394 Local E-mail
396 Webmail
398 E-mail attachments
399 Netiquette
399 QuickCheck D

400 **Section E: Web and E-mail Security**
400 Cookie Exploits
403 Spam
405 Phishing
405 Fake Sites
407 QuickCheck E

408 **Issue: Who's Reading Your E-mail?**

410 **Computers in Context: Fashion Industry**

412 **New Perspectives Labs**

413 **Review Activities**
413 Key Terms
414 Interactive Summary
416 Interactive Situation Questions
416 Interactive Practice Tests
417 Learning Objectives Checkpoints and Concept Map
418 Projects

419 **On the Web**

## CHAPTER 8

# DIGITAL MEDIA

422 **Section A: Digital Sound**
422 Digital Audio Basics
425 Digital Audio File Formats
427 MIDI Music
428 Speech Recognition and Synthesis
429 QuickCheck A

430 **Section B: Bitmap Graphics**
430 Bitmap Basics
431 Scanners and Cameras
433 Image Resolution
436 Color Depth and Palettes
439 Image Compression
442 Bitmap Graphics Formats
443 QuickCheck B

444 **Section C: Vector and 3-D Graphics**
444 Vector Graphics Basics
447 Vector-to-Bitmap Conversion
448 Vector Graphics on the Web
449 3-D Graphics
451 QuickCheck C

452 **Section D: Digital Video**
452 Digital Video Basics
453 Producing Video Footage
455 Video Transfer
456 Video Editing
457 Video Output
459 Web Video
461 DVD-Video
463 QuickCheck D

464 **Section E: Digital Rights Management**
464 DRM Basics
465 Signal Scrambling and Digital Watermarks
466 CD Copy Protection
467 DVD and Blue-ray DRM
469 DRM for Digital Downloads
471 QuickCheck E

472 **Issue: What Happened to Fair Use?**

474 **Computers in Context: Film**

476 **New Perspectives Labs**

477 **Review Activities**
477 Key Terms
478 Interactive Summary
480 Interactive Situation Questions
480 Interactive Practice Tests
481 Learning Objectives Checkpoints
and Concept Map
482 Projects

483 **On the Web**

484 CREDITS
486 GLOSSARY
506 INDEX

## NEW PERSPECTIVES LABS

CHAPTER 1 Operating a Personal Computer; Working with Binary Numbers

CHAPTER 2 Benchmarking

CHAPTER 3 Installing and Uninstalling Software

CHAPTER 4 Managing Files; Backing Up Your Computer

CHAPTER 5 Local Area Networks

CHAPTER 6 Tracking Packets; Securing Your Connection

CHAPTER 7 Browser Security Settings; Working with Cookies; Working with HTML

CHAPTER 8 Working with Bitmap Graphics

## STUDENT EDITION LABS

CHAPTER 1 Binary Numbers; Understanding the Motherboard

CHAPTER 2 Peripheral Devices; Using Input Devices

CHAPTER 3 Word Processing; Spreadsheets; Installing and Uninstalling Software; Databases; Presentation Software; Keeping Your Computer Virus Free

CHAPTER 4 Maintaining a Hard Drive; Managing Files and Folders; Backing Up Your Computer; Using Windows

CHAPTER 5 Networking Basics; Wireless Networking

CHAPTER 6 Connecting to the Internet; Protecting Your Privacy Online; Getting the Most Out of the Internet

CHAPTER 7 Creating Web Pages; E-mail; E-commerce; Web Design Principles

CHAPTER 8 Working with Graphics; Working with Video; Working with Audio

# NP2012: Get Synched!

**Synchronicity.** It's all about students and instructors tuning in to each other. And technology makes it possible. In a world of networks, e-mail, webinars, and social networking sites, technology can certainly strengthen the link between instructors and students.

*New Perspectives on Computer Concepts 2012* is the only computer concepts product with a fully integrated and truly interactive teaching and learning environment. The printed book, CourseMate Web site, BookOnCD interactive digital textbook, and WebTrack assessment help instructors and students work synchronously to understand and apply technology in their personal and professional lives. It's an engaging, multi-layered technology platform that supports diverse teaching and learning styles in today's classrooms.

Getting "Synched" means that students and instructors can communicate more often, more easily, and more effectively than before. They can exchange information with a simple mouse click. They can sync up through NP2012's live syllabus and annotations, pre-assessments, QuickChecks, practice tests, Chirps, and more. Instructors can monitor progress and check comprehension; students can hone in on expectations and make sure they master objectives.

**New for this edition.** In NP2012, you'll find information on cutting-edge hardware technologies such as **LED SCREENS**, **ALL-IN-ONE COMPUTERS**, **GESTURE TOUCHPADS**, and the **LATEST MOBILE DEVICES**. There's coverage of **HTML5**, **WEBM**, **MIFI**, **MOTION CAPTURE**, **WINDOWS 7 LIBRARIES**, and **HOMEGROUPS**. This edition has current statistics on **SOFTWARE PIRACY** and the effect of computers on the **ENVIRONMENT**, as well as a breakdown of the latest technical jargon you need when shopping for computer gear.

NP2012 covers multiple operating system platforms. Whether you use a PC running **WINDOWS 7, VISTA, OR XP** or a Mac running **MAC OS X**, all the TRY IT! instructions in the Orientation and at the beginning of every chapter are designed to work on your computer. Mac users can even download the **MACPAC** to convert the BookOnCD into Mac format.

Be sure to check out the **ORIENTATION** with tips for **ONLINE RESEARCH** and guidelines to help you **STAY SAFE ONLINE**. Don't forget about all the NP2012 study and learning tools! The **BOOKONCD** digital textbook contains videos, software tours, and lots of ways to discover if you're ready for the next test. When you purchase access to the the new NP2012 **COURSEMATE WEB SITE**, you'll get a complete **EBOOK**, online games, CourseCasts, and other review activities.

# CREATE YOUR OWN LEARNING PLAN

It's easy! Use the NP2012 printed textbook, NP2012 CourseMate Web site, and NP2012 BookOnCD digital textbook in **ANY WAY THAT'S RIGHT FOR YOU**. The Orientation helps you get acquainted with the extensive array of NP2012 technology that's at your command.

## Your BookOn Plan—Seven Easy Steps

1. Use the digital textbook to take the **PRE-ASSESSMENT** and gauge what you already know.

2. Work on the Chapter opener **TRY IT ACTIVITY** for a hands-on introduction to the chapter topics.

3. Read a chapter and complete the **QUICKCHECKS** at the end of each section. Use **CHIRPS** while you're reading to send questions to your instructor.

4. Work with **NEW PERSPECTIVES LABS** to apply your knowledge.

5. Complete **REVIEW ACTIVITIES** using your digital textbook.

6. Take a **PRACTICE TEST** to see if you're ready for the exam.

7. Transmit your results to your instructor on **WEBTRACK**.

## Your CourseMate Plan—Seven Steps Online

1. Listen to a **COURSECAST OVERVIEW** of chapter highlights.

2. Read a chapter in the online ebook.

3. Work with the **STUDENT EDITION LABS** to apply your knowledge.

4. Have some fun reviewing with **ONLINE GAMES**.

5. Use **AUDIO AND TECHTERM FLASHCARDS** to review terminology from the chapter.

6. Check the **DETAILED LEARNING OBJECTIVES** to make sure you've mastered the material.

7. Take the **CONCEPT QUIZ** to see if you understand key concepts; your scores are automatically recorded by the Engagement Tracker.

## Your Own Plan

**MIX AND MATCH** any of your favorite activities from the printed book, digital textbook, or Web site.

## THE BOOK

*New Perspectives on Computer Concepts 2012* gives you the straight story on today's technology. The style has been carefully honed to be clear, concise, and visual.

### Easy to read

Each chapter is divided into five **SECTIONS**, offering a chunk of information that's easy to assimilate in one study session. **FAQS** answer commonly asked questions about technology and help you follow the flow of the presentation.

### Keeps you on track

**QUICKCHECKS** at the end of each section help you find out if you understand the most important concepts. As you read the chapter, look for the answers to the questions posed as Learning Objectives, then try your hand at the **LEARNING OBJECTIVES CHECKPOINTS** at the end of each chapter to make sure you've retained the key points. Additional review activities include **KEY TERMS, INTERACTIVE CHAPTER SUMMARIES, INTERACTIVE SITUATION QUESTIONS**, and **CONCEPT MAPS**.

### Helps you explore

The **ISSUE** section in each chapter highlights controversial aspects of technology. In the **COMPUTERS IN CONTEXT** section, you'll discover how technology plays a role in careers such as film-making, architecture, banking, and fashion design. **INFOWEBLINKS** lead you to Web-based information on chapter topics. Work with **NP2012 PROJECTS** to apply the concepts you learned, explore technology, consider globalization, build your resume, work with a team, and experiment with multimedia.

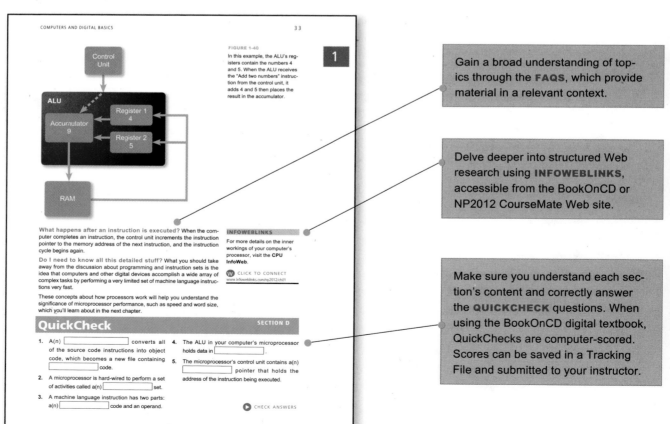

Gain a broad understanding of topics through the **FAQS**, which provide material in a relevant context.

Delve deeper into structured Web research using **INFOWEBLINKS**, accessible from the BookOnCD or NP2012 CourseMate Web site.

Make sure you understand each section's content and correctly answer the **QUICKCHECK** questions. When using the BookOnCD digital textbook, QuickChecks are computer-scored. Scores can be saved in a Tracking File and submitted to your instructor.

## THE INTERACTIVE BOOKONCD

The **BOOKONCD** is a digital version of your textbook with multimedia and interactive activities designed to enhance your learning experience.

### Works alone or with the book

Every page of the digital textbook **MIRRORS THE PRINTED TEXTBOOK**, so use the tool that's most convenient and that best suits your learning style.

### Brings concepts to life

In the digital textbook, photos turn into **VIDEOS**. Illustrations become **ANIMATED DIAGRAMS**. Screen shots activate guided **SOFTWARE TOURS**, so you can see how applications and operating systems work even if they aren't installed on your computer.

### Makes learning interactive

Before you read a chapter, take the **PRE-ASSESSMENT** to find out how to best focus your study time. You can master hundreds of computer concepts using the **NEW PERSPECTIVES LABS**. When you complete a chapter, try the interactive, **COMPUTER-SCORED ACTIVITIES**. Take some **PRACTICE TESTS** to gauge how well you'll perform on exams. Use **WEBTRACK** to easily transmit your scores to your instructor. If you have questions as you're reading, use **CHIRPS** to send questions anonymously to your instructor.

The digital textbook is easy to use. It is packed with **MULTIMEDIA**, and offers plenty of **COMPUTER-SCORED ACTIVITIES**.

Interactive **NEW PERSPECTIVES LABS** give you hands-on experience with concepts and software.

## THE NP2012 COURSEMATE WEB SITE WITH EBOOK

The NP2012 CourseMate Web site is packed full of information and includes an online ebook plus activities to accompany each chapter. Follow the directions in Section E of the Orientation chapter to sign up for an account and access the NP2012 CourseMate.

### Lets you study anywhere

CourseMate includes an **ONLINE EBOOK**, so you can access your textbook from any computer that's connected to the Internet.

### Gives you options

Want to have fun while you review? Try an **ONLINE GAME** that packages chapter concepts into an entertaining quiz show or action game. When you're ready for some serious exam preparation, work with the **CONCEPT QUIZZES** to see how well you understand key concepts. Need some last-minute review? Load up your portable music player with a **CHAPTER OVERVIEW COURSECAST** and **AUDIO FLASHCARDS**.

### Reinforces your understanding

**STUDENT EDITION LABS** give you hands-on experience with key concepts and skills. **DETAILED LEARNING OBJECTIVES** help you determine if you've mastered all the requirements for completing a chapter.

### Keeps track of your progress

CourseMate's **ENGAGEMENT TRACKER** records the time you spend on various activities, saves your scores, and shares them with your instructor.

Now you can listen to CourseCasts on your computer or download them to your portable music player. Audio chapter overviews and flashcards help you study while you're out and about.

**ONLINE EBOOK** lets you access your textbook from any computer that's connected to the Internet.

Labs, concept quizzes, games, and more provide many ways to explore and review.

Listen to chapter highlights or practice key terms with handy chapter overviews and flashcard **COURSECASTS**.

## INSTRUCTOR RESOURCES

New Perspectives instructional resources and technologies provide instructors with a wide range of tools that enhance teaching and learning. These tools and more can be accessed from the NP Community Web site www.cengage.com/ct/npconcepts.

The **NP COMMUNITY SITE** is designed to be an instructor's one-stop point of access for **TEACHING TOOLS** and **TECHNICAL SUPPORT**.

### Instructor's Manual: Help is only a few keystrokes away

The special Instructor's Manual offers bullet point lecture notes for each chapter, plus classroom activities and teaching tips, including how to effectively use and integrate CourseMate Web site content, BookOnCD content, and labs.

### Technology Guide

Want the details about how to use WebTrack, the BookOnCD, and the CourseMate Web site? We now offer instructors a Technology Guide that provides step-by-step instructions for collecting WebTrack data, adding your own annotations to the digital textbook, exporting student scores, and much more.

**ANNOTATIONS!** Instructors can create their own text, graphical, or video annotations that students will see as they read their digital textbook. Find out more about this innovative feature in the Technology Guide.

### WebTrackIII Instructor's Page

### WebTrack

Monitoring student progress is easy. With WebTrack's store-and-forward system, a student can transmit scores to an instructor, who can download them at any time. Newly downloaded scores are consolidated with previous scores and can be displayed, printed, or exported in a variety of report formats.

**WEBTRACKIII** is now available as a portable app that instructors can carry on a USB flash drive and use on their classroom, office, or home computer.

### Chirps

Would you like to know the questions students have while reading their textbooks? Chirps let you find out! Similar to tweets, our Chirps feature allows students to send questions to instructors from within their digital textbook. Instructors can also use Chirps as an in-class polling system, or as an asynchronous polling tool for online students. To learn about this versatile new NP technology, refer to the Technology Guide.

## Clicker Questions

Want to find out if your students are awake in class? Use clicker questions that are supplied with the Instructor Manual and included in the NP2012 PowerPoint presentations. Each question is numbered so you can collect results using Chirps or a third-party course polling system.

## Course Presenter

Instructors can deliver engaging and visually impressive lectures for each chapter with the professionally designed Course Presenter. Course Presenter is a PowerPoint presentation enhanced with screentours, animations, and videos.

## Engagement Tracker

For courses that take advantage of the activities on the NP2012 CourseMate Web site, the Engagement Tracker monitors student time on task and records scores that help instructors keep track of student progress.

## BlackBoard Learning System™ Content

We offer a full range of content for use with the BlackBoard Learning System to simplify using NP2012 in distance education settings.

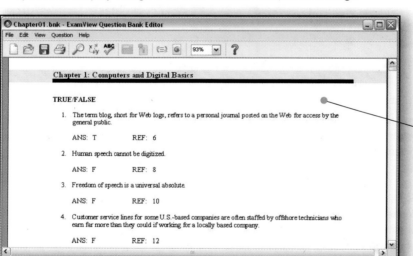

ExamView test banks for New Perspectives on Computer Concepts 2012 make test creation a snap.

## ExamView: Testbanks and powerful testing software

With ExamView, instructors can generate printed tests, create LAN-based tests, or test over the Internet. Examview testbanks cover the same material as Practice Tests and Test Yourself testbanks, but the questions are worded differently so that the ExamView testbanks contain a unique collection of questions for graded tests and exams.

## SAM

SAM (Skills Assessment Manager) is a robust assessment, training, and project-based system that enables students to be active participants in learning valuable Microsoft Office skills. A set of testbank questions ties directly to each applicable chapter in this book. Let SAM be an integral part of your students' learning experience! Please visit www.cengage.com/samcentral.

## FROM THE AUTHORS

Many of today's students have substantially more practical experience with computers than their counterparts of 15 years ago, and yet other students enter college with inadequate technology preparation. The goal of New Perspectives on Computer Concepts is to bring every student up to speed with computer basics, and then go beyond basic computer literacy to provide students with technical and practical information that every college-educated person would be expected to know.

In producing the 2012 edition of this very popular textbook, we incorporated significant technology trends that affect computing and everyday life. Concerns for data security, personal privacy, and online safety, controversy over digital rights management, interest in open source software and portable applications, the popularity of the iPad, and the skyrocketing sales of Macs are just some of the trends that have been given expanded coverage in this edition of the book.

Whether you are an instructor or a student, we hope that you enjoy the learning experience provided by our text-based and technology-based materials.

## ACKNOWLEDGEMENTS

The book would not exist—and certainly wouldn't arrive on schedule—were it not for the efforts of our media, editorial, and production teams. We thank Deb Kaufmann for her developmental edit and tireless work on every detail of the project; Kate Russillo for masterfully managing the complex coordination for this edition; Suzanne Huizenga for a miraculously detailed copy edit; Marie L. Lee for her executive leadership of the New Perspectives series; Jennifer Goguen McGrail for managing production; artist Derek Bedrosian for great illustrations; Abigail Reip for photo research; Julia Leroux-Lindsay for managing the book's ancillaries; Jacqueline Lacaire for assisting the editorial team; and Ryan DeGrote and his team for encouraging instructors to adopt this book for their intro courses.

The MediaTechnics team worked tirelessly and we can't offer enough thanks to Donna Mulder for managing the lab revisions and revising the screentours; Tensi Parsons for her extraordinary devotion to desktop publishing; Keefe Crowley for his versatile skills in producing the BookOnCD, creating videos, taking photos, and maintaining the InfoWebLinks site; Chris Robbert for his clear narrations; and Debora Elam, Jaclyn Kangas, Kevin Lappi, Joseph Smit, Marilou Potter, Michael Crowley, and Renee Gleason for checking and double-checking the alpha and beta CDs.

We also want to give special thanks to Officer David Zittlow of the City of Fond du Lac Police Department for providing photos of computer technology used in law enforcement; Bob Metcalf for giving us permission to use his original sketch of Ethernet; The University of Illinois for supplying photos of PLATO; Rob Flickenger for providing the photo of his Pringles can antenna; and Joe Bush for his distinctive photo work.

In addition, our thanks go to the New Perspectives Advisory Committee members and reviewers listed on the next page, who have made a tremendous contribution to New Perspectives. Thank you all!

June Parsons and Dan Oja

## ACADEMIC, TECHNICAL, AND STUDENT REVIEWERS

Thank you to the many students, instructors, Advisory Committee members, and subject-matter experts who provided valuable feedback and who have influenced the evolution of New Perspectives on Computer Concepts:

Dr. Nazih Abdallah, University of Central Florida; Beverly Amer, Northern Arizona University; Ken Baldauf, Florida State University; Dottie Baumeister, Harford Community College; Paula Bell, Lock Haven University of Pennsylvania; Mary Burke, Ocean County College; Barbara Burns, St. Johns River Community College; Mary Caldwell, Rollins College; Chuck Calvin, Computer Learning Centers; Wendy Chisholm, Barstow College; Linda Cooper, Macon State College; Dave Courtaway, Devry University, Ponoma; Becky Curtin, William Rainey Harper College; Eric Daley, University of New Brunswick; Sallie Dodson, Radford University; Leonard Dwyer, Southwestern College of Business; Robert Erickson, University of Vermont; Mark Feiler, Merritt College; Alan Fisher, Walters State Community College; Pat Frederick, Del Mar College; Michael Gaffney, Century College; John Gammell, St. Cloud State University; Ernest Gines, Tarrant Count College SE; Ione Good, Southeastern Community College; Tom Gorecki, College of Southern Maryland; Steve Gramlich, Pasco-Hernando Community College; Michael Hanna, Colorado State University; Dorothy Harman, Tarrant County College Northeast; Bobbye Haupt, Cecil Community College; Heith Hennel, Valencia Community College; Gerald Hensel, Valencia Community College; Patti Impink, Macon State College; Bob Irvine, American River College; Ernie Ivey, Polk Community College; Joanne Lazirko, University of Wisconsin; Stan Leja, Del Mar College; Martha Lindberg, Minnesota State University; Richard Linge, Arizona Western College; Terry Long, Valencia Community College; Karl Smart Lyman, Central Michigan University; Dr. W. Benjamin Martz, University of Colorado, Colorado Springs; Deann McMullen, Western Kentucky Community and Technical College; Dori McPherson, Schoolcraft College; Saeed Molki, South Texas College; Robert Moore, Laredo Community College; Ed Mott, Central Texas College; Cindi Nadelman, New England College; Karen O'Connor, Cerro Coso Community College; Dr. Rodney Pearson, Mississippi State University; Catherine Perlich, St. Thomas; Tonya Pierce, Ivy Tech College; David Primeaux, Virginia Commonwealth University; Ann Rowlette, Liberty University; Lana Shyrock, Monroe County Community College; Betty Sinowitz, Rockland Community College; Martin Skolnik, Florida Atlantic University; Karl Smart, Central Michigan University; Jerome Spencer, Rowan University; Ella Strong, Hazard Community and Technical College; Gregory Stefanelli, Carroll Community College; Shane Thomas, Victor Valley College Martha; J. Tilmann, College of San Mateo; Michael Wiemann, Blue River Community College; Kathy Winters, University of Tennessee, Chattanooga; John Zamora, Modesto Junior College; Mary Zayac, University of the Virgin Islands; Matt Zullo, Wake Tech Community College; Student Reviewers Kitty Edwards and Heather House; Technical Reviewers Jeff Harrow, Barbra D. Letts, John Lucas, Ramachandran Bharath, and Karl Mulder.

# Computer Concepts 2012

Parsons :: Oja

# Orientation

## Chapter Contents

**SECTION A:**
**GETTING STARTED**
Computer Equipment
How to Turn Your Computer
    On and Off
Turn Your Computer On
Windows Basics
Mac OS X Basics
Mouse Basics
Use Your Mouse
Keyboard Basics
Working with Windows Software
Start Microsoft Paint
Use the Toolbar or Ribbon
Use the Ribbon or Menu Bar
Use the Sizing Buttons
Working with Mac Software
Find Out Which Programs Are
    in the Dock
Use Finder to Start a Program
Use a Menu and Dialog Box
Close a Program
Help

**SECTION B:**
**DOCUMENTS, BROWSERS,**
    **AND E-MAIL**
Creating Documents
Create a Document
Save a Document
Print a Document, Close It,
    and Exit Your Word
    Processing Application
Internet and Web Basics
Start Your Browser
How to Use a Web Browser
    and Search Engine
Use a Search Engine
Check Out Wikipedia
Working with E-mail
Get a Web-based E-mail Account
Create and Send E-mail

**SECTION C:**
**SECURITY AND PRIVACY**
Securing Your Computer and Data
Check the Accounts on
    Your Computer
Avoiding Viruses
Get Familiar with Your
    Antivirus Software
Preventing Intrusions
Check Your Windows Computer's
    Firewall
Check Your Mac Computer's
    Firewall
Blocking Spyware and Pop-up Ads
Check Internet Security and Privacy
    Options
Protecting E-commerce Transactions
Identify a Secure Connection
Avoiding E-mail Scams
Arm Yourself Against E-mail
    Scams
Protecting Your Privacy
Check Your Privacy
Safe Social Networking
Check Your Social Networking
    Sites
Online Privacy and Safety Guidelines

**SECTION D:**
**BOOKONCD**
BookOnCD Basics
Start the BookOnCD
Start the MacBookOnCD
Open a Chapter and Navigate
    the BookOnCD
Multimedia and Computer-
    scored Activities
Explore Multimedia and Computer-
    scored Activities
New Perspectives Labs
Open a New Perspectives Lab
Tracking Your Scores
Create a Tracking File
Complete a Practice Test
View the Contents of Your
    Tracking File
Send Your Tracking Data and
    Send a Chirp

**SECTION E:**
**NP2012 COURSEMATE WEB SITE**
Web Site Resources
Web Site Access
Access the NP2012 CourseMate
CourseMate Web Site Tour
Explore the NP2012 CourseMate
Student Edition Labs
Work with Student Edition
    Labs

---

### InfoWebLinks

Visit the InfoWebLinks site to access additional resources ⓦ that accompany this chapter.

### Multimedia and Interactive Elements

When using the BookOnCD or CourseMate eBook, the ▶ icons are clickable to access multimedia resources.

## Apply Your Knowledge The information in this chapter will give you the background to:

- Start your computer, use the keyboard, and operate the mouse
- Work with Windows or Mac OS
- Use word processing software
- Carry out research on the Web using a search engine and other resources such as Wikipedia
- Send e-mail

- Take effective steps to guard your privacy and safety online
- Use BookOnCD resources, such as pre-assessments, practice tests, labs, and interactive summaries
- Access the NP2012 CourseMate Web site for labs, concept quizzes, CourseCasts, and online games

## Try It

### WHAT DO I NEED TO GET STARTED?

To complete the activities in the Orientation, you'll need access to a computer, the BookOnCD packaged with your textbook (or other digital versions of the textbook), Internet access, your e-mail address, and your instructor's e-mail address.

To be sure you have what you need, use the following checklist. Check off the boxes for each item that you have.

☐ Access to a computer. If you're using your own computer, you might need a user ID and password to log in. Don't write your password down, but make sure you know what it is.

☐ Access to a school computer network. You might need a user ID and password if you use a lab computer or access your school's network. Check with your instructor or lab manager to learn how your school handles network access.

☐ The interactive, digital version of the textbook, such as the BookOnCD. The BookOnCD requires a computer CD or DVD drive to run. If your computer does not have this type of drive, check with your instructor. eBook versions of your textbook require a browser. Your school network might provide access to the NP2012 BookOnCD or eBook from lab computers.

☐ Your e-mail address. Your instructor should explain how you can obtain an e-mail address if you don't already have one. Write your e-mail address here:

_____

☐ Your instructor's e-mail address. To correspond with your instructor, you'll need your instructor's e-mail address. Write it here:

_____

☐ Your instructor's WebTrack address. If your instructor will be collecting your scores with WebTrack, make sure you have your instructor's WebTrack address. Write it here:

_____

*NEW PERSPECTIVES*

Computer Concepts 2012

CONTAINS A
BookOnCD
FOR A FULLY INTERACTIVE
LEARNING EXPERIENCE

Parsons :: Oja

# Getting Started

WHEN YOU USE the *New Perspectives on Computer Concepts* textbook, you will not only learn about computers; you'll also use computers as learning tools. Therefore, it is a good idea to have a basic understanding of how to use your computer. Section A is designed to get computer novices quickly up to speed with computing basics, such as turning on computer equipment, working with Windows or Mac OS, using a mouse and computer keyboard, and accessing Help. Read through this section while at a computer so that you can do the TRY IT! activities.

## COMPUTER EQUIPMENT

**What do I need to know about my computer?** Your computer—the one you own, the one you use in a school lab, or the one provided to you at work—is technically classified as a microcomputer and sometimes referred to as a personal computer. A computer runs software applications (also called programs) that help you accomplish a variety of tasks. A typical computer system consists of several devices—you must be able to identify these devices to use them.

**What are the important components of my computer system?** The system unit contains your computer's circuitry, including the microprocessor that is the "brain" of your computer and memory chips that temporarily store data. It also contains storage devices, such as a hard disk drive.

Your computer system includes basic hardware devices that allow you to enter information and commands, view work, and store information for later retrieval. Devices for entering information include a keyboard and mouse or touchpad. A display device, sometimes called a monitor, allows you to view your work, a printer produces "hard copy" on paper, and speakers produce beeps and chimes that help you pay attention to what happens on the screen.

**Where are the important components of a desktop computer system?** A desktop computer is designed for stationary use on a desk or table. Figure 1 shows the key components of a desktop computer system.

### PC OR MAC?

Microcomputers are sometimes divided into two camps: PCs and Macs. PCs are manufactured by companies such as Dell, Lenovo, Acer, and Hewlett-Packard. Macs are manufactured by Apple.

Most PCs and some Macs use an operating system called Microsoft Windows. The BookOnCD is designed for use with computers that run Microsoft Windows.

To determine whether your computer runs Windows, look for screens similar to those shown in Figure 4 on page O-6. If you have a Mac that does not run Windows, you can go to the NP2012 Web site and download a MacPac to convert your CD to a format that runs on your Mac. You'll find full instructions on the site.

**FIGURE 1**

A desktop computer system includes several components, usually connected by cables.

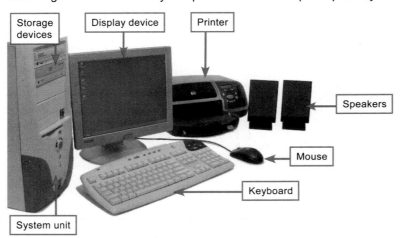

- Storage devices
- Display device
- Printer
- Speakers
- Mouse
- Keyboard
- System unit

**Where are the important components of a notebook computer system?** Notebook computers (sometimes called laptops) are small, lightweight computers designed to be carried from place to place. The components of a notebook computer system, except the printer, are housed in a single unit, as shown in Figure 2.

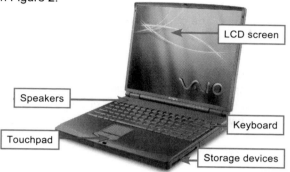

**FIGURE 2**

A notebook computer includes a flat-panel screen, keyboard, speakers, and touchpad in the same unit that contains the microprocessor, memory, and storage devices. An external mouse is sometimes used instead of the touchpad.

**How do I identify my computer's storage devices?** Your computer contains a hard disk housed inside the system unit. It is also likely to have a USB connector and some type of drive that works with CDs and DVDs. Figure 3 can help you identify your computer's storage devices and their uses.

**FIGURE 3**

You should use the hard disk to store most of your data; but to transport or back up data, you can use CDs, DVDs, or USB flash drives.

**CD drive**

CD drives can play CD-ROMs, but can't change the data they contain. CD drives can store data on CD-Rs, CD+Rs, or CD-RWs.

**DVD drive**

DVD drives read CD-ROMs and DVD-ROMs, but can't change the data on them. Most of today's DVD drives can write data on CD-Rs, CD-RWs, DVD-Rs, and DVD-RWs.

**USB flash drive**

A USB flash drive is about the size of a highlighter and plugs directly into the computer system unit. Capacities range from 32 million to 64 billion characters.

## HOW TO TURN YOUR COMPUTER ON AND OFF

**How do I turn it on?** A notebook computer typically has one switch that turns on the entire system. Look for the switch along the sides of the computer or above the keyboard. When using a desktop computer, turn on the monitor, printer, and speakers before you turn on the system unit.

Most computers take a minute or two to power up, and you might be required to log in by entering a user ID and password. Your computer is ready to use when the Windows or Mac OS desktop (Figure 4 and Figure 5 on the next two pages) appears on the computer screen and you can move the arrow-shaped pointer with your mouse.

**How do I turn it off?** Your computer is designed to turn itself off after you initiate a shutdown sequence. When using a Windows computer, click the on-screen Start button, select Shut Down or Turn Off Computer, and follow the instructions on the screen. When using a Mac, click the Apple icon in the upper-left corner of the screen and select Shut Down. After the computer shuts off, you can turn off the monitor, speakers, and printer. When using computers in a school lab, ask about the shutdown procedure. Your lab manager might ask that you log out but do not turn the computer off.

**TRY IT!**

**Turn your computer on**

**1.** Locate the power switch for any devices connected to your computer and turn them on.

**2.** Locate the power switch for your computer and turn it on.

**3.** If a message asks for your user ID and/or password, type them in, and then press the **Enter** key on your computer's keyboard.

**4.** Wait for the desktop to appear.

## WINDOWS BASICS

**What is Windows?** Microsoft Windows is an example of a type of software called an operating system. The operating system controls all the basic tasks your computer performs, such as running application software, manipulating files on storage devices, and transferring data to and from printers, digital cameras, and other devices. The operating system also controls the user interface—the way software appears on the screen and the way you control what it does.

**What is the Windows desktop?** The Windows desktop is the base of operations for using your computer. It displays small pictures called icons that help you access software, documents, and the components of your computer system. The design of the Windows desktop depends on the version of Windows you're using. Figure 4 shows the important elements of the three most recent versions: Windows XP, Windows Vista, and Windows 7.

FIGURE 4

Windows desktop components as they appear in Windows XP (top), Windows Vista (middle), and Windows 7 (bottom).

**Desktop icons** can represent programs, documents, folders, or other electronic tools.

The **taskbar** contains the Start button and Notification area. Taskbar buttons help you keep track of programs that are in use.

The **Start button** displays the Start menu, which lists programs installed on your computer.

The **Start menu** lists application and utility programs installed on your computer.

The **Notification area** displays the current time and the status of programs, devices, and Internet connections.

## MAC OS X BASICS

**What is Mac OS?** Mac OS is the operating system used on many of today's Macintosh computers. The most recent version of this operating system is Mac OS X, featured in Figure 5.

**How similar are the Mac and Windows desktops?** The Mac and Windows desktops have many similarities, such as the use of icons, menus, and rectangular on-screen windows. However, there are notable differences in the two desktops, such as the Mac desktop's dock, Apple icon, and fixed menu bar. If you switch between computers running Windows and Mac OS X, you should be aware of these differences.

**What is the dock?** The dock is a collection of icons that represent programs, files, and other activities. Usually the dock is located at the bottom of the screen, but it can be configured to appear on the left side or right side of the screen if that better suits the way you work. You can add icons to the dock for programs you use frequently so they are easily accessible.

**What is the Apple icon?** The Apple icon is the first icon on the menu bar located at the top of the Mac desktop. It is always visible, regardless of the program you're using. Clicking the Apple icon displays a menu that you can use to configure preferences for your computer display and devices. The Apple icon menu also includes options for logging out and shutting down your computer.

**How does the fixed menu bar work?** The Mac desktop contains a menu bar that remains at the top of the screen. The options on this menu bar change according to the program you are using. In contrast, the menus for Windows programs are incorporated into individual program windows; so if you have more than one window open, each program window displays a menu.

**FIGURE 5**

The Mac OS X desktop includes icons, a fixed menu bar, and a dock.

**Desktop icons** can represent devices, programs, documents, folders, or other electronic tools.

The **dock** displays icons for frequently used programs and files.

The **menu bar** contains the Apple icon and menu options for the active program.

The **Apple icon** is used to display a menu of options for setting preferences, moving the dock, logging in, and shutting down.

## MOUSE BASICS

**What is a mouse?** A mouse is a device used to manipulate items on the screen, such as the buttons and icons displayed on the Windows desktop. The mouse controls an on-screen pointer. The pointer is usually shaped like an arrow ⟨, but it can change to a different shape, depending on the task you're doing. For example, when the computer is busy, the arrow shape turns into an hourglass ⧖ or circle ⟲, signifying that you should wait for the computer to finish its current task before attempting to start a new task.

PC-compatible mice have at least two buttons, typically located on top of the mouse. Most mice also include a scroll wheel mounted between the left and right mouse buttons. Other mice include additional buttons on the top or sides (Figure 6).

**How do I use a mouse?** Hold the mouse in your right hand as shown in Figure 7. When you drag the mouse from left to right over your mousepad or desk, the arrow-shaped pointer on the screen moves from left to right. If you run out of room to move the mouse, simply pick it up and reposition it. The pointer does not move when the mouse is not in contact with a flat surface.

**FIGURE 6**

For basic mousing, you only need to use the mouse buttons, but the scroll wheel is also handy.

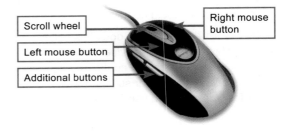

Scroll wheel
Left mouse button
Additional buttons
Right mouse button

There are several ways you can manipulate on-screen objects. Although you might not be able to manipulate every object in all possible ways, you'll soon learn which mouse actions are allowed for each type of control. The following list describes your repertoire of mouse actions.

| Action | How to | Result |
|--------|--------|--------|
| Click | Press the left mouse button once, and then immediately release it. | Select an object |
| Double-click | Press the left mouse button twice in rapid succession without moving the body of the mouse. | Activate an object |
| Right-click | Press the right mouse button once, and then immediately release it. | Display a shortcut menu |
| Drag | Hold the left mouse button down while you move the mouse. | Move an object |

**FIGURE 7**

Rest the palm of your right hand on the mouse. Position your index finger over the left mouse button and your middle finger over the right mouse button.

⌨ **TRY IT!**

**Use your mouse**

**1.** With your computer on and the desktop showing on the screen, move your mouse around on the desk and notice how mouse movements correspond to the movement of the arrow-shaped pointer.

**2.** Move the mouse to position the pointer on the Start button or Apple icon.

**3.** Click the left mouse button to open the Start menu or Apple menu.

**4.** Click the **Start** button or **Apple** icon again to close the Start menu.

## KEYBOARD BASICS

**What are the important features of a computer keyboard?** You use the computer keyboard to input commands, respond to prompts, and type the text of documents. An insertion point that looks like a flashing vertical bar indicates where the characters you type will appear. You can change the location of the insertion point by using the mouse or the arrow keys. Study Figure 8 for an overview of important computer keys and their functions.

**FIGURE 8**

Computer keyboards typically include special function keys.

A. The **Esc** (Escape) key cancels an operation.

B. **Function keys** activate commands, such as Save, Help, and Print. The command associated with each key depends on the software you are using.

C. The **Print Screen** key prints the contents of the screen or stores a copy of the screen in memory that you can print or manipulate with graphics software.

D. The **Windows** key on a PC opens the Start menu.

E. The **Page Up** key displays the previous screen of information. The **Page Down** key displays the next screen of information.

F. The **Backspace** key deletes one character to the left of the insertion point.

G. The **Insert** key switches between insert mode and typeover mode.

H. The **Home** key takes you to the beginning of a line or the beginning of a document, depending on the software you are using.

I. The **Tab** key can move your current typing location to the next tab stop or the next text-entry box.

J. The **Caps Lock** key capitalizes all the letters you type when it is engaged, but does not produce the top symbol on keys that contain two symbols. This key is a toggle key, which means that each time you press it, you switch between uppercase and lowercase modes.

K. The **Shift** key capitalizes letters and produces the top symbol on keys that contain two symbols.

L. You hold down the **Ctrl** key while pressing another key. On a Mac, the Command key, marked with an Apple or ⌘ symbol, works the same way. The result of Ctrl or Alt key combinations depends on the software you are using.

M. You hold down the **Alt** key while you press another key.

N. The **Enter** key is used to indicate that you have completed a command or want to move your typing position down to the next line.

O. The **Delete** key deletes the character to the right of the insertion point.

P. The **End** key takes you to the end of a line or the end of a document, depending on the software you are using.

Q. The **right-click** key accomplishes the same task as right-clicking a mouse button, and usually opens a shortcut menu.

R. The **arrow keys** move the insertion point.

S. The **numeric keypad** produces numbers or moves the insertion point, depending on the status of the Num Lock key shown by indicator lights or a message on the screen.

**What do Alt and Ctrl mean?** The Alt and Ctrl keys work with the letter keys. If you see <Ctrl X>, Ctrl+X, [Ctrl X], Ctrl-X, or Ctrl X on the screen or in an instruction manual, it means to hold down the Ctrl key while you press X. For example, Ctrl+X is a keyboard shortcut for clicking the Edit menu, and then clicking the Cut option. A keyboard shortcut allows you to use the keyboard rather than the mouse to select menu commands.

**What if I make a mistake?** Everyone makes mistakes. The first rule is don't panic! Most mistakes are reversible. The hints and tips in Figure 9 should help you recover from mistakes.

FIGURE 9

Most mistakes are easy to fix.

| What Happened | What to Do |
|---|---|
| Typed the wrong thing | Use the Backspace key to delete the last characters you typed. |
| Selected the wrong menu | Press the Esc key to close the menu. |
| Opened a window you didn't mean to | Click the X button in the upper corner of the window. |
| Computer has "hung up" and no longer responds to mouse clicks or typed commands | Hold down the Ctrl, Shift, and Esc keys, and then follow instructions to close the program. |
| Pressed the Enter key in the middle of a sentence | Press the Backspace key to paste the sentence back together. |

## WORKING WITH WINDOWS SOFTWARE

**How do I start Windows programs?** When using Windows, you can click the Start button to launch just about any software that's installed on your computer. The Start menu includes a list of recently accessed programs. Clicking the All Programs option displays a list of every program installed on your computer. You can run a program from this list simply by clicking it. Follow the instructions in the TRY IT! box to start Microsoft Paint (assuming it is installed on your computer).

### TRY IT!

**Start Microsoft Paint**

**1.** Make sure your computer is on and it is displaying the Windows desktop.

**2.** Click the **Start** button to display the Start menu.

**3.** Click **All Programs** to display a list of all software installed on your computer.

**4.** Click **Accessories**, and then click **Paint**.

**5.** Wait a few seconds for your computer to display the main screen for Microsoft Paint, shown below in Windows XP and Vista (top) or Windows 7 (bottom). Leave Paint open for use with the next TRY IT!.

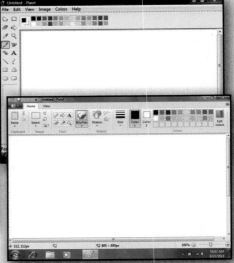

**How do I tell the software what I want to do?** Word processing, photo editing, and other software designed for use on computers running the Windows operating system is referred to as Windows software. Most Windows software works in a fairly uniform way and uses a similar set of controls.

Each software application appears within a rectangular area called a window, which can include a title bar, a menu bar, a ribbon, a work-space, and various controls shown in Figure 10.

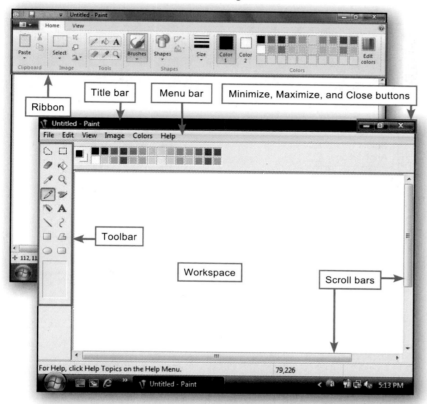

**FIGURE 10**

The **title bar** displays the title of the software, the name of the current data file, and the window sizing buttons.

The **Minimize button** shrinks the window to a button at the bottom of the screen.

The **Maximize button** stretches the window to fill the screen.

The **Close button** closes the window and exits the program.

A **menu bar** displays the titles of menus you can click to select commands.

A **toolbar** displays a series of tools for accomplishing various tasks.

A **ribbon** combines the options of a menu and toolbars into a single set of controls.

A **scroll bar** can be clicked or dragged to see any material that does not fit in the displayed window.

The **workspace** is the area in which your document or drawing is displayed.

If you're unfamiliar with Windows controls, take a few minutes to complete the steps in the TRY IT! box below.

**TRY IT!**

**Use the toolbar or ribbon**

**1.** As shown below, click the **Brushes** button on the Paint toolbar or ribbon.

**2.** Move the pointer to the work-space, hold down the left mouse button, and drag the mouse to paint a shape.

**3.** Release the mouse button when the shape is complete.

**Use the ribbon or menu bar**

**1.** Click the arrow next to **Rotate**, then click **Flip vertical**.

In old versions of Paint, click **Image**, click **Flip/Rotate**, click **Flip Vertical**, then click the **OK** button.

Your shape is now upside down.

**Use the sizing buttons**

**1.** Click the ▬ **Minimize** button.

**2.** The Paint window shrinks down to a button on the taskbar at the bottom of the screen.

**3.** Click the taskbar button to make the Paint window reappear.

**4.** Click the ▬×▬ **Close** button to close the Paint program and remove its window from the screen. If you see a message asking if you want to save changes, click the Don't Save button.

## WORKING WITH MAC SOFTWARE

**How do I start programs on the Mac?** When using Mac OS X, you can click icons in the dock to easily start programs. For programs that are not in the dock, you can click the Finder icon and then click the Applications option. If you are using a Mac and need to brush up on its controls, follow the instructions in the TRY IT! box below.

### TRY IT!

**Find out which programs are in the dock**

1. Position the mouse pointer over each of the icons in the dock and wait for the program name to appear.

**Use Finder to start a program**

1. Click the ![Finder] **Finder** icon on the left side of the dock.

2. When the Finder window (similar to one at right) appears, click the **Applications** option.

3. Double-click the **iCal** option to start the iCal calendar program and display the iCal window shown at right.

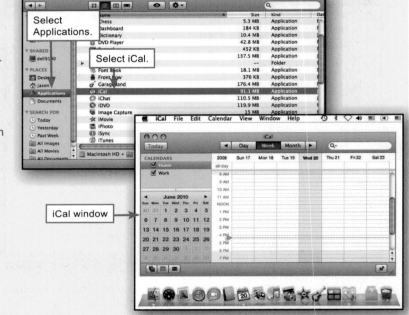

Select Applications.

Select iCal.

iCal window

**Use a menu and dialog box**

1. Click **iCal** on the menu bar at the top of the screen.

2. Click **Preferences** to display a dialog box.

3. Click the ![button] button next to *Start week on* to change the day to Monday.

4. Click the ⊗ **Close** button to close the Preferences dialog box.

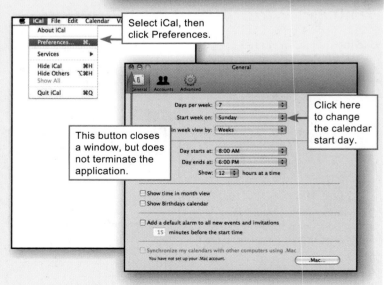

Select iCal, then click Preferences.

This button closes a window, but does not terminate the application.

Click here to change the calendar start day.

**Close a program**

1. Click **iCal** on the menu bar.

2. Click **Quit iCal** to close the window and terminate the application.

## HELP

**How can I get help using software?** If you've had problems using software, you're not alone! Everyone has questions at one time or another. Most software offers several sources of help, such as the following:

● Message boxes. When using software, it is important to pay attention to any message boxes displayed on the screen. Make sure you carefully read the options they present. If the box doesn't seem to apply to what you want to do, click its Cancel button to close it. Otherwise, set the options the way you want them, and then click the OK button to continue.

● User manual. Whether you're a beginner or a power user, the manual that comes with software can be an excellent resource. User manuals can contain quick-start guides, tutorials, detailed descriptions of menu options, and tips for using features effectively. Many manuals are offered online along with tools you can use to browse through them or look for the answer to a specific question.

● Help menu. The Help menu provides access to on-screen documentation, which can contain detailed instructions, tips, and FAQs. Answers to specific questions can be found by entering search terms, consulting the index, or browsing through a table of contents (Figure 11).

**FIGURE 11**

Clicking the 🔘 Help button or the Help menu produces a list of help options, where you can enter search terms or browse through topics.

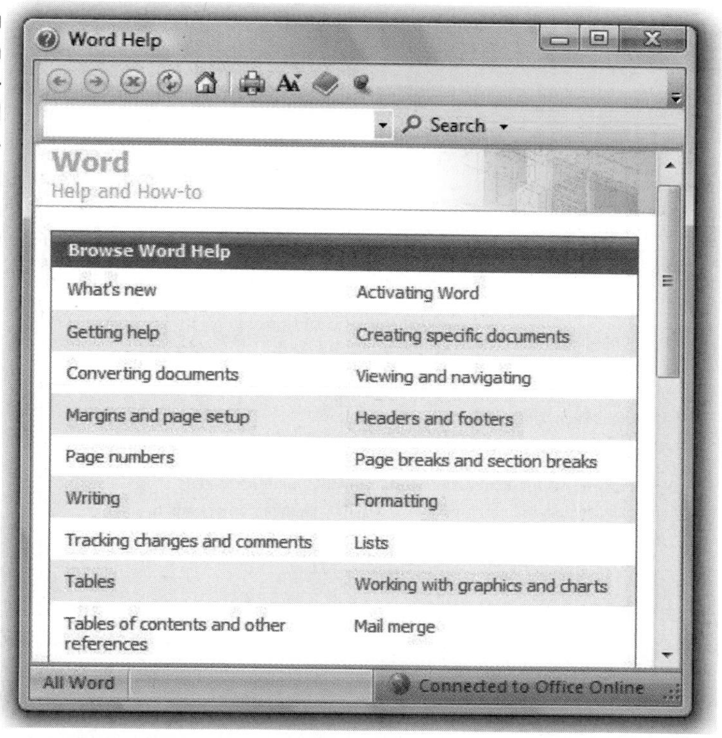

# QuickCheck

1. The case that holds a computer's circuitry and storage devices is called a(n) [_____] unit.

2. Instead of using the on/off switch to turn off a computer, you should instead use the Shut Down option from the Start menu or Apple menu. True or false? [_____]

3. On the Mac desktop, the [_____] displays a row of program icons.

4. Some programs include a ribbon of commands, whereas other programs present commands on a(n) [_____] bar.

5. The [_____] key can be used to delete the last character you typed.

▶ CHECK ANSWERS

# Documents, Browsers, and E-mail

**TO COMPLETE ASSIGNMENTS** for your course, you should be able to work with documents, browsers, and e-mail. Section B walks you through the basics.

## CREATING DOCUMENTS

**How do I create and save a document?** To create a document, simply type text in the workspace provided by word processing software such as Microsoft Word, OpenOffice Writer, Apple iWork Pages, or NeoOffice Writer. The flashing vertical insertion point (Figure 12) indicates your place in the document. Figure 13 explains how to save a document.

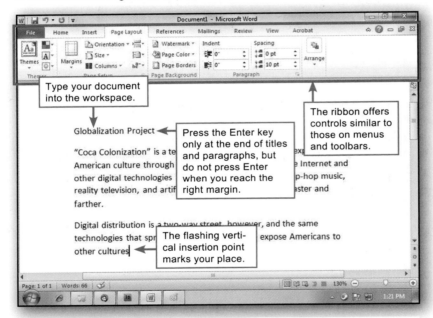

**FIGURE 12**

When typing text, you can use the following keys to move within a document and make revisions:

- **Backspace:** Delete the character to the left of the insertion point.

- **Delete:** Delete the character to the right of the insertion point.

- **Enter:** End a paragraph and begin a new line.

- **Arrow keys:** Move the insertion point up, down, right, or left.

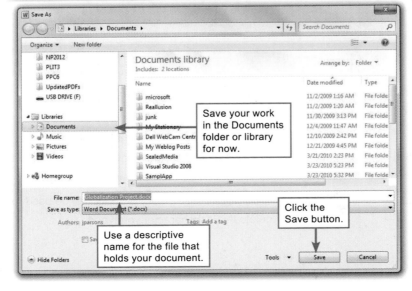

**FIGURE 13**

It is a good idea to save your document every few minutes, even if it is not finished. When you save a document, use the 💾 Save icon at the top of the screen. Your computer is probably configured to save documents on the hard disk in a library called Documents or a folder called My Documents. There is no need to change that until you gain more experience. File names can be several words long; just do not use the * / \ " ' : symbols in the file name.

**How do I print a document?** To print a document, simply click the File tab, File menu, or Office button and then select Print. Your computer displays a window containing a series of print options. If you want to print a single copy of your document, these settings should be correct, so you can click the Print or OK button to send your document to the printer.

**Can I send a document to my instructor?** You can e-mail a document by using the Send option accessed from the File tab, File menu, or Office button (Figure 14). To do so, you must know your instructor's e-mail address. Documents that you send along with e-mail messages are referred to as attachments. You'll learn more about e-mail later in the Orientation, but keep this option in mind because it is a handy way to submit assignments, such as projects and term papers.

**How do I find my documents again in the future?** If you want to revise a document sometime in the future, simply start your word processing software, click the File tab, File menu, or Office button, and then click Open. Your computer should display a list of documents stored in the Documents folder. Locate the one you want to revise and double-click it.

**What should I do when I'm done?** When you're ready to quit, you can close the document by clicking the Close option from the File tab, File menu, or Office button. When you want to close your word processing software, click the [X] Close button (Windows) or click the program name on the menu bar and then select Quit (Mac).

**FIGURE 14**

Most word processing programs offer an option for sending a document as an e-mail attachment.

• In Word 2010, click the File tab, select Save & Send, and then select Send as Attachment (shown below).

• In Word 2007, click the Office button, point to Send, and then select E-mail.

• In Word 2003, OpenOffice Writer, or NeoOffice Writer, click File, and then select Send or Send To.

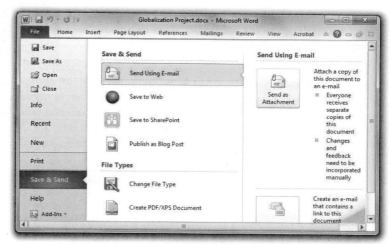

## TRY IT!

**Create a document**

**1.** Click the **Start** button (Windows) or click the **Finder** icon and select the Applications option (Mac).

**2.** Look for Microsoft Word, OpenOffice Writer, or iWork Pages. Click the name of your word processing software to open it.

**3.** Click the workspace to position the insertion point in the upper-left corner.

**4.** Type a paragraph. Refer to Figure 12 for keys to use while typing and revising your work.

**5.** When the first paragraph is complete, press the **Enter** key to begin a new paragraph.

**6.** Type a second paragraph of text.

**Save a document**

**1.** Click the [icon] **Save** icon located near the top of the window.

**2.** Make sure the Documents library or folder is selected. If not, click the [▸] button next to your user name at the top of the window and then click the Documents folder from the list. (Or use the [▾] button next to the Save In box to display a list of folders.)

**3.** In the *File name* box, type a name for your document.

**4.** Click the **Save** button.

**5.** When the Save As dialog box closes, your document is saved.

**Print a document, close it, and exit your word processing application**

**1.** Click the **File** tab, **File** menu, or **Office** button and then click **Print**.

**2.** Make sure the page range is set to **All**.

**3.** Make sure number of copies is set to **1**.

**4.** Click the **Print** or **OK** button and wait a few seconds for the printer to produce your document.

**5.** Close the document by clicking the **File** tab, **File** menu, or **Office** button and then clicking **Close**. The workspace should become blank.

**6.** Exit your word processing software by clicking the [X] **Close** button (Windows) or clicking the program name on the menu bar, then selecting **Quit** (Mac).

## INTERNET AND WEB BASICS

**What is the Internet?** The Internet is the largest computer network in the world, carrying information from one continent to another in the blink of an eye (Figure 15). The computers connected to this network offer many types of resources, such as e-mail, instant messaging, social networking, popular music downloads, and online shopping.

**What is the Web?** Although some people use the terms *Internet* and *Web* interchangeably, the two are not the same. The Internet refers to a communications network that connects computers all around the globe. The Web—short for World Wide Web—is just one of the many resources available over this communications network.

The Web is a collection of linked and cross-referenced information available for public access. This information is accessible from Web sites located on millions of computers. The information is displayed as a series of screens called Web pages. You'll use the Web for general research and for specific activities designed to accompany this textbook. To use the Web, your computer must have access to the Internet.

**How do I access the Internet?** Most computers can be configured to connect to the Internet over telephone, cell phone, satellite, or cable television systems. Internet access can be obtained from school computer labs, local service providers such as your cable television company, and national Internet service providers such as AOL, AT&T, Comcast, Verizon, and EarthLink.

To expedite your orientation, it is assumed that your computer has Internet access. If it does not, consult your instructor, or ask an experienced computer user to help you get set up.

**How do I know if my computer has Internet access?** The easiest way to find out if your computer can access the Internet is to try it. You can quickly find out if you have Internet access by starting software called a browser that's designed to display Web pages.

Browser software called Internet Explorer is supplied with Microsoft Windows. Mac OS X includes a browser called Safari. Other browsers, such as Firefox and Chrome, are also available. Follow the steps in the TRY IT! box to start your browser.

## HOW TO USE A WEB BROWSER AND SEARCH ENGINE

**How do I use a browser?** A browser lets you enter a unique Web page address called a URL, such as *www.google.com*. You can also jump from one Web page to another by using links. Links are usually underlined; and when you position the arrow-shaped mouse pointer over a link, it changes to a hand shape.

**FIGURE 15**

The Internet communications network stretches around the globe.

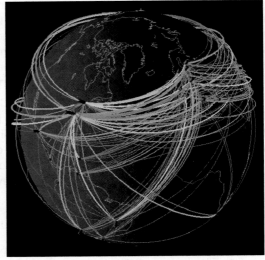

### TRY IT!

**Start your browser**

1. Click the [icons] icon for your browser. It is usually located near the Start button or on the dock.

2. Your computer should soon display the browser window.

If your computer displays a Connect to box, click the **Dial** button to establish a dial-up connection over your telephone line.

You'll need to cancel the browser command and consult an experienced computer user if:

- Your computer displays a "working off line" message.
- Your computer displays an Internet Connection Wizard box.

Although browsers offer many features, you can get along quite well using the basic controls shown in Figure 16.

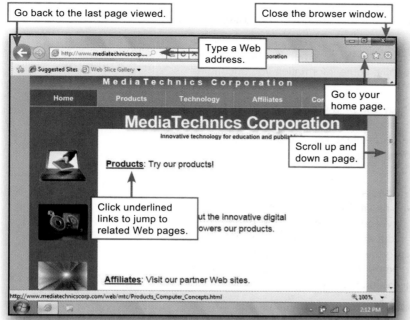

Go back to the last page viewed.

Close the browser window.

Type a Web address.

Go to your home page.

Scroll up and down a page.

Click underlined links to jump to related Web pages.

**FIGURE 16**

Using a Browser

A full Web address might look like this:
http://www.mediatechnicscorp.com
It is not necessary to type the *http://*, so to access the MediaTechnics Corporation page shown here, you would type:
**www.mediatechnicscorp.com**
When typing a Web address, do not use any spaces, and copy upper- and lowercase letters exactly.

**How do I find specific information on the Web?** If you're looking for information and don't know the Web site where it might be located, you can use a search engine to find it. Follow the steps in the TRY IT! box to "google it" by using the Google search engine.

**TRY IT!**

**Use a search engine**

1. Make sure the browser window is open.

2. Click the Address box and type:

www.google.com

3. Press the **Enter** key. Your browser displays the Web page for the Google search engine.

4. Click the blank search box and then type **national parks**.

5. Press the **Enter** key. Google displays a list of Web pages that relate to national parks.

6. Click the underlined **National Park Service** link. Your browser displays the Park Service's home page.

7. Leave your browser open for the next TRY IT!.

**What are the best sources of information on the Web?** The best sources of information are easy to access, dependable, and preferably free. Sites such as Wikipedia, Answers.com, WhatIs.com, and HowStuffWorks are great sources for general information and researching topics for computer courses.

When you're looking for information on the Web, remember that virtually anyone can post anything. Consequently, some information you encounter might not be accurate.

To check the quality of information provided by a Web site, you can cross-check facts with other sites. Be sure to check when the material was posted or updated to determine if it is current. You might also consider the information source. Blogs and YouTube videos often express opinions rather than facts.

**How does Wikipedia work?** Wikipedia is an encyclopedia that is written and maintained by the people who use it. More than ten million in-depth articles on a vast range of topics have been submitted and updated by users, many of them experts. Wikipedia information tends to be accurate because users are continually reading the articles and correcting inaccurate or biased information. However, some vandalism occurs and from time to time a few articles contain false or misleading information.

Most Wikipedia articles include a History tab that tracks changes. Check the date of the last change to determine if the information is current. Articles also include a Discussion tab that can help you spot controversial aspects of the information. Use the TRY IT! below to see how Wikipedia works.

## TRY IT!

**Check out Wikipedia**

1. In the Address bar of your browser, type **www.wikipedia. org** and then press the **Enter** key.

2. When the Wikipedia window appears, enter **cyberspace** in the search box and then press **Enter**.

3. Read a bit of the article to get an idea of its scope and detail. Do you detect any bias in the article?

4. Click the **History** tab. Look at the last few updates. Does this article seem up to date?

5. Click the **Discussion** tab. What is the status of the article? Does it contain controversial statements? Can you envision how you might use Google or other Web resources to explore specific controversies?

6. Click the **Article** tab to return to the Cyberspace article.

7. You can leave your browser open for the next TRY IT!.

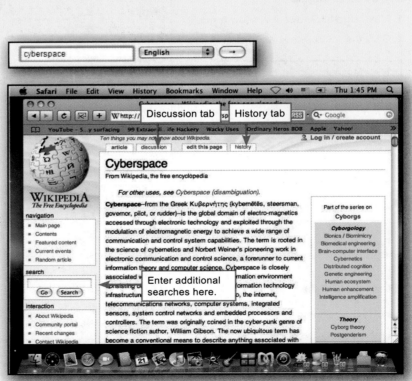

# WORKING WITH E-MAIL

**What is e-mail?** E-mail is a form of communication that relies on computer networks, such as the Internet, to transmit messages from one computer to another. Like regular mail, e-mail messages are sent to a mailbox where they are kept until the recipient retrieves the message. Messages might arrive at their destination within seconds, or might not arrive for a few hours. Once sent, e-mail messages cannot be retrieved.

**What do I need to use e-mail?** To send and receive e-mail, you need an Internet connection, an e-mail account, and software that enables you to compose, read, and delete e-mail messages. An e-mail account consists of an e-mail address (Figure 17), a password, and a mailbox. You can usually obtain an e-mail account from your Internet service provider, your school, or a Webmail provider, such as Hotmail, Yahoo! Mail, or Gmail.

Webmail providers store your mail online. To access your mail, simply use your browser. In contrast, local mail, such as Microsoft Outlook, transfers mail to your computer and requires you to use special e-mail software instead of a browser.

**How do I get a Webmail account?** Registering for a Webmail account is easy and many online e-mail providers offer free basic service. Work with the TRY IT! below to see how.

**FIGURE 17**

E-mail Addresses

An e-mail address consists of a user ID followed by an @ symbol and the name of a computer that handles e-mail accounts. Ask your instructor for his or her e-mail address. It is likely similar to the following:

**instructor@school.edu**

When typing an e-mail address, use all lowercase letters and do not use any spaces.

## TRY IT!

**Get a Web-based e-mail account**

**1.** In the Address bar of your browser, enter **www.gmail.com**.

**2.** When the Gmail window appears, click the button labeled **Create an account**.

**3.** Follow the directions to enter your first name, last name, and login name.

**4.** Click the **check availability!** button. If the login name you want is already in use, you'll have to try a different one, again clicking the check availability! button.

**5.** When you've selected a valid login name, continue down the page to create a password. Try not to use a name, date, or any dictionary word as your password.

**6.** Continue down the page to complete the rest of the registration form.

**7.** Before finalizing your registration, review the information you've entered and jot down your login name and password.

**8.** Read the Terms of Service, and if you agree, click the **I accept** button. That's it! You now have a Gmail account.

New to Gmail? It's free and easy.

**Create an account »**

About Gmail    New features!

**Get started with Gmail**

First name: John

Last name: Adams

Desired Login Name: JohnXAdams    @gmail.com
Examples: JSmith, John.Smith

check availability!    ← You might have to try several login names to find one that is available.

**JohnXAdams** is available

Choose a password: ••••••••••    Password strength:    Strong
Minimum of 8 characters in length.

Re-enter password: ••••••••••    Try to choose a strong password.

☑ Remember me on this computer.

Creating a Google Account will enable Web History. Web History is a feature that will provide you with a more personalized experience on Google that includes more relevant search results and recommendations. Learn More
☐ Enable Web History. ←    You can uncheck this box for better privacy.

By clicking on 'I accept' below you are agreeing to the Terms of Service above and both the Program Policy and the Privacy Policy.

I accept. Create my account.

**Is Webmail better than local e-mail?** Both Web-based and local e-mail have their advantages and disadvantages. Webmail accounts are definitely easier to set up and you can use them from any computer with an Internet connection. Webmail accounts are also ideal for "throw-away" accounts.

**What is a throw-away e-mail account?** Whether you use local mail or Webmail for your regular correspondence, you might consider creating one or two throw-away accounts for occasions when you have to give an e-mail address, but you don't want any continued correspondence from that source. Later in the chapter, you'll learn more about how e-mail scams and online marketing contribute to all the junk e-mail you receive. Your throw-away e-mail address can become the recipient for lots of those messages, and eventually you can simply delete the throw-away account and all the junk it contains.

**How do I create and send an e-mail message?** Many e-mail systems are available, and each uses slightly different software, making it impossible to cover all options in this short orientation. You might want to enlist the aid of an experienced computer user to help you get started. The steps in the TRY IT! box pertain to Gmail, but other e-mail packages work in a similar way.

## TRY IT!

**Create and send e-mail**

**1.** If Gmail is not open, open your browser and type **www.gmail.com** in the address box. Log in to your Gmail account.

**2.** Click the **Compose Mail** link to display a form like the one below.

**3.** Follow steps 4 through 6 as shown below.

**7.** When your message is complete, click the **Send** button and Gmail sends the message.

**8.** You can continue to experiment with e-mail. When done, use the **Sign out** link, then close your browser.

**Note:** With some local e-mail configurations, the Send button places the e-mail in an Outbox and you have to click the **Send/Receive** button on the toolbar to ship the message out from your computer.

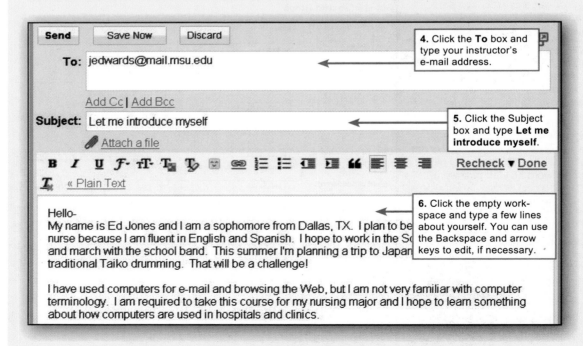

**How do I get my e-mail?** As with sending mail, the way you get mail depends on your e-mail system. In general, clicking the Send/Receive button collects your mail from the network and stores it in your Inbox. Your e-mail software displays a list of your messages. The new ones are usually shown highlighted or in bold type. You can click any message to open it, read it, and reply to it, as shown in Figure 18.

**How do I log off?** When working with a Webmail account, it is important to use the Log out or Sign out link before you close your browser. Taking this extra step makes your e-mail less vulnerable to hackers.

**FIGURE 18**

When e-mail software displays your Inbox, you can:

- Open a message and read it.
- Reply to a message.
- Delete unwanted messages (a good idea to minimize the size of your mailbox).
- Forward a message to someone else.

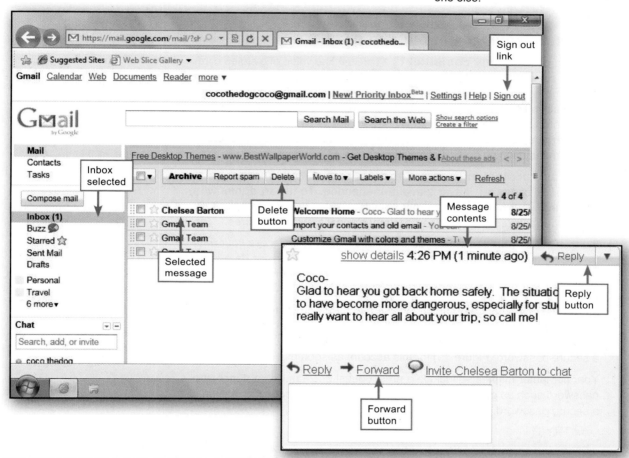

## QuickCheck

SECTION B

1. Documents that you send along with e-mail messages are referred to as [          ].

2. Popular [          ] software includes Internet Explorer, Chrome, and Firefox.

3. When looking for information on the Web, you can use a(n) [          ] engine to produce a list of links to Web pages that might contain the information you seek.

4. An e-mail [          ] looks something like student@school.edu.

5. To access Webmail, you use a browser; but to access [          ] e-mail, you use e-mail software such as Microsoft Outlook.

 CHECK ANSWERS

# Security and Privacy

AS WITH MOST OTHER facets of modern life, computing has its share of troublemakers, scam artists, and identity thieves. Section C offers some tips on navigating through the sometimes rough neighborhoods of cyberspace, while keeping your data safe and your identity private.

## SECURING YOUR COMPUTER AND DATA

**What's at risk if my computer is stolen?** The value of a stolen computer is not so much in the hardware as in the data it contains. With stolen data such as your bank account numbers and PINs, a thief can wipe out your checking and savings accounts. With your credit card numbers, a thief can go on a spending spree. Even worse, a criminal can use stolen data to assume your identity, run up debts, get into legal difficulties, ruin your credit rating, and cause you no end of trouble.

**How can I protect my computer data from theft?** When you carry a notebook computer, never leave it unattended. To thwart a thief who breaks into your home or dorm room, anchor your computer to your desk with a specially designed lock you can buy at most electronics stores.

If a thief steals your computer, you can make it difficult to access your data by setting up a password. Until the password is entered, your data is off limits. A thief might be able to boot up the desktop, but should not be able to easily look at the data in your folders.

Many new computers are shipped with a standard administrator password that everyone knows. If you are the only person using your computer, you can use the administrator account for your day-to-day computing, but create a secure password (Figure 19) for this account as soon as you can.

Your computer might also include a preset guest account with a nonsecure password such as *guest*. You should disable this guest account or assign it a secure password.

**FIGURE 19**

To create a secure password:

- Use at least eight characters, mixing numbers with letters, as in 2by4lumber.

- Do not use your name, the name of a family member, or your pet's name.

- Do not use a word that can be found in the dictionary.

- Do not forget your password!

### TRY IT!

**Check the accounts on your computer**

**1.** To access accounts on Windows, click the **Start** button, then select **Control Panel**.

For Windows Vista and Windows 7, select **User Accounts and Family Safety**, select **User Accounts**, and then select **Manage another account**. (You might be required to enter an administrator password.) For Windows XP, select **User Accounts**.

On a Mac, click the **Apple** icon, select **System Preferences**, and **Accounts**.

**2.** Check the password protection on all accounts. If you are working on a school lab computer, do not make changes to the account settings. If you are using your own computer, click the Administrator account and make sure it has a secure password.

## AVOIDING VIRUSES

**What's so bad about computer viruses?** The term *virus* has a technical meaning, but many people use the term loosely when referring to malicious programs that circulate on disks, in e-mail attachments, and on the Internet. This malware, as it is sometimes called, can steal your data, destroy files, or create network traffic jams. It might display an irritating message to announce its presence, or it might work quietly behind the scenes to spread itself to various files on your computer or mail itself out to everyone in your e-mail address book.

After a virus takes up residence in your computer, it is often difficult to disinfect all your files. Rather than wait for a virus attack, you should take steps to keep your computer virus free.

**How can I keep viruses out of my computer?** It helps to avoid risky behaviors, such as downloading pirated software, opening e-mail attachments from unknown senders, installing random social networking plug-ins, gambling online, and participating in illegal file sharing. Windows users should install antivirus software such as the packages listed in Figure 20. Because fewer viruses target Macs, OS X users who don't engage in risky online activities sometimes opt to work without antivirus software.

If you use antivirus software, configure it to run continuously whenever your computer is on. You should make sure your antivirus software is set to scan for viruses in incoming files and e-mail messages. At least once a week, your antivirus software should run a full system check to make sure every file on your computer is virus free.

As new viruses emerge, your antivirus software needs to update its virus definition file. It gets this update as a Web download. If you've selected the auto update option, your computer should automatically receive updates as they become available.

**FIGURE 20**

Popular Antivirus Software

Norton AntiVirus Plus
McAfee VirusScan
Kaspersky Anti-Virus
F-Secure Antivirus
Panda Antivirus
Trend Micro Antivirus
AVG Anti-Virus
avast!

### TRY IT!

**Get familiar with your antivirus software**

**1.** In Windows, click the **Start** button, and then select **All Programs**. On the Mac, use **Finder** to access the Applications folder. Look for antivirus software (refer to Figure 20 for a list). Open your antivirus software by clicking it.

**Can't find any?** If you are using your own computer and it doesn't seem to have antivirus software, you can connect to an antivirus supplier's Web site and download it.

**2.** Each antivirus program has unique features. The figure on the right shows the main screen for avast! antivirus software. Explore your antivirus software to make sure it is configured to do the following:

• Scan incoming e-mail.

• Run continuously in the background—a feature sometimes called Auto Protect.

• Block malicious scripts.

**3.** Check the date of your last full system scan. If it was more than one week ago, you should check the settings that schedule antivirus scans.

**4.** Check the date when your computer last received virus definitions. If it was more than one week ago, you should make sure your antivirus software is configured to receive automatic live updates.

## PREVENTING INTRUSIONS

**Is it risky to go online?** The Internet offers lots of cool stuff—music downloads, movie reviews and trailers, online shopping and banking, consumer information, blogs, social networking sites, news, sports, weather, and much more. Most Internet offerings are legitimate, but some downloads contain viruses, and shady characters called hackers control programs that lurk about waiting to snatch your personal data or infiltrate your computer. The longer your computer remains connected to the Internet, the more vulnerable it is to a hacker's infiltration attempts.

If a hacker gains access to your computer, he or she can look through your files, use your computer as a launching platform for viruses and network-jamming attacks, or turn your computer into a server for pornography and other unsavory material. Hackers have even found ways to turn thousands of infiltrated computers into "zombies," link them together, and carry out coordinated attacks to disrupt online access to Microsoft, Bank of America, and other Internet businesses.

**How do hackers gain access to my computer?** Intruders gain access by exploiting security flaws in your computer's operating system, browser, and e-mail software. Software publishers are constantly creating updates to fix these flaws. As part of your overall security plan, you should download and install security updates as they become available.

**How can I block hackers from infiltrating my computer?** Firewall software and Internet security suites, such as those listed in Figure 21, provide a protective barrier between a computer and the Internet. If your computer is directly connected to the Internet, it should have active firewall software. If your computer connects to a local area network for Internet access, the network should have a device called a router to block infiltration attempts.

When a firewall is active, it watches for potentially disruptive incoming data called probes. When a probe is discovered, your firewall displays a warning and asks what to do. If the source looks legitimate, you can let it through; if not, you should block it (Figure 22).

**Where do I get a firewall?** Mac OS X and Windows include built-in firewalls. Third-party Internet security suites also include firewall modules.

**FIGURE 21**

Popular Firewall Software and Internet Security Suites

Emsisoft Online Armor
McAfee Internet Security
ZoneAlarm Internet Security
Norton Internet Security
Mac OS X Firewall
Agnitum Outpost Firewall
Windows Firewall
Comodo Firewall Pro
Symantec Internet Security
Kaspersky Internet Security
Trend Micro Internet Security Pro

**FIGURE 22**

When your firewall software encounters new or unusual activity, it asks you what to do.

### 🖮 TRY IT!

**Check your Windows computer's firewall**

**1.** Click the **Start** button, then click **Control Panel**. For Windows Vista, click the **Security** link; for Windows 7, click the **System and Security** link; or for Windows XP, double-click the **Security Center** icon. Click the **Windows Firewall** link.

**2.** If the Windows firewall is not active, you should check to see if a third-party firewall is protecting your computer.

**3.** Click the **Start** button, click **All Programs**, and then look through the program list for firewalls such as those in Figure 21. If you find a firewall listed, start it and explore to see if it has been activated.

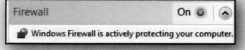

**Check your Mac computer's firewall**

**1.** Click the **Apple** icon, and then select **System Preferences**.

**2.** Click the **Security** icon and then click the **Firewall** button.

**3.** Click the third option, **Set access for specific services and applications**, to turn on the firewall.

**4.** Click the **Advanced** button and make sure both items are checked. Click **OK** and then close the Security dialog box.

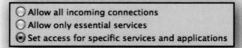

## BLOCKING SPYWARE AND POP-UP ADS

**Are some Web sites dangerous?** When you access Web sites, data is transferred to your computer and displayed by your browser. Most of this data is harmless, but malicious HTML scripts, rogue ActiveX components, and spyware have the potential to search your computer for passwords and credit card numbers, monitor your Web-browsing habits for marketing purposes, block your access to legitimate Web sites, or surreptitiously use your computer as a staging area for illicit activities.

Spyware is the most insidious threat. It often piggybacks on pop-up ads and activates if you click the ad window. Some spyware can begin its dirty work when you try to click the Close button to get rid of an ad.

**How can I block spyware?** The first line of defense is to never click pop-up ads—especially those with dire warnings about your computer being infected by a virus or spyware! (Figure 23.) To close an ad, right-click its button on the taskbar at the bottom of your screen, and then select the Close option from the menu that appears. Most browsers can be configured to block spyware and pop-up ads (Figure 24). Your antivirus software might offer similar options.

**What other steps can I take to browse the Web safely?** Most browsers include security features. You should take some time to become familiar with them. For example, Internet Explorer allows you to specify how you want it to deal with ActiveX components. You can also specify how to deal with HTML scripts, cookies, security certificates, and other Web-based data. If you don't want to be bothered by these details, however, Internet Explorer offers several predefined configurations for Low, Medium, and High security. Most Internet Explorer users set security and privacy options to Medium.

**FIGURE 23**

Some pop-up ads contain fake warnings about viruses, spyware, and intrusion attempts.

**FIGURE 24**

Check your browser's settings to make sure it is blocking pop-up ads.

### ⌨ TRY IT!

**Check Internet security and privacy options**

1. Start your browser and look for its security settings.

**Internet Explorer:** Click **Tools**, then select **Internet Options**. Click the **Security** tab. Typically, your security setting should be Medium. Click the **Privacy** tab. Typically, your privacy setting should be Medium. If your version of IE offers a Pop-up Blocker, make sure its box contains a check mark so that it is activated.

**Firefox:** Click **Tools**, select **Options**, and then click **Content**. Make sure there is a check mark in the box for **Block pop-up windows**.

**Safari:** Click **Safari** on the menu bar. Make sure there is a check mark next to **Block Pop-Up Windows**.

**Chrome:** Click the **Wrench** (Tools) icon, select **Options**, and then click **Under the Hood** and click the **Content settings** button. Under Pop-ups, make sure that the **Do not allow** option is selected.

2. If your browser does not seem to offer antispyware and pop-up blocking, you can use the Start button to see if one of the security suites listed in Figure 21 has been installed. If your computer seems to have no antispyware or ad-blocking software, you might want to download some and install it.

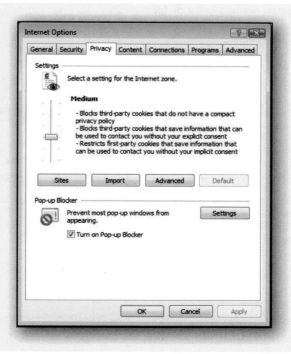

## PROTECTING E-COMMERCE TRANSACTIONS

**Is online shopping safe?** Online shopping is generally safe. From time to time, shoppers encounter fake storefronts designed to look like legitimate merchants but that are actually set up to steal credit card information. You can avoid these fakes by making sure you enter correctly spelled URLs when connecting to your favorite shopping sites.

**How safe is my credit card information when I'm shopping online?** Online shopping is not much more dangerous than using your credit card for a telephone order or giving it to a server when you've finished eating in a restaurant. Anyone who handles your card can copy the card number, jot down the expiration date, and try to make unauthorized charges.

That's not to say that credit cards are risk free. Credit cards are surprisingly vulnerable both online and off. Thieves can break into merchant computers that store order information. Thieves might even pick up your credit card information from discarded order forms. Despite these risks, we continue to use credit cards.

Many people are concerned about their credit card data getting intercepted as it travels over the Internet. As you wrap up an online purchase and submit your credit card information, it is transmitted from your computer to the merchant's computer. Software called a packet sniffer, designed for legitimately monitoring network traffic, is occasionally used by unscrupulous hackers to intercept credit card numbers and other data traveling over the Internet.

**How can I keep my credit card number confidential?** When you submit credit card information, make sure the merchant provides a secure connection for transporting data. Typically, a secure connection is activated when you're in the final phases of checking out—as you enter your shipping and credit card information into a form and click a Submit button to send it. A secure connection encrypts your data. Even if your credit card number is intercepted, it cannot be deciphered and used. To make sure you have a secure connection, look for the lock icon. The Address box should also display a URL that begins with *https://* (Secure HTTP) or contains ssl (Secure Sockets Layer).

### 🖳 TRY IT!

**Identify a secure connection**

**1.** Start your browser and connect to the site **www.bestbuy.com**.

**2.** Select any item and use the **Add to Cart** button to place it in your online shopping cart.

**3.** Click the **Checkout** button, then at the next screen click the **Checkout as Guest** button to reach the screen where you enter your billing information.

**4.** At the Billing Address screen, do you see any evidence that you're using a secure connection?

**5.** Close your browser so that you don't complete the transaction.

## AVOIDING E-MAIL SCAMS

**What are e-mail scams?** From time to time, you hear about con artists who have bilked innocent consumers out of their life savings. The Internet has its share of con artists, too, who run e-mail scams designed to collect money and confidential information from unsuspecting victims. E-mail scams are usually distributed in mass mailings called spam.

**What do I need to know about spam?** The Internet makes it easy and cheap to send out millions of e-mail solicitations. In the United States, the CAN-SPAM Act requires mass-mail messages to be labeled with a valid subject line. Recipients are supposed to be provided with a way to opt out of receiving future messages.

Legitimate merchants and organizations comply with the law when sending product announcements, newsletters, and other messages. Unscrupulous spammers ignore the law and try to disguise their solicitations as messages from your friends, chat room participants, or co-workers (Figure 25).

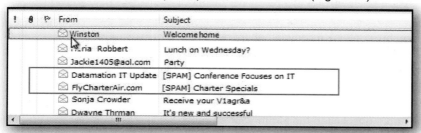

**FIGURE 25**

Some e-mail systems use spam filters to flag suspected spam by adding [SPAM] to the subject line. Spam filters are not perfect, however. Some spam is not flagged and occasionally legitimate mail is mistaken for spam.

**Is spam dangerous?** Some mass mailings contain legitimate information, including daily or weekly newsletters to which you've subscribed. Many mass mailings, however, advertise illegal products. Others are outright scams to get you to download a virus, divulge your bank account numbers, or send in money for products you'll never receive.

Beware of e-mail containing offers that seem just too good to be true. Messages about winning the sweepstakes or pleas for help to transfer money out of Nigeria (Figure 26) are scams to raid your bank account.

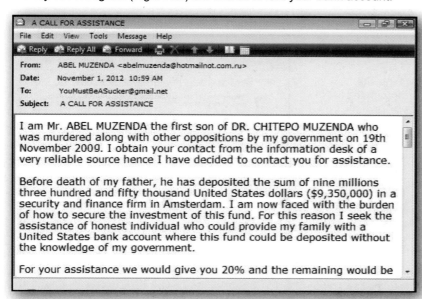

**FIGURE 26**

Many variations of this African money-transfer fraud—complete with deliberate grammatical errors—have circulated on the Internet for years. Victims who respond to these preposterous e-mails have found their bank accounts raided, their credit ratings destroyed, and their reputations ruined. According to the FBI, some victims have even been kidnapped!

**What's phishing?** Phishing (pronounced "fishing") is a scam that arrives in your e-mailbox looking like official correspondence from a major company, such as Microsoft, PayPal, eBay, MSN, Yahoo!, or AOL. The e-mail message is actually from an illegitimate source and is designed to trick you into divulging confidential information or downloading a virus.

Links in the e-mail message often lead to a Web site that looks official, where you are asked to enter confidential information such as your credit card number, Social Security number, or bank account number.

The following are examples of phishing scams you should be aware of:

• A message from Microsoft with an attachment that supposedly contains a security update for Microsoft Windows. Downloading the attachment infects your computer with a virus.

• A message that appears to come from PayPal, complete with official-looking logos, that alerts you to a problem with your account. When you click the Billing Center link and enter your account information, it is transmitted to a hacker's computer.

• A message that's obviously spam, but contains a convenient opt-out link. If you click the link believing that it will prevent future spam from this source, you'll actually be downloading a program that hackers can use to remotely control your computer for illegal activities.

**How do I avoid e-mail scams?** If your e-mail software provides spam filters, you can use them to block some unsolicited mail from your e-mailbox. Spam filters are far from perfect, however, so don't assume everything that gets through is legitimate. Use your judgment before opening any e-mail message or attachment.

Never reply to a message that you suspect to be fraudulent. If you have a question about its legitimacy, check whether it's on a list of known scams. Never click a link provided in an e-mail message to manage any account information. Instead, use your browser to go directly to the company's Web site and access your account as usual. Microsoft never sends updates as attachments. To obtain Microsoft updates, go to *www.microsoft.com* and click Security & Updates.

**TRY IT!**

**Arm yourself against e-mail scams**

**1.** Start your browser and connect to the site **www.millersmiles.co.uk**. Browse through the list of recent phishing attacks.

**2.** Open your e-mail software and find out if it includes spam filters. You can usually find this information by clicking **Help** on the menu bar and then typing **spam filter** in the search box.

**3.** Explore your options for configuring spam filters. If you use Windows Live Mail (shown at right), you can find these settings by clicking the **Menus** button and then clicking **Safety options**. Check the settings for spam filters on the Options tab, and then check the settings on the Phishing tab.

Spam filters sometimes catch legitimate mail and group it with junk mail. You might want to keep tabs on your spam filters when they are first activated to make sure they are set to a level that eliminates most unwanted spam without catching too much legitimate mail.

## PROTECTING YOUR PRIVACY

**How much information about me has been collected online?** Information about you is stored in many places and has the potential to be consolidated by government agencies, private businesses, and criminals. Some databases are legitimate—those maintained by credit bureaus and medical insurance companies, for example. By law, you have the right to ask for a copy of these records and correct any errors you find. Many other databases, such as those maintained at e-commerce sites and those illegally acquired by hackers, are not accessible, and you have no way of checking the data they contain.

**What's the problem with having my personal information in a few databases?** The problem is that many companies share their databases with third parties. Your personal data might start in a single legitimate database, but that data can be sold to a continuous chain of third parties who use it to generate mass mailings that clog up your Inbox with marketing ploys, unwanted newsletters, and promotions for useless products.

**Can I control who collects information about me?** To some extent, you can limit your exposure to future data collection by supplying personal data only when absolutely necessary. When filling out online forms, consider whether you want to or need to provide your real name and address. Avoid providing merchants with your e-mail address even if you're promised a $5 coupon or preferred customer status. A small reward might not be worth the aggravation of an Inbox brimming with spam and e-mail scams. You should also be careful when using public computers (Figure 27).

**Can I opt out?** Some mass e-mailings give you a chance to opt out so that you don't receive future messages. Opting out is a controversial practice. On mailings from reputable businesses, clicking an opt-out link might very well discontinue unwanted e-mail messages. However, opting out does not necessarily remove your name from the database, which could be sold to a third party that disregards your opt-out request.

Scammers use opt-out links to look for "live" targets, perhaps in a database that contains lots of fake or outdated e-mail addresses. By clicking one of these opt-out links, you've played right into the hands of unscrupulous hackers—this action lets them know that your e-mail address is valid. Most experts recommend that you never use opt-out links, but instead go to the sender's Web site and try to opt out from there. If you are tempted to use an opt-out link directly from an e-mail message, carefully examine the link's URL to make sure you'll connect to a legitimate Web site.

### 🖮 TRY IT!

**Check your privacy**

**1.** Start your browser and go googling by connecting to **www.google.com**. Enter your name in the Search box. What turns up?

**2.** Connect to **www.peopledata.com**. Enter your name and state of residence. Click the **Search** button. Notice all the information that's offered.

**3.** Connect to **www.ciadata.com** and scroll down the page to view the kind of information anyone can obtain about you for less than $100.

**4.** Read about your rights to view credit reports at the Federal Trade Commission site:
**www.ftc.gov/bcp/menus/consumer/credit/rights.shtm**

**FIGURE 27**

Using public computers poses security risks from people looking over your shoulder, spyware that collects your keystrokes, and the footprint you leave behind in cookies and temporary Internet pages.

To minimize risks when using public computers:

● Be sure to log out from all sites and close all browser windows before quitting.

● Delete cookies and browser history.

● Avoid using public computers for financial transactions such as filing your taxes.

● Reboot the computer before you quit.

● If you're using your own portable apps from a USB drive, make sure your computer is running antivirus software.

Orientation

## SAFE SOCIAL NETWORKING

**What's the risk at sites like Twitter, Facebook, and LinkedIn?**
A prolific Twitter user with 650 "friends" had a nasty surprise one morn-
ing. She discovered that private messages she'd sent to specific friends
were showing up on her public feed for everyone to see. Although this is an
extreme example of how things can go wrong on social networking sites,
embarrassing incidents are all too frequent.

The more information you reveal at social networking sites, the more you
increase your susceptibility to identity theft, stalking, and other embarrassing moments, such as when a prospective employer happens to see those
not-so-flattering photos of you on your spring break.

**How do I stay safe and keep my stuff private when using
social networking sites?** The first rule of social networking safety is
never share your Social Security number, phone number, or home address.
Unfortunately, everyone has access to Web-based tools for finding
addresses and phone numbers, so withholding that information provides
only a thin security blanket.

Most social networking sites depend on references and friends-of-friends
links to establish a trusted circle of contacts. *Trusted* is the key word here.
When using social networking sites, make sure you understand what
information is being shared with friends, what information is available to
strangers on the site, and what data is available publicly to search engines.

Be careful about revealing personal information at social networking sites,
including blogs, chat rooms, and virtual worlds such as Second Life. Many
online participants are not who they appear to be. Some people are just
having fun with fantasy identities, but others are trying to con people by
telling hard luck stories and faking illnesses. Resist the temptation to meet
face to face with people you've met online without taking precautions, such
as taking along a group of friends.

**And what about the site itself?** Social networking sites, like any
online business, are always looking for ways to make a profit. Every participant is a valuable commodity in a database that can be used for marketing
and research. Before you become a member, read the site's privacy policy
to see how your personal data could be used. Remember, however, that
privacy policies can change, especially if a site goes out of business and
sells its assets.

You should also find out if you can remove your data from a site. Although
most sites allow you to deactivate your information, some sites never actually remove your personal information from their databases, leaving it open
to misuse in the future.

### 📟 TRY IT!

**Check your social networking sites**

**1.** Log in to any social networking site you use.

**2.** Locate the site's privacy policy and read it. Are you comfortable with the
ways in which the site protects your personal information?

**3.** If you are not familiar with the site's options for designating who can view
your personal data, find out how you can limit its public exposure.

**4.** Find out if you can delete your data from the site.

## ONLINE PRIVACY AND SAFETY GUIDELINES

**What should I do?** Online safety and privacy are becoming one of the most important aspects of computer use today. The average consumer has to remain constantly vigilant to detect if his or her personal data has been misused or has fallen into the wrong hands.

Cyberthreats are becoming more troubling. Who would imagine that the webcam at the top of your notebook computer screen could be remotely controlled by hackers to capture video of you without your knowledge?

If you recognize that anything on the Web or in e-mail messages is not necessarily private, you've got the right outlook. You can use the guidelines in Figure 28 to keep track of your personal data and stay safe online.

**FIGURE 28**

Online Privacy and Safety Guidelines

- Use a password to protect your data in case your computer is stolen.

- Don't leave your computer unattended in public places.

- Run antivirus software and keep it updated.

- Install software service packs and security patches as they become available, but make sure they are legitimate.

- Install and activate firewall software, especially if your computer is directly connected to the Internet by an ISDN, DSL, satellite, or cable connection.

- Do not publish or post personal information, such as your physical address, passwords, Social Security number, phone number, or account numbers, on your Web site, in your online resume, in your blog, or in other online documents.

- Be wary of contacts you make in public chat rooms and social networking sites.

- Don't click pop-up ads.

- Install and activate antispyware and ad-blocking software.

- Do not reply to spam.

- Ignore e-mail offers that seem too good to be true.

- Establish a throw-away e-mail account and use it when you have to provide your e-mail address to marketers and other entities whom you don't want to regularly correspond with.

- Make sure you control who has access to the data you post at social networking sites.

- Do not submit data to a social networking site until you've read its privacy policy and have made sure that you can remove your data when you no longer want to participate.

- Avoid using opt-out links in mass mailings unless you are certain the sender is legitimate.

- When using public computers, avoid financial transactions if possible. Make sure you log out from password-protected sites. Delete cookies and Internet history. Reboot the computer at the end of your session.

- Regard e-mail messages as postcards that can be read by anyone, so be careful what you write!

- Cover the webcam on your computer with a piece of tape when it is not in use.

## QuickCheck

1. Internet security suites usually include antivirus and antispyware tools. True or false? [          ]

2. [          ] software can block intrusion attempts such as hacker probes.

3. Most Web browsers include settings for blocking pop-up ads. True or false? [          ]

4. E-mail scams are usually distributed in mass mailings called [          ].

5. Using opt-out links is the most secure and dependable way to reduce the amount of spam you receive. True or false? [          ]

 CHECK ANSWERS

# BookOnCD

**ELECTRONIC VERSIONS** of your textbook are designed to be portable, interactive learning environments. This section offers an interactive overview of the popular BookOnCD.

## BOOKONCD BASICS

**What is the BookOnCD?** The BookOnCD is a multimedia version of your textbook with photos that come to life as videos, diagrams that become animations, screenshots that open to guided software tours, and computer-scored activities that can help improve your test scores.

**What's the most effective way to use the BookOnCD?** If you're accustomed to reading documents and Web pages on your computer screen, you can use the BookOnCD for most of your reading and studying. As you work through a chapter, you'll be able to view the multimedia elements in context and take QuickChecks at the end of each section. If you prefer to read from your printed textbook, you can start the BookOnCD whenever you want to view a multimedia element or work with a computer-scored activity.

**How do I start the BookOnCD?** To start the BookOnCD on any Windows computer, follow the instructions in the TRY IT! box below. If you have an OS X Mac, skip to the instructions on the next page.

## TRY IT!

**Start the BookOnCD**

**1.** Insert the BookOnCD into your computer's CD or DVD drive, label side up.

**2.** Wait a few seconds until the BookOnCD has loaded.

**3.** When the main Computer Concepts screen appears, proceed to step 4.
● If an Autoplay box appears, select *Run BookOnCD.exe.*
● If the CD does not start automatically, click the Start button, click Computer, and then double-click the CD or DVD drive icon.

The BookOnCD allows you to save your scores for QuickChecks, practice tests, and other activities, but for this session you do not need to track this data.

**4.** To disable tracking for now, make sure the box next to *Save Tracking data* is empty. If the box contains a check mark, click the box to empty it.

**5.** Click the **OK** button. The Tracking Options dialog box closes and the BookOnCD displays the first page of Chapter 1.

To disable tracking for a session, make sure this box is empty.

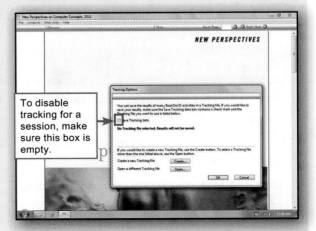

**What if I have a Mac?** If you have a Mac that runs Parallels or Boot Camp, that means you have access to the Windows operating system on your Mac. Boot up your Mac in Windows mode and then use the BookOnCD just as you would on a Windows computer.

If your Mac runs only OS X, you can still access the digital textbook by performing a simple conversion process. It takes just a few minutes; and when the process is complete, you'll have all the BookOnCD files on your Mac's hard drive. You can launch the book right from there, or you can copy the files to a CD or USB flash drive if that is more convenient.

**How do I convert the BookOnCD so it works on a Mac?** Make sure you have the BookOnCD supplied with your textbook, then use your browser to connect to *www.mediatechnicscorp.com/pub/samples/ NP2012MacPac.htm* and follow the instructions. When the MacPac page appears, you might want to print out the instructions so that you can easily follow them.

The MacPac file is about the size of two or three iTunes songs, so it does not take long to download it. Once the file is downloaded, follow the rest of the instructions to get your MacBookOnCD ready to go.

**How do I start the MacBookOnCD?** The setup process puts a MacBookOnCD folder icon on your desktop. The TRY IT! below guides you through the startup process.

**TRY IT!**

**Start the MacBookOnCD**

THESE INSTRUCTIONS ARE FOR MAC OS X USERS ONLY!

**1.** Make sure you have an NP2012 BookOnCD folder icon on your Mac desktop. If not, refer to the material at the top of this page for instructions on how to convert your BookOnCD to run on the Mac.

**2.** Double-click the **NP2012 BookOnCD** desktop icon.

**3.** When the Finder window appears, look for the MacBookOnCD program.

NOTE: You might also have a *BookOnCD.exe* program, but that is NOT the program that runs on the Mac. This is the Windows version of the BookOnCD.

**4.** Double-click **MacBookOnCD** and your digital textbook should open and display the Tracking Options dialog box.

The BookOnCD allows you to save your scores for QuickChecks, practice tests, and other activities, but for this session you do not need to track this data.

**5.** To disable tracking for now, make sure the box next to *Save Tracking data* is empty. If the box contains a check mark, click the box to empty it.

**6.** Click the **OK** button. The Tracking Options dialog box closes and the BookOnCD displays the first page of Chapter 1.

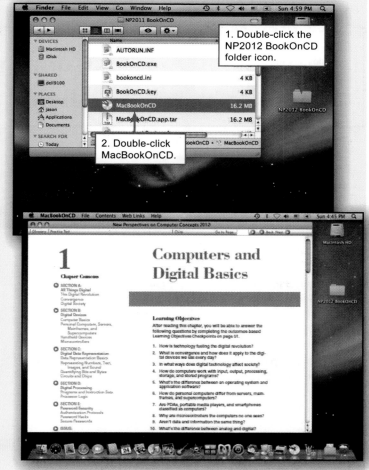

**How do I navigate through the book?** The BookOnCD menu and toolbar, near the top of the screen, contain tools you can use for navigation. The Next and Back buttons turn one page at a time. To get to the first page of any chapter, you can select it from the Contents menu.

The BookOnCD pages mirror the pages in the printed book. So if you want to take the QuickCheck that's on page 21 of your printed textbook, for example, you can use the Go to Page option on the toolbar to jump right to it.

**What are the other menu and navigation options?** The menu bar includes a Web Links menu with options that open your browser and connect to InfoWebLinks, the NP2012 Web site, and the Course Technology Web site. The menu bar also includes a Help menu where you can access instructions and troubleshooting FAQs. The Glossary button provides access to definitions for key terms. An Annotation button appears when your instructor has posted comments or lecture notes. If your instructor has not posted annotations, the button will not appear.

**How do I exit the BookOnCD?** When you have completed a session and want to close the BookOnCD, you can click the [X] button in the upper-right corner of the title bar (Windows). On Mac OS X, you can click MacBookOnCD on the menu bar and select Quit. Figure 29 helps you locate the Close button and BookOnCD navigation tools.

### FLASH PLAYER

The BookOnCD requires Adobe Flash Player for displaying labs. The Flash Player is installed on most computers. If the BookOnCD cannot find your Flash Player when it starts, you'll be directed to go online to download and install it.

**FIGURE 29**

Key Features of the BookOnCD Menu Bar and Toolbar

The Contents menu takes you to the first page of any chapter you select.

The Back button displays the previous page.

The Next button displays the next page.

The Glossary button helps you look up key terms.

To jump to a specific page, enter the page number in the box, then click the ➤ button.

The Close button closes the BookOnCD on Windows computers.

### 🖥 TRY IT!

**Open a chapter and navigate the BookOnCD**

**1.** Click **Contents** on the menu bar. The Contents menu appears.

**2.** Click **Chapter 2**.

**3.** When Chapter 2 appears, click the **Next** button twice until you see page 56.

**4.** Click the **Back** button twice to go back to the first page of Chapter 2.

**5.** Click the white box on the right side of Go to Page. Type **89**, then click the **Go to Page** ➤ button.

**6.** Click the ➤ **Go to Page** button. Now you should be back at the first page of Chapter 2.

**7.** Scroll down the page until you can see the Chapter Contents listing. As shown at right, you can use this list to quickly jump to Sections A, B, C, D, or E; Issues; Computers in Context; labs; and end-of-chapter activities.

**8.** Click ▶ **Section D** to jump to Section D.

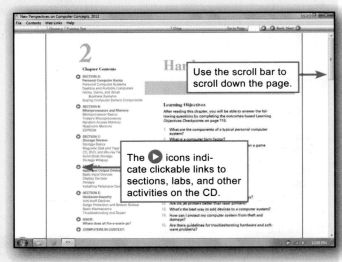

Use the scroll bar to scroll down the page.

The ▶ icons indicate clickable links to sections, labs, and other activities on the CD.

## MULTIMEDIA AND COMPUTER-SCORED ACTIVITIES

**What kinds of multimedia are included in the BookOnCD?** Figures in your book marked with the ▶ icon morph into multimedia screentours, animations, and videos. A screentour takes you on a guided software tour—even if you don't have the software installed on your computer! Animations and videos visually expand on the concepts presented in the text.

**How do I access screentours and other multimedia?** To access multimedia elements, simply click the ▶ icon while using the BookOnCD.

**Which activities are computer scored?** Figure 30 lists the BookOnCD activities that are computer scored. You can use these activities to gauge how well you remember and understand the material you read in the textbook.

Suppose you're reading Chapter 2. Work with the TRY IT! below to see how multimedia and computer-scored activities work.

**FIGURE 30**

BookOnCD Computer-scored Activities

**Pre-assessment Quiz**

**Interactive Summary**

**Interactive Situation Questions**

**Practice Tests**

**Concept Map**

**QuickChecks**

**Lab QuickChecks**

### ⌨ TRY IT!

**Explore multimedia and computer-scored activities**

**1.** Use the **Go to Page** control to jump to page 79.

**2.** On page 79, Figure 2-24 contains an ▶ icon. Click any line of the figure caption to launch the video.

**3.** When you want to stop the video, click any blank area of the BookOnCD page. To restart the video, click the ▶ icon again.

**4.** Now, try a computer-scored QuickCheck. Use the **Go to Page** control to get to page 87 and scroll down the page until you can see the entire set of QuickCheck questions.

**5.** Click the answer box for question 1, and then type your answer. Most answers are a single word. Upper- and lowercase have no effect on the correctness of your answer.

**6.** Press the **Tab** key to jump to question 2, and then type your answer. Don't worry if you don't know the answer; you haven't actually read Chapter 2 yet. Just make a guess for now.

**7.** When you have answered all the questions, click the ▶ CHECK ANSWERS icon. The computer indicates whether your answer is correct or incorrect.

**8.** Continue to click **OK** to check the rest of your answers.

**9.** When you've reviewed all your answers, the computer presents a score summary. Click **OK** to close the dialog box.

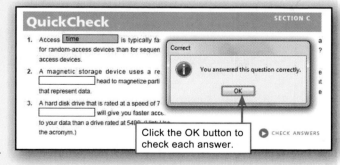

## NEW PERSPECTIVES LABS

**What about labs?** Your textbook gives you access to two kinds of labs. New Perspectives Labs are part of the BookOnCD. Student Edition Labs are located at the NP2012 CourseMate Web site. You'll learn how to access Student Edition Labs in Section E.

New Perspectives Labs give you hands-on experience applying concepts and using software discussed in each chapter. Labs on the BookOnCD are divided into topics, and each topic ends with a QuickCheck so that you can make sure you understand key concepts.

In addition to lab QuickChecks, each New Perspectives Lab also includes a set of assignments located in the Lab section of each chapter. Your instructor might require you to complete these assignments. You can submit them on paper, on disc, or as an e-mail message, according to your instructor's directions.

**How do I launch a lab?** First, navigate to the lab page using the New Perspectives Labs option from the Chapter Contents list or type in the corresponding page number from the printed book. Click the lab's ▶ icon to start it, as explained in the TRY IT! below.

### ⌨ TRY IT!

**Open a New Perspectives Lab**

**1.** Click **Contents** on the BookOnCD menu bar and select **Chapter 1**.

**2.** Scroll down to the Chapter Contents list and click ▶ **New Perspectives Labs**.

**3.** When the New Perspectives Labs page appears, click ▶ **Operating a Personal Computer**.

**4.** The lab window opens. Click the ⏩ button to view objectives for Topic 1.

**5.** Click the ⏩ button again to view page 1 of the lab. Read the information on the page, and then continue through the lab, making sure to follow any numbered instructions.

**6.** After page 8, you will encounter the first QuickCheck question. Click the correct answer, and then click the **Check Answer** button. After you find out if your answer was correct, click the ⏩ button to continue to the next question. Complete all the QuickCheck questions for Topic 1.

**7.** For this TRY IT! you don't have to complete the entire lab. When you are ready to quit, click the ⏺ button.

**8.** Click the ⏺ button again. Your Lab QuickCheck results are displayed.

**9.** Click the **OK** button to return to the BookOnCD.

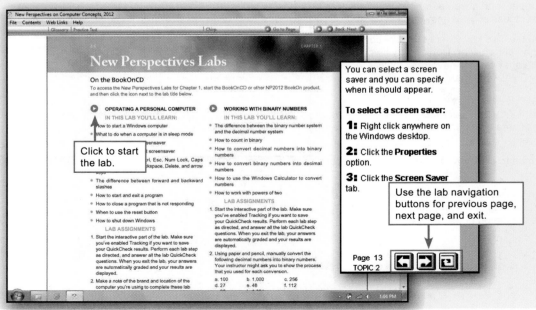

## TRACKING YOUR SCORES

**Can I save scores from QuickChecks, labs, and other activities?**
To save your scores, you have to create a Tracking file. The file can be located on a rewritable CD, your computer's hard disk, a USB flash drive, or a network drive where you have permission to store files.

**How do I make a Tracking file?** The Tracking Options dialog box lets you create a Tracking file and designate where you want to store it. Work with the TRY IT! below to create a Tracking file.

### TRY IT!

**Create a Tracking file**

**1.** Make sure your BookOnCD is open.

**2.** Click **File** on the BookOnCD menu bar, then click **Change Tracking Options**.

**3.** When the Tracking Options dialog box appears, click the **Create** button.

**4.** When the Create Tracking File dialog box appears, enter the requested data (see illustration at right), then click **Continue**. The Save As (Windows) or Save (Mac) dialog box appears.

**5.** Use the dialog box to specify the location and name for your Tracking file. (See the illustration at right for Windows or the illustration below for Macs.)

**6.** After selecting a name and location for your Tracking file, click the **Save** button.

**7.** Back at the Tracking Options dialog box, make sure there is a check mark in the box labeled *Save Tracking data*, then click the **OK** button. Now your Tracking file is ready to receive your scores.

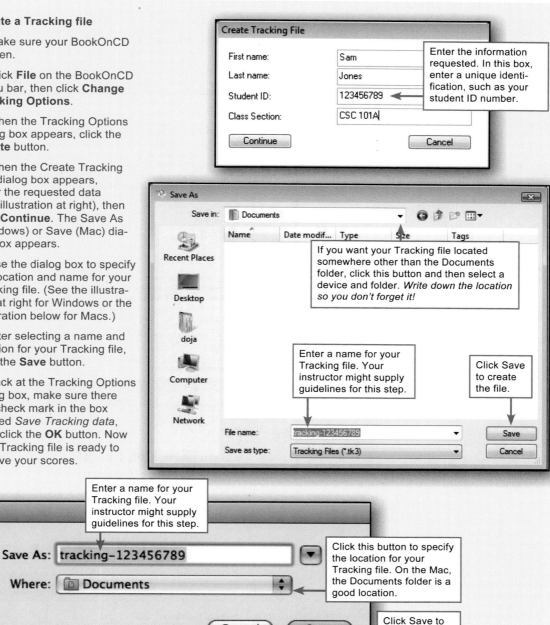

**How do I get scores into my Tracking file?** Whenever the Save Tracking data box is checked, all scored activities are automatically saved in your Tracking file. In the previous TRY IT!, you activated tracking; so until you go back into Tracking Options and remove the check mark from Tracking Options, your scores will be saved.

**What happens if I do an activity twice?** While tracking is active, all your scores are saved. If you do an activity twice, both scores are saved. Your scores are dated, so you and your instructor can determine which scores are the most recent.

**Can I review my scores?** You can see all your scores in a Tracking Report.

**Can I delete or change my scores?** No. Your Tracking data is encrypted and cannot be changed.

Work with the TRY IT! below to see how easy it is to save scores and view your Tracking Report.

**TRY IT!**

### Complete a Practice Test

To start tracking your scores, you can complete a Practice Test.

**1.** Click the **Practice Test** button located on the BookOnCD toolbar.

**2.** The first question of a ten-question Practice Test appears. Answer the question, then click the **Next** button.

**3.** Answer the remaining questions, then click the **Check Answers** button.

**4.** When you see your score summary, click the **OK** button. You can then step through each of your answers or view a study guide.

**5.** Click the **Study Guide** button. A browser window opens to display each Practice Test question, your answers, and corresponding page numbers in your textbook.

**6.** Close the Study Guide by clicking the ☒ button on your browser window (Windows) or clicking the browser name in the Mac menu bar and then selecting Quit.

**7.** Click the **Close** button on the Practice Test window to close it and save your scores.

### View the contents of your Tracking file

**1.** Click **File** on the BookOnCD menu bar.

**2.** Click **View Tracking Report**. Your computer opens your browser and displays a summary score for the Practice Test you completed. The list of summary scores grows as you save additional Practice Tests, QuickChecks, Interactive Summaries, Interactive Situation Questions, and Lab QuickChecks.

**3.** To close the Tracking Report, close the browser window (Windows) or the TextEdit window (Mac).

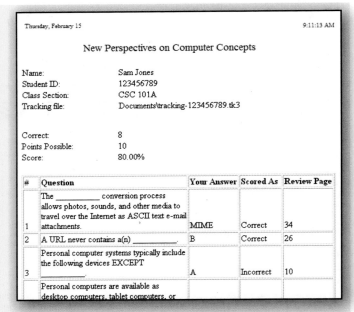

Thursday, February 15 — 9:11:13 AM

New Perspectives on Computer Concepts

Name: Sam Jones
Student ID: 123456789
Class Section: CSC 101A
Tracking file: Documents\tracking-123456789.tk3

Correct: 8
Points Possible: 10
Score: 80.00%

| # | Question | Your Answer | Scored As | Review Page |
|---|----------|-------------|-----------|-------------|
| 1 | The _____ conversion process allows photos, sounds, and other media to travel over the Internet as ASCII text e-mail attachments. | MIME | Correct | 34 |
| 2 | A URL never contains a(n) _____. | B | Correct | 26 |
| 3 | Personal computer systems typically include the following devices EXCEPT _____. | A | Incorrect | 10 |
| | Personal computers are available as desktop computers, tablet computers, or | | | |

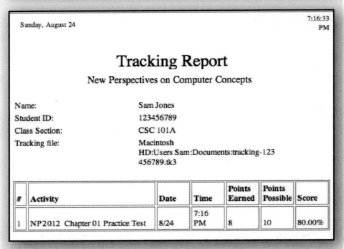

Sunday, August 24 — 7:16:33 PM

# Tracking Report

**New Perspectives on Computer Concepts**

Name: Sam Jones
Student ID: 123456789
Class Section: CSC 101A
Tracking file: Macintosh HD:Users Sam:Documents:tracking-123 456789.tk3

| # | Activity | Date | Time | Points Earned | Points Possible | Score |
|---|----------|------|------|---------------|-----------------|-------|
| 1 | NP2012 Chapter 01 Practice Test | 8/24 | 7:16 PM | 8 | 10 | 80.00% |

**How do I submit scores from my Tracking file?** You can use the Submit Tracking Data option on the File menu to send your scores to your instructor. The files are sent over an Internet service called WebTrack.

**Are the scores erased from my Tracking file when they are sent?** No. Your scores remain in your file—a copy is sent to your instructor. If your instructor's computer malfunctions and loses your data, you can resubmit your Tracking file. It is a good idea to back up your Tracking file using the Back Up Tracking File option on the File menu.

**What are chirps?** A chirp is a short message, similar to a Twitter-style tweet. You can use chirps to send queries to your instructor. Your instructor might also use chirps as a classroom polling system. Chirps work through WebTrack.

### TRY IT!

**Send your Tracking data and send a chirp**

**1.** Click **File** on the BookOnCD menu bar, then click **Submit Tracking Data**.

**2.** Make sure your instructor's WebTrack address is correctly displayed in the Tracking Data Destination dialog box, then click **Continue**.

**3.** Your computer opens a browser window, makes an Internet connection, and contacts the WebTrack server.

**4.** When the WebTrack screen appears, make sure the information displayed is correct, then click the **Submit** button.

**5.** When you see a message that confirms your data has been submitted, you can close the browser window.

**6.** To send a chirp, click the **Chirp** button on the BookOnCD toolbar.

**7.** When the Chirps panel appears, enter your message in the box labeled Your Message.

**8.** Click the **Send** button.

**9.** Close your BookOnCD.

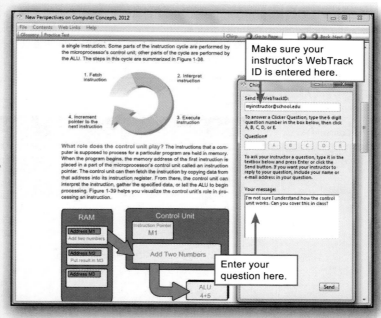

## QuickCheck

**1.** Figures in the book marked with an & sign morph into multimedia screentours, animations, and videos. True or false? [ ]

**2.** When you use the NP2012 BookOnCD, a(n) [ ] button appears if your instructor has posted comments or lecture notes.

**3.** To save your scores, you have to create a(n) [ ] file.

**4.** New Perspectives [ ] are divided into topics and each topic ends with a QuickCheck.

**5.** WebTrack provides a way to submit scores to your instructor. True or false? [ ]

 CHECK ANSWERS

# NP2012 CourseMate Web Site

THE INTERNET offers access to information that's useful to just about everyone, and New Perspectives students are no exception. When you purchase access to the New Perspectives NP2012 CourseMate Web site, you'll find targeted learning materials to help you understand key concepts and prepare for exams.

## WEB SITE RESOURCES

**What's on CourseMate?** The New Perspectives NP2012 CourseMate Web site includes an eBook, concept quizzes, games, and even audio files that you can download to your iPod or other portable device. Figure 31 highlights the features you'll find on the NP2012 CourseMate.

**FIGURE 31**

NP2012 CourseMate Features

### eBook
The NP2012 eBook gives you access to your textbook from any computer connected to the Internet.

### Detailed Objectives
Access an expanded version of the Learning Objectives that are included at the beginning of each chapter.

### TechTerm Flashcards
Make sure you understand all of the technical terms presented in the chapter.

### Chapter Overview CourseCasts
Listen to a five-minute audio presentation of chapter highlights on your computer or download the files to your MP3 player to study on the go.

### Audio Flashcards
Interact with downloadable audio flashcards to review key concepts terms from the chapter.

### Concept Quizzes
Check your understanding and ability to apply concepts.

### Student Edition Labs
Get hands-on practice with key topics presented in a chapter.

### Games
Have some fun while refreshing your memory about key concepts that might appear on the exam.

### Glossary
Get a quick overview of all the key terms presented in each chapter.

Orientation

## WEB SITE ACCESS

**How do I access the NP2012 CourseMate?** You can get to the site by opening your browser and typing *www.cengagebrain.com.*

**Do I need a password?** The first time you connect to CengageBrain, sign up for an account. When you have completed the short registration process, enter the ISBN for your book, and if you have an access code, enter it, too. Your materials are added to your dashboard for easy access. Click the link for the NP2012 CourseMate. From there, you can click links to each chapter's activities and information.

 **TRY IT!**

### Access the NP2012 CourseMate

**1.** Start your browser.

**2.** Click the address box and type:

Make sure to use all lowercase letters, insert no spaces, and use the / slash, not the \ slash.

**3.** Press the **Enter** key. The CengageBrain screen is displayed.

**4.** If you are accessing CengageBrain for the first time, click the **Sign Up** tab and follow the instructions to create your account.

**5.** Once you've created a CengageBrain account, you can log in by entering your user name and password, then clicking the **log in** button.

**6.** In the *Add a title to your bookshelf* box, enter the ISBN for your book and follow the links to add it to your bookshelf.

**7.** Once the title is added, you can look for the link to the CourseMate on the right side of the dashboard. The NP2012 CourseMate Welcome screen contains links to activities for each chapter of the textbook. Use the **Select Chapter** button to access Chapter 1. Your browser displays links to activities for the first chapter in your textbook.

**8.** You can always return to the Welcome screen by clicking the Home button on the Chapter toolbar. Click the **Home** button now.

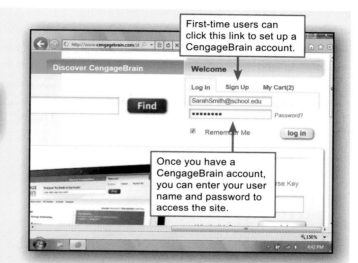

First-time users can click this link to set up a CengageBrain account.

Once you have a CengageBrain account, you can enter your user name and password to access the site.

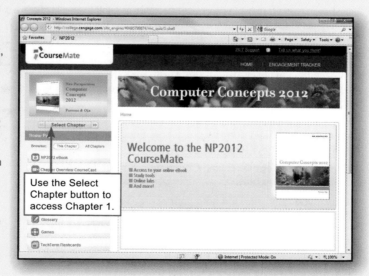

Use the Select Chapter button to access Chapter 1.

## COURSEMATE WEB SITE TOUR

**How do I use the resources at the NP2012 Web site?** The NP2012 CourseMate Web site is designed to help you review chapter material, prepare for tests, and extend your understanding of various topics.

The Chapter eBook contains text and figures from the printed textbook, videos, guided software tours, and InfoWebLinks.

The Chapter Overview presents a high-level introduction to chapter highlights. Use it as an orientation or as a quick refresher before an exam.

If you like a challenge, use the online games as a review activity; you'll get high scores if you understand the chapter material.

Concept quizzes are a great way to make sure that you understand and can apply key concepts presented in a chapter.

For last-minute review, load up your iPod with the Audio Flashcards. You can listen to them for a quick refresher on your way to the test!

**Can I submit scores from CourseMate activities to my instructor?** Your results from various CourseMate activities are automatically recorded for your instructor using the Engagement Tracker. You do not have to take any additional steps to send scores.

Follow the steps in the box below to explore the NP2012 CourseMate and find out how to view a summary of your scores.

### ▧ TRY IT!

**Explore the NP2012 CourseMate**

**1.** Connect to the NP2012 CourseMate, and use the **Select Chapter** button to access Chapter 1.

**2.** To listen to a CourseCast on your computer, click the **Chapter Overview CourseCast** link. You might have to wait a bit for the overview to begin, depending on the speed of your Internet connection. If you want to store a CourseCast on your computer or portable music player, right-click the link, click **Download Audio**, and then select a location for the CourseCast file. When you are ready to continue the tour, close the audio window.

**3.** Click the **Games** link and select the one of the games. Try your hand at a few questions, and then go back to the Chapter 1 page.

**4.** Click the **Concept Quiz** link. Complete a quiz and then click the **Done** button.

**5.** Check your answers and note your score. You can click the magnifying glass icon to see more details for each question. Your score is saved by the Engagement Tracker.

**6.** Look for the link to the eBook and click it. Use the Next page and Previous page buttons to navigate page by page.

**7.** Jump to page 6 and scroll down the page, if necessary, until you can see Figure 1-4.

**8.** Click to start the software tour.

**9.** When the tour ends, make sure that you can see the CourseMate menu.

Online games provide a fun way to review chapter material.

## STUDENT EDITION LABS

**How do I access Student Edition Labs?** Student Edition Labs help you review the material presented in the textbook and extend your knowledge through demonstrations and step-by-step practice.

### ⌨ TRY IT!

**Work with Student Edition Labs**

1. Make sure you're connected to the NP2012 CourseMate, and use the **Select Chapter** button to access Chapter 1.

2. Click the link for **Student Edition Labs**.

3. Take a few minutes to walk through the section **Guide to Student Edition Labs**.

4. Click **Select a Lab** and then click **Understanding the Motherboard** to start the lab.

5. Complete the first section of the lab, including the Intro, Observe, Practice, and Review activities.

6. When you've completed the review activity, a report containing your results is displayed. Use the Print button to print your report, or return to the NP2012 CourseMate.

7. Exit the lab by clicking the **Exit** button in the upper-right corner of the lab window.

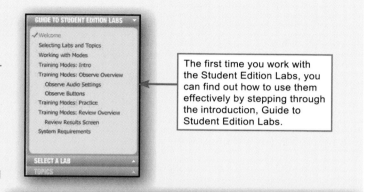

The first time you work with the Student Edition Labs, you can find out how to use them effectively by stepping through the introduction, Guide to Student Edition Labs.

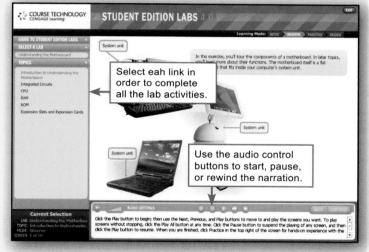

Select eah link in order to complete all the lab activities.

Use the audio control buttons to start, pause, or rewind the narration.

# QuickCheck                                                    SECTION E

1. To access the NP2012 CourseMate, you need a user name and password. True or false? [        ]

2. The [            ] Tracker automatically records your scores.

3. When you're at the NP2012 CourseMate, you can use the [            ] button to display the Welcome screen.

4. The Chapter Overview [            ] is a five-minute audio presentation of chapter highlights.

5. The Student Edition [            ] help you review through demonstrations and step-by-step practice.

 CHECK ANSWERS

# Computer Concepts 2012

Parsons :: Oja

# 1

# Computers and Digital Basics

## Chapter Contents

▶ **SECTION A:**
**ALL THINGS DIGITAL**
The Digital Revolution
Convergence
Digital Society

▶ **SECTION B:**
**DIGITAL DEVICES**
Computer Basics
Personal Computers, Servers,
   Mainframes, and
   Supercomputers
Handheld Devices
Microcontrollers

▶ **SECTION C:**
**DIGITAL DATA REPRESENTATION**
Data Representation Basics
Representing Numbers, Text,
   Images, and Sound
Quantifying Bits and Bytes
Circuits and Chips

▶ **SECTION D:**
**DIGITAL PROCESSING**
Programs and Instruction Sets
Processor Logic

▶ **SECTION E:**
**PASSWORD SECURITY**
Authentication Protocols
Password Hacks
Secure Passwords

▶ **ISSUE:**
**ARE YOU BEING TRACKED?**

▶ **COMPUTERS IN CONTEXT:**
**MARKETING**

▶ **NEW PERSPECTIVES LABS**

▶ **REVIEW ACTIVITIES**

▶ **ON THE WEB**

## Learning Objectives

After reading this chapter, you will be able to answer the following questions by completing the outcomes-based Learning Objectives Checkpoints on page 51.

1. How is technology fueling the digital revolution?

2. What is convergence and how does it apply to the digital devices we use every day?

3. In what ways does digital technology affect society?

4. How do computers work with input, output, processing, storage, and stored programs?

5. What's the difference between an operating system and application software?

6. How do personal computers differ from servers, mainframes, and supercomputers?

7. Are PDAs, portable media players, and smartphones classified as computers?

8. Why are microcontrollers the computers no one sees?

9. Aren't data and information the same thing?

10. What's the difference between analog and digital?

11. How do digital devices use 1s and 0s to work with numbers, text, images, and sound?

12. Why is there so much jargon pertaining to bits and bytes?

13. What hardware components manipulate the bits that represent data?

14. Why do computers need programs?

15. How do a microprocessor's ALU and control unit work?

16. How do hackers steal passwords?

17. How can I create secure passwords?

## InfoWebLinks

Visit the InfoWebLinks site to access additional resources **ⓦ** that accompany this chapter.

## Multimedia and Interactive Elements

When using the BookOnCD or CourseMate eBook, the ▶ icons are clickable to access multimedia resources.

## Pre-Assessment Quiz

Take the pre-assessment quiz to find out how much you know about the topics in this chapter. ▶

### Apply Your Knowledge The information in this chapter will give you the background to:

- Inventory the digital devices you own
- Put digital technology in the context of history, pop culture, and the global economy
- Read computer ads with an understanding of technical terminology

- Select secure passwords for protecting your computer and Internet logins
- Use a password manager to keep track of all your passwords
- Use digital devices with an awareness of how they might infringe on your privacy

## Try It

### WHAT'S MY DIGITAL PROFILE?

The average American consumer owns more than 24 digital devices. Before you begin Chapter 1, take an inventory of your digital equipment to find the brands, models, and serial numbers. Tuck this information in a safe place. It can come in handy when you need to call technical support, arrange for repair services, or report missing equipment.

**1.** Fill in the following table for any digital equipment you own, rent, lease, or use.

|  | Brand | Model | Serial Number |
|---|---|---|---|
| Computer |  |  |  |
| Keyboard |  |  |  |
| Mouse |  |  |  |
| Monitor |  |  |  |
| Printer |  |  |  |
| Digital camera |  |  |  |
| Digital music player |  |  |  |
| Internet or network device |  |  |  |
| Mobile phone |  |  |  |
| Game console |  |  |  |
| Other (list) |  |  |  |

# All Things Digital

**IN A SIMPLER TIME** of poodle skirts, saddle shoes, and ponytails, consumers used a telephone to communicate, switched on a radio for music, watched the television for news, went to a movie theater for entertainment, trudged to the library for research, and headed to the nearest pizza joint for a game of pinball. Today, technology offers an unprecedented number of choices for entertainment, information, and communication. It has changed the fabric of life in significant ways. We're using innovative new products, adjusting to industries in transformation, watching new markets emerge, and grappling with complex issues that have the potential to influence culture, politics, and economics on a global scale. Section A offers an overview of digital technology within the context of social and economic change.

## THE DIGITAL REVOLUTION

**What is the digital revolution?** The **digital revolution** is an ongoing process of social, political, and economic change brought about by digital technology, such as computers and the Internet. The digital revolution became a significant factor in the 1980s, as computers and other digital devices became popular and as the Internet opened global communications.

The term *digital revolution* was probably coined as a parallel to the term *industrial revolution*, and in that sense it promises to bring about a similar level of social and economic change. The digital revolution is creating an Information Society, in which owning, generating, distributing, and manipulating information becomes a significant economic and cultural activity.

The digital revolution is happening now. Every day new digital innovations challenge the status quo and require societies to make adjustments to traditions, lifestyles, and legislation.

**What technologies are fueling the digital revolution?** The digital revolution revolves around a constellation of technologies, including digital electronics, computers, communications networks, the Web, and digitization. Before you learn about these technologies in greater detail later in the book, the following overview explains the big picture.

**What's the significance of digital electronics?** Digital electronics use electronic circuits to represent data. In the 1940s and 1950s, engineers began to develop digital electronic devices and refine the electronic components used to build them. Transistors and then integrated circuits, which we call computer chips, were key factors in making electronic devices increasingly smaller and less expensive (Figure 1-1).

Consumers first became acquainted with digital electronics through digital watches that appeared in 1972, and then with handheld electronic calculators popularized by Texas Instruments in 1973. Today, digital electronic devices include computers, portable media players such as iPods, digital cameras and camcorders, cell phones, radios and televisions, GPSs (global positioning systems), DVD and CD players, e-book readers, digital voice recorders, and handheld gaming consoles. Even cars and appliances, such as microwave ovens, refrigerators, and washing machines, include digital electronics for control, monitoring, and fault diagnosis.

TERMINOLOGY NOTE

The word *digital* comes from the root *digit*. In Latin, the word *digitus* means finger or toe. The modern use of the term *digital* is probably derived from the idea of counting on your fingers.

**FIGURE 1-1**

Digital devices, such as this wireless mouse, are built from solid state circuit boards and computer chips, making them small, light, responsive, inexpensive, and durable.

Without digital electronics, you'd be listening to bulky vacuum-tube radios instead of toting sleek iPods; computers would be huge machines, priced far beyond the reach of individuals; and your favorite form of entertainment would probably be foosball.

**When did computers enter the picture?** Engineers built the first digital computers during World War II for breaking codes and calculating missile trajectories. By the 1950s, a few computers were being used for business data processing applications, such as payroll and inventory management. Businesses adopted computers with increasing enthusiasm as benefits for cutting costs and managing mountains of data became apparent.

During the antiestablishment era of the 1960s, the digital revolution was beginning to transform organizations, but had little effect on ordinary people. As with many technologies, computers were initially viewed with some measure of suspicion by consumers, who worried that impersonal data processing machines were treating people simply as numbers (Figure 1-2).

When the first personal computers became available in 1976, sales got off to a slow start. Without compelling software applications, personal computers, such as the Apple II, seemed to offer little for their $2,400 price. As the variety of software increased, however, consumer interest grew. In 1982, *TIME* magazine's annual Man of the Year award went to the computer, an indication that computers had finally gained a measure of acceptance by the person in the street.

As generations of computer users since that time have discovered, computers are handy devices. They displaced typewriters for creating documents, obsoleted mechanical calculators for number crunching, and took games to an entirely new dimension. Ambitious parents snapped up computers and educational software for their children and school systems set about equipping schools with computer labs.

In 1982, computers might have gained recognition in *TIME* magazine, but fewer than 10% of U.S. households had a computer. Working on a standalone computer wasn't for everyone. People without interest in typing up corporate reports or school papers, crunching numbers for accounting, or playing computer games weren't tempted to become active soldiers in the digital revolution. Social scientists even worried that people would become increasingly isolated as they focused on computer activities rather than social ones. Computer ownership increased at a gradual pace until the mid-1990s, and then it suddenly accelerated as shown in the graph in Figure 1-3.

TERMINOLOGY NOTE

Prices noted in this text are in U.S. dollars. For currency conversions, go to any currency conversion Web site, such as *gocurrency.com* or *xe.com*.

FIGURE 1-2

In the 1950s and 1960s, data used by government and business computers was coded onto punched cards that contained the warning "Do not fold, tear, or mutilate this card." Similar slogans were used by protesters who were concerned that computers would have a dehumanizing effect on society.

*Do not fold, bend, spindle, or mutilate*

FIGURE 1-3

Household ownership of personal computers in the United States

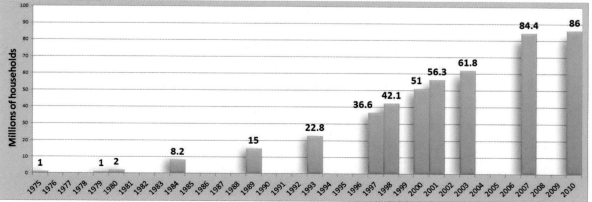

*Source: U.S. Census Bureau and Consumer Electronics Association*

**What caused the sudden upswing in computer ownership?**
The second phase of the digital revolution materialized when the Internet was opened to public use. The **Internet** is a global computer network originally developed as a military project, then handed over to the National Science Foundation for research and academic use.

When commercial Internet use was first allowed in 1995, companies such as AOL and CompuServe began to offer Internet access and e-mail to a quickly growing list of subscribers. **E-mail**, a form of electronic communication, was an application for the masses and finally a reason to buy a computer and join the digital revolution.

In addition to e-mail, the Internet offers many ways for people to communicate and interact. The Internet has turned the old idea of social isolation on its head; instead of computers reducing human interaction, computer networks seem to encourage new types of interpersonal communications and relationships.

Electronic communication can be divided into two categories. **Synchronous communication** takes place in real time similar to a phone conversation. Chat groups, Web conferencing, and Internet telephony, such as Skype, are examples of synchronous communications.

**Asynchronous communication** does not require both parties to be online at the same time. Instead, one person can post a message, which can later be accessed by one or more other people. Blogs (short for Web logs) and your Facebook wall are examples of asynchronous communications.

**Online social networks**, such as Classmates and Facebook (Figure 1-4), have become wildly popular. They offer a variety of ways to interact and communicate, including e-mail, blogs, chat, and posts. Your Facebook page contains posts that your friends can access asynchronously.

Other social networking options include Twitter, a service for posting short text messages from the Twitter Web site or from compatible applications on mobile phones or other handheld devices. Messages cannot exceed 140 characters. They are posted publicly unless you restrict posts to a list of authorized recipients, called followers.

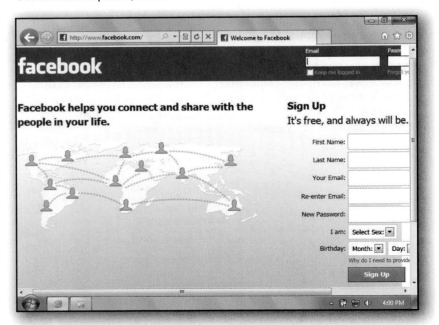

**FIGURE 1-4**

Online social networks offer netizens a place to look up old friends and meet friends of friends. ▶ When using a digital version of your textbook, such as the BookOnCD, click the round icon in this figure for an overview of social networking sites.

The Internet allows people to share resources as well as interact. Individuals' computers can be linked together in grid networks with powerful processing capabilities. One of the most ambitious grid computing efforts, SETI@home, uses the Internet to connect personal computers of more than 3 million volunteers from all over the world to analyze deep space radio signals in the search for extraterrestrial life.

A **computer network** is a group of computers linked by wired or wireless technology to share data and resources. Network technology existed before the Internet became popular, but the first computer networks were mainly deployed in schools and businesses. They were complicated to set up, unreliable, and offered only local connectivity. Network technology eventually became consumer-friendly, allowing homeowners to connect multiple computers for sharing printers, files, and an Internet connection.

Wireless networks offer even more advantages. Wi-Fi hotspots provide access to the Internet in coffee shops and many other locations. Whereas the Internet enhances communications, wireless network technology offers convenience and makes digital information as accessible as radio stations.

**What about the Web?** When historians look back on the digital revolution, they are certain to identify the Web as a major transformative influence. The **Web** (short for *World Wide Web*) is a collection of linked documents, graphics, and sounds that can be accessed over the Internet. The Web has changed centuries-old business models, revolutionized the flow of information, and created a new virtual world.

Online stores pioneered by Amazon.com transformed the face of retailing. Rummage sales have gone global with Web sites such as eBay. Consumers now have more direct access to products and services, such as music downloads and airline reservations.

The publisher of telephone's ubiquitous Yellow Pages used to advertise "Let your fingers do the walking." That catchphrase has never been more true as Web surfers' fingers jog miles over their keyboards each day to find answers, read the news, get sports scores, and check the weather forecast. In 2010, there were more than 234 million Web sites, each with hundreds or thousands of pages containing information.

Fallout from the massive pool of Web-based information includes the proliferation of misinformation and disinformation. Anyone can post virtually anything on the Web, so researchers and ordinary netizens who use the Web have had to develop strategies to sift for the truth.

A key aspect of the Web is that it adds content and substance to the Internet. Without the Web, the Internet would be like a library without any books or a railroad without any trains. From storefronts to online magazines to multiplayer games, the Web has made Internet access a compelling digital technology for just about everyone.

**Cyberspace** is a term that refers to entities that exist largely within computer networks (Figure 1-5). The virtual world isn't reality in the sense of bricks and mortar, or flesh and blood. You might envision online stores as similar to shops in your local mall, but in reality they are simply a collection of data and images stored at a Web site. The Web defines much of the landscape of cyberspace, and its graphics and sounds make things seem real.

**How does digitization factor into the digital revolution?** **Digitization** is the process of converting text, numbers, sound, photos, and video into data that can be processed by digital devices. Some of the most obvious effects of the digital revolution can be attributed to digitization.

**FIGURE 1-5**

The term *cyberspace* was coined by science fiction writer William Gibson in his novelette *Burning Chrome*.

Digital images have changed the photographic industry. More than 99% of all cameras sold are digital, and the market for camera film is dwindling rapidly. One-hour photo processing labs, so popular in the 1990s, are disappearing from the strip-market landscape now that consumers can easily print their snapshots at home or from a Walmart photo kiosk. Digital images can also be easily modified, encouraging all sorts of creative uses, but rendering photographic evidence somewhat less authoritative than it was in the pre-digital past.

Digital imaging, such as computed tomography used in CT scans, has had profound effects in medicine. The advantage of digital images is that they can be easily stored and transmitted. For example, rather than sending an X-ray to a consulting physician by overnight mail, a digital X-ray can be quickly transmitted over the Internet.

Digital video is responsible for special effects in movies, new trends in 3-D animation, portable video, and surging consumer interest in home video. The film industry has become much more technology oriented and job openings reflect the need for specialists in graphics and motion video. Feature-length 3-D animated films are responsible for stunning technology breakthroughs, such as the ability to realistically depict the movement of clothing on a moving character and animate individual strands of hair or fur (Figure 1-6).

At the consumer level, computer gaming is probably the most significant force driving research into faster computers and more sophisticated graphics processing.

Digital music first became popular when Internet-based file-sharing networks like Napster offered free music downloads. The term **download** refers to the practice of copying a file from a remote computer to a local computer, such as when you copy a song from the Internet to your computer's hard disk. By disregarding copyrights and enabling users to pirate copyrighted music, file-sharing networks ran afoul of the law and many were forced to shut down. Apple and other astute companies saw a business opportunity in digital music, and online music stores, such as iTunes, quickly became popular.

Online music stores are transforming the industry by changing the way music is marketed, bought, and played. The ability to purchase a single song, rather than an entire album, is making recording artists reconsider some of the shovelware they've been producing to bulk up albums.

Human speech can also be digitized. Weather reports on weatherband radio are read by computerized voice synthesizers. Automated telephone systems understand caller comments by using voice recognition. United Airlines' sophisticated telephone-based automated reservation system can handle an entire reservation by collecting customers' verbal responses to computerized questions about routes and travel dates.

## CONVERGENCE

**What is convergence?** Your cell phone has a camera. Your clock has a radio. Your watch functions as a compass. You can watch movies on your iPod touch. All these are examples of technological **convergence**, a process by which several technologies with distinct functionalities evolve to form a single product.

In the pre-digital days, convergence often meant combining two technologically different devices in a single box. Old clock radios, for example,

**FIGURE 1-6**

Animators at Pixar Animation Studios created software called Fizt to individually simulate each of the 3 million hairs that flow and flutter on furry animated characters.

combined a transistor radio and wind-up clock into a single case. Digital technology makes convergence much easier. Modern digital clock radios use a single microchip programmed for clock and radio functionality.

Convergence is currently working its magic on cell phones, PDAs, computers, portable media players, digital cameras, GPSs, watches, and e-book readers. These devices are gradually acquiring overlapping features and seem to be headed toward becoming a single device.

Another technology in convergence is voice communication. The current mix of land lines, cell phones, and Voice over IP burdens consumers with multiple handsets, numbers, and rate plans. Most people would like to have a single telephone number that can be used while at home, at work, or traveling. The phone must have a full set of features, such as emergency 911, caller ID, and voice mail. One vision for voice communication convergence is a Voice over IP phone that operates over home-, school-, or work-based broadband Internet connections, and switches automatically to a mobile network for use in other locations.

**How does convergence affect consumers?** Convergence tends to offer enhanced functionality and convenience. An average consumer owns more than 24 digital devices. Rather than juggle a cell phone, portable media player, camera, GPS, and computer, combining their features puts your data in a single device with a single charger.

**Why does convergence seem to take so long?** Technology sometimes outstrips society's ability to deal with it. Many aspects of the digital revolution challenge the adaptability of societies and individuals. Laws and customs tend to change more slowly than technology; therefore technologies might be ready for deployment, but people and institutions are not ready to use them productively or responsibly.

Apple's foray into handheld computers illustrates the barriers that can hinder convergence. In 1993, Apple introduced a handheld device called the Newton that featured a small screen, personal organizer software, e-mail, and network connectivity (Figure 1-7). You'll recognize these features as being similar to today's iPod. Unfortunately, the Newton was too large to fit in a shirt pocket and its handwriting module failed to recognize all but the most painstakingly printed characters. But the real problem was that people just didn't have much use for the product and so it was discontinued.

In 2004, Apple risked another foray into the handheld market, this time with a portable media player called the iPod. In contrast to the Newton, the iPod became an immediate hit because a huge population of young music lovers immediately recognized its value.

Technologies don't necessarily develop evenly and sometimes bottlenecks prevent or delay convergence. In an ideal world, an iPhone could be used as a mobile phone, portable media player, GPS, and Web browser. It might also be used to serve as a wireless link between a full-size portable computer and the Internet. But as many users have discovered, today's batteries are quickly drained by watching a movie or providing Internet service to other devices.

iPhone-based activities are also limited by cell service capacity. If you aren't in a 4G service area, access to the Internet can be slow. By the time GPS maps appear, you might have traveled so far that you are outside of the map's boundaries.

Convergence successfully takes place only when a series of technologies come into alignment, and when a clear social or economic necessity exists.

TERMINOLOGY NOTE

*Voice over IP (VoIP)* refers to voice conversations that are routed over the Internet, rather than over land lines or cellular phones. It is also called IP telephony or Internet telephony.

**FIGURE 1-7**

The Apple Newton was an early attempt to develop a handheld computing device that combined an appointment book, contact manager, clock, alarm, and calculator. It lacked a key element for success, which turned out to be the ability to work with digital music.

## DIGITAL SOCIETY

**How does digital technology affect freedom and democracy?**
Freedom of speech is the cornerstone of democracy. It can be defined as being able to speak freely without censorship or fear of reprisal. The concept is not limited to speaking, but includes all forms of expression, including writing, art, and symbolic actions. The more inclusive term *freedom of expression* is sometimes used instead of *freedom of speech*.

Freedom of speech is not an absolute. Most societies prohibit or repress some types of expression, such as hate speech, libel, pornography, and flag burning. Although freedom of expression is guaranteed under the U.S. Constitution, the European Convention on Human Rights, and the Universal Declaration of Human Rights, these documents recognize the necessity for some restrictions, which might vary from one society to the next. Incidents ranging from the controversy over teaching evolution in schools to the Arab world's fury over cartoons of Mohammed illustrate that societies draw the freedom of speech line in different places. The types of expression that are allowed or prohibited in a particular country are, in many respects, a reflection of its culture (Figure 1-8).

FIGURE 1-8

The 1960 movie *Inherit the Wind* was based on the trial of John Scopes, who was accused of violating a state law that prohibited teaching evolution in state-funded schools.

Digital technologies and communications networks make it easy to cross cultural and geographic boundaries. News, television shows, music, and art from all over the globe are accessible on the Internet. The Internet has the potential to expand freedom of speech by offering every person on the globe a forum for personal expression using personal Web sites, blogs, chat groups, and collaborative Wikis. Anonymous Internet sites such as Freenet and **anonymizer tools** that cloak a person's identity even make it possible to exercise freedom of speech in situations where reprisals might repress it.

Internet information that seems innocuous in some cultures is not acceptable in others. Governments, parents, and organizations sometimes find it necessary to censor the Internet by limiting access and filtering content. China has some of the most draconian Internet censorship in the world. It blocks access to Web sites such as the BBC, The New York Times, Amnesty International, and Human Rights Watch. U.S. firms allegedly supplied the Chinese government with software necessary to erect its sophisticated filtering system.

Chinese Internet censorship might seem excessive, but it is by no means the only instance of free speech suppression. eBay has banned listings for any merchandise that could "promote or glorify hatred, violence or racial intolerance, or items that promote organizations with such views (e.g., KKK, Nazis, neo-Nazis, Skinhead Aryan Nation)." Parents frequently use filtering software such as Net Nanny and Safe Eyes. The U.S. Digital Millennium Copyright Act essentially censors technical information by making it a crime to publish information about cracking DVD and CD copy protection.

Despite attempts to censor and filter speech on the Internet, it seems clear that digital technology opens the door to freedom of expression in unprecedented ways. Limitations on Internet speech are likely to change, too, as technology evolves and as societies come to grips with the balance between freedom and responsibility.

**TERMINOLOGY NOTE**

A Wiki is one or more collaborative documents posted on the Web that can be viewed and changed by users. For example, Wikipedia is a collection of documents that form an encyclopedia. Visitors to the Wikipedia Web site can view definitions and information on a huge variety of topics and make changes to entries that are not correct or complete.

**Has digital technology changed the way we view privacy?**
Citizens of free societies have an expectation of privacy, which in the
words of Supreme Court Justices Warren and Brandeis is "the right to be
let alone." Digital technology use has exerted substantial pressure to dimin-
ish privacy by making it possible to easily collect and distribute data about
individuals without their knowledge or consent.

In the United States, the expectation of privacy is derived from Fourth
Amendment protections against unreasonable searches and seizures. The
Fourth Amendment was formulated long before digital technologies such
as e-mail and GPS devices. Legislation and court decisions pertaining to
new technologies do not always strike the right balance between privacy
and competing principles, such as free speech or free trade.

Privacy also encompasses confidentiality—the expectation that personal
information will not be collected or divulged without permission. Internet
marketers have a whole bag of tricks for getting personal information, and
hackers are adept at breaking into sensitive databases to obtain confidential information.

Surveillance is viewed by many people as an invasion of privacy. Digital
technology, such as GPS devices embedded in cell phones and cars,
makes it much too easy to track people without their knowledge.

Some individuals dismiss the erosion of privacy saying, "I have nothing to
hide, so I don't care." But even they typically don't want stores, hackers,
and curious onlookers to have access to data about what they buy, read,
and watch, who they call, where they travel, and what they say.

Digital technology has not so much changed the way we view privacy—
most citizens still have a reasonable expectation that their private lives will
remain so. Instead, technology may help us develop a better appreciation
for privacy and an understanding of the nuances that differentiate private
and public spaces.

**How does digital technology affect**
**intellectual property? Intellectual property**
refers to the ownership of certain types of information, ideas, or representations. It includes
patented, trademarked, and copyrighted material, such as music, photos, software, books,
and films. In the past, such works were difficult
and expensive to copy.

Digital technology has made it easy to produce
copies with no loss in quality from the original.
Pirating—illegal copying and distribution of
copyrighted material—is simple and inexpensive. It has caused significant revenue loss
for software publishers, recording studios, and
film producers. The fight against piracy takes many forms, from passing
strict anti-piracy laws, to scrambling, encryption, digital rights management schemes that physically prevent copying, and anti-piracy videos
(Figure 1-9).

Digital technology adds complexity to intellectual property issues. For
example, artists used to think nothing of cutting out various photos from
magazines and pasting them together to form a collage. It is even easier

**FIGURE 1-9**

Most moviegoers have seen the
rock-video style "Don't Copy"
trailer. Consumer education
is one front in the war against
piracy. ▶ You can view this
video from your digital textbook.

to download digital images from the Web and paste them into reports, add them to Web pages, and incorporate them into works of art. Without permission, however, such digital cut and paste is not allowed.

Some films contain scenes that parents would rather their children not see. Even some scenes from family-oriented Harry Potter films might be too intense for young viewers. So, why not simply edit them out digitally to make a new DVD that the little tykes can watch? Such modifications are not allowed under current U.S. law, even for private viewing.

In the U.S. it is legal to make a backup copy of software CDs or DVDs that you own. However, if a CD, for example, is copy protected to prevent you from making a copy, it is against the law to break the copy protection. So, legally you have a right to a backup, but you don't have the right to circumvent the copy protection to legally create one!

Bucking protectionist trends are **open source** projects that promote copying, free distribution, peer review, and user modification. Linux is an open-source computer operating system that can be modified and freely distributed. Open source application software includes the popular OpenOffice.org suite, Firefox Web browser, Thunderbird e-mail, and ClamWin antivirus.

Digital technology makes it possible to copy and modify films, music, software, and other data, but a tricky balancing act is required to allow consumers flexibility to use data while protecting the income stream to artists, performers, and publishers.

**What effect does digital technology have on the economy?** Digital technology is an important factor in global and national economies, in addition to affecting the economic status of individuals. **Globalization** can be defined as the worldwide economic interdependence of countries that occurs as cross-border commerce increases and as money flows more freely among countries. Consumers gain access to a wide variety of products, including technology products manufactured in locations scattered all over the globe. Countries that benefit from significant technology output include the United States, Japan, China, India, South Korea, and Finland (Figure 1-10).

Global communications technology offers opportunities for teleworkers in distant countries. Customer service lines for U.S.-based companies, such as IBM, Dell, and Hewlett-Packard, are often staffed by offshore technicians who earn far more than they could if working for a company in their home country.

Globalization, fueled by digital technology, has controversial aspects, however. Worker advocates object to the use of cheap offshore labor that displaces onshore employees.

Some individuals are affected by the **digital divide**, a term that refers to the gap between people who have access to technology and those who do not. Typically, digital have-nots face economic barriers. They cannot afford

FIGURE 1-10

Finland is a world leader in wireless technology. Its flagship technology company, Nokia, is responsible for about 25% of the country's exports.

computers, cell phones, and Internet access, or they are located in an economically depressed region where electricity is not available to run digital devices, power satellite dishes, and pick up Internet signals. But technology offers opportunity even to digital have-nots. For example, the Village Phone Project provides a small loan to entrepreneurs known as "village phone ladies" who sell minutes on their cell phones to neighbors who cannot afford their own land lines or cell phones (Figure 1-11).

Globalization is an ongoing process that will have far reaching effects on people in countries with developed technologies and those with emerging economies. Digital technology will be called upon to open additional economic opportunities without disrupting the lifestyles of currently prosperous nations.

**So what's the point?** Learning about digital technology is not just about circuits and electronics, nor is it only about digital gadgets, such as computers and portable music players. Digital technology permeates the very core of modern life. Understanding how this technology works and thinking about its potential can help you comprehend many issues related to privacy, security, freedom of speech, and intellectual property. It will help you become a better consumer and give you insights into local and world events.

You might even come to realize that some people who are responsible for making decisions about technology have only a vague idea of how it works. Without a solid grasp of technology problems, business leaders have little hope of finding effective solutions and politicians will be unable to make valid decisions pertaining to technology legislation.

As you continue to read this textbook, don't lose sight of the big picture. On one level, in this course you might be simply learning about how to use a computer and software. On a more profound level, however, you are accumulating knowledge about digital technology that applies to broader cultural and legal issues that are certain to affect your life far into the future.

**FIGURE 1-11**

In less technically developed countries such as Uganda and Bangladesh, women make a living by selling cell phone time to their neighbors.

# QuickCheck                                              SECTION A

1. Transistors and [_____] circuits were responsible for making electronic devices smaller and less expensive.

2. The [_____] revolution was fueled by technologies such as computers and the Internet.

3. A computer [_____] is a group of computers linked together to share data and resources.

4. The process of converting text, numbers, sound, photos, or video into data that can be processed by a computer is called [_____].

5. A(n) [_____] is one or more collaborative documents, such as an encyclopedia, posted on the Web that can be viewed and changed by the public.

▶ CHECK ANSWERS

# Digital Devices

**WHETHER YOU REALIZE IT** or not, you already know a lot about the devices that fuel the digital revolution. You've picked up information from commercials and news articles, from books and movies, from conversations and correspondence—perhaps even from using a variety of digital devices and trying to figure out why they don't always work! The quintessential digital device is the computer. Section B provides an overview that's designed to help you start organizing what you know about digital devices, beginning with computers.

## COMPUTER BASICS

**What is a computer?** The word *computer* has been part of the English language since 1646; but if you look in a dictionary printed before 1940, you might be surprised to find a computer defined as a person who performs calculations! Prior to 1940, machines designed to perform calculations were referred to as calculators and tabulators, not computers. The modern definition and use of the term *computer* emerged in the 1940s, when the first electronic computing devices were developed.

Most people can formulate a mental picture of a computer, but computers do so many things and come in such a variety of shapes and sizes that it might seem difficult to distill their common characteristics into an all-purpose definition. At its core, a **computer** is a multipurpose device that accepts input, processes data, stores data, and produces output, all according to a series of stored instructions (Figure 1-12).

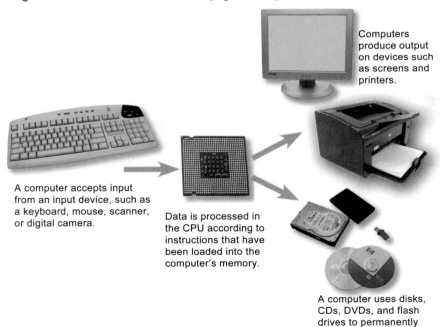

**FIGURE 1-12**

A computer can be defined by its ability to accept input, process data, store data, and produce output, all according to a set of instructions from a computer program.

Computers produce output on devices such as screens and printers.

A computer accepts input from an input device, such as a keyboard, mouse, scanner, or digital camera.

Data is processed in the CPU according to instructions that have been loaded into the computer's memory.

A computer uses disks, CDs, DVDs, and flash drives to permanently store data.

**What is input?** Computer **input** is whatever is typed, submitted, or transmitted to a computer system. Input can be supplied by a person, by the environment, or by another computer. Examples of the kinds of input that computers can accept include words and symbols in a document, numbers for a calculation, pictures, temperatures from a thermostat, audio signals from a microphone, and instructions from a computer program. An input device, such as a keyboard or mouse, gathers data and transforms it into a series of electronic signals for the computer to store and manipulate.

**What is output?** **Output** is the result produced by a computer. Some examples of computer output include reports, documents, music, graphs, and pictures. Output devices display, print, or transmit the results of processing.

**What does *process data* mean?** Technically speaking, **data** refers to the symbols that represent facts, objects, and ideas. Computers manipulate data in many ways, and this manipulation is called **processing**. Some of the ways that a computer can process data include performing calculations, modifying documents and pictures, keeping track of your score in a fast-action game, drawing graphs, and sorting lists of words or numbers (Figure 1-13).

In a computer, most processing takes place in a component called the **central processing unit** or **CPU**. The CPU of most modern computers is a **microprocessor**, which is an electronic component that can be programmed to perform tasks based on data it receives. You'll learn more about microprocessors later in the chapter. For now, visualize a microprocessor as the little black box that's the brain of a digital device.

**How do computers store data?** A computer stores data so that it will be available for processing. Most computers have more than one place to put data, depending on how the data is being used. **Memory** is an area of a computer that temporarily holds data waiting to be processed, stored, or output. **Storage** is the area where data can be left on a permanent basis when it is not immediately needed for processing.

Data is typically stored in files. A computer file, usually referred to simply as a **file**, is a named collection of data that exists on a storage medium, such as a hard disk, CD, DVD, or flash drive. A file can contain data for a term paper, Web page, e-mail message, or music video. Some files also contain instructions that tell the computer how to perform various tasks.

**What's so significant about a computer's ability to store instructions?** The series of instructions that tells a computer how to carry out processing tasks is referred to as a **computer program**, or simply a program. These programs form the **software** that sets up a computer to do a specific task. When a computer *runs* software, it performs the instructions to carry out a task.

Take a moment to think about the way you use a simple handheld calculator to balance your checkbook each month. You're forced to do the calculations in stages. Although you can store data from one stage and use it in the next stage, you cannot store the sequence of formulas—the program—required to balance your checkbook. Every month, therefore, you have to perform a similar set of calculations. The process would be much simpler if your calculator remembered the sequence of calculations and just asked you for this month's checkbook entries.

**FIGURE 1-13**

An unsorted list is input into the computer, where it is processed in the CPU and output as a sorted list.

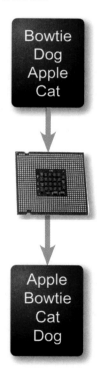

The idea of a **stored program** means that a series of instructions for a computing task can be loaded into a computer's memory. These instructions can easily be replaced by a different set of instructions when it is time for the computer to perform another task. This ability to switch programs makes computers multipurpose machines.

The stored program concept allows you to use your computer for one task, such as word processing, and then easily switch to a different type of computing task, such as editing a photo or sending an e-mail message. It is the single most important characteristic that distinguishes a computer from other simpler and less versatile digital devices, such as watches, calculators, and pocket-sized electronic dictionaries.

**What kinds of software do computers run?** Computers run two main types of software: application software and system software. A computer can be applied to many tasks, such as writing, number crunching, video editing, and online shopping. **Application software** is a set of computer programs that helps a person carry out a task. Word processing software, for example, helps people create, edit, and print documents. Personal finance software helps people keep track of their money and investments. Video editing software helps people create and edit home movies—and even some professional films.

Whereas application software is designed to help a person carry out a task, the primary purpose of **system software** is to help the computer system monitor itself in order to function efficiently. An example of system software is a computer **operating system** (OS), which is essentially the master controller for all the activities that take place within a computer. Although an operating system does not directly help people perform application-specific tasks, such as word processing, people do interact with the operating system for certain operational and storage tasks, such as starting programs and locating data files.

## PERSONAL COMPUTERS, SERVERS, MAINFRAMES, AND SUPERCOMPUTERS

**Are computers categorized in any way?** At one time it was possible to define three distinct categories of computers. Mainframes were housed in large, closet-sized metal frames. Minicomputers were smaller, less expensive, and less powerful computers that were able, nevertheless, to provide adequate computing power for small businesses. Microcomputers were clearly differentiated from computers in other categories because their CPUs consisted of a single microprocessor chip.

Today, microprocessors are no longer a distinction between computer categories because just about every computer uses one or more microprocessors as its CPU. The term *minicomputer* has fallen into disuse and the terms *microcomputer* and *mainframe* are used with less and less frequency.

Computers are versatile machines that can perform a truly amazing assortment of tasks, but some computers are better suited than others for certain tasks. Categorizing computers is a way of grouping them according to criteria such as usage, cost, size, and capability. Experts don't necessarily agree on the categories or the devices placed in each category, but commonly used computer categories include personal computers, servers, mainframes, and supercomputers.

---

**TERMINOLOGY NOTE**

The term *personal computer* is sometimes abbreviated as *PC*. However, *PC* can also refer to a specific type of personal computer that descended from the original IBM PC and runs Windows software.

In this book, *PC* refers to IBM PC descendants. It is not used as an abbreviation for *personal computer*.

**What is a personal computer?** A **personal computer** is a microprocessor-based computing device designed to meet the computing needs of an individual. It typically provides access to a wide variety of computing applications, such as word processing, photo editing, and e-mail.

Personal computers are available as desktop or portable models, and in a variety of shapes, sizes, and colors. You'll learn more about the wide variety of personal computer in the Hardware chapter. For now, simply remember that computers like those pictured in Figure 1-14 are classified as personal computers.

Personal computer designs run the gamut from drab gray boxes to colorful curvy cases.

**What is a workstation?** The term **workstation** has two meanings. It can simply refer to an ordinary personal computer that is connected to a network. A second meaning refers to powerful desktop computers used for high-performance tasks, such as medical imaging and computer-aided design, that require a lot of processing speed. Some workstations contain more than one microprocessor, and most have circuitry specially designed for creating and displaying three-dimensional and animated graphics. Workstations, such as the one pictured in Figure 1-15, typically cost a bit more than an average personal computer.

**Is an Xbox a personal computer?** A **videogame console**, such as Nintendo's Wii, Sony's PlayStation, or Microsoft's Xbox, is not generally referred to as a personal computer because of its history as a dedicated game device. Videogame consoles originated as simple digital devices that connected to a TV set and provided only a pair of joysticks for input.

Today's videogame consoles contain microprocessors that are equivalent to any found in a fast personal computer, and they are equipped to produce graphics that rival those on sophisticated workstations. Add-ons such as keyboards, DVD players, and Internet access make it possible to use a videogame console to watch DVD movies, send and receive e-mail, and participate in online activities such as multiplayer games. Despite these features, videogame consoles like the one in Figure 1-16 fill a specialized niche and are not considered a replacement for a personal computer.

A workstation resembles a desktop computer, but typically features more processing power and storage capacity.

A videogame console includes circuitry similar to a personal computer's, but its input and output devices are optimized for gaming.

**What makes a computer a server?** In the computer industry, the term *server* has several meanings. It can refer to computer hardware, to a specific type of software, or to a combination of hardware and software. In any case, the purpose of a **server** is to serve computers on a network (such as the Internet or a home network) by supplying them with data.

Any software or digital device, such as a computer, that requests data from a server is referred to as a **client**. For example, on the Internet, a server might respond to a client's request for a Web page. Servers also handle the steady stream of e-mail that travels among clients from all over the Internet. A server might also allow clients within a home, school, or business network to share files or access a centralized printer.

Remarkably, just about any personal computer, workstation, mainframe, or supercomputer can be configured to perform the work of a server. That fact should emphasize the concept that a server does not require a specific type of hardware. Nonetheless, computer manufacturers such as IBM, SGI, HP, and Dell offer devices called blade servers and storage servers (Figure 1-17) that are especially suited for storing and distributing data on a network. Server prices vary, depending on configuration, but tend to be more similar to workstation prices than personal computer prices. Despite impressive performance on server-related tasks, these machines do not offer features such as sound cards, DVD players, and other fun accessories, so they are not a suitable alternative to a personal computer.

**What's so special about a mainframe computer?** A **mainframe computer** (or simply a mainframe) is a large and expensive computer capable of simultaneously processing data for hundreds or thousands of users. Mainframes are generally used by businesses or governments to provide centralized storage, processing, and management for large amounts of data. Mainframes remain the computer of choice in situations where reliability, data security, and centralized control are necessary.

The price of a mainframe computer typically starts at $100,000 and can easily exceed $1 million. Its main processing circuitry is housed in a closet-sized cabinet (Figure 1-18); but after large components are added for storage and output, a mainframe computer system can fill a good-sized room.

**How powerful is a supercomputer?** A computer falls into the **supercomputer** category if it is, at the time of construction, one of the fastest computers in the world (Figure 1-19).

**FIGURE 1-17**

Some servers look like personal computers, whereas others are housed in industrial-looking cases.

**FIGURE 1-18**

This IBM z10 E12 mainframe computer weighs 2,807 pounds and is about 6.5 feet tall.

**FIGURE 1-19**

In 2010, a Cray XT5HE computer named Jaguar was the fastest supercomputer. Using more than 18,000 processors, the Jaguar clocks peak performance speeds of 2.3 petaflops or 2.3 quadrillion operations per second.

Because of their speed, supercomputers can tackle complex tasks and compute-intensive problems that just would not be practical for other computers. A **compute-intensive** problem is one that requires massive amounts of data to be processed using complex mathematical calculations. Molecular calculations, atmospheric models, and climate research are all examples of projects that require massive numbers of data points to be manipulated, processed, and analyzed.

Common uses for supercomputers include breaking codes, modeling worldwide weather systems, and simulating nuclear explosions. One impressive simulation, which was designed to run on a supercomputer, tracked the movement of thousands of dust particles as they were tossed about by a tornado.

At one time, supercomputer designers focused on building specialized, very fast, and very large CPUs. Today, most supercomputer CPUs are constructed from thousands of microprocessors. Of the 500 fastest supercomputers in the world, the majority use microprocessor technology.

## HANDHELD DEVICES

**Are handheld devices computers?** Handheld digital devices include familiar gadgets such as iPhones, iPods, Garmin GPSs, Blackberry Torches, and Kindles. These devices incorporate many computer characteristics. They accept input, produce output, process data, and include storage capabilities. Handheld devices vary in their programmability and their versatility. Technically, most of these devices could be classified as computers, but they are customarily referred to by function, for example, as mobile phones or portable media players.

**What is a PDA?** The first handheld digital devices were PDAs. A **PDA** (personal digital assistant) is a pocket-sized digital appointment book with a small keyboard or a touch-sensitive screen, designed to run on batteries and be used while holding it. PDAs synchronize appointment data and contact lists with desktop computers by exchanging data over a dedicated wired or wireless connection. Originally, PDAs were not equipped for voice communications, which distinguished them from cell phones. The term *PDA* is falling into disuse now that mobile phones offer scheduling and contact management features.

**How do mobile phones fit into the picture?** Cell phones were originally designed exclusively for voice communications. They have since evolved into devices such as those in Figure 1-20 that offer sophisticated features such as touch screen, full qwerty keypad, text messaging, e-mail, Web access, removable storage, camera, FM radio, digital music player, GPS navigation, and a wide selection of applications and maps.

**FIGURE 1-20**

Many mobile phones feature a small keyboard, others accept handwriting input, and some work with touch screen icons.

Feature rich mobile phones are sometimes called **smartphones**. These devices contain a microprocessor and have many characteristics of computers, but they are not usually referred to as computers because of their origins as simple cell phones.

**How are iPods classified?** iPods are enhanced MP3 players. The basic idea behind MP3 players is to store music that has been converted into digital format from CDs or downloaded from the Web. The music is stored in a type of file called MP3, which stands for MPEG-1 Audio Layer-3.

Sharing MP3 files on the Web became hugely popular despite its questionable legality. After many music sharing sites were shut down, Apple created a legal Web-based music store called iTunes where music is stored in a proprietary, copy-protected file format and sold by the song or by the album. The iPod (Figure 1-21) was designed as a portable music player, and enhanced versions of the device now store and play video and photos as well.

iPods and similar devices are classified as **portable media players** because their main strength is playing music, showing videos, and storing photos. Like other handheld digital devices, these players have many computer characteristics. An iPod, for example, contains a microprocessor, accepts input, has significant storage capacity on its built-in hard disk, and outputs stored music, video, and images. Some portable media players have limited programmability. They are not designed for users to add software and their lack of a keyboard or touch screen puts severe limits on data entry.

**What about apps?** When iPhone ads say "There's an app for that," it means that the device is programmable and, like a full-size computer, can run various **apps** (applications) that include games, calendars, stock market trackers, tour guides, highway traffic monitors, and news feeds. Devices such as the iPhone, iPod touch, iPad, and Android phones are programmable and can run apps.

Apps for handheld devices are typically more limited than the applications available for full-size desktop or notebook computers. Small screens and tiny keyboards impose some limits on the types of applications that function effectively. Hardware limitations from memory and storage capacity, processor speed, and battery life also limit the sophistication of apps for handheld devices.

## MICROCONTROLLERS

**What is a microcontroller?** Have you ever wondered how a guided missile reaches its target or how your refrigerator knows when to initiate a defrost cycle? What controls your microwave oven, digital video recorder, washing machine, and watch? Many common appliances and machines are controlled by embedded microcontrollers. A **microcontroller** is a special-purpose microprocessor that is built into the machine it controls. A microcontroller is sometimes called a computer-on-a-chip or an embedded computer because it includes many of the elements common to computers.

**How does a microcontroller work?** Consider the microcontroller in a Sub-Zero refrigerator. It accepts user input for desired temperatures in the refrigerator and freezer compartments. It stores these desired temperatures in memory. Temperature sensors collect additional input of the actual temperatures. The microcontroller processes the input data by comparing the actual temperature to the desired temperature. As output, the microcontroller sends signals to activate the cooling motor as necessary. It also generates a digital readout of the refrigerator and freezer temperatures.

**Is a microcontroller really a computer?** Recall that a computer is defined as a multipurpose device that accepts input, produces output, stores data, and processes it according to a stored program. A microcontroller seems to fit the input, processing, output, and storage criteria that define computers. Some microcontrollers can even be reprogrammed to perform different tasks.

Technically, a microcontroller could be classified as a computer, just as mobile phones and portable media players can be. Despite this technicality, however, microcontrollers tend to be referred to as processors rather than as computers because in practice they are used for dedicated applications, not as multipurpose devices.

**Why are microcontrollers significant?** Microcontrollers, such as the one in Figure 1-22, can be embedded in all sorts of everyday devices, enabling machines to perform sophisticated tasks that require awareness and feedback from the environment. When combined with wireless networks, devices with embedded processors can relay information to Web sites, cell phones, and a variety of data collection devices. Machines and appliances with embedded processors tend to be smarter about their use of resources—such as electricity and water—which makes them environmentally friendly.

Perhaps the most significant effect of microcontrollers is that they are an almost invisible technology, one that doesn't require much adaptation or learning on the part of the people who interact with microcontrolled devices. However, because microcontrollers remain mostly out-of-sight and out-of-mind, it is easy for their use to creep into areas that could be detrimental to quality of life, privacy, and freedom. That innocuous GPS chip in your cell phone, for example, can be useful if you're lost and need 911 assistance, but it could potentially be used by marketers, law enforcement, and others who want to track your location without your consent.

**FIGURE 1-22**

A microcontroller is usually mounted on a circuit board and then installed in a machine or appliance using wires to carry input and output signals.

# QuickCheck

1. A computer is a digital device that processes data according to a series of [        ] instructions.

2. Computer data is temporarily stored in [        ], but is usually transferred to [        ] where it can be left on a more permanent basis.

3. [        ] computers are available in desktop and portable models.

4. A digital device, such as a computer, is called a(n) [        ] when it requests data from a server.

5. A(n) [        ] is a special-purpose microprocessor that is built into the machine it controls.

▶ CHECK ANSWERS

# Digital Data Representation

**COMPUTERS AND OTHER DIGITAL DEVICES** work with all sorts of "stuff," including text, numbers, music, images, speech, and video. The amazing aspect of digital technology is that it distills all these different elements down to simple pulses of electricity and stores them as 0s and 1s. Understanding the data representation concepts presented in Section C will help you grasp the essence of the digital world and get a handle on all the jargon pertaining to bits, bytes, megahertz, and gigabytes.

## DATA REPRESENTATION BASICS

**What is data?** As you learned earlier in the chapter, *data* refers to the symbols that represent people, events, things, and ideas. Data can be a name, a number, the colors in a photograph, or the notes in a musical composition.

**Is there a difference between data and information?** In everyday conversation, people use the terms *data* and *information* interchangeably. Nevertheless, some technology professionals make a distinction between the two terms. They define data as the symbols that represent people, events, things, and ideas. Data becomes information when it is presented in a format that people can understand and use. As a general rule, remember that (technically speaking) data is used by machines, such as computers; information is used by humans.

**What is data representation?** **Data representation** refers to the form in which data is stored, processed, and transmitted. For example, devices such as mobile phones, iPods, and computers store numbers, text, music, photos, and videos in formats that can be handled by electronic circuitry. Those formats are data representations. Data can be represented using digital or analog methods.

**What's the difference between analog and digital?** For a simple illustration of the difference between analog and digital, consider the way you can control the lights in a room using a traditional light switch or a dimmer switch (Figure 1-23). A traditional light switch has two discrete states: on and off. There are no in-between states, so this type of light switch is digital. A dimmer switch, on the other hand, has a rotating dial that controls a continuous range of brightness. It is, therefore, analog.

**Digital data** is text, numbers, graphics, sound, and video that has been converted into discrete digits such as 0s and 1s. In contrast, **analog data** is represented using an infinite scale of values.

**How does digital data work?** Imagine that you want to send a message by flashing a light. Your light switch offers two states: on and off. You could use sequences of ons and offs to represent various letters of the alphabet. To write down the representation for each letter, you can use 0s and 1s. The 0s represent the off state of your light switch; the 1s indicate the on state. For example, the sequence on on off off would be written 1100, and you might decide that sequence represents the letter *A*.

TERMINOLOGY NOTE

The word *data* can be correctly treated either as a plural noun or as an abstract mass noun, so phrases such as "The data are being processed" and "The data is being processed" are both correct usage. In this textbook, data is treated as in the latter case and is paired with singular verbs and modifiers.

FIGURE 1-23

A computer is a digital device, more like a standard light switch than a dimmer switch.

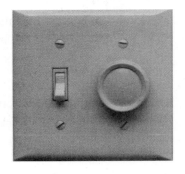

Digital devices are electronic and so you can envision data flowing within these devices as pulses of light. In reality, digital signals are represented by two different voltages, such as +5 volts and 0 volts. They can also be represented by two different tones as they flow over a phone line. Digital data can also take the form of light and dark spots etched onto the surface of a CD or the positive and negative orientation of magnetic particles on the surface of a hard disk. Regardless of the technology, however, digital data is always represented by two states denoted as 0 and 1.

The 0s and 1s used to represent digital data are referred to as binary digits. It is from this term that we get the word *bit*—*bi*nary digi*t*. A **bit** is a 0 or 1 used in the digital representation of data.

## REPRESENTING NUMBERS, TEXT, IMAGES, AND SOUND

**How do digital devices represent numbers?** **Numeric data** consists of numbers that might be used in arithmetic operations. For example, your annual income is numeric data, as is your age. The price of a bicycle is numeric data. So is the average gas mileage for a vehicle, such as a car or an SUV. Digital devices can represent numeric data using the binary number system, also called base 2.

The **binary number system** has only two digits: 0 and 1. No numeral like 2 exists in this system, so the number two is represented in binary as 10 (pronounced *one zero*). You'll understand why if you think about what happens when you're counting from 1 to 10 in the familiar decimal system. After you reach 9, you run out of digits. For ten, you have to use the digits 10—zero is a placeholder and the 1 indicates one group of tens.

In binary, you just run out of digits sooner—right after you count to 1. To get to the next number, you have to use the zero as a placeholder and the 1 indicates one group of 2s. In binary then, you count 0 (zero), 1 (one), 10 (one zero), instead of counting 0, 1, 2 in decimal. If you need to brush up on binary numbers, refer to Figure 1-24 and to the lab at the end of the chapter.

The important point to understand is that the binary number system allows digital devices to represent virtually any number simply by using 0s and 1s. Digital devices can then perform calculations using these numbers.

| Decimal (Base 10) | Binary (Base 2) |
|---|---|
| 0 | 0 |
| 1 | 1 |
| 2 | 10 |
| 3 | 11 |
| 4 | 100 |
| 5 | 101 |
| 6 | 110 |
| 7 | 111 |
| 8 | 1000 |
| 9 | 1001 |
| 10 | 1010 |
| 11 | 1011 |
| 1000 | 1111101000 |

**FIGURE 1-24**

The decimal system uses ten symbols to represent numbers: 0, 1, 2, 3, 4, 5, 6, 7, 8, and 9. The binary number system uses only two symbols: 0 and 1.

## How do digital devices represent words and letters?

**Character data** is composed of letters, symbols, and numerals that are not used in arithmetic operations. Examples of character data include your name, address, and hair color. Just as Morse code uses dashes and dots to represent the letters of the alphabet, a digital computer uses a series of bits to represent letters, characters, and numerals. Figure 1-25 illustrates how a computer can use 0s and 1s to represent the letters and symbols in the text *HI!*

Digital devices employ several types of codes to represent character data, including ASCII, EBCDIC, and Unicode. **ASCII** (American Standard Code for Information Interchange, pronounced *ASK* ee) requires only seven bits for each character. For example, the ASCII code for an uppercase *A* is 1000001. ASCII provides codes for 128 characters, including uppercase letters, lowercase letters, punctuation symbols, and numerals.

A superset of ASCII, called **Extended ASCII**, uses eight bits to represent each character. For example, Extended ASCII represents the uppercase letter *A* as 01000001. Using eight bits instead of seven bits allows Extended ASCII to provide codes for 256 characters. The additional Extended ASCII characters include boxes and other graphical symbols. Figure 1-26 lists the Extended ASCII character set.

**FIGURE 1-25**

A computer treats the letters and symbols in the word *HI!* as character data, which can be represented by a string of 0s and 1s.

01001000   01001001   00100001

**FIGURE 1-26**

The Extended ASCII code uses eight 1s and 0s to represent letters, symbols, and numerals. The first 32 ASCII characters are not shown in the table because they represent special control sequences that cannot be printed. The two blank entries are space characters.

| Char | Code | Char | Code | Char | Code | Char | Code | Char | Code | Char | Code | Char | Code | Char | Code |
|---|---|---|---|---|---|---|---|---|---|---|---|---|---|---|---|
|  | 00100000 | > | 00111110 | \ | 01011100 | z | 01111010 | ÿ | 10011000 | ╢ | 10110110 | ╘ | 11010100 | ≥ | 11110010 |
| ! | 00100001 | ? | 00111111 | ] | 01011101 | { | 01111011 | Ö | 10011001 | ╖ | 10110111 | ╒ | 11010101 | ≤ | 11110011 |
| " | 00100010 | @ | 01000000 | ^ | 01011110 | \| | 01111100 | Ü | 10011010 | ╕ | 10111000 | ╓ | 11010110 | ⌠ | 11110100 |
| # | 00100011 | A | 01000001 | _ | 01011111 | } | 01111101 | ¢ | 10011011 | ╣ | 10111001 | ╫ | 11010111 | ⌡ | 11110101 |
| $ | 00100100 | B | 01000010 | ` | 01100000 | ~ | 01111110 | £ | 10011100 | ║ | 10111010 | ╪ | 11011000 | ÷ | 11110110 |
| % | 00100101 | C | 01000011 | a | 01100001 | ⌂ | 01111111 | ¥ | 10011101 | ╗ | 10111011 | ┘ | 11011001 | ≈ | 11110111 |
| & | 00100110 | D | 01000100 | b | 01100010 | Ç | 10000000 | ₧ | 10011110 | ╝ | 10111100 | ┌ | 11011010 | ° | 11111000 |
| ' | 00100111 | E | 01000101 | c | 01100011 | ü | 10000001 | ƒ | 10011111 | ╜ | 10111101 | █ | 11011011 | ∙ | 11111001 |
| ( | 00101000 | F | 01000110 | d | 01100100 | é | 10000010 | á | 10100000 | ╛ | 10111110 | ▄ | 11011100 | · | 11111010 |
| ) | 00101001 | G | 01000111 | e | 01100101 | â | 10000011 | í | 10100001 | ┐ | 10111111 | ▌ | 11011101 | √ | 11111011 |
| * | 00101010 | H | 01001000 | f | 01100110 | ä | 10000100 | ó | 10100010 | └ | 11000000 | ▐ | 11011110 | ⁿ | 11111100 |
| + | 00101011 | I | 01001001 | g | 01100111 | à | 10000101 | ú | 10100011 | ┴ | 11000001 | ▀ | 11011111 | ² | 11111101 |
| , | 00101100 | J | 01001010 | h | 01101000 | å | 10000110 | ñ | 10100100 | ┬ | 11000010 | α | 11100000 | ■ | 11111110 |
| - | 00101101 | K | 01001011 | i | 01101001 | ç | 10000111 | Ñ | 10100101 | ├ | 11000011 | ß | 11100001 |  | 11111111 |
| . | 00101110 | L | 01001100 | j | 01101010 | ê | 10001000 | ª | 10100110 | ─ | 11000100 | Γ | 11100010 |  |  |
| / | 00101111 | M | 01001101 | k | 01101011 | ë | 10001001 | º | 10100111 | ┼ | 11000101 | π | 11100011 |  |  |
| 0 | 00110000 | N | 01001110 | l | 01101100 | è | 10001010 | ¿ | 10101000 | ╞ | 11000110 | Σ | 11100100 |  |  |
| 1 | 00110001 | O | 01001111 | m | 01101101 | ï | 10001011 | ⌐ | 10101001 | ╟ | 11000111 | σ | 11100101 |  |  |
| 2 | 00110010 | P | 01010000 | n | 01101110 | î | 10001100 | ¬ | 10101010 | ╚ | 11001000 | µ | 11100110 |  |  |
| 3 | 00110011 | Q | 01010001 | o | 01101111 | ì | 10001101 | ½ | 10101011 | ╔ | 11001001 | τ | 11100111 |  |  |
| 4 | 00110100 | R | 01010010 | p | 01110000 | Ä | 10001110 | ¼ | 10101100 | ╩ | 11001010 | Φ | 11101000 |  |  |
| 5 | 00110101 | S | 01010011 | q | 01110001 | Å | 10001111 | ¡ | 10101101 | ╦ | 11001011 | Θ | 11101001 |  |  |
| 6 | 00110110 | T | 01010100 | r | 01110010 | É | 10010000 | « | 10101110 | ╠ | 11001100 | Ω | 11101010 |  |  |
| 7 | 00110111 | U | 01010101 | s | 01110011 | æ | 10010001 | » | 10101111 | ═ | 11001101 | δ | 11101011 |  |  |
| 8 | 00111000 | V | 01010110 | t | 01110100 | Æ | 10010010 | ░ | 10110000 | ╬ | 11001110 | ∞ | 11101100 |  |  |
| 9 | 00111001 | W | 01010111 | u | 01110101 | ô | 10010011 | ▒ | 10110001 | ╧ | 11001111 | φ | 11101101 |  |  |
| : | 00111010 | X | 01011000 | v | 01110110 | ö | 10010100 | ▓ | 10110010 | ╨ | 11010000 | ε | 11101110 |  |  |
| ; | 00111011 | Y | 01011001 | w | 01110111 | ò | 10010101 | │ | 10110011 | ╤ | 11010001 | ∩ | 11101111 |  |  |
| < | 00111100 | Z | 01011010 | x | 01111000 | û | 10010110 | ┤ | 10110100 | ╥ | 11010010 | ≡ | 11110000 |  |  |
| = | 00111101 | [ | 01011011 | y | 01111001 | ù | 10010111 | ╡ | 10110101 | ╙ | 11010011 | ± | 11110001 |  |  |

An alternative to the 8-bit Extended ASCII code, called **EBCDIC** (Extended Binary-Coded Decimal Interchange Code, pronounced *EB seh dick*), is usually used only by older, IBM mainframe computers.

**Unicode** (pronounced *YOU ni code*) uses sixteen bits and provides codes for 65,000 characters—a real bonus for representing the alphabets of multiple languages. For example, Unicode represents an uppercase *A* in the Russian Cyrillic alphabet as 0000010000010000.

**Why do ASCII and Extended ASCII provide codes for 0, 1, 2, 3, 4, 5, 6, 7, 8, and 9?** While glancing at the table of ASCII codes in Figure 1-26, you might have wondered why the table contains codes for 0, 1, 2, 3, and so on. Aren't these numbers represented by the binary number system? A computer uses Extended ASCII character codes for 0, 1, 2, 3 , etc. to represent numerals that are not used for calculations. For example, you don't typically use your Social Security number in calculations, so it is considered character data and represented using Extended ASCII. Likewise, the numbers in your street address can be represented by character codes rather than binary numbers.

**How can bits be used to store images?** Images, such as photos, pictures, line art, and graphs, are not small, discrete objects like numbers or the letters of the alphabet. To work with images, they must be digitized.

Images can be digitized by treating them as a series of colored dots. Each dot is assigned a binary number according to its color. For example, a green dot might be represented by 0010 and a red dot by 1100, as shown in Figure 1-27. A digital image is simply a list of color numbers for all the dots it contains.

**How can bits be used to store sound?** Sound, such as music and speech, is characterized by the properties of a sound wave. You can create a comparable wave by etching it onto a vinyl platter—essentially how records were made in the days of jukeboxes and record players. You can also represent that sound wave digitally by sampling it at various points, and then converting those points into digital numbers. The more samples you take, the closer your points come to approximating the full wave pattern. This process of sampling, illustrated in Figure 1-28, is how digital recordings are made.

**FIGURE 1-27**

An image can be digitized by assigning a binary number to each dot.

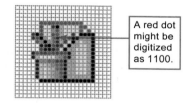

A red dot might be digitized as 1100.

**FIGURE 1-28**

A sound wave can be sampled at fraction-of-a-second time intervals. Each sample is recorded as a binary number and stored.

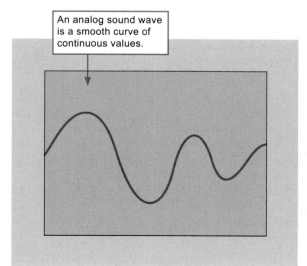

An analog sound wave is a smooth curve of continuous values.

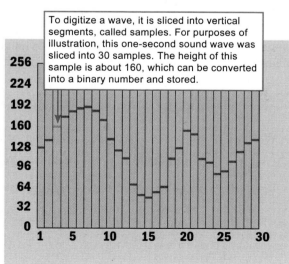

To digitize a wave, it is sliced into vertical segments, called samples. For purposes of illustration, this one-second sound wave was sliced into 30 samples. The height of this sample is about 160, which can be converted into a binary number and stored.

## QUANTIFYING BITS AND BYTES

**How can I tell the difference between bits and bytes?** The ads for digital devices typically include lots of abbreviations relating to bits and bytes. A few key concepts can help you understand what these abbreviations mean. Even though the word *bit* is an abbreviation for *binary digit*, it can be further abbreviated, usually as a lowercase *b*.

On older digital devices, bits were handled in groups, and terminology from that era is still used. A group of eight bits is called a **byte** and is usually abbreviated as an uppercase *B*.

Transmission speeds are typically expressed in bits, whereas storage space is typically expressed in bytes. For example, a cable Internet connection might transfer data from the Internet to your computer at 8 mega*bits* per second. In an iPod ad, you might notice that it can store up to 60 giga*bytes* of music and video.

**What do the prefixes *kilo-, mega-, giga-,* and *tera-* mean?** When reading about digital devices, you'll frequently encounter references such as 50 kilobits per second, 1.44 megabytes, 2.8 gigahertz, and 2 terabytes. Kilo, mega, giga, tera, and similar terms are used to quantify digital data.

In common usage, *kilo*, abbreviated as K, means a thousand. For example, $50K means $50,000. In the context of computers, however, 50K means 51,200. Why the difference? In the decimal number system we use on a daily basis, the number 1,000 is 10 to the third power, or $10^3$. For digital devices where base 2 is the norm, a kilo is precisely 1,024, or $2^{10}$. A **kilobit** (abbreviated Kb or Kbit) is 1,024 bits. A **kilobyte** (abbreviated KB or Kbyte) is 1,024 bytes. Kilobytes are often used when referring to the size of small computer files.

The prefix *mega* means a million, or in the context of bits and bytes, precisely 1,048,576 (the equivalent of $2^{20}$). A **megabit** (Mb or Mbit) is 1,048,576 bits. A **megabyte** (MB or MByte) is 1,048,576 bytes. Megabytes are often used when referring to the size of medium to large computer files.

In technology lingo, the prefix *giga* refers to a billion, or precisely 1,073,741,824. As you might expect, a **gigabit** (Gb or Gbit) is approximately 1 billion bits. A **gigabyte** (GB or GByte) is 1 billion bytes. Gigabytes are typically used to refer to storage capacity.

Computers—especially mainframes and supercomputers—sometimes work with huge amounts of data, and so terms such as *tera* (trillion), *peta* (thousand trillion), and *exa* (quintillion) are also handy. Figure 1-29 summarizes the terms commonly used to quantify computer data.

What's a kibibyte? Some computer scientists have proposed alternative terminology to dispel the ambiguity in terms such as *mega* that can mean 1,000 or 1,024. They suggest the following prefixes:

Kibi = 1,024

Mebi = 1,048,576

Gibi = 1,073,741,824

| | | | |
|---|---|---|---|
| Bit | One binary digit | Gigabit | $2^{30}$ bits |
| Byte | 8 bits | Gigabyte | $2^{30}$ bytes |
| Kilobit | 1,024 or $2^{10}$ bits | Terabyte | $2^{40}$ bytes |
| Kilobyte | 1,024 or $2^{10}$ bytes | Petabyte | $2^{50}$ bytes |
| Megabit | 1,048,576 or $2^{20}$ bits | Exabyte | $2^{60}$ bytes |
| Megabyte | 1,048,576 or $2^{20}$ bytes | | |

**FIGURE 1-29**

Quantifying Digital Data

## CIRCUITS AND CHIPS

**How do digital devices store and transport all those bits?**
Because most digital devices are electronic, bits take the form of electrical
pulses that can travel over circuits in much the same way that electricity
flows over a wire when you turn on a light switch. All the circuits, chips,
and mechanical components that form a digital device are designed to work
with bits.

At the simplest level, you can envision bits as two states of an electric circuit; the state used for a 1 bit would be on and the state for a 0 bit would be
off. In practice, the 1 bit might be represented by an elevated voltage, such
as +5 volts, whereas a 0 bit is represented by a low voltage, such as 0.

**What's inside?** If it weren't for the miniaturization made possible by
digital electronic technology, computers, cell phones, and portable media
players would be huge, and contain a complex jumble of wires and other
electronic gizmos. Instead, today's digital devices contain relatively few
parts—just a few wires, some microchips, and one or more circuit boards.

**What's a computer chip?** The terms *computer chip*, *microchip*, and
*chip* originated as technical jargon for integrated circuit. An **integrated circuit** (IC), such as the one pictured in Figure 1-30, is a super-thin slice of
semiconducting material packed with microscopic circuit elements, such as
wires, transistors, capacitors, logic gates, and resistors.

**Semiconducting materials** (or semiconductors), such
as silicon and germanium, are substances with properties
between those of a conductor (like copper) and an insulator
(like wood). To fabricate a chip, the conductive properties
of selective parts of the semiconducting material can be
enhanced to essentially create miniature electronic pathways
and components, such as transistors.

Integrated circuits are packaged in protective carriers that
vary in shape and size. Figure 1-31 illustrates some chip carriers, including small rectangular DIPs (dual in-line packages) with caterpillar-like
legs protruding from a black, rectangular body; and pincushion-like PGAs
(pin-grid arrays).

**INFOWEBLINKS**

Learn more about digital
electronics at the **Integrated
Circuits InfoWeb**.

 CLICK TO CONNECT
www.infoweblinks.com/np2012/ch01

**FIGURE 1-30**

The first computer chips
contained fewer than 100 min-
iaturized components, such as
diodes and transistors. The chips
used as the CPUs for today's
computers and cutting edge
graphics cards contain billions of
transistors.

A DIP has two rows of pins
that connect the IC circuitry
to a circuit board.

A PGA is a square chip
package with pins arranged in
concentric squares, typically
used for microprocessors.

**FIGURE 1-31**

Integrated circuits can be used
for microprocessors, memory,
and support circuitry. They are
housed within a ceramic carrier.
These carriers exist in several
configurations, or chip packages, such as DIPs and PGAs.

**How do chips fit together?** The electronic components of most digital devices are mounted on a circuit board called a system board, motherboard, or main board. The **system board** houses all essential chips and provides connecting circuitry between them. In Figure 1-32, you can see what's inside a typical desktop computer, a handheld computer, and a cell phone.

**FIGURE 1-32**

The electronic components of computers and handheld devices have many similar elements, including microchips and circuit boards. Circuit boards are usually green, whereas microchips are usually black.

# QuickCheck

1. Data [ ] refers to the format in which data is stored, processed, and transferred.

2. Digital devices often use the [ ] number system to represent numeric data.

3. Most computers use Unicode or Extended [ ] code to represent character data. (Hint: Use the acronym.)

4. KB is the abbreviation for [ ].

5. Integrated circuits are fabricated from [ ] materials that have properties of a conductor and an insulator.

 CHECK ANSWERS

# Digital Processing

**SECTION D**

**COMPUTERS AND OTHER DIGITAL DEVICES** process data, but how do they know what to do with it? The instructions you issue aren't 0s and 1s that a digital device can work with. So what goes on inside the box? Section D explains the programs that make digital devices tick. You'll discover that although digital devices appear to perform very complex tasks, under the hood they are really performing some very simple operations, but doing them at lightning speed.

## PROGRAMS AND INSTRUCTION SETS

**How do digital devices process data?** Computers, portable media players, PDAs, and smartphones all work with digital data. That data is manipulated under the control of a computer program, or software. But how do digital circuits know what those program instructions mean? Let's take a closer look at programs to see how they are created and how digital devices work with them.

**Who creates programs?** Computer programmers create programs that control digital devices. These programs are usually written in a high-level **programming language**, such as C, BASIC, COBOL, or Java.

Programming languages use a limited set of command words such as *Print*, *If*, *Write*, *Display*, and *Get* to form sentence-like statements designed as step-by-step directives for the processor chip. An important characteristic of most programming languages is that they can be written with simple tools, such as a word processor, and they can be understood by programmers. A simple program to select a song on your iPod might contain the statements shown in Figure 1-33.

```
Display Playlist

Get Song

Play Song
```

**FIGURE 1-33**

The program for an iPod displays a list of songs that the user can choose to play. A program works behind the scenes to display the list, get your selection, process it, and play the song.

The human-readable version of a program, like the one above, created in a high-level language by a programmer is called **source code**. Source code is an important first step in programming application software, batch files, and scripts that you'll learn about in later chapters. However, just as a digital device can't work directly with text, sounds, or images until they have been digitized, source code has to be converted into a digital format before the processor can use it.

**How does source code get converted?** The procedure for translating source code into 0s and 1s can be accomplished by a compiler or an interpreter. A **compiler** converts all the statements in a program in a single batch, and the resulting collection of instructions, called **object code**, is placed in a new file (Figure 1-34). Most of the program files distributed as software contain object code that is ready for the processor to execute.

**FIGURE 1-34**

A compiler converts statements written in a high-level programming language into object code that the processor can execute.
▶ Watch a compiler in action.

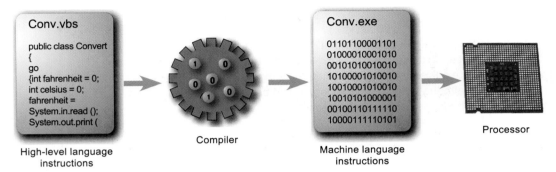

High-level language instructions — Compiler — Machine language instructions — Processor

As an alternative to a compiler, an **interpreter** converts and executes one statement at a time while the program is running. After a statement is executed, the interpreter converts and executes the next statement, and so on (Figure 1-35).

**FIGURE 1-35**

An interpreter converts high-level statements one at a time as the program is running.
▶ Watch an interpreter in action.

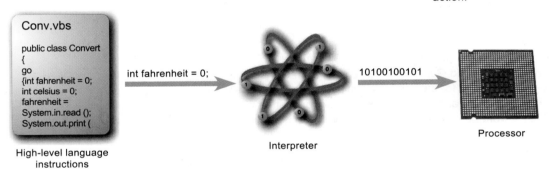

High-level language instructions — int fahrenheit = 0; — Interpreter — 10100100101 — Processor

Compilers and interpreters don't simply convert the characters from source code into 0s and 1s. For example, in the first line of the iPod program, Display Playlist, a compiler would not simply convert the *D* into its ASCII equivalent. No, computers are a little trickier than that.

**What does the conversion process produce?** A microprocessor is hard-wired to perform a limited set of activities, such as addition, subtraction, counting, and comparisons. This collection of preprogrammed activities is called an **instruction set**. Instruction sets are not designed to carry out any specific task, such as word processing or playing music. Instead, an instruction set is designed to be general purpose so that programmers can use it in creative ways for the wide variety of tasks performed by all kinds of digital devices.

Each instruction has a corresponding sequence of 0s and 1s. For example, 00000100 might correspond to *Add*. The list of codes for a microprocessor's instruction set, called **machine language**, can be directly executed by the processor's circuitry. A set of machine language instructions for a program is called **machine code**.

A machine language instruction has two parts: the op code and the operands. An **op code**, which is short for *operation code*, is a command word for an operation such as add, compare, or jump. The **operand** for an instruction specifies the data, or the address of the data, for the operation. In the following instruction, the op code means add and the operand is 1, so the instruction means Add 1.

| Op code | → 00000100 | 00000001 ← | Operand |

A single high-level instruction very often converts into multiple machine language instructions. Figure 1-36 illustrates the number of machine language instructions that correspond to a simple high-level program.

```
#include <stdio.h>
int main ()
{
int i;

for (i=1; i<=100; i=i+1)
  printf("%d\t",i);
return(0);
}
```

```
00100111101111011111111111100000
10101111101111110000000000010100
10101111101001000000000000100000
10101111101001010000000000100100
10101111101000000000000000011000
10101111101000000000000000011100
10001111101011100000000000011100
10001111101110000000000000011000
00000001110011100000000000011001
00100101110010000000000000000001
00101001000000010000000001100101
10101111101010000000000000011100
00000000000000000111100000010010
00000011000011111100100000100001
00010100001000011111111111110111
10101111101110010000000000011000
00111100000000010000010000000000
10001111101001010000000000011000
00001100000010000000000000111101100
00100100100001000000000100001100000
```

FIGURE 1-36

The source code program on the left prints numbers from 1 to 100. This source code is converted to machine language instructions shown in the right column that the computer can directly process.

To summarize what you should now know about programs and instruction sets, a programmer creates human-readable source code using a programming language. A compiler or interpreter converts source code into machine code. Machine code instructions are a series of 0s and 1s that correspond to a processor's instruction set.

## PROCESSOR LOGIC

**What happens inside a computer chip?** A microprocessor contains miles of microscopic circuitry and millions of miniature components divided into different kinds of operational units, such as the ALU and the control unit.

The **ALU** (arithmetic logic unit) is the part of the microprocessor that performs arithmetic operations, such as addition and subtraction. It also performs logical operations, such as comparing two numbers to see if they are the same. The ALU uses **registers** to hold data that is being processed, just as you use a mixing bowl to hold the ingredients for a batch of cookies.

The microprocessor's **control unit** fetches each instruction, just as you get each ingredient out of a cupboard or the refrigerator. Data is loaded into the ALU's registers, just as you add all the ingredients to the mixing bowl. Finally, the control unit gives the ALU the green light to begin processing, just as you flip the switch on your electric mixer to begin blending the cookie ingredients. Figure 1-37 illustrates a microprocessor control unit and an ALU preparing to add 2 + 3.

FIGURE 1-37

The control unit fetches the ADD instruction, then loads data into the ALU's registers where it is processed.

**What happens when a computer executes an instruction?** The term **instruction cycle** refers to the process in which a computer executes a single instruction. Some parts of the instruction cycle are performed by the microprocessor's control unit; other parts of the cycle are performed by the ALU. The steps in this cycle are summarized in Figure 1-38.

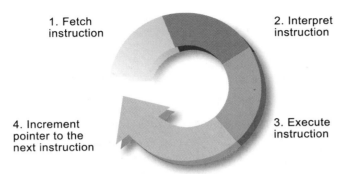

1. Fetch instruction

2. Interpret instruction

4. Increment pointer to the next instruction

3. Execute instruction

**FIGURE 1-38**

The instruction cycle includes four activities.

**What role does the control unit play?** The instructions that a computer is supposed to process for a particular program are held in memory. When the program begins, the memory address of the first instruction is placed in a part of the microprocessor's control unit called an instruction pointer. The control unit can then fetch the instruction by copying data from that address into its instruction register. From there, the control unit can interpret the instruction, gather the specified data, or tell the ALU to begin processing. Figure 1-39 helps you visualize the control unit's role in processing an instruction.

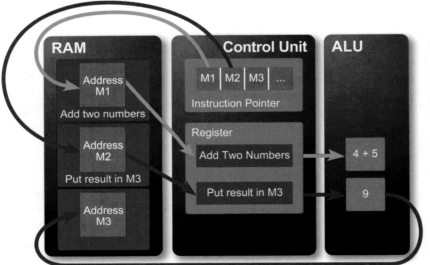

RAM

Address M1

Add two numbers

Address M2

Put result in M3

Address M3

Control Unit

M1 | M2 | M3 | ...

Instruction Pointer

Register

Add Two Numbers

Put result in M3

ALU

4 + 5

9

**FIGURE 1-39**

The control unit's instruction pointer indicates M1, a location in memory. The control unit fetches the "Add two numbers" instruction from M1. This instruction is then sent to the ALU. The instruction pointer then changes to M2. The processor fetches the instruction located in M2, moves it to a register, and executes it

**When does the ALU swing into action?** The ALU is responsible for performing arithmetic and logical operations. It uses registers to hold data ready to be processed. When it gets the go-ahead signal from the control unit, the ALU processes the data and places the result in an accumulator. From the accumulator, the data can be sent to memory or used for further processing. Figure 1-40 on the next page helps you visualize what happens in the ALU as the computer processes data.

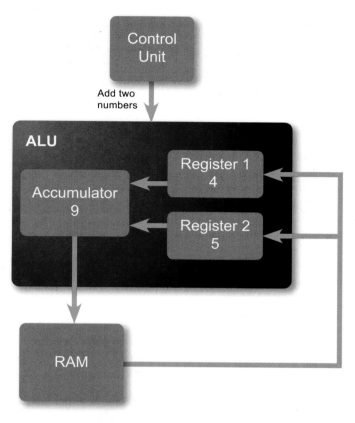

FIGURE 1-40

In this example, the ALU's registers contain the numbers 4 and 5. When the ALU receives the "Add two numbers" instruction from the control unit, it adds 4 and 5 then places the result in the accumulator.

**What happens after an instruction is executed?** When the computer completes an instruction, the control unit increments the instruction pointer to the memory address of the next instruction, and the instruction cycle begins again.

**Do I need to know all this detailed stuff?** What you should take away from the discussion about programming and instruction sets is the idea that computers and other digital devices accomplish a wide array of complex tasks by performing a very limited set of machine language instructions very fast.

These concepts about how processors work will help you understand the significance of microprocessor performance, such as speed and word size, which you'll learn about in the next chapter.

**INFOWEBLINKS**

For more details on the inner workings of your computer's processor, visit the **CPU InfoWeb**.

W CLICK TO CONNECT
www.infoweblinks.com/np2012/ch01

# QuickCheck

SECTION D

1. A(n) [_____] converts all of the source code instructions into object code, which becomes a new file containing [_____] code.

2. A microprocessor is hard-wired to perform a set of activities called a(n) [_____] set.

3. A machine language instruction has two parts: a(n) [_____] code and an operand.

4. The ALU in your computer's microprocessor holds data in [_____].

5. The microprocessor's control unit contains a(n) [_____] pointer that holds the address of the instruction being executed.

 CHECK ANSWERS

# Password Security

**USER IDS,** passwords, and personal identification numbers (PINs) are a fact of everyday life in the information age. They are required for activities such as using ATMs and debit cards, logging into Windows, accessing wireless networks, making an iTunes purchase, instant messaging, reading e-mail, and file sharing. Many Web sites encourage you to sign up for membership by choosing a user ID and password. Section E provides information about selecting secure passwords and managing the mountain of passwords you collect and tend to forget.

## AUTHENTICATION PROTOCOLS

**What is an authentication protocol?** Security experts use the term **authentication protocol** to refer to any method that confirms a person's identity using something the person knows, something the person possesses, or something the person is. For example, a person might know a password or PIN. A person might possess an ATM card or a credit card. A person can also be identified by **biometrics**, such as a fingerprint, facial features (photo), or a retinal pattern (Figure 1-41).

Authentication protocols that use more than one means of identification are more secure than others. Two-factor authentication, which verifies identity using two independent elements of confirmation such as an ATM card and PIN, is more secure than single-factor authentication, such as a password. Computer-related security is primarily based on passwords associated with user IDs. The level of protection offered by single-factor authentication depends on good password selection and management on the part of users.

**What is a user ID?** A **user ID** is a series of characters—letters and possibly numbers or special symbols—that becomes a person's unique identifier, similar to a Social Security number. It is also referred to as a user name, login, screen name, online nickname, or handle. User IDs are typically public. Because they are not secret, they do not offer any level of security.

User IDs are significant because they are the name on an account, such as e-mail or iTunes, that requires a password. When you first apply for or set up an account, you might be supplied with a user ID or you might be asked to create one. Often a user ID is a variation of your name. Brunhilde Jefferson's user ID might be bjeffe, bjefferson, brunhilde_jefferson, or bjeff0918445. It is also becoming common to use your e-mail address as a user ID.

The rules for creating a user ID are not consistent throughout all applications, so it is important to read instructions carefully before finalizing your user ID. For example, spaces might not be allowed in a user ID. Hence, the underline in brunhilde_jefferson is used instead of a space. There might be a length limitation, so Ms. Jefferson might have to choose a short user ID, such as bjeffe.

**FIGURE 1-41**

Biometric authentication protocols include retinal scans that identify unique patterns of blood vessels in the eye.

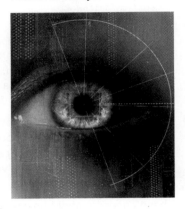

Some computers that host password-protected resources don't differentiate between uppercase and lowercase letters, and would consider the user IDs B_Jefferson and b_jefferson to be the same. Other computers are **case sensitive** and differentiate between uppercase and lowercase. On such computers, if Ms. Jefferson selected Brun_Jeff as her user ID, she would not be able to gain access by typing brun_jeff. To avoid such problems, most people stick to lowercase letters for their user IDs.

**What is a password?** A **password** is a series of characters that verifies a user ID and guarantees that you are the person you claim to be. Although you might be assigned a password, typically you are asked to provide your own. In some situations you might be given a temporary password, and then asked to change it as soon as you successfully log in for the first time. Passwords and user IDs are typically created on a registration or enrollment screen similar to the one in Figure 1-42.

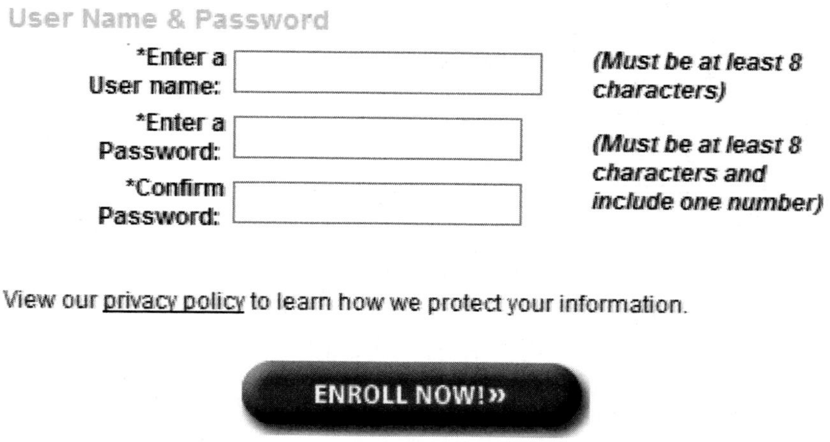

User Name & Password

| *Enter a User name: | [_____] | (Must be at least 8 characters) |
| *Enter a Password: | [_____] | (Must be at least 8 characters and include one number) |
| *Confirm Password: | [_____] | |

View our privacy policy to learn how we protect your information.

**ENROLL NOW!»**

**FIGURE 1-42**

When you create an account, you are typically asked to enter a user ID and password.

**What if I forget my password?** Login screens for many applications provide a "forgot my password" link. Clicking this link checks your identity using your answer to a personal question. If your identity checks out, your password is e-mailed to you. A personal question provides an alternative authentication protocol to ensure that you are not a hacker pretending to be a legitimate user who has lost a password.

Personal questions and answers are usually set up at the same time you create an account. After selecting a password, you are required to choose a question that you must answer before your forgotten password is e-mailed to you. This question might be something like: *What is your mother's maiden name?*, *What is your favorite color?*, or *Where were you born?* You should be careful about the question you choose because public information like your mother's maiden name or the town of your birth can be researched by any hacker.

**What is the difference between a password and a PIN?** Both passwords and PINs are classified as *something-the-user-knows* authentication methods. In practice, PINs tend to be a short sequence of numbers that can be entered using a numeric keypad, whereas passwords tend to be longer sequences of letters, numbers, and special characters that require a full qwerty keyboard for entry. PINs are typically used with two-factor authentication protocols, whereas passwords are used in conjunction with single-factor authentication protocols.

For example, ATMs require a bank card (something you possess) and a PIN (something you know). In contrast, passwords are associated with single-factor authentication used for networks, Web sites, and other situations in which the hardware for dealing with ID cards is not available.

## PASSWORD HACKS

**How serious is password theft?** To a hacker, obtaining the password for a specific user ID can be even more rewarding than a burglar figuring out the combination to a house safe. Once hackers get into a user account, a wealth of personal information can be at their fingertips. This information could be anything from juicy e-mail gossip to Social Security numbers, credit card numbers, bank account numbers, health data, and other private details. When someone gains unauthorized access to your personal data and uses it illegally, it is called **identity theft**. Victims of this increasingly common crime often don't realize what is happening until it's too late.

Armed with your password and other personal data, a cybercriminal can rack up bills using your credit card, apply for a mortgage using your financial data, create fake accounts in your name, send embarrassing e-mail messages, or wreak havoc on your bank account. Once a thief breaks into an online account, he or she can also change your password and you will no longer be able to log in. Password theft is serious and pervasive, so it is important to understand how hackers get passwords and how you can protect yours.

**How can hackers get my password?** Hackers employ a whole range of ways to steal passwords. Some primitive means include shoulder surfing, which is looking over your shoulder as you type in your password, and dumpster diving, which is going through your trash.

Password thieves can easily find your password if you write it down on a yellow sticky note hidden under your keyboard or in plain sight on top of your monitor. If a hacker doesn't have physical access to your work area but your computer is connected to a network, your password can be discovered by a hacker using a remote computer and software tools that systematically guess your password, intercept it, or trick you into revealing it.

A **dictionary attack** helps hackers guess your password by stepping through a dictionary containing thousands of the most commonly used passwords. Password dictionaries can be found on black hat sites and packaged with password-cracking software, such as John the Ripper. Unfortunately, dictionary attacks are often enough to break a password because many users choose passwords that are easy to remember and likely to be in the most commonly used list (Figure 1-43).

### TERMINOLOGY NOTE

*Hacker* can refer to a skilled programmer or to a person who manipulates computers with malicious intent. The terms *black hat* and *cracker* are also used to refer to a malicious or criminal hacker.

**FIGURE 1-43**

Some of the most commonly used passwords are included in the dictionaries packaged with password-cracking software. These passwords (listed in order of popularity) should not be used.

| | | | | | |
|---|---|---|---|---|---|
| 12345 | internet | jordan | alex | newyork | jonathan |
| abc123 | service | michael | apple | soccer | love |
| password | canada | michelle | avalon | thomas | marina |
| computer | hello | mindy | brandy | wizard | master |
| 123456 | ranger | patrick | chelsea | Monday | missy |
| tigger | shadow | 123abc | coffee | asdfgh | monday |
| 1234 | baseball | andrew | dave | bandit | monkey |
| a1b2c3 | donald | bear | falcon | batman | natasha |
| qwerty | harley | calvin | freedom | boris | ncc1701 |
| 123 | hockey | changeme | gandalf | dorothy | newpass |
| xxx | letmein | diamond | golf | eeyore | pamela |
| money | maggie | matthew | green | fishing | pepper |
| test | mike | miller | helpme | football | piglet |
| carmen | mustang | ou812 | linda | george | poohbear |
| mickey | snoopy | tiger | magic | happy | pookie |
| secret | buster | trustno1 | merlin | iloveyou | rabbit |
| summer | dragon | 12345678 | molson | jennifer | rachel |

The **brute force attack** also uses password-cracking software, but its range is much more extensive than the dictionary attack. Because it exhausts all possible combinations of letters to decrypt a password, a brute force attack can run for days or even as long as a week to crack some passwords.

If hackers can't guess a password, they can use another technique called **sniffing**, which intercepts information sent out over computer networks. Sniffing software is used legitimately by network administrators to record network traffic for monitoring and maintenance purposes. The same software can also be used for illicit activities. If your user ID and password travel over a network as unencrypted text, they can easily fall into the hands of a password thief.

An even more sophisticated approach to password theft is **phishing**, in which a hacker poses as a legitimate representative of an official organization such as your ISP, your bank, or an online payment service in order to persuade you to disclose highly confidential information. Mostly through e-mail or instant messaging, a fake customer representative or administrator asks you to visit a Web page to confirm billing information or verify your account by providing your password, credit card number, or Social Security number.

If you examine phishing messages more closely, you might realize that the Web sites referred to are fake. However, seasoned hackers try to make the URLs look as close as possible to the official Web sites they claim to represent (Figure 1-44).

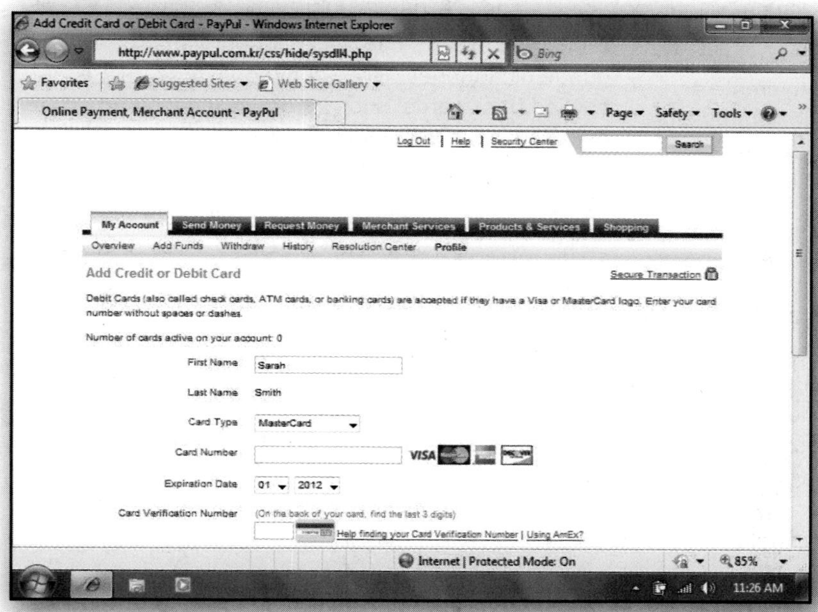

**FIGURE 1-44**

A fake Web site can look very similar to the real thing, but this fraudulent site originates in Korea. You should avoid clicking links in e-mail messages that attempt to get you to confirm or renew account data.

As users became better at identifying phishing messages, password thieves resorted to the use of keyloggers. Short for *keystroke logging*, a **keylogger** is software that secretly records a user's keystrokes and sends the information to a hacker. A keylogger is a form of malicious code called a Trojan horse, or Trojan. Trojans are computer programs that seem to perform one function while actually doing something else. They can be embedded in e-mail attachments, software downloads, and even files. Trojans are discussed in more detail in the security section of the Software chapter.

## SECURE PASSWORDS

**How do I create a secure password?** With password theft becoming more and more widespread, security experts recommend using a strong, secure password for financial transactions such as those that involve PayPal or bank accounts. A strong, secure password is one that is easy to remember but difficult to crack. Figure 1-45 offers guidelines for selecting secure passwords and avoiding ones that are easily crackable.

FIGURE 1-45

Tips for Creating Secure Passwords

- Use passwords that are at least eight characters in length. The longer the password, the tougher it is to crack.

- Use a combination of letters, numbers, and special characters such as $, #, if permitted.

- Use uppercase and lowercase letters if the hosting computer is case sensitive.

- Use a passphrase, that is, one that is based on several words or the first letters of a verse from a favorite poem or song. For example, the words from the nursery rhyme "Jack and Jill went up the hill" can be converted to jjwuth. You can then insert special characters and numbers, and add some uppercase letters to create a password that still makes sense to you personally, such as J&J w^th!ll. This type of password appears random to anyone else but you.

- Do not use a password based on public information such as your phone number, Social Security number, driver's license number, or birthday. Hackers can easily find this information, and other personal facts such as names of your spouse, children, or pets.

- Avoid passwords that contain your entire user ID or part of it. A user ID of bjeffe coupled with a password of bjeffe123 is an easy target for password thieves.

- Steer clear of words that can be found in the dictionary, including foreign words. Dictionary attacks can utilize foreign language dictionaries. Even common words spelled backwards, such as *drowssap* instead of *password*, are not tricky enough to fool password-cracking software.

**How do I protect my password?** Once you have selected a strong password, you must take steps to keep it safe. Do not share your password with anyone. Avoid writing down a password. If possible, memorize it. If you must write down a password, do not leave it in an obvious place such as under your keyboard or mouse pad. Recording passwords in an unencrypted file stored on your computer is risky, too, especially if you have more than one password. A hacker who gains access to that file can use the passwords to access all your accounts.

If you think one of your passwords has been compromised, change it immediately. Even if you have no evidence of password tampering, security experts recommend that you change passwords periodically, say every six months. When you change your passwords, do not just make a slight variation to your current one. For example, do not change just4Me1 to just4Me2. You should not reuse your old passwords either, so it's best to keep a password history list.

Aside from good password maintenance habits, computer maintenance is also essential. Make sure that your entire computer is protected by security software, which is explained in the Software chapter.

**How do I deal with all my passwords and user IDs?** You can accumulate many passwords and user IDs—for logging into Windows, accessing online banking, using e-mail, shopping online, downloading music, and getting into your Facebook account. The more passwords and user IDs you have, the more difficult they become to remember.

How many times have you had to click on the "I forgot my password" link when you logged in to an online account? Your passwords provide the most protection if they are unique, but accessing even 25 different Web sites that require 25 different user IDs and 25 corresponding passwords requires quite a memory. To add to the confusion, you must also regularly change passwords to your critical accounts!

Instead of using 25 different user IDs and passwords, you need some way to reduce the number of things you have to memorize. First, strive to select a unique user ID that you can use for more than one site. Remember that people with your name who selected user IDs before you might have already taken the obvious user IDs. For example, when John Smith selects a user ID, you can bet that other people have already used johnsmith, jsmith, and john_smith. To keep his user ID unique, John might instead select jsl2wm (the first letters in "John Smith loves 2 watch movies").

Next, you can maintain two or three tiers of passwords—the top level for high security, the second level for medium security, and the third level for low security. If you do not have too many accounts, you can opt for just two tiers—for high and low security. You can then select two passwords. Use the high-security password for accessing critical data, such as online banking, for managing an online stock portfolio, or for your account at an online bookstore that stores a copy of your billing and credit card information.

Use your low-security password in situations where you don't really care if your security is compromised. Some places on the Internet want you to establish an account with a user ID and password just so that they can put you on a mailing list. At other sites, your user ID and password provide access to information, but none of your critical personal or financial data is stored there. It is not necessary to change your low-security password very often. Figure 1-46 provides more information about tiered passwords.

**Tier 1:** High security
**Password:** BBx98$$NN26
**Uses:**
Online banking
PayPal
iTunes
Amazon.com

**Tier 2:** Low security
**Password:** Rover
**Uses:**
New York Times archive
Google
Wikipedia
photoSIG

**FIGURE 1-46**

Tiered passwords reduce the number of user IDs and passwords that you have to remember; however, the disadvantage is that a hacker who discovers one of your passwords will be able to use it to access many of your accounts.

**Can my computer help me to remember passwords?** Your computer's operating system, Web browser, or other software might include a password manager to help you keep track of user IDs and passwords. A **password manager** stores user IDs with their corresponding passwords and automatically fills in login forms. For example, when you register at a Web site while using a browser such as Internet Explorer, the browser stores your new ID and password in an encrypted file on your computer's hard disk. The next time you visit the Web site, your ID and password are automatically filled in on the login screen (Figure 1-47).

The drawback to password managers that are built into browsers, operating systems, or other software is that if you switch to different software or to a different computer, you will not have access to the stored passwords. Standalone password manager software offers a more inclusive approach to creating and retrieving passwords.

**What is password manager software?** A standalone password manager is a software application that feeds passwords into login forms regardless of the software you're using. As with built-in password managers, a standalone password manager stores user IDs and passwords in an encrypted file. You can access this file using a master password. This type of password manager can be moved from one computer to another, for example, if you purchase a new computer.

A standalone password manager can also generate secure "nonsense passwords." You don't have to worry if the passwords are difficult to remember because the password manager software can keep track of them (Figure 1-48).

FIGURE 1-47

Checking the "Remember me" box saves your user ID and password for the next time you log in, but you have to be using the same browser.

FIGURE 1-48

Password managers help you keep track of all your passwords. ▶ If you've never used a password manager and want to see how one works, start the guided tour for this figure in your digital textbook.

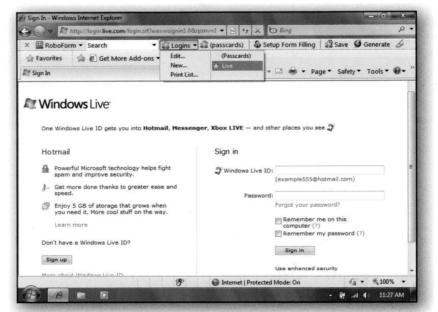

In addition to generating and tracking your passwords, most password manager software provides other features, such as password strength meters and form fillers.

A password strength meter indicates whether your passwords are secure enough—a feature that is useful if you've created your own passwords, rather than using your password manager to generate them.

Form fillers automatically enter data into online Web forms such as those that request billing data when you order at an online shopping site. Many form fillers also match a Web form's URL against a set of valid URLs that you have provided in order to avoid sending data to a fake Web site that you have been lured to visit by a phishing message. When entering passwords, form fillers are not collecting your password from the keyboard; therefore, a hacker's keylogger cannot secretly record keystrokes.

There are several free, shareware, or open source password managers, such as KeePass, RoboForm, and SurfSecret KeyPad. Some password manager software is portable, which means that it does not have to be installed on a computer before it is used. Instead, you can carry it around on a USB flash drive so that your passwords are available wherever you use a computer, such as in your school lab, at the library, or at work. When you remove the flash drive, your portable password manager leaves no traces of passwords behind (Figure 1-49).

For extra protection against intruders who might search your computer for passwords, a flash drive that contains a password manager can be unplugged when you are not accessing password protected sites. You can also remove the flash drive from your computer when you're out so that your nosy roommate can't snoop through your computer files.

New password management techniques are being developed, but some offer their own set of potential security problems. For example, Web-based password managers can be attractive targets for password thieves. By breaking into a single site, a password thief could harvest thousands of passwords. As new password management technologies appear, make sure you evaluate them carefully before trusting them with your valuable data.

**FIGURE 1-49**

Some password managers are portable so that you can carry them with you on a USB flash drive.

**INFOWEBLINKS**

Visit the **Password Management InfoWeb** to learn more about creating and managing all your user IDs and passwords.

 CLICK TO CONNECT
www.infoweblinks.com/np2012/ch01

# QuickCheck                                    SECTION E

1. An authentication [_____] is any method that confirms a person's identity using something the person knows, something the person possesses, or something the person is.

2. On a(n) [_____]-sensitive server, the user ID BJP is different than bjp.

3. A(n) [_____] attack can guess your password if you are using common passwords or everyday words.

4. A(n) [_____] scam looks like a request from your bank or an online payment service, but is actually a hacker who wants you to disclose your user ID and password.

5. Most browsers include a built-in password [_____] that remembers the user IDs and passwords you use when logging into Web sites or online e-mail.

▶ CHECK ANSWERS

# Issue: Are You Being Tracked?

**IN THE BOOK** *Harry Potter and the Prisoner of Azkaban*, Harry acquires a magical item called the Marauder's Map, which shows the location of every teacher and student at the Hogwarts School of Witchcraft and Wizardry. A group of students at the Massachusetts Institute of Technology became fascinated by the idea of a tracking map and constructed one of their own. It is rather amazing that a fictional magic device could so easily become reality.

In the context of Harry Potter, tracking technology seems fun; but in real life this apparently innocent tracking technology could be used by governments, corporations, and possibly criminals to monitor the daily activities of ordinary people. Location privacy can be defined as the ability to prevent other parties from learning one's current or past location. Tracking technology could have a significant effect on our ability to keep our daily lives private.

A location-enabled device (sometimes referred to as a location-aware device) is one that can determine its geographic location. Most are handheld mobile devices, but tracking chips can also be embedded in items as varied as cars, shipping cartons, product labels, clothing, and passports. Three technologies are used to equip devices with location awareness: GPS, cellular networks, and RFID (radio frequency identification).

A global positioning system, or GPS, uses a receiver inside a mobile device to triangulate a location based on signals from three or more Earth-orbiting satellites. GPS technology is used for handheld GPS locator devices and automobile tracking services such as OnStar.

GPS is a one-way technology; data travels to the GPS device, but the device does not transmit its position back to a satellite. However, coordinates from a GPS can be transmitted over a different network, such as the cellular phone system or wireless network. For example, a tourist might rent a virtual tour guide device that narrates points of interest on a walking tour. The device collects information from a GPS satellite and when the tourist reaches an attraction, begins narrating. Unbeknownst to the tourist, however, the device can transmit its location to the tour operator's office. Not only does the tour operator know the tourist's location, but that information could be passed to a third-party marketer or to immigration officials.

Wireless networks, such as a cellular phone system, can determine location based on the antenna to which they broadcast. An antenna's coverage area ranges from a few miles up to 20 miles. The location of a mobile device and the person using it can be roughly determined to be within the range of the antenna it is currently transmitting to. A more precise location can be triangulated using multiple antennas. With current technology, triangulation from cellular phone antennas is less accurate than with GPS; current technology pinpoints a location to within 50–150 meters. Locations can be tracked only within range of cell towers. In contrast, GPS tracking is essentially worldwide.

Wireless transmissions are bi-directional; unlike one-way GPS, most mobile devices can transmit a location back to a base station. Cellular phone companies originally used this capability to determine when customers were roaming out of their home coverage area.

Currently, location data from cellular phones is also available for use by emergency responders to locate people in need of assistance. More controversially, bi-directional tracking devices have been embedded in rental cars to determine whether the car is exceeding the speed limit or is being used for unauthorized travel across state lines.

New child-tracking services offered by cellular phone carriers allow parents to track their cell-phone equipped children on a Web-based map. Parents can even set up boundaries and if their child crosses out of the approved area, an alarm sounds on the parent's computer or cell phone.

Law enforcement agencies have tried to gain access to location information to track suspected criminals. In some states, motor vehicle officials are considering plans to implant tracking devices in license plates.

RFID technology is based on a special-purpose computer chip equipped with a microscopic antenna that receives and responds to radio-frequency queries from a transceiver. Whenever the chip is within range of a transceiver, its signal can be picked up. RFID chips are so small that they are almost unnoticeable. They can be implanted in animals or people, incorporated into a credit card or passport, and tucked away in clothing labels or commercial products.

RFID product labels were originally designed to streamline warehouse and retail store operations, so that products could be scanned without removing them from shipping crates or shopping carts. They became controversial because consumers were not necessarily able to locate or remove the RFID device. Further, RFID-enabled items could be linked to a specific individual if an RFID labeled item was purchased with a credit card. It also seemed possible that unauthorized people could hijack RFID signals and track a person by, for example, picking up the signals emitted by her Benetton sweater.

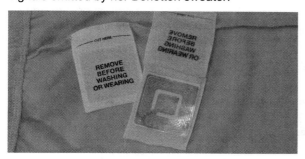

Tracking technology has many uses. Employers can use location data to make sure employees are not spending too much time in the smoking area or break room. Cell phone carriers can collaborate with aggressive marketers to turn your cell phone into a handheld carnival barker who tries to coax you into nearby stores or restaurants. Data from a location-enabled device could be correlated with health clinics, bars, or adult bookstores allowing trackers to make inferences about a person's lifestyle.

The use of tracking technology is spreading and it seems clear that laws and regulations are necessary to prevent abusive practices. The Communications Act of 1934 requires that carriers only use a customer's confidential information for providing services specifically requested by that customer. The so-called E911 Act that required wireless service providers to equip phones with GPS capability added location data to the list of information that is supposed to be kept confidential, and it prohibited certain marketing uses of customers' location data. Unfortunately, a bill that was proposed in 2001, requiring location-based services to obtain permission from customers before disclosing location information, was not passed into law.

Privacy advocates are demanding strict protocols for collecting, using, storing, and distributing location information. They face opposition, however, from law enforcement officials who would like to explore ways location technology can be used to track criminals and prevent terrorism. Commercial interest in this technology for marketing and advertising is also high and consumers might be willing to give up some measure of privacy for economic incentives, such as free OnStar service in exchange for listening to location-based advertising while driving.

The outcome of conflicting interests will determine if location-tracking technology can be implemented in such a way that the rights and privacy of individuals are protected.

**INFOWEBLINKS**

You'll find lots more information about tracking devices at the **Digital Surveillance InfoWeb**.

ⓦ CLICK TO CONNECT
www.infoweblinks.com/np2012/ch01

# What Do You Think?

ISSUE

1. Should users of location-enabled devices be informed when location tracking is in use?

  ◯ Yes   ◯ No   ◯ Not sure

2. Do you think most people are aware of the privacy issues associated with location-enabled devices?

  ◯ Yes   ◯ No   ◯ Not sure

3. Should users of location-aware devices be permitted to enable and disable tracking features on their devices?

  ◯ Yes   ◯ No   ◯ Not sure

▶ SAVE RESPONSES

# Computers in Context: **Marketing**

**WALKING OUT THE GATE** of ancient Pompeii, you might have come across an eye-catching sign extolling the virtues of a popular tavern in the next town. The sign was a clever bit of marketing designed to target thirsty travelers and drum up business. Throughout the centuries, handbills, newspaper ads, television commercials, radio spots, and mass mail campaigns were all important tools of the marketing industry. Now, computers have opened new vistas for communicating with consumers.

The American Marketing Association defines marketing as an organizational function and a set of processes for creating, communicating, and delivering value to customers and for managing customer relationships in ways that benefit the organization and its stakeholders. A person-in-the-street definition might simply be that marketing is an attempt to sell products.

Computers first played a role in marketing as a research tool for quickly crunching numbers from consumer surveys and sales figures. Statistics derived from that data helped companies focus development efforts on the most promising products and market them effectively. Marketing research data made one fact very clear: even the most effective advertising cannot convince everyone to buy a particular product. A costly prime-time television ad, for example, might be seen by millions of viewers, but many of them have no interest in the advertised product. To better target potential buyers, marketers turned to direct marketing.

Direct marketing attempts to establish a one-to-one relationship with prospective customers rather than waiting for them to learn about a product from general, impersonal forms of advertising, such as billboards, radio spots, television commercials, and newspaper ads. The first direct marketing techniques included personalized let-

ters, catalogs, and telemarketing. Customer names, addresses, and phone numbers were mined from computer databases maintained by mailing list brokers. Lists could be tailored in rudimentary ways to fit target markets. Selling snow tires? Get a list of consumers in northern states. Looking for Peace Corps volunteers? Get a list of college students.

"Dear Carmen Smith, you might already have won…" Just about everyone in America has received a personalized sweepstakes mailing. Initially, personalized names were crudely inserted using dot matrix printers, but today high-speed laser printers dash off thousands of personalized letters per hour and use graphics capabilities to affix signatures that appear to have been hand-signed in ink.

Telemarketing is a technique for telephone solicitation. Computerized autodialers make it possible for telemarketers to work efficiently. An autodialer is a device that can dial telephone numbers stored in a list. It can also generate and dial telephone numbers using a random or sequential number generator.

A smart autodialer, called a predictive dialer, increases a telemarketer's efficiency even more by automatically calling several numbers at the same time and only passing a call to the marketer when a person answers.

If you've picked up the telephone only to hear silence or a disconnect, it was likely an autodialer that connected to more than one person at the same time and dropped your call. Predictive dialers eliminate telemarketing time that would be otherwise wasted with busy signals, answering machines, and so on.

The Internet opened up dramatic new horizons in direct marketing by providing an inexpensive conduit for collecting information about potential customers and distributing targeted direct marketing. According to author Jim Sterne, "The Internet and the World

Wide Web have become the most important new communication media since television, and ones that are fundamentally reshaping contemporary understanding of sales and marketing." Today, a vast amount of information flows over the Internet and marketers are trying to harness that information to most efficiently communicate their messages to prospective customers.

Market analysts are interested in consumer opinions about companies and products. Analysts for companies like Ford, Microsoft, and Sony track opinions on the Internet by monitoring message boards, discussion sites, and blogs.

E-commerce Web sites offer a global distribution channel for small entrepreneurs as well as multinational corporations. Consumers can locate e-commerce sites using a search engine. Some search engines allow paid advertising to appear on their sites. Clever marketers use search engine optimization techniques to get their Web sites to the top of search engine lists.

Another way to drive traffic to an e-commerce site is banner advertising that clutters up Web pages with inviting tag lines for free products. Clicking the ad connects consumers to the site. The cost of placing a banner ad depends on the click-through rate—the number of consumers who click an ad. Sophisticated banner ad software displays the banner ad across an entire network and monitors click-through rates. Not only does this software keep track of click throughs for billing purposes, it can automatically adjust the sites that carry each ad to maximize click-through rates.

Internet marketing is often associated with the tidal wave of spam that's currently crashing into everyone's Inbox. These mass spam e-mails, however bothersome, are a very crude form of direct marketing. Typically, spammers use unscrubbed mailing lists containing many expired, blocked, and invalid e-mail addresses. This hit-or-miss strategy is cheap. Ten million e-mail addresses can be rented for as low as $100 and server bandwidth provided by e-mail brokers costs about $300 per million messages sent.

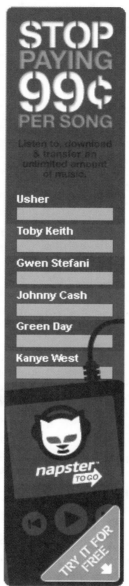

Marketing professionals regard massive e-mail spamming with some degree of scorn because most lists don't narrow the focus to the most promising customers. Worse yet, consumers react by installing spam filters. Some spammers try to evade spam filters. More than one Web site offers marketers a free service that analyzes mass e-mail solicitations using a spam filter simulator. If the solicitation can't get through the filter, the service offers suggestions on what to change so the message slips through.

In contrast to gratuitous spammers, marketing professionals have learned that opt-in mailing lists have much higher success rates. Consumers who have asked for information more often appreciate receiving it and act on it. Opt-in consumers are also more willing to divulge information that develops an accurate profile of their lifestyle so marketers can offer them the most appropriate products.

Most consumers would agree that the marketing industry needs professionals who are socially responsible. In describing the qualifications for marketing professionals, the Bureau of Labor Statistics states the obvious when it says, "Computer skills are vital because marketing, product promotion, and advertising on the Internet are increasingly common."

In preparing for a marketing career, a knowledge of computers, the Web, and the Internet are important. Equally important is preparation in statistical analysis, psychology, and ethics, along with coursework that covers legal and regulatory aspects of the technology-driven marketing industry.

**INFOWEBLINKS**

You'll find additional information about this Computers in Context topic by visiting the **Computers and Marketing InfoWeb**.

W CLICK TO CONNECT
www.infoweblinks.com/np2012/ch01

# New Perspectives Labs

## On the BookOnCD

To access the New Perspectives Labs for Chapter 1, start the BookOnCD and then click the icon next to the lab title below.

▶ **OPERATING A PERSONAL COMPUTER**

### IN THIS LAB YOU'LL LEARN:

- How to start a Windows computer
- What to do when a computer is in sleep mode
- How to deactivate a screensaver
- How to select a different screensaver
- How to use the Alt, Ctrl, Esc, Num Lock, Caps Lock, Windows, Fn, Backspace, Delete, and arrow keys
- The difference between forward and backward slashes
- How to start and exit a program
- How to close a program that is not responding
- When to use the reset button
- How to shut down Windows

### LAB ASSIGNMENTS

1. Start the interactive part of the lab. Make sure you've enabled Tracking if you want to save your QuickCheck results. Perform each lab step as directed, and answer all the lab QuickCheck questions. When you exit the lab, your answers are automatically graded and your results are displayed.

2. Make a note of the brand and location of the computer you're using to complete these lab assignments.

3. Use the Start button to access your computer's Control Panel folder. Describe the status of your computer's power saver settings.

4. Preview the available screensavers on the computer you use most frequently. Select the screensaver you like the best and describe it in a few sentences.

5. What is the purpose of an Fn key? Does your computer keyboard include an Fn key? Explain why or why not.

6. In your own words, describe what happens when you (a) click the Close button, (b) hold down the Ctrl, Alt, and Del keys, (c) press the reset button, and (d) select the Shut Down option.

▶ **WORKING WITH BINARY NUMBERS**

### IN THIS LAB YOU'LL LEARN:

- The difference between the binary number system and the decimal number system
- How to count in binary
- How to convert decimal numbers into binary numbers
- How to convert binary numbers into decimal numbers
- How to use the Windows Calculator to convert numbers
- How to work with powers of two

### LAB ASSIGNMENTS

1. Start the interactive part of the lab. Make sure you've enabled Tracking if you want to save your QuickCheck results. Perform each lab step as directed, and answer all the lab QuickCheck questions. When you exit the lab, your answers are automatically graded and your results are displayed.

2. Using paper and pencil, manually convert the following decimal numbers into binary numbers. Your instructor might ask you to show the process that you used for each conversion.

   a. 100       b. 1,000       c. 256
   d. 27        e. 48          f. 112
   g. 96        h. 1,024

3. Using paper and pencil, manually convert the following binary numbers into decimal numbers. Your instructor might ask you to show the process that you used for each conversion.

   a. 100       b. 101         c. 1100
   d. 10101     e. 1111        f. 10000
   g. 1111000   h. 110110

4. Describe what is wrong with the following sequence:

   10  100  110  1000  1001  1100  1110  10000

5. What is the decimal equivalent of $2^0$? $2^1$? $2^8$?

# Key Terms

Make sure you understand all the boldfaced key terms presented in this chapter. With the NP2012 BookOnCD, you can use this list of terms as an interactive study activity. First, try to define a term in your own words, and then click the term to compare your definition with the definition presented in the chapter. Online, try your hand at the TechTerm Flashcards.

ALU, 31
Analog data, 22
Anonymizer tools, 10
Application software, 16
Apps, 20
ASCII, 24
Asynchronous communication, 6
Authentication protocol, 34
Binary number system, 23
Biometrics, 34
Bit, 23
Brute force attack, 37
Byte, 26
Case sensitive, 35
Central processing unit, 15
Character data, 24
Client, 18
Compiler, 30
Compute-intensive, 19
Computer, 14
Computer network, 7
Computer program, 15
Control unit, 31
Convergence, 8
CPU, 15
Cyberspace, 7
Data, 15
Data representation, 22
Dictionary attack, 36
Digital data, 22
Digital divide, 12
Digital revolution, 4
Digitization, 7

Download, 8
EBCDIC, 25
E-mail, 6
Extended ASCII, 24
File, 15
Gigabit, 26
Gigabyte, 26
Globalization, 12
Identity theft, 36
Input, 15
Instruction cycle, 32
Instruction set, 30
Integrated circuit, 27
Intellectual property, 11
Internet, 6
Interpreter, 30
Keylogger, 37
Kilobit, 26
Kilobyte, 26
Machine code, 30
Machine language, 30
Mainframe computer, 18
Megabit, 26
Megabyte, 26
Memory, 15
Microcontroller, 20
Microprocessor, 15
Numeric data, 23
Object code, 30
Online social networks, 6
Op code, 31
Open source, 12
Operand, 31

Operating system, 16
Output, 15
Password, 35
Password manager, 40
PDA, 19
Personal computer, 17
Phishing, 37
Portable media players, 20
Processing, 15
Programming language, 29
Registers, 31
Semiconducting materials, 27
Server, 18
Smartphone, 20
Sniffing, 37
Software, 15
Source code, 29
Storage, 15
Stored program, 16
Supercomputer, 18
Synchronous communication, 6
System board, 28
System software, 16
Unicode, 25
User ID, 34
Videogame console, 17
Web, 7
Workstation, 17

# Interactive Summary

To review important concepts from this chapter, fill in the blanks to best complete each sentence. When using the NP2012 BookOnCD, click the Check Answers buttons to automatically score your answers.

**SECTION A:** The [_____] revolution is an ongoing process of social, political, and economic change brought about by technologies such as computers and networks. The [_____] is a global computer network originally developed as a military project, adapted for research and academic use, and then for commercial use. [_____], a form of electronic communication, was an application for the masses and finally a reason to buy a computer and join the digital revolution. Another aspect of the digital revolution is [_____], a process by which several technologies with distinct functionalities evolve to form a single product. Technology has the potential to spread ideas, such as freedom and democracy, but it might have a chilling effect on [_____], or "the right to be left alone." It might also affect intellectual [_____] because digital technology has made it easy to produce copies with no loss in quality from the original. And although technology-driven [_____] has an effect on the economy, activists worry about the digital [_____] that separates people who have access to technology and those who do not.

▶ CHECK ANSWERS

**SECTION B:** A(n) [_____] is a multipurpose device that accepts input, processes data, stores data, and produces output according to a series of stored instructions. The data a computer is getting ready to process is temporarily held in [_____]. This data is then processed in the central processing [_____]. The series of instructions that tells a computer how to carry out processing tasks is referred to as a computer [_____], which forms the [_____] that sets up a computer to do a specific task. Data is typically stored in a(n) [_____] which is a named collection of data that exists on a storage medium, such as a hard disk, CD, DVD, Blu-ray disc, or USB flash drive. The idea of a [_____] program means that a series of instructions for a computing task can be loaded into a computer's memory. [_____] software is a set of computer programs that helps a person carry out a task. [_____] software helps the computer system monitor itself in order to function efficiently. For example, a computer [_____] system (OS) is essentially the master controller for all the activities that take place within a computer. Computers can be grouped into categories. A(n) [_____] computer is a type of microcomputer designed to meet the needs of an individual. The term [_____] can refer to an ordinary personal computer that is connected to a network or to a powerful desktop computer designed for high-performance tasks. A(n) [_____] is, at the time of its construction, one of the fastest computers in the world. A(n) [_____] computer is large, expensive, and capable of simultaneously processing data for hundreds or thousands of users. Mobile phones and portable media players can be classified as [_____] digital devices. A(n) [_____] is a special-purpose microprocessor that can control a device, such as a refrigerator or microwave oven.

▶ CHECK ANSWERS

## SECTION C:

[_____] data is processed, stored, and transmitted as a series of 1s and 0s. Each 1 or 0 is called a(n) [_____] . A series of eight 0s and 1s, called a(n) [_____] , represents one character—a letter, number, or punctuation mark. Data becomes [_____] when it is presented in a format that people can understand and use. [_____] data consists of numbers that might be used in arithmetic operations. It can be represented digitally using the [_____] number system. [_____] data is composed of letters, symbols, and numerals that are not used in arith-metic operations. Computers represent this type of data using [_____] , EBCDIC, or Unicode. Data is quantified using terms such as [_____] or kibibyte (1024 bytes), and prefixes, such as [_____] or mebi (1,048,576), and giga or [_____] (1,073,741,824). The bits that represent data travel as electronic pulses through [_____] circuits, sometimes called computer chips. These chips are made from [_____] materials and are housed in chip carriers that can be plugged into the [_____] board of a digital device. ▶ CHECK ANSWERS

## SECTION D:

Software is usually written in high-level languages, such as C, BASIC, COBOL, and Java. The human-readable version of a program, created in a high-level language by a programmer, is called [_____] code. A(n) [_____] or an interpreter converts this high-level code into [_____] code. A microprocessor is hard-wired to perform a limited set of activities, such as addition, subtraction, counting, and comparisons. This collection of preprogrammed activities is called a(n) [_____] set. Each instruction begins with a(n) [_____] code, which is a command word for an operation such as add, subtract, compare, or jump. Most instructions also include a(n) [_____] that specifies the data, or the address of the data, for the operation. The processor's ALU uses [_____] to hold data that is being processed. The processor's [_____] unit fetches each instruction, sends data to the registers, and then signals the ALU to begin processing. ▶ CHECK ANSWERS

## SECTION E:

Passwords and user IDs are the most common authentication [_____] . Password theft has become a serious security problem that has led to many cases of [_____] theft, when unauthorized individuals gain access to personal data. Hackers guess, discover, and steal passwords using a variety of techniques. A(n) [_____] attack tries passwords from a list of commonly used passwords. A(n) [_____] force attack tries every possible combination of letters and numbers. [_____] intercepts information sent out over computer networks. [_____] uses fraudulent Web sites or e-mail messages to fool unsuspecting readers into entering passwords and other personal information. A(n) [_____] is software that secretly records a user's keystrokes and sends them to a hacker. To keep passwords safe, you should consider using tiered passwords or standalone password [_____] software that generates secure passwords and keeps track of which password corresponds to each site you access. ▶ CHECK ANSWERS

# Interactive Situation Questions

Apply what you've learned to some typical computing situations. When using the NP2012 BookOnCD, you can type your answers, and then use the Check Answers button to automatically score your responses.

1. Suppose that you walk into an office and see the devices pictured to the right. You would probably assume that they are the screen, keyboard, and mouse for a(n) [_____] computer, workstation, or server.

2. You receive an e-mail message asking you to join a circle of friends. You assume that the message was generated in conjunction with an online [_____] network, such as Facebook, and if you become a member, you will be able to socialize online.

3. You go to the iTunes music store and purchase an album. When you see the [_____] message at the top of the screen, you know that the songs are being transferred from the remote iTunes server to your local computer.

4. You're visiting an antique shop and notice a collection of old fashioned radios. They actually feature a dial for tuning in different radio stations. You immediately recognize this as a(n) [_____] device because it deals with an infinite scale of values, rather than discrete values.

5. While attending a meeting at work, you hear one of the executives wondering if "unit code" would be helpful. After a moment of puzzlement, you realize that the executive really meant [_____], and that it would allow your company software to be translated into the Cyrillic alphabet used by the Russian language.

6. You have a new storage device that offers 2 GB of storage space. It is currently empty. Your friend wants to give you a large digital photo that's 16 MB. Will it fit on your storage device? [____]

7. Your bank is giving customers the choice of using a four-digit PIN or a password that can contain up to ten letters and numbers. The [_____] is more secure, so that's what you decide to use.

8. You need to select a password for your online PayPal account. Which of the following passwords would be the LEAST secure: jeff683, hddtmrutc, gargantuan, fanhotshot, bb#ii22jeffry, or high348? [_____]

▶ CHECK ANSWERS

# Interactive Practice Tests

Practice tests that consist of ten multiple-choice, true/false, and fill-in-the-blank questions are available on both the NP2012 BookOnCD and the NP2012 CourseMate Web site. BookOnCD test questions are selected at random from a large test bank, so each time you take a test, you'll receive a different set of questions. Your tests are scored immediately, and you can print study guides that help you find the correct answers for any questions that you missed. Online, you'll find a Practice Test for each section of the chapter. Your results from online tests are saved by Engagement Tracker. ▶ CLICK TO START

# Learning Objectives Checkpoints

Learning Objectives Checkpoints are designed to help you assess whether you have achieved the major learning objectives for this chapter. You can use paper and pencil or word processing software to complete most of the activities.

1. List five technologies that are fueling the digital revolution.

2. Define the term *convergence* and provide examples of at least five devices that are converging.

3. Describe at least two social, political, and economic effects of the digital revolution.

4. Draw a diagram to explain how a computer makes use of input, processing, storage, memory, output, and stored programs.

5. Describe the difference between system software, an operating system, application software, and a computer program.

6. List, briefly describe, and rank (in terms of computing capacity) the characteristics of each computer category described in Section B of this chapter.

7. List the characteristics that smartphones, PDAs, and portable media players have in common with personal computers, and list factors by which they differ.

8. Define the term *microcontroller* and provide three examples of devices in which microcontrollers are found.

9. Explain the technical difference between data and information.

10. Provide three examples of digital devices and three examples of analog devices.

11. List the ASCII representation for *B* and the binary representation for 18; draw a stepped waveform showing a digital sound; and draw a diagram showing how color is represented in a graphic.

12. List and define all the chapter terms, such as bit, byte, and kibibyte, that pertain to quantifying data.

13. Use the terms *integrated circuits*, *microprocessor*, and *system board* in a meaningful sentence.

14. Describe how compilers and interpreters work with high-level programming languages, source code, and object code.

15. Make a storyboard showing how a microprocessor's ALU would add the numbers 2 and 8.

16. Explain how hackers use dictionary and brute force attacks.

17. Provide examples of five secure passwords and five passwords that might be easy to crack.

Study Tip: Make sure you can use your own words to correctly answer each of the red focus questions that appear throughout the chapter.

# Concept Map

Fill in the blanks to show that you understand the relationships between programming concepts presented in the chapter.

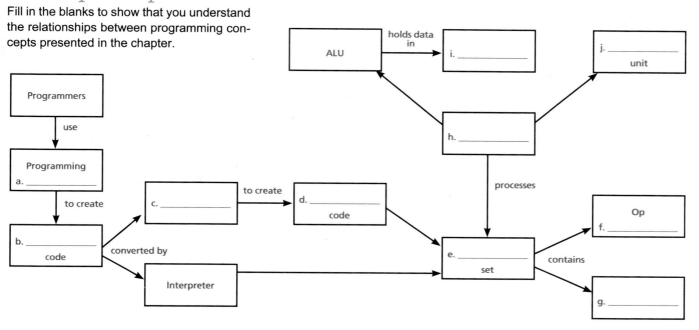

 CHECK ANSWERS

# Projects

##  CRITICAL THINKING

Whether you're taking this course to fulfill a graduation requirement, to improve your career options, or just for fun, take a few minutes to evaluate what you expect to gain from this course. Look through the table of contents of this textbook and select the five sections that you think will be most interesting, and the five sections that seem to be the least relevant to you. Incorporate your thoughts in two or three paragraphs that you e-mail to your instructor.

##  GROUP PROJECT

Form a group with four or five other students. Each student in the group should ask at least five friends if they have 1) a computer, 2) a cell phone, 3) a portable music player, 4) dial-up Internet access, 5) high-speed Internet access. Consolidate the data from all members of your group into an Excel spreadsheet, and then graph it. How do your statistics coincide with nationwide statistics for digital ownership? Graph or write a summary and make sure you cite your sources for national statistics.

##  CYBERCLASSROOM

Your instructor should provide each student with the e-mail addresses of four or five other students who will form a team, and designate a team leader. The team leader should find a news story about a technology issue from a source such as *news.google.com* and send it to one of the other students on the team. That student should add his or her opinion and comments, then send the message to another student in the group. Each student should use a different font color and initial their comments. When the message has circulated to all team members, it should be sent to your instructor. Make sure every member of the team is using antivirus software because, as you learned in the chapter, hackers can take advantage of unprotected computers.

##  MULTIMEDIA PROJECT

Screenshots can be useful tools for learning, documentation, and troubleshooting. Any time you need to show someone what's displayed on your computer screen, you can press the Print Screen (PrtScr) key, which stores a copy of the screen into memory. On a Mac, hold down the Command (Apple) key while you press the Shift key and the 3 key. From there, you can paste the screenshot into a document you're creating with a word processor. You can also paste it into a graphics program, such as Microsoft Paint, and then edit it. For this project, take a screenshot and paste it into a Word document. Under the screenshot, enter a description of the software and the purpose of the screen you captured.

##  RESUME BUILDER

Several Web sites offer career aptitude assessments that claim to help you select a career that's suited to your personality and background. Use a search engine to locate three free Web-based career aptitude tests. Take the tests. If you are asked to sign up, make sure you exercise caution in the amount of personal information you divulge. After completing the tests, compare the results. Do they all point you in a similar career direction? What is your reaction to the results? Which test do you think was the most valid and why? Provide your instructor with your analysis, along with the URLs for the Web sites that provided the tests.

##  GLOBALIZATION

Although the Internet provides a global communications network, communication between people still depends on finding a common language. For this project, explore the Web and experiment with ways in which technology is being used to close the language gap. You might start at Google or Wikipedia and look at the selection of languages they offer. Chronicle your exploration, making sure to document the Web sites you visited. What are your conclusions about Internet use by non-English speakers?

##  ISSUE

The Issue section of this chapter focused on the increasing use of digital devices that can track a person's location. Tracking technology has advantages and disadvantages. It has been used to track down terrorists and to find missing children, but it can also be abused by government and private companies. For this project, begin by scanning some of the links at the Digital Surveillance InfoWeb. Add to your knowledge by using a search engine, such as Google, to scan recent information about location-aware devices. Make a list of at least ten legitimate and useful applications of digital tracking. Make another list of ten abusive uses of tracking technology. Cite your sources for each item you list.

##  COMPUTERS IN CONTEXT

The Computers in Context section highlighted new technologies used in the marketing industry. Think of a product that you recently bought. Now, suppose you work for the company that produces the product and you've been assigned to create a marketing campaign. Create a table in which the first column contains a short description of every way you can think of to market the product. In the second column of the table, indicate the main technology used to communicate the marketing message. In column 3, indicate which of the methods would be considered direct marketing. In column 4, rank the marketing methods from most expensive (10) to least expensive (1). (You can use the Web to get estimated costs for various types of advertising.) Finally, in column 5, rank the marketing methods from most effective (10) to least effective (1). Submit your table following your instructor's guidelines for format and style.

# On the Web

## STUDENT EDITION LABS

When you purchase access to the NP2012 CourseMate Web site, you'll find targeted learning materials to help you understand key concepts and prepare for exams. See page O-41 in the Orientation Chapter for login instructions.

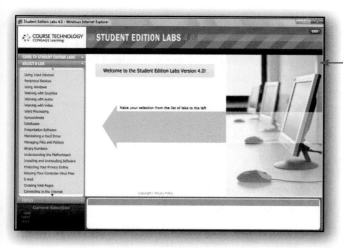

Work hands-on in structured simulations practicing important skills and concepts

### BINARY NUMBERS

In the Binary Numbers Student Edition Lab, you will learn about the following topics:

- Comparing binary numbers to decimal numbers
- Adding binary numbers manually
- Converting binary numbers to decimal equivalents

### UNDERSTANDING THE MOTHERBOARD

In the Understanding the Motherboard Student Edition Lab, you will learn about the following topics:

- Identifying components of the motherboard, such as integrated circuits, the CPU, RAM, ROM, and expansion slots and cards
- Modifying the way Windows handles virtual memory on a system
- Installing expansion cards into a PC

 **CHAPTER OVERVIEW COURSECAST**

Use your computer or iPod to hear a five-minute audio presentation of chapter highlights.

 **PRACTICE TESTS**

Review chapter material by taking these ten-question tests. Your results are saved by Engagement Tracker.

 **AUDIO FLASHCARDS**

Interact with audio flashcards to review key concepts from the chapter.

 **ONLINE GAMES**

Have some fun while refreshing your memory about key concepts that might appear on the next test.

 **DETAILED OBJECTIVES**

Make sure that you've achieved all the objectives for a chapter before it's time for your test!

**AND MORE!**

At the NP2012 CourseMate Web site you'll also find the NP2012 eBook, TechTerm Flashcards, Online Glossary, and What Do You Think? opinion polls.

# 2 Computer Hardware

## Chapter Contents

▶ SECTION A:
**PERSONAL COMPUTER BASICS**
Personal Computer Systems
Desktop and Portable Computers
Home, Game, and Small
    Business Systems
Buying Computer System Components

▶ SECTION B:
**MICROPROCESSORS AND MEMORY**
Microprocessor Basics
Today's Microprocessors
Random Access Memory
Read-only Memory
EEPROM

▶ SECTION C:
**STORAGE DEVICES**
Storage Basics
Magnetic Disk and Tape Technology
CD, DVD, and Blu-ray Technology
Solid State Storage
Storage Wrapup

▶ SECTION D:
**INPUT AND OUTPUT DEVICES**
Basic Input Devices
Display Devices
Printers
Installing Peripheral Devices

▶ SECTION E:
**HARDWARE SECURITY**
Anti-theft Devices
Surge Protection and Battery Backup
Basic Maintenance
Troubleshooting and Repair

▶ ISSUE:
**WHERE DOES ALL THE E-WASTE GO?**

▶ **COMPUTERS IN CONTEXT:**
**MILITARY**

▶ **NEW PERSPECTIVES LABS**

▶ **REVIEW ACTIVITIES**

▶ **ON THE WEB**

## Learning Objectives

After reading this chapter, you will be able to answer the following questions by completing the outcomes-based Learning Objectives Checkpoints on page 115.

1. What are the components of a typical personal computer system?
2. What is a computer form factor?
3. Is a home computer more or less desirable than a game console or small business computer?
4. What's the best way to select a computer?
5. Are PCs and Macs compatible?
6. Is it a good idea to upgrade an old computer?
7. How does a microprocessor work?
8. Why are some computers faster than others?
9. Why does a computer need memory?
10. What is the best type of storage for my data?
11. What factors affect a computer's screen display?
12. Are ink jet printers better than laser printers?
13. What's the best way to add devices to a computer system?
14. How can I protect my computer system from theft and damage?
15. Are there guidelines for troubleshooting hardware and software problems?

---

**InfoWebLinks**
Visit the InfoWebLinks site to access additional resources ⓦ that accompany this chapter.

**Multimedia and Interactive Elements**
When using the BookOnCD or CourseMate eBook, the ▶ icons are clickable to access multimedia resources.

## Pre-Assessment Quiz

Take the pre-assessment quiz to find out how much you know about the topics in this chapter. ▶

**Apply Your Knowledge** The information in this chapter will give you the background to:

- Identify all the components of a typical personal computer system
- Purchase a new computer based on features, performance, and price
- Upgrade your current computer
- Mod a computer
- Change your computer's boot settings in EEPROM

- Select a microprocessor based on performance specifications
- Select storage devices for your computer
- Change the resolution of your monitor
- Install peripheral devices
- Perform basic maintenance on your computer and troubleshoot hardware problems

## Try It

### HOW POWERFUL IS MY COMPUTER?

As you read Chapter 2, you'll learn that some computers are more powerful than others because they can store more data and process data faster. To find out how your home, work, or lab computer stacks up, you'll need to know a few of its specifications. Check your computer's specifications by starting your computer and then doing the following:

**1. Windows:** Click the **Start** button, then click **Control Panel**.

Select the **System** icon or link to open the System Properties dialog box. (If you're in Category View, click System and Maintenance first.)

If you see a window with tabs, make sure the General tab is displayed.

**MAC OS X:** Click the 🍎 **Apple** icon on the menu bar located at the top of the desktop. Select **About this Mac**.

**2.** Record information about your computer similar to the information provided for the sample computer in the table below.

**3.** Then, just to get an idea of the other equipment you've got attached to your Windows computer, click the link or icon for **Device Manager**. (You might have to click the Hardware tab first.) For more information about your Mac hardware, click the More Info button.

**4.** Browse through the list. When you're done, close all the dialog boxes.

**5.** If your computer has Windows 7, click **Check the Windows Experience Index**. Make a note of your computer's base score and subscores, then click the link to find out what the numbers mean.

|  | Sample Computer | Your Computer |
|---|---|---|
| **Computer Manufacturer** | Dell | |
| **Computer Model** | Studio 17 | |
| **Processor Manufacturer** | Intel | |
| **Processor Type** | Core i7 | |
| **Processor Speed** | 1.60 GHz | |
| **Operating System** | Windows 7 | |
| **RAM Capacity** | 6 GB | |

# Personal Computer Basics

**WHETHER YOU ARE SHOPPING** for a new computer, using your trusty laptop, or troubleshooting a system glitch, it is useful to have some background about computer system components and how they work. Section A begins with a framework for understanding the vast number of options available for putting together a personal computer system, and then wraps up with some tips on interpreting the jargon in computer ads and negotiating the digital marketplace.

## PERSONAL COMPUTER SYSTEMS

**What's a personal computer system?** The term *personal computer system* has at least two meanings. It can broadly refer to any computer system that uses personal computers for core processing operations. Such systems would include school labs and small business networks. In a more limited context, the term *personal computer system* refers to a personal computer, software, and peripheral devices that can be connected together for use by a single individual. This chapter focuses on computers in the latter context to make sure you're familiar with the hardware tools that make a computer system tick.

**What are the components of a typical personal computer system?** The centerpiece of a personal computer system is, of course, a personal computer. In addition, most systems include peripheral devices. The term **peripheral device** designates input, output, and storage equipment that might be added to a computer system to enhance its functionality. Popular peripheral devices include printers, digital cameras, scanners, joysticks, and speakers.

A personal computer system usually includes the components shown in Figure 2-1. These components are described briefly on the next page. They are defined and discussed in more detail later in the chapter.

**FIGURE 2-1**

A typical personal computer system includes the system unit and a variety of storage, input, and output devices. ▶ The components of a typical desktop system are shown here. To compare the components of desktops with portable computers, watch the video for this figure in your digital textbook.

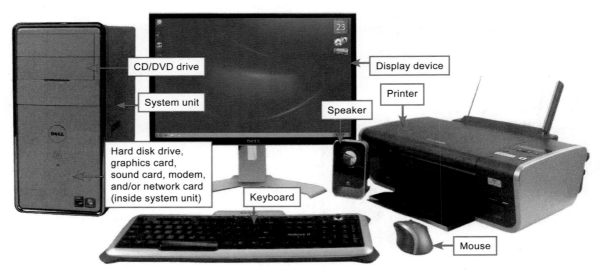

CD/DVD drive

Display device

Printer

System unit

Speaker

Hard disk drive, graphics card, sound card, modem, and/or network card (inside system unit)

Keyboard

Mouse

- System unit. The **system unit** is the case that holds the computer's main circuit boards, microprocessor, memory, power supply, and storage devices. Depending on the computer design, the system unit might also include other built-in devices, such as a keyboard and speakers.

- Keyboard. Most personal computer systems are equipped with a keyboard as the primary input device.

- Mouse. A mouse is an input device designed to manipulate on-screen graphical objects and controls.

- Hard disk drive. A hard disk drive is the main storage device on a personal computer system. It is usually mounted inside the computer's system unit and can store billions of characters of data. A small external light indicates when the drive is reading or writing data.

- Optical drive. An optical drive is a storage device that works with CDs, DVDs, Blu-ray discs, or some combination of these storage media. Optical drives are handy for playing audio CDs, DVD movies, and Blu-ray movies. They can also be used to store computer data on writable CDs, DVDs, and Blu-ray discs.

- Other storage. In the past, personal computers included a low-capacity storage device called a floppy disk drive. Today, these drives have been replaced by solid state storage options, such as USB flash drives and memory cards (Figure 2-2).

- Sound system. The sound system for a personal computer can output digital music, digitally recorded speech, and a variety of sound effects called system sounds designed to draw your attention to various messages and events. To produce sounds, a computer uses a circuit board called a sound card, which is typically housed in the system unit. A computer's sound card sends signals to speakers, which can be external devices or built into the system unit.

- Display system. A personal computer display system consists of two parts. Circuitry, called a graphics card, converts raw digital data into images that can be shown on a display device. Display devices, often called computer screens or monitors, present visual output, such as documents, photos, and videos. Personal computer systems can use several types of display technologies, including LCDs and LEDs. Display devices are usually integrated with the system unit of portable computers, but exist as standalone devices for computers that spend most of their time on a desk.

- Network and Internet access. Many personal computer systems include built-in circuitry for wired or wireless connections to a computer network. Networking circuitry is useful for constructing a home network or connecting to public networks in coffee shops and airports. Most Internet connections require a modem. Modems that establish an Internet connection using a standard telephone line are sometimes built into the system unit. Modems for cable, satellite, and other types of Internet access are usually separate components.

- Printer. A computer printer is an output device that produces computer-generated text or graphical images on paper.

The word peripheral is a relatively old part of computer jargon that dates back to the days of mainframes when the CPU was housed in a giant box and all input, output, and storage devices were housed separately. Technically speaking, a peripheral is any device that is not part of the CPU.

In the world of personal computers, however, the use of the term peripheral varies and it is often used to refer to any components that are not housed inside the system unit. Many personal computer owners do not think of a hard disk drive as a peripheral device, but technically it is one.

**FIGURE 2-2**

Computers provide sockets called ports for solid state storage such as these SD cards and USB flash drives.

## DESKTOP AND PORTABLE COMPUTERS

**What is the significance of different computer designs?** The industrial design principle that "form follows function" applies to computers. If you need a computer that's functional for mobile applications, you would not consider hauling around a large, heavy unit designed to remain on a desk. Instead, you would look for a computer "form" that suits your mobile "function."

In the computer industry, the term **form factor** refers to the size and dimensions of a component, such as a system board or system unit. Personal computers are available in all sorts of form factors; some are small and some are large; some are designed to remain on a desk, whereas others are designed to be portable.

**What are the characteristics of desktop computers?** A **desktop computer** fits on a desk and runs on power from an electrical wall outlet. The main component of a typical desktop computer is a system unit that houses the processor, memory, storage devices, display circuitry, and sound circuitry. A desktop computer's keyboard, mouse, and display screen are typically separate components that are connected to the main unit by cables or wireless technology.

The first personal computers were desktop models, and this style remains popular for offices, schools, and homes. Because their components can be manufactured economically, desktop computers typically provide the most computing power for your dollar. The price of an entry-level desktop computer starts at US$300 or a bit less, but most consumers select more powerful models that cost between $700 and $1,100.

A desktop computer's system unit can be housed in a vertical case or a horizontal case. Most horizontal units are placed under the display device to save desk space. Horizontal system units were once the most common desktop computer form factor; however, they are much less popular now that manufacturers offer a wider variety of options.

One of those options is a vertical system unit, which can be placed on the desk, on the floor, or in a cubbyhole beneath the desk. The case for a vertical system unit is often referred to as a *tower*. A **tower case** provides plenty of space for gamers and "modders" who want to soup up their machines by adding storage devices, lighted power cables, or accelerated graphics cards. Tower units are also the form factor of choice for computer owners who might want to upgrade components in the future because it is easy to get inside the case and swap out parts.

Another desktop computer option is a cube-shaped **mini case**, which is smaller than a tower unit and sometimes sports a handle. Mini cases are popular with gamers because they can be easily carried to LAN parties where they are networked together for multiplayer games.

Some manufacturers eliminate the separate system unit by incorporating computer circuitry in the back of a flat-panel screen. Dubbed an **all-in-one computer**, this form factor is handy, but has limited space for expansion. Figure 2-3 illustrates some popular desktop form factors.

**FIGURE 2-3**

A desktop computer fits on a desk and is tethered to a wall outlet.

A tower unit can be placed on the desk or on the floor.

A small form factor desktop is easy to carry, but is not classified as a portable computer because it requires power from a wall outlet and does not run on batteries.

The circuitry for this desktop all-in-one model is integrated into the case that holds the screen.

How do portable computers differ from desktops? A **portable computer** is a small, lightweight personal computer with screen, keyboard, storage, and processing components integrated into a single unit that runs on power supplied by an electrical outlet or a battery. Portable computers are ideal for mobile uses because they are easy to carry and can be used outdoors, in airports, and in classrooms without the need for a nearby electrical outlet. Portable computers are classified as notebooks, netbooks, and tablets (Figure 2-4).

What is a notebook computer? A **notebook computer** (also referred to as a laptop) is a small, lightweight portable computer that opens like a clamshell to reveal a screen and keyboard. Notebook computers tend to cost a bit more than desktop computers with similar computing power and storage capacity.

Notebook computers are popular with students because they don't take up too much space in crowded dorm rooms and they are fairly easy to carry around campus. On average, a notebook computer weighs about five pounds. The price of an entry-level notebook computer starts around $400. Consumers often spend between $700 and $1,000, however, to get the features and performance they want. A fully loaded notebook computer with widescreen display can cost more than $2,500.

What is a netbook? An increasingly popular type of personal computer called a **netbook** offers even more portability than a standard notebook computer. Classified as subnotebooks and sometimes referred to as mini-laptops, these small form factor computers are scaled-down versions of standard clamshell-style notebook computers. They are typically only seven or eight inches wide and weigh about two pounds. The small form factor doesn't have space for a CD or DVD drive, but one can be connected externally if needed to install software or play DVDs. Some netbooks run Windows, but Linux is also a popular operating system for these fully functional computers priced under $300.

What is a tablet computer? A **tablet computer** is a portable computing device featuring a touch-sensitive screen that can be used as a writing or drawing pad. A convertible tablet computer is constructed like a notebook computer, but the screen folds face up over the keyboard to provide a horizontal writing surface.

A slate tablet configuration resembles a high-tech clipboard and lacks a built-in keyboard (although one can be attached). The Apple iPad is a variation of the slate tablet design and fills a niche similar to netbooks. The iPad is smaller than a full-size tablet and has a more limited feature set. For example, the iPad does not have a built-in CD or DVD drive.

Tablet computers shine for applications that involve handwritten input. Most tablet computers are also configured to accept voice input. These capabilities are particularly useful for insurance adjusters who do most of their work at the scene of accidents and natural disasters, real estate agents who need access to data while out with clients, and health care workers who are moving quickly from one patient to the next.

When tablet computers were first introduced in 2002, they were priced significantly higher than notebook computers with similar processors and memory capacity. Currently, however, full-size tablet computers are priced only slightly higher than equivalent notebook computers, while iPad-sized tablets cost about $500.

**FIGURE 2-4**

Portable computers can run on batteries and incorporate the screen, drive, and CPU into a single unit.

A notebook computer is small and lightweight, giving it the advantage of portability. It can be plugged into an electrical outlet, or it can run on battery power.

Netbooks are scaled-down versions of standard notebook computers. They are lightweight, small, and very portable.

A convertible tablet computer is similar to a notebook computer, but the screen can swivel over the keyboard to provide a writing surface.

A slate is a type of tablet computer that's similar in size to a notebook computer, but features a touch-sensitive screen that can be used for input instead of a keyboard.

2

## HOME, GAME, AND SMALL BUSINESS SYSTEMS

**What's the significance of designations, such as home, small business, or game systems?** When studying computer ads and browsing vendor Web sites, you're likely to see some computer systems designated as home systems, whereas others are designated as game systems or small business systems. These designations are created by computer vendors to help consumers sort through the sometimes mind-boggling variety of configuration options.

**What differentiates a home computer from other types?** The idea of a home computer system probably developed because Microsoft offered Home and Professional versions of the Windows operating system. Windows Home version targeted less sophisticated users and originally was not meant to be used extensively for networking.

Today, the term **home computer system** encompasses a vast array of computer configurations designed to accommodate consumers who use computers for personal tasks. These systems also work for dual-use environments where a computer might be needed for general computing activities and also for home office tasks. Netbooks, as well as notebooks, tablets, and many desktop computers, are marketed as home computer systems.

The prices and features of home computer systems vary. Basic, inexpensive home systems offer adequate, but not super-charged, support for most computer applications, including Web browsing, e-mail, working with photos, downloading music, and working with general productivity applications, such as word processing. Software applications run at an acceptable speed, but graphics and games might be a bit slow.

A basic home computer system can also function for home office tasks with the addition of accounting software or other business applications.

Upscale home computer systems include cutting-edge computers, large-screen displays, and entertainment components to stream music throughout the house and display movies in a home theater (Figure 2-5).

**FIGURE 2-5**

Many high-end home computers are configured to function as the command center for watching movies and listening to music.

**NEW** **HP Pavilion dv8t series**

★★★★☆ **3.9 out of 5 stars** (111 reviews)

**iCore performance, Blu-ray, ultrawide display with 1080p and a 16:9 ratio, this 18" laptop is ready to bring you power and extreme entertainment. Includes discrete graphics**

• <u>Genuine</u> Windows 7 Home Premium 64-bit

• Intel(R) Core(TM) i5-450M Dual Core processor (2.40GHz, 3MB L3 Cache) with Turbo Boost up to 2.66 GHz

• FREE Upgrade to 6GB DDR3 System Memory (2 Dimm)

• 640GB 7200RPM SATA Dual Hard Drive (320GB x 2) with HP ProtectSmart Hard Drive Protection

• 1GB Nvidia GeForce GT 230M

• SuperMulti 8X DVD+/-R/RW with Double Layer Support

• SRS audio + Altec Lansing speakers

**What's so great about a gaming PC?** Some of the most cutting-edge computers are designed for gaming. Not only do these machines feature the fastest processors, they are also stuffed with memory, include state-of-the-art sound capabilities, and feature multiple graphics processors (Figure 2-6).

Although some manufacturers produce gaming notebook computers, most serious gamers tend to select desktop models because they are easier to customize and offer a little more power per dollar. The technophile features of a gaming computer come with a steep price premium. Computers start at $2,000 and quickly climb past the $4,000 price point.

**What are the characteristics of small business computers?** Computers marketed for small business applications tend to be middle-of-the-line models pared down to essentials. A medium-speed processor, moderate amount of RAM, and sensible disk capacity are adequate for basic business applications, such as word processing, spreadsheet analysis, accounting, and e-mail. Easy networking options allow small business computers to connect with other computers in an office environment.

Tower and all-in-one units are popular for in-office use, whereas notebook computers are a practical solution for employees who are on the go.

With price tags under $1,000, small business computers like those advertised in Figure 2-7 remain cost-effective because they are not loaded with memory, fancy graphics cards, or audio systems typical on home computers. Small business computers might not include a CD or DVD drive and often do not include speakers.

**FIGURE 2-6**

Inside the system unit, game computers feature state-of-the-art components for processing, graphics, and audio.

2

**FIGURE 2-7**

Small business owners want a cost-effective solution without bells and whistles.

## Vostro 230 Desktop

### Reliable, Expandable Solution for Small Business

From its scalable design to its ability to integrate with the latest Dell business hardware and services, the Vostro 230 desktop provides a strong foundation for your small business to grow on.

- **Smart, Scalable Design:** Just the right size for the office; easily set up and expandable for "future-proof" performance
- **Affordable Desktop Solution:** "Plug-and-play" compatibility with a range of affordable Dell business printers and monitors
- **Backed by Dell Services:** Full-service support options that can be customized to meet the unique needs of your small business

## BUYING COMPUTER SYSTEM COMPONENTS

**How do I get started?** The process of buying your own computer system is not cut and dried. Some experts advocate assessing your computing needs first, whereas other experts suggest researching features and prices. The trick is to do your homework for the entire system before jumping into a purchase of any one component. Remember that you will be purchasing peripherals, software, and accessories in addition to a computer. To prepare for a computer purchase, you should complete the following activities:

- Browse through computer magazines and online computer stores to get a general idea of features and prices.

- Decide on a budget and stick to it.

- Make a list of the ways you plan to use your computer.

- Select a platform.

- Decide on a form factor.

- Select peripherals, software, and accessories.

**Where can I find product information?** You can start by looking at ads in current computer magazines, such as *CPU*, *PCWorld*, and *Macworld*. You might visit computer stores online or in a nearby mall to get a general idea of prices and features.

**How can I make sense of all the jargon in computer ads?** Computer ads are loaded with jargon and acronyms, such as RAM, ROM, GHz, GB, and USB. You're sure to spot lots of this computer lingo in ads like the one in Figure 2-8.

When you complete this chapter, you should be able to sort out the terminology used in a typical computer ad. For terms you encounter that are not covered in this textbook, you can google the term or refer to online dictionaries and encyclopedias, such as Webopedia, Whatis.com, or Wikipedia.

**What can I expect to pay for a new computer?** Computers are sold at price points ranging from a few hundred dollars to several thousand dollars. Computer price points can be roughly grouped into three categories.

A computer priced higher than $1,500 is the computer equivalent of a luxury automobile. Computers in this price range contain one or more fast processors, a generous amount of RAM, and a copious amount of disk space. These computers contain state-of-the-art components and should not have to be replaced as quickly as less expensive computers. Computer game enthusiasts and anyone planning to work extensively with video editing, graphics, and desktop publishing are likely to require a high-end computer that costs over $1,200.

Computers that retail for between $500 and $1,200 might be considered the four-door sedans of the computer marketplace because a majority of buyers select computers in this price range. These popular computers lack the flashy specifications of their state-of-the-art cousins, but provide ample computing power to meet the needs of an average user.

**FIGURE 2-8**

A typical computer ad provides specifications couched in lots of computer jargon.

- Intel Core i5-520M processor 2.4 GHz 1066 MHz FSB
- 3 MB L2 cache
- 4 GB DDR3-800 MHz dual channel SDRAM
- 500 GB SATA HD (7200 rpm)
- 8x CD/DVD burner (Dual Layer DVD+/-R)
- 15.6" High Def (720p) LCD display screen
- 512 MB NVIDIA GeForce graphics card
- HD Audio 2.0 Support SRS Sound
- Integrated 1.3 megapixel Webcam
- 4 USB ports
- 1 IEEE 1394 port
- VGA and HDMI graphics ports
- 5-in-1 Media card reader
- Wireless networking 802.11 g/n
- Integrated 10/100 network card
- Windows 7 Home Premium 64-bit operating system
- Home/small business software bundle
- 1-year limited warranty

In the computer industry, the equivalent of a compact car is a sub-$500 computer. The technology in these computers is usually a year or two old and you can expect reduced processor speed, memory capacity, and drive capacity. Nevertheless, budget computers feature many of the same components that owners coveted in their state-of-the-art computers a few years back. You might have to replace a budget computer sooner than a more expensive computer, but it should be serviceable for typical applications.

**Why is it important to figure out how I'm going to use my new computer?** Computers can help you perform such a wide variety of tasks that it can be impossible to predict all the ways you might use your new machine in the future. You can, however, make a list of the ways you plan to immediately use your computer and that list can help you think about the features you'll need.

Some computer-based activities require more processing or storage capacity than others. Therefore, if you have some ideas about your computer usage, you're more likely to buy the right computer and not have to purchase expensive upgrades for it later. Figure 2-9 offers some guidelines to help you evaluate how your plan for using a computer might affect your purchase decision.

**FIGURE 2-9**

Situations such as those listed in the left column help to narrow down the mind-boggling number of choices offered to computer shoppers.

| Usage Plan | Purchase Recommendation |
|---|---|
| You plan to use your computer for popular tasks such as e-mail, browsing the Web, playing a few games, managing your checkbook, downloading digital music, and writing school papers. | A mid-priced computer with standard features might meet your needs. |
| You're on a budget. | A budget-priced computer will handle the same applications as a mid-priced computer, but some tasks might run more slowly. |
| You plan to work on accounting and budgeting for a small business. | Consider one of the business systems offered by a local or an online computer vendor. |
| You spend lots of time playing computer games. | Buy a computer with the fastest processor and graphics card you can afford. |
| You plan to work extensively with video editing or desktop publishing. | Select a computer system with a fast processor, lots of hard disk capacity, and a graphics card loaded with memory. |
| Someone who will use the computer has special needs. | Consider purchasing appropriate adaptive equipment, such as a voice synthesizer or one-handed keyboard. |
| You plan to use specialized peripheral devices. | Make sure the computer you purchase can accommodate the devices you plan to use. |
| Your work at home overlaps your work at school or on the job. | Shop for a computer that's compatible with those you use at school or work. |
| You want to work with specific software, such as a game or graphics tool. | Make sure you select a computer that meets the specifications listed on the software box or Web site. |
| You're buying a new computer to replace an old one. | If you have a big investment in software, you should select a new computer that's compatible with the old one. |

**How important is compatibility?** Suppose that you want to do some assignments at home using the same software provided by your school lab. Maybe you want to transport data back and forth between your job and home. Or, perhaps your children want to use a computer at home similar to those they use at school. Computers that operate in essentially the same way and use the same software are said to be compatible. To assess whether two computers are compatible, check their operating systems. Computers with the same operating systems can typically use the same software and peripheral devices.

Today, there are three personal computer platforms: PC, Mac, and Linux. The **PC platform** is based on the design for one of the first personal computer superstars—the IBM PC. The great grandchildren of the IBM PC are on computer store shelves today—a huge selection of personal computer brands and models manufactured by companies such as Lenovo, Hewlett-Packard, Dell, and Sony. The Windows operating system was designed specifically for these personal computers and, therefore, the PC platform is sometimes called the Windows platform.

The **Mac platform** is based on a proprietary design for a personal computer called the Macintosh (or Mac), manufactured almost exclusively by Apple Inc. The Mac lineup includes the iMac, MacBook, MacBook Air, MacBook Pro, Mac mini, Mac Pro, and iPad computers, all running the Mac OS operating system.

The **Linux platform** can use a standard PC or Mac running the Linux operating system. A variety of software is available for this platform, though it tends to be more specialized but not as polished as software for Windows and Mac operating systems.

At one time, the PC, Mac, and Linux platforms were not compatible because of hardware and operating system differences. Application software designed for Macs did not typically work on other platforms and vice versa.

The compatibility situation has changed because many Mac computers now use the same microprocessor as PCs. If you have a Mac computer with an Intel processor (sometimes called an Intel Mac), you can install Windows on it and run Windows software. You can also configure it to run Linux software.

The ability to run Windows offers Mac owners access to software from the PC and Mac platforms, and makes it possible to use the Mac OS to run one application, then switch to Windows to run another application. This capability can come in handy, for example, if a parent who uses Windows software is sharing a computer with an elementary-school student who is working with Macs at school.

**What about software?** Most computers are sold with a preinstalled operating system, which typically includes a Web browser and e-mail software. Some computers are bundled with application software that you can use to create documents, crunch numbers, and produce presentations. Check the software situation carefully. The trend today is for manufacturers to install trial software that you can use free for a few months. To continue using the software beyond the trial period, however, you have to pay for it. Such software is "included" but not "free." Buyer beware.

If you're purchasing a computer to do a task that requires specialized software, you should factor its cost into the cost of your computer system. Check the specifications listed on the software box to make sure your new computer has enough memory and processing speed to run it.

**TERMINOLOGY NOTE**

Computers that are compatible with the PC platform are usually referred to simply as PCs. Computers in the Mac platform are referred to as Macs.

Can I upgrade a computer to make it more powerful? When shopping for a computer system, your budget might not stretch to cover the cost of all the equipment you want. Or, you might wonder if you can extend the life of your current computer by upgrading key components. Some components are easy to add or change, whereas others are not. Figure 2-10 summarizes the most popular computer equipment upgrades, and indicates their average time for completion, cost, difficulty level, and accessibility.

**FIGURE 2-10**

Popular upgrades at a glance; in the Accessibility column, internal upgrades require you to open the system unit.

2

| Upgrade | Time | Cost (US$) | Difficulty | Accessibility |
|---|---|---|---|---|
| Replace processor | 1–5 hours | $200–$600 | Difficult and not recommended | Internal |
| Add memory | 30–60 minutes | $50–$300 | Moderate | Internal |
| Add external hard drive | 10–15 minutes | $100–$300 | Easy | External |
| Replace internal hard disk drive | 1–2 hours | $50–$500 | Somewhat difficult | Internal |
| Replace graphics card | 1 hour | $150–$500 | Moderate | Internal |
| Switch to wireless keyboard and mouse | 15 minutes | $50–$100 | Easy | External |
| Add USB port or digital camera memory card reader | 15 minutes | $20–$200 | Easy | External |
| Add second display screen | 5–10 minutes | $120–$500 | Easy | External |
| Add or replace speakers | 5–10 minutes | $50–$500 | Easy | External |
| Replace CD or DVD drive | 1–2 hours | $50–$150 | Moderate | Internal |

**What is a mod?** Upgrades and add-ons, such as those listed in Figure 2-10, are usually sanctioned and approved by computer manufacturers and vendors. However, some creative computer owners, called modders, work with unsanctioned modifications. In the context of computing, a **mod** is a custom hand-built modification to a computer system component.

Mods are analogous to hot rods in many ways. Just as hot rod construction begins with a standard car chassis, a computer mod begins with standard, off-the-shelf components. Hot rods can be chopped and jacked, fenders removed, windows added, engines chromed, and chassis painted in sparkling colors. Computer mods often include custom paint jobs, glowing lights, and clear Plexiglas side panels that offer a view of the system board.

**Where do modders find components?** Modders have built computers using discarded microwave ovens, vintage televisions, gumball machines, LEGOS, suitcases, and toys—all items that can be picked up in thrift stores or rummage sales.

Electronic components, such as cold cathode lights and neon string lights, can be scavenged from a variety of sources. RadioShack offers a collection of products for modders, but a much more extensive selection of modding components can be found at Web sites that specialize in modding. Figure 2-11 illustrates a creative mod that uses see-through and lighting effects.

**Where is the best place to buy a computer?** Consumers have many choices for computer vendors. Manufacturers such as Dell and Apple sell computers online at company Web sites, where you can easily configure a computer system with various features and get a price quote. The Web hosts a wide array of computer vendors. Make sure you are dealing with a reputable vendor before finalizing your purchase and providing your credit card number.

Computers and peripherals are also sold at office stores, such as OfficeMax, and electronics stores, such as Best Buy. You might have the option of working with a locally owned computer boutique. Most consumer advocates suggest shopping around to compare prices, service, and warranties.

Before you make a final decision on computer equipment or software, ask the following questions: Does your new equipment or software come with technical support? How long does the support last? How can you contact technical support? Is it free? Is the support staff knowledgeable? What is the duration of the equipment warranty? Does it cover the cost of parts and labor? Where do repairs take place? Who pays shipping costs for equipment that is sent to the manufacturer for repair? How long do repairs typically take? With the answers to these questions in hand along with your decisions about budget, form factor, and platform, you can be confident that you're making a savvy computer purchase.

**FIGURE 2-11**

Mods are customized computers that sport radical modifications, such as see-through cases and lighted cables.

---

## QuickCheck

1. A computer [_____] unit houses the main circuit board, microprocessor, storage devices, and network card.

2. Personal computers are available in a variety of [_____] factors, such as tower units, mini-cases, and all-in-one units.

3. The iPad is an example of a classification of portable computers called [_____].

4. Small [_____] computers are typically middle-of-the-line models that are not loaded with memory, fancy graphics cards, or audio systems.

5. There are three personal computer [_____]: PCs, Macs, and Linux.

▶ CHECK ANSWERS

# Microprocessors and Memory

**2**

**A TYPICAL COMPUTER AD** contains a long list of specifications that describe a computer's components and capabilities. Savvy shoppers understand how these specifications affect computer performance and price. Most computer specifications begin with the microprocessor type and speed. Computer manufacturers want consumers to think that faster is better, but is there a point at which you can pay for speed you won't need? Computer ads also contain information about a computer's memory capacity. Lots of memory can add hundreds of dollars to the cost of a computer. Consumers are right to ask "How much RAM is enough?" Section B explains how microprocessors and memory affect computer performance and price.

## MICROPROCESSOR BASICS

**What exactly is a microprocessor?** As you learned in Chapter 1, a microprocessor (sometimes simply referred to as a processor) is an integrated circuit designed to process instructions. It is the most important, and usually the most expensive, component of a computer. Although a microprocessor is sometimes mistakenly referred to as a computer on a chip, it can be more accurately described as a CPU on a chip because it contains—on a single chip—circuitry that performs essentially the same tasks as the central processing unit of a classic mainframe computer.

**What does it look like?** Looking inside a computer, you can usually identify the microprocessor because it is the largest chip on the system board, although it might be hidden under a cooling fan. Most of today's microprocessors are housed in a pin grid array chip package, as shown in Figure 2-12.

**What makes one microprocessor perform better than another?** Computer ads typically include microprocessor specifications related to performance. For example, an ad might describe a microprocessor as "Intel® Core i7 720QM 1.60 GHz, 1066 MHz FSB, 3 MB L2 Cache." A microprocessor's performance is affected by several factors, including clock speed, bus speed, word size, cache size, instruction set, number of cores, and processing techniques.

**What do MHz and GHz have to do with computer performance?** A specification, such as 2.4 GHz, that you see in a computer ad indicates the speed of the **microprocessor clock**—a timing device that sets the pace for executing instructions. Most computer ads specify the speed of a microprocessor in gigahertz. **Gigahertz** (GHz) means a billion cycles per second.

A cycle is the smallest unit of time in a microprocessor's universe. Every action a processor performs is measured by these cycles. It is important, however, to understand that the clock speed is not equal to the number of instructions a processor can execute in one second. In many computers, some instructions occur within one cycle, but other instructions might require multiple cycles. Some processors can even execute several instructions in a single clock cycle.

**FIGURE 2-12**

Today's microprocessors are typically housed in a PGA chip package.

A specification such as 1.60 GHz means that the microprocessor's clock operates at a speed of 1.6 billion cycles per second. If you are curious about the speed of the processor in your computer, Figure 2-13 can help you find it.

You might expect a computer with a 1.60 GHz processor to perform slower than a computer with a 2.40 GHz processor. This is not necessarily the case. Clock speed comparisons are only valid when comparing processors within the same chip family. As you might expect, a 1.87 GHz i7 840QM processor is faster than a 1.6 GHz i7 720QM processor.

Suppose, however, that you're shopping for a notebook computer and you have the option of an Intel i7 720QM 1.60 GHz processor or an i5 520M 2.4 GHz processor. You might be surprised that the i7 1.60 GHz processor is faster than the i5 2.4 GHz processor. Why? Because factors other than clock speed contribute to the overall performance of a microprocessor. In multi-core processors, the number of cores affects performance.

**What's a multi-core processor?** A single microprocessor that contains circuitry for more than one processing unit is called a **multi-core processor**. More cores usually produce faster performance. The i5 processor has two cores, giving it the equivalent of 4.8 GHz performance, where as the i7 processor has four cores, giving it the equivalent of 6.4 GHz performance.

**FIGURE 2-13**

You can discover your computer processor's specs using operating system utilities or third-party software, such as CPU-Z. If you are using a Mac, click the Apple icon and then select About This Mac. When using Windows, click the Control Panel button to access System Information.

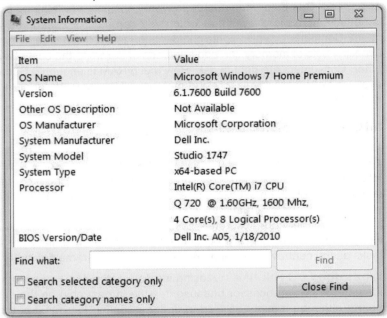

**What is FSB?** FSB stands for **front side bus**, a term that refers to the circuitry that transports data to and from the microprocessor. A fast front side bus moves data quickly and allows the processor to work at full capacity. FSB speed (technically its frequency) is measured in megahertz. **Megahertz** means one million cycles per second. Today's computers have FSB speeds ranging from 1000 MHz to 1600 MHz. Higher numbers indicate faster FSB speeds.

**How does the cache size affect performance?** **CPU cache** (pronounced "cash") is special high-speed memory that allows a microprocessor to access data more rapidly than from memory located elsewhere on the system board. A large cache can increase computer performance.

CPU cache is structured into several levels. Level 1 cache (L1) is the fastest, whereas Level 2 (L2) and Level 3 (L3) are slightly slower, but still faster than accessing main memory or disk storage. Cache capacity is usually measured in megabytes.

**What impact does word size have on performance?** **Word size** refers to the number of bits that a microprocessor can manipulate at one time. Word size is based on the size of registers in the ALU and the capacity of circuits that lead to those registers. A **64-bit processor**, for example, has 64-bit registers and processes 64 bits at a time. A large word size gives processors the ability to handle more data during each processing cycle—a factor that leads to increased computer performance. Today's personal computers typically contain 32-bit or 64-bit processors.

**How does an instruction set affect performance?** As chip designers developed various instruction sets for microprocessors, they added increasingly complex instructions, each requiring several clock cycles for execution. A microprocessor with such an instruction set uses **CISC** (complex instruction set computer) technology. A microprocessor with a limited set of simple instructions uses **RISC** (reduced instruction set computer) technology. A RISC processor performs most instructions faster than a CISC processor. It might, however, require more of these simple instructions to complete a task than a CISC processor requires for the same task.

Most processors in today's personal computers use CISC technology. Many processors used in handheld devices, such as iPods, Droids, and BlackBerrys, are ARM (advanced RISC Machine) processors.

A processor's ability to handle graphics can be enhanced by adding specialized graphics and multimedia instructions to a processor's instruction set. 3DNow!, MMX, AVX, and SSE5 are examples of instruction set enhancements sometimes mentioned in computer ads. Although instruction set enhancements have the potential to speed up games, graphics software, and video editing, they offer speed enhancements only with software designed to utilize these specialized instructions.

**Can a microprocessor execute more than one instruction at a time?** Some processors execute instructions "serially"—that is, one instruction at a time. With **serial processing**, the processor must complete all steps in the instruction cycle before it begins to execute the next instruction. However, using a technology called **pipelining**, a processor can begin executing an instruction before it completes the previous instruction. Many of today's microprocessors also perform **parallel processing**, in which multiple instructions are executed at the same time. Pipelining and parallel processing, illustrated in Figure 2-14, enhance processor performance.

To get a clearer picture of serial, pipelining, and parallel processing technology, consider an analogy in which computer instructions are pizzas. Serial processing executes only one instruction at a time, just like a pizzeria with one oven that holds only one pizza. Pipelining is similar to a pizza conveyor belt. A pizza (instruction) starts moving along the conveyor belt into the oven; but before it reaches the end, another pizza starts moving along the belt. Parallel processing is similar to a pizzeria with many ovens. Just as these ovens can bake more than one pizza at a time, a parallel processor can execute more than one instruction at a time.

**FIGURE 2-14**

Microprocessor designers have developed techniques for serial processing, pipelining, and parallel processing.

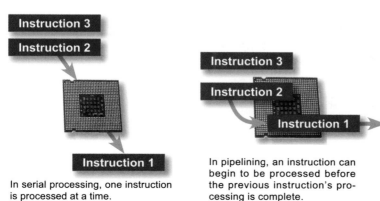

In serial processing, one instruction is processed at a time.

In pipelining, an instruction can begin to be processed before the previous instruction's processing is complete.

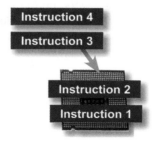

In parallel processing, multiple instructions can be processed at the same time.

**With so many factors to consider, how can I compare microprocessor performance?** Various testing laboratories run a series of tests to gauge the overall speed of a microprocessor. The results of these tests—called **benchmarks**—can then be compared to the results for other microprocessors. The results of benchmark tests are usually available on the Web and published in computer magazine articles.

Windows 7 offers a set of benchmarks called the Windows Experience Index that scores a computer's overall performance, and the performance of components such as its processor, memory, graphics, and storage system (Figure 2-15).

**FIGURE 2-15**

To access the Windows Experience Index, enter "Windows Index" in the Start menu's Search box.

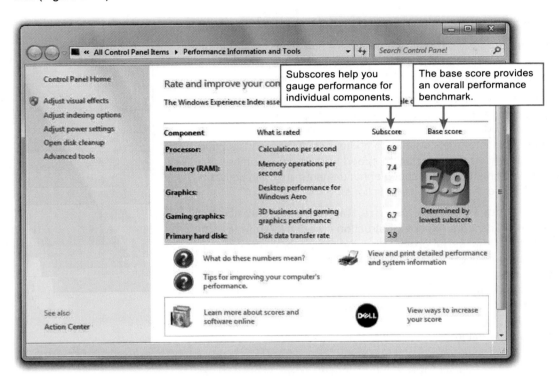

Subscores help you gauge performance for individual components.

The base score provides an overall performance benchmark.

**What do the Windows Experience Index scores mean?** Windows determines the performance subscores for five computer components: processor speed, memory transfer speed, ability to display the Aero desktop, 3-D and animated graphics performance, and disk drive data transfer rate. Scores range from a low of 1.0 to a high score of 7.9.

The base score is determined by the lowest subscore because the component with the worst performance sets the limit on overall performance. Computers with a base score lower than 3 might be fine for basic applications, but base scores above 6.0 are desirable for computers used for multiplayer and 3-D games, teleconferencing, and HDTV playback.

**INFOWEBLINKS**

For updates on popular microprocessors, you can connect to the **Microprocessor Update InfoWeb**.

 CLICK TO CONNECT
www.infoweblinks.com/np2012/ch02

## TODAY'S MICROPROCESSORS

**Which companies produce most of today's popular microprocessors?** Intel is the world's largest chipmaker and supplies a sizeable percentage of the microprocessors that power PCs. In 1971, Intel introduced the world's first microprocessor—the 4004. Intel's 8088 processor powered the original IBM PC. Since the debut of the IBM PC in 1985, Intel has introduced numerous microprocessors that have been used by most major computer manufacturers.

AMD (Advanced Micro Devices) is Intel's chief rival in the PC chip market. AMD's Phenom processors are direct competitors to Intel's Core 2 Quad line; AMD's Athlon X2 processors compete directly with Intel's Core 2 Duo processors (Figure 2-16). AMD processors are less expensive than comparable Intel models and have a slight performance advantage according to some benchmarks.

ARM processors are designed and licensed by ARM Holdings, a British technology company founded by Acorn Computers, Apple Inc., and VLSI Technology. Its RISC processors are used in many mobile phones and other handheld devices, such as the Apple iPad.

**Which microprocessor is best for my PC?** The microprocessor that's best for you depends on your budget and the type of work and play you plan to do. The microprocessors marketed with the current crop of computers can handle most business, educational, and entertainment applications. You'll want to consider the fastest processor offerings if you typically engage in processing-hungry activities, such as 3-D animated computer games, desktop publishing, multitrack sound recording, or video editing.

**Can I replace my computer's microprocessor with a faster one?** It is technically possible to upgrade your computer's microprocessor, but computer owners rarely do so. The price of the latest, greatest microprocessor can often get you more than halfway to buying an entirely new computer system. Technical factors also discourage microprocessor upgrades. A microprocessor operates at full efficiency only if all components in the computer can handle the faster speeds. In many cases, installing a new processor in an old computer can be like attaching a huge outboard engine to a canoe. In both cases, too much power can lead to disaster.

**What is overclocking?** **Overclocking** is a technique for increasing the speed of a computer component, such as a processor, graphics card, system board, or memory. When successful, overclocking can increase the processing power of a slow component to match that of a faster, more expensive component. Overclocking is popular with gamers who want to squeeze every bit of processing speed out of their computers.

**Why doesn't everyone overclock?** Overclocking is very risky. Additional electrical power pumped into a component increases heat output. Overclocked components can overheat and even catch fire. To maintain safe operating temperatures, modders install supplemental cooling systems, sometimes using heavy-duty heatsinks, big fans, liquid oxygen, dry ice, or other refrigerants.

**FIGURE 2-16**

Today's Popular Server, Desktop, and Mobile Microprocessor Families

| Processor | Application |
|---|---|
| **(intel)** | |
| Core i7 and i5 | Desktops and Notebooks |
| Pentium | Desktops |
| Celeron | Desktops and Notebooks |
| Xeon | Servers and Workstations |
| Itanium | Servers |
| Atom | Netbooks and Handhelds |
| **AMD** | |
| Phenom | Desktops |
| Athlon | Desktops and Notebooks |
| Sempron | Desktops and Notebooks |
| Turion | Notebooks |
| Opteron | Servers and Workstations |
| **ARM** | |
| ARM7 | Handhelds |
| Cortex | Mobile Phones |
| Cortex | PDAs |

## RANDOM ACCESS MEMORY

**What is RAM?** **RAM** (random access memory) is a temporary holding area for data, application program instructions, and the operating system. In a personal computer, RAM is usually several chips or small circuit boards that plug into the system board within the computer's system unit. A computer's RAM capacity is invariably included in the list of specifications in a computer ad (Figure 2-17).

The amount of RAM in a computer can affect the overall price of a computer system. To understand how much RAM your computer needs and to understand computer ad terminology, it is handy to have a little background on how RAM works and what it does.

**Why is RAM so important?** RAM is the "waiting room" for the computer's processor. It holds raw data waiting to be processed as well as the program instructions for processing that data. In addition, RAM holds the results of processing until they can be stored more permanently on disk or tape.

Let's look at an example. When you use personal finance software to balance your checkbook, you enter raw data for check amounts, which is held in RAM. The personal finance software sends to RAM the instructions for processing this data. The processor uses these instructions to calculate your checkbook balance and sends the results back to RAM. From RAM, your checkbook balance can be stored on disk, displayed, or printed.

In addition to data and application software instructions, RAM also holds operating system instructions that control the basic functions of a computer system. These instructions are loaded into RAM every time you start your computer, and they remain there until you turn off your computer.

**How does RAM differ from hard-disk storage?** RAM and hard disk storage both hold data. They are typically "hidden" inside the system unit and they can both be measured in gigabytes. To differentiate between RAM and hard-disk storage, remember that RAM holds data in circuitry that's directly connected to the system board, whereas hard-disk storage places data on magnetic media. RAM is temporary storage; hard-disk storage is more permanent. In addition, RAM usually has less storage capacity than hard-disk storage.

**How does RAM work?** In RAM, microscopic electronic parts called **capacitors** hold the bits that represent data. You can visualize the capacitors as microscopic lights that can be turned on or off. A charged capacitor is "turned on" and represents a "1" bit. A discharged capacitor is "turned off" and represents a "0" bit. Each bank of capacitors holds eight bits—one byte of data. A RAM address on each bank helps the computer locate data, as needed, for processing (Figure 2-18).

### FIGURE 2-17

A computer ad typically specifies the amount and type of RAM.

- Intel Core i7 720QM processor 1.60 GHz 1600 MHz FSB
- 6 MB L2 cache
- 4 GB DDR2-800 MHz dual channel SDRAM
- 500 GB SATA HD (7200 rpm)
- 16X max. DVD+/-R/RW SuperMulti drive

### FIGURE 2-18

Each RAM location has an address and uses eight capacitors to hold the eight bits that represent a byte. ▶ Your digital textbook shows you how RAM works with bits that represent data.

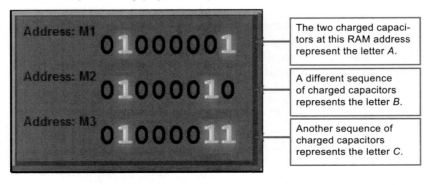

Address: M1  01000001 — The two charged capacitors at this RAM address represent the letter *A*.

Address: M2  01000010 — A different sequence of charged capacitors represents the letter *B*.

Address: M3  01000011 — Another sequence of charged capacitors represents the letter *C*.

In some respects, RAM is similar to a chalkboard. You can use a chalkboard to write mathematical formulas, erase them, and then write an outline for a report. In a similar way, RAM can hold numbers and formulas when you balance your checkbook, and then can hold the outline of your English essay when you use word processing software. RAM contents can be changed just by changing the charge of the capacitors.

Unlike disk storage, most RAM is **volatile**, which means it requires electrical power to hold data. If the computer is turned off, if the battery runs out of juice, or if a desktop computer is accidentally unplugged or experiences a power failure, all data stored in RAM instantly and permanently disappears.

**How much RAM does my computer need?** RAM capacity is expressed in gigabytes. Today's personal computers typically feature 2–8 GB of RAM. The amount of RAM your computer needs depends on the software you use. RAM requirements are routinely specified on the outside of a software package (Figure 2-19). If you need more RAM, you can purchase and install additional memory until you reach the maximum limit. For good basic performance, a computer running Windows 7 should have at least 1 GB of RAM. Games, desktop publishing, graphics, and video applications tend to run more smoothly with at least 2 GB of RAM.

**Can my computer run out of memory?** Suppose that you want to work with several programs and large graphics at the same time. Will your computer eventually run out of memory? The answer is "probably not." Today's personal computer operating systems are quite adept at allocating RAM space to multiple programs. If a program exceeds its allocated space, the operating system uses an area of the hard disk, called **virtual memory**, to store parts of programs or data files until they are needed. By selectively exchanging the data in RAM with the data in virtual memory, your computer effectively gains almost unlimited memory capacity.

Too much dependence on virtual memory can slow down your computer's performance, however, because getting data from a mechanical device, such as a hard disk drive, is much slower than getting data from an electronic device, such as RAM. To minimize virtual memory use, load up your computer with as much RAM as possible.

**How do I add RAM?** First, check how much RAM is currently installed, and then check the maximum RAM limit to make sure RAM can be added. Check your computer documentation or the manufacturer's Web site for information on the type and speed of RAM required.

Most of today's personal computers use SDRAM (synchronous dynamic RAM), which is fast and relatively inexpensive. SDRAM (shown in Figure 2-20) is further classified as DDR, DDR2, or DDR3. Make sure that you purchase the right type.

RAM speed is often expressed in nanoseconds or megahertz. One nanosecond (ns) is one-billionth of a second. In the context of RAM speed, lower **nanosecond** ratings are better because it means the RAM circuitry can react faster to update the data it holds. For example, 8 ns RAM is faster than 10 ns RAM.

RAM speed can also be expressed in MHz (millions of cycles per second). Just the opposite of nanoseconds, higher MHz ratings mean faster speeds. For example, 1066 MHz RAM is faster than 800 MHz RAM.

After purchasing RAM, follow your computer manufacturer's instructions for opening the system unit and inserting the RAM modules.

**FIGURE 2-19**

Minimum RAM requirements are typically displayed on the package of a software product.

Minimum System Requirements:
- Windows 7 or Vista
- 1 GB of RAM
- 450 MB hard drive space
- CD drive for installation
- Mouse
- Internet connection (optional)
- Printer (optional)
- Scanner or digital camera with 32-bit twain interface (optional)

**FIGURE 2-20**

SDRAM is the most popular type of RAM in today's computers. It is typically available on a small circuit board. When adding memory to a computer, check with the computer manufacturer to make sure you purchase the correct RAM type and speed.

## READ-ONLY MEMORY

**How is ROM different from RAM?** **ROM** (read-only memory) is a type of memory circuitry that holds the computer's startup routine. ROM is housed in a single integrated circuit—usually a fairly large, caterpillar-like DIP package—which is plugged into the system board.

Whereas RAM is temporary and volatile, ROM is permanent and non-volatile. ROM holds "hard-wired" instructions that are a permanent part of the circuitry and remain in place even when the computer power is turned off. This is a familiar concept to anyone who has used a handheld calculator that includes various hard-wired routines for calculating square roots, cosines, and other functions. The instructions in ROM are permanent, and the only way to change them is to replace the ROM chip.

**If a computer has RAM, why does it need ROM too?** When you turn on your computer, the microprocessor receives electrical power and is ready to begin executing instructions. As a result of the power being off, however, RAM is empty and doesn't contain any instructions for the microprocessor to execute. Now ROM plays its part. ROM contains a small set of instructions called the **ROM BIOS** (basic input/output system). These instructions tell the computer how to access the hard disk, find the operating system, and load it into RAM. After the operating system is loaded, the computer can understand your input, display output, run software, and access your data.

## EEPROM

**Where does a computer store its basic hardware settings?** To operate correctly, a computer must have some basic information about storage, memory, and display configurations. For example, your computer needs to know how much memory is available so that it can allocate space for all the programs you want to run.

RAM goes blank when the computer power is turned off, so configuration information cannot be stored there. ROM would not be a good place for this information, either, because it holds data on a permanent basis. If, for example, your computer stored the memory size in ROM, you could never add more memory—well, you might be able to add it, but you couldn't change the size specification in ROM. To store some basic system information, your computer needs a type of memory that's more permanent than RAM, but less permanent than ROM. EEPROM is just the ticket.

**EEPROM** (electrically erasable programmable read-only memory) is a non-volatile chip that requires no power to hold data. EEPROM replaces CMOS technology that required power from a small battery integrated into the system board.

When you change the configuration of your computer system—by adding RAM, for example—the data in EEPROM must be updated. Some operating systems recognize such changes and automatically perform the update. You can manually change EEPROM settings by running your computer's setup program, as described in Figure 2-21 on the next page.

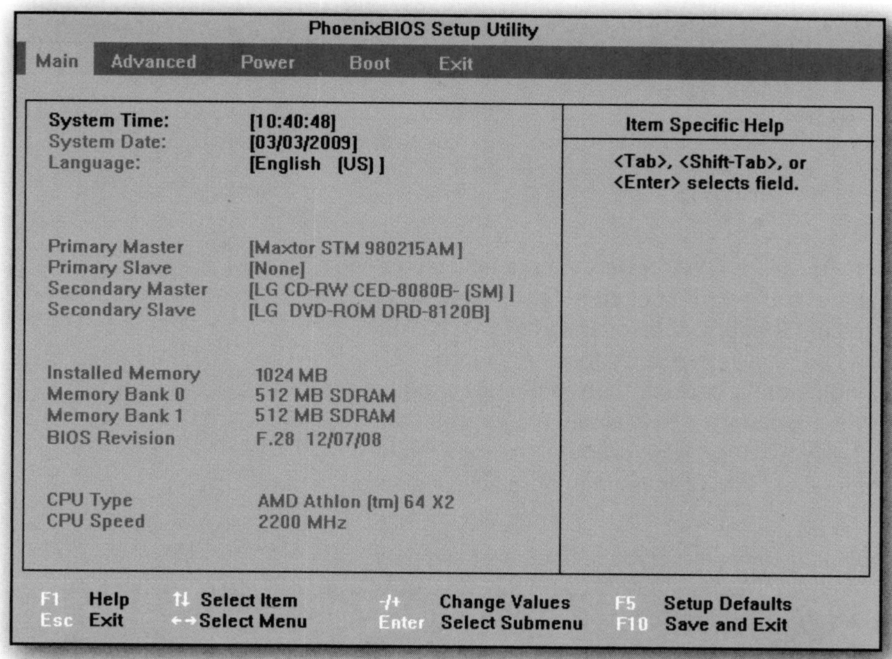

```
                    PhoenixBIOS Setup Utility
  ┌──────────────────────────────────────────────────────────────┐
  │ Main  Advanced  Power   Boot   Exit                           │
  ├──────────────────────────────────────┬───────────────────────┤
  │                                       │                       │
  │ System Time:      [10:40:48]          │   Item Specific Help  │
  │ System Date:      [03/03/2009]        │                       │
  │ Language:         [English  [US]]     │  <Tab>, <Shift-Tab>, or│
  │                                       │  <Enter> selects field.│
  │                                       │                       │
  │ Primary Master    [Maxtor STM 980215AM]│                      │
  │ Primary Slave     [None]              │                       │
  │ Secondary Master  [LG CD-RW CED-8080B- [SM]]                  │
  │ Secondary Slave   [LG  DVD-ROM DRD-8120B]                     │
  │                                       │                       │
  │ Installed Memory    1024 MB           │                       │
  │ Memory Bank 0       512 MB SDRAM      │                       │
  │ Memory Bank 1       512 MB SDRAM      │                       │
  │ BIOS Revision       F.28  12/07/08    │                       │
  │                                       │                       │
  │ CPU Type            AMD Athlon (tm) 64 X2                     │
  │ CPU Speed           2200 MHz          │                       │
  │                                       │                       │
  ├──────────────────────────────────────┴───────────────────────┤
  │ F1   Help    ↑↓ Select Item    -/+   Change Values  F5  Setup Defaults │
  │ Esc  Exit    ←→ Select Menu   Enter  Select Submenu F10 Save and Exit  │
  └──────────────────────────────────────────────────────────────┘
```

**FIGURE 2-21**

EEPROM holds computer configuration settings, such as the date and time, hard disk capacity, number of floppy disk drives, and RAM capacity. To access the EEPROM setup program, hold down the F1 key as your computer boots. But be careful! If you make a mistake with these settings, your computer might not be able to start.

If you mistakenly enter the setup program, follow the on-screen instructions to exit and proceed with the boot process. The Esc (Escape) key typically allows you to exit the setup program without making any changes to the EEPROM settings.

**What information about memory performance is most important?** Even though ROM and EEPROM have important roles in the operation of a computer, RAM capacity really makes a difference you can notice. With lots of RAM, you'll find that documents scroll faster, games respond more quickly, and many graphics operations take less time than with a computer that has a skimpy RAM capacity.

Most ads specify RAM capacity, speed, and type. Now when you see the specification "2 GB Dual Channel DDR2 SDRAM at 800 MHz (max 4 GB)" in a computer ad, you'll know that the computer's RAM capacity is 2 gigabytes (enough to run Windows 7), that it operates at 800 megahertz (fairly fast), and that it uses dual-channel, double data rate SDRAM. You'll also have important information about the maximum amount of RAM that can be installed in the computer—4 GB, which is more than enough for the typical computer owner who does a bit of word processing, surfs the Web, and plays computer games.

# QuickCheck

1. A personal computer with an Intel Core i7 microprocessor is likely to operate at a speed of 1.86 _____ . (Hint: Use the abbreviation.)

2. A(n) _____ side bus is circuitry that transports data to and from the processor.

3. 4004, 8088, Athlon, and Pentium are all types of _____ .

4. *DDR2*, *virtual*, and *volatile* are terms that apply to _____ . (Hint: Use the acronym.)

5. The instructions for loading the operating system into RAM when a computer is first turned on are stored in _____ . (Hint: Use the acronym.)

▶ CHECK ANSWERS

# Storage Devices

**COMPUTER MANUFACTURERS** typically try to entice consumers by configuring computers with a variety of storage devices, such as a hard disk drive, solid-state card readers, and some sort of CD or DVD drive. What's the point of having so many storage devices? As it turns out, none of today's storage technologies is perfect. One technology might provide fast access to data, but it might also be susceptible to problems that could potentially wipe out all your data. A different technology might be more dependable, but it might have the disadvantage of relatively slow access to data.

Smart shoppers make sure their new computers are equipped with a variety of storage devices. Informed computer owners understand the strengths and weaknesses of each storage technology so that they can use these devices with maximum effectiveness. In this section, you'll find guidelines that can make you a smart storage technology buyer and owner. The storage technologies you'll learn about are now used in a variety of devices—from digital cameras to player pianos—so an understanding of storage technology can be useful even outside the boundaries of personal computing.

## STORAGE BASICS

**What are the basic components of a data storage system?** A data storage system has two main components: a storage medium and a storage device. A **storage medium** (*storage media* is the plural) is the disk, tape, CD, DVD, paper, or other substance that contains data. A **storage device** is the mechanical apparatus that records and retrieves data from a storage medium. Storage devices include hard disk drives, floppy disk drives, tape drives, CD drives, DVD drives, and flash drives. The term *storage technology* refers to a storage device and the media it uses.

**How does a storage device interact with other computer components?** You can think of your computer's storage devices as having a direct pipeline to RAM. Data gets copied from a storage device into RAM, where it waits to be processed. After data is processed, it is held temporarily in RAM, but it is usually copied to a storage medium for more permanent safekeeping.

As you know, a computer's processor works with data that has been coded into bits that can be represented by 1s and 0s. When data is stored, these 1s and 0s must be converted into some kind of signal or mark that's fairly permanent, but can be changed when necessary.

Obviously, the data is not literally written as "1" or "0." Instead, the 1s and 0s must be transformed into something that can remain on the surface of a storage medium. Exactly how this transformation happens depends on the storage technology. For example, hard disks store data in a different way than CDs. Three types of storage technologies are commonly used for personal and handheld computers: magnetic, optical, and solid state.

**Which storage technology is best?** Each storage technology has its advantages and disadvantages. If one storage system was perfect, we wouldn't need so many storage devices connected to our computers! To compare storage devices, it is useful to apply the criteria of versatility, durability, speed, and capacity.

**How can one storage technology be more versatile than another?** The hard disk drive sealed inside a computer's system unit is not very versatile; it can access data only from its fixed disk platters. More versatile devices can access data from several different media. For example, a DVD drive is versatile because it can access computer DVDs, DVD movies, audio CDs, computer CDs, and CD-Rs.

**What makes a storage technology durable?** Most storage technologies are susceptible to damage from mishandling or environmental factors, such as heat and moisture. Some technologies are more susceptible than others to damage that could cause data loss. CDs and DVDs tend to be more durable than hard disks, for example.

**What factors affect storage speed?** Quick access to data is important, so fast storage devices are preferred over slower devices. **Access time** is the average time it takes a computer to locate data on the storage medium and read it. Access time for a personal computer storage device, such as a disk drive, is measured in milliseconds (thousandths of a second). One millisecond (ms) is one-thousandth of a second. Lower numbers indicate faster access times. For example, a drive with a 6 ms access time is faster than a drive with an access time of 11 ms.

Access time is best for random-access devices. **Random access** (also called direct access) is the ability of a device to "jump" directly to the requested data. Floppy disk, hard disk, CD, DVD, and solid state drives are random-access devices, as are the memory cards used in digital cameras. A tape drive, on the other hand, must use slower **sequential access** by reading through the data from the beginning of the tape. The advantage of random access becomes clear when you consider how much faster and easier it is to locate a song on a CD (random access) than on a cassette tape (sequential access).

**Data transfer rate** is the amount of data a storage device can move per second from the storage medium to the computer. Higher numbers indicate faster transfer rates. For example, a hard disk drive with a 57 MBps (megabits per second) data transfer rate is faster than one with a 50 MBps transfer rate.

**What's important about storage capacity?** In today's computing environment, higher capacity is almost always preferred. Storage capacity is the maximum amount of data that can be stored on a storage medium, and it is measured in bytes; usually in gigabytes (GB), or terabytes (TB).

Storage capacity is directly related to **storage density**, the amount of data that can be stored in a given area of a storage medium, such as the surface of a disk. The higher the storage density, the more data is stored. Storage density can be increased by making the particles representing bits smaller, by layering them, packing them closer together, or standing them vertically (Figure 2-22).

**FIGURE 2-22**

Vertical storage produces higher storage capacities than horizontal storage.

With horizontal storage, particles are arranged end to end, and use of the disk surface is not optimized.

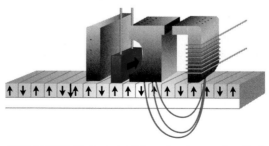

With vertical storage, particles stand on end so that many more can be packed on the disk surface.

2

## MAGNETIC DISK AND TAPE TECHNOLOGY

**What is magnetic disk and tape technology?** Hard disk, floppy disk, and tape storage technologies can be classified as **magnetic storage**, which stores data by magnetizing microscopic particles on a disk or tape surface. The particles retain their magnetic orientation until that orientation is changed, thereby making disks and tapes fairly permanent but modifiable storage media. A **read-write head** mechanism in the disk drive can magnetize particles to write data, and sense the particles' polarities to read data. Figure 2-23 shows how a computer stores data on magnetic media.

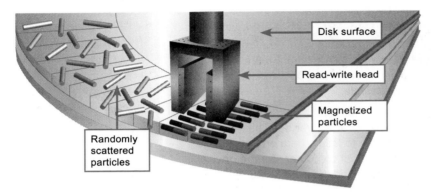

Disk surface

Read-write head

Magnetized particles

Randomly scattered particles

**FIGURE 2-23**

Before data is stored, particles on the surface of the disk are scattered in random patterns. The disk drive's read-write head magnetizes the particles, and orients them in a positive (north) or negative (south) direction to represent 0 and 1 bits.

Data stored magnetically can be easily changed or deleted simply by changing the magnetic orientation of the appropriate particles on the disk surface. This feature of magnetic storage provides lots of flexibility for editing data and reusing areas of a storage medium containing unneeded data.

Data stored on magnetic media can be unintentionally altered by magnetic fields, dust, mold, smoke particles, heat, and mechanical problems with a storage device. Over time, magnetic media gradually lose their magnetic charge, resulting in lost data. Some experts estimate that the reliable life span of data stored on magnetic media is about three years. They recommend that you refresh your data every two years by recopying it.

**Why are hard disk drives so popular?** Hard disk technology is the preferred type of main storage for most computer systems for three reasons. First, it provides lots of storage capacity. Second, it provides fast access to files. Third, a hard disk is economical. The cost of storing 40 megabytes of data is about a penny. You'll find hard disk drives in all kinds of digital devices, including personal computers, iPod classics, and TiVo digital video recorders (DVRs).

**How does hard disk technology work?** As the main storage device on most computers, a **hard disk drive** contains one or more platters and their associated read-write heads. A **hard disk platter** is a flat, rigid disk made of aluminum or glass and coated with magnetic iron oxide particles. More platters mean more data storage capacity. The platters rotate as a unit on a spindle, making thousands of rotations per minute.

Each platter has a read-write head that hovers over the surface to read data. The head hovers only a few microinches above the disk surface, as shown in Figure 2-24 on the next page.

**TERMINOLOGY NOTE**

You might hear the term *fixed disk* used to refer to hard disks. You often see the terms *hard disk* and *hard disk drive* used interchangeably, although technically *hard disk* refers to the platters sealed inside the hard disk drive.

Spindle

Read-write head

Platters

**FIGURE 2-24**

Hard disk platters and read-write heads are sealed inside the drive case or cartridge to screen out dust and other contaminants. ▶ The video for this figure in your digital textbook shows how a hard drive works and what happens when a hard disk crashes.

Personal computer hard disk platters are typically 3.5" in diameter, with storage capacities ranging from 40 GB to 2 TB. Miniature hard drives, such as Hitachi's 1" Microdrive featured on Apple's iPod, store 30 to 160 GB.

Hard disk access times of 6 to 11 ms are not uncommon, whereas a CD takes about half a second to spin up to speed and find data. Hard disk drive speed is sometimes measured in revolutions per minute (rpm). The faster a drive spins, the more rapidly it can position the read-write head over specific data. For example, a 7,200 rpm drive is able to access data faster than a 5,400 rpm drive.

Computer ads typically specify the capacity, access time, and speed of a hard disk drive. So "160 GB 8 ms 7200 RPM HD" means a hard disk drive with 160 gigabyte capacity, access time of 8 milliseconds, and speed of 7,200 revolutions per minute. Ads rarely specify the amount of data that a hard drive can transfer, but the average data transfer rate is about 57,000 KBps (also expressed as 57 MBps or MB/s).

**What's all this business about Ultra ATA, EIDE, SCSI, and DMA?** Computer ads use these acronyms to describe hard disk drive technology. A hard drive mechanism includes a circuit board called a **hard disk controller** that positions the disk, locates data, and interfaces with components on the system board. Disk drives are classified according to their controllers. Popular types of drive controllers include SATA, Ultra ATA, EIDE, and SCSI. Although computer ads often specify the hard drive controller type, consumers don't really have much choice. If you want a 160 GB drive, for example, your hardware vendor is likely to offer only one brand of drive with one type of controller. Figure 2-25 shows a typical controller mounted on a hard disk drive.

The storage technology used on many PCs transfers data from a disk, through the controller, to the processor, and finally to RAM before it is actually processed. Computer ads sometimes specify this technology. DMA (direct memory access) technology allows a computer to transfer data directly from a drive into RAM, without intervention from the processor. This architecture relieves the processor of data-transfer duties and frees up processing cycles for other tasks. UDMA (ultra DMA) is a faster version of DMA technology.

**TERMINOLOGY NOTE**

Data transfer rates can be specified in bits or bytes, so read the specifications carefully.

50 Mbps or MB/s means 50 mega*bits* per second.

50 MBps or MB/s means 50 mega*bytes* per second.

Also stay alert for the difference between kilo (K) and mega (M), remembering that mega is 1,000 times more than kilo.

**FIGURE 2-25**

A hard disk controller circuit board is typically mounted in the hard disk drive case.

**What's the downside of hard disk storage?** Hard disks are not as durable as many other storage technologies. The read-write heads in a hard disk hover a microscopic distance above the disk surface. If a read-write head runs into a dust particle or some other contaminant on the disk, it might cause a **head crash**, which damages some of the data on the disk. To help prevent contaminants from contacting the platters and causing head crashes, a hard disk is sealed in its case. A head crash can also be triggered by jarring the hard disk while it is in use. Although hard disks have become considerably more rugged in recent years, you should still handle and transport them with care. You should also make backup copies of the data stored on your hard disk in case of a head crash.

**Can I use a second hard disk drive to increase storage space?** You can increase the storage capacity of your computer by adding a second hard disk drive, which can also provide a backup for your primary drive. Hard disk drives are available as internal or external units. Internal drives are inexpensive and can be easily installed in a desktop computer's system unit. External drives are slightly more expensive and connect to a desktop or notebook computer using a cable.

**What is floppy disk technology?** At one time, just about every personal computer included a floppy disk drive (Figure 2-26) that stored data on **floppy disks** (also called floppies or diskettes). This storage technology is no longer used because a floppy disk's 1.44 MB capacity is not sufficient for today's media-intensive applications. Many MP3 music files and photos are too large to fit on a floppy. In the past, floppy disks were extensively used to distribute software. CDs and DVDs offer more capacity for distributing the huge files for today's software applications. Web downloads offer more convenience.

**FIGURE 2-26**

A standard floppy disk drive reads and writes data on a 3.5" floppy disk.

**Do computers still store data on tapes?** Next time you watch a movie from the 1950s or 1960s that shows a computer, look for the big reels of tape used as storage devices. Tape storage, once used to store mainframe data and also used for personal computer backups, is too slow for modern computing.

## CD, DVD, AND BLU-RAY TECHNOLOGY

**How do CD, DVD, and Blu-ray technologies differ?** Today, most computers come equipped with one or more drives designed to work with CD, DVD, and Blu-ray technologies.

**CD** (compact disc) technology was originally designed to hold 74 minutes of recorded music. The original CD standard was adapted for computer storage with capacity for 650 MB of data. Later improvements in CD standards increased the capacity to 80 minutes of music or 700 MB of data.

**DVD** (digital video disc or digital versatile disc) is a variation of CD technology that was originally designed as an alternative to VCRs, but was quickly adopted by the computer industry to store data. The initial DVD standard offered 4.7 GB (4,700 MB) of data storage; that's about seven times as much capacity as a CD. Subsequent improvements in DVD technology offer even more storage capacity. A **double layer DVD** has two recordable layers on the same side and can store 8.5 GB of data.

**Blu-ray** is a high-capacity storage technology with a 25 GB capacity per layer. The name *Blu-ray* is derived from the blue-violet colored laser used to read data stored on Blu-ray discs. DVD technology uses a red laser; CD technology uses a near infrared laser.

**How do CD, DVD, and Blu-ray drives work?** CD, DVD, and Blu-ray technologies are classified as **optical storage**, which stores data as microscopic light and dark spots on the disc surface. The dark spots, shown in Figure 2-27, are called **pits**. The lighter, non-pitted surface areas of the disc are called **lands**.

Optical drives contain a spindle that rotates the disc over a laser lens. The laser directs a beam of light toward the underside of the disc. The dark pits and light lands on the disc surface reflect the light differently. As the lens reads the disc, these differences are translated into the 0s and 1s that represent data (Figure 2-28).

**FIGURE 2-27**

As seen through an electron microscope, the pits on an optical storage disc look like small craters. Each pit is less than 1 micron (one-millionth of a meter) in diameter—1,500 pits lined up side by side are about as wide as the head of a pin.

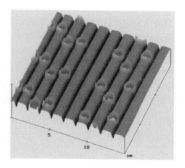

**FIGURE 2-28**

CD, DVD, and Blu-ray drives use a laser to read data from the underside of a disc.

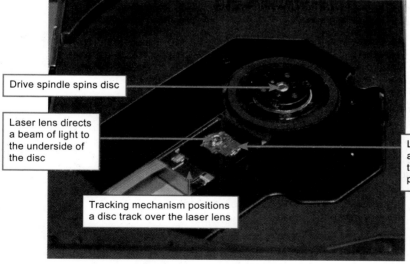

Drive spindle spins disc

Laser lens directs a beam of light to the underside of the disc

Laser pickup assembly senses the reflectivity of pits and lands

Tracking mechanism positions a disc track over the laser lens

The surface of an optical disc is coated with clear plastic, making the disc quite durable and less susceptible to environmental damage than data recorded on magnetic media. An optical disc, such as a CD, is not suscepti- ble to humidity, fingerprints, dust, magnets, or spilled soft drinks. Scratches on the disc surface can interfere with data transfer, but a good buffing with toothpaste can erase the scratch without damaging the underlying data. An optical disc's useful life is estimated to be more than 30 years. Figure 2-29 illustrates the layers of an optical disc.

**FIGURE 2-29**

CDs, DVDs, and Blu-ray discs are constructed with one or more layers of recording sur- face sandwiched between protective plastic.

**How fast are CD, DVD, and Blu- ray drives?** The original CD drives could access 150 kilobytes per second (150 KBps) of data. The next genera- tion of drives doubled the data transfer rate and were consequently dubbed "2X" drives. Transfer rates seem to be continually increasing. A 52X CD drive, for example, transfers data at 7,800 KBps, which is still relatively slow com- pared to an average hard disk drive's transfer rate of 57,000 KBps.

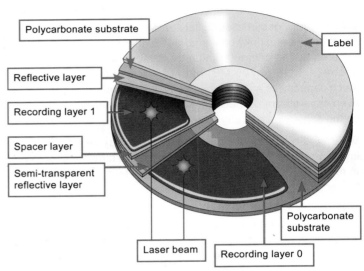

The speed of a DVD drive is measured on a different scale than a CD drive. A 1X DVD drive is about the same speed as a 9X CD drive. Today's DVD drives typically have 24X speeds for a data transfer rate of about 3,600 KBps.

Blu-ray drive speed is measured on an even different scale. A 1X Blu-ray drive transfers data at 4,500 KBps.

**What's the significance of ROM, R, and RW?** Optical technologies are grouped into three categories: read-only, recordable, and rewritable.

**Read-only technology** (ROM) stores data permanently on a disc, which cannot be subsequently added to or changed. Read-only discs, such as CD-ROMs, CDDAs, DVD-Video, and DVD-ROMs, are typically pre-pressed during mass production and used to distribute software, music, and movies.

**Recordable technology** (R) uses a laser to change the color in a dye layer sandwiched beneath the clear plastic disc surface. The laser creates dark spots in the dye that are read as pits. The change in the dye is permanent, so data cannot be changed once it has been recorded.

**Rewritable technology** (RW) uses phase change technology to alter a crystal structure on the disc surface. Altering the crystal structure creates patterns of light and dark spots similar to the pits and lands on a CD. The crystal structure can be changed from light to dark and back again many times, making it possible to record and modify data much like on a hard disk. The term *rerecordable* (RE) is sometimes used instead of *rewritable*.

**What are my choices for CD, DVD, and Blu-ray media?** Several CD and DVD formats are currently popular for use in personal computers:

TERMINOLOGY NOTE

The letter *D* in acronyms for optical media such as CDs and DVDs formally means *disc*. In common usage, however, you will often see it spelled *disk*.

- **CDDA** (compact disc digital audio), more commonly known as audio CD, is the format for commercial music CDs. Music is typically recorded on audio CDs by the manufacturer, but can't be changed by the consumer.

- **DVD-Video** (digital versatile disc video) is the format for commercial DVDs that contain feature-length films.

- **CD-ROM** (compact disc read-only memory, pronounced "cee dee rom") was the original optical format for computer data. Data is stamped on the disc at the time it is manufactured. Data cannot be added, changed, or deleted from these discs.
- **DVD-ROM** (digital versatile disc read-only memory) contains data stamped onto the disc surface at the time of manufacture. Like CD-ROMs, the data on DVD-ROMs is permanent, so you cannot add or change data.
- **CD-R** (compact disc recordable) discs store data using recordable technology. The data on a CD-R cannot be erased or modified once you record it. However, most CD-R drives allow you to record your data in multiple sessions. For example, you can store two files on a CD-R disc today, and add data for a few more files to the disc at a later time.
- **DVD+R** or **DVD-R** (digital versatile disc recordable) discs store data using recordable technology similar to a CD-R, but with DVD storage capacity.
- **CD-RW** (compact disc rewritable) discs store data using rewritable technology. Stored data can be recorded and erased multiple times, making it a very flexible storage option.
- **DVD+RW** or **DVD-RW** (DVD rewritable) discs store data using rewritable technology similar to CD-RW, but with DVD storage capacity.
- **BD-ROM** (Blu-ray read-only memory) is used for movies; **BD-R** (Blu-ray recordable) can be written to once; **BD-RE** (Blu-ray rerecordable) can record and erase data multiple times.

**TERMINOLOGY NOTE**

Even though *CD-ROM* and *ROM BIOS* both contain the word *ROM*, they refer to quite different technologies. ROM BIOS is a chip on the system board that contains permanent instructions for the computer's boot sequence. A CD-ROM drive is an optical storage device that's usually installed in one of the system unit's drive bays.

**Are rewritable CD, DVD, or Blu-ray drives an acceptable replacement for a hard disk?** A rewritable CD, DVD, or Blu-ray drive is a fine addition to a computer system, but is not a good replacement for a hard disk drive. Unfortunately, the process of accessing, saving, and modifying data on a rewritable disc is relatively slow compared to the speed of hard disk access.

**Can I use a single drive to work with any CD, DVD, or Blu-ray media?** Most CD drives can read CD-ROM, CD-R, and CD-RW discs, but cannot read DVDs or BDs. Most DVD drives can read CD and DVD formats. Storing computer data and creating music CDs require a recordable or rewritable device. As you can see from the table in Figure 2-30, the most versatile optical storage device is a Blu-ray DVD writer.

**FIGURE 2-30**

CD and DVD Capabilities

| | Play Audio CDs | Play DVD Movies | Read CD Data | Read DVD Data | Create Music CDs | Store Data on CDs | Store Data on DVDs | Store Data on BDs |
|---|---|---|---|---|---|---|---|---|
| **CD-ROM Drive** | ✔ | | ✔ | | | | | |
| **CD-R Drive** | ✔ | | ✔ | | ✔ | ✔ | | |
| **CD-RW Drive** | ✔ | | ✔ | | ✔ | ✔ | | |
| **DVD/CD-RW Drive** | ✔ | ✔ | ✔ | ✔ | ✔ | ✔ | | |
| **DVD-R/RW/ CD-RW Drive** | ✔ | ✔ | ✔ | ✔ | ✔ | ✔ | ✔ | |
| **Blu-ray Drive** | ✔ | ✔ | ✔ | ✔ | | | | ✔ |
| **Blu-ray/DVD Writer** | ✔ | ✔ | ✔ | ✔ | ✔ | ✔ | ✔ | ✔ |

## SOLID STATE STORAGE

**What is solid state storage?** **Solid state storage** (sometimes called flash memory) is a technology that stores data in erasable, rewritable circuitry, rather than on spinning disks or streaming tape. It is widely used in portable consumer devices, such as digital cameras, portable media players, PDAs, iPads, and cell phones. It is also used as an alternative for hard disk storage in some notebook computers and netbooks.

Solid state storage is removable and provides fairly fast access to data. It is an ideal solution for storing data on mobile devices and transporting data from one device to another.

**How does solid state storage work?** Solid state storage contains a gridwork of circuitry. Each cell in the grid contains two transistors that act as gates. When the gates are open, current can flow and the cell has a value that represents a "1" bit. When the gates are closed by a process called Fowler-Nordheim tunneling, the cell has a value that represents a "0" bit.

Very little power is required to open or close the gates, which makes solid state storage ideal for battery-operated devices, such as digital cameras and media players. Once the data is stored, it is **non-volatile**—the chip retains the data without the need for an external power source.

Solid state storage provides fast access to data because it includes no moving parts. This storage technology is very durable—it is virtually impervious to vibration, magnetic fields, or extreme temperature fluctuations. On the downside, the capacity of solid state storage does not currently match that of hard disks. The cost per megabyte of solid state storage is slightly higher than for magnetic or optical storage.

**What are my options for solid state storage?** Several types of solid state storage are available to today's consumers. The formats for small, flat memory cards include CompactFlash, MultiMedia, Secure Digital (SD), xD-Picture Cards, and SmartMedia. A **card reader** is a device that reads and writes data on solid state storage. Sometimes referred to as 5-in-1, 7-in-1, or all-in-one card readers, these combination devices work with multiple types of solid state storage formats (Figure 2-31).

Because digital photography is so popular, many notebook and desktop computers have a built-in card reader to make it simple to transfer photos from your camera to your computer. Moving data in the other direction, a computer can download MP3 or iTunes music files and store them on a solid state memory card. That card can be removed from the computer and inserted into a portable media player, so you can listen to your favorite tunes while you're on the go.

For even more versatility, solid state drives and USB flash drives can be used to store computer data files and programs. A **solid state drive** (SSD) can be used as a substitute for a hard disk drive in handheld devices and netbooks. A **USB flash drive** is typically used for storing data files and programs that you want to use on various computers; for example, on your home computer and at work or in a school lab.

FIGURE 2-31

Most personal computers are equipped with a card reader for transferring data to and from solid state memory cards.

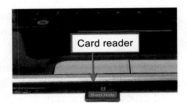

**Do I need a solid state drive?** Solid state drives like the one in Figure 2-32 are sometimes available as an alternative to a conventional hard disk drive. Like hard disk drives, SSDs offer fast data transfer rates and are fixed in place. Although they use the same technology as USB flash drives, SSDs cannot be easily removed from a computer.

When shopping for a netbook or notebook computer, you might have the choice of a hard disk drive or SSD. The SSD option would be attractive for customers who use computers in rugged conditions. Currently, solid state drives are not a popular option for adding storage capacity to existing computers.

**What is the best use for USB flash drives?** A USB flash drive is a portable storage device that plugs directly into a computer's system unit using a built-in connector (Figure 2-33).

Also called thumb drives, pen drives, jump drives, keychain drives, or UFDs, USB flash drives are about the size of a highlighter pen and so durable that you can literally carry them on your key ring. USB flash drives have capacities ranging from 16 MB to 256 GB.

USB flash drive data transfer speeds average 10–35 MBps (10,000–35,000 KBps). At these speeds, flash drives are slower than hard disk drives, so you might notice a bit of hesitation, especially when working with large files.

Files stored on a USB flash drive can be opened, edited, deleted, and run just as though those files were stored on magnetic or optical media. You might say that USB flash drives are the new floppy disks because not only can you access files as if they were stored on disks, but you can carry them from one computer to another and you can run software from them, too.

When a USB flash drive is inserted, your computer automatically detects it. Macs display a flash drive icon on the desktop. Windows detects the flash drive and displays the AutoPlay window shown in Figure 2-34 so that you can quickly access files.

**FIGURE 2-32**

Solid state drives store data in erasable, rewritable circuitry.

**FIGURE 2-33**

A USB flash drive plugs directly into a computer's system unit.

**FIGURE 2-34**

To view the files and programs stored on a USB flash drive, insert it into the computer. Windows displays the AutoPlay window that you can use to quickly view the files stored on the USB device.

## STORAGE WRAPUP

**Can I add storage to my computer?** You can increase storage capacity by adding hard drives and you can add storage flexibility by installing additional types of storage devices.

External storage devices, such as external hard disk drives, CD drives, DVD drives, and USB flash drives, simply plug into connectors built into your computer's system unit. They can be easily detached when you want to move your computer or if your external drive contains a backup that you want to store away from your computer.

Before you disconnect any storage device, make sure you understand the manufacturer's instructions for doing so. On PCs, you usually have to use the Safely Remove Hardware icon on the Windows taskbar. Macs usually provide an eject icon next to the drive listing.

As an alternative to an external drive, you can install storage devices inside your computer's system unit case in "parking spaces" called **drive bays**. An external drive bay provides access from outside the system unit—a necessity for a storage device with removable media, such as floppy disks, CDs, and DVDs.

Internal drive bays are located deep inside the system unit and are designed for hard disk drives, which don't use removable storage media. Most desktop and notebook computers include at least one internal drive bay and one or more external bays (Figure 2-35).

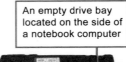

An empty drive bay located on the side of a notebook computer

**FIGURE 2-35**

Most notebook computers provide bays for one hard disk drive and one CD or DVD drive.

Most desktop computers have several drive bays, some accessible from outside the case, and others—designed for hard disk drives—without any external access. Empty drive bays are typically hidden from view with a face plate.
▶ Watch the video for this figure to find out how to install internal and external drives.

**What are the relative advantages and disadvantages of each type of computer storage device?** Earlier in the chapter, you read that no storage technology is perfect. While hard disk drives offer fast and inexpensive access, they are not the most durable technology. CD and DVD technology is durable, but slow, and flash drive storage is expensive when compared to other storage media. The table in Figure 2-36 summarizes the relative advantages and disadvantages of each storage technology covered in this section.

**FIGURE 2-36**

Storage Technology Comparison

2

| Storage Device | Cost of Device | Capacity | Cost of Media (Disk/Tape) | Data Transfer Rate | Technology | Removable |
|---|---|---|---|---|---|---|
| USB Flash Drive | $15–$500 | 2–256 GB | | 10–35 MBps | Solid state | Yes |
| CD-RW | $30–$60 | 700 MB | $0.64 in bulk | 7.8 MBps (52X) | Optical | Yes |
| DVD+RW | $40–$400 | 8.5 GB | $0.45 in bulk | 3.6 MBps (24X) | Optical | Yes |
| Blu-ray Writer | $90–$300 | 50 GB | $15.00 | 4.5 MBps (1X) | Optical | Yes |
| Floppy Disk Drive | $15–$30 | 1.44 MB | $0.17 | 62.5 KBps | Magnetic | Yes |
| Hard Drive (Internal) | $50–$400 | 80 GB–2 TB | | 50–100 MBps | Magnetic | No |
| Hard Drive (External) | $70–$250 | 80 GB–2 TB | | 12–480 MBps | Magnetic | Yes |
| Solid State Drive (Internal) | $120–$1,000 | 32 GB–256 GB | | 100–200 MBps | Solid state | No |
| Tape Drive | $300–$1,000 | 4 GB–800 GB compressed | $3–$150 in bulk | 2–160 MBps | Magnetic (sequential) | No |

# QuickCheck

1. Access [_____] is typically faster for random-access devices than for sequential-access devices.

2. A magnetic storage device uses a read-[_____] head to magnetize particles that represent data.

3. A hard disk drive that is rated at a speed of 7200 [_____] will give you faster access to your data than a drive rated at 5400. (Hint: Use the acronym.)

4. CD-R technology allows you to write data on a disc, and then change that data. True or false? [_____]

5. A(n) [_____] uses the same storage technology as a USB flash drive, but is not designed to be removable. (Hint: Use the acronym.)

▶ CHECK ANSWERS

# Input and Output Devices

**THIS SECTION** provides an overview of the most popular input and output devices for personal computers. It begins with input devices, including keyboards, mice, trackpads, joysticks, and touch screens. Next, a survey of computer display devices helps you understand their features and settings. A guide to printers describes today's most popular printer technologies. You'll also take a look at the computer's expansion bus—the components that carry data to peripheral devices. With an understanding of how the expansion bus works, you'll be able to select, install, and use all kinds of peripherals.

## BASIC INPUT DEVICES

**What devices can I use to get data into a computer?** Most computer systems include a keyboard and pointing device, such as a mouse, for basic data input. Touch-sensitive screens offer an additional input option. Other input devices, such as scanners, digital cameras, and graphics tablets, are handy for working with graphical input. Microphones and electronic instruments provide input capabilities for sound and music.

**What's special about a computer keyboard's design?** The design of most computer keyboards is based on the typewriter's qwerty layout, which was engineered to keep the typewriter's mechanical keys from jamming. In addition to a basic typing keypad, desktop and notebook computer keyboards include a collection of keys such as Alt, Ctrl, and Print Screen, designed for computer-specific tasks.

Most desktop computer keyboards include a calculator-style numeric keypad, plus an editing keypad with keys such as End, Home, and Page Up, to efficiently move the screen-based insertion point. You can even find tiny keyboards on handheld devices—entering text and numbers is an important part of most computing tasks.

**What does a pointing device do?** A **pointing device** allows you to manipulate an on-screen pointer and other screen-based graphical controls. The most popular external pointing devices for personal computers include mice, trackballs, and joysticks. External pointing devices, such as those in Figure 2-37 can be connected to the computer with a cable or with a wireless connection.

**Which pointing device should I choose?** Most desktop computer systems include a **mouse** as the primary pointing device. Many computer owners also add a mouse to their notebook computers. A mouse includes one or more buttons that can be clicked to input command selections, such as "Start" and "Shut down."

A **trackball** consists of a ball resting in a stationary base. Controlling a trackball uses a different set of muscles than controlling a mouse, so some computer owners periodically switch to a trackball to prevent stress injuries.

A **joystick** looks like a small version of a car's stick shift. Moving the stick provides input to on-screen objects. Some joysticks are designed for people who have physical disabilities that prevent them from using a mouse.

**FIGURE 2-37**

An optical mouse uses an onboard chip to track a light beam as it bounces off a surface, such as a desk, clipboard, or mouse pad.

With a trackball, you use your fingers or palm to roll the ball and move the pointer. Buttons on the base serve the same function as the buttons on a mouse.

Joysticks can include several sticks and buttons for arcade-like control when playing computer games.

**When do I need a trackpad?** A **trackpad** (or touchpad) is a touch-sensitive surface on which you can slide your fingers to move the on-screen pointer. Trackpads also include buttons that serve the same function as mouse buttons. Trackpads are typically supplied with notebook and net-book computers so that it is not necessary to carry a mouse as an extra component.

The act of moving your fingers on the surface of a trackpad is called a ges-ture. On a standard trackpad, sliding a single finger moves the pointer. With a multi-touch trackpad, additional gestures are possible (Figure 2-38).

FIGURE 2-38

Touchpad Gestures

2

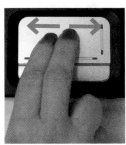

Zoom in: Move two fingers apart to zoom in and enlarge photos or documents.

Zoom out: Move two fingers closer to each other to reduce the size of images or documents.

Horizontal scrolling: Move two fingers to the right or left.

Vertical scrolling: Move two fingers up or down.

Rotate: Turn two fingers on the trackpad to rotate an image.

Tap: Tapping the trackpad performs the same function as clicking a mouse button.

Two-finger tap: Tapping the trackpad with two fingers generates a right-click.

Swipe: Move three fingers horizontally to step through a series of photos, album covers, or windows.

**How does a touch screen work?** Tablet computers, handheld devices, retail store self checkouts, and information kiosks collect input from a **touch screen**, which overlays a display screen. The most commonly used touch screen technology is a transparent panel coated with a thin layer of electrically conductive material that senses a change in the electri-cal current when touched. This "resistive" technology is fairly durable. It is not susceptible to dust or water, but it can be damaged by sharp objects. Processing technology can interpret a single touch or more complex input such as handwriting.

The coordinates for a touch event are processed in essentially the same way as a mouse click. For example, if you touch your iPad screen at the location of a button labeled Calendar, the area you touch generates coor-dinates and sends them to the processor. The processor compares the coordinates to the image displayed on the screen to find out what is at the coordinates, and then responds, in this case by opening your appointment calendar. A popular use for touch screens is to display a keyboard on the screen of a handheld device, as shown in Figure 2-39.

FIGURE 2-39

Most touch screens use resis-tive technology that registers a change in electrical current when touched.

## DISPLAY DEVICES

**What are my options for display devices?** A computer display device, sometimes referred to as a monitor, that simply displays text and images is classified as an output device. Touch-sensitive screens, however, can be classified as both input and output devices because they accept input and display output. Two technologies are commonly used for computer display devices: LCD and LED.

An **LCD display** (Figure 2-40) produces an image by filtering light through a layer of liquid crystal cells. Modern LCD (liquid crystal display) technology is compact in size, lightweight, and provides an easy-to-read display. LCDs are standard equipment on notebook computers. Standalone LCDs, referred to as LCD monitors or flat panel displays, are popular for desktop computers. The advantages of LCD monitors include display clarity, low radiation emission, portability, and compactness. Most new computers ship with LCD displays.

The source of the light that filters through the LCD is referred to as backlighting. In a standard LCD screen, the source of this light is typically a series of cold cathode fluorescent lamps (CCFLs), which are not environmentally friendly. Gradually, CCFL backlighting technology is being replaced by low-power light-emitting diodes (LEDs). A computer screen that uses this technology is sometimes referred to as an **LED display**.

**Can I watch DVDs and television on a computer display?** Computer display devices can be equipped with NTSC (standard American television) or HDTV (high-definition television) circuitry so they accept television signals from an antenna or cable. This technology lets you switch between your computer desktop and television stations, or simultaneously view computer data and television on the same display device using split-screen or picture-in-picture format.

**What factors affect image quality?** Image quality is a factor of screen size, dot pitch, width of viewing angle, response rate, resolution, and color depth. Screen size is the measurement in inches from one corner of the screen diagonally across to the opposite corner. Screen sizes range from 11" on netbooks to 60" or more for home entertainment systems.

**Dot pitch** (dp) is a measure of image clarity. A smaller dot pitch means a crisper image. Technically, dot pitch is the distance in millimeters between like-colored **pixels**—the small dots of light that form an image. A dot pitch between .26 and .23 is typical for today's display devices.

A display device's **viewing angle width** indicates how far to the side you can still clearly see the screen image. With a wide viewing angle of 170 degrees or more, you can view the screen from various positions without compromising image quality.

**Response rate** is the time it takes for one pixel to change from black to white then back to black. Display devices with fast response rates display a crisp image with minimal blurring or "ghosting" of moving objects. Response rate is measured in milliseconds (ms). For gaming systems, a response rate of 5 ms or less is desirable.

The number of colors a monitor can display is referred to as **color depth** or bit depth. Most PC display devices have the capability to display millions of colors. When set at 24-bit color depth (sometimes called True Color), your PC can display more than 16 million colors—and produce what are considered photographic-quality images.

**FIGURE 2-40**

LCD screens are used with most desktop and portable computers.

**What should I know about screen resolution?** The number of horizontal and vertical pixels that a device displays on the screen is referred to as **screen resolution**. Standard resolutions are optimized for 4:3 aspect ratio in which the width is slightly larger than the height. Widescreen displays with 16:9 aspect ratios carry a W designation. Common screen resolutions are listed in Figure 2-41.

HDTV broadcast systems use resolutions of 1280 x 720 (720p) or 1920 x 1080 (1080p). For HDTV compatibility, make sure your computer monitor is compatible with one of these formats.

**Should I set my computer on its highest resolution?** At higher resolutions, text and other objects appear smaller, but the computer can display a larger work area, such as an entire page of a document. At lower resolutions, text appears larger, but the work area is smaller. Enlarged text sometimes looks blurry because a letter that required one row of dots might now require additional dots to fill it in. Most displays have a recommended resolution at which images are clearest and text is crispest.

The two screens in Figure 2-42 help you compare a display set at 1280 x 800 resolution with a display set at 800 x 600 resolution.

**FIGURE 2-41**

Common Screen Resolutions

| VGA | 640 x 480 |
|------|------------|
| SVGA | 800 x 600 |
| XGA | 1024 x 768 |
| SXGA | 1280 x 1024 |
| UXGA | 1600 x 1200 |
| WUXGA | 1920 x 1200 |
| WQXGA | 2560 x 1600 |

**FIGURE 2-42**

The screen on the left shows 1280 x 800 resolution. Notice the size of text and other screen-based objects. The screen on the right shows 800 x 600 resolution. Text and other objects appear larger on the low-resolution screen, but you see a smaller portion of the screen desktop.

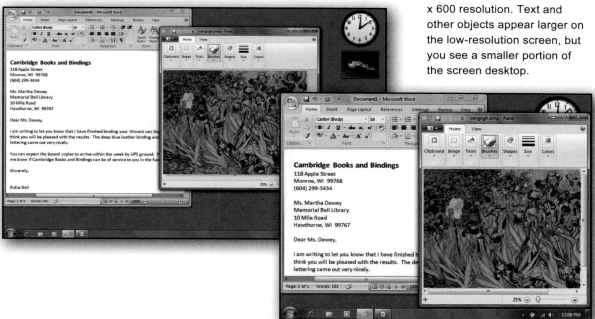

**What are the components of a typical computer display system?** In addition to a display device, such as a monitor, a computer display system also requires graphics circuitry that generates the signals for displaying an image on the screen. One type of graphics circuitry, referred to as integrated graphics, is built into a computer's system board. Graphics circuitry can also be supplied by a small circuit board called a **graphics card** (graphics board or video card), like the one in Figure 2-43.

A graphics card typically contains a **graphics processing unit** (GPU) and special video memory, which stores screen images as they are processed but before they are displayed. Lots of video memory is the key to lightning-fast screen updating for fast action games, 3-D modeling, and graphics-intensive desktop publishing. In addition to video memory, most graphics cards contain special graphics accelerator technology to further boost performance.

**FIGURE 2-43**

A graphics card is a small circuit board that plugs into the system board.

## PRINTERS

**What printer technologies are available for personal computers?**
Printers are one of the most popular output devices available for personal
computers. Today's best-selling printers typically use ink jet or laser technology in multifunction devices that can also serve as scanners, copiers,
and fax machines.

**How does an ink jet printer work?** An **ink jet printer** has a nozzle-
like print head that sprays ink onto paper to form characters and graphics.
The print head in a color ink jet printer consists of a series of nozzles, each
with its own ink cartridge. Most ink jet printers use CMYK color, which
requires only cyan (blue), magenta (pink), yellow, and black inks to create a
printout that appears to have thousands of colors. Alternatively, some printers use six or eight ink colors to print midtone shades that create slightly
more realistic photographic images.

**FIGURE 2-44**

Ink jet printers spray ink from a
series of ink cartridges.

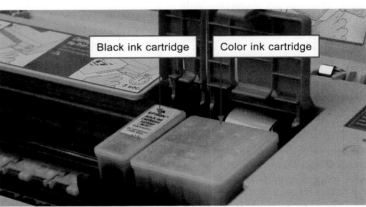

Black ink cartridge    Color ink cartridge

Ink jet printers, such as the one in
Figure 2-44, outsell all other types
of printers because they are inexpensive and produce both color and
black-and-white printouts. They work
well for most home and small business applications. Small, portable ink
jet printers meet the needs of many
mobile computer owners. Ink jet
technology also powers many photo
printers, which are optimized to print
high-quality images produced by digital cameras and scanners.

**How do laser printers compare to ink jet printers?** A **laser printer**
uses the same technology as a photocopier to paint dots of light on a light-
sensitive drum. Electrostatically charged ink is applied to the drum and then
transferred to paper. Laser technology is more complex than ink jet technology, which accounts for the higher price of laser printers.

A basic laser printer like the one in Figure 2-45 produces only black-and-
white printouts. Color laser printers are available, but are somewhat more
costly than basic black-and-white models. Laser printers are often the
choice for business printers, particularly for applications that produce a high
volume of printed material.

Toner
cartridge

**FIGURE 2-45**

Laser printers electrostatically
collect toner on a drum, then
the toner is transferred onto
paper. ▶ Find out more about
laser printers by watching the
video for this figure in your digital textbook.

**What is a dot matrix printer?** When PCs first appeared in the late 1970s, dot matrix printers were the technology of choice, and they are still available today. A **dot matrix printer** produces characters and graphics by using a grid of fine wires. As the print head noisily clatters across the paper, the wires strike a ribbon and paper in a pattern prescribed by your PC (Figure 2-46).

**FIGURE 2-46**

Unlike laser and ink jet technologies, a dot matrix printer actually strikes the paper and, therefore, can print multipart carbon forms.

Print head contains a matrix of thin wires

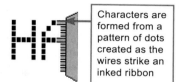

Characters are formed from a pattern of dots created as the wires strike an inked ribbon

Dot matrix printers can print text and graphics—some even print in color using a multicolored ribbon. Today, dot matrix printers are used primarily for "back-office" applications that demand low operating cost and dependability, but not high print quality.

**What features should I look for in a printer?** Printers differ in resolution, speed, duty cycle, operating costs, duplex capability, and memory.

● Resolution. The quality or sharpness of printed images and text depends on the printer's resolution—the density of the gridwork of dots that create an image. Printer resolution is measured by the number of dots printed per linear inch, abbreviated as dpi. At normal reading distance, a resolution of about 900 dpi appears solid to the human eye, but a close examination reveals a dot pattern. If you want magazine-quality printouts, 900 dpi is sufficient resolution. If you are aiming for resolution similar to expensive coffee-table books, look for printer resolution of 2,400 dpi or higher.

● Print speed. Printer speeds are measured either by pages per minute (ppm) or characters per second (cps). Color printouts typically take longer than black-and-white printouts. Pages that contain mostly text tend to print more rapidly than pages that contain graphics. Typical speeds for personal computer printers range between 6 and 30 pages of text per minute. A full-page 8.5 x 11 photo can take about a minute to print.

● Duty cycle. In addition to printer speed, a printer's **duty cycle** determines how many pages a printer is able to churn out. Printer duty cycle is usually measured in pages per month. For example, a personal laser printer has a duty cycle of about 3,000 pages per month (ppm)—that means roughly 100 pages per day. You wouldn't want to use it to produce 5,000 campaign brochures for next Monday, but you would find it quite suitable for printing 10 copies of a five-page outline for a meeting tomorrow.

● Operating costs. The initial cost of a printer is only one of the expenses associated with printed output. Ink jet printers require frequent replacements or refills for relatively expensive ink cartridges. Laser printers require toner cartridge refills or replacements. Dot matrix printers require replacement ribbons. When shopping for a printer, you can check online resources to determine how often you'll need to replace printer supplies and how much they are likely to cost.

- Duplex capability. A **duplex printer** can print on both sides of the paper. This environmentally friendly option saves paper but can slow down the print process, especially on ink jet printers that pause to let the ink dry before printing the second side.

- Memory. A computer sends data for a printout to the printer along with a set of instructions on how to print that data. **Printer Control Language** (PCL) is the most widely used language for communication between computers and printers, but **PostScript** is an alternative printer language that many publishing professionals prefer. The data that arrives at a printer along with its printer language instructions require memory. Laser printers do not start printing until all the data for a page is received. You can add memory to most laser printers if necessary for your print jobs.

- Networkability. If your personal computer system is not networked to other computers in your house, apartment, or dorm, you can attach a printer directly to your computer. If your computer is part of a network, you can share your printer with other network users, who essentially send their print jobs to your computer's printer for output. Another way to configure network printing for multiple users is to purchase a network-enabled printer that connects directly to the network, rather than to one of the computers on a network. The network connection can be wired or wireless. The advantage of a network-ready printer is that it can be placed in a location convenient for all the network users.

**Should I refill or recycle?** Ink and toner cartridges are expensive and you can save some money by refilling them yourself or taking them to an ink refilling station at a local office store. Remanufactured and discount printer supplies are available online, too. Before you try one of these options, read the instructions and warranty for your printer. Inexpensive printer supplies don't always get stellar ratings from consumers. If cartridge and toner refills are not available, find out how to responsibly recycle them (Figure 2-47).

### INSTALLING PERIPHERAL DEVICES

**How does a computer move data to and from peripheral devices?** When you install a peripheral device, you are basically creating a connection for data to flow between the device and the computer. Within a computer, data travels from one component to another over circuits called a **data bus**. One part of the data bus, referred to as the local bus or internal bus, runs between RAM and the microprocessor. The segment of the data bus to which peripheral devices connect is called the **expansion bus** or external bus. As data moves along the expansion bus, it can travel through expansion slots, expansion cards, ports, and cables (Figure 2-48).

**FIGURE 2-47**

When you replace printer components, check to see if the manufacturer has a recycle program.

**Return HP inkjet or LaserJet print cartridges to HP authorized retail recycling locations**

Find a location near you and get additional information.

**FIGURE 2-48**

The expansion bus connects the computer system board to peripheral devices.

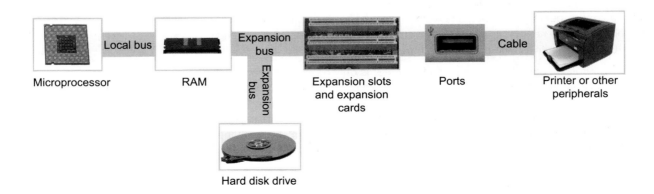

Microprocessor — Local bus — RAM — Expansion bus — Expansion slots and expansion cards — Ports — Cable — Printer or other peripherals

Hard disk drive

**What's an expansion slot?** An **expansion slot** is a long, narrow socket on the system board into which you can plug an expansion card. An **expansion card** is a small circuit board that gives a computer the capability to control a storage device, an input device, or an output device. Expansion cards are also called expansion boards, controller cards, or adapters.

Expansion slots are typically used for installing high-end graphics cards in desktop computers configured for gaming, desktop publishing, and graphics applications. Figure 2-49 shows how to plug an expansion card into an expansion slot.

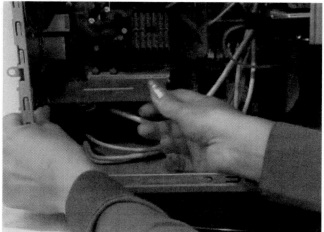

**FIGURE 2-49**

An expansion card simply slides into an expansion slot. Before you install an expansion card, be sure to unplug the computer and ground yourself—that's technical jargon for releasing static electricity by using a special grounding wristband or by touching both hands to a metal object. ▶ Your digital textbook explains how to install expansion cards in a desktop computer.

**What is an expansion port?** An **expansion port** is any connector that passes data into and out of a computer or peripheral device. It is similar to an electrical outlet because you can plug things in to make a connection.

Expansion ports are usually incorporated in the system board. Computer system units are designed with openings that make these ports accessible from outside the case. As shown in Figure 2-50, the built-in ports supplied with today's computers usually include graphics ports for connecting display devices, an Ethernet port for connecting to a wired network, eSATA and FireWire ports for high-speed external data storage, audio ports for microphone and speakers, and USB ports for connecting a mouse, keyboard, printer, and other peripherals.

**FIGURE 2-50**

When this system board is installed in a computer, the expansion ports will be accessible from outside the system unit.

Graphics ports        FireWire port        Ethernet network port

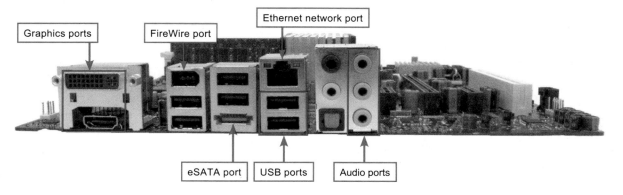

eSATA port        USB ports        Audio ports

**Is it difficult to install a new peripheral device?** At one time, installing computer peripherals required a screwdriver and extensive knowledge of ports, slots, boards, and various electronic gizmos. Today, most peripheral devices connect to an external **USB** (universal serial bus) port, located on the front, sides, or back of the computer system unit (Figure 2-51).

Many kinds of peripheral devices—including mice, scanners, and joysticks—are available with USB connections. Transmitters for wireless devices, such as wireless mice, also plug into USB slots. Several types of storage devices, such as USB flash drives and external hard disk drives, use USB connections, too.

**What if I run out of USB ports?** You can easily add USB ports to your computer by using an inexpensive **USB hub**, which contains several auxiliary USB ports. The hub plugs into one of your computer's USB ports and you can then insert multiple USB devices into the ports supplied by the hub.

Self-powered USB hubs require power from an external power supply, such as a wall outlet. Bus-powered USB hubs (sometimes called unpowered hubs) draw their power from the computer. A bus-powered USB hub can be used for low-power devices, such as card readers and mice. A self-powered USB hub is required if the hub is used for connecting scanners, printers, and some external hard drives. Figure 2-52 illustrates how a USB hub can be used to connect several devices to a single USB port on a computer.

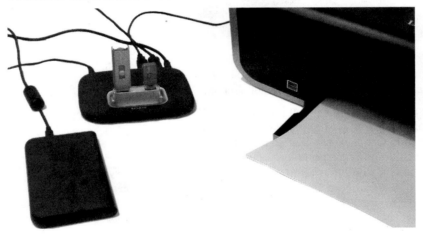

**When do I use other kinds of ports?** **FireWire** ports (also called IEEE 1394 ports) are used for external storage devices and for transferring data from digital video cameras to a computer for editing, printing, or storage. **eSATA** is another type of port, popular for connecting high-speed external storage devices.

**VGA** (Video Graphics Array), **DVI** (Digital Visual Interface), and **HDMI** (High-Definition Multimedia Interface) ports are designed for audiovisual devices. They are primarily used for connecting a monitor to a desktop computer, and for connecting an external monitor to a notebook computer. Figure 2-53 illustrates ports that can be used for connecting display devices.

VGA

DVI

HDMI

**FIGURE 2-51**

A USB connector is shaped like a flat rectangle. Make sure you know which side of the plug is up; the top is usually labeled with the USB logo.

**FIGURE 2-52**

This self-powered USB hub connects two USB flash drives, an external hard drive, and a printer to a single USB port on the host computer.

**FIGURE 2-53**

A variety of ports are available for connecting an external monitor to a desktop or notebook computer.

**What is hot-plugging?** When you connect or disconnect a peripheral device while the computer is operating, you are **hot-plugging**, a practice that's allowed with USB and FireWire devices. Before you unplug a device, such as a USB flash drive, however, your computer might require notification. In Windows, you can give notification using the Safely Remove Hardware icon in the notification area of the taskbar. With a Mac, hold down the Control key, click the device icon, and then select Eject (Figure 2-54).

**FIGURE 2-54**

Before removing USB devices when the computer is operating, issue a notification. For Windows (left), use the Safely Remove Hardware icon. On Macs (below), hold down the Control key, click, and select Eject.

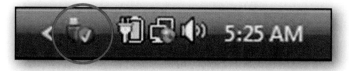

**Why do some peripheral devices include a disk or CD?** Some devices require software to establish communication with your computer. The directions supplied with your peripheral device include instructions on how to install the software. Typically, you use the installation CD one time to get everything set up, and then you can put the CD away in a safe place. You'll learn more about this software, called a device driver, in the next chapter.

Long-time computer techies probably remember the days when installing a peripheral device meant messing around with little electronic components called dip switches and a host of complex software settings called IRQs. Fortunately, today's computers include a feature called **Plug and Play** that automatically takes care of these technical details.

Plug and Play works quite well for most popular peripheral devices. If your computer does not recognize a newly connected device or is unable to correctly exchange data with it, check the manufacturer's Web site for a device driver update, or call the manufacturer's technical support department. Plug and Play detects new devices that are connected to a computer and attempts to establish the settings necessary for sending data between them.

# QuickCheck                                                    SECTION D

1. On a multi-touch trackpad, you can use various [_____] to move the pointer, zoom, and scroll.

2. A widescreen computer display with a 16:9 [_____] carries a W designation.

3. One type of graphics circuitry, referred to as [_____] graphics, is built into a computer's system board.

4. Most ink jet printers use [_____] color that requires four ink colors. (Hint: Use the acronym.)

5. A(n) [_____] port provides one of the fastest, simplest ways to connect peripheral devices. (Hint: Use the acronym.)

▶ CHECK ANSWERS

# Hardware Security

THE INFORMATION that computers contain and process has become practically priceless to every PC owner. Just about everyone depends on a computer for information and communication. A stolen computer, even if it's low-priced, can be a huge loss if it holds valuable financial data or months of research. A broken PC can easily cost hundreds of dollars to repair, especially if the data is damaged and needs to be recovered. For trouble-free computer use, it is important to secure and regularly maintain your computer equipment, just as you would your home and car.

## ANTI-THEFT DEVICES

**What can I do to prevent my computer from being stolen?** Computers have rapidly become prime targets for thieves. Many security breaches have been traced to stolen computers. The portability of notebook, netbook, and slate computers makes them particularly easy for a thief to grab, just as a wallet or a handbag would be. Figure 2-55 contains important tips for protecting your portable computer from theft.

**FIGURE 2-55**

Tips for Preventing Computer Theft

- Never leave your portable computer unattended, especially when you are at a coffee shop, the library, or the airport.
- If you have to leave your portable computer in your car, never leave it in plain view. Lock it up in the trunk or cover it up.
- Carry your portable computer in an inconspicuous carrying case.
- Record your portable computer's make, model, and serial number and store them away from the computer. Many recovered computers cannot be returned to their owners because this tracking information is not supplied to police.
- Consider securing your portable computer with an anti-theft device.

**How do computer anti-theft devices work?** Several computer anti-theft devices are available. Most can be used for both desktops and notebook computers.

The Kensington Security Slot is a security mechanism that's factory-installed on many personal computers. It is a small, reinforced oblong hole into which you can insert a special lock that can be attached to a cable. The cable can be fastened to a desk to prevent theft as shown in Figure 2-56.

**FIGURE 2-56**

The Kensington Security Slot is an industry standard way to secure a computer to a desk.

Notebook computers can also be fastened with tie-down brackets or stored in a specially designed locker that can be installed under a desk or in a closet. Another option for securing notebook computers is a security plate that's affixed to the underside of the computer or to a desk (Figure 2-57).

Computer motion sensor alarms, similar to those for automobiles, can be installed on desktop or notebook computers and armed so that any movement triggers audible alarm sounds or recorded verbal warnings.

**If my computer is stolen, can authorities recover it?** Your chances of recovering a stolen computer improve if you have taken some steps in advance, such as recording the computer's serial number, affixing a tracking label, or installing tracking software.

STOP (Security Tracking of Office Property) plates leave an indelible tattoo on your computer equipment. It takes 800 pounds of force to remove a plate, which contains a unique ID number, a warning message, and a toll-free number to report a stolen computer. Each plate ID number is registered in the international STOP database, thereby making it virtually impossible for a thief to resell a computer that has a STOP label.

**FIGURE 2-57**

Security plates are designed to lock a computer to a desk.

Tracking and recovery software, such as CyberAngel and LoJack for Laptops, secretly sends a message as soon as a thief uses a stolen computer to log onto the Internet. This message contains the computer's exact location and is directed to a tracking or monitoring center. Some tracking software products can be configured to delete the data on the stolen computer.

## SURGE PROTECTION AND BATTERY BACKUP

**What is a power surge?** To ensure that your computer stays in good running condition, it is essential that you protect it from power surges that endanger many electrical appliances and digital equipment. A **power surge** is a sudden increase in electrical energy affecting the current that flows to electrical outlets. Power surges often occur before or after power failures, which also put your computer and data at risk.

Computers and peripheral devices require stable current and are particularly sensitive to these sudden bursts of electrical energy. A powerful surge can ruin computer circuitry. Smaller surges can slowly damage your computer's circuit boards and other electrical components. Over time, even small, repeated power surges can shorten your PC's life.

Power surges originate from a number of sources: downed power lines, power grid switching by the electric company, faulty wiring, and large appliances like refrigerators and air conditioners powering on and off. Lightning causes extremely large power surges and consequently poses a real threat to your computer equipment.

**How can I protect my computer from power surges?** You can protect your computer equipment from power surges by plugging it into a surge strip instead of directly into a wall outlet. For added protection during thunderstorms, shut down your computer, turn off all your peripheral devices, and unplug the surge strip and all computer-related cables from wall outlets, including the cable for your modem.

**What is a surge strip and how does one work?** A **surge strip** (also called a surge suppressor or surge protector) is a device that contains electrical outlets protected by circuitry that blocks surges. Some surge strips also have sockets for modem connections that prevent surges from traveling down telephone or cable lines and into your computer.

A surge strip like the one in Figure 2-58 monitors the electrical current that passes from an outlet to all the devices plugged into the strip. When it detects a surge, it redirects the extra current to a grounded circuit.

**FIGURE 2-58**

Surge strips should be connected directly to a wall outlet. Plugging one surge strip into another surge strip reduces their effectiveness.

A big power surge can burn out a surge strip while it tries to protect your equipment. Some surge strips have an indicator light that warns you if the surge strip is no longer functioning properly. Check the manufacturer's documentation to determine if you should discard the depleted strip, reset it, or install a new fuse.

**What is a UPS?** A **UPS** (uninterruptible power supply) is a device that not only provides surge protection, but also furnishes desktop computers and network devices with battery backup power during a power outage. If your computer is connected to a UPS when a power outage occurs, the battery backup allows you to save what you're doing and shut down your PC properly. Depending on your system's configuration, a UPS with a high-performance battery might give you enough backup power to keep your computer up and running for several hours, allowing you to continue to work during the entire power outage.

Portable computers run on battery power and so the data you're working on is not immediately affected by a power outage. However, if you want to access your local area network or Internet connection, you might consider plugging your network devices and Internet modem into a UPS so that they continue to operate during an outage.

As shown in Figure 2-59, most UPSs have two types of sockets: one type offers battery backup plus surge protection, and the other offers only surge protection. The surge-only sockets are for printers, which use so much power that they can quickly drain the battery. At the Web site for American Power Conversion, you'll find tips for choosing a UPS based on your system's configuration and the amount of run time you want during a power outage.

Surge and battery backup outlets

Surge-only outlets

**FIGURE 2-59**

An uninterruptible power supply (UPS) not only protects electronic equipment from power surges, it also provides battery power during power outages.

## BASIC MAINTENANCE

**Can I prevent hardware problems?** Computer component failures can be caused by manufacturing defects and other circumstances beyond your control. You can, however, undertake some preventive maintenance that can add years to the life of your computer equipment, just as regular tune-ups lengthen the life of your car.

Preventive maintenance can save you more than the cost of repairs; you also save the time you would've lost while tracking down problems and arranging for repairs. Regular cleaning of your PC's components and peripheral devices helps to keep your system in good condition.

**How do I clean the keyboard?** Always shut down your PC before you clean your keyboard so that you don't inadvertently type in commands that you don't want your system to execute. Also, disconnect your keyboard and remember where the connection is located. Flip the keyboard over and shake it gently to get rid of any small pieces of dirt between the keys. A can of compressed air is effective for blowing off the dust and dislodging larger debris. A vacuum cleaner can pop off and suck away the keys on your keyboard, so be very careful if you use one to clean your keyboard.

You can use cotton swabs just slightly moistened with a mild cleaning fluid to clean the sides of keys. Wipe the tops of the keys with a soft cloth, again slightly dampened with a mild cleaning solution. Allow your keyboard to dry before you reconnect it to your PC. Keep drinks away from your computer to avoid spilling liquids onto the keyboard. Figure 2-60 provides more information on cleaning your computer keyboard.

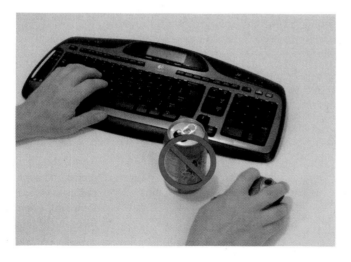

**FIGURE 2-60**

Carefully use a cotton swab and a can of compressed air or a vacuum cleaner to remove dust and debris from your keyboard. Sticky liquids are difficult to remove. That can of pop? Keep it away from your keyboard. ▶ Watch the video in your digital textbook to see how to safely clean your computer keyboard.

**How do I get dust and fingerprints off my computer screen?** Dust and fingerprint smudges can easily accumulate on your computer screen and make it quite difficult to read. You should clean your screen on a regular basis, at least weekly. It's always best to turn off your display device before you clean because a blank screen will reveal all the smudges, dust, and dirt.

Follow manufacturer's instructions for cleaning your computer screen, using the recommended cleaning product. Spray the cleaner on a lint-free, soft cloth, but never directly on the screen. Don't scrub. The membrane covering many screens is delicate and can be easily damaged.

**Should I be concerned about my computer's operating temperature?** High-performance processors, hard drives, graphics cards, and several other computer components generate a lot of heat. Overheating can shorten the lifespan of internal components and chips.

Most desktop computers have a fan mounted on the power supply that runs continuously to maintain the proper temperature inside of the system unit. Additional cooling fans might also be used to cool the microprocessor or graphics card. Notebook computers also have cooling fans, but the fans come on only after the processor reaches a certain temperature (Figure 2-61).

**FIGURE 2-61**

Fans that cool your computer vent outside the case. Keep the area around your computer clear for good air circulation.

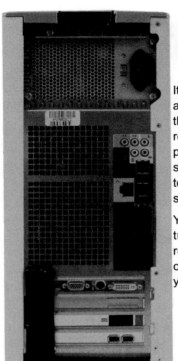

It is important to be aware of the ventilation around your computer system and ensure that the fans are able to draw air from the room and blow it across the internal components. If your computer is in an enclosed space, such as a cabinet, you might need to cut out a hole at the back to give your PC some room to "breathe."

You should also be aware of the temperature in the room in which your computer resides. Several vendors sell cooling mats containing fans that can be placed under your notebook computer (Figure 2-62).

**FIGURE 2-62**

If your notebook or netbook computer case usually feels warm, consider placing it on a chill mat containing fans that can lower the computer's temperature and potentially increase its lifespan.

Dust particles, dirt, and even your pet's hair can collect on and around the cooling fans and impede their performance. You should regularly use a can of compressed air or a vacuum cleaner hose to clean out debris from the vents and fans.

You should, however, exercise extreme caution when you clean out your computer's system case. First, make sure that you've turned off your PC, display device, and all other related devices. Stay a couple of inches away from all components as you dust, especially if you're using a vacuum cleaner hose. Do not touch the system board, and be sure not to knock any cables loose.

**Are there any other components that need TLC?** To avoid read or write errors, you want your optical drives to function properly. Retailers provide cleaning kits for many types of storage devices and media. Also examine your CDs and DVDs for scratches and fingerprints. Clean them with a soft cloth slightly dampened with water. If the smudges don't come off, a little isopropyl alcohol might help.

**What is a good computer maintenance routine?** Aside from cleaning your computer equipment on a regular basis, you should do the preventive maintenance tasks listed in Figure 2-63. You'll learn how to do these tasks in later chapters.

**FIGURE 2-63**

Tips for Regular Computer Maintenance

- Back up your files regularly, particularly those that are most important to you. You might want to perform daily incremental backups of critical data and monthly backups of all your files. You should also test your backup procedures periodically.

- Run utilities that ensure peak performance for your hard disk drive. In Windows, these utilities include Disk Cleanup and Disk Defragmenter. It's best to do this maintenance on a weekly basis.

- Delete your browser's history and cache files on a monthly basis in order to free up space for your temporary files. The free space results in faster downloads from the Internet.

- Apply the latest operating system, driver, and security updates.

- Scan your computer for viruses and spyware once a week.

- Keep antivirus and spyware definitions updated.

## TROUBLESHOOTING AND REPAIR

**How can I tell if something is wrong with my computer?** There are several telltale signs that your computer is in trouble. The most obvious one is your PC's failure to power up. A loud beep at startup time can also indicate a problem. If your computer's screen remains blank or error messages appear, you might have a hardware problem.

Hardware problems can also show up as unexpected restarts at random intervals, or as a peripheral device that stops working. Some problems are intermittent and might seem to be resolved only to come back when they are least convenient to deal with.

Many seasoned Windows users have encountered the **blue screen of death** (also called BSoD) that suddenly replaces the usual graphical screen display with an enigmatic error message written in white text against a blue background. The blue screen of death indicates that the operating system has encountered an error from which it cannot recover, and the computer no longer accepts any commands.

Hardware problems can quickly escalate and some can eventually make your computer non-functional or make your data impossible to access. Any computer problem that prevents you from working as usual should be taken seriously. A little time spent troubleshooting can save you lots of annoyance down the road.

**How do I troubleshoot a hardware problem?** You might be able to solve many hardware problems by simply following the basic guidelines for troubleshooting listed in Figure 2-64.

FIGURE 2-64

Troubleshooting Tips

- Stay calm and don't jump to any conclusions until you've thought everything through.
- Write down all error messages and any other information that goes with them.
- Make sure all components are plugged in and that there are no loose cables. For example, if your display device's cable is loose, the indicator light will be off and your screen will be blank.
- If you can, try to duplicate the problem by going through the same steps that led you to it.
- Look for troubleshooting and repair tips in your user's manual, on your vendor's Web site, or even through a search engine. If you search the Internet by typing in the error message number or keywords in the error message, you might discover that at least one person has already found a solution to your problem.
- Run your spyware and antivirus software. Lurking viruses, worms, Trojan horses, and spyware (discussed in the next chapter) can cause strange and unexplainable occurrences in your computer system. For example, spyware can cause your computer to keep displaying a pop-up ad no matter how you try to close it.
- A simple reboot of your computer might clear up the problem. Windows always requires a reboot when it displays the blue screen of death. However, a more serious problem underlying the BSoD will not be resolved with a reboot. To reboot a PC, hold down the Ctrl, Alt, and Del keys at the same time. When the next screen appears, click the red Shut Down button in the lower-right corner.

Troubleshooting and diagnostic tools can help you find the source of a problem and fix it. For example, Windows offers interactive troubleshooting tools formatted as a series of simple questions, answers, and recommendations (Figure 2-65). You might have to borrow a computer to run these tools if your computer is totally out of commission.

**FIGURE 2-65**

To access a Windows troubleshooter, enter "troubleshoot" in the Start menu's Search box, then select the Troubleshooting option.

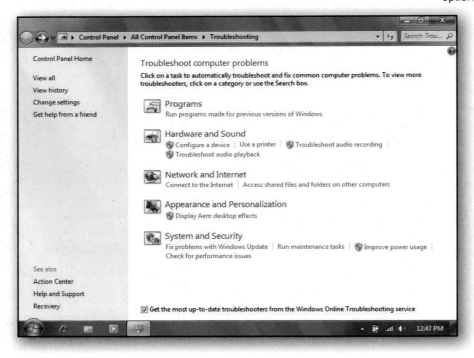

**What is Safe Mode?** If Windows encounters a critical problem that is keeping it from operating normally, it starts up in Safe Mode the next time you reboot your computer. **Safe Mode** is a limited version of Windows that allows you to use your mouse, screen, and keyboard, but no other peripheral devices (Figure 2-66). While in Safe Mode you can use the Control Panel's Add/Remove Programs to uninstall recently added programs or hardware that might be interfering with the operation of other components.

**FIGURE 2-66**

To enter Safe Mode, you can press the F8 function key as your PC boots.

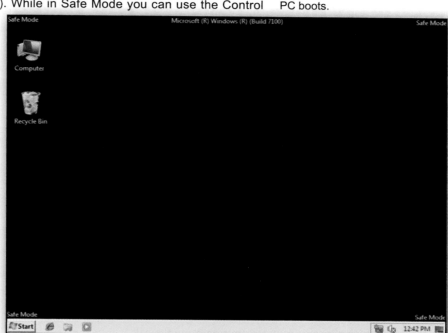

**What if I can't solve the problem myself?** If you are unable to fix a hardware problem yourself, you might have to call the technical support center for the device or component that is malfunctioning. You can also consider asking for help from a knowledgeable person or from computer repair professionals like the Geek Squad.

When seeking outside technical help, make sure you've checked your warranty, and know the purchase date, serial number, brand, model, and operating system. You should also have a written copy of error messages and a description of the steps that led to the problem.

Once the problem is resolved, write down the solution. You never know when you might need it again!

## QuickCheck                                                                SECTION E

1. A power [                    ] is a sudden increase or spike in electrical energy, affecting the current that flows to electrical outlets.

2. A(n) [                    ] can provide power to keep your computer, network, and Internet connection operational during a power outage. (Hint: Use the acronym.)

3. If your computer's built-in fans don't provide an adequate level of cooling, you can place it on a chill mat. True or false? [                    ]

4. When using Windows, you can troubleshoot hardware problems by logging into the BSoD. True or false? [                    ]

5. [                    ] Mode is a stripped-down version of Windows that is designed for troubleshooting.

● CHECK ANSWERS

# Issue: Where Does All the E-waste Go?

**IT IS CALLED** e-waste, e-garbage, or techno-trash—unwanted and outdated computers, monitors, printers, cell phones, PDAs, disk drives, disks, CDs, and DVDs. According to Greenpeace, 50 million tons of it is discarded every year. In the United States alone, almost eight printer cartridges are discarded every second. A recycling company called GreenDisk estimates that about 1 billion floppy disks, CDs, and DVDs end up in landfills every year.

U.S. landfills already hold more than 2 million tons of computer and electronic parts, which contain toxic substances such as lead, cadmium, and mercury. An Environmental Protection Agency (EPA) report describes the situation: "In this world of rapidly changing technology, disposal of computers and other electronic equipment has created a new and growing waste stream."

*Recycled Computer Creations by Gregory Steele, Marquette, MI*

E-waste is a global problem. As countries struggle to deal with discarded electronic components, an alarming amount of e-waste is shipped to developing countries where villagers, working for pennies a day, are exposed to toxic chemicals as they attempt to reclaim resalable metals from discarded equipment. Documentaries produced by Greenpeace and media investigative reporters have exposed the appalling working conditions and environmental devastation created by these recycling sweat shops.

Many computers end up in landfills because their owners are unaware of potential environmental hazards and simply toss them in the garbage. In addition, PC owners typically are not given information on options for disposing of their old machines. When it is time to dispose of your computer, is there a way to do it in an environmentally safe way?

Instead of throwing away your old computer, you might be able to sell it; donate it to a local school, church, or community program; have it hauled away by a professional recycling firm; or send it back to the manufacturer. Some artists even accept old computers and use parts in jewelry and craft projects.

With the growing popularity of Internet auctions and dedicated computer reclamation sites, you might be able to get some cash for your old computer. At Web sites such as craigslist.org, you can post an ad for your old equipment. Off the Web, you can find businesses that refurbish and sell old computers. Goodwill stores in many communities accept old computer equipment and arrange for it to be reused or recycled.

Donating your old computer to a local organization doesn't actually eliminate the disposal problem, but it does delay it. Unfortunately, finding a new home for an old computer is not always easy. Most schools and community organizations have few resources for repairing broken equipment, so if your old computer is not in good working order, it could be more of a burden than a gift. In addition, your computer might be too old to be compatible with the other computers in an organization.

It helps if you can donate software along with your old computer. To ensure a legal transfer, include the software distribution disks, manuals, and license agreement. And remember, once you donate the software, you cannot legally use it on your new computer unless it is freeware or shareware.

If you cannot find an organization to accept your computer donation, look in your local Yellow Pages or on the Internet for an electronics recycling firm, which will haul away your computer and recycle any usable materials.

Despite private sector options for selling, donating, or recycling old computers, many governments are worried that these voluntary efforts will not be enough to prevent massive dumping of an ever-growing population of obsolete computers.

Many states have taken legislative action to curtail the rampant disposal of obsolete computer equipment. For example, Massachusetts has banned televisions and computer monitors from its landfills. In Maine it is illegal to dispose of computers or monitors—they have to be recycled in an environmentally sound way. But recycling can be costly—equipment needs to be collected, sorted, disassembled, and shipped to processing or disposal plants.

Basic to the issue of reducing electronic waste is the question of "Who pays?" Should it be the taxpayer, the individual consumer, the retailer, or the computer manufacturer?

When Californians were faced with the prospect of tax hikes to deal with alarming increases in electronic waste, activists questioned if tax increases were fair to individual taxpayers who generate very little electronic waste. Now, consumers buying computers in California have to pay a recycling fee at the time of purchase.

Other lawmakers propose to make manufacturers responsible for recycling costs and logistics. "Extended producer responsibility" refers to the idea of holding manufacturers responsible for the environmental effects of their products through the entire product life cycle, which includes taking them back, recycling them, or disposing of them. Maryland requires computer manufacturers to ante up an annual fee for electronic waste disposal.

The economics of mandatory take-back programs can increase product costs, however, if manufacturers pass recycling costs through to consumers.

The EPA advocates a national plan in which consumers, retailers, and manufacturers can cooperate to reduce electronic waste. Its Plug-In To eCycling Web site makes the point that "No national infrastructure exists for collecting, reusing, and recycling electronics."

Most experts agree that an effective approach to controlling e-waste involves a partnership between manufacturers and consumers.

Manufacturers should minimize the use of toxic materials both in the production process and in finished products. Manufacturers should also offer low-cost, convenient recycling options.

Consumers can select "green" products and purchase equipment from environment-friendly manufacturers. Check out Greenpeace's Green Ranking to find out which digital equipment manufacturers have the greenest recycling policies and manufacturing methods. Consumers can also help to keep the planet green by recycling unwanted electronic equipment instead of throwing it in the trash.

**INFOWEBLINKS**

You'll find much more information about how you can recycle an old computer by connecting to the **Computer Recycling InfoWeb**.

(W) CLICK TO CONNECT
www.infoweblinks.com/np2012/ch02

## What Do You Think?

ISSUE

1. Have you ever thrown away an old computer or other electronic device?  ◯ Yes  ◯ No  ◯ Not sure

2. Are you aware of any options for recycling electronic equipment in your local area?  ◯ Yes  ◯ No  ◯ Not sure

3. Would it be fair for consumers to pay a recycling tax on any electronic equipment that they purchase?  ◯ Yes  ◯ No  ◯ Not sure

 SAVE RESPONSES

# Computers in Context: Military

**IN THE BOOK ENGINES OF THE MIND,** Joel Shurkin writes, "If necessity is the mother of invention, then war can be said to be its grandmother." The military, an early pioneer in computer and communication technologies, continues to be the driving force behind technologies that have revolutionized everyday life.

During World War II, the U.S. military initiated a classified research program, called Project PX, to develop an electronic device to calculate artillery firing tables; by hand, each table required weeks of grueling calculations. Project PX produced ENIAC (Electrical Numerical Integrator And Computer), one of the first general-purpose electronic computers. When ENIAC was completed in 1946, the war was over, but ENIAC's versatile architecture could be used for other calculations, such as designing hydrogen bombs, predicting weather, and engineering wind tunnels. ENIAC's technology evolved into the computers used today.

After Project PX, the military continued to support computer research. Like most large corporations, the military used mainframe computers to maintain personnel, inventory, supply, and facilities records. This data was distributed to terminals at other locations through rudimentary networks.

Because all data communication flowed through the mainframe, a single point of failure for the entire system was a possible risk. A malfunction or an enemy "hit" could disrupt command and control, sending the military into chaos. Therefore, the armed forces created the Advanced Research Projects Agency (ARPA) to design a distributed communications system that could continue operating without a centralized computer.

The result was ARPANET, which paved the way for the data communications system we know today as the Internet. ARPANET was activated in 1967, but the .mil domain that designates U.S. military Web sites was not implemented until 1984.

The U.S. Department of Defense (DoD) currently maintains several data communications networks, including SIPRNet, a classified (secret-level) network, and NIPRNet, which provides unclassified services. The DoD's public Web site, called DefenseLINK, provides official information about defense policies, organizations, budgets, and operations.

Computers and communications technology have also become an integral part of high-tech military operations. U.S. Apache helicopters, for example, are equipped with computer-based Target Acquisition Designation Sights, laser range finder/designators, and Pilot Night Vision Sensors.

The U.S. Army's BCT Modernization project includes high-tech vehicles, sensors, and equipment, coordinated by a network of computers, software, and radios. According to United States Army General George W. Casey Jr., "The network links Soldiers on the battlefield with space-based and aerial sensors, robots, and command posts. This provides the situational awareness necessary to apply lethal and non-lethal force with the precision demanded by the security environment."

BCT, which stands for Brigade Combat Team, includes "software-defined" radios that are less vulnerable to cyberthreats than conventional radios. Soldiers can use these radios to communicate voice and data.

A small handheld device with a touch-sensitive screen allows soldiers to control unmanned robots and drones. A solar backpack supplements the battery-powered device. BCT equipment also includes wearable devices, such as helmet-mounted displays and communications devices.

The military has conducted research in computer simulations that are similar to civilian computer games. "Live" military training is dangerous—weapons are deadly and equipment costs millions of dollars. With computer simulations, however, troops can train in a true-to-life environment without physical harm or equipment damage.

Flying an F-16 fighter, for example, costs thousands of dollars an hour, but flying an F-16 simulator costs only a few hundred dollars per hour. The military uses simulators to teach Air Force pilots to fly fighter jets, Navy submarine officers to navigate in harbors, and Marine infantry squads to handle urban combat. Military trainers agree that widespread use of computer games helps prepare troops to adapt quickly to simulations.

A 24-year-old preflight student at Pensacola Naval Air Station modified the Microsoft Flight Simulator game to re-create a T-34C Turbo Mentor plane's controls. After logging 50 hours on the simulator, the student performed so well on a real plane that the Navy used his simulation to train other pilots. Today, a growing cadre of computer and communications specialists is needed to create and maintain increasingly complex military systems such as the Defense Department's Distributed Common Ground System (DCGS) for sharing surveillance imagery and intelligence.

Armies once depended primarily on their infantry divisions, but today's high-tech armies also depend on database designers, computer programmers, and network specialists. Even previously low-tech military jobs, such as mechanics and dietitians, require some computer expertise. Happily, new recruits are finding military computer systems easy to learn, based on their knowledge of civilian technologies, such as the Internet and computer games.

Although most citizens recognize that an adequate national defense is necessary, the cost of defense-related equipment, personnel, and cutting-edge research remains controversial. In 1961, President Dwight Eisenhower warned "We must guard against the acquisition of unwarranted influence, whether sought or unsought, by the military-industrial complex."

Some socially motivated citizens and pacifists tried to withhold tax dollars from the military-industrial complex that Eisenhower cautioned against. In retrospect, however, military funding contributed to many technologies we depend on today.

For example, detractors tried to convince the government that Project PX was doomed to failure, but without ENIAC research, computers might not exist today. Skeptics saw no future for the fruits of ARPANET research, but it led to the Internet, which has changed our lives significantly.

# New Perspectives Labs

## On the BookOnCD

To access the New Perspectives Lab for Chapter 2, start the BookOnCD and then click the icon next to the lab title below.

### ▶ BENCHMARKING

#### IN THIS LAB YOU'LL LEARN:

- Which computer performance factors can be measured by benchmark tests

- How to run a test that identifies a computer's processor type, RAM capacity, and graphics card type

- How to run benchmarking software that analyzes a computer's processor speed and graphics processing speed

- How to interpret the results of a benchmark test

- How to compare the results from benchmark tests that were performed on different system configurations

- When benchmark tests might not provide accurate information on computer performance

#### LAB ASSIGNMENTS

1. Start the interactive part of the lab. Make sure you've enabled Tracking if you want to save your QuickCheck results. Perform each lab step as directed, and answer all the lab QuickCheck questions. When you exit the lab, your answers are automatically graded and your results are displayed.

2. Use the System Information utility to analyze the computer you typically use. If you are using a Windows 7 computer, also check the results of the Windows Experience Index. Provide the results of the analysis along with a brief description of the computer you tested and its location (at home, at work, in a computer lab, and so on).

| PROCESSOR BENCHMARKS | | |
|---|---|---|
| Processor | Quake III Arena | PCMark |
| "Supernova EE" | 548 | 5198 |
| "Pulsar FX" | 551 | 5020 |

3. Based on the Processor Benchmarks table above, which fictional processor appears to be faster at graphics processing? Which processor appears to be better at overall processing tasks?

4. Explain why you might perform a benchmark test on your own computer, but get different results from those stated in a computer magazine, which tested the same computer with the same benchmark test.

5. Use a search engine on the Web to find benchmark ratings for one of Intel's Core processors and one of AMD's Athlon 64 processors. Are the benchmarks different? What would account for the benchmark results?

# Key Terms

Make sure you understand all the boldfaced key terms presented in this chapter. With the NP2012 BookOnCD, you can use this list of terms as an interactive study activity. First, try to define a term in your own words, and then click the term to compare your definition with the definition presented in the chapter. Online, try your hand at the TechTerm Flashcards.

2

64-bit processor, 68
Access time, 77
All-in-one computer, 58
BD-R, 83
BD-RE, 83
BD-ROM, 83
Benchmarks, 70
Blue screen of death, 103
Blu-ray, 81
Capacitors, 72
Card reader, 84
CD, 81
CDDA, 82
CD-R, 83
CD-ROM, 83
CD-RW, 83
CISC, 69
Color depth, 90
CPU cache, 68
Data bus, 94
Data transfer rate, 77
Desktop computer, 58
Dot matrix printer, 93
Dot pitch, 90
Double layer DVD, 81
Drive bays, 86
Duplex printer, 94
Duty cycle, 93
DVD, 81
DVD+R, 83
DVD+RW, 83
DVD-R, 83
DVD-ROM, 83
DVD-RW, 83
DVD-Video, 82
DVI, 96
EEPROM, 74
eSATA, 96
Expansion bus, 94
Expansion card, 95
Expansion port, 95
Expansion slot, 95
FireWire, 96
Floppy disks, 80
Form factor, 58

Front side bus, 68
Gigahertz, 67
Graphics card, 91
Graphics processing unit, 91
Hard disk controller, 79
Hard disk drive, 78
Hard disk platter, 78
HDMI, 96
Head crash, 80
Home computer system, 60
Hot-plugging, 97
Ink jet printer, 92
Joystick, 88
Lands, 81
Laser printer, 92
LCD display, 90
LED display, 90
Linux platform, 64
Mac platform, 64
Magnetic storage, 78
Megahertz, 68
Microprocessor clock, 67
Mini case, 58
Mod, 65
Mouse, 88
Multi-core processor, 68
Nanosecond, 73
Netbook, 59
Non-volatile, 84
Notebook computer, 59
Optical storage, 81
Overclocking, 71
Parallel processing, 69
PC platform, 64
Peripheral device, 56
Pipelining, 69
Pits, 81
Pixels, 90
Plug and Play, 97
Pointing device, 88
Portable computer, 59
PostScript, 94
Power surge, 99
Printer Control Language, 94
RAM, 72

Random access, 77
Read-only technology, 82
Read-write head, 78
Recordable technology, 82
Response rate, 90
Rewritable technology, 82
RISC, 69
ROM, 74
ROM BIOS, 74
Safe Mode, 105
Screen resolution, 91
Sequential access, 77
Serial processing, 69
Solid state drive, 84
Solid state storage, 84
Storage density, 77
Storage device, 76
Storage medium, 76
Surge strip, 100
System unit, 57
Tablet computer, 59
Touch screen, 89
Tower case, 58
Trackball, 88
Trackpad, 89
UPS, 100
USB, 96
USB flash drive, 84
USB hub, 96
VGA, 96
Viewing angle width, 90
Virtual memory, 73
Volatile, 73
Word size, 68

# Interactive Summary

To review important concepts from this chapter, fill in the blanks to best complete each sentence. When using the NP2012 BookOnCD, click the Check Answers buttons to automatically score your answers.

**SECTION A:** The core of a personal computer system includes the computer system [_____], display device, keyboard, and mouse. Personal computers come in several varieties of [_____] factors. A(n) [_____] computer fits on a desk, runs on power from an electrical wall outlet, and can be housed in a horizontal case or vertical [_____] case. A(n) [_____] computer is a small, lightweight personal computer with screen, keyboard, storage, and processing components integrated into a single unit that runs on power supplied by an electrical outlet or a battery. Three categories of these computers are notebook computers, netbooks, and [_____] computers. Personal computers are sometimes designated as home, small business, or game systems to help consumers select the computer that's right for their needs. Although the Mac platform was not previously [_____] with the PC platform, the situation is changing now that Intel Macs use the same [_____] as PCs. Consumers can sometimes save money by installing upgrades after purchase; however, replacing a(n) [_____] is difficult and not recommended. Some computer owners make unauthorized modifications called [_____] to their computer systems. For information on the latest computers, mods, and prices, consumers can check computer magazines and Web sites. ▶ CHECK ANSWERS

**SECTION B:** The microprocessor and memory are two of the most important components in a computer. The microprocessor is a(n) [_____] circuit, which is designed to process data based on a set of instructions. Microprocessor performance can be measured by the speed of the microprocessor [_____]. A specification such as 3.33 GHz means that the microprocessor operates at a speed of 3.33 [_____] cycles per second. Other factors affecting overall processing speed include word size, cache size, instruction set complexity, parallel processing, and pipelining. Most personal computers only contain one main microprocessor, but today's multi-[_____] processors contain the circuitry for multiple microprocessors. Computers contain various kinds of memory. Random [_____] memory is a special holding area for data, program instructions, and the [_____] system. It stores data on a temporary basis until the processor makes a data request. The speed of RAM circuitry is measured in [_____] or in megahertz (MHz). RAM is different from disk storage because it is [_____], which means that it can hold data only when the computer power is turned on. Computers also contain Read [_____] memory, which is a type of memory that provides a set of "hardwired" instructions that a computer uses to boot up. A third type of memory, called by its acronym [_____], is a non-volatile chip that contains configuration settings, such as hard disk size and RAM capacity. ▶ CHECK ANSWERS

**SECTION C:** Today's personal computers use a variety of storage technologies. [_____] storage technologies, such as hard disks, floppy disks, and tapes, store data as magnetized particles. A hard disk drive provides multiple [_____] for data storage that are sealed inside the drive case to prevent airborne contaminants from interfering with the read-write heads. Hard disks are less durable than many other types of storage, so it is important to make a copy of the data they contain. [_____] storage technologies store data as a series of [_____]

and lands on the surface of CDs, DVDs, or BDs. Storage technologies, such as CD-[_____], are often used for distributing software, but you cannot alter the disc's contents. [_____] technology allows you to write data on a CD, DVD, or BD, but you cannot delete or change that data. Rerecordable or [_____] technology allows you to write and erase data on a CD, DVD, or BD. [_____] state storage technologies, such as USB flash drives, store data by activating electrons in a microscopic grid of circuitry. ▶ CHECK ANSWERS

**SECTION D:** Most computer systems include a keyboard and some type of [_____] device for basic data [_____]. For output, most computers include a display device. [_____] technology produces an image by filtering light through a layer of liquid crystal cells. Image quality for a display device is a factor of resolution, screen size, dot [_____], viewing angle width, response [_____], and color [_____]. A typical computer display system consists of the display device and a(n) [_____] card. For printed output, most personal computer owners select [_____] jet

printers, although [_____] printers are a popular option when low operating costs and high duty cycle are important. A(n) [_____] matrix printer is sometimes used for back-office applications and printing multipart forms. Installing a peripheral device is not difficult when you remember that it uses the [_____] bus to make a connection between the computer and peripheral device. Many of today's peripherals connect to a(n) [_____] port. If the right type of port is not built into your computer, you might have to add a(n) [_____] card. ▶ CHECK ANSWERS

**SECTION E:** For trouble-free computer use, it is important to secure and regularly [_____] your computer equipment. Anti-theft devices include computer locks and tie-down brackets. Computers can be protected from power [_____] by connecting to a surge strip. A(n) [_____] power supply can also protect against surges, plus it can supply backup power in case of a power outage. Keeping your computer's [_____] vents

free of dust can help to keep its temperature within operational levels. You can also clean dust off the screen and shake dirt out of the keyboard. Problems such as the blue screen of [_____] require troubleshooting. Windows offers interactive troubleshooting tools formatted as a series of simple questions, answers, and recommendations. Booting into [_____] Mode can also be a helpful step in the troubleshooting process. ▶ CHECK ANSWERS

# Interactive Situation Questions

Apply what you've learned to some typical computing situations. When using the NP2012 BookOnCD, you can type your answers, and then use the Check Answers button to automatically score your responses.

1. Suppose you're reading a computer magazine and you come across the ad pictured to the right. By looking at the specs, you can tell that the microprocessor was manufactured by which company? _____

2. The capacity of the hard disk drive in the ad is _____ GB and the memory capacity is _____ GB.

3. The computer in the ad appears to have a(n) _____ controller card for the hard disk drive.

4. You are thinking about upgrading the microprocessor in your four-year-old computer, which has a 2.6 GHz Pentium microprocessor and 512 MB of RAM. Would it be worthwhile to spend $500 to install an Intel Core i5 processor? Yes or no? _____

5. You're in the process of booting up your computer and suddenly the screen contains an assortment of settings for date and time, hard disk drive, and memory capacity. From what you've learned in this chapter, you surmise that these settings are stored in _____ , and that they are best left unmodified.

6. You're looking for a portable storage device that you can use to transport a few files between your home computer and your school computer lab. The school lab computers have no floppy disk drives, but do have USB ports. You should be able to transport your files using a USB _____ drive.

7. You want to add a storage device to your computer that reads CD-ROMs, DVD-ROMs, DVD-Videos, and CD-Rs. A DVD/CD-RW will do the job. True or false? _____

---

### SUP-R GAME DESKTOP MODEL EEXL

- Intel® Core™ i7-920
- 6 GB Tri-Channel DDR3 at 1066 MHz
- 500 GB - SATA-II (7200 rpm)
- 16x CD/DVD burner
- 21.5" HD widescreen monitor
- NVIDIA® GeForce™
- Creative Sound Blaster® X-Fi Titanium
- Altec Lansing speakers
- Gigabit Ethernet port
- 3-year limited warranty
- Windows 7

### $1400

---

8. Suppose that you want to purchase a new monitor. A(n) _____ screen offers a more environmentally friendly choice than a(n) _____ screen.

9. Suppose that you volunteer to produce a large quantity of black-and-white leaflets for a charity organization. It is fortunate that you have access to a(n) _____ printer with a high duty cycle and low operating costs.

▶ CHECK ANSWERS

## Interactive Practice Tests

Practice tests that consist of ten multiple-choice, true/false, and fill-in-the-blank questions are available on both the NP2012 BookOnCD and the NP2012 CourseMate Web site. BookOnCD test questions are selected at random from a large test bank, so each time you take a test, you'll receive a different set of questions. Your tests are scored immediately, and you can print study guides that help you find the correct answers for any questions that you missed. Online, you'll find a Practice Test for each section of the chapter. Your results from online tests are saved by Engagement Tracker. ▶ CLICK TO START

# Learning Objectives Checkpoints

2

Learning Objectives Checkpoints are designed to help you assess whether you have achieved the major learning objectives for this chapter. You can use paper and pencil or word processing software to complete most of the activities.

1. Draw a sketch of your computer system and label at least six of its components. Make a table with three columns, labeled Input, Output, and Storage/Memory. Page through the chapter and for each device you encounter, place it in one or more of the columns as appropriate.

2. Draw a set of quick sketches that show each of the following form factors: desktop tower, desktop horizontal, small form factor desktop, notebook, slate tablet, convertible tablet, and netbook. List the advantages of each form factor.

3. Create a short consumer brochure that lists five characteristics that would help consumers choose among a home, game, or small business computer system.

4. List important factors to consider when shopping for a new computer. Describe the three price points for personal computers and indicate which price point best fits your computing needs.

5. Explain how Intel Macs are changing the old idea that PCs and Macs are not compatible.

6. List at least six computer upgrades and rank each as easy, moderate, or difficult for computer owners to perform.

7. Refer to Section D of Chapter 1 and create a sequence of sketches that shows what happens in a microprocessor's ALU and control unit when an instruction is processed.

8. List and describe the factors that affect microprocessor performance. Name three companies that produce microprocessors, and list some of the models that each company produces.

9. List four types of memory and briefly describe how each one works.

10. Describe the advantages and disadvantages of magnetic storage, optical storage, and solid state storage using criteria such as versatility, durability, capacity, access time, and transfer rate.

11. Summarize what you know about how a graphics card can affect a display device's resolution.

12. Compare and contrast the technologies and applications for ink jet, laser, and dot matrix printers.

13. Create your own diagram to illustrate how the data bus connects RAM, the microprocessor, and peripheral devices. Explain the hardware compatibility considerations, device drivers, and procedures involved in installing a peripheral device.

14. List ways you can protect your computer system hardware from theft and damage.

15. Think about the last time you had a problem with computer hardware or software. Would any of the steps in Figure 2-64 have helped you solve the problem faster? If not, what guidelines would you add to the list in the figure?

Study Tip: Make sure you can use your own words to correctly answer each of the red focus questions that appear throughout the chapter.

## Concept Map

Fill in the blanks to show the hierarchy of system unit components.

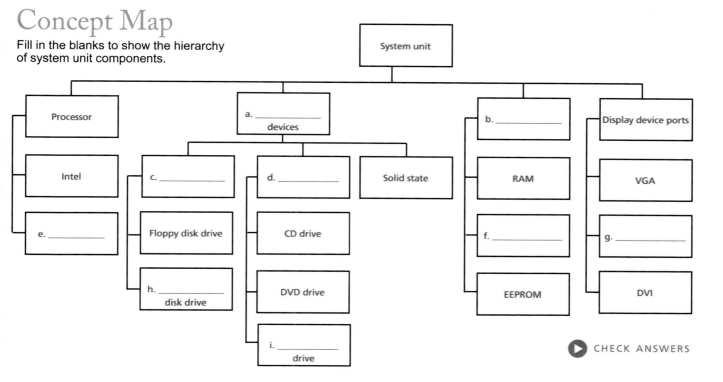

CHECK ANSWERS

# Projects

##  CRITICAL THINKING

Steve Jobs, co-founder of Apple Inc., coined the idea that computers should be consumer appliances like toasters that could be set up easily, used by anyone, and "democratically priced" so they are affordable to everyone. An opposing philosophy, championed by many PC owners, is that computers should be flexible modular systems that can be easily customized, upgraded, and modified by anyone with a moderate degree of technical savvy. Which philosophy do you personally prefer? What do you think is the preference of the majority of computer shoppers? If you were a computer designer, how would you provide your customers with flexibility while making it approachable for non-techies? Incorporate your ideas in a one-page e-mail message or attachment and submit it to your instructor.

##  GROUP PROJECT

For this project, work in groups of three or four. The group should select a digital device, such as a printer, scanner, digital camera, Web camera, digital video camera, digital music player, video capture card, digitizing tablet, or accelerated 3-D graphics card. If a member of your group owns the device, that's a plus. Create promotional materials for a trade show booth featuring your product. You might include a product photo, a list of specifications, and a short instruction manual. If time permits, your instructor might ask your group to present your sales pitch or a demonstration to the rest of the class.

##  CYBERCLASSROOM

E-mail the other members of your team a technical support question based on a hypothetical problem you're having with your computer. They should try to solve the problem using their current expertise and relevant Web sites. At the end of the project, evaluate your team's success rate based on the difficulty of the problems and the efficiency of their troubleshooting.

##  MULTIMEDIA PROJECT

Search the Web for "modding" and collect ideas for souping up your computer system unit, keyboard, and mouse. Make sure you check out options for clear Lexan and metallic cases, along with lighting options. Download photos from the Web and print them out, keeping track of sources. Using ideas from your collection of photos, sketch out plans for your ultimate modded computer. Submit your plan along with a list of the sources you used to get ideas and images.

##  RESUME BUILDER

Use the Web and other resources to learn about the computers and other technologies used in your career field or a profession of interest to you. Develop the information you find into a format similar to the Computers in Context section of each chapter in this textbook. Make sure you select two photos to accompany your narrative and include a list of relevant InfoWebLinks.

##  GLOBALIZATION

Computer ownership is growing worldwide and providing access to productivity tools and a global communications infrastructure. For this project, look for statistics and graphs showing the increase in computer ownership over time. How does it compare to telephone, television, and radio ownership? Are any aspects of this data unexpected or surprising? Gather your graphs and analysis into a two- to three-page executive summary.

##  ISSUE

The Issue section of this chapter focused on the potential for discarded computers and other electronic devices to become a significant environmental problem. For this project, write a two- to five-page paper about recycling computers, based on information you gather from the Internet. To begin this project, consult the Computer Recycling InfoWeb (see page 107) and link to the recommended Web pages to get an in-depth overview of the issue. Next, determine the specific aspect of the issue you will present in your paper. You might, for example, decide to focus on toxic materials that end up in landfills or barriers that discourage shipping old computers across national borders. Whatever aspect of the issue you present, make sure you can back up your discussion with facts and references to authoritative articles and Web pages. Follow your professor's instructions for formatting citations and for submitting your paper by e-mail or as a printed document.

##  COMPUTERS IN CONTEXT

The Computers in Context section of this chapter focused on computer and communication technologies pioneered by the military and then adopted into civilian use. For this project, research one of two topics:

• The use of notebook computers in combat environments and how design innovations for military use might affect the design of your next computer

• Developments in wearable computers and how soldiers and civilians might use them

To begin the project, survey the material in the Computers and the Military InfoWeb (page 109). Use a Web search engine to locate additional material relevant to the topic you've selected. Then write a two- to four-page paper about your findings and include graphics to illustrate your points. Make sure you cite sources for your material. Follow your professor's instructions for formatting and submitting your paper.

# On the Web

## STUDENT EDITION LABS

When you purchase access to the NP2012 CourseMate Web site, you'll find targeted learning materials to help you understand key concepts and prepare for exams. See page O-41 in the Orientation Chapter for login instructions.

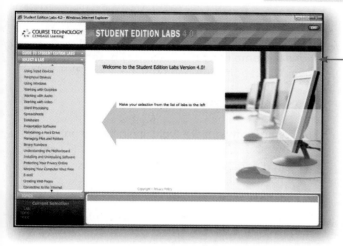

Work hands-on in structured simulations practicing important skills and concepts

### PERIPHERAL DEVICES

In the Peripheral Devices Student Edition Lab, you will learn about the following topics:

- Identifying commonly used peripheral devices, such as display devices, printers, scanners, digital cameras, and storage devices

- Adjusting display properties on a monitor and printer settings on a printer

- Identifying storage devices and their appropriate uses

### USING INPUT DEVICES

In the Using Input Devices Student Edition Lab, you will learn about the following topics:

- Using a keyboard, including using the function keys and the numeric keypad

- Using a mouse, including double-clicking, right-clicking, and dragging objects

- Identifying other input devices, such as touchpads, styluses, microphones, and digital video cameras

 **CHAPTER OVERVIEW COURSECAST**

Use your computer or iPod to hear a five-minute audio presentation of chapter highlights.

 **PRACTICE TESTS**

Review chapter material by taking these ten-question tests. Your results are saved by Engagement Tracker.

 **AUDIO FLASHCARDS**

Interact with audio flashcards to review key concepts from the chapter.

 **ONLINE GAMES**

Have some fun while refreshing your memory about key concepts that might appear on the next test.

 **DETAILED OBJECTIVES**

Make sure that you've achieved all the objectives for a chapter before it's time for your test!

 **AND MORE!**

At the NP2012 CourseMate Web site you'll also find the NP2012 eBook, TechTerm Flashcards, Online Glossary, and What Do You Think? opinion polls.

# 3

# Computer Software

## Chapter Contents

▶ SECTION A:
**SOFTWARE BASICS**
Software Categories
Application Software
Utility Software
Device Drivers

▶ SECTION B:
**POPULAR APPLICATIONS**
Document Production Software
Spreadsheet Software
"Number Crunching" Software
Database Software
Graphics Software
Music Software
Video Editing and DVD Authoring
    Software
Educational Software
Entertainment Software
Business Software

▶ SECTION C:
**BUYING SOFTWARE**
Consumer Basics
Software Copyrights and Licenses

▶ SECTION D:
**INSTALLING SOFTWARE AND
    UPGRADES**
Installation Basics
Installing Local Applications
Installing Portable Software and
    Web Apps
Software Upgrades and Updates
Uninstalling Software

▶ SECTION E:
**SECURITY SOFTWARE**
Security Software Basics
Security Suites
Antivirus Modules

▶ ISSUE:
**HOW SERIOUS IS SOFTWARE
    PIRACY?**

▶ **COMPUTERS IN CONTEXT:
JOURNALISM**

▶ **NEW PERSPECTIVES LABS**

▶ **REVIEW ACTIVITIES**

▶ **ON THE WEB**

## Learning Objectives

After reading this chapter, you will be able to answer the following questions by completing the outcomes-based Learning Objectives Checkpoints on page 179.

1. What are the most popular types of application software?

2. What kinds of system software are typically installed on personal computers?

3. What are the main differences between word processing, desktop publishing, and Web authoring software?

4. How does spreadsheet software work?

5. In addition to spreadsheets, what other types of "number crunching" software are available?

6. Why are there different types of graphics software?

7. What do software shoppers need to know?

8. What is a EULA?

9. How does local software differ from portable software and Web apps?

10. Is installing downloaded software different from installing software from a distribution CD?

11. What are the differences between proprietary software, commercial software, shareware, open source software, freeware, and public domain software?

12. What are software patches and service packs?

13. What's malware?

14. How does antivirus software work?

## InfoWebLinks

Visit the InfoWebLinks site to access additional resources Ⓦ that accompany this chapter.

## Multimedia and Interactive Elements

When using the BookOnCD or CourseMate eBook, the ▶ icons are clickable to access multimedia resources.

## Pre-Assessment Quiz

Take the pre-assessment quiz to find out how much you know about the topics in this chapter. ▶

## Apply Your Knowledge
The information in this chapter will give you the background to:

- Set up and use desktop gadgets and widgets
- Find, view, and update device drivers for printers and other devices
- Use word processing, desktop publishing, and Web page editing software
- Use a spreadsheet
- Select new software for your computer

- Find open source software
- Read a software license so that you know how to use it legally
- Download and install software
- Work with portable application software
- Uninstall software
- Install and use antivirus software

## Try It

**IS MY SOFTWARE UP TO DATE?**

Chapter 3 introduces you to basic concepts about computer software. Before you begin reading, take a glance at the software installed on your home, work, or school computer. Want to know if your software is up to date? You can use the "About" feature of any software package to find its version number and discover if a service pack (SP) has been installed.

**1. Windows:** Click the **Start** button. Click the **All Programs** option to display a list of installed software. Point to items in the list that have a ▶ symbol to see a sublist of software programs.

**Mac:** Click the 🖥 **Finder** icon and then click **Applications** from the list on the left side of the Finder window.

**2.** As you read through the list of installed software, jot down the names of any that you're not familiar with. When you read the chapter, you might find out what they do.

**3.** Open any one of your applications.

**4.** To find the current version of the application in Windows, click the **Help** menu, then click **About**. For Microsoft Office applications, click **File**, then click **Help**. On the Mac, click the program name from the menu bar at the top of the screen, then select **About**.

**5.** A dialog box appears. It contains a version number like 6.0 or 7.0, and it might also contain a service pack number like SP2. You'll learn the significance of version numbers and service packs when you read the chapter.

**6.** Close the About window. Close the program by clicking the 🗙 button (Windows) or clicking the program name on the menu bar, and then selecting **Quit** (Mac).

**7.** Check the version numbers for other software that is installed on your computer. Do some programs provide more information than others in the About window?

# Software Basics

**COMPUTER SOFTWARE** determines the tasks a computer can help you accomplish. Some software helps you create documents, while other software helps you block viruses or fine-tune your computer's performance. Section A delves into the characteristics of application software, utilities, and device drivers.

## SOFTWARE CATEGORIES

**What is software?** As you learned in Chapter 1, the instructions that tell a computer how to carry out a task are referred to as a computer program. These programs form the software that prepares a computer to do a specific task, such as document production, photo editing, virus protection, file management, or Web browsing.

**How is software categorized?** The two main categories are system software and application software. System software is designed for computer-centric tasks, whereas application software is designed to help people accomplish real-world tasks. For example, you would use system software to diagnose a problem with your hard disk drive or Internet connection, but you would use application software to edit a photo or write a term paper.

Application software can be divided into subcategories according to its use. System software includes operating systems (discussed in detail in Chapter 4), utilities, and device drivers. System software and application software subcategories are shown in Figure 3-1.

**TERMINOLOGY NOTE**

The term *software* was once used for all non-hardware components of a computer. In this context, software referred to computer programs and to the data the programs used. It could also refer to any data that existed in digital format, such as documents or photos. Using today's terminology, however, the documents and photos you create are usually referred to as *data files* rather than as software.

**FIGURE 3-1**

Software can be classified into categories.

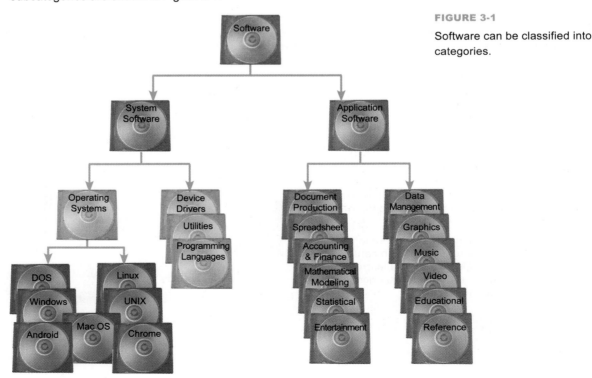

## APPLICATION SOFTWARE

**Why is it called application software?** When you hear the word *application*, your first reaction might be to envision a financial aid application or a form you fill out to apply for a job, a club membership, or a driver's license. The word *application* has other meanings, however. One of them is a synonym for the word *use*. A computer certainly has many uses, such as creating documents, crunching numbers, drawing designs, and editing videos. Each use is considered an application, and the software that provides the computer with instructions for each use is called application software, an application, or simply an app.

There are thousands of useful software applications designed for personal use or business use. You'll get a detailed look at some of the most popular application software later in the chapter.

**What is productivity software?** Some types of application software are referred to as productivity software. Many different definitions exist for this popular term. In general, however, **productivity software** can be defined as any type of application software that has the potential to help people do their work more efficiently.

The term might have originated in reference to software tools used by businesses to increase secretarial efficiency at routine office tasks, such as typing, filing, and basic bookkeeping. The applications that are most commonly associated with productivity software include word processing, spreadsheets, schedulers, and database management systems. Graphics software, presentation software, and desktop publishing software are also sometimes classified as productivity applications.

**What is groupware?** Another type of application software, called **groupware**, is designed to help several people collaborate on a single project using local networks or Internet connections. Groupware usually provides the capability to maintain schedules for group members, automatically select meeting times for the group, facilitate communication by e-mail or other channels, distribute documents according to a prearranged schedule or sequence, and allow multiple people to contribute to a single document.

**How do I run application software?** Techniques for running applications depend on your computer's operating system; but on most personal computers, you can double-click a desktop icon or select the application from a menu, as shown in Figure 3-2.

**FIGURE 3-2**

When using a PC, you can usually start application software using the Start menu or a desktop icon. ▶ Use your digital textbook to take a tour of ways to start programs and create desktop shortcuts.

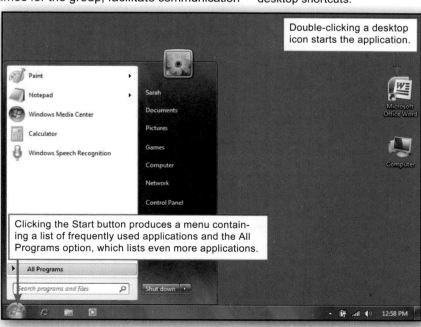

Double-clicking a desktop icon starts the application.

Clicking the Start button produces a menu containing a list of frequently used applications and the All Programs option, which lists even more applications.

## UTILITY SOFTWARE

**What is utility software?** A type of system software called **utility software** is designed to help you monitor and configure settings for your computer system equipment, the operating system, or application software.

Like all system software, utilities focus on computer-centric tasks such as blocking viruses or diagnosing hard disk errors, rather than real-world tasks such as document production or accounting. Examples of utility software include setup wizards, communications programs, security software, and diagnostic tools.

In recent years, antivirus products, such as Norton AntiVirus, McAfee VirusScan Plus, and avast! Antivirus, have been a popular category of utility software. With the recent influx of nuisance ads, intrusion attempts, and spam, utilities such as pop-up ad blockers, personal firewalls, and spam filters have also become best-sellers.

Other security-related utilities include file-encryption software, such as PGP, that scrambles file contents for storage or transmission. For people who are nervous about the trail of Web sites they leave behind, utilities supplied by your browser or operating system remove Internet history lists, files, and graphics from locations that can be scattered in many parts of the hard disk. Filtering software, such as Net Nanny, is used by parents to block their children from viewing objectionable Web sites.

**FIGURE 3-3**

Utility software includes diagnostics that track down file errors and other problems that prevent computers from running at peak efficiency.

Another popular category of utility software is system utilities, such as TuneUp Utilities, Advanced System Optimizer, and System Mechanic. These utilities can track down and fix disk errors, repair corrupted files, and give your PC a performance-enhancing tune-up (Figure 3-3).

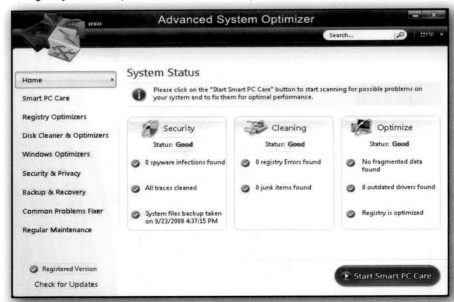

Adobe Reader (formerly known as Acrobat Reader) is a popular utility that works with files stored in standard PDF format. For example, a document created with expensive desktop publishing software can be converted into PDF format. Once converted, the document can be read or printed using Adobe Reader instead of the expensive desktop publishing software.

Computer owners like to customize their screen-based desktops with screensavers that display clever graphics when the machine is idle. Skins that customize the look and feel of media players and DVD burners are also popular (Figure 3-4).

Another group of utilities worth mentioning is designed for backing up files, cleaning up hard disks, and shredding files so they can't be recovered. Utilities such as Eraser, Windows File Shredder, and Lavasoft File Shredder can help you delete files before you donate or recycle your old computers.

**What are desktop widgets?** A **desktop widget** (sometimes called a gadget, dashboard widget, or control) is a specialized utility program that appears on a computer's screen-based desktop, looks like a control, and might display a snippet of information. Some examples of desktop widgets include clocks, calendars, calculators, news aggregators, sticky notes, and weather stations. Widgets can be configured to autostart when a computer boots up, and remain on the desktop until the computer is shut down. Widgets can also be corralled in a sidebar or dashboard.

Widgets are sometimes designed to be transparent so that they don't obscure other objects. Figure 3-5 illustrates some popular desktop widgets.

**FIGURE 3-4**

Skins that change the appearance of Windows Media Player are an example of popular utilities.

**FIGURE 3-5**

Desktop widgets are available on PCs and Macs for all kinds of tasks.

▶ Click to learn how to select, install, and use widgets.

**Where can I get utilities and widgets?** Most desktop operating systems offer basic utility software and a few essential widgets. Third-party software companies offer additional products that extend and improve upon those supplied by the operating system.

## DEVICE DRIVERS

**What is a device driver?** A **device driver** is software that helps a peripheral device establish communication with a computer. This type of system software is used by printers, monitors, graphics cards, sound cards, network cards, modems, storage devices, mice, and scanners. Once installed, a device driver automatically starts when it is needed. Device drivers usually run in the background, without opening a window on the screen.

Suppose you connect a new printer to your computer. You might also have to install a printer driver or select a preinstalled driver. After the device driver is installed, it runs in the background to send data to the printer whenever you initiate a print job. The printer driver signals you only if it runs into a problem, such as if the printer is not connected or it runs out of paper.

On a PC, if you need to change the settings for a device driver or update it, you can usually access the driver by using the Start menu's Control Panel option and then opening the System icon. Then use the Device Manager option to view a list of your computer system hardware and corresponding device drivers, as shown in Figure 3-6.

**FIGURE 3-6**

The Windows Device Manager offers access to device drivers. You can typically check if they are working and change settings. You can also check the device driver's version number and compare it with the most recent version posted online.

## QuickCheck

1. The category of software that is designed for computer-centric tasks is [                ] software.

2. [                ] software helps you carry out tasks such as creating documents, editing graphics, and conducting mathematical modeling.

3. [                ] software can be defined as any type of software that has the potential to help people do their work more efficiently.

4. Antivirus software, file shredders, and desktop widgets are categorized as [                ] software.

5. A(n) [                ] driver is designed to help a peripheral device establish communication with a computer.

 CHECK ANSWERS

# Popular Applications

3

**MOST COMPUTERS INCLUDE** basic word processing, e-mail, and Internet access software, but computer owners invariably want additional software to increase productivity, run a business, learn new things, and just have fun. Section B provides an overview of the vast array of application software that's available for personal computers.

## DOCUMENT PRODUCTION SOFTWARE

**How can my computer help me with my writing?** Whether you are writing a ten-page paper, generating software documentation, designing a brochure for your new startup company, or laying out the school newspaper, you will probably use some form of **document production software**. This software assists you with composing, editing, designing, printing, and electronically publishing documents. The three most popular types of document production software are word processing, desktop publishing, and Web authoring (Figure 3-7).

**Word processing software** has replaced typewriters for producing many types of documents, including reports, letters, memos, papers, and book manuscripts. Word processing packages, such as Microsoft Word, iWork Pages, and OpenOffice Writer, give you the ability to create, spell-check, edit, and format a document on the screen before you commit it to paper.

**Desktop publishing software** (abbreviated DTP) takes word processing software one step further by helping you use graphic design techniques to enhance the format and appearance of a document. Although today's word processing software offers many page layout and design features, DTP software products, such as QuarkXPress and Adobe InDesign, have sophisticated features to help you produce professional-quality output for newspapers, newsletters, brochures, magazines, and books.

**Web authoring software** helps you design and develop customized Web pages that you can publish electronically on the Internet. Only a few years ago, creating Web pages was a fairly technical task that required authors to insert HTML tags, such as <a href="contents.htm">. Now Web authoring software products, such as Amaya, iWeb, and Adobe Dreamweaver, help nontechnical Web authors by providing easy-to-use tools for composing the text for a Web page, assembling graphical elements, and automatically generating HTML tags.

**How does document production software help me turn my ideas into sentences and paragraphs?** Document production software makes it easy to let your ideas flow because it automatically handles many tasks that might otherwise distract you. For example, you don't need to worry about fitting words within the margins. A feature called *word wrap* determines how your text flows from line to line by automatically moving words down to the next line as you reach the right margin. Imagine that the sentences in your document are ribbons of text; word wrap bends the ribbons. Changing the margin size just means bending the ribbon in different

**TERMINOLOGY NOTE**

*OpenOffice.org* is the official name of this free software suite, but it is commonly referred to simply as *OpenOffice*.

**FIGURE 3-7**

Popular document production software includes Microsoft Word, QuarkXPress, and Adobe Dreamweaver CS5.

places. Even after you type an entire document, adjusting the size of your right, left, top, and bottom margins is simple.

**What if I'm a bad speller?** Most document production software includes a **spelling checker** that marks misspelled words in a document (Figure 3-8). You can easily correct a misspelled word as you type, or you can run the spelling checker when you finish entering all the text. Some software even has autocorrecting capability that automatically changes a typo, such as *teh*, to the correct spelling (*the*).

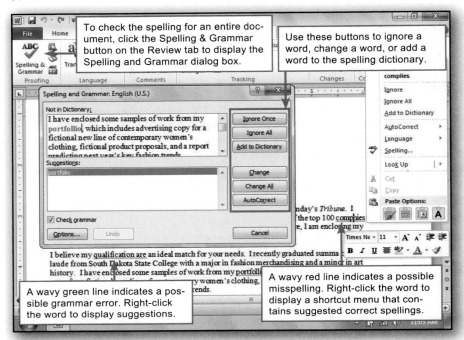

**FIGURE 3-8**

Document production software can check your spelling and grammar. ▶ Refer to your digital textbook for an overview of using your word processor's thesaurus, spelling checker, grammar checker, and readability statistics.

Although your software's spelling checker helps you correct misspellings, it cannot guarantee an error-free document. A spelling checker works by comparing each word from your document to a list of correctly spelled words that is stored in a data file called a **spelling dictionary**. If the word from your document is in the dictionary, the spelling checker considers the word correctly spelled. If the word is not in the dictionary, the word is counted as misspelled. Sounds okay, right? But suppose your document contains a reference to the city of Negaunee. This word is not in the dictionary, so the spelling checker considers it misspelled, even though it is spelled correctly. Proper nouns and scientific, medical, and technical words are likely to be flagged as misspelled, even if you spell them correctly, because they are not included in the spelling checker's dictionary.

Now suppose that your document contains the phrase a *pear of shoes*. Although you meant to use *pair* rather than *pear*, the spelling checker will not catch your mistake because *pear* is a valid word in the dictionary. Your spelling checker won't help if you have trouble deciding whether to use *there* or *their*, *its* or *it's*, or *too* or *to*. Remember, then, that a spelling checker cannot substitute for a thorough proofread.

**Can document production software improve my writing?** Because word processing software tends to focus on the writing process, it offers several features that can improve the quality of your writing. These features may not be available in desktop publishing software or Web authoring software, which focus on the format of a document.

Your word processing software is likely to include a **thesaurus**, which can help you find a synonym for a word so that you can make your writing more varied and interesting. A **grammar checker** reads through your document and points out potential grammatical trouble spots, such as incomplete sentences, run-on sentences, and verbs that don't agree with nouns.

Your word processing software might also be able to analyze the reading level of your document using a standard **readability formula**, such as the Flesch-Kincaid reading level. You can use this analysis to find out if your writing matches your target audience, based on sentence length and vocabulary.

**Can document production software help me break bad writing habits?** Most word processing, DTP, and Web authoring software includes a **Search and Replace** feature. You can use this feature to hunt down mistakes that you typically make in your writing. For example, you might know from experience that you tend to overuse the word *typically*. You can use Search and Replace to find each occurrence of *typically*, and then you can decide whether you should substitute a different word, such as *usually* or *ordinarily*.

**How do I get my documents to look good?** The term **document format** refers to the way that all the elements of a document—text, pictures, titles, and page numbers—are arranged on the page. The final format of your document depends on how and where you intend to use it. A school paper, for example, simply needs to be printed in standard paragraph format—perhaps double spaced and with numbered pages. Your word processing software has all the features you need for this formatting task.

A brochure, newsletter, or corporate report, on the other hand, might require more ambitious formatting, such as columns that continue on noncontiguous pages and text labels that overlay graphics. You might consider transferring your document from your word processing software to your desktop publishing software for access to more sophisticated formatting tools. For documents that you plan to publish on the Web, Web authoring software usually provides the most useful set of formatting tools.

The look of your final document depends on several formatting factors, such as font style, paragraph style, and page layout. A **font** is a set of letters that share a unified design. Font size is measured as **point size**, abbreviated pt. (One point is about 1/72 of an inch.) Figure 3-9 illustrates several popular fonts included with document production software.

| | |
|---|---|
| Times New Roman Font | 8 pt. |
| Times New Roman Font | 10 pt. |
| Times New Roman Font | 12 pt. |
| Times New Roman Font | 16 pt. |
| **Times New Roman Font** | **16 pt. Bold** |
| Times New Roman Font | 16 pt. Green |
| Arial Font | 16 pt. |
| Comic Sans MS | 16 pt. |
| Georgia Font | 16 pt. Bold Gold |
| Dotto | 24 pt. Orange |

**FIGURE 3-9**

You can vary the font style by selecting character formatting attributes, such as bold, italics, underline, superscript, and subscript. You can also select a color and size for a font. The font size for the text in a typical paragraph is set at 8, 10, or 12 pt. Titles might be as large as 72 pt.

**Paragraph style** includes the alignment of text within the margins and the space between each line of text. **Paragraph alignment** refers to the horizontal position of text—whether it is aligned at the left margin, aligned at the right margin, or **fully justified** so that the text is aligned evenly on both the right and left margins. Your document looks more formal if it is fully justified, like the text in this paragraph, than if it has an uneven or ragged right margin. The spacing between lines of text is called **leading** (pronounced "LED ding"). Documents are typically single spaced or double spaced, but word processing and DTP software allows you to adjust line spacing in 1 pt. increments.

Instead of individually selecting font and paragraph style elements, document production software typically allows you to select a **style** that lets you apply several font and paragraph characteristics with a single click. You can select a predefined style or you can create your own styles. For example, instead of applying bold and italics to every heading, changing the font to Arial, and then adjusting the font size to 18 pt., you can define a Heading style as 18 pt., Arial, bold, italic. You can then apply all four style characteristics at once simply by selecting the Heading style (Figure 3-10).

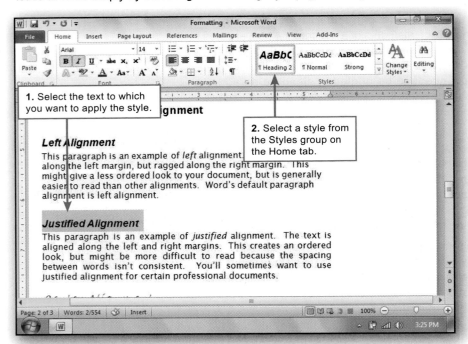

**FIGURE 3-10**

In this document, headings were formatted by selecting a style with a single click instead of individually selecting a font color, font size, and font style. Now if the Heading style is changed to green, for example, all the headings will automatically change from black to green. ▶ Your digital textbook walks you through the process of defining and using styles.

**Page layout** refers to the physical position of each element on a page. In addition to paragraphs of text, these elements might include:

- Headers and footers. A **header** is text that you specify to automatically appear in the top margin of every page. A **footer** is text that you specify to automatically appear in the bottom margin of every page. You might put your name and the document title in the header or footer of a document so that its printed pages won't get mixed up with those of another printed document.

- Page numbers. Word processing and DTP software automatically numbers the pages of a document according to your specifications, usually placing the page number within a header or footer. A Web page, no matter what its length, is all a single page, so Web authoring software typically doesn't provide page numbering.

- Graphical elements. Photos, diagrams, graphs, and charts can be incorporated in your documents. **Clip art**—a collection of drawings and photos designed to be inserted in documents—is a popular source of graphical elements.

- Tables. A **table** is a grid-like structure that can hold text or pictures. For printed documents, tables are a popular way to produce easy-to-read columns and rows of data and to position graphics. It may sound surprising, but for Web pages, tables provide one of the few ways to precisely position text and pictures. As a result, Web page designers make extensive and very creative use of tables.

Most word processing software is page-oriented, meaning that it treats each page as a rectangle that can be filled with text and graphics. Text automatically flows from one page to the next. In contrast, most DTP software is frame-oriented, allowing you to divide each page into several rectangular-shaped **frames** that you can fill with text or graphics. Text flows from one frame to the next, rather than from page to page (Figure 3-11).

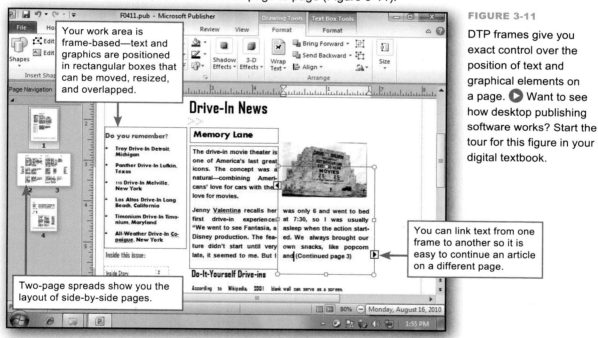

**FIGURE 3-11**

DTP frames give you exact control over the position of text and graphical elements on a page. ▶ Want to see how desktop publishing software works? Start the tour for this figure in your digital textbook.

**Does document production software increase productivity?**
Word processing software, in particular, provides several features that automate tasks and allow you to work more productively. For example, suppose that you want to send prospective employers a letter and your resume. Instead of composing and addressing each letter individually, your software can perform a **mail merge** that automatically creates personalized letters by combining the information in a mailing list with a form letter. Some additional capabilities of word processing software include:

- Automatically generating a table of contents and an index for a document

- Automatically numbering footnotes and positioning each footnote on the page where it is referenced

- Providing document templates and document wizards that show you the correct content and format for a variety of documents, such as business letters, fax cover sheets, and memos

- Exporting a document into HTML format for use on the Web

# SPREADSHEET SOFTWARE

**What is a spreadsheet?** A **spreadsheet** uses rows and columns of numbers to create a model or representation of a real situation. For example, your checkbook register is a type of spreadsheet because it is a numerical representation of cash flowing into and out of your bank account.

**Spreadsheet software**, such as Microsoft Excel, iWork Numbers, or OpenOffice Calc, provides tools to create electronic spreadsheets. It is similar to a smart piece of paper that automatically adds up the columns of numbers you write on it. You can use it to make other calculations, too, based on simple equations that you write or more complex, built-in formulas. As an added bonus, spreadsheet software helps you turn your data into colorful graphs. It also includes special data-handling features that allow you to sort data, search for data that meets specific criteria, and print reports.

Spreadsheet software was initially popular with accountants and financial managers who dealt with paper-based spreadsheets, but found the electronic version far easier to use and less prone to errors than manual calculations. Other people soon discovered the benefits of spreadsheets for projects that require repetitive calculations—budgeting, maintaining a grade book, balancing a checkbook, tracking investments, calculating loan payments, and estimating project costs.

Because it is so easy to experiment with different numbers, spreadsheet software is particularly useful for **what-if analysis**. You can use what-if analyses to answer questions such as "What if I get an A on my next two economics exams? But what if I get only Bs?" or "What if I invest $100 a month in my retirement plan? But what if I invest $200 a month?"

**What does a computerized spreadsheet look like?** You use spreadsheet software to create an on-screen **worksheet**. A worksheet is based on a grid of columns and rows. Each **cell** in the grid can contain a value, label, or formula. A **value** is a number that you want to use in a calculation. A **label** is any text used to describe data. For example, suppose that your worksheet contains the value $486,000. You could use a label to identify this number as Projected Income (Figure 3-12).

**INFOWEBLINKS**

For links to today's best-selling spreadsheet software, connect to the **Spreadsheet InfoWeb**.

 CLICK TO CONNECT
www.infoweblinks.com/np2012/ch03

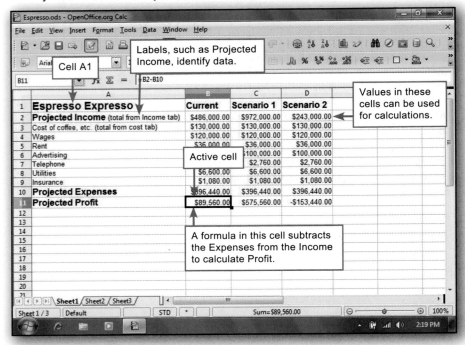

**FIGURE 3-12**

In a worksheet, each column is lettered and each row is numbered. The intersection of a column and a row is called a cell. Each cell has a unique cell reference, or address, derived from its column and row location. For example, A1 is the cell reference for the upper-left cell in a worksheet because it is in column A and row 1. You can designate the active cell by clicking it. Once a cell is active, you can enter data into it.
▶ Click for an overview of spreadsheet software.

You can format the labels and values on a worksheet in much the same way as you would format text in a word processing document. You can change fonts and font size, select a font color, and select font styles, such as bold, italics, and underline.

**How does spreadsheet software work?** The values contained in a cell can be manipulated by formulas placed in other cells. A **formula** works behind the scenes to tell the computer how to use the contents of cells in calculations. You can enter a simple formula in a cell to add, subtract, multiply, or divide numbers. More complex formulas can be designed to perform just about any calculation you can imagine. Figure 3-13 illustrates how a formula might be used in a simple spreadsheet to calculate savings.

**3**

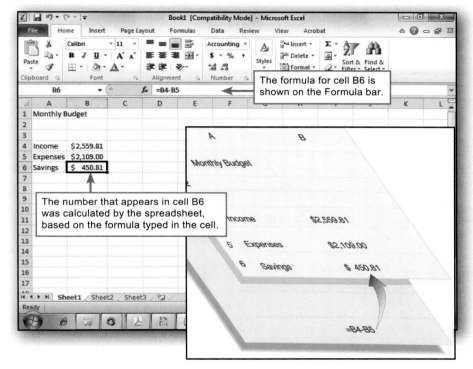

**FIGURE 3-13**

When a cell contains a formula, it displays the result of the formula rather than the formula itself. To view and edit the formula, you use the Formula bar. You can think of the formula as working behind the scenes to perform calculations and then to display the result.

▶ Why is it important to use a formula such as =B4-B5 instead of a formula with the actual numbers? To find out, start the tour for this figure in your digital textbook.

**FIGURE 3-14**

Functions are special formulas provided by spreadsheet software.

A formula, such as =D4-D5+((D8/B2)*110), can contain **cell references** (like D4 and D5), numbers (like 110), and **mathematical operators**, such as the multiplication symbol (*), the division symbol (/), the addition symbol, and the subtraction symbol. Parts of a formula can be enclosed in parentheses to indicate the order in which the mathematical operations should be performed. The operation in the innermost set of parentheses—in this case, (D8/B2)—should be performed first.

You can enter a formula from scratch by typing it into a cell, or you can use a built-in preset formula called a **function**, provided by the spreadsheet software. To use a function, you simply select one from a list, as shown in Figure 3-14, and then indicate the cell references of any values you want to include in the calculation.

**What happens when I modify a worksheet?** When you change the contents of any cell in a worksheet, all the formulas are recalculated. This **automatic recalculation** feature ensures that the results in every cell are accurate for the information currently entered in the worksheet.

Your worksheet is also automatically updated to reflect any rows or columns that you add, delete, or copy within the worksheet. Unless you specify otherwise, a cell reference is a **relative reference**—that is, a reference that can change from B4 to B3, for example, if row 3 is deleted and all the data moves up one row.

If you don't want a cell reference to change, you can use an absolute reference. An **absolute reference** never changes when you insert rows, or copy or move formulas. Understanding when to use absolute references is one of the key aspects of developing spreadsheet design expertise. Figure 3-15 and its associated tour provide additional information about relative and absolute references.

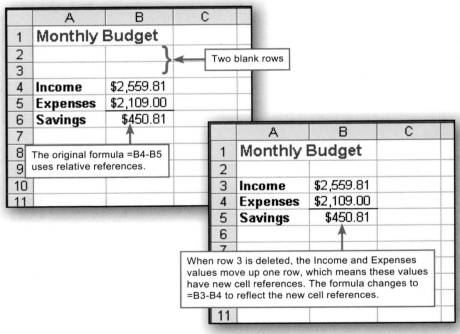

**FIGURE 3-15**

As shown in the examples, a relative reference within a formula can change when you change the sequence of a worksheet's rows and columns. An absolute reference is anchored so that it always refers to a specific cell. ▶ For some dynamic examples of absolute and relative references, watch the tour for this figure in your digital textbook.

**How will I know which formulas and functions to use when I create a worksheet?** To create an effective and accurate worksheet, you typically must understand the calculations and formulas that are involved. If, for example, you want to create a worksheet that helps you calculate your final grade in a course, you need to know the grading scale and understand how your instructor plans to weight each assignment and test.

Most spreadsheet software includes a few templates or wizards for pre-designed worksheets, such as invoices, income-expense reports, balance sheets, and loan payment schedules. Additional templates are available on the Web. These templates are typically designed by professionals and contain all the necessary labels and formulas. To use a template, you simply plug in the values for your calculation.

## "NUMBER CRUNCHING" SOFTWARE

**Aside from spreadsheets, what other "number crunching" software is available?** Spreadsheet software provides a sort of blank canvas on which you can create numeric models by simply painting values, labels, and formulas. The advantage of spreadsheet software is the flexibility it provides—flexibility to create customized calculations according to your exact specifications. The disadvantage of spreadsheet software is that—aside from a few predesigned templates—you are responsible for entering formulas and selecting functions for calculations. If you don't know the formulas or don't understand the functions, you're out of luck.

In contrast to the blank canvas approach provided by spreadsheet software, other number crunching software works more like paint by numbers. It provides a structured environment dedicated to a particular number crunching task, such as statistical analysis, mathematical modeling, or money management.

**Statistical software** helps you analyze large sets of data to discover relationships and patterns. Products such as IBM SPSS Statistics and StatSoft STATISTICA are helpful tools for summarizing survey results, test scores, experiment results, or population data. Most statistical software includes graphing capability so that you can display and explore your data visually.

**Mathematical modeling software** provides tools for solving a wide range of math, science, and engineering problems. Students, teachers, mathematicians, and engineers, in particular, appreciate how products such as Mathcad and Mathematica help them recognize patterns that can be difficult to identify in columns of numbers (Figure 3-16).

**INFOWEBLINKS**

For more information about popular "number crunching" software, take a look at the **Numeric Software InfoWeb**.

 CLICK TO CONNECT
www.infoweblinks.com/np2012/ch03

**3**

**FIGURE 3-16**

Mathematical modeling software helps you visualize the product of complex formulas. Here the points from a sphere are graphed onto a plane to demonstrate the principles behind the Astronomical Clock of Prague.

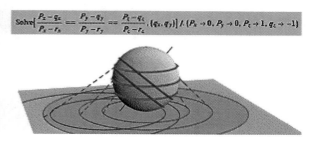

**Money management software** offers a variety of tools for tracking monetary transactions and investments. In this software category, **personal finance software**, such as MechCAD AceMoney and Intuit Quicken, is designed to keep records of income, expenses, assets, and liabilities using a simple checkbook-like user interface. This software also automates routine financial tasks, such as budgeting, investing, check writing, and bill paying. Many personal financial software products provide direct links to online banking services, so you can use them to check account balances, transfer funds, and pay bills.

Personal finance software produces reports and graphs that show you where your money goes. For example, you can analyze various aspects of your cash flow, such as how much you spent on entertainment last month and how that compares to the previous month.

**Tax preparation software** is a specialized type of personal finance software designed to help you gather your annual income and expense data, identify deductions, and calculate tax payments. Popular products, such as Intuit TurboTax, even accept data directly from personal finance software to eliminate hours of tedious data entry.

## DATABASE SOFTWARE

**What is a database?** The term *database* has evolved from a special-ized technical term into a part of our everyday vocabulary. In the context of modern usage, a **database** is simply a collection of data that is stored on one or more computers. A database can contain any sort of data, such as a university's student records, a library's card catalog, a store's inventory, an individual's address book, or a utility company's customers. Databases can be stored on personal computers, network servers, Web servers, main-frames, and even handheld computers.

**What is database software?** **Database software** helps you enter, find, organize, update, and report information stored in a database. Microsoft Access, FileMaker Pro, and OpenOffice Base are three examples of popular database software for personal computers. Oracle and MySQL are popular server database software packages. For PDAs and iPhones, popular choices include HanDBase, StoreIt, and Bento.

**How does a database store data?** Database software stores data as a series of records, which are composed of fields that hold data. A **record** holds data for a single entity—a person, place, thing, or event. A **field** holds one item of data relevant to a record. You can envision a record as a Rolodex card or an index card. A series of records is often presented as a table (Figure 3-17).

**TERMINOLOGY NOTE**

Database software is also referred to as database man-agement software (DBMS).

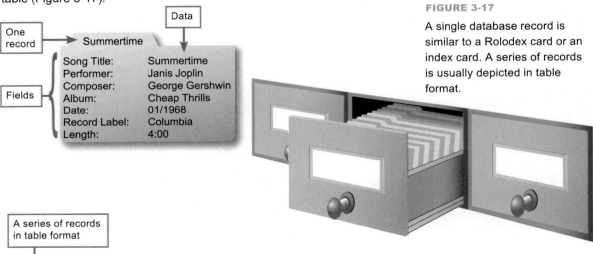

**FIGURE 3-17**

A single database record is similar to a Rolodex card or an index card. A series of records is usually depicted in table format.

| Song Title | Performer | Composer | Album | Date | Label | Length |
|---|---|---|---|---|---|---|
| Chasing Pirates | Norah Jones | Jones | The Fall | 11/17/2009 | Blue Note | 2:40 |
| Even Though | Norah Jones | Jones, Harris | The Fall | 11/17/2009 | Blue Note | 3:52 |
| Summertime | Janis Joplin | George Gershwin | Cheap Thrills | 08/12/1968 | Columbia | 4:00 |
| Summertime | Sarah Vaughan | George Gershwin | Compact Jazz | 06/22/1987 | PolyGram | 4:34 |

Some database software provides tools to work with more than one collec-tion of records, as long as the records are somehow related to each other. For example, MTV might maintain a database pertaining to jazz music. One series of database records might contain data about jazz songs. It could contain fields such as those shown in Figure 3-17. Another series of records might contain biographical data about jazz performers, including name, birth date, and home town. It might even include a field for the per-former's photo.

These two sets of records can be related by the name of the performing artist, as shown in Figure 3-18.

**JAZZ PERFORMERS**

| Performer | Birth Date | Home Town |
|---|---|---|
| Ella Fitzgerald | 04/25/1917 | Newport News, VA |
| Norah Jones | 03/30/1979 | New York, NY |
| Billie Holiday | 04/07/1915 | Baltimore, MD |
| Lena Horne | 06/30/1917 | Brooklyn, NY |

**JAZZ SONGS**

| Song Title | Performer | Composer | Album | Date | Label | Length |
|---|---|---|---|---|---|---|
| Chasing Pirates | Norah Jones | Jones | The Fall | 11/17/2009 | Blue Note | 2:40 |
| Even Though | Norah Jones | Jones, Harris | The Fall | 11/17/2009 | Blue Note | 3:52 |
| Summertime | Janis Joplin | George Gershwin | Cheap Thrills | 08/12/1968 | Columbia | 4:00 |
| Summertime | Sarah Vaughan | George Gershwin | Compact Jazz | 06/22/1987 | PolyGram | 4:34 |

**FIGURE 3-18**

The two sets of records are related by the Performer field. The relationship allows you to select Norah Jones from the Jazz Performers table and locate two of her songs in the Jazz Songs table.

3

**How do I create records?** Database software provides the tools you need to define fields for a series of records. Figure 3-19 shows a simple form you might use to specify the fields for a database.

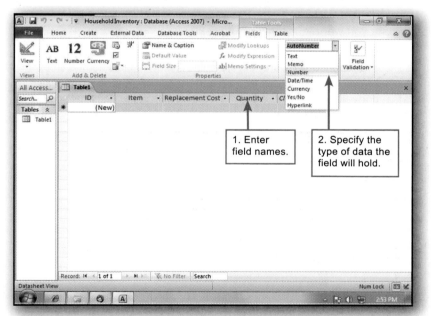

1. Enter field names.

2. Specify the type of data the field will hold.

**FIGURE 3-19**

Database software provides tools for specifying fields for a series of records. ▶ Your digital textbook shows you how to use database software to create a handy household database.

**When can I enter data?** After you've defined fields for a series of records, you can enter the data for each record. Your database software provides a simple-to-use data entry form that allows you to easily fill in the data for each field. Instead of typing data into a database, you can also import data from a commercial database, such as a customer mailing list. You can even download databases from the Web, and then import the data into fields you have defined with your database software.

**How do I locate specific data?** Many databases contain hundreds or thousands of records. If you want to find a particular record or a group of records, scrolling through every record is much too cumbersome. Instead, you can enter a query to perform a search, and the computer will quickly locate the records you seek.

A **query** is a description of the information that you want to find. Queries can take several forms, based on query languages, keywords, or examples.

Most database software provides one or more methods for making queries. A **query language**, such as SQL (Structured Query Language), provides a set of commands for locating and manipulating data. To locate all performances of *Summertime* before 1990 from a Jazz Songs database, you might enter a query such as:

Select * from JazzSongs where SongTitle = 'Summertime' and Date < '1990'

In addition to a formal query language, some database software provides **natural language query** capabilities. To make such queries, you don't have to learn an esoteric query language. Instead, you can simply enter questions, such as:

Who performed Summertime before 1990?

Another query option is the use of a **keyword search**, popular with search engines such as Google. Simply enter words relevant to your search, like this:

Summertime song performer <1990

As an alternative to a query language or a natural language query, your database software might allow you to **query by example** (QBE), simply by filling out a form with the type of data you want to locate. Figure 3-20 illustrates a query by example for Summertime performances before 1990.

**How can I use search results?** Your database software can typically help you print reports, export data to other programs (such as to a spreadsheet where you can graph the data), convert the data to other formats (such as HTML so that you can post the data on the Web), and transmit data to other computers.

Whether you print, import, copy, save, or transmit the data you find in databases, it is your responsibility to use it appropriately. Never introduce inaccurate information into a database. Respect copyrights, giving credit to the person or organization that compiled the data. You should also respect the privacy of the people who are the subject of the data. Unless you have permission to do so, do not divulge names, Social Security numbers, or other identifying information that might compromise someone's privacy.

**FIGURE 3-20**

When you query by example, your database software displays a blank form on the screen, and you enter examples of the data that you want to find.

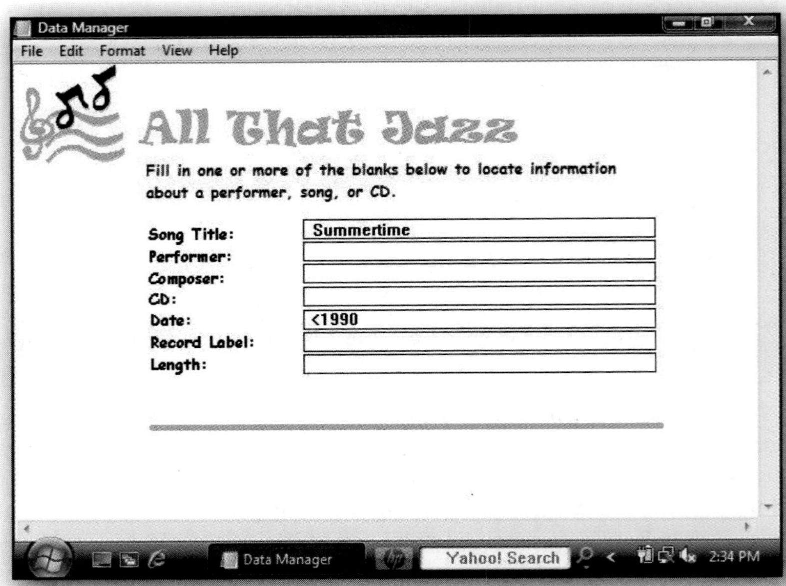

## GRAPHICS SOFTWARE

**What kind of software do I need to work with drawings, photos, and other pictures?** In computer lingo, the term **graphics** refers to any picture, drawing, sketch, photograph, image, or icon that appears on your computer screen. **Graphics software** is designed to help you create, manipulate, and print graphics. Some graphics software products specialize in a particular type of graphic, while others allow you to work with multiple graphics formats. If you are really interested in working with graphics, you will undoubtedly end up using more than one graphics software product.

**Paint software** (sometimes called image editing software) provides a set of electronic pens, brushes, and paints for painting images on the screen. A simple program called Microsoft Paint is included with Windows. More sophisticated paint software products include Corel Painter and Paint.NET. Many graphic artists, Web page designers, and illustrators use paint software as their primary computer-based graphics tool.

**Photo editing software**, such as Adobe Photoshop, includes features specially designed to fix poor-quality photos by modifying contrast and brightness, cropping out unwanted objects, and removing red eye. Photos can also be edited using paint software, but photo editing software typically offers tools and wizards that simplify common photo editing tasks.

**Drawing software** provides a set of lines, shapes, and colors that can be assembled into diagrams, corporate logos, and schematics. The drawings created with tools such as Adobe Illustrator and CorelDRAW tend to have a flat cartoon-like quality, but they are very easy to modify and look good at just about any size. Figure 3-21 illustrates a typical set of tools provided by drawing software.

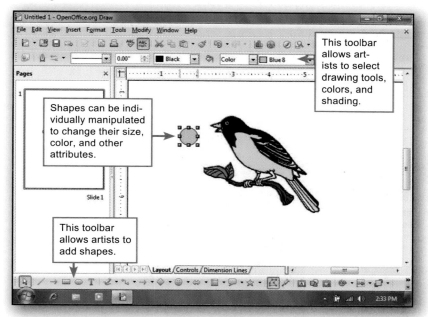

**FIGURE 3-21**

Drawing software provides tools for creating and manipulating graphics.

**3-D graphics software** provides a set of tools for creating wireframes that represent three-dimensional objects. A wireframe acts much like the framework for a pop-up tent. Just as you would construct the framework for the tent and then cover it with a nylon tent cover, 3-D graphics software can cover a wireframe object with surface texture and color to create a graphic of a 3-D object (Figure 3-22 on the next page).

FIGURE 3-22

3-D graphics software provides tools for creating a wireframe that represents a 3-D object. Some 3-D software specializes in engineering-style graphics, while other 3-D software specializes in figures.

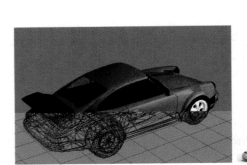

**CAD software** (computer-aided design software) is a special type of 3-D graphics software designed for architects and engineers who use computers to create blueprints and product specifications. AutoCAD is one of the best-selling professional CAD products. TurboCAD is a low-cost favorite. Scaled-down versions of professional CAD software provide simplified tools for homeowners who want to redesign their kitchens, examine new landscaping options, or experiment with floor plans.

**Presentation software** (Figure 3-23) supplies the tools you need for combining text, photos, clip art, graphs, animations, and sound into a series of electronic slides. You can display electronic slides on a color monitor for a one-on-one presentation or use a computer projection device for group presentations. You can also output the presentation as overhead transparencies, paper copies, or 35 mm slides. Popular presentation software products include Microsoft PowerPoint, iWork Keynote, and OpenOffice Impress.

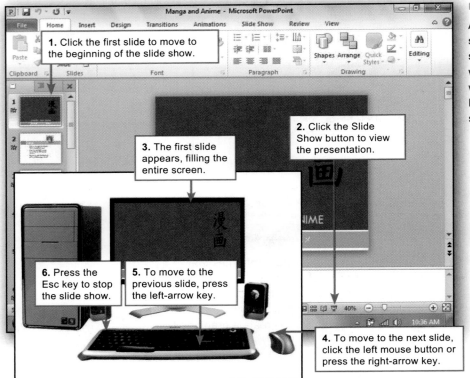

**FIGURE 3-23**

A computer-based presentation consists of a series of slides created with presentation software. ▶ Click to find out how to use presentation software.

## MUSIC SOFTWARE

**Why would I need music software?** You don't have to be a musician or composer to have a use for music software. Many types of music software are available. You might be surprised to find out how many of them come in handy.

It is possible—and easy—to make your own digital voice and music recordings, which you store on your computer's hard disk. Your operating system might supply **audio editing software**, such as Sound Recorder, or you can download open source software, such as Audacity (Figure 3-24).

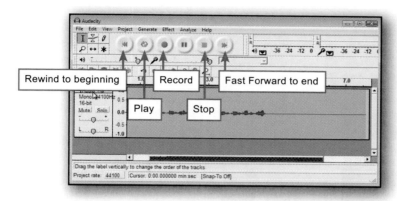

**FIGURE 3-24**

Audio editing software provides controls much like those on a tape recorder. Menus offer additional digital editing features, such as speed control, volume adjustments, clipping, and mixing.

Audio editing software typically includes playback as well as recording capabilities. A specialized version of this software called karaoke software integrates music files and on-screen lyrics—everything you need to sing along with your favorite tunes.

Music can be stored in a variety of digital formats on a computer or on a portable media player, such as Apple's iPod. Digital music formats, such as MP3 and AAC, are not the same formats used to store music on commercial audio CDs. These file formats take up much less storage space than on the original CD.

Audio editing software and audio playback software, such as iTunes, can be used to convert music from commercial CDs for use on computers and portable audio players. Such software can also convert audio files from one format to another. For example, you can convert a larger WAVE file to a smaller WMV file.

**Ear training software** targets musicians and music students who want to learn to play by ear, develop tuning skills, recognize notes and keys, and develop other musical skills. **Notation software** is the musician's equivalent of a word processor. It helps musicians compose, edit, and print the notes for their compositions. For non-musicians, **computer-aided music software** is designed to generate unique musical compositions simply by selecting the musical style, instruments, key, and tempo. **MIDI sequencing software** and software synthesizers are an important part of the studio musician's toolbox. They're great for sound effects and for controlling keyboards and other digital instruments.

**INFOWEBLINKS**

At the **Music Software InfoWeb**, you'll find detailed information on popular software in this category.

 CLICK TO CONNECT
www.infoweblinks.com/np2012/ch03

## VIDEO EDITING AND DVD AUTHORING SOFTWARE

**What can video editing software do?** The popularity of computer-based video editing can be attributed to video editing software, such as Windows Movie Maker and Apple iMovie, now included with just about every new computer. **Video editing software** provides a set of tools for transferring video footage from a camcorder to a computer, clipping out unwanted footage, assembling video segments in any sequence, adding special visual effects, and adding a soundtrack. Despite an impressive array of features, video editing software is relatively easy to use, as explained in Figure 3-25.

**INFOWEBLINKS**

Learn more about Apple iMovie and similar products at the **Video Editing Software InfoWeb**.

 CLICK TO CONNECT
www.infoweblinks.com/np2012/ch03

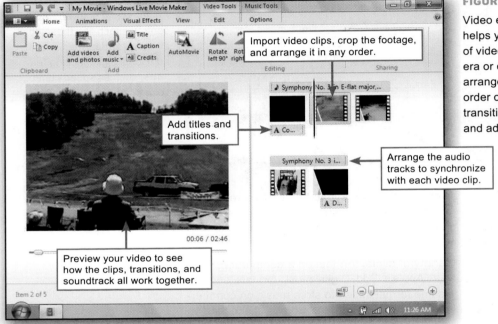

**FIGURE 3-25**

Video editing software helps you import a series of video clips from a camera or other video source, arrange the clips in the order of your choice, add transitions between clips, and add an audio track.

Desktop video authors now want to transfer their productions to DVDs and watch them on standard DVD players connected to television sets or projectors. **DVD authoring software** offers tools for creating DVDs with Hollywood-style menus. Just like commercial movies, desktop videos can now include menu selections such as Play Movie, Scene Selection, and Special Features. You can use the remote control for your DVD player to scroll through and select menu options. Examples of DVD authoring software include Roxio DVDit Pro 6, ULead DVD MovieFactory, and Apple iDVD.

## EDUCATIONAL SOFTWARE

**How can I use my computer for learning new things?** **Educational software** helps you learn and practice new skills. For the youngest students, educational software, such as MindTwister Math and Carmen Sandiego Word Detective, teaches basic arithmetic and reading skills. Instruction is presented in game format, and the levels of play are adapted to the player's age and ability.

For older students and adults, software is available for such diverse educational endeavors as learning languages, training yourself to use new software, learning how to play the piano or guitar, improving keyboarding skills, and even learning managerial skills for a diverse workplace. Exam

**INFOWEBLINKS**

What can you learn on your computer? Check out the **Educational Software InfoWeb**.

 CLICK TO CONNECT
www.infoweblinks.com/np2012/ch03

preparation software is available for standardized tests such as the SAT, GMAT, and LSAT. Web-based learning management systems, such as Blackboard and Moodle, help instructors keep track of student progress and provide students with interactive study and testing activities.

## ENTERTAINMENT SOFTWARE

**What's the best-selling entertainment software?** Computer games are the most popular type of entertainment software. Over $1 billion of computer and video games are sold each month in North America. Computer games are generally classified into subcategories, such as role-playing, action, adventure, puzzles, simulations, sports, and strategy/war games, as described in Figure 3-26.

**How do multiplayer games work?** Multiplayer games provide an environment in which two or more players can participate in the same game. Even some of the earliest computer games, like Pong, supplied joysticks for two players. Today's multiplayer games are a far cry from those simplistic games. Now numerous players can use Internet technology to band together or battle one another in sophisticated virtual environments.

Large-scale multiplayer games, such as World of Warcraft, Halo, and EverQuest, operate on multiple Internet servers, each one with the capacity to handle thousands of players at peak times. A new twist in online multiplayer games is persistent metaworlds, in which objects remain even when play ends. If one player drops an object, for example, it will be there when other players pass by.

3

**FIGURE 3-26**

Game Categories

| Type of Game | Description | Examples |
|---|---|---|
| Role-playing | Based on a detailed story line—often one that takes place in a medieval world populated with dastardly villains and evil monsters—the goal is to build a character into a powerful entity that can conquer the bad guys and accumulate treasure. | Diablo, EverQuest, World of Warcraft, Final Fantasy |
| Action | Like arcade games, action games require fast reflexes as you maneuver a character through a maze or dungeon. | Quake, Doom, Unreal Tournament, Halo, Tomb Raider |
| Adventure | Similar to role-playing games except that the focus is on solving problems rather than building a character into a powerful wizard or fighter. | Secret Files, Still Life, 3 Cards to Midnight |
| Puzzle | Include computerized versions of traditional board games, card games, and Rubik's Cube-like challenges. | Tetris, Minesweeper |
| Simulation | Provide a realistic setting, such as the cockpit of an airplane. Players must learn to manipulate controls using the keyboard, joystick, or special-purpose input device. A great way to get your adrenaline pumping without expenses or risks. | The Sims, Guitar Hero, Rock Band, Flight Simulator, NASCAR Racing |
| Sports | Place participants in the midst of action-packed sports events, such as a football game, baseball game, hockey final, soccer match, or golf tournament. Most sports games offer arcade-like action and require quick reflexes. | Wii Fit, Madden NFL, NBA Live, MVP Baseball |
| Strategy | Players (one player might be the computer) take turns moving characters, armies, and other resources in a quest to capture territory. | Age of Empires, World of Warcraft |

## BUSINESS SOFTWARE

**Do businesses use specialized software?** *Business software* is a broad term that describes vertical and horizontal market software, which helps businesses and organizations accomplish routine or specialized tasks.

**What is vertical market software?** **Vertical market software** is designed to automate specialized tasks in a specific market or business. Examples include patient management and billing software that is specially designed for hospitals, job estimating software for construction businesses, and student record management software for schools. Today, almost every business has access to some type of specialized vertical market software designed to automate, streamline, or computerize key business activities.

**What is horizontal market software?** **Horizontal market software** is generic software that just about any kind of business can use. **Payroll software** is a good example of horizontal market software. Almost every business has employees and must maintain payroll records. No matter what type of business uses it, payroll software must collect similar data and make similar calculations to produce payroll checks and W-2 forms.

Accounting software and project management software are additional examples of horizontal market software. **Accounting software** helps a business keep track of the money flowing into and out of various accounts. **Project management software** is an important tool for planning large projects, scheduling project tasks, and tracking project costs.

## QuickCheck                                                    SECTION B

1.  _____ publishing software uses frames to hold text and graphics.

2.  _____ software is useful for performing "what-if" analyses.

3.  When using database software, you can search for data by entering a keyword or a natural language _____ .

4.  _____ software is a special type of 3-D graphics software designed for architects and engineers who use computers to create blueprints and product specifications. (Hint: Use the acronym.)

5.  Payroll, accounting, and project management software are examples of a category of business software called _____ market software.

▶ CHECK ANSWERS

# Buying Software

3

SAVVY SOFTWARE SHOPPERS have a good sense of what to buy and where to find it. Section C offers some shopping tips for expanding your computer's software repertoire. The section ends with a discussion of software copyrights—important information that will help you understand the difference between legal and illegal software use.

## CONSUMER BASICS

**What are the most essential applications and utilities to have?** In addition to an operating system, your computer should have browser software, an e-mail client, word processing software, a security suite, a graphics viewer, and software that lets you burn files onto CDs and DVDs. You will probably also want compression software that lets you shrink big graphics files before e-mailing them, graphics software for editing photos, and some type of diagnostic software for troubleshooting hardware and software problems. For entertainment, you might want sound recording and playback software, as well as a few computer games.

**Should I use the apps and utilities that come with the operating system?** Most operating systems include a handful of small applications and a good variety of useful utility software. You'll want to thoroughly explore what your operating system has to offer before you spend money on third-party software. Figure 3-27 contains a list of the most frequently used apps and utilities offered by the Microsoft Windows operating system.

| Software | Function |
|----------|----------|
| Internet Explorer | Browse the Web |
| Windows Explorer | Keep track of files and folders; shrink file size |
| WordPad | Perform basic word processing |
| Notepad | Perform basic text editing |
| Calculator | Add, subtract, and calculate basic functions |
| Paint | Edit bitmap images, such as photos |
| Sound Recorder | Digitize music and voice input from a microphone |
| Windows Media Player | Play music and videos |
| Backup | Make backups of hard disk files |
| Disk Defragmenter | Arrange data on hard disk for optimal efficiency |
| Security Center | Set security levels for Internet and network access |
| Windows Firewall | Block intrusion attempts |
| Windows Movie Maker | Edit videos |
| Windows Photo Gallery | View digital photos |

**FIGURE 3-27**

The Windows operating system includes many useful applications and utilities. You can evaluate these offerings before considering whether to supplement them with third-party versions.

If you want utilities other than those included with your computer's operating system, you can explore software offered by third-party vendors. As it turns out, third-party vendors also offer utilities designed for the same tasks as those packaged with operating systems and you might want to consider those as well.

There are two reasons why some computer owners prefer utilities produced by third-party vendors over those packaged with an operating system. First, operating system utilities are sometimes not as dependable as third-party utilities designed by companies that specialize in media, system maintenance, or security.

For example, Symantec's Norton SystemWorks has a long track record of producing dependable diagnostic utilities, and McAfee's security software was successfully protecting computers from viruses and intrusions long before Microsoft developed its own set of Security Center utilities.

Additionally, some operating system utilities are not as full featured as third-party versions. For example, although Windows supplies a file compression utility that reduces file size for quick transmission or efficient storage, many computer owners prefer to use third-party utilities, such as WinZip, IZArc, Quick Zip, or PKZIP, that offer a variety of compression options.

**What is the advantage of a software suite?** A **software suite** is a collection of software applications sold as a single package. Office suites, such as Microsoft Office, Apple iWork, and OpenOffice, include applications to boost basic productivity: word processing, spreadsheet, and e-mail software. Graphics suites, such as Adobe Creative Suite and CorelDRAW Graphics Suite, typically include paint, draw, and Web graphics tools. Media suites such as Roxio Creator and CyberLink DVD suite provide tools for creating music CDs and video DVDs. Security suites include tools to scan your computer for viruses, block online intrusions, and prevent identity theft.

Purchasing a software suite is usually much less expensive than purchasing the applications separately. Another advantage is usability. Because all the applications in a suite are produced by the same software publisher, they tend to use similar user interfaces and provide an easy way to transport data from one application to another. The disadvantage of a software suite is that you might pay for applications you don't need. Figure 3-28 lists the components of several popular software suites.

**FIGURE 3-28**

Software suites are available in many application categories, such as productivity, antivirus, graphics, and media.

| Microsoft Office Professional | ZoneAlarm Internet Security Suite | Adobe Creative Suite | CyberLink Media Suite |
|---|---|---|---|
| Word | Antivirus/Spyware Scan | InDesign | PowerDVD |
| Excel | Two-way Firewall | Photoshop | PowerProducer |
| Outlook | Credit Bureau Monitor | Illustrator | PowerDirector |
| PowerPoint | Download Protection | Flash Professional | Power2Go |
| OneNote | Parental Controls | Acrobat Pro | MediaShow |
| Publisher | Antispam | Flash Catalyst | and more ... |
| Access | OS Firewall | Dreamweaver | |
| | | Fireworks | |

### How do I know if a software program will work on my computer?
Tucked away at the software publisher's Web site or printed on the software package (Figure 3-29) you'll find **system requirements**, which specify the operating system and minimum hardware capacities necessary for a software product to work correctly.

**System Requirements**

Operating Systems: Windows 7/Vista/XP
Processor: Intel Pentium or Core or equivalent
Memory: 1 GB or more
Hard Disk Space: 10 MB for installation
Network Protocol: TCP/IP
Network Connection: 10/100 Ethernet LAN/WAN, cable modem, DSL router, ISDN router, or dial-up modem

### Where can I find out about the latest, greatest software?
New software appears so quickly that it can seem impossible to keep up with it. However, a collection of publications and Web sites can help you keep abreast of software developments that might improve your computing experience.

Computer and technology magazines, such as *Wired*, *Macworld*, and *CPU Magazine*, usually include software reviews in every issue. Some magazines focus on games, while others specialize in business or power apps; but if you find a computer magazine that you enjoy reading, it is likely to include information about software that interests you.

Most computer magazines have companion Web sites and some of those significantly extend the material offered in the magazine's printed pages. ZDNet and CNET (*reviews.cnet.com*), for example, offer in-depth comparison reviews written by experts and tested under laboratory conditions.

Consumer-oriented Web sites also offer reviews. For example, the site *toptenreviews.com* contains easy-to-understand, in-depth checklists that make it easy to compare the features of popular software packages.

User reviews and consumer ratings can be found at several download sites, such as *download.cnet.com*, and comparison shopping sites that include *bizrate.com*, *Amazon.com*, and *newegg.com*. You might also find a blog or news feed that focuses on the type of software you typically use.

### Where can I get software?
Software is sold in some surprising places. You might find graphics software at your local art supply store. Your favorite home improvement store might carry software to help you select a paint color for your living room.

Software is also available from traditional sources, including office stores, computer superstores, electronics stores, and discount stores as well as local computer stores and mail-order catalogs. Today, however, most software is sold online from the software publisher's Web site or software download sites.

**What's included in a typical software package?** The key ingredients necessary to install new software are the files that contain the programs and data. These files might be supplied on **distribution media**—one or more CDs or DVDs that are packaged in a box, along with an instruction manual. The files might also be supplied as an Internet download that contains program modules and the text of the instruction manual.

**Is it better to buy software in a box or download it?** Boxed software can be purchased in a store or shipped to you by mail. The box usually includes distribution CDs and an installation manual. It might also include a more extensive user manual, but many software publishers have cut costs by supplying user manuals online or as an extra cost item. The advantage of distribution CDs is their availability in case your hard disk fails and you have to reinstall your software. Boxed software can give you a physical record of your registration code, serial number, and certificate of authenticity, which might be necessary for reinstallation.

You can download software from a Web site instead of buying it in a box. Downloading can be convenient. It saves you a trip to the store and you don't have to wait for a mail order package to arrive. Depending on the speed of your Internet connection, however, downloads can tie up your computer for a few hours. Even with a fast connection, a download can be interrupted and you might have to call customer service to restart it without paying for the product again.

Downloading can be risky. Some download sites display an irritating number of ads and are sometimes exploited by hackers. Software downloaded from less reputable sites might contain viruses. When possible, you should download directly from the software publisher's Web site or from a download site operated by a reputable business, such as a computer magazine or retailer. In any case, it is good practice to scan downloaded files for viruses before installing them.

Prices for boxed software and Web downloads can vary, so if you have the time to shop around, you are likely to save some money.

## SOFTWARE COPYRIGHTS AND LICENSES

**What is a software copyright?** After you purchase a software package, you might assume that you can install it and use it in any way you like. In fact, your purchase entitles you to use the software only in certain prescribed ways. In most countries, computer software, like a book or movie, is protected by a copyright.

A **copyright** is a form of legal protection that grants the author of an original work an exclusive right to copy, distribute, sell, and modify that work. Purchasers do not have this right except under the following special circumstances described by copyright laws:

- The purchaser has the right to copy software from distribution media or a Web site to a computer's hard disk in order to install it.

- The purchaser can make an extra, or backup, copy of the software in case the original copy becomes erased or damaged, unless the process of making the backup requires the purchaser to defeat a copy protection mechanism designed to prohibit copying.

- The purchaser is allowed to copy and distribute sections of a software program for use in critical reviews and teaching.

Most software displays a **copyright notice**, such as © *2012 eCourse Corporation*, on one of its screens. This notice is not required by law, however, so programs without a copyright notice are still protected by copyright law. People who circumvent copyright law and illegally copy, distribute, or modify software are sometimes called software pirates, and their illegal copies are referred to as **pirated software**.

**Can I tell if software is pirated?** Software pirates are getting more and more aggressive, and pirated software is not always easy to identify. Some unsuspecting consumers have inadvertently obtained pirated software, even when paying full price from a reputable source. According to the Software & Information Industry Association (SIIA), the attributes in Figure 3-30 could indicate that a software product is pirated.

Widespread pirating of Microsoft products has led to preventive measures such as Certificates of Authenticity and expensive-to-duplicate holographic images on CD labels.

If you suspect that software is pirated, it is best not to buy it or install it. If you have questions about a product's authenticity, you can contact the SIIA or the legitimate software publisher.

**What is a software license?** In addition to copyright protection, computer software is often protected by the terms of a software license. A **software license**, or license agreement, is a legal contract that defines the ways in which you may use a computer program. Software licenses can impose additional restrictions on software use, or they can offer additional rights to consumers. For example, most software is distributed under a **single-user license** that limits use to one person at a time. However, some software publishers offer licenses for multiple users to schools, organizations, and businesses.

A **site license** is generally priced at a flat rate and allows software to be used on all computers at a specific location. A **multiple-user license** is priced per user and allows the allocated number of people to use the software at any time. A **concurrent-use license** is priced per copy and allows a specific number of copies to be used at the same time.

**Where is the license?** For personal computer software, you can find the license on the outside of the package, on a separate card inside the package, on the CD packaging, or in one of the program files. Most legal contracts require signatures before the terms of the contract take effect. This requirement becomes unwieldy with software—imagine having to sign a license agreement and return it before you can use new software. To circumvent the signature requirement, software publishers typically use two techniques to validate a software license: shrink-wrap licenses and EULAs.

**What is a shrink-wrap license?** When you purchase computer software, the distribution media are usually sealed in an envelope, a plastic box, or shrink wrapping. A **shrink-wrap license** goes into effect as soon as you open the packaging. Figure 3-31 explains more about the mechanics of a shrink-wrap license.

**FIGURE 3-30**

According to the Software & Information Industry Association, pirated software can sometimes be identified by these characteristics:

- Software sold in a clear CD-ROM jewel case with no accompanying documentation, license, registration card, or Certificate of Authenticity
- Software marked as an "Academic" product, but not purchased through an authorized dealer
- Software marked as "OEM" or "For Distribution Only With New PC Hardware"
- Software CD-ROMs with handwritten labels
- Backup discs that you receive from a computer retailer containing handwritten labels
- Poor graphics and coloring of labels, disc jackets, or documentation
- Multiple programs from many different publishers on a single CD-ROM (commonly referred to as Compilation CDs)
- If a computer retailer loads software on your PC and you request the original manual, but the dealer responds by telling you to purchase a third-party book (e.g., *Photoshop for Dummies*)
- Photocopied manuals

**FIGURE 3-31**

When software has a shrink-wrap license, you agree to the terms of the software license by opening the package. If you do not agree with the terms, you should return the software in its unopened package.

**What is a EULA?** A **EULA** (end-user license agreement) is displayed on-screen when you first install software. After reading the software license on the screen, you can indicate that you accept the terms of the license by clicking a designated button—usually labeled OK, I agree, or I accept. If you do not accept the terms, the software does not load and you will not be able to use it.

**When I accept a software license, what am I agreeing to do?** Software licenses are often lengthy and written in legalese, but your legal right to use the software continues only as long as you abide by the terms of the software license. Therefore, you should understand the software license for any software you use. To become familiar with a typical license agreement, you can read through the one in Figure 3-32.

### Software License Agreement

**Important - READ CAREFULLY:** This License Agreement ("Agreement") is a legal agreement between you and eCourse Corporation for the software product, eCourse GraphWare ("The SOFTWARE"). By installing, copying, or otherwise using the SOFTWARE, you agree to be bound by the terms of this Agreement. The SOFTWARE is protected by copyright laws and international copyright treaties. The SOFTWARE is licensed, not sold.

**GRANT OF LICENSE.** This Agreement gives you the right to install and use one copy of the SOFTWARE on a single computer. The primary user of the computer on which the SOFTWARE is installed may make a second copy for his or her exclusive use on a portable computer.

**OTHER RIGHTS AND LIMITATIONS.** You may not reverse engineer, decompile, or disassemble the SOFTWARE except and only to the extent that such activity is expressly permitted by applicable law.

The SOFTWARE is licensed as a single product; its components may not be separated for use on more than one computer. You may not rent, lease, or lend the SOFTWARE.

You may permanently transfer all of your rights under this Agreement, provided you retain no copies, you transfer all of the SOFTWARE, and the recipient agrees to the terms of this Agreement. If the software product is an upgrade, any transfer must include all prior versions of the SOFTWARE.

You may receive the SOFTWARE in more than one medium. Regardless of the type of medium you receive, you may use only one medium that is appropriate for your single computer. You may not use or install the other medium on another computer.

**WARRANTY.** eCourse warrants that the SOFTWARE will perform substantially in accordance with the accompanying written documentation for a period of ninety (90) days from the date of receipt. TO THE MAXIMUM EXTENT PERMITTED BY APPLICABLE LAW, eCourse AND ITS SUPPLIERS DISCLAIM ALL OTHER WARRANTIES AND CONDITIONS EITHER EXPRESS OR IMPLIED, INCLUDING, BUT NOT LIMITED TO, IMPLIED WARRANTIES OF MERCHANTABILITY, FITNESS FOR A PARTICULAR PURPOSE, TITLE, AND NON-INFRINGEMENT, WITH REGARD TO THE SOFTWARE PRODUCT.

**FIGURE 3-32**

When you read a software license agreement, look for answers to the following questions:

Am I buying the software or licensing it?

When does the license go into effect?

Under what circumstances can I make copies?

Can I rent the software?

Can I sell the software?

What if the software includes a distribution CD and a set of distribution floppy disks?

Does the software publisher provide a warranty?

Can I loan the software to a friend?

**Are all software licenses similar?** From a legal perspective, there are two categories of software: public domain and proprietary. **Public domain software** is not protected by copyright because the copyright has expired, or the author has placed the program in the public domain, making it available without restriction. Public domain software may be freely copied, distributed, and even resold. The primary restriction on public domain software is that you are not allowed to apply for a copyright on it.

**Proprietary software** has restrictions on its use that are delineated by copyright, patents, or license agreements. Some proprietary software is distributed commercially, whereas some of it is free. Based on licensing rights, proprietary software is distributed as commercial software, demoware, shareware, freeware, and open source software.

**What is commercial software?** **Commercial software** is typically sold in computer stores or at Web sites. Although you buy this software, you actually purchase only the right to use it under the terms of the software license. A license for commercial software typically adheres closely to the limitations provided by copyright law, although it might give you permission to install the software on a computer at work and on a computer at home, provided that you use only one of them at a time.

**What is demoware?** Some commercial software is available as a trial version, sometimes called demoware. **Demoware** is distributed for free and often comes pre-installed on new computers, but it is limited in some way until you pay for it.

Demoware publishers can use a variety of techniques to limit the software. It might remain functional for a set number of days before expiring and requiring payment. It might run for a limited amount of time—for example, 60 minutes—each time you launch it. Demoware could be configured so that you can run it for only a limited number of times. Or, key features, such as printing, might be disabled.

Demoware publishers usually take steps to prevent users from uninstalling and reinstalling the demo to circumvent time limitations. Users who want to unlock the full version of a demo can typically do so by following links to the software publisher's Web site and using a credit card to purchase a registration code. The software can then be restarted and used without further interruption after the registration code is entered.

**Is shareware the same as demoware?** The characteristics of shareware sound very similar to those of demoware. **Shareware** is copyrighted software marketed under a try-before-you-buy policy. It typically includes a license that permits you to use the software for a trial period. To use it beyond the trial period, you are supposed to pay a registration fee. The original idea behind shareware was that payment would be on the honor system. Unlike feature- or time-limited demoware, shareware was supposed to be fully-functioning software.

Shareware was conceived as a low-cost marketing and distribution channel for independent programmers. Thousands of shareware programs are available, encompassing just about as many applications as commercial software. A shareware license usually encourages you to make copies of the software and distribute them to others. Copying, considered a bad thing by commercial software publishers, can work to the advantage of shareware authors, but only if users pay for the product. Unfortunately, many shareware authors collect only a fraction of the money they deserve for their programming efforts.

3

Today, many shareware authors use demoware techniques to limit their programs until payment is received. The term *shareware* is used today to refer to programs distributed by independent programmers, whereas *demoware* tends to be used when referring to trial versions of software from big software firms, such as Microsoft, Adobe Systems, and Symantec.

**What about freeware?** **Freeware** is copyrighted software that—as you might expect—is available for free. It is fully functional and requires no payment for its use. Because the software is protected by copyright, you cannot do anything with it that is not expressly allowed by copyright law or by the author. Typically, the license for freeware permits you to use the software, copy it, and give it away, but does not permit you to alter it or sell it. Many utility programs, device drivers, and some games are available as freeware.

**What is open source software?** **Open source software** makes uncompiled program instructions—the source code—available to programmers who want to modify and improve the software. Open source software may be sold or distributed free of charge in compiled form, but it must, in every case, also include the source code.

Linux is an example of open source software, as is FreeBSD—a version of UNIX designed for personal computers. OpenOffice—a full-featured productivity suite—is another popular example of open source software. You can search for open source applications at the *sourceforge.net* Web site.

Despite the lack of restrictions on distribution and use, open source software is copyrighted and is not in the public domain. Many open source characteristics also apply to free software (not to be confused with freeware, which you are not supposed to modify or resell). Both open source and free software can be copied an unlimited number of times, distributed for free, sold, and modified.

The philosophies behind open source and free software are slightly different, but their licenses are really quite similar. Two of the most common open source and free software licenses are BSD and GPL. The **BSD license** originated as the Berkeley Software Distribution license for a UNIX-like operating system. The license is simple and short (Figure 3-33).

**FIGURE 3-33**

Open source and free software applications are plentiful. Many have a very simple BSD license that ensures the source code is distributed along with the compiled software. ● Click to find out how to participate in open source software development projects and download free open source software.

| Software | Function |
| --- | --- |
| OpenOffice | Productivity |
| Thunderbird | E-mail |
| Firefox | Browser |
| Pidgin | Instant messenger |
| GIMP | Graphics editing |
| Gallery | Photo viewer |
| Blender | 3-D modeling and game design |
| Audacity | Sound editing and effects |
| MediaPortal | PC/TV media center |
| 7-Zip | Compression |
| ClamWin | Antivirus |

open source ™

The **GPL** (General Public License) was developed for a free operating system called GNU. The GPL is slightly more restrictive than the BSD license because it requires derivative works to be licensed. That means if you get a really cool computer game that's licensed under a GPL and you modify the game to create a new level, you have to distribute your modification under the GPL. You cannot legally market your modification under a commercial software license. There are currently three versions of the GPL. Their differences are of interest primarily to software developers.

**Should a software license affect my purchase decision?** Savvy software buyers typically consider software licenses before they make a purchase. Understanding a software license helps you stay on the right side of the law and can save you money.

Before purchasing software, make sure the license allows you to use the software the way you want to. If you plan to install the software on more than one computer or introduce modifications, make sure the license allows you to do so.

Some commercial software, such as security software, requires annual renewal. If you don't want to pay the fee every year, you might consider freeware or open source security software instead. Informed consumers tend to make better buying decisions. Just remember that many software programs exist and you can usually find alternatives with similar features offered under various licensing terms.

**INFOWEBLINKS**

To learn more about open source software and for a list of the most popular open source download sites, connect to the **Open Source Software InfoWeb**.

Ⓦ CLICK TO CONNECT
www.infoweblinks.com/np2012/ch03

# QuickCheck                                                          SECTION C

1. Most computer operating systems include some applications and [_____] software for file compression, editing text, and making backups.

2. Software [_____] from less-than-reputable Web sites sometimes contains viruses.

3. [_____] law allows you to make an extra, or backup, copy of software as long as you do not defeat any copy protection mechanisms.

4. [_____] that expires after a set period of time is often factory-installed on new computers.

5. OpenOffice and Linux are examples of [_____] source software that can be legally modified and redistributed.

▶ CHECK ANSWERS

# Installing Software and Upgrades

**IT'S SURPRISING HOW QUICKLY** your collection of software can grow as you discover new ways to use your computer for school, work, and play. Before you can use software, you have to install it on your computer. As you read Section D, you'll find out how to install software from CDs or from downloads, how to upgrade your software, and how to eliminate some of the software you no longer need.

## INSTALLATION BASICS

**What's included in a typical software package?** Whether it's on a CD or downloaded from the Web, today's software is typically composed of many files. For example, the eVideo-In Pro software includes numerous files as shown in Figure 3-34.

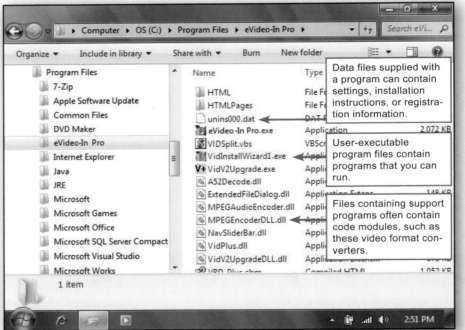

**FIGURE 3-34**

The files required by the eVideo-In Pro software contain user-executable programs, support programs, and data.

At least one of the files included in a software package is an **executable file** designed to be started by users or automatically launched by the operating system. These programs are sometimes referred to as EXE files (pronounced "E-X-E") because of the .exe file extension appended to the program name.

Other files supplied with a software package contain support programs for the computer to use in conjunction with the main executable file. A support program can be "called," or activated, by the main program as needed. In the context of Windows software, support programs often have a .dll file extension.

### TERMINOLOGY NOTE

A file extension is a three-letter suffix, such as .doc, that is appended to a file name to indicate the kind of information the file contains. Operating systems on PCs and Macs often hide file extensions, requiring users to adjust settings to see them.

In addition to program files, many software packages also include data files. As you might expect, these files contain any data that is necessary for a task, but not supplied by the user, such as Help documentation, a word list for an online spelling checker, synonyms for a thesaurus, or graphics for the software's toolbar icons. The data files supplied with a software package sport file extensions such as .txt, .bmp, and .hlp. Figure 3-35 can help you visualize how multiple files work together as one software application.

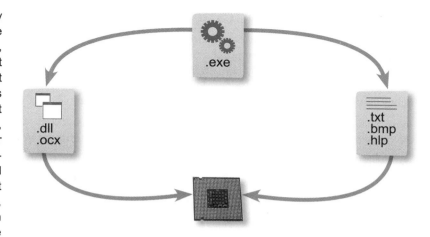

**FIGURE 3-35**

The main executable file provides the primary set of instructions for the computer to execute and calls various support programs and data files as needed.

With some operating systems, including Windows, one software program might share some common files with other software. These shared files are often supplied by the operating system and perform routine tasks, such as displaying the Print dialog box, which allows you to select a printer and specify how many copies you want to print. Shared files are not typically distributed with software because they should already exist on your computer. The installation routine attempts to locate these files. It then notifies you if any files are missing, and provides instructions for installing them.

**Why does software require so many files?** The use of a main executable file plus several support programs and data files offers a great deal of flexibility and efficiency for software developers. Support programs and data files from existing programs can usually be modified by developers for other programs without changing the main executable file. This modular approach can significantly reduce the time required to create and test the main executable file, which usually contains a long and fairly complex program. The modular approach also allows software developers to reuse their support programs in multiple software products and adapt preprogrammed support modules for use in their own software.

Modular programming techniques are of interest mainly to people who create computer programs; however, these techniques affect the process of installing and uninstalling software. It is important, therefore, to remember that computer software typically consists of many files; some contain user-executable programs or support programs, whereas other files contain data used by the program.

**Is it necessary to install software?** **Software installation** (sometimes referred to as setup) is a process that places a program into a computer so that it can be run or executed. Installation can simply be a matter of copying files to a computer or plugging in a USB flash drive, or it can be a more formal process that requires a series of steps and configurations. Installation procedures depend on your computer's operating system and whether the software is a local, Web, or portable application.

For the purposes of this discussion, we'll look at software installation under the Windows operating system. The procedure involves some quirks and complexities that don't exist with the Mac and Linux platforms; and because Windows is so pervasive, understanding how to install software on a PC is useful and practical.

## INSTALLING LOCAL APPLICATIONS

**What is a local application?** A **local application** is software that is designed to reside on a computer's hard disk. When you install a local application, its files are placed in the appropriate folders on your computer's hard disk, and then your computer performs any software or hardware configurations necessary to make sure the program is ready to run.

Most local applications contain a **setup program** that guides you through the installation process. During the installation process, the setup program usually performs the following activities:

- Copies files from distribution media or downloads files to specified folders on the hard disk

- Uncompresses files that have been distributed in compressed format

- Analyzes the computer's resources, such as processor speed, RAM capacity, and hard disk capacity, to verify that they meet or exceed the minimum system requirements

- Analyzes hardware components and peripheral devices to select appropriate device drivers

- Looks for any system files and players, such as Internet Explorer or Windows Media Player, that are required to run the program but are not supplied on the distribution media or download

- Updates necessary system files, such as the Windows Registry and the Windows Start menu, with information about the new software

**What is the Windows Registry?** The **Windows Registry** is a database that keeps track of your computer's peripheral devices, software, preferences, and settings. You'll learn more about the Registry in the operating system chapter; but the important concept to understand is that when you install software on the hard disk, information about the software is recorded in the Registry.

**Are all the software files installed in the same folder?** Most executable files and data files for new software are placed in the folder you specify. Some support programs for the software, however, might be stored in other folders, such as Windows\System. The location for these files is determined by the software installation routine. Figure 3-36 maps out the location of files for a typical Windows software installation.

### TERMINOLOGY NOTE

Although the term *local application* seems to imply application software as opposed to system software, it is also used in a broader sense to refer to any system or application software that is installed locally on the hard disk.

**FIGURE 3-36**

When you install software, its files might end up in different folders. Files for the eVideo-In Pro software are installed in two folders.

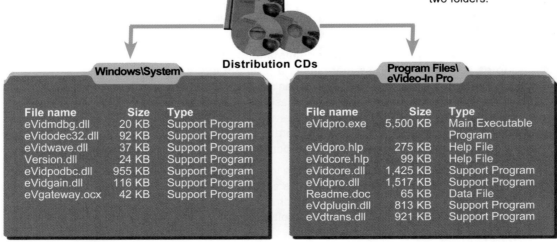

**Distribution CDs**

| Windows\System | | |
|---|---|---|
| File name | Size | Type |
| eVidmdbg.dll | 20 KB | Support Program |
| eVidodec32.dll | 92 KB | Support Program |
| eVidwave.dll | 37 KB | Support Program |
| Version.dll | 24 KB | Support Program |
| eVidpodbc.dll | 955 KB | Support Program |
| eVidgain.dll | 116 KB | Support Program |
| eVgateway.ocx | 42 KB | Support Program |

| Program Files\ eVideo-In Pro | | |
|---|---|---|
| File name | Size | Type |
| eVidpro.exe | 5,500 KB | Main Executable Program |
| eVidpro.hlp | 275 KB | Help File |
| eVidcore.hlp | 99 KB | Help File |
| eVidcore.dll | 1,425 KB | Support Program |
| eVidpro.dll | 1,517 KB | Support Program |
| Readme.doc | 65 KB | Data File |
| eVdplugin.dll | 813 KB | Support Program |
| eVdtrans.dll | 921 KB | Support Program |

**How do I install local applications from CDs and DVDs?** The process of installing a local application from distribution CDs or DVDs is quite straightforward. You insert the CD or DVD and close the tray. A setup program should autostart and then guide you through the process of selecting the hard disk location for the program files and acknowledging the EULA. Figure 3-37 shows what to expect when you use a setup program to install local applications from CDs or DVDs.

**FIGURE 3-37**

Installing from Distribution Media

**1** Insert the first distribution CD or DVD. The setup program should start automatically. If it does not, look for a file called Setup.exe and then run it.

**2** Read the license agreement, if one is presented on the screen. By agreeing to the terms of the license, you can proceed with the installation.

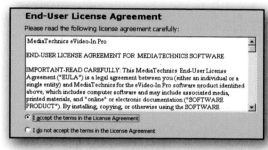

**3** Select the installation option that best meets your needs. If you select a full installation, the setup program copies all files and data from the distribution medium to the hard disk of your computer system. A full installation gives you access to all features of the software.

If you select a custom installation, the setup program displays a list of software features for your selection. After you select the features you want, the setup program copies only the selected program and data files to your hard disk. A custom installation can save space on your hard disk.

**4** Follow the prompts provided by the setup program to specify a folder to hold the new software program. You can use the default folder specified by the setup program or a folder of your own choosing. You can also create a new folder during the setup process.

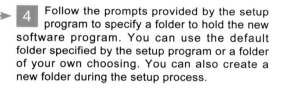

**5** If the software includes multiple distribution CDs, insert each one in the specified drive when the setup program prompts you to do so.

**6** When the setup is complete, start the program you just installed to make sure it works.

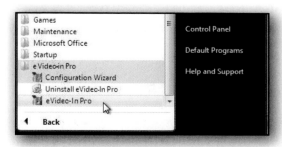

**How do I install downloaded software?** The installation process is slightly different for Windows software that you download. Usually all the files needed for the new software are **zipped** to consolidate them into one large file, which is compressed to decrease its size and reduce the download time. As part of the installation process, this downloaded file must be reconstituted, or **unzipped**, into the original collection of files.

It is a good idea to store original unzipped files for downloaded software on a CD or in a hard disk folder that you back up periodically. If your computer's hard drive malfunctions, you can use these files to reconstitute your software without having to download all of it again. Figure 3-38 maps out the process of downloading and installing local apps.

**FIGURE 3-38**

Installing Downloaded Software

**1** At the distribution Web site, locate any information pertaining to installing the software. Read it. You might also want to print it.

**2** Click the download link.

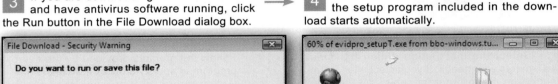

**3** If you are downloading from a trusted site and have antivirus software running, click the Run button in the File Download dialog box.

**4** Wait for the download to finish. Typically, the setup program included in the download starts automatically.

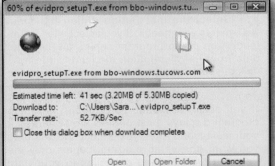

**5** Use the setup program to specify a folder to hold the new software program. You can use the default folder specified by the setup program or a folder of your own choosing. You can also create a new folder during the setup process.

**6** Wait for the setup program to uncompress the downloaded file and install the software in the selected directory. During this process, respond to the license agreement and other prompts. When the installation is complete, test the software to make sure it works.

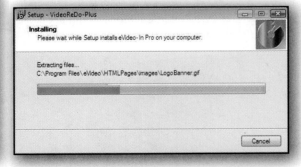

Downloadable software products can be provided in several different formats. Some automatically install themselves, but others require manual installation procedures. A downloadable file typically is set up as a **self-installing executable file**, **self-extracting zip file**, or **non-executing zip file** (Figure 3-39).

FIGURE 3-39

Downloadable File Formats

### Self-installing Executable Files

Under the most automated installation system, the process of downloading new software automatically initiates the entire installation process.

The software download is packaged as one large file with an .exe extension. This file automatically unzips itself and starts the setup program. You simply follow the setup program prompts to acknowledge the license agreement, indicate the folder for the software files, and complete the installation.

### Self-extracting Zip Files

Downloaded files with .exe extensions do not always install themselves. Some are simply self-extracting zip files, which automatically unzip the software's files, but do not automatically start the setup program.

To install software from a self-extracting zip file, you start the executable file to unzip the files for the new software. One of these files will be the Setup.exe program. Next, you manually start the setup program and follow its prompts to complete the installation.

### Non-executing Zip Files

If you download software and it arrives as one huge file with a .zip extension, you must locate this file on your hard disk and then use Windows or a program such as WinZip to unzip it.

After unzipping the file, you must run the setup program to acknowledge the license agreement, indicate the folder for the software files, and complete the installation.

3

**What if my software requires activation?** **Product activation** is a means of protecting software from illegal copying by requiring users to enter a product key or activation code before the software can be used. Activation is usually part of the software installation process, but it can also occur when demoware times out. Failure to enter a valid code prohibits the program from launching.

Product activation is not the same as registration, which is designed to collect demographic information from consumers, although a few software publishers tie activation and registration together.

Software can be activated over the phone or more commonly on the Internet. Usually a message appears on the screen instructing you to enter a serial number or validation code supplied on the distribution medium, packaging material, or download site, or in an e-mail message. The information you enter is either checked against a database or used to create a hash value.

Checking an activation code against a database makes sure that the code you've entered has not been used before. If the code is a duplicate, the license for that copy of the software is being used by someone else and you will have to call customer service to straighten out the problem.

A **hash value** is a unique number derived from encoding one or more data sets, such as names, serial numbers, and validation codes. Product validation can create a hash value based on your validation code and your computer's internal serial number, effectively tying the software to use on one specific computer.

Validation codes are very important. You should keep a list of them in a safe place, along with other configuration information for your computer system.

## INSTALLING PORTABLE SOFTWARE AND WEB APPS

**What is portable software?** **Portable software** is designed to run from removable storage, such as a CD or USB flash drive. Program files are not installed on the hard disk, no configuration data is stored on the hard disk, and no entries need to be made in the Windows Registry. When the media containing the portable software is removed from the computer, no trace of it is left there.

Your BookOnCD is an example of portable software. To use it, you simply insert the CD containing the program files. Other examples of portable applications include OpenOffice Portable, Thunderbird (e-mail), Firefox (browser), and FileZilla (upload and download), which are designed to run from USB flash drives.

**How do I install portable software?** Portable software is so simple to install that it is sometimes referred to as install-free software. Installation is simply a matter of getting program files to the media on which they are supposed to run. For example, suppose that you want to run OpenOffice Portable from a USB flash drive. You can download the OpenOffice Portable zip file and then simply unzip it so that the files end up on the USB flash drive (Figure 3-40).

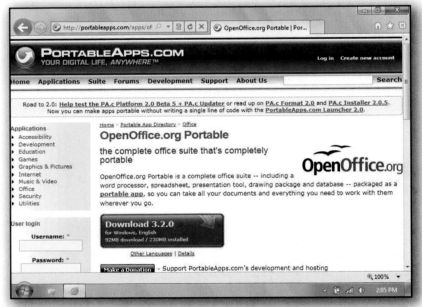

**FIGURE 3-40**

OpenOffice.org Portable includes word processing, spreadsheet, database, graphics, and presentation modules. ▶ Find out how to work with portable software from your USB flash drive.

**What are Web apps?** A **Web application** (or Web app) is software that is accessed with a Web browser. Instead of running locally, much of the program code for the software runs on a remote computer connected to the Internet or other computer network. Web apps are available for many of the same applications that run locally, such as e-mail, calendars, databases, photo sharing, project management, maps, games, and even word processing. Google offers popular spreadsheet, word processing, and presentation Web apps that allow group collaboration on projects from participants in multiple locations.

**How do I install Web apps?** Some Web apps, such as Gmail and Yahoo! Mail, require no installation at all on your local computer. These applications use browser software as the e-mail client software, making it possible to access your e-mail from any computer that has a browser and an Internet connection.

Some Web applications, such as Google Earth, require a client-side program to be installed on your local computer. The Internet sites that host Web apps typically include instructions if installation is necessary. You can print the instructions if they look somewhat tricky. Once installed, you can access most Web apps from your browser (Figure 3-41).

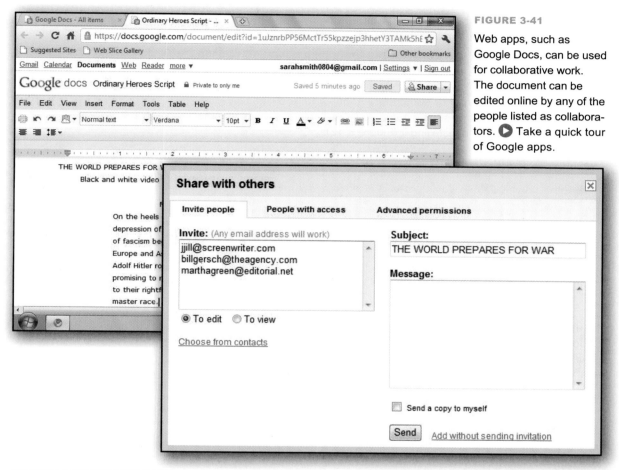

**FIGURE 3-41**

Web apps, such as Google Docs, can be used for collaborative work. The document can be edited online by any of the people listed as collaborators. ▶ Take a quick tour of Google apps.

**3**

## SOFTWARE UPGRADES AND UPDATES

**What are updates, patches, and service packs?** Software publishers regularly revise their software to add new features, fix bugs, and improve its security. These revisions are offered to consumers as new versions, patches, or service packs.

Periodically, software publishers replace older versions of a software product with a new version that's sometimes referred to as a **software upgrade**. To keep these upgrades straight, each one carries a version or revision number. For example, version 1.0 might be replaced by a newer version, such as version 2.0. Upgrading to a new version usually involves a fee, but it is typically less costly than purchasing the new version off the shelf.

A **software update** (sometimes called a software patch) is a small section of program code that replaces part of the software you currently have installed. The term **service pack**, which usually applies to operating system updates, is a set of patches designed to correct problems and address security vulnerabilities. Software updates and service packs are usually free. They are typically numbered using decimal places; for example, an update might change version 2.0 to version 2.01.

**How do I get updates?** Software publishers have various ways of notifying customers about updates. Many allow you to set your preferences for how you would like to receive notifications and updates. If you have registered your software—usually by connecting to the publisher's Web site during or after an installation—you might receive an e-mail notice when an update is available. Alternatively, you can check the publisher's Web site from time to time.

Some software provides an Automatic Update option that periodically checks the software publisher's Web site for updates, then downloads updates automatically and installs them without user intervention. The advantage of Automatic Update is convenience. The disadvantage is that changes can be made to your computer without your knowledge. Some software checks the Web to see if an update is available and gives you the option of downloading and installing it (Figure 3-42).

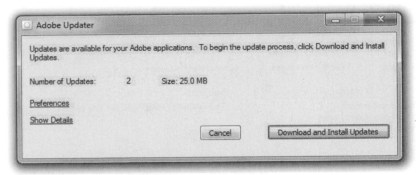

**FIGURE 3-42**

If you prefer not to have software updates automatically installed, look for an option or preference that lets you choose which updates to install and decide when to install them. ▶ Work with the tour to find out how to manually launch updates.

**When should I update or upgrade my software?** It is always a good idea to install updates and service packs when they become available. The revised code they contain often addresses security vulnerabilities and the sooner you patch up those holes, the better.

Version upgrades are a slightly different story. Many savvy computer owners wait to upgrade for a few weeks or months after new software versions become available. The reason they wait is to find out how other users like the new version. If Internet chatter indicates some major flaws, it can be prudent to wait until the publisher is able to address them with patches.

**How do I install an upgrade?** A new version upgrade usually installs in a similar way as you installed the original version, by activating a setup program, displaying a license agreement, and adding updated entries to your computer's Start menu. To combat piracy, many software publishers require users to enter a validation code to complete an upgrade.

**When I install updates and upgrades, what happens to the old version?** The result of an update or upgrade depends on several factors. Most updates and service pack installations cannot be reversed. New version upgrades typically overwrite the old version, but you might have the option to keep the old version just in case you have trouble with the new one and need to revert back to the previous version. The documentation for the upgrade should explain your options for retaining or overwriting old versions.

## UNINSTALLING SOFTWARE

**How do I know what software is installed on my computer?**
Mac users can find a list of installed software by opening the Macintosh HD and then selecting Applications. When working with a PC, there are several places you can look to see what software is installed. The All Programs menu lists most installed applications. A few applications might not appear on this list if they were installed in a non-standard way.

**How do I get rid of software?** With some operating systems, such as DOS, you can remove software simply by deleting its files. Other operating systems, such as Windows and Mac OS, include an **uninstall routine** (Figure 3-43), which deletes the software's files from various folders on your computer's hard disk. The uninstall routine also removes references to the program from the desktop and from operating system files, such as the file system and, in the case of Windows, the Windows Registry.

3

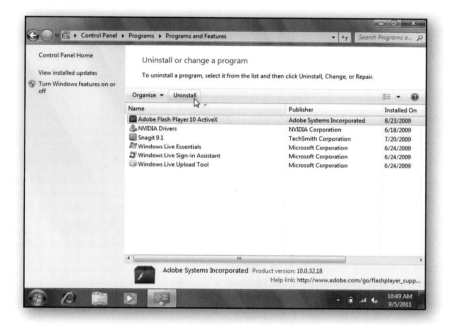

**FIGURE 3-43**

The Uninstall utility provided by Windows 7 lists installed software and gives you the option to select a program for deletion. ▶ Make sure you know how to uninstall software by watching the tour for this figure in your digital textbook.

## QuickCheck

1. Computer software typically includes many files that contain user- [＿＿＿＿] programs, support programs, and data.

2. Most local software applications include a(n) [＿＿＿＿] program that guides you through the installation process.

3. Usually all the files for downloaded software are [＿＿＿＿] into one large file that is also compressed to decrease its size and reduce download time.

4. When you activate software, the process might create a(n) [＿＿＿＿] value based on your validation code and your computer's internal serial number.

5. A(n) [＿＿＿＿] pack is a set of patches that correct problems and address security vulnerabilities.

 CHECK ANSWERS

# Security Software

THE DAYS WHEN VIRUSES were the greatest threat to computers are long gone. Today, a virus is just one of many categories of malicious software, or malware, that can wreak havoc on computer systems and networks. Deluged with such a huge assortment of threats to their systems and often unable to distinguish one type of threat from another, individual computer users and businesses have had to defend themselves by purchasing all kinds of security software. Section E explains how you can use security software to combat malicious software that threatens your computer.

## SECURITY SOFTWARE BASICS

**What is security software?** **Security software** is designed to protect computers from various forms of destructive software and unauthorized intrusions. One of the first security software offerings was created by Dr. Peter Tippett, an emergency room physician who took a page from conventional medicine and applied it to computer viruses. The security software developed by Dr. Tippett was sold to Symantec Corporation in 1992 and incorporated into the popular Norton AntiVirus software.

Security software can be classified into various types: antivirus, anti-spyware, anti-spam, and firewalls. Each type focuses on a specific security threat.

**What are malware threats?** The terms **malicious software** and **malware** refer to any computer program designed to surreptitiously enter a computer, gain unauthorized access to data, or disrupt normal processing operations. Malware includes viruses, worms, Trojans, bots, and spyware.

Malware is created and unleashed by individuals referred to as hackers, crackers, black hats, or cybercriminals. The motivation behind malware is varied. Some malware is intended to be a relatively harmless prank or mildly annoying vandalism. Other malware is created to distribute political messages or to disrupt operations at specific companies. In an increasing number of cases, the motivation is monetary gain. Malware designed for identity theft or extortion has become a very real threat to individuals and corporations. Organized crime bosses, drug traffickers, and terrorists are joining forces with cybercriminals to increase the sophistication of their activities (Figure 3-44).

Emerging security threats often combine and refine old exploits, blurring the lines between viruses, worms, and other kinds of malware. For example, a Trojan horse might carry a bot that turns a victim's computer into a distribution point for a mass-mailing worm. Security experts use the term **blended threat** to describe malware that combines more than one type of malicious program. Although the nuances of blended threats are beyond the scope of this chapter, it is important to understand the threats posed by malware if you hope to avoid identity theft and other inconvenient computing incidents.

**FIGURE 3-44**

Security breaches were once little more than pranks, but today's threats from organized crime and terrorists are serious concerns for individuals as well as for corporations and governments.

**What is a virus?** A **computer virus** is a set of program instructions that attaches itself to a file, reproduces itself, and spreads to other files. A common misconception is that viruses spread themselves from one computer to another. They don't. Viruses can replicate themselves only on the host computer. A key characteristic of viruses is their ability to lurk in a computer for days or months, quietly replicating themselves. While this replication takes place, you might not even know that your computer has contracted a virus; therefore, it is easy to inadvertently spread infected files to other people's computers.

In addition to replicating itself, a virus usually delivers a payload, which can be as harmless as displaying an annoying message or as devastating as trashing the data on your computer's hard disk. It can corrupt files, destroy data, or otherwise disrupt computer operations. A trigger event, such as a specific date, can unleash some viruses. For example, the now defunct Michelangelo virus triggered on March 6, the birthday of artist Michelangelo. Viruses that deliver their payloads on a specific date are sometimes referred to as time bombs. Viruses that deliver their payloads in response to some other system event are referred to as logic bombs.

Viruses spread when people distribute infected files by exchanging disks and CDs, sending e-mail attachments, exchanging music on file-sharing networks, and downloading software from the Web.

**What is a worm?** A **computer worm** is a self-replicating program designed to carry out some unauthorized activity on a victim's computer. Worms can spread themselves from one computer to another without any assistance from victims.

Worms can enter a computer through security holes in browsers and operating systems, as e-mail attachments, and by victims clicking on infected pop-up ads or links contained in e-mails. A mass-mailing worm called Ackantta is hidden in an attachment to an e-mail message that's a fake Twitter invitation. Clicking the attachment activates the worm.

A **mass-mailing worm** spreads by sending itself to every address in the address book of an infected computer. Your friends receive these messages and, thinking that they are from a trusted source, open the infected attachment, spreading the worm to their computers and on to their friends.

Although e-mail is currently the primary vehicle used to spread worms, hackers have also devised ways to spread worms over file-sharing networks, instant messaging links, and mobile phones.

**What is a Trojan horse?** A **Trojan horse** (sometimes simply called a Trojan) is a computer program that seems to perform one function while actually doing something else. Unlike a worm, a Trojan is not designed to spread itself to other computers. Also differing from viruses and worms, Trojans are not typically designed to replicate themselves. Trojans are standalone programs that masquerade as useful utilities or applications, which victims download and install unaware of their destructive nature.

Trojans are notorious for stealing passwords using a keylogger that records keystrokes as you log in to your computer and various online accounts. Another type of Trojan called a **Remote Access Trojan** (RAT) has backdoor capabilities that allow remote hackers to transmit files to victims' computers, search for data, run programs, and use a victim's computer as a relay station for breaking into other computers.

3

**What is a bot?** Any software that can automate a task or autonomously execute a task when commanded to do so is called an intelligent agent. Because an intelligent agent behaves somewhat like a robot, it is often called a **bot**.

Good bots perform a variety of helpful tasks such as scanning the Web to assemble data for search engines like Google. Some bots offer online help, while others monitor online discussions for prohibited behavior and language. Bad bots, on the other hand, are controlled by hackers and designed for unauthorized or destructive tasks. They can be spread by worms or Trojans. Most bad bots are able to initiate communications with a central server on the Internet to receive instructions. A computer under the control of a bad bot is sometimes referred to as a **zombie** because it carries out instructions from a malicious leader.

Like a spider in its web, the person who controls many bot-infested computers can link them together into a network called a **botnet**. Experts have discovered botnets encompassing more than 1 million computers. Botmasters who control botnets use the combined computing power of their zombie legions for many types of nefarious tasks such as breaking into encrypted data, carrying out denial-of-service attacks against other computers, and sending out massive amounts of spam.

**What is spyware?** **Spyware** is a type of program that secretly gathers personal information without the victim's knowledge, usually for advertising and other commercial purposes. Once it is installed, spyware starts monitoring Web-surfing and purchasing behavior, and sends a summary back to one or more third parties. Just like Trojans, spyware can monitor keystrokes and relay passwords and credit card information to cybercriminals.

Spyware can get into a computer using exploits similar to those of Trojans. It can piggyback on seemingly legitimate freeware or shareware downloads. You can also inadvertently allow spyware into your computer by clicking innocuous but infected pop-up ads or surfing through seemingly valid and secure Web sites that have been compromised by hackers.

**What does malware do?** Once viruses, worms, bots, Trojans, and spyware enter your computer, they can carry out a variety of unauthorized activities, such as those listed in Figure 3-45.

> ## TERMINOLOGY NOTE
>
> A denial-of-service attack is designed to generate a lot of activity on a network by flooding its servers with useless traffic—enough traffic to overwhelm the server's processing capability and essentially bring all communications and services to a halt.

**FIGURE 3-45**

Malware Activities

- Display irritating messages and pop-up ads
- Delete or modify your data
- Encrypt your data and demand ransom for the encryption key
- Upload or download unwanted files
- Log your keystrokes to steal your passwords and credit card numbers
- Propagate malware and spam to everyone in your e-mail address book or your instant messaging buddy list
- Disable your antivirus and firewall software
- Block access to specific Web sites and redirect your browser to infected Web sites
- Cause response time on your system to deteriorate
- Allow hackers to remotely access data on your computer
- Allow hackers to take remote control of your machine and turn it into a zombie
- Link your computer to others in a botnet that can send millions of spam e-mails or wage denial-of-service attacks against Web sites
- Cause network traffic jams

**How do I know if my computer is infected?** Watch out for the symptoms of an infected computer listed in Figure 3-46.

- Irritating messages or sounds
- Frequent pop-up ads, at times with pornographic content
- The sudden appearance of a new Internet toolbar on your browser's home page
- An addition to your Internet favorites list that you didn't put there
- Prolonged system start-up
- Slower than usual response to mouse clicks and keyboard strokes
- Browser or application crashes
- Missing files
- Your computer's security software becomes disabled and cannot be restarted
- Periodic network activity when you are not actively browsing or sending e-mail
- Your computer reboots itself frequently

**FIGURE 3-46**

Symptoms of Infection

Some malware does a good job of cloaking itself, so victims are unaware of its presence. Cloaking techniques are great defense mechanisms because when victims aren't aware of malware, they won't take steps to eradicate it. Many victims whose computers were part of massive botnets never knew their computers were compromised.

Some hackers cloak their work using rootkits. The term **rootkit** refers to software tools used to conceal malware and backdoors that have been installed on a victim's computer. Rootkits can hide bots, keyloggers, spyware, worms, and viruses. With a rootkit in place, hackers can continue to exploit a victim's computer with little risk of discovery. Rootkits are usually distributed by Trojans.

**How do I avoid security threats?** The Orientation section at the beginning of this book listed some techniques for safe computing. That list is worth repeating (Figure 3-47).

- Install and activate security software on every computing device you own.
- Keep software patches and operating system service packs up to date.
- Do not open suspicious e-mail attachments.
- Obtain software only from reliable sources, and before running it use security software to scan for malware.
- Do not click pop-up ads—to make an ad go away, right-click the ad's taskbar button and select the Close option.
- Avoid unsavory Web sites.
- Disable the option *Hide extensions for known file types in Windows* so you can avoid opening files with more than one extension, such as a file called game. exe.zip.

**FIGURE 3-47**

Avoiding Security Threats

**What's a virus hoax?** Some virus threats are very real, but you're also likely to get e-mail messages about so-called viruses that don't really exist. A **virus hoax** usually arrives as an e-mail message containing dire warnings about a supposedly new virus on the loose. When you receive an e-mail message about a virus or any other type of malware, don't panic. It could be a hoax.

You can check one of the many antivirus software Web sites to determine whether you've received a hoax or a real threat. The Web sites also provide security or virus alerts, which list all of the most recent legitimate malware threats. If the virus is a real threat, the Web site can provide information to determine whether your computer has been infected. You can also find instructions for eradicating the virus. If the virus threat is a hoax, by no means should you forward the e-mail message to others.

**What if my computer gets infected?** If you suspect that your computer might be infected by a virus or other malware, you should immediately use security software to scan your computer and eradicate any suspicious program code.

## SECURITY SUITES

**What is a security suite?** A **security suite** integrates several security modules to protect against the most common types of malware, unauthorized access, and spam. Security suites might include additional features such as Wi-Fi detection that warns of possible intrusions into your wireless network, and parental controls for monitoring and controlling children's Internet usage. A security suite, like the one in Figure 3-48, typically includes antivirus, firewall, and anti-spyware modules.

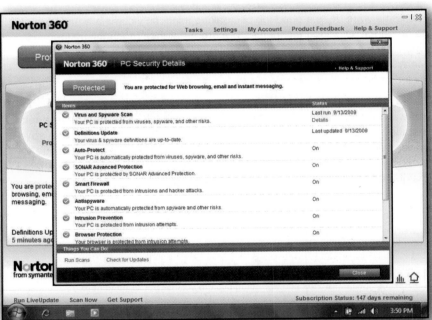

**What are the advantages and disadvantages of a security suite?** A security suite costs less than purchasing standalone security modules. In addition, a single interface for accessing all of the security suite's features is much less complex than having to learn how to configure and run several different products.

When installing a security suite, you are typically required to uninstall or disable all other antivirus, anti-spyware, and firewall software on your computer. Most security suites cannot run concurrently with standalone security products, and overlapping security coverage from two similar products can cause glitches. Therefore, one disadvantage of security suites is that you become dependent on your security package's vendor, which becomes the sole protector of your computer from malicious code. In addition, suites may not have the best individual security components, but you cannot pick and choose. However, competition between security suite vendors tends to increase the quality of security offerings.

**FIGURE 3-48**

The Norton security suite includes modules for scanning viruses, detecting spyware, and activating a firewall against unauthorized intrusions. ▶ Take a tour of these modules by using your digital textbook.

**Where can I purchase a security suite?** The most popular security suites include Symantec Norton Internet Security, McAfee Internet Security Suite, ALWIL avast!, and Trend Micro Internet Security. They can be purchased in most office, electronics, and computer stores, or downloaded from the Web.

It is also worth looking into your ISP's free security offerings. For example, Comcast provides its customers with Norton security products, all accessible through Comcast's Security Web page. AOL offers its customers the McAfee Internet Security Suite.

A security suite is often pre-installed on a new computer. However, it is usually demoware, so you have the option of purchasing it after the trial period, normally 60 days. Typically, there is also an annual subscription fee for continued use and regular updates. When you renew your subscription, you might have an option to upgrade to a newer version for an extra US$10–$20. There are also open source and freeware versions of antivirus software, which do not require annual subscription fees.

**Is open source security software as dependable as commercial security suites?** Open source security software, like all open source software, is distributed with its source code. Because the source code is open for examination, black hats can view the code and look for security holes. They can potentially plot strategies to disable security protection or sneak past its defenses. Proponents of open source software, however, claim that because the code is open, security holes are likely to be discovered and fixed by white hats before they can be exploited by hackers. Vulnerabilities have been discovered in both open source and commercial security products.

Whether open source products such as ClamWin (Figure 3-49) or commercial security software, each security suite has unique strengths and weaknesses, which can change as the suites are updated. Before you purchase a security suite, read current reviews and check user ratings at consumer Web sites.

## ANTIVIRUS MODULES

**What is antivirus software?** **Antivirus software** is a type of utility software that looks for and eradicates viruses, Trojan horses, worms, and bots. Some antivirus software also scans for spyware, although several security software publishers offer spyware detection as a separate module. Antivirus software is included in security suites or can be purchased as a standalone module. Antivirus software is available for all types of computers and data storage devices, including handhelds, personal computers, USB flash drives, and servers.

**How does antivirus software work?** Modern antivirus software attempts to identify malware by searching your computer's files and memory for virus signatures. A **virus signature** is a section of program code, such as a unique series of instructions, that can be used to identify a known malicious program, much as a fingerprint is used to identify an individual.

Antivirus software scans for virus signatures in programs, data files, incoming and outgoing e-mail and attachments, and inbound instant message attachments. Antivirus software can also watch for unusual activity such as a considerably large number of e-mail messages being sent out from your computer by a mass-mailing worm or bot.

**3**

FIGURE 3-49

Open source antivirus software ClamWin comes in a portable version to protect USB flash drives.

Most antivirus programs can also scan for virus signatures in zip files, which is important when downloading zipped software and receiving zipped e-mail attachments.

**How do I activate and deactivate my antivirus software?** Installation and activation procedures vary for each virus protection product. However, once you have installed your antivirus software, the best and safest practice is to keep it running full time in the background so that it checks every e-mail message as it arrives and scans all files the moment you access them. The scanning process requires only a short amount of time, which creates a slight delay in downloading e-mail and opening files.

When installing some application or utility software, you might be instructed to deactivate your antivirus software. You can usually right-click the icon on your computer's taskbar that corresponds to your antivirus software and then select the exit or disable option. Do not forget to reactivate your antivirus software as soon as the installation is completed.

**How should I configure my antivirus software?** For the most extensive protection from malware, you should look for and enable the features of your antivirus software listed in Figure 3-50.

**FIGURE 3-50**

You might want to take a few minutes to check these settings for your computer's antivirus software.

- Start scanning when the computer boots.
- Scan all programs when they are launched and document files when they are opened.
- Scan other types of files, such as graphics, if you engage in some risky computing behaviors and are not concerned with the extra time required to open files as they are scanned.
- Scan incoming mail and attachments.
- Scan incoming instant message attachments.
- Scan outgoing e-mail for worm activity such as mass-mailing worms.
- Scan zipped (compressed) files.
- Scan for spyware, sometimes called pups (potentially unwanted programs).
- Scan all files on the computer's hard disk at least once a week.

**How do I keep my antivirus software up to date?** Two aspects of your antivirus software periodically need to be updated. First, the antivirus program itself might need a patch or update to fix bugs or improve features. Second, the list of virus signatures must be updated to keep up with the latest malware developments.

Virus signatures and other information that antivirus software use to identify and eradicate malware are stored in one or more files usually referred to as **virus definitions** (or a virus database). Antivirus program updates and revised virus definitions are packaged into a file that can be manually or automatically downloaded. If your antivirus software is part of a security suite, the update might also include patches for other security software modules, such as the spyware module or firewall.

Most antivirus products are preconfigured to regularly check for updates, download them, and install them without user intervention. If you would rather control the download and installation process yourself, you can configure your antivirus software to alert you when updates are ready. In any case, you should manually check for updates periodically just in case the auto-update function has become disabled.

**How often should I run a system scan?** Most experts recommend that you configure your antivirus software to periodically scan all the files on your computer. With the proliferation of malware attacks, it's best to schedule a weekly system scan. Because a full system scan can significantly slow down your computer, schedule the scan for a time when you are not usually using your computer, but it is turned on.

You can also run a manual scan of your entire computer or of specific files. For example, suppose you download a program and you want to make sure it is virus free before you install and run it. You can use Windows Explorer to locate and right-click the downloaded file, then select the Scan option from the pop-up menu (Figure 3-51).

**What does quarantine mean?** If, during the scanning process, your virus protection software identifies a virus, worm, Trojan horse, or bot in a file or attachment, it can try to remove the infection, put the file into quarantine, or simply delete the file.

A **quarantined file** typically contains suspicious code, such as a virus signature. For your protection, most antivirus software encrypts the file's contents and isolates it in a quarantine folder, so it can't be inadvertently opened or accessed by a hacker. If the infected file ends up on a quarantine list, your antivirus software might give you the option of trying to disinfect the file or deleting it.

**How dependable is antivirus software?** Today's antivirus software is quite dependable, but not infallible. A fast-spreading worm can reach your computer before a virus definition update arrives, some spyware can slip through the net, and cloaking software can hide some viral exploits. Despite occasional misses, however, antivirus software and other security software modules are constantly weeding out malware that would otherwise infect your computer. It is essential to use security software, but also important to take additional precautions, such as making regular backups of your data.

**FIGURE 3-51**

Before installing and running a downloaded file, you can scan it by right-clicking the file name and selecting the Scan option.

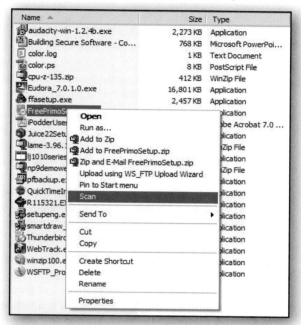

3

# QuickCheck

1. A computer [_____] can lurk in a computer for days or months, quietly replicating itself.

2. A mass-mailing [_____] spreads to other computers by sending itself to all the addresses stored in the local e-mail client.

3. A group of zombie computers controlled by a hacker is called a(n) [_____] .

4. A virus [_____] is a unique section of malicious code that can be identified by antivirus software.

5. A(n) [_____] file is suspected of containing a virus, so your antivirus software usually encrypts the file and stores it in a special folder.

 CHECK ANSWERS

# Issue: How Serious Is Software Piracy?

**SOFTWARE IS EASY TO STEAL.** You don't have to walk out of a Best Buy store with a box of expensive software under your shirt. You can simply copy the software from your friend's computer. It seems so simple that it couldn't be illegal. But it is.

Piracy takes many forms. End-user piracy includes friends loaning distribution discs to each other and installing software on more computers than the license allows. Although it is perfectly legal to lend a physical object, such as a sweater, to a friend, it is not legal to lend digital copies of software and music because, unlike a sweater that can be worn by only one person at a time, copies of digital things can be simultaneously used by many people.

Software counterfeiting is the large-scale illegal duplication of software distribution media, and sometimes even its packaging. According to Microsoft, many software counterfeiting groups are linked to organized crime and money-laundering schemes that fund a diverse collection of illegal activities, such as smuggling, gambling, extortion, and prostitution. Counterfeit software is sold in retail stores and through online auctions—often the packaging looks so authentic that buyers have no idea they have purchased illegal goods.

Internet piracy uses the Web as a way to illegally distribute unauthorized software. In Net jargon, the terms *appz* and *warez* (pronounced as "wares" or "war EZ") refer to pirated software. Some warez has even been modified to eliminate serial numbers, registration requirements, expiration dates, or other forms of copy protection. Web sites, peer-to-peer file sharing networks, and auction sites sell or distribute hundreds of thousands of pirated software products.

In many countries, including the United States, software pirates are subject to civil lawsuits for monetary damages and criminal prosecution, which can result in jail time and stiff fines. Nonetheless, software piracy continues to have enormous impact. According to a Business Software Alliance (BSA) and IDC Piracy Study, $130 billion of software was legitimately purchased worldwide, but software worth a whopping $53 billion was pirated.

A small, but vocal, minority of software users, such as members of GNU (which stands for "Gnu's Not UNIX"), believes that data and software should be freely distributed. Richard Stallman writes in the GNU Manifesto, "I consider that the golden rule requires that if I like a program I must share it with other people who like it. Software sellers want to divide users and conquer them, making each user agree not to share with others. I refuse to break solidarity with other users in this way. I cannot in good conscience sign a nondisclosure agreement or a software license agreement."

Is software piracy really damaging? Who cares if you use a program without paying for it? According to industry experts, software piracy has a negative effect on the economy. Software production makes a major contribution to the United States economy, employing more than 250,000 people and accounting for billions of dollars in corporate revenue. It fuels economic development in countries such as India and China. A BSA economic impact study concluded that lowering global piracy by 10 percentage points in the next four years would add more than 500,000 jobs and $141 billion in worldwide economic growth.

Decreases in software revenues can have a direct effect on consumers, too. When software publishers are forced to cut corners, they tend to reduce customer service and technical support. As a result, you, the consumer, get put on hold when you call for technical support, find fewer free technical support sites, and encounter customer support personnel who are only moderately knowledgeable about their products. The bottom line—software piracy negatively affects customer service.

As an alternative to cutting support costs, some software publishers might build the cost of software piracy into the price of the software. The unfortunate result is that those who legitimately license and purchase software pay an inflated price.

The BSA and IDC reported about 43% of the software currently in use is pirated. Georgia, Zimbabwe, Bangladesh, and Moldova have the world's highest piracy rates. More than 90% of the software used in those countries is believed to be pirated. In China the piracy rate is 79%, down from 92% in 2003. In the United States, an estimated 20% of software is pirated. In Japan, the rate is 21%.

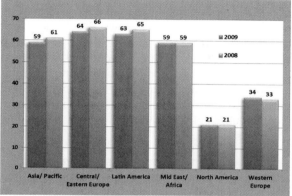

*Source: Seventh Annual BSA/IDC Global Software Piracy Study*

Overall, piracy appears to be growing by one or two percentage points each year. Analysts fear that the Internet is a major factor in piracy growth. As Internet access becomes more widely available, piracy is likely to increase, rather than decrease. To make matters worse, access to high-speed Internet connections makes it much easier to quickly download large software files.

As a justification of high piracy rates, some observers point out that people in many countries simply might not be able to afford software priced for the U.S. market. This argument could apply to China,

where the average annual income is equivalent to about US$5,420, and in North Korea, where the average income is only US$2,820. A Korean who legitimately purchases Microsoft Office for US$250 would be spending about one-eighth of his or her annual income.

Annual income rates do not necessarily correlate with piracy, however. India—which has a fairly large computer-user community, but relatively low per capita income—is not among the top 20 countries with high rates of software piracy.

Economics appears to be a factor that contributes to high rates of piracy, but it is not the only one. The incidence of piracy seems to be higher among small businesses and individual users than corporations and government agencies. According to one study, two-thirds of college and university students see nothing unethical about swapping or downloading digital copyrighted software, music, and movie files without paying for them, and more than half of the people surveyed for the study believe it is acceptable to do so in the workplace.

Some analysts suggest that people need more education about software copyrights and the economic implications of piracy. Other analysts believe that copyright enforcement must be increased by implementing more vigorous efforts to identify and prosecute pirates.

**INFOWEBLINKS**

You can read the GNU Manifesto and other thought-provoking articles about software piracy by going to the **Copyright and Piracy InfoWeb**.

**W** CLICK TO CONNECT
www.infoweblinks.com/np2012/ch03

## What Do You Think?

1. Do you believe that software piracy is a serious issue?   ◯Yes  ◯ No  ◯ Not sure

2. Do you know of any instances of software piracy?   ◯Yes  ◯ No  ◯ Not sure

3. Do you think that most software pirates understand that they are doing something illegal?   ◯Yes  ◯ No  ◯ Not sure

4. Should software publishers try to adjust software pricing for local markets?   ◯Yes  ◯ No  ◯ Not sure

▶ SAVE RESPONSES

# Computers in Context: Journalism

**IN THE ANCIENT WORLD,** news spread by word of mouth, relayed by bards and merchants who traveled from town to town—in essence, they were the first reporters to broadcast the news. The news business is all about gathering and disseminating information quickly. Technology has played a major role in news reporting's evolution from its bardic roots to modern 24-hour news networks and Web sites.

Johann Gutenberg's printing press (ca. 1450), the first technological breakthrough in the news business, made it feasible to publish news as printed notices tacked to walls in the town square. As paper became more economical, resourceful entrepreneurs sold broadsheets to people eager for news, and the concept of a newspaper was born. The first regularly published newspapers appeared in Germany and Holland in 1609, and the first English newspaper, the *Weekly News*, was published in 1622.

But the news spread slowly. In the early 1800s, it took four weeks for newspapers in New York to receive reports from London. With the advent of the telegraph in 1844, however, reporters from far-flung regions could wire stories to their newspapers for publication the next day. The first radio reporters in the 1920s offered live broadcasts of sports events, church services, and variety shows. Before the 1950s, black-and-white newsreels shown in movie theaters provided the only visual imagery of news events, but television gave viewers news images on a nightly basis.

Technology has benefited print journalism, too. For decades, typesetters transferred reporters' handwritten stories into neatly set columns of type. Today, reporters use computers and word processing software to tap out their stories and run a preliminary check of spelling and grammar.

Stories are submitted by computer network to editors, who also use word processing software to edit stories to fit time and space constraints. The typesetting process has been replaced by desktop publishing software and computer to plate (CTP) technology. Digital pages produced with desktop publishing software are sent to a raster image processor (RIP), which converts the pages into dots that form words and images. After a page has been RIPed, a plate-setter uses lasers to etch the dots onto a physical plate, which is then mounted on the printing press to produce printed pages. CTP is much faster and more flexible than typesetting, so publishers can make last-minute changes to accommodate late-breaking stories.

Personal computers have also added a new dimension to the news-gathering process. Reporters were once limited to personal interviews, observation, and fact gathering at libraries, but can now make extensive use of Internet resources and e-mail. Web sites and online databases provide background information on all sorts of topics. Other resources include newsgroups and chat rooms, where reporters can monitor public opinion on current events and identify potential sources.

Most major networks maintain interactive Web sites that offer online polls and bulletin boards designed to collect viewers' opinions. Although online poll respondents are not a representative sample of the population, they can help news organizations gauge viewer opinions and determine whether news coverage is comprehensive and effective.

News organizations also accept news, images, and videos from amateur "citizen journalists" who happen upon news events armed with a cell phone or digital camera. And even CNN now reports on news stories that originate on blogs such as *slashdot.org*.

E-mail has changed the way reporters communicate with colleagues and sources. It's often the only practical method for contacting people in remote locations or distant time zones, and it's useful with reluctant sources, who feel more comfortable providing information under the cloak of anonymous Hotmail or Yahoo! accounts. Vetting e-mail sources—verifying credentials such as name, location, and occupation—can be difficult, however, so reporters tend not to rely on these sources without substantial corroboration.

For broadcast journalism, digital communications play a major role in today's live-on-the-scene television reporting. Most news organizations maintain remote production vans, sometimes called satellite news gathering (SNG) trucks, that travel to the site of breaking news, raise their antennas, and begin to broadcast. These complete mobile production facilities include camera control units, audio and video recording equipment, and satellite or microwave transmitters.

On-the-scene reporting no longer requires a truck full of equipment, however. Audiovisual editing units and video cameras have gone digital, making them easier to use and sized to fit in a suitcase. A new breed of backpack journalists carry digital video cameras, notebook computers, and mobile phones.

Backpack journalists can transfer video footage to their notebook computers and then edit the footage with consumer-level video editing software. The resulting video files are compressed and sent to newsroom technicians, who decompress the videos and then broadcast them—all in a matter of seconds.

One drawback of backpack journalists' use of digital cameras and compression is that the video quality usually isn't as crisp as images filmed with studio cameras. News organizations with high standards were once hesitant to use this lower quality video, but have found that viewers would rather see a low-quality image now than a high-quality image later. To many viewers, a few rough edges just make the footage seem more compelling—more like you are there.

A memorable tour de force in SNG was the brainchild of David Bloom, an NBC reporter embedded with the U.S. Army 3rd Infantry Division during Operation Iraqi Freedom. He helped modify an M-88 tank recovery vehicle into a high-tech, armored SNG vehicle. The $500,000 Bloommobile featured a gyrostabilized camera that could produce jiggle-free video as the tank blasted over sand dunes at 50 mph. Tragically, Bloom died while covering the conflict; but many viewers vividly remember his exhilarating reports as the Bloommobile raced down desert roads, trundled along with Army supply convoys, and narrowly escaped enemy fire.

Video-enabled mobile phones ushered in another era of news gathering. Citizen journalists who are on the spot during news-making events simply point, shoot, and e-mail footage to media Web sites, such as CNN.com and FOXNews.com. During the tragic 2008 terrorist attacks in Mumbai, eyewitness accounts and updates flooded over social networking sites such as Facebook and Twitter. The first images of the attacks spread through social networking sites minutes before they appeared on mainstream news channels.

Computers, the Internet, and communications technology make it possible to instantly broadcast live reports across the globe, but live reporting is not without controversy. Reporters and amateur journalists who arrive at the scene of a disaster with microphones, cameras, or cell phones in hand have little time for reflection, vetting, and cross-checking, so grievous errors, libelous images, or distasteful video footage sometimes find their way into news reports.

Jeff Gralnick, former executive producer for ABC News, remarks, "In the old days, we had time to think before we spoke. We had time to write, time to research and time to say, 'Hey, wait a minute.' Now we don't even have the time to say, 'Hey, wait a nanosecond.' Just because we can say it or do it, should we?" Technology has given journalists a powerful arsenal of tools for gathering and reporting the news, but has also increased their accountability for accurate, socially responsible reporting.

**INFOWEBLINKS**

You'll find lots more information related to this topic at the **Computers and Journalism InfoWeb**.

CLICK TO CONNECT
www.infoweblinks.com/np2012/ch03

# New Perspectives Labs

## On the BookOnCD

To access the New Perspectives Lab for Chapter 3, start the BookOnCD and then click the icon next to the lab title below.

 **INSTALLING AND UNINSTALLING SOFTWARE**

### IN THIS LAB YOU'LL LEARN:

- How to use a setup program to install Windows application software from a distribution CD

- The difference between typical, compact, and custom installation options

- How to specify a folder for a new software installation

- How to install downloaded software

- How to install an upgrade

- How to uninstall a Windows application

- What happens, in addition to deleting files, when you uninstall a software application

- How to locate the program that will uninstall a software application

- Why you might not want to delete all of the files associated with an application

### LAB ASSIGNMENTS

1. Start the interactive part of the lab. Make sure you've enabled Tracking if you want to save your QuickCheck results. Perform each lab step as directed, and answer all the lab QuickCheck questions. When you exit the lab, your answers are automatically graded and your results are displayed.

2. Browse the Web and locate a software application that you might like to download. Use information supplied by the Web site to answer the following questions:

   a. What is the name of the program and the URL of the download site?

   b. What is the size of the download file?

   c. According to the instructions, does the download file appear to require manual installation, is it a self-executing zip file, or is it a self-installing executable file?

3. On the PC you typically use, look through the list of programs (click Start, then select All Programs to see a list of them). List the names of any programs that include their own uninstall routines.

4. On the PC you typically use, open the Control Panel and then select the Uninstall a Program option. List the first ten programs shown.

# Key Terms

Make sure you understand all the boldfaced key terms presented in this chapter. With the NP2012 BookOnCD, you can use this list of terms as an interactive study activity. First, try to define a term in your own words, and then click the term to compare your definition with the definition presented in the chapter. Online, try your hand at the TechTerm Flashcards.

Absolute reference, 132
Automatic recalculation, 132
Blended threat, 162
Bot, 164
Botnet, 164
BSD license, 150
Cell, 130
Cell references, 131
Clip art, 129
Commercial software, 149
Computer virus, 163
Computer worm, 163
Concurrent-use license, 147
Copyright, 146
Copyright notice, 147
Database, 134
Demoware, 149
Desktop widget, 123
Device driver, 124
Distribution media, 146
Document format, 127
EULA, 148
Executable file, 152
Field, 134
Font, 127
Footer, 128
Formula, 131
Frames, 129
Freeware, 150
Fully justified, 128
Function, 131
GPL, 151
Grammar checker, 127
Graphics, 137
Groupware, 121
Hash value, 157
Header, 128

Keyword search, 136
Label, 130
Leading, 128
Local application, 154
Mail merge, 129
Malicious software, 162
Malware, 162
Mass-mailing worm, 163
Mathematical operators, 131
Multiple-user license, 147
Natural language query, 136
Non-executing zip file, 157
Open source software, 150
Page layout, 128
Paragraph alignment, 128
Paragraph style, 128
Pirated software, 147
Point size, 127
Portable software, 158
Product activation, 157
Productivity software, 121
Proprietary software, 149
Public domain software, 149
Quarantined file, 169
Query, 136
Query by example, 136
Query language, 136
Readability formula, 127
Record, 134
Relative reference, 132
Remote Access Trojan, 163
Rootkit, 165
Search and Replace, 127
Security suite, 166
Self-extracting zip file, 157
Self-installing executable file, 157
Service pack, 159

Setup program, 154
Shareware, 149
Shrink-wrap license, 147
Single-user license, 147
Site license, 147
Software installation, 153
Software license, 147
Software suite, 144
Software update, 159
Software upgrade, 159
Spelling checker, 126
Spelling dictionary, 126
Spreadsheet, 130
Spyware, 164
Style, 128
System requirements, 145
Table, 129
Thesaurus, 127
Trojan horse, 163
Uninstall routine, 161
Unzipped, 156
Utility software, 122
Value, 130
Virus definitions, 168
Virus hoax, 166
Virus signature, 167
Web application, 158
What-if analysis, 130
Windows Registry, 154
Worksheet, 130
Zipped, 156
Zombie, 164

*See page 178 for a list of key software applications

3

# Interactive Summary

To review important concepts from this chapter, fill in the blanks to best complete each sentence. When using the NP2012 BookOnCD, click the Check Answers buttons to automatically score your answers.

**SECTION A:** Computer software can be grouped into two main categories. [_____] software is designed for computer-centric tasks, whereas [_____] software is designed to help people accomplish real-world tasks. These two main categories can be further divided into subcategories. [_____] software is designed to help you monitor and configure settings for your computer system equipment, the operating system, or application software. Many software packages in this category appear as desktop [_____] that display controls and snippets of information for clocks, calendars, calculators, news aggregators, sticky notes, and weather stations. Device [_____] are a type of system software that helps a computer establish communication with peripheral devices. [_____] software can be defined as any type of application software that has the potential to help people do their work more efficiently. [_____] is designed to help several people collaborate on a single project using local networks or Internet connections.

▶ CHECK ANSWERS

**SECTION B:** Document [_____] software assists you with composing, editing, designing, printing, and electronically publishing documents. The three most popular types of document production software are word processing, desktop publishing, and Web authoring. [_____] software is similar to a smart piece of paper that automatically adds up the columns of numbers you write on it. You can use it to make other calculations, too, based on simple equations that you write or more complex, built-in formulas. Because it is so easy to experiment with different numbers, this type of software is particularly useful for [_____] analyses. [_____] software helps you store, find, organize, update, and report information stored in one or more tables.

When two sets of records are [_____], database software allows you to access data from both tables at the same time. [_____] software, including paint, photo editing, drawing, 3-D, and presentation software, is designed to help you create, manipulate, and print images. Music and video editing software, educational software, and entertainment software round out the most popular categories of personal computer software.

For businesses, [_____] market software is designed to automate specialized tasks in a specific market or business. [_____] market software is generic software that can be used by just about any kind of business.

▶ CHECK ANSWERS

## SECTION C:

Most new computers include an operating system, essential utilities, and some basic application software. If you want utilities other than those included with your computer's operating system, you can explore software offered by [          ]-party vendors. When shopping for application software, consider software [          ], which are a collection of software applications sold as a single package. All the bundled applications usually have similar controls, and data can be easily transferred from one application to another. Software can be purchased in a box containing [          ] media, such as CDs or DVDs, or as a download. [          ] software, such as commercial software, is protected by copyright that grants to its author an exclusive right to copy, distribute, sell, and modify that work. Public [          ] software is not protected by copyright. A software [          ] can extend or limit the rights granted by copyright. Demoware and [          ] are distributed free of charge, but require payment for continued use. Freeware is copyrighted software that can be used for free, but cannot be altered or resold. [          ] source software is distributed with its source code, and can be modified, sold, and redistributed.

▶ CHECK ANSWERS

## SECTION D:

The process of [          ] software places a program into a computer so that it can be executed or run. The main program is stored in a(n) [          ] file that might call additional programs as necessary. Most programs are [          ] applications, designed to be installed or "loaded" on a hard disk. A(n) [          ] program, included with the software, guides you through the installation process. For downloaded software, the first step in the installation process is usually to [          ] the distribution file that was compressed to conserve space and reduce download time. In contrast to local applications, [          ] software is designed to run from removable storage, such as a CD or USB flash drive. On PCs, these apps require no entries in the Windows Registry. [          ] applications are designed to be accessed with a browser. Some require no installation on your local computer, whereas others require a small client-side program. Software publishers regularly update their software to add new features, fix bugs, and update its security. A software [          ] is a small section of program code that replaces part of the software you currently have installed. The term service [          ], which usually applies to operating system updates, is a set of patches that correct problems and address security vulnerabilities. To remove software from a PC, it is important to use a(n) [          ] routine, rather than simply deleting program files.

▶ CHECK ANSWERS

## SECTION E:

Security software can be classified into various types: antivirus, anti-spyware, anti-spam, and firewalls. Each type focuses on a specific security threat. A computer [          ] is a set of program instructions that attaches itself to a file, reproduces itself, and spreads to other files. A computer [          ] is a self-replicating program designed to carry out some unauthorized activity on a victim's computer. In the context of computing, a Trojan [          ] is a computer program that seems to perform one function while actually doing something else. For example, it might steal passwords using a type of program called a [          ] that records keystrokes. A Remote Access Trojan sets up [          ] capabilities that allow remote hackers to access files on victims' computers. [          ] programs can turn computers into zombies and link them together into [          ]. [          ] is a type of program that secretly gathers personal information without the victim's knowledge, usually for advertising and other commercial purposes. To combat malware, it is important to use [          ] software that looks for virus signatures. Most computer owners obtain this software as one module in a security [          ].

▶ CHECK ANSWERS

# Software Key Terms

3-D graphics software, 137
Accounting software, 142
Antivirus software, 167
Audio editing software, 139
CAD software, 138
Computer-aided music software, 139
Database software, 134
Desktop publishing software, 125
Document production software, 125
Drawing software, 137
DVD authoring software, 140
Ear training software, 139

Educational software, 140
Graphics software, 137
Horizontal market software, 142
Mathematical modeling software, 133
MIDI sequencing software, 139
Money management software, 133
Notation software, 139
Paint software, 137
Payroll software, 142
Personal finance software, 133
Photo editing software, 137
Presentation software, 138

Project management software, 142
Security software, 162
Spreadsheet software, 130
Statistical software, 133
Tax preparation software, 133
Vertical market software, 142
Video editing software, 140
Web authoring software, 125
Word processing software, 125

## Interactive Situation Questions

Apply what you've learned to some typical computing situations. When using the NP2012 BookOnCD, you can type your answers, and then use the Check Answers button to automatically score your responses.

1. You've volunteered to create some graphics for a nonprofit organization, but you'll need a variety of graphics software tools for the organization's computer. Your first choice is to consider a graphics _____ that bundles together paint, draw, and Web graphics software.

2. Suppose that you've been hired to organize a professional skateboard competition. When you consider how you'll need to use computers, you realize that you must collect information on each competitor and keep track of every competitive event. With at least two types of related records, you'll probably need to use _____ software.

3. Imagine that you just purchased a new software package. You insert the distribution CD, but nothing happens. No problem—you can manually run the _____ program, which will start the install routine.

4. You are preparing to download a new software program from the Web. The download consists of one huge file with an .exe extension. You recognize this file as a self-_____ executable file that will automatically unzip itself and start the installation routine.

5. You download an open source software program from the Web. You assume that the download includes the uncompiled _____ code for the program as well as the _____ version.

6. You're in the process of receiving some e-mail messages when your antivirus software displays an alert. You assume that it has discovered a virus _____ in an attachment for one of the e-mail messages. The message also states that the file has been _____ ; that is, moved to an area where it cannot cause more harm.

 CHECK ANSWERS

## Interactive Practice Tests

Practice tests that consist of ten multiple-choice, true/false, and fill-in-the-blank questions are available on both the NP2012 BookOnCD and the NP2012 CourseMate Web site. BookOnCD test questions are selected at random from a large test bank, so each time you take a test, you'll receive a different set of questions. Your tests are scored immediately, and you can print study guides that help you find the correct answers for any questions that you missed. Online, you'll find a Practice Test for each section of the chapter. Your results from online tests are saved by Engagement Tracker. ▶ CLICK TO START

# Learning Objectives Checkpoints

Learning Objectives Checkpoints are designed to help you assess whether you have achieved the major learning objectives for this chapter. You can use paper and pencil or word processing software to complete most of the activities.

1. List ten examples of application software and make sure that you include at least three examples of productivity software and one example of groupware.

2. List at least three examples of system software and five examples of utility software.

3. Compare the strengths of word processing, DTP, and Web authoring software. Explain how a spelling checker works and why it is not a substitute for proofreading.

4. Draw a sketch of a simple worksheet and label the following: columns, rows, cell, active cell, values, labels, formulas, and Formula bar. Explain the difference between an absolute reference and a relative reference, giving an example of each.

5. List five types of "number crunching" software that you can use in addition to spreadsheet software.

6. Describe how you would use each of the six types of graphics software described in this chapter.

7. List five guidelines that are important for software shoppers.

8. Read the license agreement in Figure 3-32 and answer each of the questions in the corresponding figure caption.

9. Explain the procedures for installing local software, portable software, and Web apps.

10. Write a set of step-by-step instructions for installing software from a distribution CD and another set of instructions for installing downloaded software. Explain the differences between self-installing executable files, self-extracting zip files, and non-executing zip files.

11. Explain the differences between proprietary software, commercial software, shareware, open source software, freeware, and public domain software.

12. Explain the purpose of a software patch and describe how it differs from a service pack.

13. Create a table that summarizes the differences between various types of malware based on their method of distribution and exploits.

14. Draw a story board to illustrate how antivirus software works.

Study Tip: Make sure you can use your own words to correctly answer each of the red focus questions that appear throughout the chapter.

3

# Concept Map

Fill in the blanks to show the hierarchy of software described in this chapter.

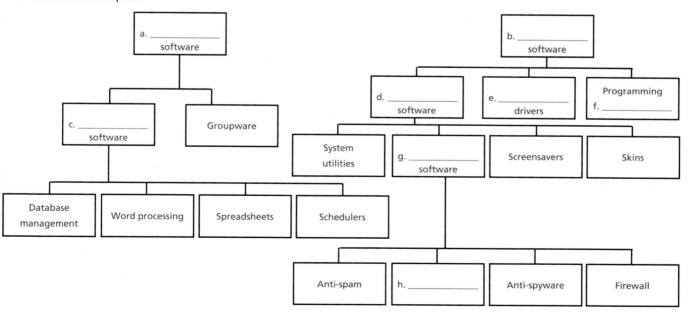

 CHECK ANSWERS

# Projects

## CRITICAL THINKING

Have you heard about the "24-hour rule" for software that says you can legally use any software for free for 24 hours without paying for it? How about your right to use so-called abandoned software that's no longer supported or that was created by a company now out of business? Both the 24-hour rule and the concept of abandoned software are urban legends and have no basis in copyright law. Does it seem to you that most people don't have the facts about copyrights? How strong a factor is that in the proliferation of software piracy? What are your thoughts about the connection between knowing the copyright rules and following them? Put your thoughts in order, write them up, and send them to your instructor.

## GROUP PROJECT

Form a group with at least two of your classmates. Now imagine that your college (or business) has decided to negotiate with software publishers to offer students (or employees) a bundled software package at a greatly discounted price. Your group's job is to select the 15 software products for the bundle. Your group must make sure the software effectively meets the major needs of the students at your school (or employees in your workplace). Use Internet resources to look at the range of software available and make your selections. Make sure you take advantage of group members' expertise and experience with software products. Arrange your final list into categories like those in Figure 3-1.

## CYBERCLASSROOM

Some productivity packages, such as Microsoft Word, include features designed for group collaboration. Learn how to use revision marks. Create a document at least three paragraphs long about your favorite computer software and circulate it to all team members as an e-mail attachment for comment using revision marks.

## MULTIMEDIA PROJECT

Find a photo from one of your old albums or at an antique store. Scan the photo into digital format. Use graphics software to improve the photo quality. Your instructor might run a contest to see which students can most dramatically improve their original photos.

## RESUME BUILDER

Use the Web and other resources to compile a list of the software used in your current or future career field. Are there standard packages that job applicants should know how to use? If so, what can you find out about those packages on the Web? If your career field does not use any standard software packages, explain why you think that is the case. Also, make a list of the software packages you're familiar with. As you consider your school and career goals for the next year, list at least five additional software packages you would like to learn. Explain why they would be helpful. Submit your lists to your instructor by e-mail.

## GLOBALIZATION

Computer games are big business. They are exported worldwide and accessed by communities of online players around the globe. For this project, gather information about the most internationally popular computer games. Try some of them yourself to see what they're all about. What effect, if any, would you expect these games to have on individual players living in the cultures of 1) industrialized countries, 2) Middle-Eastern countries, and 3) developing countries? Summarize your ideas in one or two pages.

## ISSUE

The Issue section of this chapter focused on copyrights and software piracy. For this project, you will write a two- to five-page paper about this issue based on information you gather from the Internet. To begin this project, consult the Copyright and Piracy InfoWeb, and link to the recommended Web pages to get an in-depth overview of the issue. Armed with this background, select one of the following viewpoints and statements and argue for or against it:

• Free software advocates: As an enabling technology, software should be freely distributed, along with its modifiable source code.

• Librarians: Copyright laws, especially the Digital Millennium Copyright Act, minimize the needs of the public and go too far in their efforts to protect the rights of software authors.

• Software & Information Industry Association: Strong copyright laws and enforcement are essential for companies to publish and support high-quality software.

## COMPUTERS IN CONTEXT

The Computers in Context section of this chapter focused on computer and communications technology used by reporters and journalists. Technology has had a major effect on backpack journalists who use small-scale digital devices to gather and report the news. For this project, use a Web search engine to collect information on the advantages and disadvantages of backpack journalism. In your research, you should explore technical issues, such as the cost of equipment, video quality, and transmission capabilities. Also explore ethical issues pertaining to on-the-spot news reporting. Summarize your research in a two- to four-page paper.

# On the Web

## STUDENT EDITION LABS

When you purchase access to the NP2012 CourseMate Web site, you'll find targeted learning materials to help you understand key concepts and prepare for exams. See page O-41 in the Orientation Chapter for login instructions.

### WORD PROCESSING

In the Word Processing Student Edition Lab, you will learn about the following topics:

- Opening, saving, and printing a document
- Moving the insertion point, and entering and editing text
- Moving and deleting blocks of text
- Inserting graphics and formatting your document
- Checking your document for spelling errors

### SPREADSHEETS

In the Spreadsheets Student Edition Lab, you will learn about the following topics:

- Entering labels, values, and formulas
- Selecting and naming ranges
- Inserting functions
- Formatting a worksheet
- Creating a chart

### INSTALLING AND UNINSTALLING SOFTWARE

In the Installing and Uninstalling Software Student Edition Lab, you will learn about the following topics:

- Installing software from a distribution CD
- Installing downloaded software
- Understanding the differences between upgrades, updates, and patches
- Uninstalling software applications

### DATABASES

In the Databases Student Edition Lab, you will learn about the following topics:

- Entering and editing data
- Understanding the relationships between tables
- Sorting data
- Creating an index
- Creating queries
- Applying filters
- Creating and modifying reports

### PRESENTATION SOFTWARE

In the Presentation Software Student Edition Lab, you will learn about the following topics:

- Adding text, graphics, animations, and sound to slides
- Using slide layouts and design templates
- Understanding the slide master
- Previewing, viewing, and printing a presentation

### KEEPING YOUR COMPUTER VIRUS FREE

In the Keeping Your Computer Virus Free Student Edition Lab, you will learn about the following topics:

- Using antivirus software
- Virus detection and prevention

 **CHAPTER OVERVIEW COURSECAST**

Use your computer or iPod to hear a five-minute audio presentation of chapter highlights.

 **AUDIO FLASHCARDS**

Interact with audio flashcards to review key concepts from the chapter.

 **DETAILED OBJECTIVES**

Make sure that you've achieved all the objectives for a chapter before it's time for your test!

 **PRACTICE TESTS**

Review chapter material by taking these ten-question tests. Your results are saved by Engagement Tracker.

 **ONLINE GAMES**

Have some fun while refreshing your memory about key concepts that might appear on the next test.

 **AND MORE!**

At the NP2012 CourseMate Web site you'll also find the NP2012 eBook, TechTerm Flashcards, Online Glossary, and What Do You Think? opinion polls.

# 4

# Operating Systems and File Management

## Chapter Contents

▶ SECTION A:
**OPERATING SYSTEM BASICS**
Operating System Activities
User Interfaces
The Boot Process

▶ SECTION B:
**TODAY'S OPERATING SYSTEMS**
Microsoft Windows
Mac OS
UNIX and Linux
DOS
Handheld Operating Systems

▶ SECTION C:
**FILE BASICS**
File Names and Extensions
File Directories and Folders
File Formats

▶ SECTION D:
**FILE MANAGEMENT**
Application-based File
 Management
File Management Utilities
File Management Metaphors
Windows Explorer
File Management Tips
Physical File Storage

▶ SECTION E:
**BACKUP SECURITY**
Backup Basics
File Copies and Synchronization
System Synchronization
File and System Backup
Bare-metal Restore and Virtual
 Machines

▶ ISSUE:
**CYBERTERRORISTS OR
 PRANKSTERS?**

▶ **COMPUTERS IN CONTEXT:
 LAW ENFORCEMENT**

▶ **NEW PERSPECTIVES LABS**

▶ **REVIEW ACTIVITIES**

▶ **ON THE WEB**

## Learning Objectives

After reading this chapter, you will be able to answer the following questions by completing the outcomes-based Learning Objectives Checkpoints on page 241.

1. What are system resources?
2. How do multitasking, multithreading, and multiprocessing work?
3. What is a memory leak?
4. When do users interact with the operating system?
5. How do GUIs differ from command line interfaces?
6. What happens during the boot process?
7. Which operating systems are typically used on personal computers, on servers, and on handheld devices?
8. What is a virtual machine?
9. Do operating systems put limits on the names that can be used for files?
10. What is a file specification or path?
11. What is a native file format?
12. Are there guidelines for managing files so that they are easy to locate and back up?
13. What happens behind the scenes when a computer stores a file?
14. How do I devise a backup plan?
15. What is the best backup device?
16. How does backup software work?
17. How do restore points, bare-metal restore, disk imaging, virtual machines, boot disks, and recovery disks relate to backup?

## InfoWebLinks

Visit the InfoWebLinks site to access additional resources ⓦ that accompany this chapter.

## Multimedia and Interactive Elements

When using the BookOnCD or CourseMate eBook, the ▶ icons are clickable to access multimedia resources.

## Pre-Assessment Quiz

Take the pre-assessment quiz to find out how much you know about the topics in this chapter. ▶

**Apply Your Knowledge** The information in this chapter will give you the background to:

- Find out which processes are running on your computer
- Use Windows, Mac OS, DOS, and Linux
- Maintain an efficient organization of files on your computer
- Use extensions to identify the software needed to open a file
- Convert files from one format to another

- Open, save, rename, move, copy, and delete files
- Burn a CD, DVD, or BD
- Defragment your computer's hard disk
- Shred computer files so they cannot be read
- Make a backup of the data on your computer's hard disk
- Get up and running after a hard disk failure

## Try It

### IS MY COMPUTER'S HARD DISK GETTING FULL?

Your computer's hard disk stores a high percentage of the programs you use and the data files you create. You might wonder if your hard disk is getting full. To find out, follow the steps below.

**Windows:**

**1.** Start your computer and make sure you can see the Windows desktop.

**2.** Click the **Start** button, and then select Computer (or My Computer if you're using Windows XP).

**3.** Right-click your **(C:)** drive to display a pop-up menu.

**4.** Click **Properties**. A Local Disk Properties dialog box should appear containing statistics about your computer's hard disk.

**5.** For the properties indicated by red underlines in the figure below, jot down the statistics for used space, free space, and capacity. Then sketch in the slices of the pie chart for your computer.

**6.** Also, use the blank provided to jot down the file system used by your computer. You'll learn the significance of your computer's file system when you read the chapter.

**Mac:**

**1.** Start your computer and make sure you can see the Mac OS X desktop, dock, and toolbar.

**2.** Locate the desktop icon labeled **Macintosh HD** and right-click it. (If your mouse has only one button, hold down the Ctrl key and click it.)

Macintosh HD

**3.** Select **Get Info** from the pop-up menu.

**4.** For the properties indicated by red underlines in the figure at right, jot down the statistics for capacity, available space, and used space in GB and bytes.

**5.** Also, jot down the file system shown on the Format line. You'll learn the significance of the file system when you read the chapter.

# Operating System Basics

**AN OPERATING SYSTEM** is an integral part of virtually every computer system. It fundamentally affects how you can use your computer. Can you run two programs at the same time? Can you connect your computer to a network? Does your computer run dependably? Does all your software have a similar look and feel, or do you have to learn a different set of controls and commands for each new program you acquire? To answer questions like these, it is helpful to have a clear idea about what an operating system is and what it does. Section A provides an overview of operating system basics.

## OPERATING SYSTEM ACTIVITIES

**What is an operating system?** An **operating system** (abbreviated OS) is a type of system software that acts as the master controller for all activities that take place within a computer system. It is one of the factors that determines your computer's compatibility and platform. Most personal computers are sold with a preinstalled operating system, such as Microsoft Windows or Mac OS (Figure 4-1). A third operating system called Linux is typically used for high-end workstations and servers, but can also be installed on personal computers. A variety of other operating systems, such as Google Chrome OS, DOS, UNIX, and OpenSolaris are also available.

**FIGURE 4-1**

Windows (left) is typically pre-installed on IBM-compatible computers manufactured by companies such as Dell and Hewlett-Packard. Mac OS (middle) is preinstalled on Apple Macintosh computers. Linux (right) is an open source operating system that's available as a free download.

**Is the Windows operating system the same as Windows software?** No. Although it is true that an operating system is software, terms such as *Windows software*, *Mac software*, or *Linux software* are used to refer to application software. Windows software, for example, refers to applications designed to run on computers that have Microsoft Windows installed as the operating system. A program called Microsoft Word for Windows is an example of Windows software; it is a word processing program designed to run under the Windows operating system. Mac software is designed to run under Mac OS and Linux software is designed to run under the Linux operating system.

**What does an operating system do?** The most obvious responsibility of your computer's operating system is to provide an environment for running software. Your computer's operating system, application software, and device drivers are organized similar to the chain of command in an army. You issue a command using application software. Application software tells the operating system what to do. The operating system tells the device drivers, device drivers tell the hardware, and the hardware actually does the work. Figure 4-2 illustrates this chain of command for printing a document or photo.

FIGURE 4-2

A command to print a document is relayed through various levels of software, including the operating system, until it reaches the printer.

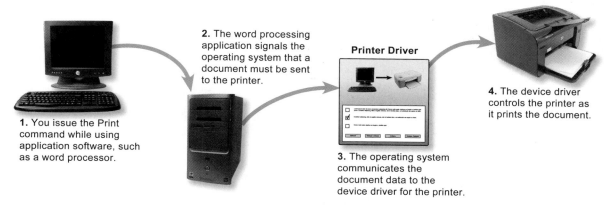

**2.** The word processing application signals the operating system that a document must be sent to the printer.

**Printer Driver**

**4.** The device driver controls the printer as it prints the document.

**1.** You issue the Print command while using application software, such as a word processor.

**3.** The operating system communicates the document data to the device driver for the printer.

The operating system interacts with application software, device drivers, and hardware to manage a computer's resources. In the context of a computer system, the term **resource** refers to any component that is required to perform work. For example, the processor is a resource. RAM (random access memory), storage space, and peripherals are also resources. While you interact with application software, your computer's operating system is busy behind the scenes with resource management tasks such as those listed in Figure 4-3.

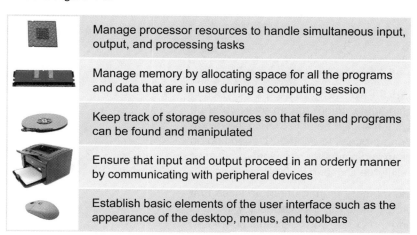

Manage processor resources to handle simultaneous input, output, and processing tasks

Manage memory by allocating space for all the programs and data that are in use during a computing session

Keep track of storage resources so that files and programs can be found and manipulated

Ensure that input and output proceed in an orderly manner by communicating with peripheral devices

Establish basic elements of the user interface such as the appearance of the desktop, menus, and toolbars

FIGURE 4-3

Operating System Tasks

**How do operating systems manage processor resources?**
Every cycle of a computer's microprocessor is a resource for accomplishing tasks. Many activities—called processes—compete for the attention of your computer's microprocessor. Commands are arriving from programs you're using, while input is arriving from the keyboard and mouse. At the same time, data must be sent to the display device or printer, and Web pages are arriving from your Internet connection.

To manage all these competing processes, your computer's operating system must ensure that each process receives its share of microprocessor cycles. You can check the processes that are being executed by the microprocessor (Figure 4-4). You'll be surprised by all the activity that's taking place. You can check processes if you suspect that a program did not close properly or that malware is working behind the scenes.

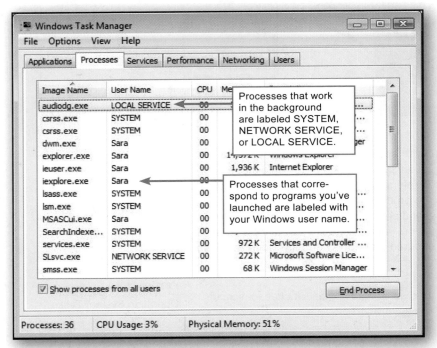

**FIGURE 4-4**

The Windows operating system displays a list of processes when you hold down the Ctrl, Shift, and Esc keys. On the Mac look for the Activity Monitor in the Utilities folder listed under Applications. Most processes are legitimate programs that run in the background to carry out tasks for the operating system, device drivers, and applications. Occasionally a bot or worm launches rogue processes. If you want to know if a process is legitimate, you can google it. ▶ Use your digital textbook to find out how to access information about the processes on your computer.

**How do operating systems handle so many processes?** During a typical computing session, your computer might run an average of 50 processes. Ideally, the operating system should be able to help the microprocessor switch seamlessly from one process to another. Depending on the capabilities of the operating system and computer hardware, processes can be managed by multitasking, multithreading, and multiprocessing.

**Multitasking** provides process and memory management services that allow two or more tasks, jobs, or programs to run simultaneously. Most of today's operating systems, including the OS on your personal computer, offer multitasking services.

Within a single program, **multithreading** allows multiple parts, or threads, to run simultaneously. For example, one thread for a spreadsheet program might be waiting for input from the user while other threads perform a long calculation in the background. Multithreading can speed up performance on single or multiple processor computers.

Many new computers include multi-core processors or multiple processors. An operating system's **multiprocessing** capability supports a division of labor among all the processing units.

**How does an operating system manage memory?** A microprocessor works with data and executes instructions stored in RAM—one of your computer's most important resources. When you want to run more than one program at a time, the operating system has to allocate specific areas of memory for each program, as shown in Figure 4-5.

When multiple programs are running, the OS should prevent a **memory leak**—a situation in which instructions and data from one area of memory overflow into memory allocated to another program. If an OS falls down on the job and fails to protect each program's memory area, data can get corrupted, programs can crash, and your computer displays error messages, such as "General Protection Fault" or "Program Not Responding." Your computer can sometimes recover from a memory leak if you access Task Manager (PCs) or Activity Monitor (Macs) to close the corrupted program.

**How does the OS keep track of storage resources?** Behind the scenes, an operating system acts as a filing clerk that stores and retrieves files from your computer's hard drive and other storage devices. It remembers the names and locations of all your files and keeps track of empty spaces where new files can be stored. Later in the chapter, you'll explore file storage in more depth and learn how the operating system affects the way you create, name, save, and retrieve files.

**Why does the operating system get involved with peripheral devices?** Every device connected to a computer is regarded as an input or output resource. Your computer's operating system communicates with device driver software so that data can travel smoothly between the computer and peripheral resources. If a peripheral device or driver is not performing correctly, the operating system makes a decision about what to do—usually it displays an on-screen message to warn you of the problem.

Your computer's operating system ensures that input and output proceed in an orderly manner, using buffers to collect and hold data while the computer is busy with other tasks. By using a keyboard buffer, for example, your computer never misses one of your keystrokes, regardless of how fast you type or what else is happening in your computer at the same time.

**Are different operating systems needed for different computing tasks?** One operating system might be better suited to some computing tasks than others. To provide clues to their strengths and weaknesses, operating systems are informally categorized and characterized using one or more of the following terms:

A **single-user operating system** expects to deal with one set of input devices—those that can be controlled by one user at a time. Operating systems for handheld computers and some personal computers fit into the single-user category. DOS is an example of a single-user operating system.

A **multiuser operating system** allows a single, centralized computer to deal with simultaneous input, output, and processing requests from many users. One of its most difficult responsibilities is to schedule all the processing requests that a centralized computer must perform. IBM's z/OS is one of the most popular multiuser operating systems.

A **server operating system** provides tools for managing distributed networks, e-mail servers, and Web hosting sites. Mac OS X Server, Windows Server 2008 R2, and Linux are examples of server operating systems. Technically, multiuser operating systems schedule requests for processing on a centralized computer, whereas a server operating system simply routes data and programs to each user's local computer where the actual

**FIGURE 4-5**

The operating system allocates a specific area of RAM for each program that is open and running. The operating system is itself a program, so it requires RAM space, too.

RAM

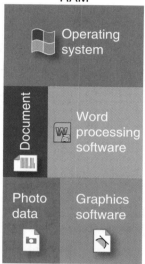

4

**TERMINOLOGY NOTE**

The term *buffer* is technical jargon for a region of memory that holds data waiting to be transferred from one device to another.

processing takes place. In practice, however, today's server OSs can be configured for centralized or distributed processing.

A **desktop operating system** is designed for a personal computer—a desktop, notebook, or tablet computer. The computer you use at home, at school, or at work is most likely configured with a desktop operating system, such as Microsoft Windows or Mac OS. Typically, these operating systems are designed to accommodate one user at a time, but also provide networking capability. Today's desktop operating systems invariably provide multitasking capabilities so that users can run more than one application at a time.

Some operating system vendors characterize their products as home or professional versions. The home version usually has fewer network management tools than the professional version.

**Do I ever interact directly with the OS?** Although its main purpose is to control what happens behind the scenes of a computer system, many operating systems provide helpful tools, called operating system utilities, that you can use to control and customize your computer equipment and work environment. For example, Microsoft Windows offers its users controls to do the following activities:

● Launch programs. When you start your computer, Windows displays graphical objects, such as icons, the Start button, and the Programs menu, which you can use to start programs.

● Manage files. A useful utility, called Windows Explorer, allows you to view a list of files, move them to different storage devices, copy them, rename them, and delete them.

● Get help. Windows offers a Help system you can use to find out how various commands work.

● Customize the user interface. The Windows Control Panel, which is accessible from the Start menu, provides utilities that help you customize your screen display and work environment.

● Configure equipment. The Control Panel also provides access to utilities that help you set up and configure your computer's hardware and peripheral devices (Figure 4-6).

**FIGURE 4-6**

Many Windows utilities can be accessed from the Control Panel. You'll find it by clicking the Start button. The Classic View displays Control Panel utilities as icons; Category View (shown here) organizes the utilities into groups. ▶ Use your digital textbook to take a tour of handy Control Panel options.

## USER INTERFACES

**What is a user interface?** A **user interface** can be defined as the combination of hardware and software that helps people and computers communicate with each other. Your computer's user interface includes a display device, mouse, and keyboard that allow you to view and manipulate your computing environment. It also includes software elements, such as icons, menus, and toolbar buttons.

**How does the operating system affect the user interface?** The operating system's user interface defines the so-called look and feel of compatible software. For example, application software that runs under Mac OS uses a standard set of menus, buttons, and toolbars based on the operating system's user interface. Originally, computers had a **command-line interface** that required users to type memorized commands to run programs and accomplish tasks.

Command-line user interfaces can be accessed from most operating systems, including Windows and Mac OS. Experienced users and system administrators sometimes prefer to use a command-line interface for troubleshooting and system maintenance. Figure 4-7 illustrates the use of a command-line interface.

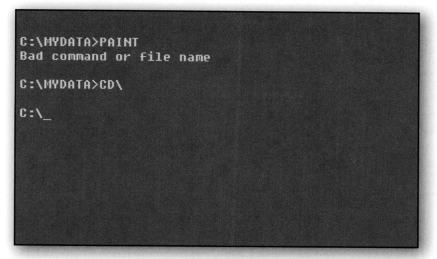

**FIGURE 4-7**

A command-line user interface requires users to type commands. Here the prompt C:\MYDATA> means the computer is looking at the MYDATA folder of drive C. The user has tried to start a program called Paint, but that program does not exist in the current folder, so the computer has produced the error message "Bad command or file name."

Most computers today feature a graphical user interface, abbreviated as GUI and pronounced as "gooey" or "gee you eye." A **graphical user interface** provides a way to point and click a mouse to select menu options and manipulate graphical objects displayed on the screen.

GUIs were originally conceived at the prestigious Xerox PARC research facility. In 1984, Apple turned the idea into a commercial success with the launch of its popular Macintosh computer, which featured a GUI operating system and applications. Graphical user interfaces didn't really catch on in the PC market until the 1992 release of Windows 3.1.

**What are the basic elements of a GUI?** GUIs are based on graphical objects that can be manipulated using a mouse or other input device. Each graphical object represents a computer task, command, or real-world object. Icons and windows can be displayed on a screen-based **desktop** as explained in Figure 4-8 on the next page. An **icon** is a small picture that represents a program, file, or hardware device. A **window** is a rectangular work area that can hold a program, data, or controls.

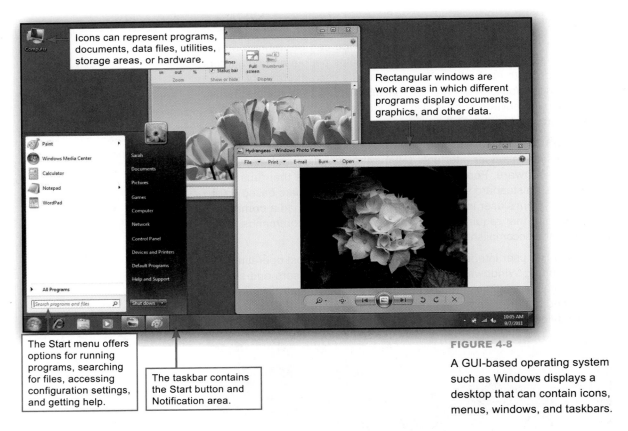

Icons can represent programs, documents, data files, utilities, storage areas, or hardware.

Rectangular windows are work areas in which different programs display documents, graphics, and other data.

The Start menu offers options for running programs, searching for files, accessing configuration settings, and getting help.

The taskbar contains the Start button and Notification area.

**FIGURE 4-8**

A GUI-based operating system such as Windows displays a desktop that can contain icons, menus, windows, and taskbars.

A **button** is a graphic—usually rectangular in shape—that can be clicked to make a selection. Buttons can be arranged in a **menu bar**, **toolbar**, **task-bar**, or **ribbon** (Figure 4-9).

**FIGURE 4-9**

Buttons and command options can be arranged on menu bars, toolbars, taskbars, or ribbons (shown top to bottom).

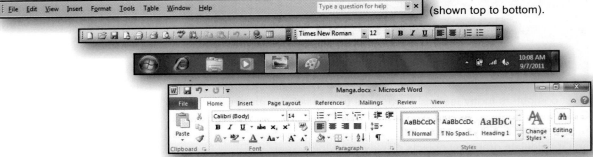

**What's the point of menus and dialog boxes?** Menus were developed as a response to the difficulties many people experienced trying to remember command words and syntax for command-line user interfaces. A **menu** displays a list of commands or options. Each line of the menu is referred to as a menu option or a menu item. Menus are popular because you simply choose the command you want from a list. Also, because all the commands on the list are valid, it is not possible to invoke invalid commands that generate errors.

You might wonder how a menu can present all the commands you might want to use. Obviously, there are many possibilities for combining command words so there could be hundreds of menu options. Two methods are generally used to present a reasonably sized list of options: submenus and dialog boxes.

A **submenu** is an additional set of commands that the computer displays after you make a selection from the main menu. Sometimes a submenu displays another submenu, providing even more command choices (Figure 4-10).

**FIGURE 4-10**

Menu options with a ▶ symbol lead to submenus.

Instead of leading to a submenu, some menu options lead to a dialog box. A **dialog box** displays the options associated with a command. You fill in the dialog box to indicate specifically how you want the command carried out. As shown in Figure 4-11, dialog boxes appear when you click a dialog box launcher or when you click a menu item that ends with an ellipsis.

**FIGURE 4-11**

Dialog boxes appear when you select corresponding menu items from the ribbon or from a menu.

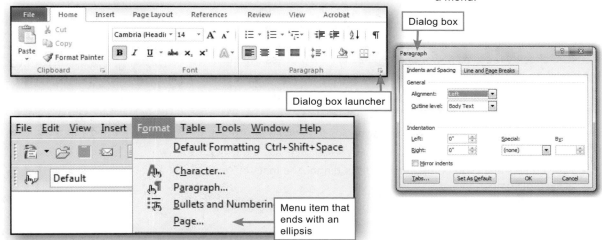

Dialog boxes display controls that you manipulate with a mouse to specify settings and other command parameters. Figure 4-12 explains how to use some of the dialog box controls that you are likely to encounter in Windows, Mac, or Linux environments.

**FIGURE 4-12**

Dialog box controls offer a variety of ways to enter specifications for tasks you'd like the software to carry out.

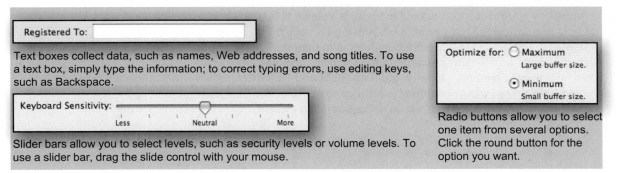

Registered To:

Text boxes collect data, such as names, Web addresses, and song titles. To use a text box, simply type the information; to correct typing errors, use editing keys, such as Backspace.

Keyboard Sensitivity:
Less    Neutral    More

Slider bars allow you to select levels, such as security levels or volume levels. To use a slider bar, drag the slide control with your mouse.

Optimize for: ○ Maximum
Large buffer size.
● Minimum
Small buffer size.

Radio buttons allow you to select one item from several options. Click the round button for the option you want.

4

How similar are the user interfaces for Windows, Mac OS, and Linux? All of the popular desktop operating systems use graphical user interfaces that are more similar than they are different. Regardless of whether you use Windows, Mac OS, or Linux, you'll encounter a fairly standard set of on-screen controls. They might differ in their visual design, but it is easy to determine how to use them. In the next section of the chapter, you'll learn more about the similarities and differences in today's popular operating systems.

## THE BOOT PROCESS

Where is the operating system stored? In some digital devices—typically handhelds and videogame consoles—the entire operating system is small enough to be stored in ROM (read-only memory). For most other computers, the operating system program is quite large, so most of it is stored on a hard disk. During the boot process, the operating system kernel is loaded into RAM. The **kernel** provides essential operating system services, such as memory management and file access. The kernel stays in RAM all the time your computer is on. Other parts of the operating system, such as customization utilities, are loaded into RAM as they are needed.

What is the boot process? The sequence of events that occurs between the time that you turn on a computer and the time that it is ready for you to issue commands is referred to as the **boot process**, or booting your computer.

Your computer's small **bootstrap program** is built into special ROM circuitry housed in the computer's system unit. When you turn on a computer, the ROM circuitry receives power and begins the boot process by executing the bootstrap program. Six major events happen during the boot process:

- Power up. When you turn on the power switch, the power light is illuminated, and power is distributed to the computer circuitry.

- Start boot program. The microprocessor begins to execute the bootstrap program that is stored in ROM.

- Power-on self-test. The computer performs diagnostic tests of several crucial system components.

- Identify peripheral devices. The computer identifies the peripheral devices that are connected and checks their settings.

- Load operating system. The operating system is copied from the hard disk to RAM.

- Check configuration and customization. The microprocessor reads configuration data and executes any customized startup routines specified by the user.

Why doesn't a computer simply leave the operating system in memory? Most of a computer's memory is volatile RAM, which cannot hold any data when the power is off. Although a copy of the operating system is housed in RAM while the computer is in operation, this copy is erased as soon as the power is turned off. In addition to RAM, computers have non-volatile memory circuitry, such as ROM and EEPROM, which can store data even when the power is off. Typically, ROM and EEPROM are not nearly large enough to store an entire operating system.

### TERMINOLOGY NOTE

The term *boot* comes from the word *bootstrap*, which is a small loop on the back of a boot. Just as you can pull on a big boot using a small bootstrap, your computer boots up by first loading a small program into memory, and then it uses that small program to load a large operating system.

Given the volatility of RAM and the insufficient size of ROM and EEPROM, computer designers decided to store the operating system on a computer's hard disk. During the boot process, a copy of the operating system is transferred into RAM, where it can be accessed quickly whenever the computer needs to carry out an input, output, or storage operation (Figure 4-13).

**How do I know when the operating system is loaded?** The operating system is loaded and the boot process is complete when the computer is ready to accept your commands. Usually, the computer displays an operating system prompt or a main screen. The Windows operating system, for example, displays the Windows desktop when the boot process is complete.

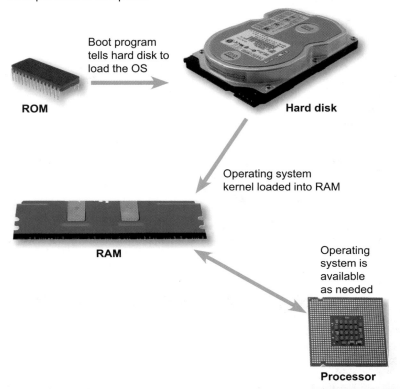

**FIGURE 4-13**

The bootstrap program copies the operating system into RAM, where it can be directly accessed by the processor to carry out input, output, or storage operations.

**4**

## QuickCheck                                          SECTION A

1. An operating system manages a computer's [_____] , such as RAM, storage, and peripherals.

2. Most personal computer operating systems have [_____] capabilities so that they can simultaneously run two or more tasks, jobs, or programs.

3. The core part of an operating system is called its [_____] .

4. Most computers today have [_____] user interfaces.

5. During the [_____] process, a program stored in ROM tells the hard disk to load the operating system into RAM.

 CHECK ANSWERS

# Today's Operating Systems

**CONSUMERS CAN SELECT** from several operating systems for their personal computers and handheld devices. What makes these operating systems different? What are their strengths and weaknesses? Section B offers an operating system overview designed to give you a basic familiarity with their features.

## MICROSOFT WINDOWS

**What's the best-selling operating system? Microsoft Windows** is installed on more than 80% of the world's personal computers. The Windows operating system gets its name from the rectangular work areas that appear on the screen-based desktop. Each work area window can display a different document or program, providing a visual model of the operating system's multitasking capabilities (Figure 4-14).

**FIGURE 4-14**

Microsoft Windows XP (top), Windows Vista (middle), and Windows 7 (bottom) use similar GUI controls, although the appearance of icons and other graphical elements is slightly different. ▶ Tour the Windows desktop.

**What do I need to know about the evolution of Windows?** The first versions of Windows, including Windows 3.1, were sometimes referred to as operating environments rather than operating systems because they required DOS to supply the operating system kernel. Windows operating environments hid the DOS command line with a point-and-click user interface, complete with graphical screen displays and mouse input. Windows operating environments evolved into today's comprehensive operating systems, which do not require the DOS kernel.

From its inception, the Windows operating system was designed to run on Intel or Intel-compatible microprocessors. As those chips evolved from 16-bit to 32-bit, and then to 64-bit architectures, Windows evolved to keep pace. In addition, Windows developers added and upgraded features, such as networking and the file system. They also refined the user interface by attempting to make it more visually attractive and easier to use. Since its introduction in 1985, Windows has evolved through several versions, listed in Figure 4-15.

**What are the strengths of Windows?** The number and variety of programs that run on Windows are unmatched by any other operating system, a fact that contributes to Windows being the most widely used desktop operating system. For the best selection of software, especially for games and vertical market business software, Windows is the operating system of choice.

The variety of hardware platforms that run Windows is also a significant strength. You can use a desktop computer, notebook, PDA, netbook, or tablet computer and see a familiar set of Windows icons and menus. Features such as handwriting recognition contribute to the versatility of Windows, allowing it to control PDAs and tablet computers with touch screens.

The Windows user community is also a strength. A vast amount of documentation, including tutorials and troubleshooting guides, can be found online and on the shelves of most bookstores. Microsoft's official site, *www.microsoft.com*, includes thousands of pages of easily searchable information. Third-party sites, such as Paul Thurrott's SuperSite for Windows, *www.winsupersite.com*, also offer tips, tools, and troubleshooting guides.

When it comes to hardware and peripheral devices, Windows offers excellent support in the form of built-in drivers and Plug and Play functionality. With the largest user base of any platform, Windows computer owners are the target market for the majority of hardware manufacturers. Many of the fastest graphics cards and the coolest joysticks are offered exclusively for the Windows platform.

**What are Windows' weaknesses?** Windows has been criticized for two major weaknesses: reliability and security. The reliability of an operating system is usually gauged by the length of time it operates without glitches. Unfortunately, Windows tends to become unstable with more frequency than other operating systems. Slow system response, programs that stop working, and error messages can be symptoms of a Windows malfunction. Rebooting usually clears the error condition and

**FIGURE 4-15**

Windows Timeline

**2009  Windows 7**
Featured 64-bit support, enhanced desktop and taskbar features, and touch-screen capabilities.

**2007  Windows Vista**
Featured 64-bit support, enhanced security, and more flexible file management. Also more powerful search capabilities and live icons that show document thumbnails.

**2001  Windows XP**
Featured an updated user interface, used the Windows 2000 32-bit kernel, and supported FAT32 and NTFS file systems.

**2000  Windows Me**
The last Windows version to use the original Windows kernel that accesses DOS.

**2000  Windows 2000**
Billed as a "multipurpose network OS for businesses of all sizes" and featured enhanced Web services.

**1998  Windows 98**
Increased stability was a big feature of this Windows version, which also included the Internet Explorer browser.

**1995  Windows 95**
Featured a revised user interface. Supported 32-bit processors, TCP/IP, dial-up networking, and long file names.

**1993  Windows NT**
Provided management and security tools for network servers and the NTFS file system.

**1992  Windows for Workgroups**
Provided peer-to-peer networking, e-mail, group scheduling, and file and printer sharing.

**1992  Windows 3.1**
Introduced program icons and the file folder metaphor.

**1990  Windows 3.0**
Introduced graphical controls.

**1987  Windows 2.0**
Introduced overlapping windows and expanded memory access.

**1985  Windows 1.0**
Divided the screen into rectangular windows that allowed users to work with several programs at the same time.

4

returns a computer to normal functionality, but the time wasted shutting down and waiting for a reboot adds unnecessary frustration to the computing experience.

Of the major desktop operating systems, Windows has the reputation for being the most vulnerable to viruses, worms, and other attacks. One reason for Windows' vulnerability is because its huge user base makes it the biggest target. In addition, anti-establishment sentiments make Microsoft a hip adversary for rebellious hackers. Even so, Windows has many security holes that are found and exploited. Although Microsoft is diligent in its efforts to patch security holes, its programmers are always one step behind the hackers; and while users wait for patches, their computers are vulnerable.

The programmers developing Windows Vista focused on improving security. Their efforts to bulletproof the operating system, however, produced another set of consequences. Compared to Windows XP, Vista's speed and response time deteriorated even though hardware requirements, such as RAM capacity, increased. Vista is not compatible with hardware drivers for some popular peripherals; Vista can disable other device drivers in an attempt to prevent the computer from displaying pirated music, movies, and other digital content. In addition, Vista frequently interrupts activities with messages asking users if they initiated an action; the feature is designed to block intrusions, but can disrupt workflow.

Because Windows 7 is built on the Vista code base, the new version does not solve all of the problems users encountered with Vista. Windows 7 can seem sluggish on less-than-cutting-edge computers. As with Vista, Windows 7 includes digital rights management that can be intrusive.

**What's the difference between desktop, server, and embedded versions of Microsoft Windows?** Microsoft typically offers several versions, called editions, of the Windows operating system for various markets. Desktop editions, such as Home, Professional, and Ultimate, are designed for personal computers. Server editions are designed for LAN, Internet, and Web servers. Embedded editions are designed for handheld devices, such as PDAs and mobile phones. Figure 4-16 categorizes some of the most popular past and present Windows offerings.

**FIGURE 4-16**

Microsoft offers several versions of Windows, designed for different computing tasks and equipment.

**Personal Computers**

Windows 7 Starter
Windows 7 Home Premium
Windows 7 Professional
Windows 7 Ultimate

**LAN, Internet, and Web Servers**

Windows Server 2008 R2
Windows Server 2003
Windows 2000 Server

**PDAs, Smartphones, and Non-personal Computer Devices**

Windows Mobile OS
Windows CE
Windows XP Embedded
Windows Phone 7

## MAC OS

**Is Mac OS similar to Windows?** **Mac OS** stands for Macintosh Operating System and it is the operating system designed for Apple Computer's Macintosh line of computer systems. Although Mac OS was developed several years before Windows, both operating systems feature multiple rectangular work areas to reflect multitasking capabilities. Both operating systems also provide basic networking services.

Unique features of the Mac desktop include the Apple icon, the Dock, and an application menu strip at the top of the screen. Figure 4-17 illustrates some basic features of the Mac desktop.

**FIGURE 4-17**

You can tell when you're using Mac OS by the Apple logo that appears on the menu bar. The Mac OS X interface includes all the standard elements of a GUI, including icons, menus, windows, and taskbars.
▶ Tour the Mac OS desktop and compare it to the Windows desktop.

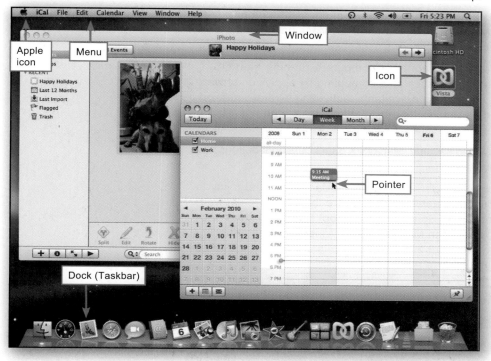

**What do I need to know about the evolution of Mac OS?** Like Windows, Mac OS has been through a number of revisions. The original Classic Mac OS was introduced in 1984 and designed for a line of Macintosh computers based on the Motorola 68000 microprocessor.

In 2001, Classic Mac OS was rewritten to run on Macintosh computers containing PowerPC microprocessors produced by IBM. The new Mac OS was called Mac OS X (the X can either be pronounced as "ten" or the letter "X"). Mac OS X was much more sophisticated than its predecessor, with better memory management and multitasking capabilities.

In 2006, Macintosh hardware changed significantly with the switch from PowerPC to Intel processors. Mac OS X was again rewritten. The first version of Mac OS X to support the Intel architecture was Mac OS X version 10.4.4, sometimes referred to as Tiger. In 2010, Apple introduced Mac OS X 10.7 (Lion), which is installed on most of today's Macs (Figure 4-18).

**FIGURE 4-18**

Mac OS X Timeline

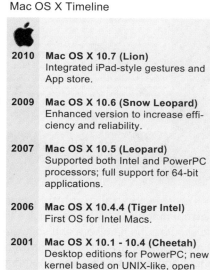

**2010** **Mac OS X 10.7 (Lion)**
Integrated iPad-style gestures and App store.

**2009** **Mac OS X 10.6 (Snow Leopard)**
Enhanced version to increase efficiency and reliability.

**2007** **Mac OS X 10.5 (Leopard)**
Supported both Intel and PowerPC processors; full support for 64-bit applications.

**2006** **Mac OS X 10.4.4 (Tiger Intel)**
First OS for Intel Macs.

**2001** **Mac OS X 10.1 - 10.4 (Cheetah)**
Desktop editions for PowerPC; new kernel based on UNIX-like, open source code.

**What are the strengths of Mac OS?** Mac OS X has a reputation for being an easy-to-use, reliable, and secure operating system. Back when PC owners were struggling with an inscrutable command-line operating system, Macintosh owners were breezing along with a point-and-click GUI. According to industry observers, Macintosh developers have always been in the lead when it comes to intuitive user interface design.

The operating system kernel of Mac OS X is based on UNIX and includes industrial-strength memory protection features that contribute to a low incidence of errors and glitches. Mac OS X inherited a strong security foundation from UNIX that tends to limit the number of security holes and the damage that can be done by hackers who manage to slip in.

Another factor that contributes to the security of computers running Mac OS is that fewer viruses are designed to target Macs because the user base is much smaller than the Windows user base.

Regardless of the relative security of computers running Mac OS X, Macintosh owners should practice safe computing by applying software and OS patches as they become available, activating wireless network encryption, not opening suspicious e-mail attachments, and not clicking links embedded in e-mail messages.

In addition to reliability and security, Mac OS X offers dual boot options and a good virtual machine platform.

**What is dual boot?** Mac OS X on an Intel Mac offers the ability to run Windows and Windows application software in addition to software designed for the Macintosh. Software called Boot Camp is a **dual boot** utility that can switch between Mac OS X and Windows. When booting, you can select either Mac OS X or Windows (Figure 4-19). To change operating systems, you have to reboot.

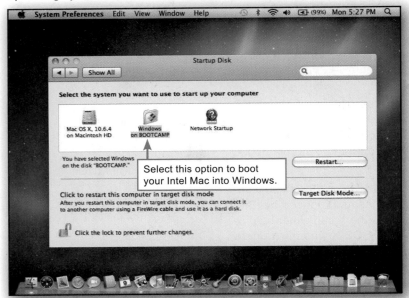

**FIGURE 4-19**

On a Macintosh computer with Boot Camp, you can boot into Mac OS X or into Windows.
▶ See how it works!

**What is a virtual machine?** Mac OS X is also a good platform for **virtual machine** (VM) technologies that allow you to use one computer to simulate the hardware and software of another. Each virtual machine has its own simulated processor (or core processor), RAM, video card, input and output ports, and operating system. Each machine can run most software that's compatible with the virtual OS platform.

Popular virtual machine software such as VMware and Parallels Desktop can run on most computers with Intel microprocessors, including Intel Macs, PCs, and generic Linux computers. The computer boots into its native OS such as Mac OS, but users can create a virtual machine running guest operating systems, such as Windows. The virtual machine's desktop appears in a window on the host desktop (Figure 4-20).

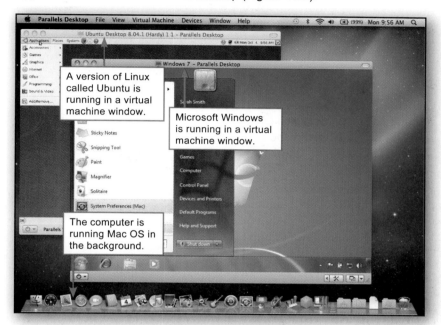

**FIGURE 4-20**

On a Mac with virtual Windows and Linux, switching from one operating system to another is as simple as selecting a window. When switched to the Windows work area, you can run games, business software, and other applications designed for the Windows OS. By clicking the Linux work area, you could run Linux applications from its vast collection of open source software. After returning to the Mac OS X desktop, you could run your collection of high-end graphics and multimedia iLife software designed exclusively for the Macintosh.

**What are the weaknesses of Mac OS?** The weaknesses of Mac OS include a somewhat limited selection of software and its use of resource forks. A decent collection of software is available for computers that run Mac OS, although the selection is not as vast as the Windows collection. Many of the most prolific software publishers produce one version of their software for Windows and another, similar version for Mac OS.

Macintosh computer owners might find that many popular software titles are not available for Mac OS X. The selection of games, for example, is much sparser than for Windows, although it should be noted that the selection of graphics software for Mac OS X is as good as or better than the selection available for Windows.

**What is a resource fork?** In most operating systems, a file is a single unit that contains data or program code. Files maintained by the Macintosh operating system, however, can have two parts, called forks. The **data fork** is similar to files in other operating systems. It contains data, such as the text for a document, the graphics for a photo, or the commands for a program. The **resource fork** is a companion file that stores information about the data in the data fork, such as the file type and the application that created it.

Although resource forks have advantages on their native Macintosh platform, they can be a nuisance when files are transferred to other platforms. When you copy a file from a Mac to a Windows computer, for example, you end up with two files, one for the data fork and one for the resource fork. The resource fork begins with a period and can usually be ignored or deleted from the Windows directory.

## UNIX AND LINUX

**Are UNIX and Linux the same?** The **UNIX** operating system was developed in 1969 at AT&T's Bell Labs. It gained a good reputation for its dependability in multiuser environments, and many versions of it became available for mainframes and microcomputers.

In 1991, a young Finnish student named Linus Torvalds developed the **Linux** (pronounced "LIH nucks") operating system. Linux was inspired by and loosely based on a UNIX derivative called MINIX, created by Andrew Tanenbaum. Linux continues to gain popularity as an operating system for personal computers, though it is not as popular for desktop applications as Windows or Mac OS.

**What are the strengths of Linux?** Linux is rather unique because it is distributed along with its source code under the terms of a GPL (General Public License), which allows everyone to make copies for their own use, to give to others, or to sell. This licensing policy has encouraged programmers to develop Linux utilities, software, and enhancements. Linux is primarily distributed over the Web.

Linux shares several technical features with UNIX, such as multitasking and multiuser capabilities. It is also secure and reliable.

**What are the weaknesses of Linux?** Linux typically requires a bit more tinkering than the Windows and Mac desktop operating systems. The comparatively limited number of programs that run under Linux also discourages many nontechnical users. A constantly growing collection of high-quality open source software is becoming available for the Linux platform, but many of these applications are targeted toward business and technical users.

**How do I get Linux?** A **Linux distribution** is a download that contains the Linux kernel, system utilities, graphical user interface, applications, and an installation routine. Beginner-friendly Linux distributions include Fedora, Mandriva, SUSE, and Ubuntu (Figure 4-21). **Google Chrome OS**, originally designed for netbooks, is built on the Linux kernel.

**FIGURE 4-21**

Linux users can choose from several graphical interfaces. Pictured here is the popular Ubuntu graphical desktop. ▶ With your digital textbook, you can tour Linux and compare it to using Windows and Mac OS.

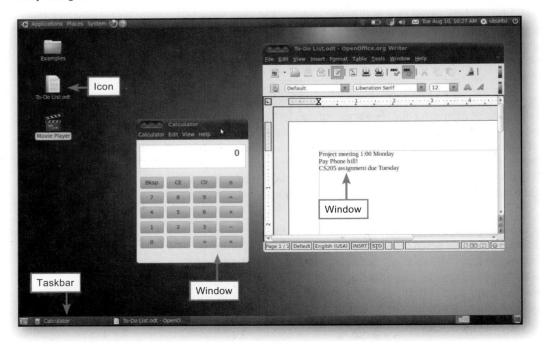

## DOS

**Why do I keep hearing about DOS?** Old-timers in the computer industry sometimes reminisce about DOS. It was the first operating system that many of them used, and its cryptic command-line user interface left an indelible impression. **DOS** (which rhymes with "toss") stands for Disk Operating System. It was developed by Microsoft—the same company that later produced Windows—and introduced on the original IBM PC in 1982. Although IBM called this operating system PC-DOS, Microsoft marketed it to other companies under the name MS-DOS.

DOS software, such as VisiCalc, used command-line interfaces and rustic menus that users controlled with the keyboard's arrow keys (Figure 4-22).

After more than 20 years, remnants of DOS still linger in the world of personal computers because it provided part of the operating system kernel for Windows versions 3.1, 95, 98, and Me.

During the peak of its popularity, thousands of software programs were produced for computers running DOS. You can occasionally find some of these programs on the Internet, and run them using the Command Prompt option accessed from the Start menu of Windows 7, Vista, or XP. DOS also offers handy troubleshooting utilities, such as Ping, Tracert, Copy, Msconfig, and Netstat, that are used by tech-savvy computer users.

**FIGURE 4-22**

When using VisiCalc, you could press the slash key (/) to call up the main menu, which simply listed the first letter of each command. For example, F was the Format command; so if you wanted to format a cell, you pressed F to see a list of letters, such as *C*, *L*, and *R*—the commands for centering, left alignment, and right alignment.

4

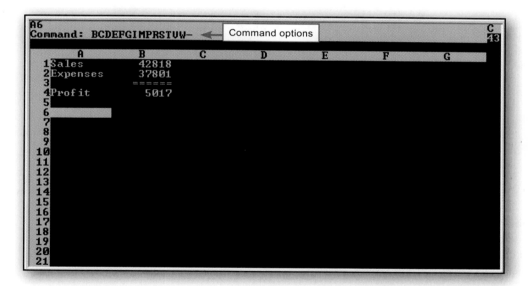

## HANDHELD OPERATING SYSTEMS

**What are the options for handheld operating systems?** Six operating systems dominate the realm of handheld computers: Palm webOS, Symbian, Windows Phone 7, BlackBerry OS, Android OS, and iOS, shown in Figure 4-23.

**FIGURE 4-23**

Operating systems for mobile devices feature graphical user interfaces with touch screen input.

Symbian^3

Windows Phone 7

BlackBerry OS

Android OS

iOS

Palm webOS

**Palm webOS** was developed for popular Palm brand PDAs and smartphones. It is based on a system of "cards" that represent applications in a multitasking environment. It is designed to seamlessly interact with social networking sites, such as Facebook and Twitter.

**Symbian** is a popular handheld operating system used with Nokia and Ericsson smartphones. In 2010, Symbian became available as an open source operating system, giving developers a free platform to use for developing Symbian mobile applications.

**Windows Phone 7** replaced Windows Mobile OS in 2010. It features a series of "tiles" that represent applications, contacts, links, or media. With the initial release, multitasking is limited to running only one third-party program at a time.

**BlackBerry OS** is a proprietary operating system produced by RIM, the Canadian company that developed the BlackBerry smartphone. A key feature of BlackBerry OS is its ability to work with corporate e-mail software systems produced by Microsoft and IBM.

**Android OS** is an open source operating system developed by Google and designed for mobile devices, such as smartphones and netbooks. It is based on the Linux kernel. Users can select from a variety of applications or create their own. Android runs on popular HTC and Motorola phones, as well as on several netbooks, tablet computers, and e-book readers.

**iOS** (formerly iPhone OS) is a version of Mac OS X written for the iPhone's ARM processor and optimized for touch-screen communications applications. iOS is also the operating system used for Apple's iPad tablet computer. It was the first handheld OS to offer routines that manage gesture inputs, such as using your fingers to "squeeze" an on-screen graphic into a smaller size. It also includes apps for stock quotes, maps, and weather reports. The iOS is an open platform, which means that programs, called iPhone apps, can be created by third-party programmers.

**How do mobile apps work?** Mobile apps are typically small, focused application software products designed for the limited screen real estate provided by a mobile phone or media player. Many mobile apps are produced by third-party developers and are submitted for approval to an apps store, such as iTunes. Apps are usually downloaded directly to a phone or other handheld device.

**Can I use mobile apps on any handheld device?** Like software designed for full-size personal computers, mobile apps work only on devices running the corresponding operating system. So, for example, an app designed for the iPhone's iOS will not work on your HTC phone running Android OS.

**Are operating systems for handheld devices similar to desktop operating systems?** Operating systems for handheld and desktop devices provide many similar services, such as scheduling processor resources, managing memory, loading programs, managing input and output, and establishing the user interface. But because handheld devices tend to be used for less sophisticated tasks, their operating systems are somewhat simpler and significantly smaller.

Today's handheld OSs typically support touch screens and include a standard set of apps for e-mail, browsing, playing media, mapping, and scheduling.

4

## QuickCheck                                              SECTION B

1. Microsoft Windows featured the first graphical user interface. True or false? [　　　　]

2. VMware and Parallels Desktop are examples of [　　　　　　] machine technology that can be used to run Windows software on a Mac.

3. An open-source operating system called [　　　　　　] is the foundation for several personal computer operating systems, such as Google Chrome and Android OS.

4. A resource [　　　　　　] is a companion file created by Mac OS to store information about a file and its data.

5. Palm webOS and iOS are examples of operating systems used for handheld devices. True or false? [　　　　]

▶ CHECK ANSWERS

# File Basics

THE TERM *FILE* WAS USED for filing cabinets and collections of papers long before it became part of the personal computer lexicon. Today, computer files in digital format offer a compact and convenient way to store documents, photos, videos, and music. Computer files have several characteristics, such as a name, format, location, size, and date. To make effective use of computer files, you'll need a good understanding of these file basics, and that is the focus of Section C.

## FILE NAMES AND EXTENSIONS

**What is a computer file?** As you learned in Chapter 1, a computer file—or simply a file—is defined as a named collection of data that exists on a storage medium, such as a hard disk, CD, DVD, or USB flash drive. A file can contain a group of records, a document, a photo, music, a video, an e-mail message, or a computer program.

When you use word processing software, the text you enter for a document is stored as a file. You can give the file a name, such as *A History of Film Noir*. A music file, such as *Bach Brandenburg Concertos* that you download over the Internet, is stored as a file, too.

**What are the rules for naming files?** Every file has a name and might also have a file extension. When you save a file, you must provide a valid file name that adheres to specific rules, referred to as **file-naming conventions**. Each operating system has a unique set of file-naming conventions. Figure 4-24 lists file-naming conventions for the current versions of Windows and Mac OS.

**Is there a maximum length for file names?** DOS and Windows 3.1 limited file names to eight characters. With that limitation, it was often difficult to create descriptive file names. A file name such as *HseBud12* might be used for a file containing a household budget for 2012. With such cryptic file names, it was not always easy to figure out what a file contained. As a result, files were sometimes difficult to locate and identify. Today, most operating systems allow you to use longer file names.

Current versions of Windows and Mac OS support file names up to 255 characters long. In practice, some of the 255 characters are used for the file's drive letter, folder designation, and extension, so the name you assign to a file should typically be quite a bit shorter. A file name limitation of 255 characters gives you the flexibility to use descriptive file names, such as *Household Budget 2012*, so that you can easily identify what a file contains.

**What is a file extension?** A **file extension** (sometimes referred to as a file name extension) is an optional file identifier that is separated from the main file name by a period, as in *Paint.exe*. As you become familiar with file extensions, they will provide a clue to the file's contents. Files with .exe extensions are executable files that your computer can run. *Paint.exe*, for example, is a graphics utility packaged with the Windows operating system. Files with .dat extensions are typically data files. Files with .doc or .docx extensions contain word processing documents.

**FIGURE 4-24**

Windows File-naming Conventions

| Case sensitive | No |
|---|---|
| Maximum length of file name | File name, path, and extension cannot exceed 255 characters |
| Spaces allowed | Yes |
| Numbers allowed | Yes |
| Characters not allowed | * \ : < > \| " / ? |
| File names not allowed | Aux, Com1, Com2, Com3, Com4, Con, Lpt1, Lpt2, Lpt3, Prn, Nul |

Macintosh File-naming Conventions

| Case sensitive | No |
|---|---|
| Maximum length of file name | File name, path, and extension cannot exceed 255 characters |
| Spaces allowed | Yes |
| Numbers allowed | Yes |
| Characters not allowed | : (the colon) |

**Why are certain characters not allowed in a file name?** If an operating system attaches special significance to a symbol, you might not be able to use it in a file name. For example, Windows uses the colon (:) character to separate the device letter from a file name or folder, as in *C:Music*. A file name that contains a colon, such as *Report:2010*, is not valid because the operating system would become confused about how to interpret the colon. When you use Windows applications, avoid using the symbols : * \ < > | " / and ? in file names.

**What are reserved words?** Some operating systems also contain a list of **reserved words** that are used as commands or special identifiers. You cannot use these words alone as a file name. You can, however, use these words as part of a longer file name. For example, under Windows, the file name *Nul* would not be valid, but you could name a file something like *Nul Committee Notes.doc* or *Null Set.exe*.

In addition to *Nul*, Windows users should avoid using the following reserved words as file names: *Aux, Com1, Com2, Com3, Com4, Con, Lpt1, Lpt2, Lpt3,* and *Prn*.

**What else should I know about creating file names?** Some operating systems are case sensitive, but not those you typically work with on personal computers. Feel free to use uppercase and lowercase letters in file names that you create on PCs and Macs.

You can also use spaces in file names. That's a different rule than for e-mail addresses where spaces are not allowed. You've probably noticed that people often use underscores or periods instead of spaces in e-mail addresses such as Madi_Jones@msu.edu. That convention is not necessary in file names, so a file name such as *Letter to Madi Jones* is valid.

## FILE DIRECTORIES AND FOLDERS

**How do I designate a file's location?** To designate a file's location, you must first specify the device where the file is stored. As shown in Figure 4-25, each of a PC's storage devices is identified by a device letter—a convention that is specific to DOS and Windows. The main hard disk drive is usually referred to as drive C. A device letter is usually followed by a colon, so C: is typically the designation for a hard disk drive.

Although the hard disk drive on a Windows computer is designated as drive C, device letters for CD, DVD, and USB flash drives are not standardized. For example, the CD writer on your computer might be assigned device letter E, whereas the CD writer on another computer might be assigned device letter R.

**What is a disk partition?** A **disk partition** is a section of a hard disk drive that is treated as a separate storage unit. Most computers are configured with a single hard disk partition that contains the operating system, programs, and data. However, it is possible to create more than one hard disk partition. For example, a PC owner might set up one partition for operating system files and another partition for programs and data. This arrangement sometimes can speed up the process of disinfecting a computer that has been attacked by malicious software.

Partitions can be assigned drive letters. In the example above, the operating system files would be stored in partition C. The program and data file partition would probably be designated as drive D. Partitions are not the same thing as folders. Partitions are more permanent, and a special utility is required to create, modify, or delete them.

**FIGURE 4-25**

The Windows operating system labels storage devices with letters, such as C: and F:.

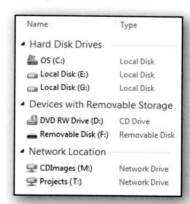

| Name | Type |
|------|------|
| ◢ Hard Disk Drives | |
|   OS (C:) | Local Disk |
|   Local Disk (E:) | Local Disk |
|   Local Disk (G:) | Local Disk |
| ◢ Devices with Removable Storage | |
|   DVD RW Drive (D:) | CD Drive |
|   Removable Disk (F:) | Removable Disk |
| ◢ Network Location | |
|   CDImages (M:) | Network Drive |
|   Projects (T:) | Network Drive |

**TERMINOLOGY NOTE**

Drive letter assignments are based on conventions that date back to the first PCs. The original IBM PCs shipped with a single floppy disk drive and it was designated drive A. An enhanced PC later shipped with two floppy disk drives, designated A and B. When hard disk drives were eventually added to PC systems, they were designated drive C.

4

**Do I have to remember where I put each file?** Your computer's operating system maintains a list of files called a **directory** for each storage disk, CD, DVD, BD, or USB flash drive. The main directory is referred to as the **root directory**. On a PC, the root directory is identified by the device letter followed by a backslash. For example, the root directory of the hard disk would be C:\. A root directory can be subdivided into smaller lists. Each list is called a **subdirectory**.

**What is a folder?** When you use Windows, Mac OS, or a Linux graphical file manager, each subdirectory is depicted as a **folder**. Folders help you envision your files as if they were stored in a filing cabinet. Each folder can hold related items, for example, a set of documents, sound clips, financial data, or photos for a school project. Windows provides a folder called My Documents that you might use to hold reports, letters, and so on. You can also create and name folders to meet your needs, such as a folder called *QuickBooks* to hold your personal finance data.

Folders can be created within other folders. You might, for example, create a Jazz folder within the Music folder to hold your jazz collection and another folder named Reggae to hold your reggae collection.

A folder name is separated from a drive letter and other folder names by a special symbol. In Microsoft Windows, this symbol is the backslash ( \ ). For example, the folder for your reggae music (within the Music folder on drive C) would be written as C:\Music\Reggae. Other operating systems use a forward slash (/) to separate folders.

A computer file's location is defined by a **file specification** (sometimes called a **path**), which includes the drive letter, folder(s), file name, and extension. Suppose that you have stored an MP3 file called *Marley One Love* in the *Reggae* folder on your hard disk. Its file specification is shown in Figure 4-26.

**FIGURE 4-26**

A file specification provides the name and location of a file.

## C:\Music\Reggae\Marley One Love.mp3

| Drive letter | Primary folder | Secondary folder | File name | File extension |

**What's the significance of a file's size?** A file contains data, stored as a group of bits. The more bits, the larger the file. **File size** is usually measured in bytes, kilobytes, or megabytes. Knowing the size of a file can be important. Compared to small files, large files fill up storage space more quickly, require longer transmission times, and are more likely to be stripped off e-mail attachments by a mail server. Your computer's operating system keeps track of file sizes and supplies that information when you request a listing of files.

**Is the file date important?** Your computer keeps track of the date that a file was created or last modified. The **file date** is useful if you have created several versions of a file and want to make sure you know which version is the most recent. It can also come in handy if you have downloaded several versions of a software package, such as your printer's device driver, and you want to make sure to install the latest version.

## FILE FORMATS

**What is a file format?** The term **file format** refers to the organization and layout of data that is stored in a file. As you might expect, music files are stored differently than text files or graphics files; but even within a single category of data, there are many file formats. For example, graphics data can be stored in file formats such as BMP, GIF, JPEG, or PNG.

The format of a file usually includes a header, data, and possibly an end-of-file marker. A **file header** is a section of data at the beginning of a file that contains information about a file—typically the date it was created, the date it was last updated, its size, and its file type.

The remaining contents of a file depend on whether it contains text, graphics, audio, or multimedia data. A text file, for example, might contain sentences and paragraphs interspersed with codes for centering, boldfacing, and margin settings. A graphics file might contain color data for each pixel, followed by a description of the color palette. Figure 4-27 illustrates the format for a Windows bitmap (BMP) file and contrasts it with the format of a GIF file.

**INFOWEBLINKS**

The **File Formats InfoWeb** provides a list of file extensions and their corresponding software.

 CLICK TO CONNECT
www.infoweblinks.com/np2012/ch04

| BMP File Format | GIF File Format |
|---|---|
| File header | File header |
| Bitmap header | Logical screen descriptor |
| Color palette | Global color table |
| | Local image descriptor |
| Image data | Local color table |
| | Image data |
| | End-of-file character |

**FIGURE 4-27**

Although BMP and GIF file formats contain graphics, the file layouts differ.

**Is a file extension the same as a file format?** No. Although a file extension is a good indicator of a file's format, it does not really define the format. You could use the Rename command to change a QuickTime movie called *Balloons.mov* to *Balloons.docx*. Despite the .docx extension, the file is still in QuickTime format because the data elements in the file are arranged in a specific configuration unique to QuickTime.

**What should I know about file formats?** Each software application works with specific file formats. When you use the Open dialog box, most applications automatically comb through your files to display a list of files that are stored in file formats they can use.

Some operating systems also do a fairly good job of shielding users from the intricacies of file formats. For example, Windows uses a file association list to link file formats with corresponding application software so that when you double-click a file name, your computer automatically opens a software application that works with the correct file format.

With all this help from the operating system and your application software, it might seem that knowing about file formats is unimportant. However, understanding file formats is useful for accomplishing tasks such as those listed in Figure 4-28.

**FIGURE 4-28**

Understanding file formats helps you perform the following tasks:

- Figure out the correct format for e-mail attachments that you send to friends or colleagues.
- Find the right player software for music and media files that you download from the Web.
- Discover how to work with a file that doesn't seem to open.
- Convert files from one format to another.

**Which file formats am I most likely to encounter?** A software program typically consists of at least one executable file with an .exe file extension. It might also include a number of support programs with extensions such as .dll, .vbx, and .ocx. Configuration and startup files usually have .bat, .sys, .ini, and .bin extensions. In addition, you'll find files with .hlp and .tmp extensions. Files with .hlp extensions hold the information for a program's Help utility.

Files with .tmp extensions are temporary files. When you open a data file with software applications, such as word processors, spreadsheets, and graphics tools, your operating system makes a copy of the original file and stores this copy on disk as a temporary file. It is this temporary file that you work with as you view and revise a file.

To the uninitiated, the file extensions associated with programs and the operating system might seem odd. Nevertheless, executable and support files—even so-called temporary files—are crucial for the correct operation of your computer system. You should not manually delete them. The table in Figure 4-29 lists the file extensions typically associated with the Windows operating system and executable files.

**FIGURE 4-29**

Executable File Extensions

| Type of File | Description | Extension |
|---|---|---|
| Batch file | A sequence of operating system commands executed automatically when the computer boots | .bat |
| Configuration file | Information about programs the computer uses to allocate the resources necessary to run them | .cfg  .sys  .mif<br>.bin  .ini |
| Help | The information displayed by on-screen Help | .hlp |
| Temporary file | A sort of scratch pad that contains data while a file is open, but is discarded when you close the file | .tmp |
| Support program | Program instructions executed along with the main .exe file for a program | .ocx  .vbx<br>.vbs  .dll |
| Program | The main executable files for a computer program | .exe  .com |

The list of data file formats is long, but becoming familiar with the most popular formats (shown in Figure 4-30) and the type of data they contain is useful, whether you are using a PC or Mac.

**FIGURE 4-30**

Data File Extensions

| Type of File | Extensions |
|---|---|
| Text | .txt  .dat  .rtf  .doc (Microsoft Word 2003)  .docx (Word 2007 and 2010)  .odt (OpenDocument text)  .wpd (WordPerfect)  .pages (iWork) |
| Sound | .wav  .mid  .mp3  .m4p  .aac  .au  .ra (RealAudio) |
| Graphics | .bmp  .tif  .wmf  .gif  .jpg  .png  .eps  .ai (Adobe Illustrator) |
| Animation/video | .flc  .swf  .avi  .mpg  .mp4  .mov (QuickTime)  .rm (RealMedia)  .wmv (Windows Media Player) |
| Web pages | .htm  .html  .asp  .vrml  .php |
| Spreadsheets | .xls (Microsoft Excel 2003)  .xlsx (Excel 2007 and 2010)  .ods (OpenDocument spreadsheet)  .numbers (iWork) |
| Database | .accdb (Microsoft Access)  .odb (OpenOffice.org Base) |
| Miscellaneous | .pdf (Adobe Acrobat)  .pptx (Microsoft PowerPoint 2007 and 2010)  .qxp (QuarkXPress)  .odp (OpenDocument presentations)  .zip (WinZip)  .pub (Microsoft Publisher) |

**How do I know which files a program will open?** A software application can open files that exist in its **native file format**, plus several additional file formats. For example, Microsoft Word opens files in its native DOC (.doc or .docx) format, plus files in formats such as HTML (.htm or .html), Text (.txt), and Rich Text Format (.rtf). Within the Windows environment, you can discover which formats a particular software program can open by looking at the list of file types in the Open dialog box, as shown in Figure 4-31.

**FIGURE 4-31**

An application's Open dialog box usually displays a list of file formats the program can open. You can also look for an Import option on the File menu.

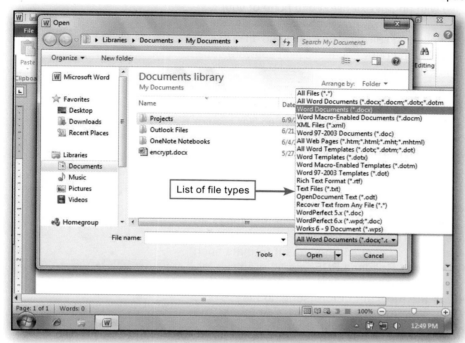

**Why can't I open some files?** Suppose you receive an e-mail attachment called *Cool.tif.* "Aha!," you say to yourself, "My Photoshop software ought to open that file." You try—several times—but all you get is an error message. When a file doesn't open, one of three things probably went wrong:

- The file might have been damaged—a techie would call it corrupted—by a transmission or disk error. Although you might be able to use file recovery software to repair the damage, it is usually easier to obtain an undamaged copy of the file from its original source.

- Someone might have inadvertently changed the file extension. While renaming the *Cool* file, perhaps the original .bmp extension was changed to .tif. If you have a little time, you can change the file extension and try to open the file. If a file contains a graphic, chances are that it should have the extension for one of the popular graphics formats, such as .bmp, .gif, .jpg, .tif, or .png. Otherwise, you should contact the source of the file to get accurate information about its real format.

- Some file formats exist in several variations, and your software might not have the capability to open a particular variation of the format. You might be able to open the file if you use different application software. For example, Photoshop might not be able to open a particular file with a .tif file extension, but Corel PaintShop Photo Pro might open it.

**What if all my software fails to open a particular file format?**
Although a computer might be able to discover a file's format, it might not necessarily know how to work with it. Just as you might be able to identify a helicopter, you can't necessarily fly it without some instructions. Your computer also requires a set of instructions to use most file formats. These instructions are provided by software. To use a particular file format, you must make sure your computer has the corresponding software.

Suppose you download a file with an .rm extension and none of your current software works with this file format. Several Web sites provide lists of file extensions and their corresponding software. By looking up a file extension in one of these lists, you can find out what application software you'll need to find, download, and install.

Many files downloaded from the Web require special player or reader software. For example, PDF text files require software called Adobe Reader, Flash video files require the Adobe Flash Player, and RM video files require the RealPlayer software. Typically, you can follow a link from the Web page that supplied your file download to find a site from which you can download the necessary player or reader software.

**How do I know what kinds of file formats I can send to other people?** Unless you know what application software is installed on your friends' computers, you won't know for certain whether they can open a particular file you've sent. There's a good chance, however, that your friends can open files saved in common document formats such as Microsoft Word's DOC or Adobe Reader's PDF format; graphics formats such as PNG, TIFF, or JPEG; and music formats such as MP3 and WAV. You should check with the recipient before sending files in less common, proprietary formats, such as Adobe Illustrator's AI format and QuarkXPress's QXP format.

**Is it possible to convert a file from one format to another?**
Perhaps you created a Word document on your PC, but you need to convert it into a format that's usable by your colleague who is using OpenOffice Writer. Or suppose you want to convert a Word document into HTML format so that you can post it on the Web. You might also want to convert a BMP graphic into GIF format so that you can include it on a Web page.

The easiest way to convert a file from one format to another is to find application software that works with both file formats. Open the file using that software, and then use the Export option, or the Save As dialog box, to select a new file format, assign the file a new name, and save it (Figure 4-32).

**FIGURE 4-32**

An easy way to convert a file from one format to another is to open it with an application that supports both file formats, and then use the Save As dialog box to select an alternative file format. ▶ Discover the native file formats for Adobe Reader and Windows Paint. Your digital textbook also shows you how to adjust the Windows setting for showing or hiding file extensions.

**Will a converted document be identical to the original?** Many file formats convert easily to another format, and the resulting file is virtually indistinguishable from the original. Some conversions, however, do not retain all the characteristics of the original file. When you convert a DOC file into HTML format, for example, the HTML page does not contain any of the headers, footers, superscripts, page numbers, special characters, or page breaks that existed in the original DOC file.

When you need a conversion routine for an obscure file format, or if you need to make conversions between many different file formats, consider specialized conversion software, available through commercial or shareware outlets.

## QuickCheck

1. .bmp, .docx, .exe, and .mov are examples of file _____ .

2. When using Windows, you cannot use a(n) _____ word, such as Aux, as a file name.

3. A disk _____ is a section of a hard disk drive that is treated as a separate storage unit.

4. A software application automatically stores files in its _____ file format unless you specify otherwise.

5. When you convert a DOC file into HTML format, the resulting file is virtually indistinguishable from the original. True or false? _____

 CHECK ANSWERS

# File Management

**FILE MANAGEMENT ENCOMPASSES** any procedure that helps you organize your computer-based files so that you can find and use them more efficiently. Depending on your computer's operating system, you can organize and manipulate files from within an application program or by using a special file management utility provided by the operating system. Section D offers an overview of application-based and operating system-based file management.

## APPLICATION-BASED FILE MANAGEMENT

**How does a software application help me manage files?** Applications, such as word processing software or graphics software, typically provide a way to open files and save them in a specific folder on a designated storage device. An application might also have additional file management capabilities, such as deleting, copying, and renaming files. Take a look at an example of the file management capabilities in a typical Windows application—Microsoft Word.

Suppose you want to write a letter about the rising tide of graffiti in your neighborhood. You open your word processing software and start typing. As you type, the document is held in RAM. When you are ready to save the document, click the File button and then select the Save As option. The Save As dialog box opens and allows you to specify a name for the file and its location on one of your computer's storage devices.

Some applications also allow you to add tags for a file. A **file tag** in the context of Windows is a piece of information that describes a file. Tags are particularly handy for files that contain photos because you can describe the location, note camera settings, and name people pictured in the shot. Figure 4-33 illustrates the process of saving a file and adding tags.

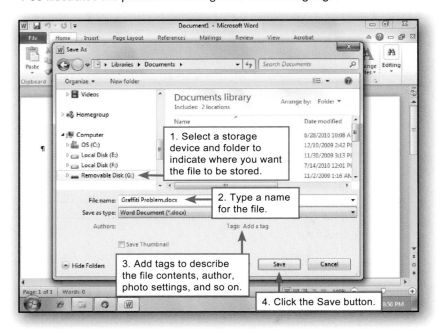

**FIGURE 4-33**

The Save As dialog box is used to name a file and specify its storage location. Here a file called Graffiti Problem is being saved on a USB flash drive. ▶ Learn more about the Save As dialog box and sort out the differences between it and the Save option.

## What's the difference between the Save option and the Save As option?
Most Windows applications provide a curious set of options on the File menu. In addition to the Save As option, the menu contains a Save option. The difference between the two options is subtle, but useful. The Save As option allows you to select a name and storage device for a file, whereas the Save option simply saves the latest version of a file under its current name and at its current location.

A potentially confusing situation occurs when you try to use the Save option for a file that doesn't yet have a name. Because you can't save a file without a name, your application displays the Save As dialog box, even though you selected the Save option. The flowchart in Figure 4-34 can help you decide whether to use the Save or Save As command.

## What other options are available in the Save As dialog box?
When you use application software, activities such as opening files and saving files require the software to interact with the operating system's file management system. When you create a file, the operating system needs to know its name. When you look for a file, the application software has to check with the operating system to get a list of available files.

You might have noticed that the Open and Save dialog boxes look the same for most of the applications that you use. That is because today's application software typically calls on the operating system to provide these dialog boxes. So, when you use Audacity, Adobe Illustrator, or other third-party Windows software, the Open and Save dialog boxes are essentially the same. Figure 4-35 illustrates some of the file management tasks you can accomplish while using the Save As dialog box.

FIGURE 4-34

Should I use the Save or Save As command?

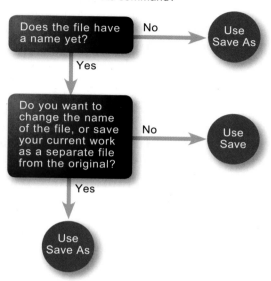

FIGURE 4-35

The Save As command of most Windows applications uses a standard dialog box provided by the operating system, so you can carry out a wide variety of file and folder tasks such as creating, renaming, and deleting files.

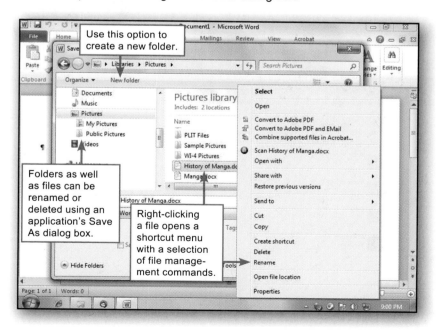

4

## FILE MANAGEMENT UTILITIES

**How does the operating system help me manage files?** Although most application software gives you access to commands you can use to save, open, rename, and delete individual files, you might want to work with groups of files or perform other file operations that are inconvenient within the Open or Save dialog boxes.

Most operating systems provide a **file management utility** that give you the big picture of the files you have stored on your disks and help you work with them. For example, Mac OS X provides a file management utility called Finder. Windows 7 provides a file management utility called Windows Explorer that can be accessed from the folder icon on the taskbar or from the first six buttons on the Start menu. Utilities such as these help you view a list of files, find files, move files from one place to another, make copies of files, delete files, discover file properties, and rename files (Figure 4-36).

**TERMINOLOGY NOTE**

Utilities called desktop search tools help you also find and access information stored in e-mails, Web pages, and contact lists in addition to data and program files. Desktop search tools are offered by third-party vendors such as Google and Yahoo!. They are also being added to operating system utilities.

**FIGURE 4-36**

Windows Explorer can be tailored to show files as lists (top), icons (middle), or tiles (bottom).
▶ The tour for this figure in your digital textbook shows you how to start Windows Explorer and use it to view files.

# FILE MANAGEMENT METAPHORS

**How can a file management utility help me visualize my computer's file storage?** File management utilities often use some sort of storage metaphor to help you visualize and mentally organize the files on your disks and other storage devices. These metaphors are also called **logical storage models** because they are supposed to help you form a mental (logical) picture of the way in which your files are stored.

**What storage metaphors are typically used for personal computers?** After hearing so much about files and folders, you might have guessed that the filing cabinet is a popular metaphor for computer storage. In this metaphor, each storage device corresponds to one of the drawers in a filing cabinet. The drawers hold folders and the folders hold files.

Another storage metaphor is based on a hierarchical diagram that is sometimes referred to as a tree structure. In this metaphor, a tree represents a storage device. The trunk of the tree corresponds to the root directory. The branches of the tree represent folders. These branches can split into small branches representing folders within folders. The leaves at the end of a branch represent the files in a particular folder. Figure 4-37 illustrates the tree lying on its side so that you can see the relationship to the metaphor shown in Figure 4-38.

The tree structure metaphor offers a useful mental image of the way in which files and folders are organized. It is not, however, particularly practical as a user interface. Imagine the complexity of the tree diagram from Figure 4-37 if it were expanded to depict branches for hundreds of folders and leaves for thousands of files.

For practicality, storage metaphors are translated into more mundane screen displays. Figure 4-38 shows how Microsoft programmers combined the filing cabinet metaphor to depict a tree structure in the Windows Explorer file management utility.

**FIGURE 4-37**

You can visualize the directory of a disk as a tree on its side. The trunk corresponds to the root directory, the branches to folders, and the leaves to files.

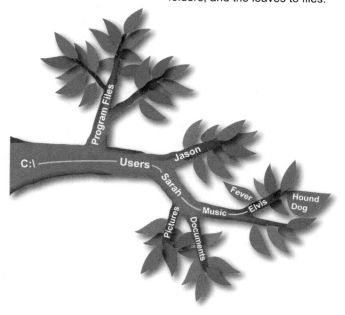

**FIGURE 4-38**

Windows Explorer borrows folders from the filing cabinet metaphor and places them in a hierarchical structure similar to a tree on its side.

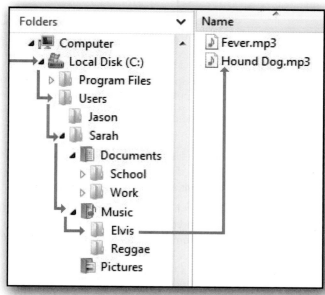

## WINDOWS EXPLORER

**How do I use a file management utility?** As an example of a file management utility, take a closer look at **Windows Explorer**, a utility program bundled with the Windows operating system and designed to help you organize and manipulate the files stored on your computer.

The Windows Explorer window is divided into several window panes. The pane on the left side of the window lists each of the storage devices connected to your computer, plus several important system objects, such as Desktop and Computer.

An icon for a storage device or other system object can be expanded by clicking its corresponding ▷ symbol. Expanding an icon displays the next level of the storage hierarchy—usually a collection of folders.

A device icon or folder can be opened by clicking directly on the icon rather than on the ▷ symbol. Once an icon is opened, its contents appear in the pane on the right side of the Windows Explorer window. Figure 4-39 illustrates how to manipulate the directory display.

**FIGURE 4-39**

Windows Explorer makes it easy to drill down through the levels of the directory hierarchy to locate a folder or file. ▶ Learn how to navigate through the hierarchy of folders by watching the tour for this figure in your digital textbook.

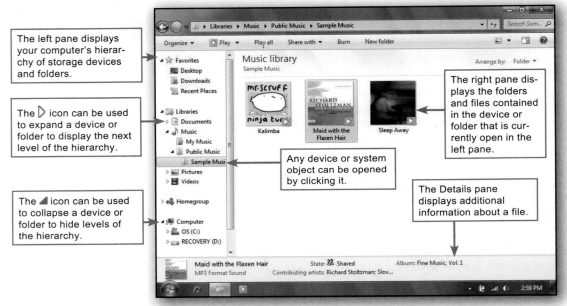

The left pane displays your computer's hierarchy of storage devices and folders.

The ▷ icon can be used to expand a device or folder to display the next level of the hierarchy.

The ◢ icon can be used to collapse a device or folder to hide levels of the hierarchy.

The right pane displays the folders and files contained in the device or folder that is currently open in the left pane.

Any device or system object can be opened by clicking it.

The Details pane displays additional information about a file.

**What can I do with the folders and files that are listed in Windows Explorer?** In addition to locating files and folders, Windows Explorer helps you manipulate files and folders in the following ways:

● Rename. You might want to change the name of a file or folder to better describe its contents.

● Copy. You can copy a file from one device to another—for example, from a USB drive to the hard disk drive. You can also make a copy of a document so that you can revise the copy and leave the original intact.

● Move. You can move a file from one folder to another or from one storage device to another. When you move a file, it is erased from its original location, so make sure you remember the new location of the file. You can also move an entire folder and its contents from one storage device to another storage device, or move it to a different folder.

● Delete. You can delete a file when you no longer need it. You can also delete a folder. Be careful when you delete a folder because most file management utilities also delete all the files within a folder.

**Can I work with more than one file or folder at a time?** To work with a group of files or folders, you must first select them. You can accomplish this task in several ways. You can hold down the Ctrl key as you click each item. This method works well if you are selecting files or folders that are not listed consecutively.

As an alternative, you can hold down the Shift key while you click the first item and the last item you want to select. By using the Shift key method, you select the two items that you clicked and all the items in between. Windows Explorer displays all the items you selected by highlighting them. After a group of items is highlighted, you can use the same copy, move, or delete procedure that you would use for a single item.

**What are personal folders?** Windows offers a set of preconfigured personal folders, such as My Documents and My Music, for storing your personal data files. Windows also supplies preconfigured Public folders, such as Public Documents and Public Pictures, that can be used to store files you want to share with other network users (Figure 4-40).

**What is a library?** In addition to folders, Windows 7 offers libraries that are handy for organizing and accessing files that you use for projects. A **library** is similar to a folder only in the sense that it can be used to group similar files; however, a library doesn't actually store files. Instead, it contains a set of links to files that are stored on various devices and in various folders.

Libraries and personal folders have similar names, which can be a bit confusing. Personal folders are labeled with "My" as in My Documents. The name of the corresponding library is simply Documents.

To understand how you might use libraries, think about a collection of music files. Some files might be stored on your hard disk in the My Music folder. Other music might be stored on an external hard drive in a folder called Jazz. Your Music library can contain links to the music files in both folders so that you can access them all from the same list (Figure 4-41).

**FIGURE 4-40**

Windows supplies a set of preconfigured personal folders and a corresponding set of Public folders.

- ▲ Libraries
  - ▲ Documents
    - ▷ My Documents
    - ▷ Public Documents
  - ▲ Music
    - ▷ My Music
    - ▷ Public Music
  - ▲ Pictures
    - ▷ My Pictures
    - ▷ Public Pictures
  - ▲ Videos
    - ▷ My Videos
    - ▷ Public Videos

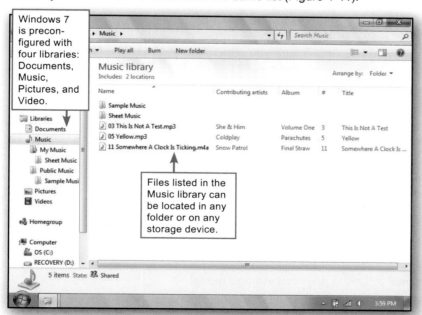

Windows 7 is preconfigured with four libraries: Documents, Music, Pictures, and Video.

Files listed in the Music library can be located in any folder or on any storage device.

**FIGURE 4-41**

A library is not a "real" location; it is more like an index in a book because it points to the location of a file.

▶ Find out how to use libraries to organize files for your projects.

## FILE MANAGEMENT TIPS

A file management utility provides tools and procedures to help you keep track of your program and data files, but these tools are most useful when you have a logical plan for organizing your files and when you follow some basic file management guidelines. Consider the following tips for managing files on your own computer. When working with files on lab computers, follow the guidelines from your instructor or lab manager.

- Use descriptive names. Give your files and folders descriptive names, and avoid using cryptic abbreviations.

- Maintain file extensions. When renaming a file, keep the original file extension so that you can easily open it with the correct application software.

- Group similar files. Separate files into folders based on subject matter. For example, store your creative writing assignments in one folder and your MP3 music files in another folder.

- Organize your folders from the top down. When devising a hierarchy of folders, consider how you want to access files and back them up. For example, it is easy to specify one folder and its subfolders for a backup. If your important data is scattered in a variety of folders, however, making backups is more time consuming.

- Consider using default folders. You should use personal folders, such as My Documents and My Music, as your main data folders. Add subfolders to these personal folders as necessary to organize your files.

- Use Public folders for files you want to share. Use the Public folders for files that you want to share with other network users.

- Do not mix data files and program files. Do not store data files in the folders that hold your software—on Windows systems, most software is stored in subfolders of the *Program Files* folder.

- Don't store files in the root directory. Although it is acceptable to create folders in the root directory, it is not a good practice to store programs or data files in the root directory of your computer's hard disk.

- Access files from the hard disk. For best performance, copy files from USB drives or CDs to your computer's hard disk before accessing them.

- Follow copyright rules. When copying files, make sure you adhere to copyright and license restrictions.

- Delete or archive files you no longer need. Deleting unneeded files and folders helps keep your list of files from growing to an unmanageable size.

- Be aware of storage locations. When you save files, make sure the drive letter and folder name specify the correct storage location.

- Back up! Back up your folders regularly.

## PHYSICAL FILE STORAGE

Is data stored in specific places on a disk? So far, you've seen how an operating system such as Windows can help you visualize computer storage as files and folders. This logical storage model, however, has little to do with what actually happens on your disk. The structure of files and folders you see in Windows Explorer is called a logical model because it is supposed to help you create a mental picture. A **physical storage model** describes what actually happens on the disks and in the circuits. As you will see, the physical model is quite different from the logical model.

Before a computer can store a file on a disk, CD, DVD, or BD, the storage medium must be formatted. The **formatting** process creates the equivalent of electronic storage bins by dividing a disk into **tracks** and then further dividing each track into **sectors**. Tracks and sectors are numbered to provide addresses for each data storage bin. The numbering scheme depends on the storage device and the operating system. On hard disks, tracks are arranged as concentric circles; on CDs, DVDs, and BDs, one or more tracks spiral out from the center of the disk (Figure 4-42).

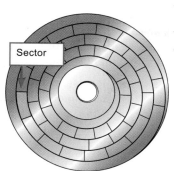

**How does a disk get formatted?** Today, most hard disks are preformatted at the factory. CDs, DVDs, and BDs are formatted by the utilities that you use when you copy data files to them. Before you write data to a CD, DVD, or BD, you usually have the option of formatting it for mastering or for packet writing (Figure 4-43).

**Disc mastering** is the process of creating a CD, DVD, or BD by selecting all the files and then copying them in a single session. The process can take some time—especially when burning a full DVD or BD. Mastered discs are compatible with the largest number of computer optical drives and standalone players. Mastering also works well if you want to burn several copies of a disc.

**Packet writing** is a recording technology that lets you record in multiple sessions. For example, you can copy a few files to a CD during one session, and then at a later date record additional files to the same CD. In Windows terminology, CDs, DVDs, and BDs formatted for packet writing are referred to as Live File System discs.

Packet writing is faster and more flexible than mastering, but discs created with packet writing might not work on all computers. A process called closing helps make the discs more compatible; but once a disc is closed, no more data can be added to it.

**How does the operating system keep track of a file's location?** The operating system uses a **file system** to keep track of the names and locations of files that reside on a storage medium, such as a hard disk. Different operating systems use different file systems. For example, Mac OS X uses the Macintosh Hierarchical File System Plus (HFS+). Ext3fs (Third Extended File System) is the native file system for Linux. Microsoft Windows 7, NT, 2000, XP, and Vista use a file system called **NTFS** (New Technology File System).

To speed up the process of storing and retrieving data, a disk drive usually works with a group of sectors called a **cluster** or a block. The number of sectors that form a cluster varies, depending on the capacity of the disk and the way the operating system works with files. A file system's primary task is to maintain a list of clusters and keep track of which are empty and which hold data. This information is stored in a special index file. If your computer uses NTFS, it is called the **Master File Table** (MFT).

**FIGURE 4-43**

CDs and DVDs can be created using mastering or packet-writing techniques. Mastering creates discs that can be used more reliably on a wide variety of computers and standalone players. Packet writing is more flexible for discs that you plan to use only on your own computer.

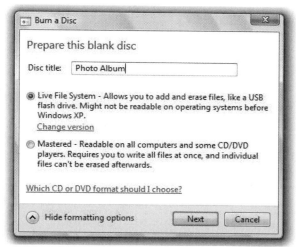

**4**

Each of your disks contains its own index file so that information about its contents is always available when the disk is in use. Unfortunately, storing this crucial file on disk also presents a risk because if the index file is damaged by a hard disk head crash or corrupted by a virus, you'll generally lose access to all the data stored on the disk. Index files become damaged all too frequently, so it is important to back up your data.

When you save a file, your PC's operating system looks at the index file to see which clusters are empty. It selects one of these empty clusters, records the file data there, and then revises the index file to include the new file name and its location.

A file that does not fit into a single cluster spills over into the next contiguous (meaning adjacent) cluster, unless that cluster already contains data. When contiguous clusters are not available, the operating system stores parts of a file in noncontiguous (nonadjacent) clusters. Figure 4-44 helps you visualize how an index file, such as the MFT, keeps track of file names and locations.

**FIGURE 4-44**

Each colored cluster on the disk contains part of a file. Bio.txt is stored in contiguous clusters. Jordan.wks is stored in noncontiguous clusters. A computer locates and displays the Jordan file by looking for its name in the Master File Table.

### Master File Table

| File | Cluster | Comment |
|------|---------|---------|
| MFT | 1 | Reserved for MFT files |
| DISK USE | 2 | Part of MFT that contains list of empty sectors |
| Bio.txt | 3, 4 | Bio.txt file stored in clusters 3 and 4 |
| Jordan.wks | 7, 8, 10 | Jordan.wks file stored noncontiguously in clusters 7, 8, and 10 |
| Pick.bmp | 9 | Pick.bmp file stored in cluster 9 |

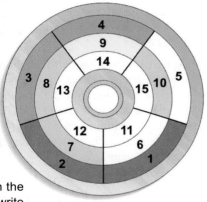

When you want to retrieve a file, the operating system looks through the index for the file name and its location. It moves the disk drive's read-write head to the first cluster that contains the file data. Using additional data from the index file, the operating system can move the read-write heads to each of the clusters containing the remaining parts of the file.

**What happens when a file is deleted?** When you click a file's icon and then select the Delete option, you might have visions of the read-write head somehow scrubbing out the clusters that contain data. That doesn't happen. Instead, the operating system simply changes the status of the file's clusters to "empty" and removes the file name from the index file. The file name no longer appears in a directory listing, but the file's data remains in the clusters until a new file is stored there.

You might think that this data is as good as erased, but it is possible to purchase utilities that recover a lot of this supposedly deleted data. Law enforcement agents, for example, use these utilities to gather evidence from deleted files on the computer disks of suspected criminals.

To delete data from a disk in such a way that no one can ever read it, you can use special **file shredder software** that overwrites supposedly empty sectors with random 1s and 0s. You might find this software handy if you plan to donate your computer to a charitable organization, and you want to make sure your personal data no longer remains on the hard disk.

**Can deleted files be undeleted?** The Windows Recycle Bin and similar utilities in other operating systems are designed to protect you from accidentally deleting hard disk files you actually need. Instead of marking a file's clusters as available, the operating system moves the file to the Recycle Bin folder. The deleted file still takes up space on the disk, but does not appear in the usual directory listing.

Files in the Recycle Bin folder can be undeleted so that they again appear in the regular directory. The Recycle Bin can be emptied to permanently delete any files it contains.

**How does a disk become fragmented?** As a computer writes files on a disk, parts of files tend to become scattered all over the disk. These **fragmented files** are stored in noncontiguous clusters. Drive performance generally declines as the read-write heads move back and forth to locate the clusters containing the parts of a file. To regain peak performance, you can use a **defragmentation utility**, such as Windows Disk Defragmenter, to rearrange the files on a disk so that they are stored in contiguous clusters (Figure 4-45).

**FIGURE 4-45**

Defragmenting a disk helps your computer operate more efficiently. Consider using a defragmentation utility at least once a month to keep your computer running in top form. ▶ Your digital textbook shows you how to defragment your computer's hard disk and how to find out how much space is available for storing files.

**4**

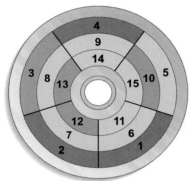

**Fragmented disk**

On the fragmented disk (left), the purple, orange, and blue files are stored in noncontiguous clusters.

When the disk is defragmented (right), the sectors of data for each file are moved to contiguous clusters.

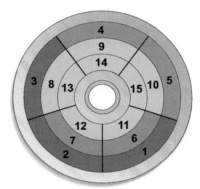

**Defragmented disk**

# QuickCheck                                                    SECTION D

1. Applications use standard Open and Save [_____] boxes provided by the operating system.

2. [_____] file storage models, such as a filing cabinet or tree metaphor, help you visualize the organization of your computer files.

3. Windows 7 offers you a preconfigured Documents [_____] that's designed to hold links to document files stored in various folders.

4. A hard disk stores data in concentric circles called [_____], which are divided into wedge-shaped [_____].

5. NTFS, HFS+, and MFT pertain to [_____] file storage models.

 CHECK ANSWERS

# Backup Security

**COMPUTER EXPERTS UNIVERSALLY RECOM-MEND** that you back up your data. It sounds pretty basic, right? Unfortunately, this advice tells you what to do, not how to do it. It fails to address some key questions, such as: Do I need special backup equipment and software? How often should I make a backup? How many of my files should I back up? What should I do with the backups? In this section, you'll find the answers to your questions about backing up data that's stored on a personal computer. You'll begin by looking at backup basics, and then review your equipment and software options. Along the way, you should pick up lots of practical tips to keep your data safe.

## BACKUP BASICS

**Why do I need to make backups?** Have you ever mistakenly copied an old version of a document over a new version? Has your computer's hard disk drive gone on the fritz? Did a virus wipe out your files? Has lightning fried your computer system? These kinds of data disasters are not rare; they can happen to everyone. You can't always prevent them, so you should have a **backup** that stores the files needed to recover data that's been wiped out by operator error, viruses, or hardware failures.

**What's the best backup plan?** A good backup plan allows you to restore your computing environment to its pre-disaster state with a minimum of fuss. Unfortunately, no single backup plan fits everyone's computing style or budget. You must devise your own backup plan that's tailored to your particular computing needs.

The list in Figure 4-46 outlines factors you should consider as you formulate your own backup plan.

**FIGURE 4-46**

Guidelines for Formulating a Backup Plan

- Decide how much of your data you want, need, and can afford to back up.
- Create a realistic schedule for making backups.
- Make sure you have a way to avoid backing up files that contain viruses.
- Find out what kind of boot disks you might need to get your computer up and running after a hard disk failure or boot sector virus attack.
- Make sure you test your restore procedure so that you can successfully retrieve the data you've backed up.
- Find a safe place to keep your backups.
- Decide what kind of storage device you'll use to make backups.
- Select software to handle backup needs.

**How often should I back up my data?** Your backup schedule depends on how much data you can afford to lose. If you're working on an important project, you might want to back up the project files several times a day. Under normal use, however, most people schedule a once-a-week backup. If you work with a To Do list, use it to remind yourself when to make a backup or verify that your automated backup has been created.

**How do I avoid backing up files that contain viruses?** Viruses can damage files to the point that your computer can't access any data on its hard disk. It is really frustrating when you restore data from a backup only to discover that the restored files contain the same virus that wiped out your original data. If your antivirus software is not set to constantly scan for viruses on your computer system, you should run an up-to-date virus check as the first step in your backup routine.

**How do I choose a backup device?** The backup device you select depends on the value of your data, your current equipment, and your budget. Many computer owners use what they have—a writable CD, DVD, or USB flash drive, but an investment in an external USB hard drive (Figure 4-47) offers the best solution for today's computer owners. If you have several backup options available, use the table in Figure 4-48 to evaluate the strengths and weaknesses of each one.

**FIGURE 4-47**

An external hard disk drive typically connects to your computer's USB port. Handy for copying data files or a full system backup, these drives can easily be disconnected when not in use and stored in a safe place.

**FIGURE 4-48**

Storage Capacities and Costs of Backup Media

4

| | Device Cost (US$) | Media Cost (US$) | Capacity | Comments |
|---|---|---|---|---|
| External hard disk | $100 (average) | N/A | 1 TB (average) | Fast, inexpensive, and convenient; but if it is damaged, all the backups it holds are lost |
| Removable hard disk | $130 (average) | $40 | 80 GB (average) | Fast, limited capacity, but disks can be removed and locked in a secure location; less dependable than a standard external or internal hard drive, but more expensive |
| External solid state drive | $120–$500 | N/A | 32–256 GB | Fast and quiet, but higher cost per GB than other media |
| Network server | $0–Depends on provider | N/A | Depends on space allocated to user | Fast and convenient, but make sure that the server is regularly backed up |
| Writable CD | $40 (average) | 15¢ | 700 MB | Limited capacity and slow, CD-RWs can be reused; CD-Rs can't be reused, long shelf life |
| Writable BD | $250 (average) | $10 | 25 GB | Good capacity, reusable, expensive very slow |
| Writable DVD | $50 (average) | 25¢ | 4.7–9.4 GB | Moderate capacity, reasonable media cost |
| USB flash drive | $15–$500 | N/A | 2–256 GB | Convenient and durable, but high-capacity models are expensive |
| Web site | N/A | $50 per year | Depends on provider | Transfer rate depends on your Internet connection; security and privacy of your data might be a concern |

**Where should I keep my backups?** If your backups are on an external hard disk or removable media, keep your backups in a safe place. Don't keep them at your computer desk because a fire or flood that damages your computer could also wipe out your backups. In addition, a thief who steals your computer might also scoop up nearby equipment and media. Storing your backups at a different location is the best idea. If offsite storage isn't practical, at least move them to a room apart from your computer.

Instead of backing up to local media, such as DVDs, flash drives, or external hard disk drives, you might consider storing your backup on a Web server. Internet sites that offer storage space for backup are called online, remote, or managed backup services. The cost of these services typically depends on the amount of storage space that's allocated to you.

Before depending on remote backups, however, be aware that the speed for backing up and restoring your data is only as fast as your Internet connection. Also, remote data is more prone to snooping by employees, hackers, and overzealous government agents; you might want to encrypt your remote backup data, but make sure you don't lose your encryption key or your backup data will be useless.

**How can I be sure that my backup works?** If your computer's hard disk crashes, you do not want to discover that your backups are blank! To prevent such a disastrous situation, it is important to enable your backup software's option to *read after write* or the option to *compare*. These options force the software to check the data in each sector as it is written to make sure it is copied without error. You should also test your backup by trying to restore one file. Restore the test file to a different drive or folder to avoid overwriting the original file.

## FILE COPIES AND SYNCHRONIZATION

**What's the easiest way to back up my important data?** The most important files on your computer contain the documents, images, and other data that you've created. These files are unique and might be difficult to reproduce. An easy way to back up your important data is simply by copying selected files to a USB flash drive or to writable CDs, DVDs, or BDs. To copy important files manually, you can use the Copy and Paste commands supplied by your computer's file management software.

Manually copying and pasting requires you to initiate the process by selecting the files you want to copy and then specifying a destination device. If you don't want to bother with manual copies, you can use file synchronization software to automatically make copies of files in specified folders. **File synchronization** (sometimes referred to as mirroring) ensures that files in two or more locations contain the same data.

Synchronization software originated with PDAs as a way to synchronize address book and scheduling data between a PDA and a personal computer. Synchronization software designed for file backup monitors the files on your hard disk, watches for changes, and automatically makes the same changes to files on your designated backup device—preferably an external hard drive.

**Which data files should I back up?** If your strategy is to back up important data files, the procedure can be simplified if you've stored all these files in one folder and its subfolders. For example, Windows users might store their data files in the preconfigured folders for their user accounts. Folders such as My Documents, My Music, and My Pictures are

**INFOWEBLINKS**

Interested in using a Web site for your backup? You can evaluate several of these sites by following the links at the **Web-based Backup InfoWeb**.

 CLICK TO CONNECT
www.infoweblinks.com/np2012/ch04

**INFOWEBLINKS**

For more detailed information on backup techniques, such as backing up the Registry, take a look at the **Backup Techniques InfoWeb**.

 CLICK TO CONNECT
www.infoweblinks.com/np2012/ch04

all stored as subfolders of your user folder. With your data files organized under the umbrella of a single folder, you are less likely to omit an important file when you make backups.

Some applications, such as financial software, create files and update them without your direct intervention. If you have the option during setup, make sure these files are stored in one of your personal folders. Otherwise, you must discover the location of the files and make sure they are backed up with the rest of your data.

In addition to data files you create, a few other types of data files might be important to you. Consider making backups of the files listed in Figure 4-49.

FIGURE 4-49

Back up these files in addition to your documents, graphics, and music files.

- **Internet connection information.** Your ISP's phone number and IP address, your user ID, and your password are often stored in an encrypted file somewhere in the Windows\System folder. Your ISP can usually help you find this file.

- **E-mail folders.** If you're using POP e-mail software, your e-mail folder contains all the e-mail messages you've sent and received, but not deleted. Check the Help menu on your e-mail program to discover the location of these files.

- **E-mail address book.** Your e-mail address book might be stored separately from your e-mail messages. To find the file on a Windows computer, use the Search or Find option on the Start menu to search for "Address Book" (XP) or "Contacts" (Windows 7 and Vista).

- **Favorite URLs.** If you're attached to the URLs you've collected in your Favorites or Bookmarks list, you might want to back up the file that contains this list. To find the file, search your hard disk for "Favorites" or "Bookmarks." As an alternative method, check your browser for an option for exporting your favorite URLs.

- **Downloads.** If you paid to download software, you might want to back it up so that you don't have to pay for it again. Downloaded software usually arrives in the form of a compressed .exe file that expands into several separate files as you install it. For backup purposes, the compressed .exe file should be all you need.

- **Validation codes and other configuration information.** If you keep a running list of validation or activation codes that correspond to your software, then it is important to copy this information in case your hard disk crashes and you have to reinstall your software. Additional configuration or procedural notes can also come in handy when it is time to reload a hard disk after a crash.

**How do I restore files from my data file backups?** Restoring from a data file backup is easy. You simply copy files from your backup to your hard disk. If, for example, you inadvertently delete an important file and discover that you have done so only after you've cleaned out your computer's Recycle Bin, then you can retrieve the file from your backup.

If your hard drive crashes and you have to install a new one, the process of retrieving your files is a bit more complex. First, you have to reload the operating system on your hard disk. That task is explained a little later in this section. Then you have to reinstall all of your software and device drivers. Make sure you have all your registration keys handy before you start reinstalling software. As the final step, you can copy your data files back to the hard disk. To avoid a lengthy manual rebuild of your hard disk, you might consider system backups and recovery disks.

**Are file backups sufficient protection against data disasters?** Your computer system contains programs in addition to your data files. Files also store your preferences, passwords, system settings, and a host of other settings for your desktop, network, and application software. Your computer setup is unique and you can't capture it by simply backing up your data files. If you want to be able to restore your computer to its current state, you need to use system synchronization software, backup software, imaging software, or virtual machine technology.

## SYSTEM SYNCHRONIZATION

**How does system synchronization differ from file synchronization?** The principle is the same, but the scope is different. Whereas file synchronization is typically used to back up selected data files, system synchronization is used to back up all the data files, program files, and system software on your computer.

**How does system synchronization software work?** A program called Time Machine supplied with Mac OS X is a good example of system synchronization software. It works by first making a **full system backup** that includes every file from the computer's primary storage device. Files are stored in non-compressed format, so the backup storage device must have capacity to handle all the space used on the primary storage device. For best results, use an external USB hard disk drive that's at least the same capacity as your computer's internal hard disk.

Every hour, Time Machine checks the files on your computer's primary storage device and synchronizes any files that have been changed. This procedure ensures that your backup is never more than an hour old. The number of backups you can retain—days', weeks', or months' worth—depends on the capacity of your external USB drive, the size of your data files, and the frequency at which you make changes.

**Can I restore individual files from these backups?** Yes. Time Machine displays a window for each hour's backup. You can go back in time to any hour or day, select a file, and restore it to your computer's primary storage device.

**What about restoring the entire computer?** Suppose your computer's hard disk fails and you have to replace it. Once you've installed a new, blank hard disk, you can insert the Mac OS setup CD and select the Time Machine option to restore the operating system, programs, preferences, and data files that existed at the time of the last Time Machine backup. Figure 4-50 explains the elements of Time Machine's interface.

**FIGURE 4-50**

Time Machine system synchronization software creates a full system backup and periodically synchronizes files to keep the backup up to date.

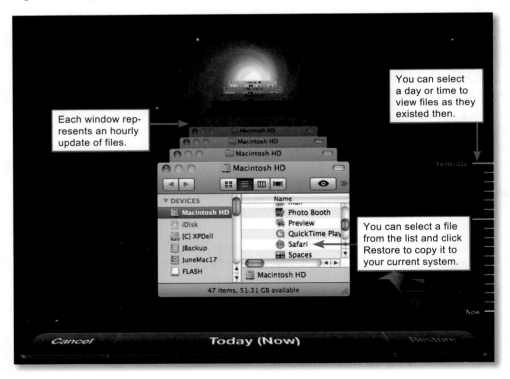

Each window represents an hourly update of files.

You can select a day or time to view files as they existed then.

You can select a file from the list and click Restore to copy it to your current system.

## FILE AND SYSTEM BACKUP

**What does backup software do?** **Backup software** is a set of utility programs designed to back up and restore some or all of the files on a computer's primary storage device. Backup software usually includes options that make it easy to schedule periodic backups, define a set of files that you want to regularly back up, and automate the restoration process.

Backup software differs from most copy and synchronization routines because it typically compresses all the files for a backup and places them in one large file. Under the direction of backup software, this file can be spread across multiple discs if necessary. The backup file is indexed so that individual files can be located, uncompressed, and restored.

Backup software is supplied with most operating systems and from third-party vendors.

**How do I use backup software?** To use backup software, you typically begin by specifying which files you want to back up, selecting the location of the backup device, and selecting the days and times for automatic backups to proceed. Because the backup process uses system resources, most people schedule backups for times when their computer is on, but when they are not typically using it (Figure 4-51).

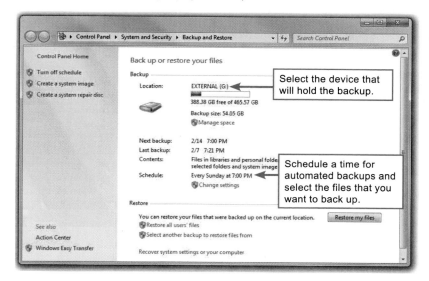

**FIGURE 4-51**

Microsoft Windows 7 includes backup software. ⊙ Discover how to use it to back up your computer's hard disk.

**What is a full backup?** When you set up your backup software, you might have a choice between full, differential, and incremental backups. A **full backup** makes a fresh copy of every file in the folders you've specified for the backup. In contrast to a full-system backup, a full backup does not necessarily contain every file on your computer. A full backup might contain only your data files, for example, if those are the files you want to regularly back up.

**What is a differential backup?** A **differential backup** makes a backup of only those files that were added or changed since your last full backup session. After making a full backup of your important files, you can make differential backups at regular intervals. If you need to restore all your files after a hard disk crash, first restore the files from your full backup, and then restore the files from your latest differential backup.

**What is an incremental backup?** An **incremental backup** makes a backup of the files that were added or changed since the last backup—not necessarily the files that changed from the last full backup, but the files that changed since any full or incremental backup.

After making a full backup of your important files, you can make your first incremental backup containing the files that changed since the full backup. When you make your second incremental backup, it will contain only the files that changed since the first incremental backup.

To restore files from an incremental backup, files from a full backup are restored first, followed by files from each incremental backup, starting with the oldest and ending with the most recent. Figure 4-52 describes the difference between differential and incremental backups.

| Full Backup on January 1: | Files Changed on January 2: | Files Changed on January 4: |
|---|---|---|
| File 1 | File 1 | File 3 |
| File 2 | File 4 | |
| File 3 | | |
| File 4 | | |
| File 5 | Incremental Backup copies only files that have changed since last backup | Incremental Backup copies only files that have changed since last backup |
| | File 1 | File 3 |
| | File 4 | |
| | Differential Backup contains any files that have changed since last full backup | Differential Backup contains any files that have changed since last full backup |
| | File 1 | File 1     File 3 |
| | File 4 | File 4 |

**FIGURE 4-52**

Suppose you have five files that you originally back up on January 1. You change two of these files on January 2. Both incremental and differential backups back up the changed files. If one additional file is changed on January 4, the incremental backup needs to only back up that one file—it is the only one that has changed since the backup on January 2. A differential backup, however, will back up three files—those that changed since the full backup.

**How many backups do I need?** Most experts recommend that you keep more than one set of backups. If you use recordable CDs or DVDs for your backups, then you simply burn a new disc each time you back up. If you are using rewritable media, such as removable hard disks or CD-RWs, then you can reuse your backups—typically by rotating three backup disks. Make sure you label each backup and note its date.

**How do I restore data from backups?** Backup software includes modules for restoring files. To restore a single file or a few files, simply start the backup software, make sure the backup device is connected, and use the Restore module to locate and retrieve the file you want. If, however, your hard disk fails, the backup process can become a bit more complex.

Whatever backup software you use, remember that it needs to be accessible when you want to restore your data. If your hard drive crashes and the only copy of your backup software exists on your backup media, you will be in a Catch-22 situation. You won't be able to access your backup software until you restore the files from your backup, but you won't be able to restore your files until your backup software is running! Make sure you keep the original distribution CD for your backup software or a disk-based copy of any backup software you downloaded from the Web.

Using a backup utility supplied by your operating system can be just as problematic. If the backup software is supplied with the OS, you'll need a copy of the OS to get the backup software running. If your computer won't boot, you'll have to reinstall the OS from distribution CDs or make sure you're using a new computer with the same OS as the one that was installed on your old system.

To recover from a hard disk crash, you have to get your computer booted up so that you can run your backup software. If your computer won't boot from the hard disk, you can use a boot disk or a recovery disk.

**What is a boot disk?** A **boot disk** is a removable storage medium containing the operating system files needed to boot your computer without accessing the hard disk. CDs, DVDs, and even USB flash drives can be used as boot disks. With current versions of Windows, the Windows installation CD is configured as a boot disk and can be used if your computer does not boot normally. When you insert the installation CD, you'll have the option of repairing Windows or reinstalling it. Try the repair option first.

**What is a recovery disk?** A **recovery disk** (sometimes referred to as a recovery CD) is a bootable CD, DVD, or other media that contains a complete copy of your computer's hard disk as it existed when the computer was new. It contains the operating system, device drivers, utilities, and even software that was bundled with your computer. You can use a recovery disk to return your computer to its factory default state. However, a recovery disk will not necessarily restore your data files, any software that you installed, or any configuration settings you've made since you unwrapped your computer from its shipping box.

**Where can I get a recovery disk?** Recovery disks are sometimes included with new computers as a CD or DVD. If you don't receive one, you should check the manufacturer's Web site for a downloadable version. The operating system might also supply a method for creating recovery disks.

Several manufacturers no longer provide recovery disks. Instead, they store an exact image of the hard disk with all factory-installed device drivers and software in a hidden partition (sometimes called a recovery partition) on the hard drive.

Recovery partitions are convenient for restoring a corrupted device driver or software module because you can simply copy or reinstall the file from the recovery partition to the main partition. The files in the recovery partition are not accessible, however, if your computer's hard disk fails. Therefore, don't be misled into thinking that a recovery partition can help you restore your computer after a hard disk failure. Computers with a recovery partition usually include a utility for copying these files to create a recovery disk that can be booted and accessed even if the hard disk is not operational.

**What about backing up the Windows Registry?** Windows users often hear a variety of rumors about backing up the Windows Registry. The Registry, as it is usually called, is an important group of files the Windows operating system uses to store configuration information about all the devices and software installed on a computer system. If the Registry becomes damaged, your computer might not be able to boot up, launch programs, or communicate with peripheral devices. It is a good idea to have an extra copy of the Registry in case the original file is damaged.

As simple as it sounds, backing up the Registry can present a bit of a problem because the Registry is always open while your computer is on. Some software that you might use for backups cannot copy open files. If you use such software, it might never back up the Registry. To get periodic copies of your computer's Registry settings, you can create restore points.

4

**What is a restore point?** A **restore point** is a snapshot of your computer settings. Restore points are essentially backups of the Windows Registry. If a hard disk problem causes system instability, you might be able to roll back to a restore point when your computer was operational.

Restore points are set automatically when you install new software. You can manually set restore points, too. For example, you might want to set a restore point before setting up a network or installing new hardware. Restore points can be set by entering "Create a Restore Point" in the Start menu Search box, then accessing the System Protection tab (Figure 4-53.)

**FIGURE 4-53**

Restore points back up personal preferences and configuration settings stored in the Windows Registry. You can manually create restore points or let Windows create them automatically whenever you add new software or hardware. ▶ Use this figure in your digital textbook to learn how to work with restore points.

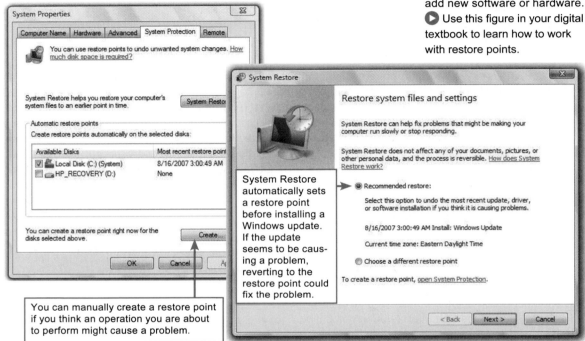

You can manually create a restore point if you think an operation you are about to perform might cause a problem.

System Restore automatically sets a restore point before installing a Windows update. If the update seems to be causing a problem, reverting to the restore point could fix the problem.

## BARE-METAL RESTORE AND VIRTUAL MACHINES

**Can I restore my computer in one simple operation?** Restoring a Windows computer usually entails several steps that can require a boot disk, recovery disk, backup disks, and file backups. The objective of this extended and sometimes frustrating process is to get optical and hard drive device drivers running so the computer can access its storage devices to get the operating system running, which can then run backup and restore software.

Some backup systems streamline the process by restoring a computer's operating system, device drivers, settings, and data in a single step—a process called **bare-metal restore**.

Bare-metal restore backup software stores the operating system, boot program, drivers, software applications, and data necessary to restore a backed up system to an entirely new computer without intermediate steps to install the operating system and device drivers. Bare-metal restore software usually works with a disk image.

**What is a disk image?** A **disk image** is a bit-by-bit copy of the data from all sectors of a disk. Disk imaging utilities create an exact clone of the original disk, unlike most backup software that makes file-by-file copies. The advantage of disk imaging is that it includes all the data from a disk, even boot information and other data locked by the operating system.

The disadvantage of disk imaging is that it copies data from the entire disk; it typically cannot be configured like traditional backup software to copy only selected files. Disk imaging takes time and is best used while other applications are not running. It is valuable for periodic backups, but a bit cumbersome for daily backups.

Popular Windows disk imaging utilities include Acronis True Image, Paragon Drive Backup, and Norton Ghost. Popular Mac disk imaging utilities include SuperDuper! and Carbon Copy Cloner.

**Are there any other backup options?** Today's trend toward the use of virtual machines offers another option for backups. Reinstalling an operating system on a blank hard disk can be a bit tricky, but you can avoid that problem if you run your operating system as a virtual machine.

For example, if you run Windows as a virtual machine on a Mac, you can simply back up the entire Windows machine as one folder or file. If a virus or corrupted file begins to disrupt the operation of Windows, instead of reformatting your hard disk and reinstalling Windows, you can simply copy the image of your Windows virtual machine from your backup device to your primary storage device and continue working.

**So what's the bottom line?** Mac users can depend on Time Machine to make easy-to-restore backups on an external hard drive. Windows users can take the following steps:

• File backups. **Make backups of your data files manually or with file synchronization software. Keep these files current so that you can restore them to your computer when necessary.**

• Restore points. **If your computer runs Windows, make sure it is set to automatically create restore points. If your computer begins to behave erratically, your first activity would be to revert back to a previous restore point.**

• Recovery disks. **Make sure you have a set of recovery disks either supplied by your computer manufacturer or that you created from a recovery partition. If devices malfunction, try restoring drivers from these disks. If your computer's hard disk fails, you can restore the computer to its factory settings.**

• System backup. **If you can afford an external hard disk drive, periodically back up your entire system on it using system synchronization or backup software. Don't leave the drive connected to your computer; but store it in a safe place to prevent it from being damaged or stolen.**

## QuickCheck

1. System _____ software, such as Time Machine, keeps your backup files up to date with the original files on your hard disk.

2. One of the best devices for home backup is a(n) _____ hard drive.

3. A(n) _____ backup makes copies of only those files that have changed since your last full backup.

4. A(n) _____ point is essentially a backup of the settings in the Windows Registry.

5. A bare-metal _____ includes the operating system, boot program, drivers, software applications, and data necessary to rebuild a replacement hard disk in one easy operation.

▶ CHECK ANSWERS

# Issue: Cyberterrorists or Pranksters?

SOME COMPUTER CRIMES require no special digital expertise. Setting fire to a computer doesn't require the same finesse as writing a stealthy virus, but both can have the same disastrous effect on data. Old-fashioned crimes, such as arson, that take a high-tech twist because they involve a computer can be prosecuted under traditional laws.

Traditional laws do not, however, cover the range of possibilities for computer crimes. Suppose a person unlawfully enters a computer facility and steals backup drives. That person might be prosecuted for breaking and entering. But would common breaking and entering laws apply to a person who remotely accesses a corporate computer system without authorization? And what if a person copies a data file without authorization? Has that file really been stolen if the original remains on the computer?

Many countries have computer crime laws that specifically define computer data and software as personal property. These laws also define as crimes the unauthorized access, use, modification, or disabling of a computer system or data. But laws don't necessarily stop criminals. If they did, we wouldn't have to deal with malicious code and intrusions.

## Computer Crime Gambits

**Data diddling:** Unauthorized alterations to data stored on a computer system, such as a student changing grades stored in a school's computer.
**Identity theft:** Unauthorized copying of personal information, such as credit card numbers, passwords, Social Security numbers, and bank account PINs.
**Salami shaving:** Redirecting small, unnoticeable amounts of money from large amounts.
**Denial of service:** An attempt to disrupt the operations of a network or computer system, usually by flooding it with data traffic.
**Information theft:** Unauthorized access to a computer system, such as military or government computers, to gain restricted information.
**Virus distribution:** Launching viruses, worms, and Trojan horses.
**Vandalism:** Intentional defacement of Web sites.

Computer crimes—costly to organizations and individuals—include a variety of gambits, such as virus distribution, data diddling, identity theft, and salami shaving.

One of the first computer crime cases involved a worm unleashed on the ARPANET in 1988 that quickly spread through government and university computer systems. The worm's author, Robert Morris, was convicted and sentenced to three years of probation, 400 hours of community service, and a $10,000 fine. This relatively lenient sentence was imposed because Morris claimed he had not intended to cripple the entire network.

A 1995 high-profile case involved a computer hacker named Kevin Mitnick, who was accused of breaking into dozens of corporate, university, government, and personal computers. Although vilified in the media, Mitnick had the support of many hackers and other people who believed that the prosecution grossly exaggerated the extent of his crimes. Nonetheless, Mitnick was sentenced to 46 months in prison and ordered to pay restitution in the amount of $4,125 during his three-year period of supervised release. The prosecution was horrified by such a paltry sum— an amount that was much less than its request for $1.5 million in restitution.

*Forbes* reporter Adam L. Penenberg took issue with the 46-month sentence imposed by Judge Mariana Pfaelzer and wrote, "This in a country where the average prison term for manslaughter is three years. Mitnick's crimes were curiously innocuous. He broke into corporate computers, but no evidence indicates that he destroyed data. Or sold anything he copied. Yes, he pilfered software—but in doing so left it behind. This world of bits is a strange one, in which you can take something and still leave it for its rightful owner. The theft laws designed for payroll sacks and motor vehicles just don't apply to a hacker."

In 2005, a German teenager confessed to creating the Sasser computer worm that was blamed for shutting down British Airways and Delta Airlines flight check-ins, hospitals and government offices in Hong Kong, part of Australia's rail network, Finnish banks, British Coast Guard stations, and millions of other computers worldwide. The teen was given a suspended sentence of 21 months and was required to perform 30 hours of community service. Microsoft paid a $250,000 reward to the two people who tipped off German police to the virus author's identity. The teen was later hired by a computer company that creates antivirus software.

Officials also made two arrests in connection with the Blaster worm. A 24-year-old Romanian citizen and an American teenager apparently downloaded copies of the worm source code, altered it slightly, and sent their versions back out again. The Romanian was allegedly mistreated by one of his professors. The American teenager was just trying to see what he could get away with.

Under Romanian law, distributing a virus can mean a 15-year prison sentence. The USA PATRIOT Act and the Cybersecurity Enhancement Act carry even stiffer penalties—anywhere from ten years to life in prison.

A CNET reporter questions the harshness of such penalties: "What bothers me most is that here in the United States, rapists serve, on average, ten years in prison. Yet if, instead of assaulting another human being, that same person had released a virus on the Net, the criminal would get the same or an even harsher sentence."

Law makers hope that stiff penalties will deter cybercriminals. U.S. Attorney John McKay is quoted as saying, "Let there be no mistake about it, cyber-hacking is a crime. It harms persons, it harms individuals, it harms businesses. We will investigate, track down, and prosecute cyber-hackers."

These cases illustrate our culture's ambivalent attitude toward computer hackers. On the one hand, they are viewed as evil cyberterrorists who are set on destroying the glue that binds together the Information Age. From this perspective, hackers are criminals who must be hunted down, forced to make restitution for damages, and prevented from creating further havoc.

From another perspective, hackers are viewed more as Casper the Friendly Ghost in our complex cybermachines—as moderately bothersome entities whose pranks are tolerated by the computer community, along with software bugs and hardware glitches. Seen from this perspective, a hacker's pranks are part of the normal course of study that leads to the highest echelons of computer expertise. "Everyone has done it," claims one hacking devotee, "even Bill Gates (founder of Microsoft) and Steve Jobs (founder of Apple Computer)."

Which perspective is right? Are hackers dangerous cyberterrorists or harmless pranksters? Before you make up your mind about computer hacking and cracking, you might want to further investigate several landmark cases by following links at the Computer Crime InfoWeb.

**INFOWEBLINKS**

Who's in the cybercrime news? How are cybercriminals caught? The **Computer Crime InfoWeb** provides answers to these questions and more.

 CLICK TO CONNECT
www.infoweblinks.com/np2012/ch04

# What Do You Think?

**ISSUE**

1. Should a computer virus distribution sentence carry the same penalty as manslaughter?

   ○ Yes  ○ No  ○ Not sure

2. Should it be a crime to steal a copy of computer data while leaving the original data in place and unaltered?

   ○ Yes  ○ No  ○ Not sure

3. Should hackers be sent to jail if they cannot pay restitution to companies and individuals who lost money as the result of a prank?

   ○ Yes  ○ No  ○ Not sure

4. Do you think that a hacker would make a good consultant on computer security?

   ○ Yes  ○ No  ○ Not sure

   ▶ SAVE RESPONSES

# Computers in Context: Law Enforcement

**SIRENS WAIL.** Blue lights flash. A speeding car slows and pulls off to the side of the road. It looks like a routine traffic stop, but the patrol car is outfitted with a mobile data computer. The police officers on this high-tech force have already checked the speeding car's license plate number and description against a database of stolen cars and vehicles allegedly used in kidnappings and other crimes.

Mounted in the dashboard of marked and unmarked police cars, a mobile data computer resembles a notebook computer with its flat-panel screen and compact keyboard. Unlike a consumer-grade notebook, however, the computers in police cruisers use hardened technology designed to withstand extreme conditions, such as high temperatures in parked vehicles. The dashboard-mounted computer communicates with an office-based server using a wireless link, such as short-range radio, mobile phone technology, or Wi-Fi. With this wireless link, police officers can access data from local, state, and national databases.

One national database, the National Crime Information Center (NCIC), is maintained by the FBI and can be accessed by authorized personnel in local, state, and federal law enforcement agencies. The system can process more than 5 million queries per day related to stolen vehicles, wanted criminals, missing persons, violent gang members, stolen guns,

and members of terrorist organizations. The officers who pulled over the speeding car received information from the NCIC that the car was stolen, so they arrested the car's occupant and took him to the police station for booking.

At the police station, digital cameras flash and the suspect's mug shot is automatically entered into an automated warrants and booking system. The system stores the suspect's complete biographical and arrest information, such as name, aliases, addresses, Social Security number, charges, and arrest date. The system also checks for outstanding warrants against the suspect, such as warrants for other thefts. Booking agents can enter those charges into the system, assign the new inmate to a cell, log his or her personal items, and print a photo ID or wrist band.

Automated warrants and booking systems have been proven to increase police productivity. New York City's system handles more than 300,000 bookings per year, with gains in productivity that have put nearly 300 officers back into action investigating crimes and patrolling neighborhoods.

As part of the booking process, the suspect is fingerprinted. A standard fingerprint card, sometimes called a ten-print card, contains inked prints of the fingers on each hand, plus name, date of birth, and other arrest information. Now, however, instead of using ink, a biometric scanning device can electronically capture fingerprints. Text information is entered using a keyboard and stored with digital fingerprint images.

The fingerprint information can be transmitted in digital format from local law enforcement agencies to the FBI's Integrated Automated Fingerprint Identification System (IAFIS). This biometric identification system uses digital imaging technology and sophisticated algorithms to analyze fingerprint data. IAFIS can classify arriving prints for storage or search for a match in its database containing 66 million criminal prints, 25 million civilian prints, and prints from 73,000 known and suspected terrorists.

Conventional crimes, such as car theft, are often solved by using standard investigative techniques with information from computer databases. To solve cybercrimes, however, the special skills of computer forensic investigators are often required.

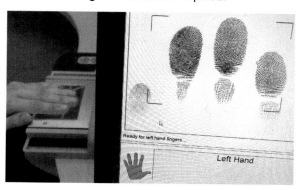

Ready for left hand fingers

Left Hand

Computer forensics is the scientific examination and analysis of data located on computer storage media, conducted to offer evidence of computer crimes in court. Computer crimes can be separated into two categories. The first includes crimes that use computers, such as transmitting trade secrets to competitors, reproducing copyrighted material, and distributing child pornography. The second includes crimes targeted at computers, such as denial-of-service attacks on servers, Web site vandalism, data theft, and destructive viruses. Computer forensics can be applied to both categories.

Whether investigators suspect that a computer is the origin of a cyber-attack or contains evidence, the first step in the forensic process is to use disk imaging software to make an exact replica of the information stored on the hard disk. The disk image is collected on a write-once medium that cannot be altered with planted evidence, and the forensic scientist begins analyzing the disk image data with simple search software that looks through files for keywords related to the crime. In the case of the Gap-Toothed Bandit who was convicted for robbing nine banks, analysis of the disk image revealed word processing files containing notes he handed to tellers demanding money.

Criminals typically attempt to delete files with incriminating evidence, but a good forensic scientist can retrieve data from deleted files with undelete software or data recovery software. Temporary Internet or cache files can also yield evidence, pointing law enforcement officers to Web sites the suspect visited that might be fronts for illegal activity.

When a computer is a target of a cyber-attack, forensic investigators use three techniques to track the source. The first option is to make an immediate image of the server's hard disk and look through its log files for evidence of activity coming from unauthorized IP addresses. A second technique is to monitor the intruder by watching login attempts, changes to log files, and file access requests. Sophisticated intruders might be able to detect such monitoring, however, and cover their tracks. A third technique is to create a honeypot—an irresistible computer system or Web site containing fake information that allows investigators to monitor hackers until identification is possible.

Despite the many techniques and tools available to forensic investigators, they have three main constraints. First, they must adhere to privacy regulations and obtain warrants to set up wiretaps or gather information from ISPs about their customers. Second, they must scrupulously document their procedures so that the evidence they produce cannot be discredited in court as planted or fabricated. Third, forensic investigators must examine a wide range of alternatives pertaining to the crime, such as the chance that an IP or e-mail address used to commit a cybercrime might belong to an innocent bystander being spoofed by the real hacker.

Privacy, documentation, and evidentiary constraints cost forensic investigators time, and failure to adhere to strict standards can sometimes allow criminals to avoid conviction and penalties. But even within these constraints, careful forensic investigation is an important aspect of catching and convicting high-tech criminals.

**INFOWEBLINKS**

For more information about police and FBI technology, connect to the **Computers in Law Enforcement InfoWeb**.

 CLICK TO CONNECT
www.infoweblinks.com/np2012/ch04

# New Perspectives Labs

## On the BookOnCD

To access the New Perspectives Labs for Chapter 4, start the BookOnCD and then click the icon next to the lab title below.

### ▶ MANAGING FILES

**IN THIS LAB YOU'LL LEARN:**

- How to access Windows Explorer
- How to expand and collapse the directory structure
- How to rename or delete a file or folder
- The basic principles for creating an efficient directory structure for your files
- How to create a folder
- How to select a single file or a group of files
- How to move files from one folder to another

**LAB ASSIGNMENTS**

1. Start the interactive part of the lab. Make sure you've enabled Tracking if you want to save your QuickCheck results. Perform each lab step, and answer all the lab QuickCheck questions.

2. Use Windows Explorer to look at the directory of the disk or USB flash drive that currently contains most of your files. Draw a diagram showing the hierarchy of folders. Write a paragraph explaining how you could improve this hierarchy, and draw a diagram to illustrate your plan.

3. On a blank USB flash drive, create three folders: Music, Web Graphics, and Articles. Within the Music folder, create four additional folders: Jazz, Reggae, Rock, and Classical. Within the Classical folder, create two more folders: Classical MIDI and Classical MP3. If you have Internet access, go on to #4.

4. Use your browser software to connect to the Internet, and then go to a Web site, such as *www. zdnet.com* or *www.cnet.com*. Look for a small graphic (perhaps 100 KB or less) and download it to your Web Graphics folder. Next, use a search engine to search for "classical MIDI music." Download one of the compositions to the Music\ Classical\Classical MIDI folder. Open Windows Explorer and expand all the directories for your USB flash drive. Open the Music\Classical\ Classical MIDI folder and make sure your music download appears. Capture a screenshot. Follow your instructor's directions to submit this screen-shot as a printout or an e-mail attachment.

### ▶ BACKING UP YOUR COMPUTER

**IN THIS LAB YOU'LL LEARN:**

- How to work with restore points
- How to create a recovery disk
- How to create a disk image
- How to make a Windows backup
- How to restore files from a backup

**LAB ASSIGNMENTS**

1. Start the interactive part of the lab. Make sure you've enabled Tracking if you want to save your QuickCheck results. Perform each lab step as directed, and answer all the lab QuickCheck questions. When you exit the lab, your answers are automatically graded and your results are displayed.

2. Describe where most of your data files are stored, and estimate how many megabytes of data (not programs) you have in all these files. Next, take a close look at these files and estimate how much data (in megabytes) you cannot afford to lose. Finally, explain what you think would be the best hardware device for backing up this amount of data.

3. Start the backup software that is provided for your computer, specify its name, and list which of the following features it provides: file backup, system image, disk image, automatic backup, manual backup. If an automatic backup is available, list the user definable options for selecting backup intervals, days, and times.

4. Explore your computer to discover how its recovery disk is provided; for example, is it a partition, a download, or a utility. Use the built-in help provided by your computer manufacturer or go to its Web site to learn how to make a recovery disk. Write a short summary of the procedure.

# Key Terms

Make sure you understand all the boldfaced key terms presented in this chapter. With the NP2012 BookOnCD, you can use this list of terms as an interactive study activity. First, try to define a term in your own words, and then click the term to compare your definition with the definition presented in the chapter. Online, try your hand at the TechTerm Flashcards.

Android OS, 203
Backup, 222
Backup software, 227
Bare-metal restore, 230
BlackBerry OS, 202
Boot disk, 229
Boot process, 192
Bootstrap program, 192
Button, 190
Cluster, 219
Command-line interface, 189
Data fork, 199
Defragmentation utility, 221
Desktop, 189
Desktop operating system, 188
Dialog box, 191
Differential backup, 227
Directory, 206
Disc mastering, 219
Disk image, 230
Disk partition, 205
DOS, 201
Dual boot, 198
File date, 206
File extension, 204
File format, 207
File header, 207
File management utility, 214
File shredder software, 220
File size, 206

File specification, 206
File synchronization, 224
File system, 219
File tag, 212
File-naming conventions, 204
Folder, 206
Formatting, 219
Fragmented files, 221
Full backup, 227
Full system backup, 226
Google Chrome OS, 200
Graphical user interface, 189
Icon, 189
Incremental backup, 228
iOS, 203
Kernel, 192
Library, 217
Linux, 200
Linux distribution, 200
Logical storage models, 215
Mac OS, 197
Master File Table, 219
Memory leak, 187
Menu, 190
Menu bar, 190
Microsoft Windows, 194
Multiprocessing, 186
Multitasking, 186
Multithreading, 186
Multiuser operating system, 187

Native file format, 209
NTFS, 219
Operating system, 184
Packet writing, 219
Palm webOS, 202
Path, 206
Physical storage model, 218
Recovery disk, 229
Reserved words, 205
Resource, 185
Resource fork, 199
Restore point, 230
Ribbon, 190
Root directory, 206
Sectors, 219
Server operating system, 187
Single-user operating system, 187
Subdirectory, 206
Submenu, 191
Symbian, 202
Taskbar, 190
Toolbar, 190
Tracks, 219
UNIX, 200
User interface, 189
Virtual machine, 198
Window, 189
Windows Explorer, 216
Windows Phone 7, 202

4

# Interactive Summary

To review important concepts from this chapter, fill in the blanks to best complete each sentence. When using the NP2012 BookOnCD, click the Check Answers buttons to automatically score your answers.

**SECTION A:** An operating system interacts with application software, device drivers, and hardware to manage a computer's [ ], such as the processor, memory, and input/output devices. To allow two or more programs to run simultaneously, an OS can offer [ ] services. Within a single program, [ ] allows multiple parts, or threads, to run simultaneously. An operating system's [ ] capability supports a division of labor among all the processing units. When multiple programs are running, the OS should prevent a memory [ ], which is a situation in which instructions and data from one area of memory overflow into memory allocated to another program. Operating systems are informally categorized and characterized using one or more of the following terms: A(n) [ ]-user operating system expects to deal with one set of input devices—those that can be controlled by one person at a time. A(n) [ ]-user operating system is designed to deal with input, output, and processing requests from many users. A(n) [ ] operating system provides management tools for distributed networks, e-mail servers, and Web site hosting. A(n) [ ] operating system is one that's designed for a personal computer—either a desktop or notebook computer.

In addition to behind-the-scenes activities, operating systems also provide tools, called operating system [ ], that you can use to control and customize your computer equipment and work environment. In addition, many operating systems also influence the "look and feel" of your software, or what's known as the user [ ]. The core part of an operating system is called the [ ], which is loaded into RAM during the [ ] process.

▶ CHECK ANSWERS

**SECTION B:** Popular [ ] operating systems include Microsoft Windows, Mac OS, and Linux. The first versions of Windows were sometimes referred to as operating [ ] rather than operating systems because they required DOS to supply the operating system kernel. Windows has evolved to keep pace with 16-bit, 32-bit, and [ ]-bit architectures. Its strengths include a huge library of Windows [ ], support for a variety of peripheral devices, and plenty of documentation. Two of the weakest features of Microsoft Windows are reliability and [ ].

Mac OS evolved from the original Classic Mac OS designed for [ ] computers based on the Motorola 68000 microprocessor. In 2001, Mac OS X was released for Apple's new line of computers using IBM's PowerPC processor. OS X was again revised for a line of computers using [ ] processors. Intel Macs can be set up to dual [ ] Mac OS and Windows. Intel Macs also offer a good platform for [ ] machine technologies that allow you to use one computer to simulate the hardware and software of another. One of the potential problems with Mac OS is its use of [ ] forks, which make cross-platform file sharing clumsy. Linux is a(n) [ ] source operating system that is used extensively for servers. One of the reasons it has not become a popular desktop OS is that it requires a bit more technical savvy than Windows or Mac OS. Developed by Microsoft and supplied on the original IBM PCs, [ ] was one of the first operating systems for personal computers. Today's handheld OSs typically support touch screens and include a standard set of [ ] for e-mail, browsing, playing media, mapping, and scheduling.

▶ CHECK ANSWERS

**SECTION C:** A computer [_____] is a named collection of data that exists on a storage medium, such as a hard disk, CD, DVD, or BD. Every file has a name and might also have a file extension. The rules that specify valid file names are called file-naming [_____]. These rules typically do not allow you to use certain characters or [_____] words in a file name. A file [_____] is usually related to a file format—the arrangement of data in a file and the coding scheme used to represent the data. A software program's [_____] file format is the default format for storing files created with that program. A file's location is defined by a file [_____] (sometimes called a path), which includes the storage device, folder(s), file name, and extension. In Windows, storage devices are identified by a drive letter, followed by a(n) [_____]. An operating system maintains a list of files called a directory for each storage disk, USB flash drive, tape, CD, or DVD. The main directory of a disk is referred to as the [_____] directory, which can be subdivided into several smaller lists called subdirectories that are depicted as [_____].

▶ CHECK ANSWERS

**4**

**SECTION D:** File [_____] encompasses any procedure that helps you organize your computer-based files so that you can find them more effectively. [_____]-based file management uses tools provided with a software program to open and save files. Additional tools might also allow you to create new folders, rename files, and delete files. The Save and Save As dialog boxes are examples of these file management tools. Most operating systems provide file management [_____] that give you the "big picture" of the files you have stored on your disks. The structure of folders that you envision on your disk is a(n) [_____] model, which is often represented by a storage [_____], such as a tree structure or filing cabinet. Windows [_____] is an example of a file management utility provided by an operating system. Windows Explorer allows you to find, rename, copy, move, and delete files and folders. In addition, it allows you to perform these file management activities with more than one file at a time. The way that data is actually stored is referred to as the [_____] storage model. Before a computer stores data on a disk, CD, or DVD, it creates the equivalent of electronic storage bins by dividing the disk into [_____], and then further dividing the disk into [_____]. This dividing process is referred to as [_____]. Each sector of a disk is numbered, providing a storage address that the operating system can track. Many computers work with a group of sectors, called a(n) [_____], to increase the efficiency of file storage operations. An operating system uses a file [_____] to track the physical location of files.

▶ CHECK ANSWERS

**SECTION E:** A backup is a copy of one or more files that has been made in case the original files become damaged. A good backup plan allows you to [_____] your computing environment to its pre-disaster state with a minimum of fuss. Your personal backup plan depends on the files you need to back up, the hardware you have available to make backups, and your backup software. In any case, it is a good idea to back up the Windows [_____] and make sure your files are free of [_____]. Backups should be stored in a safe place, away from the computer. Personal computer backups are typically recorded on writable CDs and DVDs, USB flash drives, networks, Web sites, or a second hard disk. An easy way to create a backup of important data files is to use My Computer or Windows [_____] to simply copy files to a USB flash drive. File [_____] software automates the process by keeping backup files up to date. Backup software differs from most copy routines because it [_____] all the files for a backup into one large file. A(n) [_____] backup saves time by backing up only those files that have been changed since the last backup. Restoring a Windows computer usually requires several steps, such as reinstalling the operating system, before a backup can be restored. The process can be simplified by using a backup system that offers bare-[_____] restore.

▶ CHECK ANSWERS

# Interactive Situation Questions

Apply what you've learned to some typical computing situations. When using the NP2012 BookOnCD, you can type your answers, and then use the Check Answers button to automatically score your responses.

1. While using several programs at the same time, your computer displays an error message that refers to a program that is not responding. You recognize this message as one that might result from a(n) [_____] leak and decide to close the non-responding program using the Ctrl, Shift, and Esc key combination.

2. Your friend wants to open a window on his Mac computer in which he can run Microsoft Windows and play some games designed for the Windows platform. You tell your friend to create a(n) [_____] machine using software such as Parallels Desktop.

3. Suppose you are using Microsoft Word and you want to open a file. When your software lists the documents you can open, you can expect them to be in Word's [_____] file format, which is DOC.

4. Can you use a Windows application, create a document, and store it using the file name *I L*ve NY*? Yes or no? [_____]

5. When you want to work with several files—to move them to different folders, for example—it would be most efficient to use a file management utility, such as Windows [_____].

6. When specifying a location for a data file on your hard disk, you should avoid saving it in the [_____] directory.

7. Your computer seems to be taking longer to store and retrieve files. You use a(n) [_____] utility to rearrange the files in contiguous clusters.

8. You have an old computer that you will donate to a school, but you want to make sure its hard disk contains no trace of your data. To do so, you use file [_____] software that overwrites empty sectors with random 1s and 0s.

9. You just finished making a backup on an external USB hard disk. Before you depend on this backup, you should test it to make sure you can [_____] the data in the event of a hard disk crash.

10. Your hard disk crashed for some unknown reason. Now when you switch on the computer power, all you get is an "Error reading drive C:" message. You use a(n) [_____] CD that contains the operating system files and device drivers needed to start your computer without accessing the hard disk.

 CHECK ANSWERS

## Interactive Practice Tests

Practice tests that consist of ten multiple-choice, true/false, and fill-in-the-blank questions are available on both the NP2012 BookOnCD and the NP2012 CourseMate Web site. BookOnCD test questions are selected at random from a large test bank, so each time you take a test, you'll receive a different set of questions. Your tests are scored immediately, and you can print study guides that help you find the correct answers for any questions that you missed. Online, you'll find a Practice Test for each section of the chapter. Your results from online tests are saved by Engagement Tracker.  ▶ CLICK TO START

# Learning Objectives Checkpoints

Learning Objectives Checkpoints are designed to help you assess whether you have achieved the major learning objectives for this chapter. You can use paper and pencil or word processing software to complete most of the activities.

1. List and describe the four main resources that an operating system manages.

2. Explain the significance of multitasking, multithreading, and multiprocessing.

3. Explain the term *memory leak*, and describe what you can do if one occurs on your PC.

4. Describe five tasks for which you must interact directly with the operating system.

5. Describe the basic elements of a graphical user interface and contrast them with the elements of a command-line interface.

6. Watch your computer while it boots and revise the list on page 192 so that it reflects what happens when your computer boots.

7. List four operating systems used on personal computers, two operating systems used on servers, and four operating systems used on handheld devices. List advantages and disadvantages of the three most popular personal computer operating systems.

8. Explain the difference between dual booting and virtual machine technology. Give examples of tasks that might benefit from dual booting or virtual machine capability.

9. Make a list of five file names that are valid under the file-naming conventions for your operating system. Also, create a list of five file names that are not valid, and explain the problem with each one.

10. Pick any five files on the computer that you typically use, and write out the full path for each one.

11. Describe the significance of file formats. List at least ten common formats and their extensions. Make a list of at least 20 file extensions you find on the computer you use most often. Group these extensions into the following categories: system files, graphics files, sound files, text files, other.

12. Demonstrate that you can manage files on a computer by looking at the files on your computer and locating at least five files or folders that should be renamed or relocated to improve the organization and make it easier to locate information on your computer.

13. Describe what happens in the MFT when a file is stored or deleted. Explain what it means when a file is fragmented.

14. Make a list of backup tips that you think would help people devise a solid backup plan. Demonstrate that you have a backup plan by describing how you back up your computer.

15. Discuss the pros and cons of using CDs, DVDs, BDs, USB flash drives, external hard drives, and Web sites for backups.

16. Describe the way backup software deals with the files in the backup. Explain the differences between full, differential, and incremental backups.

17. Describe the significance of restore points, bare-metal restore, disk imaging, virtual machines, boot disks, and recovery disks.

Study Tip: Make sure you can use your own words to correctly answer each of the red focus questions that appear throughout the chapter.

4

# Concept Map

Fill in the blanks to illustrate the hierarchy of OS resource management activities.

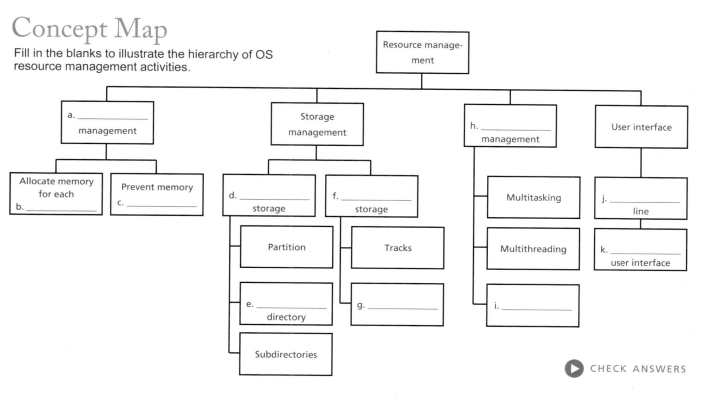

CHECK ANSWERS

# Projects

 **CRITICAL THINKING**

Think about the ways you typically interact with a computer and how the operating system factors into that interaction. What aspects of the operating system do you like? Which aspects could be improved? Organize your thoughts into an annotated list and e-mail it to your instructor.

 **GROUP PROJECT**

Keeping files and folders organized is a skill worth developing. Work with one or two other people to streamline the organization of folders and files on a computer storage device, such as a hard disk or flash drive. The storage device should contain at least 100 files. You can have the computer generate a listing of the files by connecting to *http://support.microsoft.com*, searching for article 196158, and following the instructions you find there for "How to create a text file list of the contents of a folder." Once you have a document containing the list, you can edit it to indicate how you would rearrange the files into a better structure of folders. Use a series of indents or Microsoft Word's outlining function to show the hierarchy of files and folders. Annotate your list by indicating the kinds of files you expect to be stored in each folder.

 **CYBERCLASSROOM**

Create an e-mail message that describes your backup equipment and plan along with the date of your last backup. In the subject line, include your name and the title "Original Backup Plan." Send the message to other members of your team and solicit comments and questions.

Based on the feedback you receive, use a word processor to revise your backup plan so it gives you improved protection against losing files. Using copy and paste, add the text of your Original Backup Plan and all the comments you received from your team. Your final document should contain your Revised Backup Plan, your Original Backup Plan, and your team's comments. Send this document to your instructor as an e-mail attachment.

 **MULTIMEDIA PROJECT**

Suppose you work for a software company and you are tasked with designing the user interface for a new handheld electronic toy for children ages 8–12. Write a paragraph describing how children will use the toy, then sketch out the main screen. Use callouts to describe how each of the screen elements is supposed to work.

 **RESUME BUILDER**

In today's job market, versatility is valuable. For this project, find a computer that runs an operating system different from the one you normally use. Spend at least 30 minutes working with this alternative operating system. Write a one-page description of your initial reaction, including aspects you liked and did not like.

 **GLOBALIZATION**

Computers are used worldwide, but most of the major operating systems originated in English-speaking countries. Take a look at the operating system that you use in the context of global users who might not speak English and who might not have grown up with Western customs. Describe at least five aspects of your operating system that would have to be modified to be acceptable to global users.

 **ISSUE**

The Issue section of this chapter focused on cybercrime. For this project, write a two- to five-page opinion paper about the "right to hack," based on information that you gather from the Internet. To begin this project, consult the Computer Crime InfoWeb (see page 233), and link to the recommended Web pages to get an in-depth overview of the issue. Armed with this background, select one of the following statements and argue for or against it:

• People have the right to hone their computing skills by breaking into computers.

• A person who creates a virus is perfectly justified in releasing it if the purpose is to make everyone aware of security breaches.

• Computer crimes are no different from other crimes, and computer criminals should be held responsible for the damage they cause.

Whatever viewpoint you decide to present, make sure you back it up with facts and references to authoritative articles and Web pages. Follow your professor's instructions for submitting your paper by e-mail or as a printed document.

 **COMPUTERS IN CONTEXT**

The Computers in Context section focused on computer use in law enforcement. For this project, use Web-based resources to search for cases in which computer forensic evidence was used in a criminal or civil investigation. Write a paragraph about the case's particulars, including a description of the alleged criminal activity. Next, create a list of elements, such as e-mail messages, attachments, files, and server logs, that were the focus of the forensic investigation. Follow up with a summary of the outcome. Was the suspect found guilty? Was a penalty imposed? Finally, state your opinion of how forensic evidence affected the case. Was it key evidence required to make the case, or did it simply support other physical evidence? Was the computer forensic evidence solid or open to interpretation and challenges from the defense? Make sure you include the URLs used for your research, and check with your professor for instructions on submitting this project on disc, by e-mail, or in print.

# On the Web

## STUDENT EDITION LABS

**4**

### MAINTAINING A HARD DRIVE

In the Maintaining a Hard Drive Student Edition Lab, you will learn about the following topics:

- Defragmenting a hard disk
- Running ScanDisk
- Detecting system and program failure
- Freeing up disk space

### MANAGING FILES AND FOLDERS

In the Managing Files and Folders Student Edition Lab, you will learn about the following topics:

- Using Windows Explorer to manage files and folders
- Deleting and restoring files
- Creating, naming, copying, and moving folders
- Changing folder options and properties

### BACKING UP YOUR COMPUTER

In the Backing Up Your Computer Student Edition Lab, you will learn about the following topics:

- Creating a backup
- Creating an incremental backup
- Backing up the Windows Registry
- Scheduling backup jobs
- Restoring an entire backup

### USING WINDOWS

In the Using Windows Student Edition Lab, you will learn about the following topics:

- Identifying common elements of Windows software
- Working with the taskbar and Start menu
- Using menus, toolbars, and dialog boxes

 **CHAPTER OVERVIEW COURSECAST**

Use your computer or iPod to hear a five-minute audio presentation of chapter highlights.

 **AUDIO FLASHCARDS**

Interact with audio flashcards to review key concepts from the chapter.

 **DETAILED OBJECTIVES**

Make sure that you've achieved all the objectives for a chapter before it's time for your test!

 **PRACTICE TESTS**

Review chapter material by taking these ten-question tests. Your results are saved by Engagement Tracker.

 **ONLINE GAMES**

Have some fun while refreshing your memory about key concepts that might appear on the next test.

 **AND MORE!**

At the NP2012 CourseMate Web site you'll also find the NP2012 eBook, TechTerm Flashcards, Online Glossary, and What Do You Think? opinion polls.

# 5

# LANs and WLANs

## Chapter Contents

▶ **SECTION A:**
**NETWORK BUILDING BLOCKS**
Network Classifications
LAN Standards
Network Devices
Clients, Servers, and Peers
Physical Topology
Network Links
Communications Protocols

▶ **SECTION B:**
**WIRED NETWORKS**
Wired Network Basics
Ethernet
Ethernet Equipment
Ethernet Setup

▶ **SECTION C:**
**WIRELESS NETWORKS**
Wireless Basics
Bluetooth
Wi-Fi
Wi-Fi Equipment
Wi-Fi Setup

▶ **SECTION D:**
**USING LANS**
LAN Advantages and Challenges
Sharing Files
Sharing Printers
Network Troubleshooting

▶ **SECTION E:**
**SECURITY THROUGH ENCRYPTION**
Wi-Fi Security
Encryption

▶ **ISSUE:**
**WHO'S STEALING MY SIGNALS?**

▶ **COMPUTERS IN CONTEXT:**
**EDUCATION**

▶ **NEW PERSPECTIVES LABS**

▶ **REVIEW ACTIVITIES**

▶ **ON THE WEB**

## Learning Objectives

After reading this chapter, you will be able to answer the following questions by completing the outcomes-based Learning Objectives Checkpoints on page 297.

1. What are PANs, LANs, MANs, and WANs?
2. Which devices are most common on LANs?
3. On a network, how does file sharing mode differ from client/server mode?
4. Why do networks have different topologies?
5. What is the purpose of a communications protocol?
6. Why do most networks transmit digital rather than analog signals?
7. How does data find its way over a network to a specified destination?
8. Is it easy to set up wired and wireless networks?
9. Are there different kinds of wired and wireless LANs?
10. What are the advantages and disadvantages of LANs?
11. What makes a network a security risk and how can networks be secured?
12. How does encryption work?

## InfoWebLinks

Visit the InfoWebLinks site to access additional resources ⓦ that accompany this chapter.

## Multimedia and Interactive Elements

When using the BookOnCD or CourseMate eBook, the ▶ icons are clickable to access multimedia resources.

# 5

## Pre-Assessment Quiz

Take the pre-assessment quiz to find out how much you know about the topics in this chapter. ▶

## Apply Your Knowledge The information in this chapter will give you the background to:

- Select equipment for building a wired or wireless network
- Assemble a basic network
- Configure a network router
- Use a Bluetooth device

- Share files, printers, and an Internet connection over a network
- Troubleshoot problems with your network
- Implement measures to secure your network
- Use encryption software

## Try It

### IS MY COMPUTER CONNECTED TO ANY NETWORKS?

Chapter 5 introduces computer networks and explains how handy they are for sharing files and accessing the Internet at home, at school, or in a business. Your computer might be connected to a home network or it might have access to a campus network or a local wireless hotspot. To discover the networks that your computer can access, complete the following steps:

**1. Windows:** Click **Start**, then select **Control Panel**. For **Windows 7** and **Vista**, click the **View network status and tasks** link. For **XP**, double-click the **Network Connections** icon.

   **Mac:** Click the 🍎 **Apple** icon on the menu bar, and select **System Preferences**. Click the **Network** icon.

**2.** Study the information displayed by your computer. How many networks are listed? _____

**3.** To view the status of a network in Windows 7, look for **Connections:** and click the link next to it. For Windows Vista, click the **View Status** link. For Windows XP, right-click a network, then select **Status** from the pop-up menu. For Macs, click a network.

**4.** Using applicable red lines in the screenshot at right, write down the status information for one network. Windows XP and Mac users: Your OS doesn't supply all the information; fill in as much information as you can.

**5.** After recording the information, close the dialog boxes. You'll learn more about network status as you read this chapter.

Local Area Connection Status dialog box showing General tab with Connection information (Status, Network, IPv4 Connectivity, IPv6 Connectivity, Media State, Duration, Speed, Signal Strength), a Details... button, and an Activity section showing Sent and Received Bytes, with Properties, Disable, Diagnose, and Close buttons.

# Network Building Blocks

**TODAY, NETWORKS ARE EVERYWHERE** and network technology is evolving rapidly. Just when you think you have got a handle on your home wireless network, along come technologies like MiFi, 4G, and WiMAX. Although network technology continues to evolve, it is based on a set of fairly stable concepts. If you understand the network building blocks introduced in Section A, working with new network technologies will be a piece of cake.

## NETWORK CLASSIFICATIONS

**What's the purpose of a network?** In the early years of personal computers, networks were scarce. Most personal computers functioned as standalone units, and computing was essentially a solitary activity in which one person interacted with one computer.

Some computer engineers, however, had the foresight to anticipate that personal computers could be networked to provide advantages not available with standalone computers. One of the most significant network ideas was conceived by Bob Metcalfe in 1976. His plan for transporting data between computers, shown in Figure 5-1, has become a key element in just about every computer network.

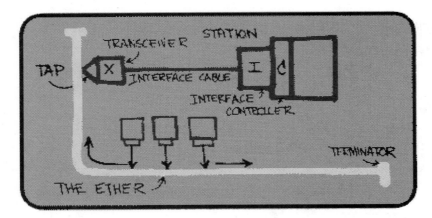

**FIGURE 5-1**

In 1976, Bob Metcalfe drew this diagram of network technology, which he called Ethernet.

**How are computer networks classified?** Networks can be classified according to their size and geographic scope.

**PAN** (personal area network) is a term sometimes used to refer to the interconnection of personal digital devices or consumer electronics within a range of about 30 feet (10 meters) and without the use of wires or cables. For example, a PAN could be used to wirelessly transmit data from a computer to a handheld device or printer; it could also transmit data from a computer to a home theater projection device.

A **LAN** (local area network) is a data communications network that connects personal computers within a very limited geographical area—usually a single building. LANs use a variety of wired and wireless technologies. School computer labs and home networks are examples of LANs.

A **MAN** (metropolitan area network) is a public high-speed network capable of voice and data transmission within a range of about 50 miles (80 km). Examples of MANs include local Internet service providers, small cable television companies, and local telephone companies.

A **WAN** (wide area network) covers a large geographical area and usually consists of several smaller networks, which might use different computer platforms and network technologies. The Internet is the world's largest WAN. Networks for nationwide banks, large cable television companies, and multi-location superstores can also be classified as WANs.

**Why is geographic scope important?** Localized networks typically include a small number of computers, which can be connected using basic equipment. As the area of network coverage expands, the number of workstations grows, specialized devices are sometimes required to boost signals, and the diversity of devices requires sophisticated management tools and strategies.

**FIGURE 5-2**

The computer network in a dorm room is a LAN.

The focus of this chapter is on LANs because you are most likely to encounter this type of network in a school lab or small business. Also, if you intend to set up or upgrade a network in your home or dorm room, you will be working with LAN technologies (Figure 5-2).

## LAN STANDARDS

**Are there different kinds of LANs?** In the past, a great diversity of LAN technologies existed as engineers pioneered various ideas to make data transport faster, more efficient, and more secure. Today, LANs are becoming more standardized, but several LAN standards remain necessary to accommodate networking environments that range from simple households to large businesses.

**What are LAN standards?** LAN technologies are standardized by the Institute of Electrical and Electronics Engineers (IEEE) Project 802 - Local Network Standards. IEEE standards exist for most types of commercial networks. An IEEE designation number, such as IEEE 802.3, is sometimes used to refer to a network standard in articles and advertisements. When you're shopping for equipment to connect your computer to a network, these designation numbers help you identify equipment that is compatible with your network technology.

**What are the most popular LAN standards?** Several LAN standards, including ARCnet, Token Ring, and FDDI, were popular in the past but are no longer in widespread use. Today, most LANs are configured with Ethernet technology and use compatible Wi-Fi standards in applications that require wireless access. These standards are popular across the board for home and business installations. You'll learn more specifics about these popular networking technologies in Sections B and C.

## NETWORK DEVICES

**What devices can be attached to a network?** You can think of a network as a spider web with many interconnecting points. Each connection point on a network is referred to as a **node**. A network node typically contains computers, networked peripherals, or network devices.

**How do computers connect to LANs?** A personal computer connected to a network is sometimes called a workstation. Other classes of computers, such as mainframes, supercomputers, servers, and handhelds, can also connect to LANs.

To connect to a LAN, a computer requires network circuitry, sometimes referred to as a **network interface card** (NIC). Network circuitry is often built into personal computers. If not, a NIC can be added to a slot in the system board or to a USB port.

**What is a networked peripheral?** A **networked peripheral**, or network-enabled peripheral, is any device that contains network circuitry to directly connect to a network. Printers, scanners, and storage devices are examples of devices that can be equipped to directly connect to a network instead of connecting to a workstation. A storage device that directly connects to a network is called **network attached storage** (NAS). Network-enabled printers and scanners are sometimes described as having "built-in networking." Some devices offer networking as an optional add-on.

**What are network devices?** A **network device** (sometimes referred to as a network appliance) is any electronic device that broadcasts network data, boosts signals, or routes data to its destination. Network devices include hubs, switches, routers, gateways, bridges, and repeaters. You will learn more about these devices later in the chapter. In the meantime, study Figure 5-3 for an example of a LAN that connects a variety of computers, networked peripherals, and network devices.

**TERMINOLOGY NOTE**

Throughout this chapter, the term *workstation* means a personal computer connected to a network.

**TERMINOLOGY NOTE**

Network interface cards are sometimes called network adapters or network cards.

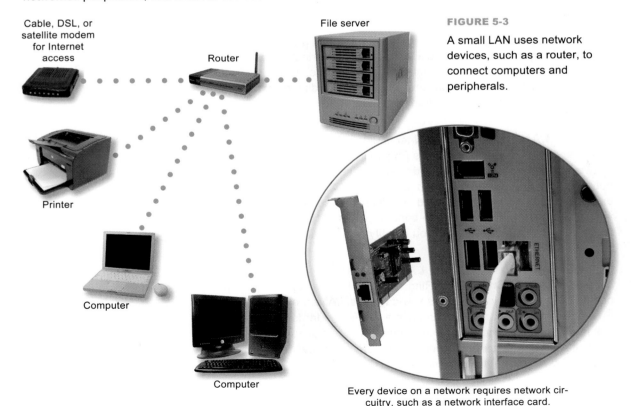

Cable, DSL, or satellite modem for Internet access

Router

File server

Printer

Computer

Computer

**FIGURE 5-3**

A small LAN uses network devices, such as a router, to connect computers and peripherals.

Every device on a network requires network circuitry, such as a network interface card.

## CLIENTS, SERVERS, AND PEERS

**What is the difference between a network client and a server?**
Network devices can function as clients or as servers. A server is a computer that provides services to other computers called clients. For example, an **application server** runs application software for network workstations. A **file server** stores files and supplies them to workstations on request. A **print server** handles jobs sent to network printers.

Servers are often dedicated to the task they perform, which means they are not assigned to users as workstations. Computers can be configured to perform both functions at the same time, but will not perform optimally in either role.

Networks that include one or more servers can operate in **client/server mode**, which you can envision as a hierarchical structure with servers at the top of the hierarchy (Figure 5-4).

**FIGURE 5-4**

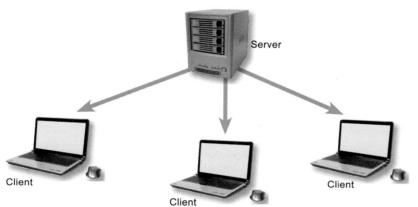

In client/server mode, a server is the most important resource. Client computers are usually personal computers that use locally installed client software, such as a browser or e-mail package, to access the server.

**Can a network function without a server?** Networks do not require servers. Files and applications can be shared among workstations operating in **peer-to-peer mode**. In this mode, workstations can share responsibility for processing, storage, printing, and communications tasks (Figure 5-5). Popular file sharing systems such as Gnutella, Kazaa, and BitTorrent operate in peer-to-peer mode.

**FIGURE 5-5**

In peer-to-peer mode, workstations serve as both clients and servers.

**Should I choose client/server or peer-to-peer?** You don't have to choose one or the other. A network can function in client/server mode when necessary and also exchange data in peer-to-peer fashion. You can, for example, share files in peer-to-peer mode with several other computers on the network during the day; then in the evening when your friends come over to play computer games, you can configure one of your computers as a server that oversees game play on the other computers in your network that operate as clients for the duration of the game.

## PHYSICAL TOPOLOGY

**How are the devices on a LAN physically arranged?** The arrangement of devices in a network is referred to as its **physical topology**. Figure 5-6 illustrates star, ring, bus, mesh, and tree topologies; the pathways shown between nodes can be linked by physical cables or wireless signals.

**What are the advantages of each topology?** A network arranged as a **star topology** features a central connection point that links cables or handles wireless broadcasts to all workstations and peripherals. Many home networks are arranged in a star topology. The advantage of this topology is that any link can fail without affecting the rest of the network. Its primary disadvantage is that it requires quite a bit of cable to link all the devices—a disadvantage that disappears with wireless networks. Although the failure of a link does not affect the rest of the network, a device with a failed link would be cut off from the network and unable to receive data.

A **ring topology** connects all devices in a circle, with each device having exactly two neighbors. Data is transmitted from one device to another around the ring. This topology minimizes cabling, but failure of any one device can take down the entire network. Ring topologies, once championed by IBM, are infrequently used in today's networks.

A **bus topology** uses a common backbone to connect all network devices. The bus spans the network and functions as a shared communication link, which carries network data. The bus stops at each end of the network with a special device called a terminator. Bus networks work best with a limited number of devices. A bus network with more than a few dozen computers is likely to perform poorly; and if the backbone cable fails, the entire network becomes unusable.

A **mesh topology** connects each network device to many other network devices. Data traveling on a mesh network can take any of several possible paths from its source to its destination. These redundant data pathways make a mesh network very robust. Even if several links fail, data can follow alternative operational links to reach its destination—an advantage over networks arranged in a star topology. The original plan for the Internet was based on mesh topology. Today, mesh topologies are used for some wireless networks. In a wireless mesh, data can be transported to nodes located far from a central access point, simply by hopping from one node to another.

A **tree topology** is essentially a blend of star and bus networks. Multiple star networks are connected into a bus configuration by a backbone. Tree topologies offer excellent flexibility for expansion—a single link to the backbone can add an entire group of star-configured devices. This link can be accomplished using the same type of hub that is used as the central connection point in a star network. Many of today's school and business networks are based on tree topologies.

**Can various networks be interconnected?** Yes. You can connect your home network to the Internet, for example. A LAN in your sorority or fraternity could be connected to your college campus network. A retail store might connect its cash register network to its financial network.

Two similar networks can be connected by a device called a **bridge**, which simply transfers data without regard to its format. Networks that use different topologies and technologies can be interconnected by using gateways.

**FIGURE 5-6**

Network Topologies

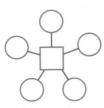

Star topology

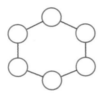

Ring topology

Bus topology

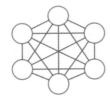

Mesh topology

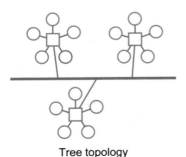

Tree topology

**Gateway** is a generic term for any device or software code used to join two networks, even if those networks use different standards. A gateway can be implemented completely in software, completely in hardware, or as a combination of the two. The device used to connect your home LAN to the Internet, for example, is a type of gateway.

## NETWORK LINKS

**What connects the nodes of a network?** Data can travel from one network device to another over a cable or through the air. A **communications channel**, or link, is a physical path or a frequency for signal transmissions. For example, Channel 12 on your TV tuner is a specific frequency used to broadcast audiovisual data for a television station. This data might also be carried over another channel, such as coaxial cable, as part of a cable TV system.

Data in a network with wired links travels from one device to another over cables (Figure 5-7). You'll learn more about wired LANs, such as Ethernet, HomePNA, and HomePlug, in Section B. Networks without wires transport data through the air, eliminating the need for cables. Section C contains more information on popular wireless network technologies, such as Wi-Fi and Bluetooth.

**FIGURE 5-7**

Wired networks transport data over cables, whereas wireless networks transmit data between devices equipped with antennas.

**What's bandwidth?** Network links must move data and move it quickly. **Bandwidth** is the transmission capacity of a communications channel. Just as a four-lane freeway can carry more traffic than a two-lane street, a high-bandwidth communications channel can carry more data than a low-bandwidth channel. For example, the coaxial cable that brings you more than 100 channels of cable TV has a higher bandwidth than your home telephone line.

The bandwidth of a channel carrying digital data is usually measured in bits per second (bps). For example, your wireless LAN might be rated for an average speed of 27 Mbps. The bandwidth of a channel carrying analog data is typically measured in hertz (Hz). For example, the copper wires that carry voice-grade telephone signals are often described as having 3,000 Hz bandwidth.

High-bandwidth communications systems, such as cable TV and DSL, are sometimes referred to as **broadband**, whereas systems with less capacity, such as dial-up Internet access, are referred to as **narrowband**. Broadband capacity is essential for networks that support many users, as well as for those that carry lots of audio and video data, such as music and movie downloads.

**TERMINOLOGY NOTE**

*Hz* is an abbreviation for hertz, which refers to the number of times a wave oscillates, or peaks, per second. Telephone signals are transmitted in the 1,200 Hz range. Many wireless networks transmit a 2.4 GHz signal that peaks 2.4 billion times per second.

5

## COMMUNICATIONS PROTOCOLS

**What is a protocol?** A protocol is a set of rules for interacting and negotiating. In some respects, it is like signals between the pitcher and catcher in a baseball game. Before the ball is thrown, the catcher and pitcher use hand signals to negotiate the speed and style of the pitch.

In the context of networks, a **communications protocol** refers to a set of rules for efficiently transmitting data from one network node to another. Just as a pitcher signals the catcher in baseball, two computers on a network might negotiate their communications protocols through a process called **handshaking**. The transmitting device sends a signal that means "I want to communicate." It then waits for an acknowledgement signal from the receiving device. The two devices negotiate a protocol that both can handle. The sounds you hear as two modems or fax machines connect are examples of handshaking.

The best-known communications protocol is probably TCP/IP. It is the protocol that regulates Internet data transport and has become a standard for LANs as well.

**What can communications protocols do?** Protocols set standards for encoding and decoding data, guiding data to its destination, and mitigating the effects of interference. Specifically, protocols are responsible for the following aspects of network communications:

- Dividing messages into packets
- Affixing addresses to packets
- Initiating transmission
- Regulating the flow of data
- Checking for transmission errors
- Acknowledging receipt of transmitted data

**How does data travel over a network?** In 1948, Claude Shannon, an engineer at the prestigious Bell Labs, published an article describing a communications system model applicable to networks of all types, including today's computer networks.

In Shannon's model, data from a source, such as a network workstation, is encoded and sent as signals over a communications channel to a destination, such as a network printer, storage device, server, or workstation. When data arrives at its destination, it is decoded. Transmission signals can be disrupted by interference called noise, which has the potential to corrupt data, making it erroneous or unintelligible (Figure 5-8).

FIGURE 5-8

A communications system basically sends information from a source to a destination. Although the path between the source and destination might appear to be straight in the diagram, the data can pass through several devices, which convert it to electrical, sound, light, or radio signals; beam it up to satellites; route it along the least congested links; or clean up parts of the signal that have been distorted by noise.

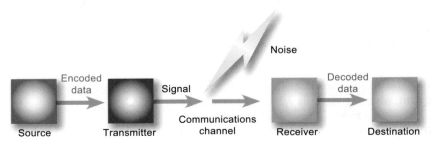

**What kind of signals travel over computer networks?** When data is transmitted over a network link, it usually takes the form of an electromagnetic signal. You can think of these signals as waves that ripple through cables or through the air. Digital signals are transmitted as bits using a limited set of frequencies. Analog signals can assume any value within a specified range of frequencies. Figure 5-9 helps you visualize the difference between digital and analog waves.

**How can a network detect if a signal has been corrupted?** Digital networks—those that transmit digital signals—can be easily monitored to determine if interference has corrupted any signals. At its most primitive level, digital equipment is sensitive to only two frequencies—one that represents 1s and one that represents 0s.

Suppose that a 0 is sent as -5 volts and a 1 is sent as +5 volts. What if, during transmission, some interference changes the voltage of a "perfect" 1 from +5 volts to +3 volts? When the signal is received, the receiving device realizes that +3 volts is not one of the two valid voltages. It guesses that a 1 bit (+5 volts) was actually transmitted, and cleans the signal by reestablishing its voltage to +5. Correcting errors is one of the responsibilities of protocols.

**What's a packet?** When you send a file or an e-mail message, you might suppose that it is transmitted as an entire unit to its destination. This is not the case. Your file is actually chopped up into small pieces called packets. A **packet** is a parcel of data that is sent across a computer network. Each packet contains the address of its sender, the destination address, a sequence number, and some data. When packets reach their destination, they are reassembled into the original message according to the sequence numbers (Figure 5-10).

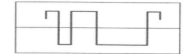

FIGURE 5-9

Digital and Analog Waves

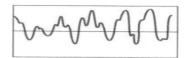

The signals carried on a digital channel are depicted as a stepped wave.

An analog signal is depicted as a smooth wave.

FIGURE 5-10

Before transmission, communications software divides messages into packets. Upon arriving at their destination, packets are reassembled into the original message.

**Why not just send an entire message?** Some communications networks, such as the telephone system, use a technology called **circuit switching**, which essentially establishes a dedicated, private link between one telephone and another for the duration of a call. This type of switching provides callers with a direct pipeline over which a stream of voice data can flow. Unfortunately, circuit switching is rather inefficient. For example, when someone is on hold, no communication is taking place—yet the circuit is reserved and cannot be used for other communications.

A more efficient alternative to circuit switching is **packet switching** technology, which divides a message into several packets that can be routed independently to their destination. Messages divided into equal-size packets are easier to handle than an assortment of small, medium, large, and huge files.

Packets from many different messages can share a single communications channel, or circuit. Packets are shipped over the circuit on a first-come, first-served basis. If some packets from a message are not available, the system does not need to wait for them. Instead, the system moves on to send packets from other messages. The end result is a steady stream of data (Figure 5-11).

FIGURE 5-11

Packet switching networks (bottom) provide a more efficient communications system than circuit switching networks (top). To see the differences between these technologies in action, click the Start icons in your digital textbook.

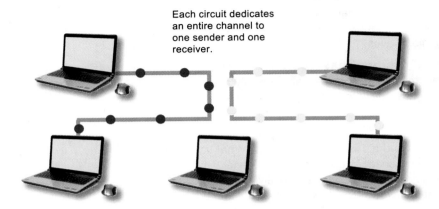

Each circuit dedicates an entire channel to one sender and one receiver.

▶ CLICK TO START

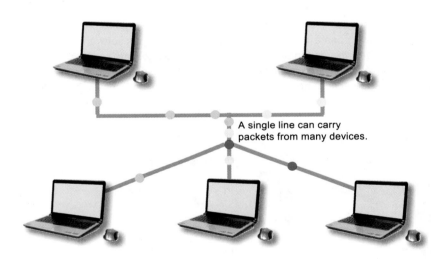

A single line can carry packets from many devices.

▶ CLICK TO START

**How are packets routed to their destinations?** Every packet that travels over a network includes the address of its destination device, similar to the way a letter contains the address of a house or mailbox. Communications protocols specify the proper format for addresses within a network. When a packet reaches a network node, a routing device examines the address and sends the packet along to its destination.

**How do devices get an address?** Network addresses are a potential source of confusion. Network devices can have a variety of addresses used for different purposes. Two commonly used addresses are MAC addresses and IP addresses.

**What is a MAC address?** In the context of networking, *MAC* stands for Media Access Control. A **MAC address** is a unique number assigned to a network interface card when it is manufactured. MAC addresses are used for some low-level network functions and can also be employed to establish network security.

**What is an IP address?** An **IP address** is a series of numbers used to identify a network device. IP addresses were originally used on the Internet, but now are the standard for assigning addresses to devices in virtually every type of computer network. IP addresses are assigned to network computers, servers, peripherals, and devices. When written, an IP address such as 204.127.129.1 is separated into four sections by periods for the convenience of human readers. Each section is called an **octet** because in binary it is represented by eight bits.

**Where do IP addresses come from?** IP addresses can be assigned by ISPs or system managers. Assigned IP addresses are semi-permanent and stay the same every time you boot your computer. If you use an assigned IP address, you have to enter it when you configure your network access.

IP addresses can also be obtained through **DHCP** (Dynamic Host Configuration Protocol), a protocol designed to automatically distribute IP addresses. Most computers are preconfigured to get an IP address by sending a query to the network device acting as the DHCP server. The IP address assigned by DHCP is good for that session. The next time you boot up, you might be assigned a different address. The fact that your IP address changes each time you boot up isn't a problem. Your network keeps track of your IP address behind the scenes; and unlike an e-mail address, your IP address is not publicized as a permanent address that people use to send files and messages to you.

**What happens when data reaches its destination?** Even on a small home network, packets might not travel from the source directly to their destination. Like travelers routed from one airline hub to another, network traffic often travels through intermediary routing devices. Some networks include protocols to keep track of each node that a packet traverses on its journey.

When data reaches its destination, it is checked for errors one last time and then the packets are reassembled into their original configuration. Tracking data is appended or stripped off, depending on the application, and then the newly delivered file is ready to be stored or viewed on the destination device.

5

## QuickCheck                                                                    SECTION A

1. The Internet covers a large geographical area and is an example of a(n) [          ] area network.

2. Each connection point on a network is referred to as a network [          ].

3. Communications [          ], such as TCP/IP, set standards for encoding and decoding data, guiding data to its destination, and mitigating the effects of noise.

4. A(n) [          ] switching network establishes a dedicated connection between two devices, whereas a(n) [          ] switching network divides messages into small parcels and handles them on a first-come, first-served basis,

5. IP addresses can be assigned by an ISP or system manager, or can be automatically obtained from a(n) [          ] server. (Hint: Use the acronym.)

▶ CHECK ANSWERS

# Wired Networks

WIRED NETWORKS offer clear advantages over their wireless counterparts for applications that require security and fast access. If you're planning to host a LAN party, for example; if you frequently transfer large video files from one computer to another; if you're nervous about the security of wireless networks; or if you're sending big graphics to a network printer, then a wired network connection should be your first choice. In Section B the focus is on wired technologies used for local area networks.

## WIRED NETWORK BASICS

**What is a wired network?** A **wired network** is one that uses cables to connect network devices. Familiar technologies such as telephone and cable television make extensive use of wired networks. Much of the Internet infrastructure is also wired. Before wireless technologies became available, local area networks were exclusively wired. Today, wired networks are used less frequently for home, school, and business networks. They remain the network technology of choice, however, for LANs that require fast and secure connectivity.

**What are the advantages of wired networks?** Wired networks are fast, secure, and simple to configure. A wired network transfers data over cables, which typically have high bandwidth and are shielded against interference. Wired connections are characteristically fast and reliable. The speed of a wired network is useful when accessing large files from a local server because file transfers on wired networks are significantly faster than on wireless networks.

Wired networks also offer a faster infrastructure for playing multiplayer computer games within a LAN (Figure 5-12). For Internet-based multiplayer games, however, the speed of the Internet connection rather than the LAN is usually the limiting factor.

Wired networks are more secure than their wireless counterparts because a computer can only join a network if it is physically connected by a cable. When you set up a wired network you don't have to worry about LAN jackers accessing your network from the sidewalk outside your house, or your neighbor stumbling across your files because your wireless signal reaches past your property line.

Today's wired LANs are easy to set up and configure. Most computers are preconfigured with the hardware and software needed to join a wired network. Whether you want to link up a desktop or notebook, PC or Mac, you can pretty much just plug in to connect.

**What are the disadvantages of wired networks?** The cables that offer speed and security for a wired network are also its main weakness. Devices tethered to cables have limited mobility. Desktop computers tend to be better candidates for wired networks, whereas notebook computers can retain their mobility when they are not tethered to a cable.

**FIGURE 5-12**

Discerning multiplayer game players prefer a fast wired connection when playing head to head on a LAN.

Cables are unsightly, tend to get tangled, and collect dust. Running cables through ceilings, walls, and floors can be tricky or banned by your landlord. Some building codes prohibit network cables from running through air conditioning and heating ducts. When drilling holes for network cables, installers should take care to avoid electrical wires and other hazards.

## ETHERNET

**Are there various types of wired networks?** In the past, many wired network technologies vied for popularity. Today, the most popular LAN technology is **Ethernet**. Most wired networks in homes, schools, and businesses use Ethernet technology that is defined by IEEE 802.3 standards.

**Why is Ethernet so popular?** Despite challenges from other technologies, Ethernet has emerged as the leading LAN technology. It is currently used in a high percentage of LANs worldwide. Ethernet's success is attributable to several factors:

● Ethernet networks are easy to understand, implement, manage, and maintain.

● As a nonproprietary technology, Ethernet equipment is available from a variety of vendors, and market competition keeps prices low.

● Current Ethernet standards allow extensive flexibility in network topology to meet the needs of small and large installations.

● Ethernet is compatible with popular Wi-Fi wireless networks, so it is easy to mix wired and wireless devices on a single network.

**How does Ethernet work?** Ethernet simultaneously broadcasts data packets to all network devices. A packet is accepted only by the device to which it is addressed (Figure 5-13).

**INFOWEBLINKS**

Ethernet is everywhere. See what the "Ether" is all about at the **Ethernet InfoWeb**.

 CLICK TO CONNECT
www.infoweblinks.com/np2012/ch05

**FIGURE 5-13**

On an Ethernet, a packet is broadcast to every device, but is accepted only by the device to which it is addressed.

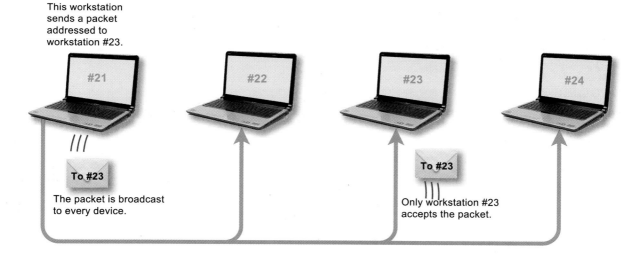

This workstation sends a packet addressed to workstation #23.

#21  #22  #23  #24

To #23

The packet is broadcast to every device.

To #23

Only workstation #23 accepts the packet.

An integral part of Ethernet technology relies on **CSMA/CD** protocol (Carrier Sense Multiple Access with Collision Detection). CSMA/CD takes care of situations in which two network devices attempt to transmit packets at the same time. A collision occurs and the signals do not reach their destination.

CSMA/CD protocol detects the collision, deletes the colliding signals, resets the network, and prepares to retransmit the data. The two devices wait for random time periods before retransmitting to prevent a collision from reoccurring (Figure 5-14).

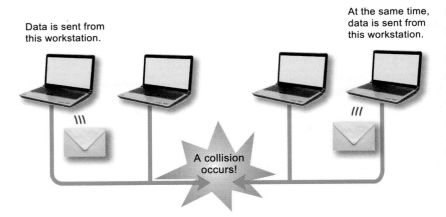

Data is sent from this workstation.

At the same time, data is sent from this workstation.

A collision occurs!

**FIGURE 5-14**

On an Ethernet, data travels on a first-come, first-served basis. If two workstations attempt to send data at the same time, a collision occurs. That data must be resent. ▶ To watch how Ethernet handles collisions, access this figure in your digital textbook.

**How fast is an Ethernet network?** The original Ethernet standard carried data over a coaxial cable bus topology at 10 Mbps. Ethernet encompasses a family of LAN technologies that offer various data transmission rates as shown in Figure 5-15. Today, most personal computers and LAN equipment work with Gigabit Ethernet.

**FIGURE 5-15**

Ethernet Standards

| Ethernet Standard | IEEE Designation | Speed |
|---|---|---|
| 10BaseT Ethernet | IEEE 802.3 | 10 Mbps |
| Fast Ethernet | IEEE 802.3u | 100 Mbps |
| Gigabit Ethernet | IEEE 802.3z | 1,000 Mbps |
| 10 Gigabit Ethernet | IEEE 802.3ae | 10 Gbps |
| 40/100 Gigabit Ethernet | IEEE 802.3ba | 40 or 100 Gbps |

## ETHERNET EQUIPMENT

**What equipment do I need for an Ethernet network?** Ethernet is the quintessential wired network technology. If you have a basic understanding of how it is installed, you can apply that knowledge to putting together just about any network.

Ethernet equipment is widely available and fairly inexpensive. For a typical home network that accesses the Internet, you need the following equipment:

- Two or more Ethernet-ready computers

- An Ethernet router

- A surge strip or UPS

- Cables for each computer

- An internet access device, such as a cable modem or DSL modem and corresponding cables

**How can I tell if a computer is Ethernet ready?** Many computers have a built-in Ethernet port located on the system case. The port looks very similar to an oversized telephone jack. If you have such a port, the next step is to determine its speed, as explained in Figure 5-16.

**FIGURE 5-16**

Most computers have a built-in Ethernet port. You can determine the speed of your computer's Ethernet adapter using networking utilities.

5

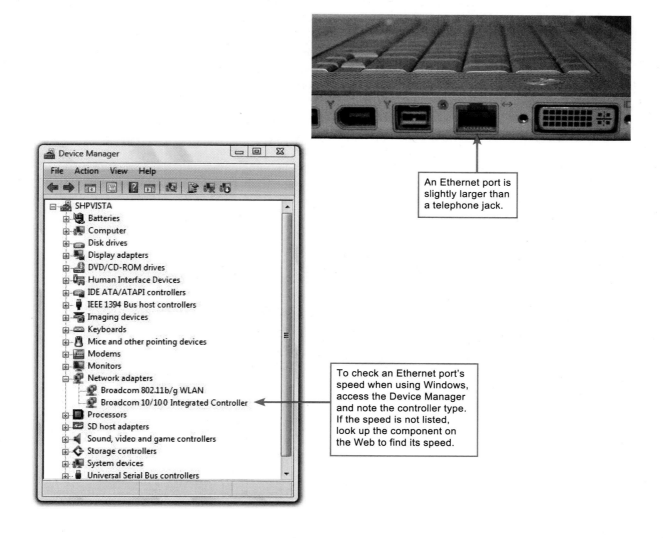

An Ethernet port is slightly larger than a telephone jack.

To check an Ethernet port's speed when using Windows, access the Device Manager and note the controller type. If the speed is not listed, look up the component on the Web to find its speed.

**What if a computer doesn't have an Ethernet port?** If your computer has no Ethernet port, you can purchase and install an **Ethernet adapter** (also called an Ethernet card or NIC). A USB Ethernet adapter plugs into a USB port and can be used with a notebook or desktop computer. You also have the option of installing an Ethernet card in an expansion slot inside the system unit of a desktop computer. Figure 5-17 illustrates some popular network adapters.

**FIGURE 5-17**
Ethernet Adapters

Ethernet adapter for USB port          Ethernet adapter for expansion slot

**Should I buy an Ethernet hub, switch, or router?** A **network hub** is a device that links two or more nodes of a wired network. On a typical network, the hub accepts data from one of the computers and then broadcasts it to all of the other network nodes. Some devices receive data that is not meant for them, but their NICs filter out any data that is not intended for that destination.

A **network switch** is a more sophisticated connection device that sends data only to the devices specified as the destination. Using a switch instead of a hub can increase a network's performance and security because data isn't flowing indiscriminately to every device on the network.

A **network router** is a network device that can ship data from one network to another. Most routers are also switches that contain ports for connecting workstations. You might see a router/switch device advertised as a "router with four-port switch." A router/switch is particularly useful for connecting a home network to the Internet; so if you are planning to connect your network to the Internet, you should consider using one as the central point of your LAN (Figure 5-18).

**FIGURE 5-18**
An Ethernet router features a collection of ports for connecting servers, workstations, and peripheral devices.

**How many ports do I need?** Your hub, switch, or router needs one port for each device you intend to wire to the network. An inexpensive router, for example, has four or five ports for network devices. It also has a WAN port that is used to connect the router to the Internet. If you want to attach more devices to a network, you can purchase an inexpensive hub that provides additional ports and connects to the router.

**What do I need to know about speed?** Ethernet routers are available at 10/100 Mbps or Gigabit speeds. If you have a Gigabit router and all the network computers have Gigabit Ethernet adapters, data will flow over all network connections at Gigabit speeds. If some computers have Gigabit adapters, whereas others have 10/100 Mbps adapters, a Gigabit router will ship data at a speed that corresponds to each adapter.

The only time you waste bandwidth is when your router is slower than one or more of the workstation network adapters. For example, suppose that you have a 10/100 Mbps router, but several of the network computers have Gigabit Ethernet adapters. In this case, the router cannot send data at Gigabit speeds, so the Gigabit adapters will send and receive data at the slower 100 Mbps rate.

Serious computer gamers who compete against each other over a LAN prefer Gigabit Ethernet equipment for adapters and routers. Some videoconferencing and streaming video applications might also benefit from high-bandwidth equipment.

**What kind of cable do I need?** The devices in an Ethernet are connected with network cables terminated at each end with a plastic **RJ45 connector** (Figure 5-19).

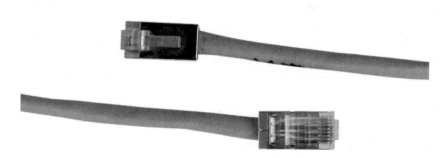

**FIGURE 5-19**

Network cables are terminated with plastic RJ45 connectors that are similar to, but larger than, the connectors used for telephones.

Network cables contain four pairs of copper wires. Each pair of wires is independently insulated and then twisted together, which is why network cable is sometimes referred to as twisted-pair cable. Shielded twisted-pair (STP) cable contains shielding, which reduces signal noise that might interfere with data transmitted over unshielded twisted-pair (UTP) cable. The shielded cable is not significantly more expensive.

When shopping for cables, look for Category 5 (Cat 5) or Category 6 (Cat 6) cables. You'll need one cable for each workstation. Network cables can be purchased in a variety of lengths. When you calculate the length of each cable, make sure you consider the path that the cable will follow as it snakes along walls from the router to the workstation. Cat 5 and Cat 6 cables have a maximum length of 328 feet (100 meters).

5

## ETHERNET SETUP

### What's the general procedure for setting up Ethernet?
Nowadays, it is easy to set up a wired network like the one in Figure 5-20.

To set up an Ethernet LAN:

- Run cables from the router to each workstation or server.
- Run a cable between the router and the device used for your Internet connection.
- Configure each workstation.
- Configure the router.

### How do I run the wiring?
Before you begin running wires, make sure the router, computers, and other devices are powered off. Connect cables between the router and the Ethernet ports on each workstation or server. Run a cable between your Internet device and the router's WAN port.

When all your devices are connected, tuck the cables out of the way. You might want to use cable tacks to carefully secure each cable to the baseboards along your walls. Use the same precautions with your network cables as you would with power cords; do not run them across walkways or under carpets.

### What about using existing wiring?
If you want the security of a wired network, but running cables is a problem, you can consider using existing telephone, cable television, or electrical wiring to connect network devices.

**HomePNA** (sometimes called HPNA) is a network technology that utilizes existing telephone wires or coaxial cables to connect network devices. Not to be confused with DSL or dial-up services that offer Internet access over your telephone lines, HomePNA uses telephone wiring already installed in your walls to connect the devices for a local area network.

A special HomePNA adapter is required to connect each workstation to a nearby telephone wall jack. Network signals then can travel from workstations, through the adapter, and over the telephone wires. An HPNA bridge device is also required so that signals can be transferred to your Ethernet router.

Another wired network option is to use premises electrical wiring. A **powerline network**, such as the HomePlug brand, transmits network data as radio signals over the wires that supply electricity to wall outlets. A powerline network adapter is required for each network device (Figure 5-21). If you install a powerline network in an apartment, make sure your apartment has a separate breaker box to prevent network signals from traveling throughout the building.

HomePNA and powerline networks can be a bit tricky to install and configure, so today most wired LANs use basic Ethernet cabling, which provides fast data transmission and is easy to install.

FIGURE 5-20

A typical wired network uses a router as a central device for connecting workstations, a file server, and an Internet access device.

FIGURE 5-21

A powerline adapter is cabled to a computer's Ethernet port and plugs into a wall outlet.

**How do I get a wired network up and running?** When you've connected cables between every network device and the router, plug in the router, preferably through a surge strip or UPS, and then turn it on. One by one, power up each network device. Figure 5-22 walks you through the basic setup.

FIGURE 5-22

Setting up a basic wired LAN requires just a few easy steps.

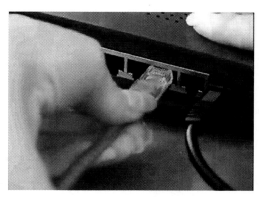

**1.** Place the router in a central location and plug it into a surge-protected outlet.

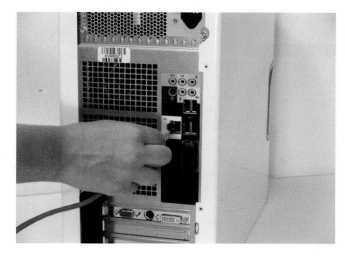

**2.** Run cables from the router to the Ethernet adapter in each workstation.

**3.** Run a cable between your Internet device and your router's WAN port.

**4.** Turn on network devices one at a time. Your operating system should automatically detect each device and establish a connection to the network.

▶ See how simple it is to set up a network!

5

**5.** Use your computer's operating system network utilities to verify each connection. When using Windows 7 or Windows Vista, access the Network and Sharing Center where you can view the status of the Local Area Connection.

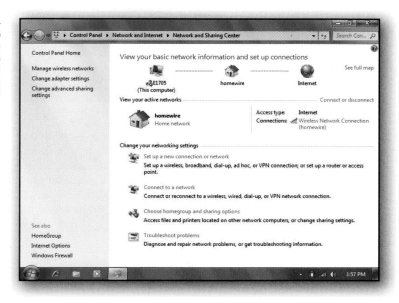

**How do I configure each workstation?** Turn on one of the workstations and wait for it to boot. Your computer's operating system should automatically sense the network connection. No additional configuration should be necessary.

**How do I configure the router?** The router's configuration data is stored in its EEPROM chip. To access the configuration data, open your browser and enter the router's address in the Address line as shown in Figure 5-23. Most routers use http://192.168.1.1 or http://192.168.1.100 as their configuration address. You can check your router's documentation to verify.

**FIGURE 5-23**

Most routers are configured using a browser. To access the router settings, enter the router address.

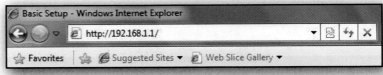

It is essential that you change the router's password to prevent unauthorized access and modifications to your network. If you are connecting your network to the Internet, additional configuration might be necessary, as explained in the Internet chapter.

**FIGURE 5-24**

Enable DHCP so that the router automatically assigns an IP address to each workstation.

**How do I set DHCP?** Each network workstation requires an IP address for sending and receiving data. Configure your router to act as a DHCP server as shown in Figure 5-24.

**How do I know when the network is ready?** Your operating system usually displays a message or icon to let you know when you are connected to a network. For example, Windows displays the Local Area Connection icon on the taskbar to indicate the status of network connections. If that icon indicates the network is connected, it is ready for use.

## QuickCheck

1. Today's most popular wired network technology is [_____] and is defined by IEEE 802.3 standards.

2. CSMA/CD is a network protocol that handles [_____] that sometimes occur when two workstations transmit data at the same time.

3. Category 5 and 6 network cables are terminated with a(n) [_____] connector.

4. A(n) [_____] with a four-port switch can be used to connect LAN devices and provide them with an Internet connection.

5. When you enable [_____] on your router, it automatically assigns IP addresses. (Hint: Use the acronym.)

CHECK ANSWERS

# Wireless Networks

**WHO WANTS LOTS OF** unsightly wires and cables snaking through their living room or office space? Today's trend is toward wireless LAN technology. Wireless LANs, dubbed WLANs, are easy to install, but it is important to secure them from intrusions. Section C supplies information on wireless LAN equipment and installation. You'll learn more about wireless security in Section E.

## WIRELESS BASICS

**What is a wireless network?** A **wireless network** transports data from one device to another without the use of cables or wires. Networks of all sizes, from PANs to LANs and WANs, can use wireless technologies, such as radio signals, microwaves, and infrared light.

**How do radio signals transport data?** Most wireless networks transport data as RF signals (radio frequency signals). **RF signals**—commonly called radio waves—are sent and received by a **transceiver** (a combination of a transmitter and a receiver) that is equipped with an antenna. Workstations, peripheral devices, and network devices can be equipped with transceivers to send and receive data on wireless networks (Figure 5-25).

**How do microwaves transport data?** **Microwaves** (the waves themselves, not your oven!) provide another option for transporting data over wireless networks. Like radio waves, microwaves are electromagnetic signals, but they behave differently. Microwaves can be aimed in a single direction and have more carrying capacity than radio waves. However, microwaves cannot penetrate metal objects and work best for line-of-sight transmission when a clear path exists between the transmitter and receiver. Microwave installations typically provide data transport for large corporate networks.

**How does infrared transport data?** Today, most people are familiar with television remote controls that use **infrared light** beams. Infrared can also carry data signals, but only for short distances and with a clear line of sight. Its most practical use seems to be for transmitting data between devices connected to a PAN.

**What are the advantages of wireless networks?** The main advantage of wireless networks is mobility. Wireless devices are not tethered to network cables, so battery-operated workstations can be easily moved from room to room, or even outdoors. With wireless networks, there are no unsightly cables, and power spikes are much less likely to run through cables to damage workstations.

**Do wireless networks have disadvantages?** In the past, wireless network equipment was quite a bit more expensive than equivalent wired equipment. With the current popularity of wireless technologies, however, prices have equalized. When compared to wired networks, the main disadvantages of wireless networks are speed, range, licensing, and security.

5

**FIGURE 5-25**

Wireless equipment often sports an antenna for transmitting and receiving data signals. The antenna is not always visible; it can be incorporated within the body of the device.

**Why is wireless slower than wired?** Wireless signals are susceptible to interference from devices such as microwave ovens, cordless telephones, and baby monitors. When interference affects a wireless signal, data must be re-transmitted, and that takes extra time.

Despite interference, wireless networks are fast enough for most applications. Even the slowest wireless LAN technologies are faster than most Internet services, so online access from a wireless LAN is usually no slower than from a wired LAN. Wireless LANs are slower for intra-LAN operations, such as exchanging files and sharing printers. When lots of computer game players compete against each other over a LAN, a fast, wired network is desirable.

**What limits the range of a wireless network?** The range of a wireless signal can be limited by the type of signal, the transmitter strength, and the physical environment. Just as radio stations fade as you move away from their broadcasting towers, data signals fade as the distance between network devices increases. Signal range can also be limited by thick walls, floors, or ceilings.

As signal strength decreases, so can speed. A weak signal usually means slow data transfers. You can monitor network signal strength from your computer's desktop (Figure 5-26).

**What's wrong with wireless security?** Wireless signals float through the air and penetrate walls. The signals that carry your wireless data can be accessed from outside your premises. Someone outside of your house, for example, could surreptitiously join your network, access files, and piggyback on your Internet connection. To make wireless network data useless to intruders, it should be encrypted. Later in the chapter, you'll learn how to use encryption to secure a wireless LAN.

**How does licensing affect wireless networks?** Signals that are sent through the air are regulated by government agencies such as the Federal Communications Commission (FCC). To broadcast at most frequencies, including those used by radio and television stations, a license is required. Only certain frequencies are unlicensed and available for public use.

Unlicensed frequencies include 2.4 GHz and 5.8 GHz used by cordless telephones and baby monitors, and the 460 MHz frequency used for two-way CB (Citizens Band) radios. Wireless networks use unlicensed frequencies so that they can be set up without applying to the FCC for permission. The few unlicensed frequencies are crowded, however, and neighboring home networks that are forced to use the same frequencies pose security risks.

**What are the most popular technologies for wireless networks?** By far the most popular wireless LAN technology is Wi-Fi. Additional wireless technologies such as Bluetooth, Wireless USB (WUSB), and Wireless HD (WiHD) are useful for PANs that include wireless game controllers, MP3 players, televisions, printers, digital cameras, and scanners. Other wireless technologies, such as WiMAX, are MAN or WAN technologies typically used for fixed Internet access. Let's take a brief look at Bluetooth technology and then examine Wi-Fi networks in more detail.

**FIGURE 5-26**

On a wireless network, signal strength varies depending on distance from a transmitter and obstacles that might interfere with the signal.

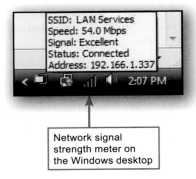

SSID: LAN Services
Speed: 54.0 Mbps
Signal: Excellent
Status: Connected
Address: 192.166.1.337

Network signal strength meter on the Windows desktop

## BLUETOOTH

**What is Bluetooth?** **Bluetooth** is a short-range wireless network technology that's designed to make its own connections between electronic devices, without wires, cables, or any direct action from a user. Bluetooth networks form automatically when two or more Bluetooth devices come within range of each other. A Bluetooth network is sometimes called a **piconet**.

To form a network, a Bluetooth device can search for other Bluetooth devices within range. When another Bluetooth device is detected, it typically broadcasts what it is; for example, a printer, a PC, or a cell phone. Before data is exchanged, the owners of the two Bluetooth devices have to exchange passkeys, or PINs (Figure 5-27). Once passkeys have been exchanged, the two Bluetooth devices form a trusted pair. Future communication between these two devices does not require the passkey to be re-entered.

**FIGURE 5-27**

Owners of Bluetooth devices can beam data to other Bluetooth device owners.

5

**Where is Bluetooth used?** Bluetooth operates at the unlicensed 2.4 GHz frequency, so anyone can set up a Bluetooth network. Bluetooth is not typically used to connect a collection of workstations into a LAN. Instead, Bluetooth connectivity replaces the short cables that would otherwise tether a mouse, keyboard, or printer to a computer.

Bluetooth can be used to link devices in a PAN, connect home entertainment system components, provide hands-free cell phone operation in an automobile, link a cell phone to a wireless headset (Figure 5-28), and synchronize PDAs with desktop base stations.

**FIGURE 5-28**

Bluetooth technology is used for wireless keyboards and mice, but it is also the technology used for wireless headsets and devices like Motorola's Bluetooth headset that clips to a motorcycle helmet so you don't miss important cell calls.

Bluetooth is built into some peripheral devices. If you want these devices to communicate with your computer, you can use a variety of add-on cards.

**What are the speed and range of Bluetooth?** Bluetooth 2.1 offers peak transmission rates of only 3 Mbps over a range of 3 to 300 feet (about 1 to 91 meters). Bluetooth 3.0 operates in the 6 to 9 GHz frequency range at peak speeds of 24 Mbps.

## WI-FI

**What is Wi-Fi?** **Wi-Fi** refers to a set of wireless networking technologies defined by IEEE 802.11 standards that are compatible with Ethernet. A Wi-Fi device transmits data as radio waves over 2.4 GHz or 5.8 GHz frequencies. When people refer to wireless networks, they are usually talking about Wi-Fi.

Wi-Fi encompasses several standards, designated by letters *b*, *a*, *g*, *n*, and *y*. Some of these standards are cross compatible, which means that you can use them on the same wireless network. Figure 5-29 summarizes the specifications for each Wi-Fi standard.

**FIGURE 5-29**

Wi-Fi Standards

| IEEE Designation | Frequency | Typical Speed | Range | Pros/Cons |
|---|---|---|---|---|
| IEEE 802.11b | 2.4 GHz | 5 Mbps | 100–300 feet | Original standard |
| IEEE 802.11a | 5 GHz | 27 Mbps | 25–75 feet | Not compatible with 802.11b, g, or n |
| IEEE 802.11g | 2.4 GHz | 27 Mbps | 100–150 feet | Faster than, but compatible with, 802.11b |
| IEEE 802.11n | 2.4/5 GHz | 144 Mbps | 100–150 feet | Faster than, but compatible with, b and g |
| IEEE 802.11y | 3.6–3.7 GHz | 27 Mbps | 3 miles | Use: wide-area commercial base stations |

**How do the speed and range of Wi-Fi compare to other network technologies?** On a wired network, the rated speed and range are usually quite close to actual performance. Wireless network speed and range, however, are often theoretical maximums because signals can easily deteriorate. Although Wi-Fi 802.11n is capable of 600 Mbps speeds, its actual performance is typically 144 Mbps, which is far slower than Gigabit Ethernet.

In a typical office environment, Wi-Fi's range varies from 25 to 150 feet (8 to 45 meters). Thick cement walls, steel beams, and other environmental obstacles can drastically reduce this range to the point that signals cannot be reliably transmitted. Wi-Fi signals can also be disrupted by interference from electronic devices operating at the same frequency, such as 2.4 GHz cordless telephones.

Wi-Fi speed and range can be improved with various technologies. For example, **MIMO** (multiple-input multiple-output) technology uses two or more antennas to essentially send multiple sets of signals between network devices (Figure 5-30).

**FIGURE 5-30**

MIMO-equipped devices usually have more than one antenna.

## WI-FI EQUIPMENT

**What equipment is required for a Wi-Fi network?** Wi-Fi equipment is widely available and fairly inexpensive. For a typical home network, you need the equipment listed in Figure 5-31.

**FIGURE 5-31**

Wireless Networking Equipment

Wireless-ready devices, such as computers and printers

Short piece of network cable to run between the router and one computer

Surge strip or UPS

Wireless router

**How can I tell if a device is wireless-ready?** Although cell phones and PDAs sometimes sport a small antenna that emphasizes their wireless communications capabilities, the antenna and transceiver for most notebook computers are hidden inside the case. You usually have to check your computer's documentation or on-screen utilities to discover if it has wireless capability (Figure 5-32).

FIGURE 5-32

Check the hardware listings to see if your computer has wireless capability. Use the Start menu to access Device Manager and look for a wireless or WLAN adapter.

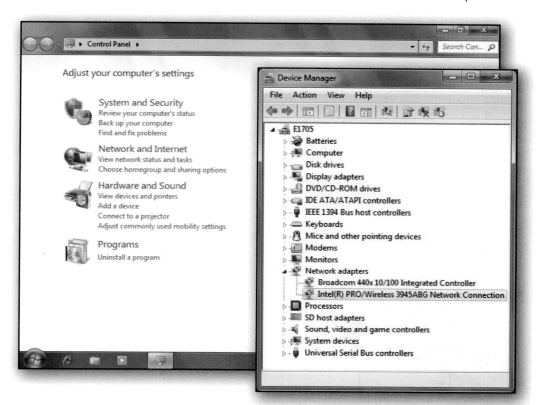

5

**Can I add Wi-Fi?** Today, most computers come equipped with Wi-Fi circuitry. Computers without Wi-Fi or those with slow Wi-Fi protocols can be upgraded using a **Wi-Fi adapter** (also called a Wi-Fi card or wireless network controller). Wi-Fi cards that plug into an expansion slot can be used to upgrade desktop computers. Wi-Fi adapters that plug into USB ports can be used to upgrade any type of computer. Figure 5-33 illustrates these two types of Wi-Fi adapters.

INFOWEBLINKS

For the latest information on Wi-Fi equipment and pricing, check out the **Wireless LAN InfoWeb**.

W CLICK TO CONNECT
www.infoweblinks.com/np2012/ch05

FIGURE 5-33

Wi-Fi Adapters

Wi-Fi adapter in PCI slot

USB Wi-Fi adapter

**Do I need a wireless router?** You can set up a wireless network in two ways (Figure 5-34). First, you can set up a **wireless ad-hoc network** in which devices broadcast directly to each other. The advantage of this configuration is cost. If your devices include factory-installed wireless networking circuitry, you don't need additional equipment.

The disadvantage of an ad-hoc network is Internet access. Although you can access the Internet from an ad-hoc network, you'll have to designate one of the network computers as the gateway device. It will require a cable connection to your Internet modem, and it will have to be left on during the time anyone on your network might want to access the Internet.

A second option called a **wireless infrastructure network** uses a centralized broadcasting device, such as a wireless access point or router. A **wireless access point** is a device that transmits and receives wireless signals. A **wireless router** is a wireless access point that also includes routing circuitry designed to connect a Wi-Fi network to the Internet.

**What about MiFi?** **MiFi** is a brand name for a compact, mobile, wireless router offered by Novatel Wireless. The term is sometimes applied to similar routers produced by other manufacturers that can form a network of about five clients, making it easy to connect notebook computers with cameras, media players, and other handheld devices.

With MiFi, you can easily assemble a small network just about anywhere, even when you are traveling. A MiFi router, like the one in Figure 5-35, is about the size of a cell phone and runs on batteries.

Wireless ad-hoc network

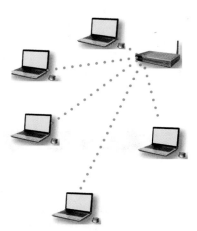

Wireless infrastructure network

**FIGURE 5-35**

MiFi routers run on batteries, so they can be used to construct portable networks. These routers are packaged with a cellular data plan for accessing the Internet.

**Can wireless routers handle wired devices, too?** Yes. Suppose that you want to use an old desktop computer as a game server or as a server for lots of video footage. You also want to be able to use a wired connection for your notebook computer when you're editing video, but you'd like the flexibility of a wireless connection so you can use your computer on the patio.

In addition to working with wireless signals, most standard wireless routers include ports for Ethernet cables and a WAN port for a cable to an Internet device, such as a cable or DSL modem (Figure 5-36).

**FIGURE 5-36**

Most wireless routers (note the antenna) also include ports for wired Ethernet connections.

## WI-FI SETUP

**What's the general procedure for setting up a Wi-Fi network?**
Standard wireless routers offer the most flexibility for Internet access and
the best security options, so most experts recommend using one as the
central point in your wireless network. The remaining information in this
section pertains to wireless infrastructure networks that use a standard
wireless router.

Setting up a Wi-Fi network like the one in Figure 5-37 involves a few simple
steps:

- Set up the router.
- Connect to the router with a computer.
- Configure the router.
- Access the router setup utility.
- Create a new router password.
- Enter an SSID for the network.
- Activate WEP, WPA, or PSK and create an encryption key.
- Set up the wireless workstations.
- Connect an Internet access device.

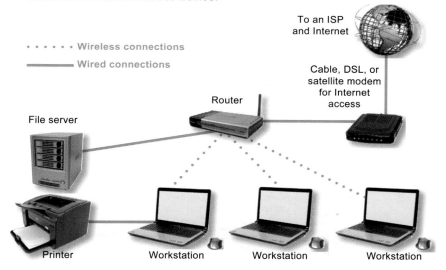

**FIGURE 5-37**

A wireless network typically
includes several workstations
connected wirelessly to a router;
an Internet device connected
by a cable to the router's WAN
port; and possibly a file server
linked with a wired or wireless
connection.

**How do I set up a wireless router?** Place the wireless router in a
central location relative to the network devices. Thick concrete walls and
floors can significantly lower signal strength; so if you encounter such
obstacles, you might have to consider adding a device to boost the signal.

Connect the wireless router to a power outlet through a surge strip or UPS.
A UPS will keep your network operational during a power outage. Your
ability to access the Internet during a power outage depends on the power
situation at your ISP, however. A network that consists of battery-operated
notebook computers and a wireless router connected to a UPS should be
able to run for several hours during a blackout.

If you want your wireless network to access the Internet, connect the router
to an Internet access device, such as a cable or DSL modem. Internet
modems are typically connected to the router's WAN port using an Ethernet
cable.

**How do I access the router's configuration utility?** Before using your wireless network, you should adjust router configuration settings for the default password, SSID, and encryption. The configuration settings are stored in the router's EEPROM memory. You'll need to log into the configuration software to adjust settings.

A router has no screen or keyboard of its own; so to access the router's configuration software, you have to connect a computer to the router. The easiest way to make this connection is with a short Ethernet cable. Although it might seem nonintuitive to use a cable to create a wireless network, the use of a cabled connection is detected automatically by Windows and that provides a direct link to the router without any preliminary setup.

Documentation for the router supplies a LAN address for the router and might also supply a default password. As you learned earlier in the chapter, a LAN address is typically something like 192.168.1.1 or 192.168.1.100. Open your browser and type http:// and the router's LAN address in the Address line.

**How do I change the default password?** Your first step after logging on to your router's configuration utility is to change the default password so that hackers can't gain access to your network and reconfigure it for their own malevolent schemes.

Locate the setting for the administrator password and create a new one. Follow the recommendations in earlier chapters for creating a strong password. This password is only used to configure the router. It does not need to be conveyed to network users who simply want to set up their computers to send and receive data over the network.

**What is an SSID?** An **SSID** (service set identifier) is the name of a wireless network. In areas where there are overlapping wireless networks, such as in a city or on a college campus, SSIDs help you log into the right network, rather than a network run by a hacker who will try to suck important information off your computer as soon as you connect.

**How do I set the SSID?** Most routers ship with an SSID predefined by the manufacturer. Predefined SSIDs are typically very simple and publicly known.

As shown in Figure 5-38, use the router configuration software to change the default SSID. When you create an SSID, think of it as a user ID, rather than a password. Examples of SSIDs would be Acme Company, Java Joe Coffee Shop, Planters Inn of Miami, or Alpha Kappa Delta Phi.

**FIGURE 5-38**

Change the default password for your router when you install a wireless network. ▶ Your digital textbook shows you how to access router settings and change the default password.

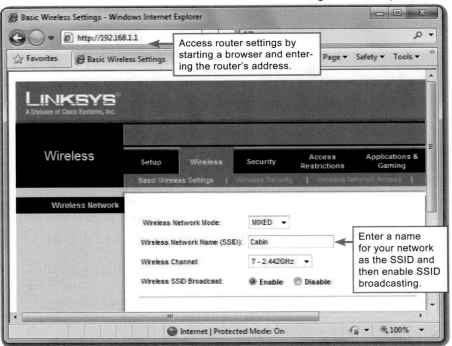

**Should I broadcast my SSID?** When SSID broadcasting is turned on, any wireless device passing by can see that a network exists. Legitimate users can easily find the network and connect to it. With SSID broadcasting turned off, the public can't see it. Unfortunately, hackers armed with the right tools can see the network even if the SSID is not broadcast.

Turning off SSID is a very weak form of security. Experts disagree about broadcasting your network's SSID. If you believe the potential for drive-by hacking is high, then you might not want to broadcast the SSID. In any case, SSID should be left on until you configure the rest of the devices that you plan to use on your network.

**Do I need to take any special steps to secure my wireless network?** Wireless networks are much more susceptible to unauthorized access and use than wired networks. Some measure of security can be gained by enabling encryption as explained in Section E.

**When is the router configuration complete?** Basic router configuration requires you to change the router password, enter an SSID, and activate encryption. Your wireless networking utility offers additional configuration options, but they are not needed for typical home and school networks. With your router configuration complete, you can close the router utility and set up the rest of the network.

**How do I connect additional workstations?** You can connect additional computers to your wireless network at any time. Simply turn on any computer with wireless capability, making sure that it is in range of your wireless router. The computer should automatically find the network SSID and ask you to enter the wireless network key or passphrase. Once the computer is approved, you can use it to exchange data with other network devices.

5

# QuickCheck                                             SECTION C

1.  A short-range, wireless network technology primarily used for PANs is called _____ .

2.  _____ is today's most popular wireless network technology for LANs.

3.  In a wireless _____ network, a centralized device, such as a router, broadcasts data to all of the workstations.

4.  A wireless _____ network does not require a router because network devices transmit directly to each other.

5.  A(n) _____ router is a battery powered device that can be used for small mobile networks.

▶ CHECK ANSWERS

# Using LANs

**LANS HAVE BECOME** an integral part of computing environments at home, at school, and at work. Many LANs are installed solely for distributing access to an Internet connection. That facet of LANs will be discussed in the next chapter. What else can you do with a LAN? Section D helps you explore the advantages and disadvantages of LANs, as well as provides practical tips on how to share files and printers.

## LAN ADVANTAGES AND CHALLENGES

**Why are LANs advantageous?** Today, the pervasiveness of LANs and other types of networks has dramatically changed the face of computing by offering **shared resources**—hardware, software, and data made available for authorized network users to access. LANs offer the following advantages:

● LANs enable people to work together. Using groupware and other specialized network application software, several people can work together on a single document, communicate by e-mail and instant messaging, take part in multiplayer computer games, and participate in online conferences and Webcasts (Figure 5-39).

**FIGURE 5-39**

LANs can be used for intra-LAN collaboration, or they can be connected to other networks for broader participation.

● Sharing networked software can reduce costs. Although purchasing and installing a single software copy for an entire LAN might be technically possible, it is typically not allowed under the terms of a single-user license agreement. However, software site licenses for network use are usually less expensive than purchasing single-user versions of a product for each network user.

● Sharing data on a LAN can increase productivity. To transfer data between standalone computers, a file is usually copied to some type of removable storage media, and then carried or mailed to the other computer where it is copied onto the hard disk. LANs can provide authorized users with access to data stored on network servers or workstations.

- Sharing networked hardware can reduce costs. In an office environment, for example, a single expensive high-speed color printer can be purchased and attached to a LAN, instead of the costly alternative of purchasing color printers for each employee who wants to generate color printouts.

- Sharing networked hardware can provide access to a wide range of services and specialized peripheral devices. A LAN can allow multiple users to access Internet services, including voice over IP, through a single Internet connection. Networked peripheral devices, such as scanners, photo printers, plotters, and high-capacity storage devices, can be accessed by any authorized LAN users. In a home environment, a LAN can offer access to surveillance and monitoring devices from inside or outside the home. LANs can control entertainment devices, and supply them with downloaded music and videos (Figure 5-40).

**FIGURE 5-40**

Music and video can stream over wireless LANs to projectors, speakers, and televisions when devices are equipped for 802.11 networking.

A wireless projector streams video signals from a remote PC.

A wireless receiver connects to an audio system, so you can listen to music from your PC in any room.

A wireless media player can stream video to your television, and play digital music on your stereo system.

**Do LANs have disadvantages?** One disadvantage of LANs is that when a network malfunctions, all the resources you're accustomed to accessing are unavailable until the network is repaired.

Another disadvantage of LANs is their vulnerability to unauthorized access. Whereas a standalone computer is vulnerable to on-premises theft or access, network computers are vulnerable to unauthorized access from many sources and locations.

Through unauthorized use of a LAN workstation, intruders can access data stored on the network server or other workstations. LANs connected to the Internet are vulnerable to intrusions from remote computers in distant states, provinces, or countries. Unsecured wireless LANs can be tapped from any computers within range of the wireless signal.

LANs are also more vulnerable than standalone computers to malicious code. Whereas the most prevalent threat to standalone computers is disk-borne viruses, networks are susceptible to an ever-increasing number of worms, Trojan horses, and blended threats. If a worm gets through LAN security, every computer on the network is at risk.

Most computer owners are enthusiastic about the benefits provided by LANs and believe that those benefits outweigh the risks of intrusions and viruses—especially if their computers can be protected by security tools, such as antivirus software and firewalls. You'll learn more about LAN security threats and countermeasures later in this chapter.

## SHARING FILES

**How do I access network resources?** If you use Windows, it automatically detects available LANs any time you turn on a workstation. Depending on your network setup, you might be asked to log in by entering a user ID and password. Once access is established, you can use any shared resources for which you have been given authorization.

You can access shared data on other workstations in a variety of ways. For example, Windows 7 users can access the Start menu's Network option to access shared resources. These resources are listed as computers, folders, or drives; their names might indicate the computer on which they reside. Figure 5-41 shows a listing of available network resources.

Another way to access network resources that works for most operating systems is to map a drive. **Drive mapping** assigns a drive letter to a storage device located on a network workstation (Figure 5-42).

**FIGURE 5-41**

The network on this Windows computer has access to five computers and one network printer.

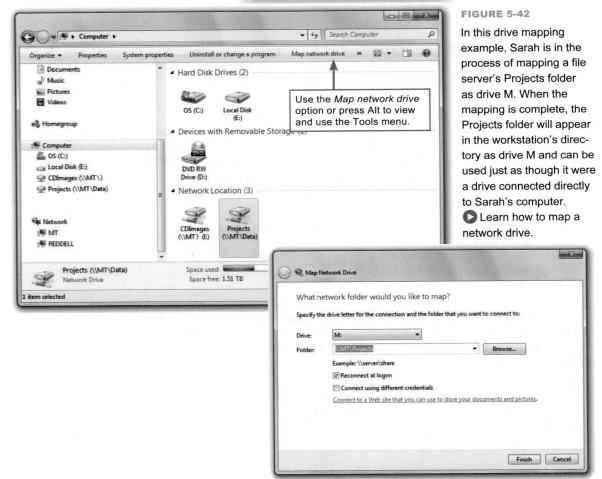

**FIGURE 5-42**

In this drive mapping example, Sarah is in the process of mapping a file server's Projects folder as drive M. When the mapping is complete, the Projects folder will appear in the workstation's directory as drive M and can be used just as though it were a drive connected directly to Sarah's computer.
▶ Learn how to map a network drive.

**How do I specify which resources can be shared by other workstations?** If your computer is part of a network, you can typically specify which of your drives and folders can be accessed from other network workstations. For security reasons, however, it is not advisable to allow shared access to the root directory of drive C on your computer.

You can allow other network users to view and edit files in the folders you've designated as shared, or you can limit access only to viewing. Figure 5-43 explains how to use Windows 7 to designate a folder as shared.

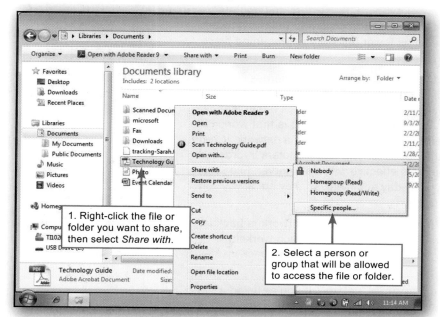

**FIGURE 5-43**

To allow other network users to access files or folders on your Windows computer, you have to designate the files as shared. ▶ Your digital textbook shows you how to adjust file sharing in Windows. You'll learn how to open your public files for sharing and how to share specific files with designated users.

**5**

**What is a homegroup?** A **homegroup** is a collection of trusted networked computers that automatically share files and folders. Access to the homegroup can be protected by password. To join a homegroup, double-click the Homegroup option in Windows Explorer's navigation pane. Figure 5-44 shows how to access files stored on homegroup computers.

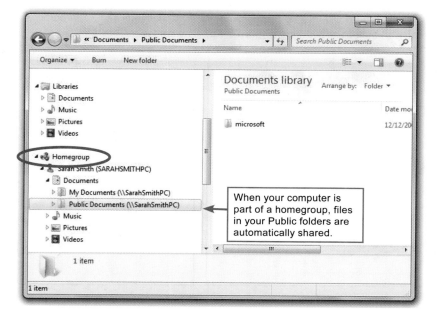

**FIGURE 5-44**

Windows 7 is preconfigured with a Homegroup that you can use to quickly link to other computers on your network and share files.

**What is a file server?** A file server is a computer whose primary purpose is to be a repository for files that can be accessed by network workstations. A file server can reside on any personal computer. For example, you might designate one of your old desktop computers as a file server and use it to store lots of big video files that you don't want clogging up your local hard disk.

A file server connects to a LAN's router just like any other network device. You can also purchase a computing device advertised as a server. A server typically has no monitor or keyboard; its system unit contains a microprocessor, memory, high-capacity hard disk, and built-in network adapter. File servers are available as tower units or rack-mounted blade servers (Figure 5-45).

**Are file servers a good idea for home networks?** Whereas file servers are an essential component of most business networks, in many home networks, files are stored on workstations in shared folders rather than on a file server. A potential problem with this arrangement is that workstations must be turned on in order to access their files over a network. If you find yourself running all over the house turning on computers in order to find files, your network could be more effective with a file server. File servers are designed to run continuously day and night, so they are always on and their files are always accessible.

Another reason to consider a file server for a home network is backup. Rather than purchasing external hard disk drives for each workstation's backup, one low-cost file server can supply enough space to back up files for several workstations.

**Do file servers require any special setup?** If you're using a file server without its own keyboard or monitor, its configuration software is accessible using a browser. To configure a file server, open a browser from any workstation, enter the file server's IP address, and provide the administrator ID and password.

## SHARING PRINTERS

**How can I set up a printer for network access?** There are three ways to set up a printer so it can be accessed from any workstation. You can set up printer sharing using a workstation printer, set up printer sharing using a print server, or install a printer with built-in networking (Figure 5-46).

**FIGURE 5-45**

Servers are sold as tower units (top) or as rack-mountable units (bottom), typically used for business applications.

**FIGURE 5-46**

Printers can be attached to LANs in various ways. The connections can be wired or wireless.

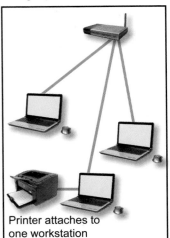

Printer attaches to one workstation

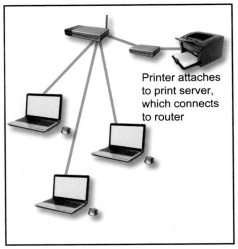

Printer attaches to print server, which connects to router

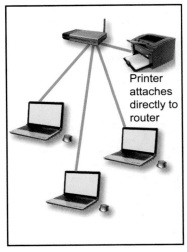

Printer attaches directly to router

**How does printer sharing work?** One way to share a printer over a network is to connect the printer to one of the workstations and then enable printer sharing. With printer sharing enabled, as long as the printer and workstation are turned on, any workstation on the network can send print jobs to the printer.

**How do I enable printer sharing?** If you're using Windows 7 and you want to allow other users to share the printer that's attached to your workstation, access Devices and Printers as shown in Figure 5-47.

**FIGURE 5-47**

You can designate the printer attached to your computer as sharable over the network.
▶ Access this figure in your digital textbook to learn how. You'll also review some security precautions that are important when sharing is turned on.

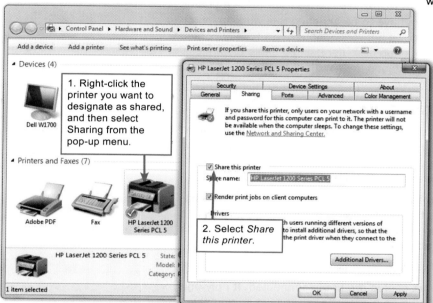

**How do I send a print job to a shared printer?** Before you can send a print job to a shared printer attached to someone else's workstation, you have to make sure that the printer driver is installed on your computer (Figure 5-48). Once you've added the printer to your list of printers and faxes, you can select the printer from your software's Print dialog box.

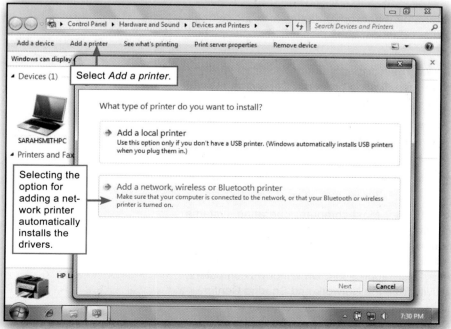

**FIGURE 5-48**

In Windows 7, selecting a network printer automatically installs the correct driver. When working with other operating systems, you might have to install the driver as a separate step.

**Can I set up a shared printer without tying up a workstation?**
You can use a network print server device to take the place of a workstation-controlled printer. By attaching a print server to a standard printer, you can access the printer from the network without going through a workstation. Print servers are available for wireless or wired networks. To set up a print server, connect it to the printer's USB port and access the configuration settings using your browser. Once the print server is configured, you can send print jobs to it using the same steps as for a shared printer.

**What about attaching a printer directly to the network?** A printer with built-in networking does not have to be attached to a workstation or a print server because it has its own network adapter. This type of printer typically connects to the network hub or router using a cable or wireless transmitter. Once configured, print jobs are sent to it just as with shared printers.

## NETWORK TROUBLESHOOTING

**What if my network stops working?** Network problems can stem from a variety of sources. Symptoms of network malfunctions are slow response time, intermittent outages, failure to access files from one workstation, and non-availability of network services to all workstations.

To troubleshoot network problems, you have to consider the possibility of a problem with a workstation's hardware or settings; network links including cables and wireless signal strength; or network devices such as routers, servers, or network adapters.

When troubleshooting network problems, consider the following possibilities:

Cables. Make sure all network cables are firmly connected. If only one workstation is not accessing the network, you can try swapping cables with another workstation.

Signal strength. In a wireless network, check the signal strength. If the signal is weak, move the workstation closer to the access point, if possible.

Security. Make sure you are using the correct password and that your password has not expired.

Interference. If you have intermittent network outages, look for sources of interference, such as cordless phones, baby monitors, or construction equipment.

Network devices. Make sure your network hub, switch, router, or wireless access point is plugged in and functioning properly. Check the activity lights to determine if data is being sent and received.

Settings. Make sure the network is enabled and then use the Control Panel to check the drivers for your network equipment.

Switches. Many portable computer include a physical switch that turns wireless networking on or off. Make sure this switch is in the On position for networking.

**Can I monitor network activity?** Most computer operating systems provide tools for monitoring the number of packets sent, received, and dropped from your network connection. This information helps you determine if data is flowing over your network. On Macs, you can view this information using the Network Utility application. On Windows computers, you can monitor network activity from the Network and Sharing Center.

**Where can I find troubleshooting utilities?** Several third-party vendors offer network monitoring and troubleshooting utilities, but check your operating system first. Windows 7, for example, offers a set of basic troubleshooters from the Network and Sharing Center (Figure 5-49).

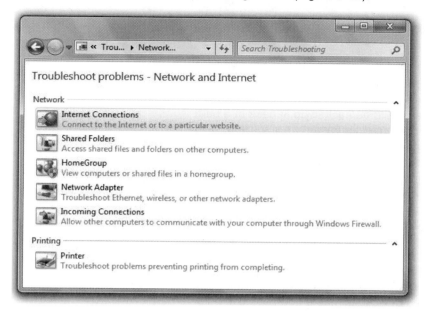

**FIGURE 5-49**

To access the network troubleshooters in Windows 7, go to the Network and Sharing Center and click *Troubleshoot problems*.

**Can I reboot my network?** Yes. When a network is not functioning correctly, you can try rebooting it. First, make sure all applications on workstation computers are closed. Then turn off the router and your Internet modem. To restart, first turn on the Internet modem. If it has a ready-to-send (RTS) status light or similar indicator, then make sure it is lit. Next, turn on your network router. Give the router a few seconds to boot, then check your network connections by trying to access another workstation or the Internet.

## QuickCheck

1. Drive _____ offers a way to designate a drive letter for a folder located on a network workstation other than your own.

2. With Windows 7, users can join a(n) _____ that automatically allows them to share files located in Public folders.

3. A(n) _____ server is a computer whose primary purpose is to be a repository for files that can be accessed by network workstations.

4. Before you can send a print job to a network printer, you have to make sure that the printer _____ is installed on your computer.

5. Many notebook computers have a physical _____ that turns wireless networking on or off.

 CHECK ANSWERS

# Security Through Encryption

**LOCAL AREA NETWORKS** are susceptible to a variety of threats. Many threats can be handled using techniques for standalone computers. Network equipment should be connected to power strips to prevent damage from power spikes. Data should be backed up in case of a hard drive failure. Workstations should be protected by antivirus software, and passwords should be required for network access. Wireless network data can also be protected by encryption. In Section E you'll learn how to enable encryption on a wireless network, you'll find out how encryption works, and you'll become familiar with other ways that encryption can be useful.

## WI-FI SECURITY

**What are the threats to my wireless network?** Compared to wired networks, wireless networks are much more susceptible to unauthorized access and use. To join a wired network, you have to gain physical access to the router and plug in a cable. To access many wireless networks, you simply boot up a wireless-enabled device such as a notebook computer within range of the wireless router. One threat to wireless network users is called an "evil twin." Users think they are logging onto a legitimate network, but its signals are being jammed by hackers who can extract passwords and credit card information from unsuspecting users.

With wireless network data floating freely through the air, hackers have an easy time intercepting signals by cruising through a business district or neighborhood with a Wi-Fi enabled notebook computer, a practice called **LAN jacking** or war driving (*war* stands for wireless access revolution).

LAN jackers can pinpoint the exact location of a wireless access point with the use of GPS receivers or legitimate network-detecting and monitoring software such as InSSIDer and NetStumbler (Figure 5-50).

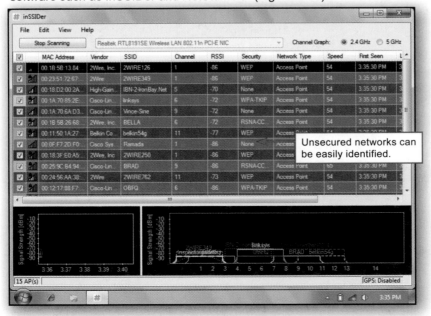

**FIGURE 5-50**

Software tools such as InSSIDer help locate and identify secured and unsecured networks. Once logged on to an unsecured wireless network, LAN jackers are free to do anything from stealing the network owner's credit card or bank information to attacking computers in other networks.

**Can I tell if someone is hacking my network?** Yes. Your network router maintains a list of clients that are accessing your network using wired or wireless connections. You can view a list of current connections as in Figure 5-51, or you can set up your router software to maintain a log over a period of hours or days.

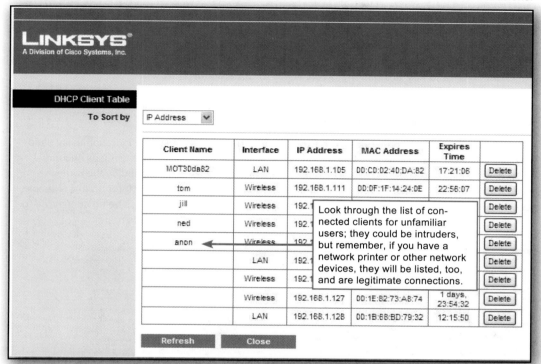

**How can I secure my wireless network?** Preventing Wi-Fi signal interception is difficult, but encrypting transmitted data makes it useless to intruders. **Wireless encryption** scrambles the data transmitted between wireless devices and then unscrambles the data only on devices that have a valid encryption key. Several types of encryption are available; some are more effective than others. You'll learn how encryption works later in the chapter.

**What are the options for wireless encryption?** The original wireless encryption was called **WEP** (Wired Equivalent Privacy) because it was designed to provide a level of confidentiality similar to that of a wired network. The original version of WEP is very easy to bypass. A second version of WEP uses stronger encryption but has several flaws that can easily be exploited by hackers.

**WPA** (Wi-Fi Protected Access) and its follow-up version, WPA2, offer stronger protection by making sure that packets have not been intercepted or tampered with in any way. **PSK** (pre-shared key), also referred to as personal mode, is a type of WPA used on most home networks. All workstations use the same key to connect to the network.

**Which type of encryption should I use?** All devices on a network must use the same type of encryption. If you have even one device on your network that only supports WEP, for example, you will have to use WEP for the entire network. Although WEP is fairly easy for hackers to neutralize, it is better than leaving a network totally unprotected. If available, you'll get better security with WPA2 or PSK2.

**How do I activate encryption?** To activate encryption for your wireless network, open the router's configuration software. Earlier in the chapter you learned that most wireless routers can be configured by opening a browser and entering the router's IP number. Use the router configuration utilities to select an encryption protocol. In addition, you must create a wireless network key.

A **wireless network key** (sometimes referred to as a network security key) is the basis for scrambling and unscrambling the data transmitted between wireless devices. The key is similar to a password, only it is often longer. Instructions for creating a valid key are usually given in the router's documentation or on-screen Help file. For example, you might be limited to using only numbers 0 to 9 and letters A to F. Alternatively, you might be allowed to use a passphrase, such as notrespassingthismeansu, as the key.

Don't use a key or passphrase that's easy for an intruder to guess. Remember the key or passphrase you use to configure the router. Later, when you set up computers and other network devices, you will enter the same key so that every device on your network can encrypt and decrypt the data flowing on the network. Figure 5-52 illustrates how to activate wireless encryption.

**FIGURE 5-52**

The configuration utility used to set up wireless security is supplied by the router manufacturer. In this example, security is being configured for a Linksys router.

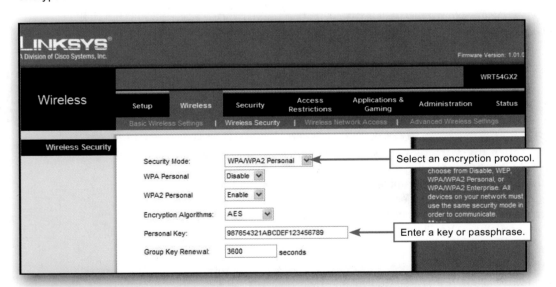

**Do I need a wireless network key for other networks I use?** Many wireless networks are not encrypted and are open to the public. You'll find these networks in coffee shops, hotels, and airports. Other networks are available for public use, but are encrypted.

To join your computer, PDA, or iPhone to an encrypted wireless hotspot on campus or at a friend's house, for example, you have to enter a wireless network key. When your computer is within range of an encrypted network, a network dialog box opens and prompts you to type the security key. Ask the person in charge of the network for the key or network password. After you enter the key, your computer can transmit and receive data over the network. Your network software stores the key, too, so that in the future you can connect without re-entering it.

# ENCRYPTION

**Exactly what is encryption?** **Encryption** transforms a message in such a way that its contents are hidden from unauthorized readers. Encryption is designed to keep messages secret. In the context of computing, encryption can be used in many ways, including the following:

- Scrambling data sent over wired or wireless networks to prevent intrusions

- Securing credit card numbers and other personal information transferred from shoppers' computers to e-commerce sites

- Encrypting computer files and databases so that data they contain is unusable if the device containing the data is lost or compromised

- Scrambling the contents of e-mail messages to maintain privacy

**How does encryption work?** An original message—one that has not yet been encrypted—is referred to as **plaintext** or cleartext. An encrypted message is referred to as **ciphertext**. The process of converting plaintext into ciphertext is called encryption. The reverse process—converting ciphertext into plaintext—is called **decryption**.

Messages are encrypted by using a cryptographic algorithm and key. A **cryptographic algorithm** is a procedure for encrypting or decrypting a message. A **cryptographic key** (usually just called a key) is a word, number, or phrase that must be known to encrypt or decrypt a message.

For example, Julius Caesar made extensive use of an encryption method called simple substitution, which could have been used to turn the plaintext message "Do not trust Brutus" into "GRQRWWUXVWEUXWXV." The cryptographic algorithm was to offset the letters of the alphabet. The key was 3 (Figure 5-53).

**FIGURE 5-53**

The algorithm for Caesar's encryption technique was to offset the letters of the alphabet—in this case, by three letters. A simple transformation table was used to encrypt or decrypt a message. For example, if a *G* appears in the encrypted message, it would be a *D* in the original unencrypted message.

**CIPHERTEXT LETTERS:**

D E F G H I J K L M N O P Q R S T U V W X Y Z A B C

**EQUIVALENT PLAINTEXT LETTERS:**

A B C D E F G H I J K L M N O P Q R S T U V W X Y Z

**What's the difference between strong and weak encryption?** Caesar's simple substitution key is an example of **weak encryption** because it is easy to decrypt even without the algorithm and key. Unauthorized decryption is sometimes referred to as breaking or cracking a code. You could crack Caesar's code in several ways. For example, you could discover the key by making 25 different transformation tables, each with a different offset (assuming that the encryption method uses the letters of the alphabet in sequence and not at random). You could also analyze the frequency with which letters appear—in English documents, *E, T, A, O,* and *N* appear most frequently—and you can piece together the message by guessing the remaining letters.

**Strong encryption** is loosely defined as "very difficult to break." **AES** (Advanced Encryption Standard), the technology used for WPA2, is one of the strongest cryptographic algorithms. With continuous advances in technology, however, strong encryption is a moving target. Several encryption methods that were considered impossible to break ten years ago have recently been cracked.

**How long does it take to break strong encryption?** Encryption methods can be broken by the use of expensive, specialized, code-breaking computers. The cost of these machines is substantial, but not beyond the reach of government agencies, major corporations, and organized crime. Encryption methods can also be broken by standard computer hardware—supercomputers, mainframes, workstations, and even personal computers. These computers typically break codes using a brute force attack, which consists of trying all possible keys (Figure 5-54).

The length of a computer-readable encryption key is measured in bits. A 32-bit key, for example, could be one of 4.2 billion ($2^{32}$) numbers. Surprisingly, it would be possible to try all these numbers and discover the key in less than a day by using an average personal computer.

To discover a 40-bit key, you would have to try about 1 trillion possible combinations—a week's worth of processing time on a personal computer. 768-bit encryption—once thought to be unbreakable by any computer in the private sector—require a lot of computing power, but have been broken by combining the power of many personal computers connected over the Internet. Most encryption today uses a 128-bit key, which is secure from casual hackers.

Another way to understand how the length of a key affects the strength of encryption is to consider this guideline: Beginning with a 40-bit key, each additional bit doubles the time it would take to discover the key. If a personal computer takes one week to crack a 40-bit key, it takes two weeks to crack a 41-bit key, four weeks to crack a 42-bit key, and eight weeks to crack a 43-bit key. A 128-bit key takes $2^{(128-40)}$ times longer to crack than a 40-bit key—that's 309,485,009,821,345,068,724,781,056 times longer!

**What's public key encryption?** Caesar's encryption method is an example of **symmetric key encryption** in which the key used to encrypt a message is also used to decrypt the message. Symmetric key encryption is used to encrypt stationary data, such as corporate financial records. It is also used to encrypt the data that travels over wireless LANs.

Symmetric keys are not practical for e-mail and other situations in which the person receiving encrypted data does not have the key beforehand. E-mailing the key would be a major security problem because of the potential for a hacker to intercept it.

**Public key encryption** (PKE) eliminates the key-distribution problem by using one key to encrypt a message, but another key to decrypt the message. Figure 5-55 illustrates how public key encryption works.

**FIGURE 5-54**

To discover a four-digit PIN by brute force, a criminal must try, at most, 10,000 possibilities. Finding the key to computer data encrypted using a 32-bit key would involve about 4.2 billion possibilities.

**FIGURE 5-55**

Public key encryption uses two keys. A public key can only encrypt a message. A private key is required to decrypt the message.

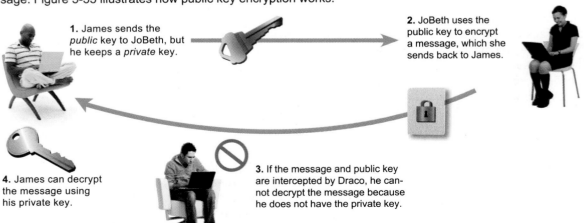

**1.** James sends the *public* key to JoBeth, but he keeps a *private* key.

**2.** JoBeth uses the public key to encrypt a message, which she sends back to James.

**3.** If the message and public key are intercepted by Draco, he cannot decrypt the message because he does not have the private key.

**4.** James can decrypt the message using his private key.

Public key encryption is a crucial technology for e-commerce and e-mail. When you use a secure connection to transmit a credit card number, the server sends a public key to your browser. Your browser uses this public key to encrypt the credit card number. After it is encrypted, no one—not even you—can use the public key to decrypt the message. The encrypted message is sent to a Web server, where the private key is used to decrypt it.

When personal computer users want to encrypt e-mail or other documents, they turn to public key encryption software, such as PGP (Pretty Good Privacy), GnuPG, or AxCrypt. When you first use PKE software, it generates a private key and a public key. You must keep your private key hidden. You can then e-mail the public key to the people you have authorized to send encrypted messages to you.

The people who receive your public key can store it and use their PKE software to encrypt messages. When they send these messages to you, you can decrypt them using your private key. Figure 5-56 contains an example of a public key generated by PGP software.

**INFOWEBLINKS**

For additional resources on using ciphertext to protect data, including PKE software that you can use on your PC, connect to the **Encryption InfoWeb**.

(W) CLICK TO CONNECT
www.infoweblinks.com/np2012/ch05

-----BEGIN PGP PUBLIC KEY BLOCK-----

Version: 5.0

mQCNAi44C30AAAEEAL1r6BylvuSAvOKlk9ze9yCK+ZPPbRZrpXlRFBb
e+U8dGPMb9XdJS4L/cy1fXr9R9j4EfFsK/rgHV6i2rE83LjWrmsDPRPSaiz
z+EQTIZi4AN99jiBomfLLZyUzmHMoUoE4shrYgOnkc0u101ikhieAFje77j
/F3596pT6nCx/9/AAURtCRBbmRyZSBCYBNhcmQgPGFiYWNhcmRAd2
VsbC5zZi5jYS51cz6JAFUCBRAuOA6O7zYZz1mqos8BAXr9AgCxCu8C
wGZRdpfSs65r6mb4MccXvvfxO4TmPi1DKQj2FYHYjwYONk8vzA7XnE5
aJmk5J/dChdvflU7NvVifV6of=GQv9

-----END PGP PUBLIC KEY BLOCK-----

**FIGURE 5-56**

PGP software generates a huge public key. Each person's public key is unique. You can e-mail this key to anyone who might want to send you an encrypted message.

**5**

# QuickCheck

1. A cryptographic [_____] is a word, number, or phrase that must be known to encrypt or decrypt a message.

2. A cryptographic [_____] is the process used to encrypt or decrypt a message.

3. WEP, WPA, and PSK refer to methods of encryption for [_____] networks.

4. [_____] key encryption uses one key to encrypt a message, but another key to decrypt the message.

5. [_____] key encryption uses the same key to encrypt a message as it does to decrypt the message.

(▶) CHECK ANSWERS

# Issue: Who's Stealing My Signals?

**A FLORIDA MAN WAS ARRESTED** and charged with unauthorized access to a computer network, a crime that's a third-degree felony and carries punishment ranging from probation to five years in prison. The accused man was allegedly piggybacking on his neighbor's wireless network to access the Internet. It was one of the first cases of its kind in the United States.

Reporters and bloggers monitoring the case reported that the fault might actually rest with the network's owner who failed to implement wireless security. An especially aggressive posting on one blog also suggested that the network equipment manufacturer could be at fault for not enabling encryption as the default security setting.

With the proliferation of home, school, and corporate wireless networks, hackers are expected to increasingly capitalize on unprotected household wireless systems to download child pornography, send threatening e-mails, and steal financial information. But what about casual interlopers who just want to borrow a little bandwidth from time to time?

One tech-savvy reporter relates that "on a trip to Colorado a fellow skier told me that although the hotel we were both staying at did not have a wireless network, an apartment complex down the street did. So I sat on their doorstep in the freezing cold to check e-mail with my laptop." He then wonders wryly if he should have rung the bell and asked if he could "please use their Wi-Fi."

Free wireless access is not unusual. You can find it in airports, hotels, and coffee shops. Free wireless access is also offered by rogue WLANs operated by public spirited individuals who are more than willing to share their bandwidth with passersby. Rogue WLAN operators typically subscribe to a high-speed Internet access service. They pay their monthly fees; but instead of limiting access to their own personal use, they distribute their connections over wireless LANs to friends, neighbors, and just about anyone who passes by with the right computer equipment.

Setting up a Wi-Fi antenna is simple and inexpensive. A basic Wi-Fi antenna can be created with a few wires and an empty Pringles container. Fancier antennas require a ravioli can—really!

The 802.11 standard uses an unlicensed telecommunications spectrum, so it is perfectly legal to set up an antenna to transmit and receive Wi-Fi signals without obtaining a broadcast license. FCC regulations even prohibit landlords from limiting tenant use of or access to wireless networks. For example, network administrators at the University of Texas at Dallas attempted to prohibit students from installing private wireless access points in their dorm rooms because the signals interfered with access to the campuswide wireless network. The university reversed its policy after reviewing FCC regulations.

Some free WLAN advocates envision a nationwide web of interconnected Wi-Fi networks that will form "a seamless broadband network built by the people, for the people." In this vision of a world connected by free WLANs, libraries can offer Internet access to people in low-income neighborhoods. Local schools could get wired without exorbitant cabling expenses. Parents, kids, and grandparents, as well as corporate executives, could exchange e-mail and instant messages from locations that include the kitchen table, the corner coffee shop, and the Little League field.

But some broadband providers, such as AT&T and Comcast, fear that every user of a free wireless network is one fewer paying customer. According to one industry analyst, "The telecom industries are addicted to the one-wire, one-customer philosophy." Sharing an Internet connection that is intended for single-user access does not coexist with this philosophy. Most subscriber agreements contain wording that limits use of a broadband connection to one user and perhaps immediate family members. Although wording varies from one provider to another, most agreements expressly prohibit subscribers from using their connections for commercial purposes. Some free WLAN operators don't believe that sharing is commercial use. "I'm sharing it with people," says one free WLAN provider, "I'm not selling it. I'm not making a profit off it."

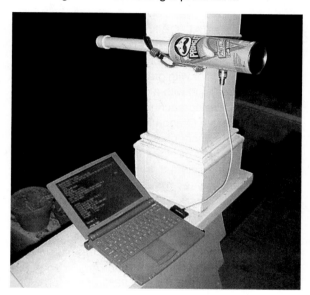

Whether or not free WLANs are legal, their benefits are tempered by several potentially negative repercussions. For example, tightening up subscriber agreements to eliminate the sharing loophole could affect many broadband subscribers who currently operate private wired or wireless networks that link several computers to a single Internet connection. Broadband providers could force private network operators to purchase more expensive multiuser licenses—an option that might be too expensive for many home network owners.

The wisdom of unregulated network availability is called into question by the proliferation of free WLANs. A publicly accessible LAN that requires no passwords or accounts can be used anonymously for a variety of illegal and dangerous activities. Like drug dealers who use public telephones to avoid taps and traces, terrorists and other criminals can simply walk into a free WLAN zone, tap into the Internet, and walk away without leaving a trace.

Widespread distribution of free WLANs can reduce the bandwidth available to paying customers. If your neighbor sets up a free WLAN that becomes popular with customers in a nearby coffee house, your previously sedate network neighborhood might suddenly become an overcrowded metropolis with major Internet access traffic jams.

Initial enthusiasm for free WLAN has wavered as projects get mired in the realities of operational costs and security problems. Equipment is not free; municipal Wi-Fi projects have been unable to recoup expenses and many cities have shut down their free networks or converted them to fee-based services.

The dream of free Wi-Fi is not dead; it has changed. Supporters now hope that access points offered by coffee shops, hotels, and other businesses will provide a blanket of free networks throughout the country.

**5**

### INFOWEBLINKS

The **Free WLAN InfoWeb** provides more details about Wi-Fi technology and renegade LANs.

 CLICK TO CONNECT
www.infoweblinks.com/np2012/ch05

## What Do You Think?

**ISSUE**

1. Have you ever accessed a free WLAN? ○ Yes ○ No ○ Not sure

2. Do you believe that rogue WLANs can survive alongside for-profit broadband ISPs? ○ Yes ○ No ○ Not sure

3. Are broadband providers justified in limiting the terms of their service agreements to "one subscription, one customer"? ○ Yes ○ No ○ Not sure

▶ SAVE RESPONSES

# Computers in Context: **Education**

**THE FIRST EDUCATIONAL** application of computers emerged in the 1960s, when huge mainframes with clunky interfaces introduced students to computer-aided instruction (CAI). Based on operant conditioning research by B. F. Skinner and Ivan Pavlov—remember dogs salivating when a bell rings?—CAI uses basic drill and practice: The computer presents a problem, the student responds, and the computer evaluates the response.

Studies in the 1970s indicated that CAI systems, such as PLATO (Programmed Logic for Automated Teaching Operations), improved student test scores, but students found the mainframe's monochrome display and the CAI's regimented drill format boring. Recent incarnations of CAI, such as an alien-invader style elementary math program, use snazzy graphics and arcade formats to grab learners' attention.

Educators looking for ways to harness computers' interactive and programmable nature arrived at the idea of computer-based training (CBT). CBT is formatted as a series of tutorials, beginning with a pretest to see whether students have the prerequisite skills and ending with a CAI-style drill and practice test to determine whether students can move on to the next tutorial segment. Today, CBT is a popular approach to learning how to use computer software.

Another educational approach, called computer-aided learning (CAL), uses the computer more as a source of information than an assessment mechanism. Students using CAL make decisions about their level of expertise, what material is relevant, and how to pace their own learning. Exploratory CAL environments include Seymour Papert's Logo programming language; students can investigate geometry concepts by using Logo to program a graphical turtle on the screen.

In addition to CAI, CBT, and CAL, simulations have become a popular educational tool. The computer mimics a real-world situation through a narrative description or with graphics. Students are given options and respond with a decision or an action. The computer evaluates each response and determines its consequences. Oregon Trail, a simulation popular with elementary school students, describes events that beset a group of pioneers traveling in a wagon train. Students respond to each event, while learning bits of history, money-handling skills, conservation, and decision making.

Most educators believe that computers can help create an individualized and interactive learning environment, which can make learning more effective and efficient. Although 99% of American public schools have computers and 93% of students use them in some way, these statistics can be deceiving. The reality falls far short of the ideal situation in which every student has access to a computer throughout the school day.

The challenge is to figure out how to achieve the computers' potential in an educational setting when supplying computers for every student is often cost prohibitive. Compromise solutions have been tried with varying degrees of success. Some schools have installed learning labs where students go for scheduled lab time. In elementary schools, often a few computers are placed in special work areas of classrooms and used for small group projects or individual drill and practice. Some schools have relegated most computers to the library, where they are connected to the Internet and used for research. In some classrooms, a single computer can be used as an effective presentation device.

A few schools without the budget for enough desktop computers have opted for inexpensive PDAs instead. "Students need to use technology just as you and I do, not just one hour a day," says one teacher in support of PDAs. Students use standard PDA software for educational tasks: tracking nutritional intake for health class, collecting data from experiments in biology class, graphing functions in math class, translating phrases for French class, and maintaining to-do lists. The biggest drawback to more widespread educational use of PDAs, however, is a lack of software specifically designed for education. The proliferation of sub-$250 netbooks might offer a software-rich alternative to PDAs.

Pioneering PDA projects led to a bevy of experiments under the umbrella of mLearning, a buzzword for *mobile learning* and defined as learning that happens across locations, or that takes advantage of learning opportunities offered by portable technologies.

Some schools—primarily colleges—have tackled the problem of computer access by requiring all incoming first-year students to purchase notebook computers. Many colleges, for example, provide Internet connections in dorm rooms and library study carrels or offer campuswide Wi-Fi service. Students can tote their notebook computers to class and take notes. They can contact instructors via e-mail, use the Internet as a research resource, and run educational software.

Another educational use of computers can be seen in distance education (DE) courses (also called distance learning). Historically, distance education meant correspondence study or courses delivered by radio or television, but the meaning has been broadened to encompass any educational situation in which students and instructors aren't in the same place. Therefore, most DE courses today require students to have access to a computer and an Internet connection. DE courses are offered to K through 12 students, college students, military personnel, businesspeople, and the general public.

Most students who choose DE courses do so because they want to learn at their own pace, at a convenient time, and in a location close to home. Single parents who deal with the realities of child care, working professionals who cannot relocate to a college town, and physically disabled students find distance education handy. Distance education has the potential of increasing the pool of students for a course by making it financially feasible; for example, an advanced Kanji course could be offered at a Midwestern university with only ten on-campus Japanese majors if enough distance education students can boost enrollment.

The Internet hosts a wide variety of DE courses, both credit-earning and noncredit courses. Several learning management systems (LMSs), such as Blackboard and Moodle, help teachers prepare and manage DE courses. These systems are popular with degree-granting institutions that offer credit-earning DE courses in their course catalogs (subject to the usual course fees and requirements).

Learning management software typically runs from a server maintained by a school system, college, or university. Using Web browsers, teachers access the LMS to post an online syllabus, develop Web pages with course content, create a database of questions for online assessment, manage e-mail, set up online discussion groups, and maintain a gradebook. Students using Internet-connected computers and standard Web browsers can access course materials, submit assignments, interact with other students, and take tests.

Computers and the Internet have opened opportunities for lifelong learning. Prospective students can use a search engine to easily find non-credit courses and tutorials for a wide range of topics, including pottery, dog grooming, radio astronomy, desktop publishing, and drumming. Some tutorials are free, and others charge a small fee.

In a society that promotes learning as a lifelong endeavor, the Internet has certainly made it possible for students of all ages to pursue knowledge and skills simply by using a computer and an Internet connection.

**INFOWEBLINKS**

You'll find lots more information related to this Computers in Context topic at the **Computers and Education InfoWeb**.

CLICK TO CONNECT
www.infoweblinks.com/np2012/ch05

# New Perspectives Labs

## On the BookOnCD

To access the New Perspectives Lab for Chapter 5, start the BookOnCD and then click the icon next to the lab title below.

 **LOCAL AREA NETWORKS**

### IN THIS LAB YOU'LL LEARN:

- The basic technology specifications for Ethernet and Wi-Fi networks
- How to identify the parts of a router
- How to open the router configuration utility
- How to change a router's default password
- How to create an SSID
- The advantages and disadvantages of WEP, WPA, and WPA2 encryption
- How to enable wireless encryption
- How to determine a computer's wired or wireless networking capability
- How to connect a LAN to the Internet
- How to make sure a router is configured for DHCP

### LAB ASSIGNMENTS

1. Start the interactive part of the lab. Perform each lab step as directed, and answer all the lab QuickCheck questions.

2. Use your computer's networking utilities to find out if your computer is LAN and/or WLAN ready. Make a note of the type and specifications of any network adapters installed in your computer.

3. Using the information you gathered from assignment 2, draw a sketch showing how your computer could be linked into a LAN.

4. Examine the networking utilities installed on your computer. If you are using Windows, you might find utilities such as Network Connections, Wireless Network Setup Wizard, and others. Look at each utility and write a one-paragraph description for each utility.

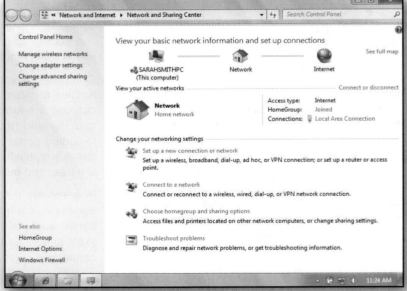

# Key Terms

Make sure you understand all the boldfaced key terms presented in this chapter. With the NP2012 BookOnCD, you can use this list of terms as an interactive study activity. First, try to define a term in your own words, and then click the term to compare your definition with the definition presented in the chapter. Online, try your hand at the TechTerm Flashcards.

AES, 285
Application server, 249
Bandwidth, 251
Bluetooth, 267
Bridge, 250
Broadband, 251
Bus topology, 250
Ciphertext, 285
Circuit switching, 253
Client/server mode, 249
Communications channel, 251
Communications protocol, 252
Cryptographic algorithm, 285
Cryptographic key, 285
CSMA/CD, 258
Decryption, 285
DHCP, 255
Drive mapping, 276
Encryption, 285
Ethernet, 257
Ethernet adapter, 260
File server, 249
Gateway, 251
Handshaking, 252
Homegroup, 277
HomePNA, 262
Infrared light, 265
IP address, 255
LAN, 247
LAN jacking, 282
MAC address, 254
MAN, 247

Mesh topology, 250
Microwaves, 265
MiFi, 270
MIMO, 268
Narrowband, 251
Network attached storage, 248
Network device, 248
Network hub, 260
Network interface card, 248
Network router, 260
Network switch, 260
Networked peripheral, 248
Node, 248
Octet, 255
Packet, 253
Packet switching, 253
PAN, 246
Peer-to-peer mode, 249
Physical topology, 250
Piconet, 267
Plaintext, 285
Powerline network, 262
Print server, 249
PSK, 283
Public key encryption, 286
RF signals, 265
Ring topology, 250
RJ45 connector, 261
Shared resources, 274
SSID, 272
Star topology, 250
Strong encryption, 285

Symmetric key encryption, 286
Transceiver, 265
Tree topology, 250
WAN, 247
Weak encryption, 285
WEP, 283
Wi-Fi, 268
Wi-Fi adapter, 269
Wired network, 256
Wireless access point, 270
Wireless ad-hoc network, 270
Wireless encryption, 283
Wireless infrastructure network, 270
Wireless network, 265
Wireless network key, 284
Wireless router, 270
WPA, 283

5

# Interactive Summary

To review important concepts from this chapter, fill in the blanks to best complete each sentence. When using the NP2012 BookOnCD, click the Check Answers buttons to automatically score your answers.

**SECTION A:** Networks can be classified by geographical scope as PANs, [                    ], MANs, and WANs. LAN technologies are standardized by the [                    ] organization. Each connection point on a network is referred to as a(n) [                    ] and can contain computers, networked [                    ], or network devices. Computers connected to a network require network circuitry, often housed on a network [                    ] card (NIC). Networks that include one or more servers can operate in [                    ] /server mode or peer-to-peer mode. Networks without a server typically operate in peer-to-peer mode. Physical network topologies include star, bus, [                    ], mesh, and tree. Network nodes are linked by communications channels. High-bandwidth channels are referred to as [                    ], whereas low-bandwidth channels are referred to as [                    ]. Communications [                    ], such as TCP/IP, divide messages into [                    ], handle addressing, and manage routing.

CHECK ANSWERS

**SECTION B:** Wired networks are fast, secure, and simple to configure. Ethernet networks use Cat 5 or Cat 6 wiring with plastic [                    ] connectors. HomePNA networks transport data over coaxial or [                    ] wiring and HomePlug networks transport data over [                    ] wiring. Ethernet uses CSMA/CD protocol to detect [                    ] . [                    ] Ethernet operates at 100 Mbps, whereas Gigabit Ethernet operates at [                    ] Mbps. Ethernet is usually wired in a(n) [                    ] topology to a central device. A network [                    ] is a device that accepts data from one workstation and broadcasts it to all of the other network nodes. A network [                    ] is a more sophisticated connection device that sends data only to the devices specified as the destination. A network [                    ] is a network device that can ship data from one network to another. You typically use your [                    ] software to access the router's configuration utilities.

CHECK ANSWERS

**SECTION C:** Most wireless LANs transport data using [_____] frequency signals. The most popular WLAN technology is Wi-Fi, but Bluetooth is used for PANs and other short-range connections. Wi-Fi is defined by the IEEE [_____] standards, and there are versions denoted by the letters *a*, *b*, *g*, *n*, and *y*. Computers on a Wi-Fi network must have wireless circuitry, such as a Wi-Fi adapter. Wireless networks can be set up as a wireless [_____] network in which devices broadcast directly to each other. Alternatively, a wireless [_____] network uses a centralized broadcasting device, such as a wireless [_____] point or a wireless router. When setting up a wireless network, it is important to change the default router password, create a(n) [_____] to uniquely identify the network, and enable wireless encryption for security.

▶ CHECK ANSWERS

**SECTION D:** LANs allow people to share network resources, such as files, printers, and Internet connections. Unfortunately, LANs are vulnerable to unauthorized access and malware. To view the files stored on other network workstations, you can use a technique called drive [_____] that assigns a drive letter and displays a remote drive's contents. Under Windows, you can designate folders and printers as [_____] if you want to allow other workstations to access them. If you have many files that need to be accessed from various workstations, you might want to add a(n) [_____] server to the network. If you would like everyone on a network to have access to a printer, but you prefer not to send print jobs through any of the workstations, you can add a(n) [_____] server or attach a network-ready printer directly to the router. Network problems can stem from a variety of sources. Symptoms of network malfunctions are slow response time, intermittent outages, failure to access files from one workstation, and non-availability of network services to all workstations. To troubleshoot network problems, you have to consider the possibility of a problem with a workstation's hardware or settings; network links including cables and wireless signal strength; or network devices such as routers, servers, or NICs. Network problems can sometimes be solved if you [_____] the network by turning off the router and Internet modem, then restarting them.

▶ CHECK ANSWERS

**SECTION E:** Compared to wired networks, wireless networks are much more susceptible to unauthorized access and use. Hackers have an easy time intercepting signals by cruising through a business district or neighborhood with a Wi-Fi enabled notebook computer, a practice called LAN [_____]. Preventing Wi-Fi signal interception is difficult, but wireless [_____] scrambles transmitted data and makes it useless to intruders. Originally, wireless networks were secured with [_____], but it proved too easy to crack. Much better security is offered by WPA protocols such as PSK. An original message—one that has not yet been encrypted—is referred to as [_____] or cleartext. An encrypted message is referred to as [_____]. Messages are encrypted by a cryptographic [_____], which is a specific procedure for encrypting or decrypting a message. A cryptographic [_____] is a word, number, or phrase that must be known to encrypt or decrypt a message. [_____] key encryption uses the same key to encrypt and decrypt a message. [_____] key encryption eliminates the key-distribution problem by using one key to encrypt a message, but another key is used to decrypt the message.

▶ CHECK ANSWERS

5

# Interactive Situation Questions

Apply what you've learned to some typical computing situations. When using the NP2012 BookOnCD, you can type your answers, and then use the Check Answers button to automatically score your responses.

1. You're installing a LAN and you decide to go with Ethernet. You'll typically use Cat 5 or Cat 6 cables to connect each workstation to a(n) [            ] .

2. You're setting up an Ethernet wired network using a router. To access the router and its configuration software, you open your [            ] and type the router's IP address.

3. You're trying to figure out if your computer has a built-in Ethernet port. You see the port pictured to the right. Is that the port you should use for your RJ45 connector? Yes or no? [            ]

4. You install an 802.11b network, but it seems to stop working at various times. To begin troubleshooting, you look for any devices, such as cordless phones, that use the [          ] GHz frequency.

5. Your PC is connected to a LAN, and you want to regularly access a file that's stored on one of the LAN workstations. You'd like to access that computer's hard disk as though it were connected to your own computer, so you decide to [            ] the workstation's hard disk drive as drive F.

6. You arrive at work and one of your co-workers tells you that the router is down. Is it correct to surmise that your workstation will not be able to access other workstations, but will be able to access the Internet? Yes or no? [            ]

7. You have a small wireless network in your house. For the past week you've seen a black SUV parked outside and its occupant seems to be using a notebook computer. The first step you should take to discover if this person has hacked into your network is: a) knock on the car window and ask; b) call the police; or c) use your router utilities to check who is connected to your network. [            ]

8. You've set up a wireless network using some new equipment and a few old Wi-Fi adapters given to you by your roommates. One of the adapters is equipped only for WEP, whereas all the other adapters support WPA2. Your roommate tells you that in order to use all the adapters, you'll have to disable wireless encryption. Is your roommate right? [            ]

▶ CHECK ANSWERS

## Interactive Practice Tests

Practice tests that consist of ten multiple-choice, true/false, and fill-in-the-blank questions are available on both the NP2012 BookOnCD and the NP2012 CourseMate Web site. BookOnCD test questions are selected at random from a large test bank, so each time you take a test, you'll receive a different set of questions. Your tests are scored immediately, and you can print study guides that help you find the correct answers for any questions that you missed. Online, you'll find a Practice Test for each section of the chapter. Your results from online tests are saved by Engagement Tracker. ▶ CLICK TO START

# Learning Objectives Checkpoints

Learning Objectives Checkpoints are designed to help you assess whether you have achieved the major learning objectives for this chapter. You can use paper and pencil or word processing software to complete most of the activities.

1. Describe the characteristics of PANs, LANs, MANs, and WANs, plus provide an example of each.

2. Create a list of network devices mentioned in this chapter. Write a brief description of each one, and indicate whether it would typically be part of the Internet, a LAN, or both.

3. Draw diagrams to show the difference between client/server mode and peer-to-peer mode.

4. Draw diagrams of star, ring, bus, mesh, and tree network topologies. Explain the advantages and disadvantages of each topology.

5. Draw a diagram of Shannon's communications model and explain how it relates to communications protocols. Apply Shannon's model to a Wi-Fi LAN by indicating which real-world devices would exist at various points in the model to originate data, encode it, transmit signals, and so on.

6. Explain the difference between an analog signal and a digital signal. Explain why most modern communications systems use digital signals.

7. Explain the difference between packet switching and circuit switching. Describe the differences between IP addresses and MAC addresses. Diagram the route of data over an Ethernet and discuss how collisions are detected and/or avoided.

8. Draw a storyboard that illustrates the process of installing a wired network. List the additional steps necessary to install a wireless network.

9. Make a list of the LAN standards described in this chapter. For each one, indicate the type of technology it uses, its maximum speed and range, and the devices available to set up network communications.

10. List five advantages and three disadvantages of computer networks.

11. Make a list of security concerns that are related to local area networks. Describe the steps that you would take to (a) secure a wired LAN and (b) secure a wireless LAN.

12. Describe the difference between symmetric encryption and public key encryption. List five uses for each one.

Study Tip: Make sure you can use your own words to correctly answer each of the red focus questions that appear throughout the chapter.

5

# Concept Map

Fill in the blanks to show the hierarchy of LAN technologies.

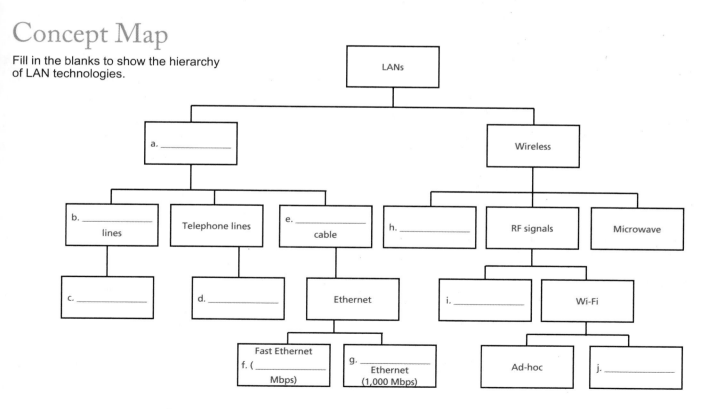

# Projects

 **CRITICAL THINKING**

Wireless technology has become quite pervasive. Not only are computing devices wireless, but most people have other devices, such as security systems, baby monitors, and entertainment systems, that could be wirelessly networked. Play the role of a futurist and think about the ultimate wireless home. Sketch out floor plans and show how you would set up wireless devices, including wireless access points.

 **GROUP PROJECT**

Form a group with three or four other students. Suppose you are all living in adjacent dorm rooms and decide to create a LAN to connect your computers. For this project, first describe the number, type, and location of the computers that will form your network. Next, decide what type of network technology you want to use: Ethernet, HomePNA, Wi-Fi, HomePlug, or a mixture. Create a diagram showing the location of each computer, the wiring path (for Ethernet), the location of electrical outlets (for HomePlug), the location of telephone outlets (for HomePNA), or potential signal interference (for wireless). Create a shopping list of the network components you need to purchase, and then use the Web to locate prices for each item on your list. Make sure you supply your instructor with the URLs for sites where you found pricing information.

 **CYBERCLASSROOM**

With a partner, research public key encryption (PKE) you could use to send encrypted e-mail back and forth. Do any utilities included with your operating system offer PKE or would you have to use third-party software? If possible, set up encryption and send your partner an encrypted e-mail message or file. Describe to your instructor the tools and procedure you used.

 **MULTIMEDIA PROJECT**

Wireless technology is increasingly being used for home entertainment systems, including stereos, television, and home theaters. For this project choose either television, stereo, or projection systems. Research the wireless options for the equipment of your choice. Write a two-page how-to article describing how to set up a cool wireless system. Be sure to describe the system's benefits as well as how to assemble the equipment.

 **RESUME BUILDER**

Bluetooth advocates champion the idea of using Bluetooth devices to exchange electronic business cards. Suppose you're working in the technology department of a corporation and your boss asks you to research the value of this concept for the company's sales representatives. After you complete your research, write a one-page memo describing your findings about cost and usefulness.

 **GLOBALIZATION**

The model for telecommunications in most technologically advanced countries depends on large telecommunications corporations for telephone and Internet access. Can you envision ways in which people in technologically underdeveloped countries could benefit from inexpensive LAN and WLAN technologies? Jot down your initial thoughts, then search the Web for additional ideas. Write a one-page executive summary that describes your ideas.

 **ISSUE**

The Issue section of this chapter focuses on the use of Wi-Fi technology to build wireless LANs that provide free Internet access. For this project, write a two- to five-page paper that examines one aspect of the free WLAN controversy. You might explore Wi-Fi technology to learn more about how it works. You might look for examples of free WLANs and try to find out what motivates their operators. You might research why free city-wide Wi-Fi projects in locations such as Philadelphia and Los Angeles failed. Or you might research how broadband providers are reacting to free WLANs. To begin this project, consult the Free WLAN InfoWeb (see page 289) to get an overview of the controversy. Using that information as background, choose the focus for your paper and continue your research. As you write your paper, make sure you can back up your statements with facts and references to authoritative articles and Web pages.

 **COMPUTERS IN CONTEXT**

The Computers in Context section focuses on the many ways computers and Internet technology are used in education. For this project, identify a topic you'd like to learn more about, such as a hobby or your academic major. Under the heading "Topic Description," write a brief description of your topic, why it interests you, and what you would like to learn about it. Next, use a search engine, such as Google, to locate online tutorials about your topic. Under the heading "Available Tutorials," write a brief description of your search results. Indicate the number of tutorials you found on the topic, provide the URLs for at least three tutorials, and write a short description of each one. Take one of the free tutorials. Under the heading "Evaluation," describe the format for the tutorial, its ease of use, and what you learned.

# On the Web

## STUDENT EDITION LABS

When you purchase access to the NP2012 CourseMate Web site, you'll find targeted learning materials to help you understand key concepts and prepare for exams. See page O-41 in the Orientation Chapter for login instructions.

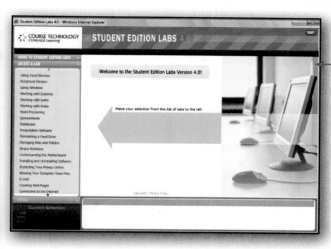

Work hands-on in structured simulations practicing important skills and concepts

### NETWORKING BASICS

In the Networking Basics Student Edition Lab, you will learn about the following topics:

- Network architecture, hardware, and software
- Network protocols and utilities
- Networked resources
- Network security

### WIRELESS NETWORKING

In the Wireless Networking Student Edition Lab, you will learn about the following topics:

- Implementing wireless networks
- Wireless security

 **CHAPTER OVERVIEW COURSECAST**

Use your computer or iPod to hear a five-minute audio presentation of chapter highlights.

 **AUDIO FLASHCARDS**

Interact with audio flashcards to review key concepts from the chapter.

 **DETAILED OBJECTIVES**

Make sure that you've achieved all the objectives for a chapter before it's time for your test!

 **PRACTICE TESTS**

Review chapter material by taking these ten-question tests. Your results are saved by Engagement Tracker.

 **ONLINE GAMES**

Have some fun while refreshing your memory about key concepts that might appear on the next test.

 **AND MORE!**

At the NP2012 CourseMate Web site you'll also find the NP2012 eBook, TechTerm Flashcards, Online Glossary, and What Do You Think? opinion polls.

# 6 The Internet

## Chapter Contents

▶ **SECTION A:**
**INTERNET TECHNOLOGY**
Background
Internet Infrastructure
Internet Protocols, Addresses,
and Domains
Connection Speed

▶ **SECTION B:**
**FIXED INTERNET ACCESS**
Dial-up Connections
DSL, ISDN, and Dedicated Lines
Cable Internet Service
Satellite Internet Service
Fixed Wireless Service
Fixed Internet Connection Roundup

▶ **SECTION C:**
**PORTABLE AND MOBILE**
**INTERNET ACCESS**
Internet to Go
Wi-Fi Hotspots
Portable and Mobile WiMAX
Portable Satellite Service
Cellular Data Service

▶ **SECTION D:**
**INTERNET SERVICES**
Real-time Messaging
Voice over IP
Forums, Wikis, Blogs, and Tweets
Cloud Computing
Grid Computing
FTP
File Sharing Networks

▶ **SECTION E:**
**INTERNET SECURITY**
Intrusion Attempts
Securing Ports
Routers and NAT
Virtual Private Networks

▶ **ISSUE:**
**WHAT'S HAPPENING TO**
**FREE SPEECH?**

▶ **COMPUTERS IN CONTEXT:**
**BANKING**

▶ **NEW PERSPECTIVES LABS**

▶ **REVIEW ACTIVITIES**

▶ **ON THE WEB**

## Learning Objectives

After reading this chapter, you will be able to answer the following questions by completing the outcomes-based Learning Objectives Checkpoints on page 355.

1. Who created the Internet?
2. How does the Internet work?
3. What is TCP/IP?
4. What are the differences between static IP addresses, dynamic IP addresses, private IP addresses, and domain names?
5. Can I find the actual speed of my Internet connection?
6. What is the best type of Internet service?
7. Is there a difference between portable Internet access and mobile Internet access?
8. How do cell phones and other handheld devices access the Internet?
9. How do chat, instant messaging, and other Internet-based communications work?
10. How does Voice over IP work?
11. What are grid and cloud computing?
12. How is FTP different from file sharing technologies such as BitTorrent?
13. How do hackers break into computers?
14. How can I protect my computer from intrusions?

## Web Site

Visit the NP2012 Web site to access additional resources Ⓦ that accompany this chapter.

## Multimedia and Interactive Elements

When using the BookOnCD or other BookOn products, the ▶ icons are clickable to access multimedia resources.

## Pre-Assessment Quiz

Take the pre-assessment quiz to find out how much you know about the topics in this chapter. ▶

**Apply Your Knowledge** The information in this chapter will give you the background to:

- Find your computer's Internet address
- Get a domain name for your Web site
- Measure the speed of your Internet connection
- Select the best Internet access services for your location and budget

- Access the Internet from a Wi-Fi hotspot
- Access the Internet from a mobile phone
- Use Internet services such as instant messaging, chat, FTP, Voice over IP, and BitTorrent
- Protect your computer from online intrusions

### Try It

**HOW FAST AND DEPENDABLE IS MY INTERNET CONNECTION?**

You can access the Internet in various ways—using your phone line, your cable TV connection, or a personal satellite dish. Is your Internet connection fast enough for activities such as downloading DVDs and playing online multiplayer games? You can discover the speed of your Internet connection by doing the following steps:

**1. Windows:** Click the **Start** button, point to **All Programs**, click **Accessories**, and then select **Command Prompt** from the list. This action opens a "DOS box." Type **Ping www.google.com** and then press the Enter key.

   **Mac:** Click the **Finder** icon, select **Applications**, **Utilities**, and **Terminal**. This action opens the Terminal window. Type **Ping -c 4 www.google.com** and then press the **Enter** key.

**2.** Your computer makes four attempts to access Google and measures the time required for each attempt. Fill in the blanks below with the Ping statistics for your computer. When you read the chapter, you'll learn how those statistics stack up for video-conferencing, Voice over IP, and online multiplayer gaming.

**3.** Close the DOS box or Terminal window.

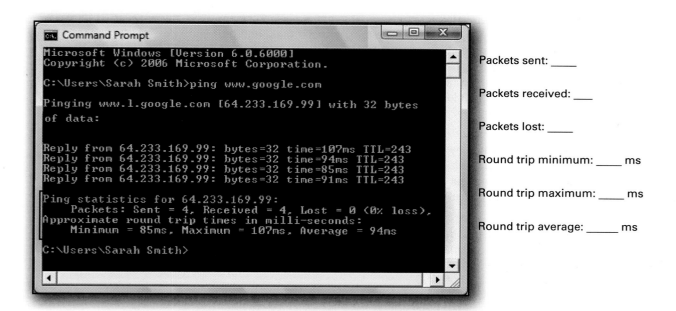

Packets sent: \_\_\_\_

Packets received: \_\_\_

Packets lost: \_\_\_\_

Round trip minimum: \_\_\_\_ ms

Round trip maximum: \_\_\_\_ ms

Round trip average: \_\_\_\_\_ ms

# Internet Technology

**TO MOST PEOPLE,** the Internet seems old hat. Even people who haven't used the Internet know a lot about it from watching the news, reading magazines, and watching movies. Using the Internet is actually pretty easy. Browsing Web sites, shopping at Amazon.com, sending e-mail, and tweeting? No problem. But what makes the Internet "tick"? How can one network offer so much information to so many people? Section A pulls back the curtain and gives you a glimpse of what happens behind the scenes on the Net.

## BACKGROUND

**How did the Internet get started?** The history of the Internet begins in 1957 when the Soviet Union launched Sputnik, the first man-made satellite. In response to this display of Soviet superiority, the U.S. government resolved to improve its scientific and technical infrastructure. One of the resulting initiatives was the Advanced Research Projects Agency (ARPA).

ARPA swung into action with a project designed to help scientists communicate and share valuable computer resources. The ARPANET, created in 1969, connected computers at UCLA, Stanford Research Institute, University of Utah, and University of California at Santa Barbara (Figure 6-1).

In 1985, the National Science Foundation (NSF) used ARPANET technology to create a larger network, linking not just a few mainframe computers, but entire LANs at each site. Connecting two or more networks creates an internetwork, or internet. The NSF network was an internet (with a lowercase *i*). As this network grew throughout the world, it became known as the Internet (with an uppercase *I*).

Early Internet pioneers—mostly educators and scientists—used primitive command-line user interfaces to send e-mail, transfer files, and run scientific calculations on Internet supercomputers. Finding information was not easy. Without search engines, Internet users relied on word of mouth and e-mail to keep informed about new data and its location. "The data you need is on the Stanford computer in a file called Chrome.txt" was typical of messages between colleagues.

**How did the Internet become so popular?** In the early 1990s, software developers created new user-friendly Internet access tools, and Internet accounts became available to anyone willing to pay a monthly subscription fee. Today, the Internet connects computers all over the globe and supplies information to people of all ages and interests.

**How big is the Internet today?** With an estimated 500 million nodes and more than 2 billion users, the Internet is huge. Although exact figures cannot be determined, it is estimated that the Internet handles more than an exabyte of data every day. An exabyte is 1.074 billion gigabytes, and that's a nearly unimaginable amount of data.

**FIGURE 6-1**

An original diagram of the ARPANET included four nodes, depicted as circles.

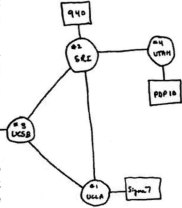

TERMINOLOGY NOTE

A few years ago, Wired News announced it would no longer capitalize the word *Internet*, a move supported by National Public Radio and several prominent linguists. Most style guides, however, still recommend that you capitalize references to the global communications network called the Internet.

## INTERNET INFRASTRUCTURE

**How is the Internet structured?** Surprisingly, the Internet is not owned or operated by any single corporation or government. It is a data communications network that grew over time in a somewhat haphazard configuration as networks connected to other networks and to the Internet backbone.

**What is the Internet backbone?** The **Internet backbone** is a network of high-capacity communications links that provides the main routes for data traffic across the Internet. At one time, the topology of the Internet backbone and interconnected networks might have resembled a spine with ribs connected along its length. Today, however, it more resembles a map of interstate highways with many junctures and redundant routes.

**How does the backbone tie the Internet together?** The Internet backbone consists of high-speed fiber-optic links connecting high-capacity routers that direct network traffic. Backbone links and routers are maintained by **network service providers** (NSPs), such as AT&T, British Telecom, Deutsche Telekom, Sprint, and Verizon. NSP equipment and links are tied together by **network access points** (NAPs), so that, for example, data can begin its journey on a Verizon link and then cross over to a Sprint link, if necessary, to reach its destination.

NSPs supply Internet connections to large Internet service providers, such as EarthLink, AOL, AT&T, and Comcast. An **Internet service provider** (ISP) is a company that offers Internet access to individuals, businesses, and smaller ISPs. Figure 6-2 shows a simplified conceptual diagram of the Internet backbone and its components.

**FIGURE 6-2**

The Internet backbone includes high-speed routers and high-speed fiber-optic links. Parts of the backbone maintained by different communications companies are connected at network access points (NAPs).

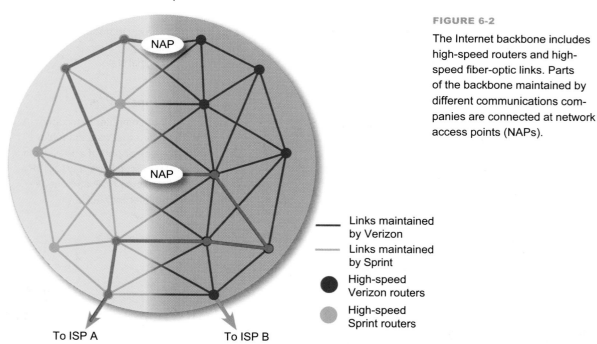

To ISP A  To ISP B

— Links maintained by Verizon
— Links maintained by Sprint
● High-speed Verizon routers
● High-speed Sprint routers

**What kinds of network devices are part of an ISP?** An ISP operates routers, communication equipment, and other network devices that handle the physical aspects of transmitting and receiving data between their subscribers and the Internet. Many ISPs also operate e-mail servers to handle incoming and outgoing mail for their subscribers. Some ISPs have Web servers for subscriber Web sites. An ISP might operate a server that translates an address, such as *www.google.com*, into a valid IP address such as 208.50.141.12. ISPs can also maintain servers for online discussions, instant messaging, music file sharing, FTP, streaming video, and other file transfer services (Figure 6-3).

**FIGURE 6-3**

ISP Equipment

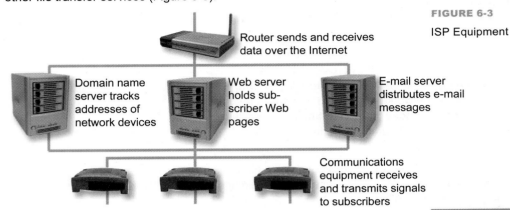

Router sends and receives data over the Internet

Domain name server tracks addresses of network devices

Web server holds subscriber Web pages

E-mail server distributes e-mail messages

Communications equipment receives and transmits signals to subscribers

### How does my computer fit into the structure of the Internet?

To communicate with an ISP, your computer uses some type of communications device, such as a modem. A **modem** contains circuitry that converts the data-carrying signals from your computer to signals that can travel over various communications channels. The kind of modem you use depends on whether you are connecting to a dial-up, wireless, cable, satellite, or DSL Internet service.

A standalone computer can communicate with an ISP directly through a modem, or through a combination of a router and modem. If your computer is part of a network, the network's router typically handles the Internet connection. Figure 6-4 illustrates the difference between standalone and LAN Internet access. You'll learn more about connecting to the Internet using telephone, cable, satellite, and cellular links in Sections B and C.

**TERMINOLOGY NOTE**

The word *modem* is derived from the words *modulate* and *demodulate*. In communications lingo, modulation means changing the characteristics of a signal, as when a dial-up modem changes a digital pulse into an analog audio signal that travels over telephone lines. Demodulation means changing a signal back to its original state.

**FIGURE 6-4**

Your computer can connect to the Internet as a standalone device or part of a LAN. Your data first travels to your ISP, then to an NSP and out over the Internet backbone.

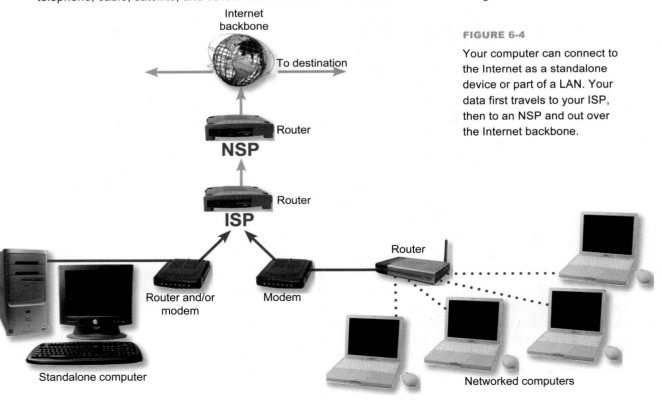

Internet backbone

To destination

Router

**NSP**

Router

**ISP**

Router and/or modem

Modem

Router

Standalone computer

Networked computers

## INTERNET PROTOCOLS, ADDRESSES, AND DOMAINS

**What protocols are used by the Internet?** The Internet uses a variety of communications protocols to support basic data transport and services, such as e-mail, Web access, and downloading. Figure 6-5 briefly describes some of the main protocols used on the Internet.

FIGURE 6-5

Protocols Used on the Internet

| Protocol | Name | Function |
|---|---|---|
| TCP | Transmission Control Protocol | Creates connections and exchanges packets of data |
| IP | Internet Protocol | Provides devices with unique addresses |
| UDP | User Datagram Protocol | An alternative data transport to TCP used for DNS, Voice over IP, and file sharing |
| HTTP | Hypertext Transfer Protocol | Exchanges information over the Web |
| FTP | File Transfer Protocol | Transfers files between local and remote host computers |
| POP | Post Office Protocol | Transfers mail from an e-mail server to a client Inbox |
| SMTP | Simple Mail Transfer Protocol | Transfers e-mail messages from client computers to an e-mail server |
| VoIP | Voice over Internet Protocol | Transmits voice conversations over the Internet |
| IRC | Internet Relay Chat | Transmits text messages in real time between online users |
| BitTorrent | BitTorrent | Distributes files using scattered clients rather than a server |

**How significant is TCP/IP?** **TCP/IP** is the primary protocol suite responsible for message transmission on the Internet. A **protocol suite** is a combination of protocols that work together. **TCP** (Transmission Control Protocol) breaks a message or file into packets. **IP** (Internet Protocol) is responsible for addressing packets so that they can be routed to their destination. From a practical perspective, TCP/IP provides a protocol standard for the Internet that is public, free, extensible, and easy to implement.

**Does the Internet use a special addressing scheme?** In the previous chapter, you learned that IP addresses can be assigned to LAN workstations. IP addresses originated on the Internet as part of the TCP/IP protocol. IP addresses are used to uniquely identify computers on the Internet as well as on LANs. In the context of the Internet, IP addresses are sometimes referred to as TCP/IP addresses or Internet addresses.

**How do IP addresses work on the Internet?** Every device on the Internet has an assigned IP address such as 128.110.192.40. In binary, the addresses are 32 bits long, but they are usually written as decimal numbers and divided by periods into four groups called octets.

The numbers in each octet correspond to network classes. For example, an IP address that begins with a number between 128 and 191 corresponds to a Class B network, such as a large college campus. When delivering a packet of data, Internet routers use the first octet to get a general idea of where to send the packet. The rest of the IP address is used to drill down to the exact destination.

**Do octets correspond to the parts of e-mail or Web site addresses?** E-mail addresses such as *imastudent@uga.edu* and Web site addresses such as *http://www.uga.edu* are separated into parts with periods, similar to the octets in an IP address. The octets do not, however,

6

TERMINOLOGY NOTE

32-bit IP—referred to as IPv4— offers about 4 billion unique addresses. When even more addresses are needed, IPv6 can offer billions and billions of addresses. An IPv6 address is 128 bits and usually written as eight groups of four hexadecimal digits, such as 2001:0db8:0:0:1319:8a2e:0370:57ab.

map to the parts of a Web site address or an e-mail address. So, although *http://www.uga.edu* has an IP address of 128.192.1.9, the first octet, 128, does not correspond to *http://*. Nor does the second octet map to *www*.

**Do I need a permanent IP address?** A computer can have a permanently assigned **static IP address** or a temporarily assigned **dynamic IP address**. As a general rule, computers on the Internet that act as servers use static IP addresses. Typically, ISPs, Web sites, Web hosting services, and e-mail servers that always need to be found at the same address require static IP addresses. Most other Internet users have dynamic IP addresses. Figure 6-6 illustrates a tool you can use to find your IP address.

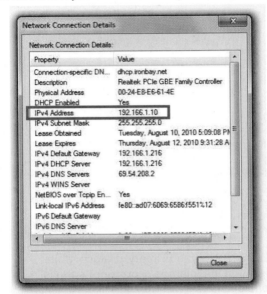

**FIGURE 6-6**

In Windows 7, you can use the Network and Sharing Center to find your computer's IP address. Other operating systems offer similar utilities. ▶ Your digital textbook shows how to find your computer's IP address using the Windows Network and Sharing Center and the command line. You'll also learn why Web-based utilities can't always identify your computer's IP address.

**Why doesn't everyone have a static IP address?** The use of 12-digit addresses such as 128.192.100.100 provides approximately 4.3 billion unique addresses, but many of these are reserved for special purposes and devices, leaving a meager number for the estimated 1.5 billion Internet users. To avoid running out of static IP addresses, dynamic addresses are used whenever possible. Dynamic IP addresses can be handed out as necessary and reused as needed.

**How do I get a dynamic IP address?** Every ISP controls a unique pool of IP addresses, which can be assigned to subscribers. If you have the type of Internet connection that requires a modem to make a telephone connection, for example, your ISP's DHCP server assigns a temporary IP address to your computer for use as long as it remains connected. When you end a session, that IP address goes back into a pool of addresses that can be distributed to other subscribers when they log in.

Your computer is rarely assigned the same dynamic IP address it had during a previous session. As an IP nomad with no permanent address, you can't feasibly run a Web site or perform other server-related activities on your computer. For example, if you try to run an online store, its address would change every time you connect to the Internet and customers would not be able to find it.

If you want to operate a server, your ISP should be able to supply you with a service plan that includes a static IP address and adequate bandwidth for server activity.

**How does a dynamic IP address relate to an always-on connection?** Most high-speed Internet connections use always-on technology. An **always-on connection** is linked to your ISP and is online whenever your computer and modem are on, even if you are not actively accessing the Internet. An always-on connection can have a static or dynamic IP address. With an always-on connection, your dynamic IP address might remain the same unless you turn off your modem, or your service provider might randomly change your IP address from time to time.

Always-on connections are convenient. You don't have to wait for a connection to be established before using your browser or sending e-mail. If you have an always-on connection, however, you should be aware that it poses a security risk. With an always-on connection, your computer is connected to the Internet for long periods of time with the same IP address, making it particularly vulnerable to hackers. In Section E you'll learn how routers and firewalls can protect computers that have always-on Internet connections.

**What's a domain name?** Although IP addresses work for communication between computers, people find it difficult to remember long strings of numbers. Therefore, most Internet servers also have an easy-to-remember name, such as *nike.com*. The official term for this name is *fully qualified domain name (FQDN)*, but most people just refer to it as a **domain name**. By convention, you should type domain names using all lowercase letters.

A domain name is a key component of Web addresses, e-mail addresses, and addresses on the Web called URLs. It is the Web server name in a Web address and the e-mail server name in an e-mail address. For example, in the Web address *www.msu.edu/infotech*, the domain name is *msu.edu*. In the e-mail address *jbillings@msu.edu*, the domain name is also *msu.edu*.

A domain name ends with an extension that indicates its **top-level domain**. For example, in the domain name *msu.edu*, *edu* indicates that the computer is maintained by an educational institution. Country codes also serve as top-level domains. Canada's top-level domain is ca; the United Kingdom's is uk; Australia's is au; the European Union uses .eu as a top-level domain. Some of the most commonly used top-level domains are listed in Figure 6-7.

**FIGURE 6-7**

Top-level Domains

6

| Domain | Description |
| --- | --- |
| biz | Unrestricted use; usually for commercial businesses |
| com | Unrestricted use; usually for commercial businesses |
| edu | Restricted to North American educational institutions |
| gov | Restricted to U.S. government agencies |
| info | Unrestricted use |
| int | Restricted to organizations established by international treaties |
| mil | Restricted to U.S. military agencies |
| mobi | Available for sites that cater to mobile devices such as smartphones |
| net | Unrestricted use; traditionally for Internet administrative organizations |
| org | Unrestricted use; traditionally for professional and nonprofit organizations |

**How are domain names related to IP addresses?** Every domain name corresponds to a unique IP address that has been entered into a huge database called the **Domain Name System** (DNS). Any computer that hosts this database is referred to as a **domain name server**. A domain name, such as *travelocity.com*, must be converted into an IP address before packets can be routed to it. For example, when you type *www.travelocity.com* into your browser, the browser's first step is to contact a domain name server to get the IP address for the Travelocity Web server, as shown in Figure 6-8.

FIGURE 6-8

A domain name request is routed through your ISP to your designated domain name server, which searches through its database to find a corresponding IP address. The IP address can then be attached to packets, such as requests for Web pages.

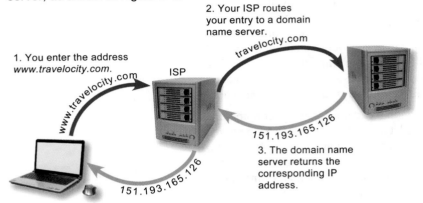

1. You enter the address *www.travelocity.com*.

2. Your ISP routes your entry to a domain name server.

3. The domain name server returns the corresponding IP address.

**Is *www* part of domain names?** No. Suppose that a corporation operates a server with an IP address of 192.150.18.61. The DNS links that address to the domain name *adobe.com*, not *www.adobe.com*. Prefixes such as *http://*, *www*, and *ftp* correspond to protocols, ports, and services offered by Internet computers.

A server can handle multiple tasks such as operating a corporate Web site, managing e-mail, and fulfilling FTP download requests. Each service uses a designated port. A **communications port** can be described as a virtual device because it is not a physical circuit or mechanism, but rather an abstract concept that allows a computer to perform more than one type of service. Port 80, for example, typically corresponds to Web services such as a corporate Web site. E-mail uses port 110. Ports 20 and 21 customarily host FTP downloads. A computer can have hundreds of ports.

When you enter *http://www.adobe.com* in a browser, the DNS gets your request as far as the adobe.com server. The server at *adobe.com* is listening to all the data packets that arrive. Packets with addresses that begin *http://www* are handled by the server's port 80, which is dedicated to Web services.

**Do I need my own domain name?** For client-style Internet activities, such as Web browsing, e-mail, and chat, you do not need your own domain name. You might, however, want a domain name if you plan to operate your own Web server or if you establish a Web site using servers provided by a Web site hosting service.

Suppose you decide to set up a Web site called Rocky Mountain Photos. For customers to access your site by typing *www.rockymtnphotos.com*, you must obtain the *rockymtnphotos.com* domain name. In contrast, if your Web site is set up on a Web server supplied by eBay, your own domain name might not be necessary because you use the domain for eBay Stores. For example, if you set up your Rocky Mountain Photos site on eBay servers, its address might be *stores.shop.ebay.com/rockymtnphotos*.

TERMINOLOGY NOTE

The communications ports used for Internet communications are sometimes simply referred to as ports. They are virtual ports, however, not physical ports like USB and FireWire ports on your computer system unit.

INFOWEBLINKS

Where can you register a domain name? What are the current fees? These questions are answered at the **Domain Name InfoWeb**.

 CLICK TO CONNECT
www.infoweblinks.com/np2012/ch06

**How do I get a domain name?** An organization called **ICANN** (Internet Corporation for Assigned Names and Numbers) is recognized by the United States and other governments as the global organization that coordinates technical management of the Internet's Domain Name System. It supervises several for-profit Accredited Domain Registrars, which handle domain name requests. You can select a domain name and register it for a minimal annual fee—currently between US$10 and $50, depending on the registration service (Figure 6-9).

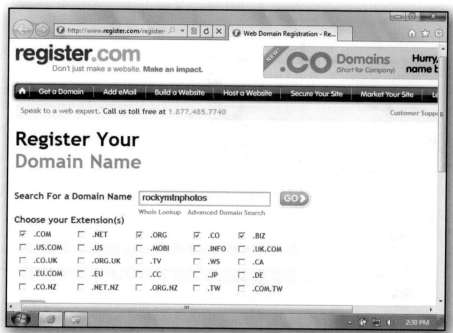

**FIGURE 6-9**

The first step in registering a domain name is to find out whether the name is currently in use or reserved for future use. If a domain name is not available, consider using a different top-level domain, such as biz instead of com. After you've found an available domain name, you can continue the registration process by filling out a simple online form.
▶ You can learn more about selecting a domain name when you access this figure in your digital textbook.

## CONNECTION SPEED

**How fast is the Internet?** Data travels over the Internet at an incredible speed. On average, data within North America usually arrives at its destination in less than 1/10th of a second (100 ms) after it is sent. Data packets usually clip along the Internet backbone at blinding speeds. Data transport can slow down, however, when usage peaks during breaking news events, or when denial-of-service attacks break through security. Such slow-downs are temporary, however, and usually last only a few hours.

The elapsed time for data to make a round trip from point A to point B and back to point A is referred to as **latency**. Typically, latency averages less than 100 ms (milliseconds) in North America. Latency increases slightly for overseas transmissions. If you want to play online multiplayer games, it is best to have less than 100 ms latency. Good quality Voice over IP and videoconferencing require latency rates of 200 ms or less.

**Can I measure speed and latency?** You can use a local Internet utility called **Ping** (Packet Internet Groper), which sends a signal to a specific Internet address and waits for a reply. If a reply arrives, Ping reports that the computer is online and displays the elapsed time for the round-trip message. You can use Ping before playing online games, using Voice over IP, or joining an online videoconference to make sure you have adequate speed for everything to run smoothly.

Ping also shows whether packets were lost in transmission. Packets can become lost when signal interference or network congestion overwhelms

Internet servers and routers. Lost packets can cause jitter in Voice over IP communications and videoconferencing. Too many lost packets during an online gaming session can cause the game to stutter or stall. And if packets don't arrive in the correct order, your game character might seem to act randomly for a few seconds.

Another utility called **Traceroute** records a packet's path in addition to its round-trip speed. You can use Traceroute to analyze the latency of your data as it hops from one Internet router to the next. Figure 6-10 contains a Traceroute report.

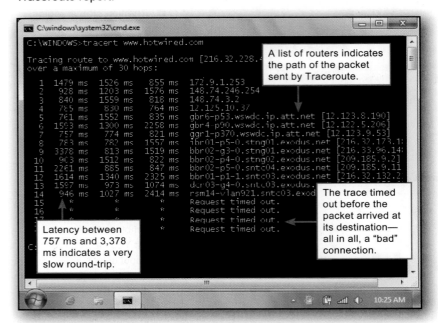

**FIGURE 6-10**

In this example, Traceroute is used to monitor an Internet connection between a small lakeside cabin in northern Michigan and the HotWired Web site. The satellite connection has extremely high latency and timed out before the Web site could be accessed. ▶ Click to learn how to launch Ping and Traceroute from the Windows command line and interpret the results.

**How fast is a typical Internet connection?** The connection speeds you see advertised by ISPs refer to the amount of data that travels between a subscriber's computer and an ISP within a given time period. Connection speed is measured in Kbps (kilobits per second) or Mbps (megabits per second).

The Internet connection speeds offered by different ISPs vary. Slow dial-up connections top out at 56 Kbps. High-speed (also called broadband) connections at 10,000 Kbps (10 Mbps) are common. High-speed connections can display graphics quickly, show smoothly streaming video, handle net-based videoconferences, and deliver high-quality Voice over IP.

**What factors affect connection speed?** Your connection speed depends on whether you connect to your ISP using a telephone, cable television, satellite, or wireless link. Actual speed can differ from maximum speed because links are susceptible to interference that can hinder signals. Upstream speed can also differ from downstream speed.

**What are upstream and downstream speeds?** **Upstream speed** is the rate of data that is uploaded from your computer to the Internet. **Downstream speed** is the rate of data downloaded to your computer. Many ISPs limit these speeds to make sure everyone gets an equal share of the bandwidth. Usually, upstream speed is slower than downstream speed.

When upstream speeds differ from downstream speeds, you have an **asymmetric Internet connection**. When upstream and downstream speeds are the same, you have a **symmetric Internet connection**.

Asymmetric connections discourage subscribers from setting up Web and e-mail servers that would transmit lots of upstream data. For most users, however, an asymmetric connection is sufficient.

You can use an Internet-based utility, such as Speedtest.net, to see if your Internet connection achieves the speed advertised by your ISP (Figure 6-11).

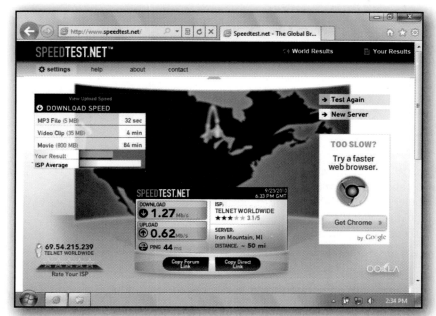

**FIGURE 6-11**

Speed tests measure the average number of bits that are transmitted per second, whereas utilities such as Ping and Traceroute measure the time required for a packet to make a round trip from your computer and back. ▶ Click to learn how to use Speedtest.net to compare the speed of your Internet connection with your ISP's advertised speed.

**What are my connection options?** Consumers have several options for connecting to the Internet. **Fixed Internet access** links your computer to an ISP from a stationary point, such as a wall socket or roof-mounted antenna. **Portable Internet access** allows you to easily move your access device, as in the case of vehicle-mounted satellite dishes that can be deployed when the vehicle is parked. **Mobile Internet access** allows you to use the Internet as you are on the go, such as using a cell phone to collect your e-mail while you are traveling by train.

You're not necessarily limited to a single Internet access option. Many consumers find it convenient to maintain fixed Internet access for home use, but use a portable or mobile method of Internet access while out and about. In Sections B and C you'll learn more about Internet access options.

# QuickCheck

1. TCP/[_____] is the primary protocol suite used on the Internet.

2. 204.127.129.1 is an example of an IPv4 address. True or false? [_____]

3. A(n) [_____] name server maintains a database of IP addresses that correspond to addresses such as *www.nike.com*.

4. If you ping Google from your computer and get a result of 46 ms, you have a relatively slow Internet connection. True or false? [_____]

5. Most ISPs offer [_____] Internet connections, meaning the downstream speed is faster than the upstream speed.

 CHECK ANSWERS

# Fixed Internet Access

ONE OF THE MOST challenging aspects of the Internet is select-ing a service provider. In this section of the chapter, you'll learn about fixed Internet access, which is typically your main link to the Internet. You'll learn to evaluate the pros and cons of various fixed Internet options, and discover why online interactive game players shun satellite Internet connections but love cable Internet service. Plus, you'll find out which types of Internet access work best for Voice over IP.

## DIAL-UP CONNECTIONS

**What is a dial-up connection?** A **dial-up connection** is a fixed Internet connection that uses a voiceband modem and telephone lines to transport data between your computer and your ISP. Many ISPs, including NetZero, AOL, PeoplePC, and EarthLink, offer dial-up Internet access. The service typically costs less than $10 per month, but access speed is slow.

**How does a dial-up connection work?** When you use a dial-up con-nection, your computer's modem places a regular telephone call to your ISP. When the ISP's computer answers your call, a dedicated circuit is established between you and your ISP—just as though you had made a voice call and someone at the ISP had picked up the phone. The circuit remains connected for the duration of your call and provides a communica-tions link that carries data between your computer and the ISP. As your data arrives at the ISP, a router sends it out over the Internet. Figure 6-12 illustrates the path of your data when you use a dial-up connection.

**FIGURE 6-12**

When you use a dial-up con-nection to access the Internet, your data travels over local telephone lines to your ISP, which sends it onto the Internet.

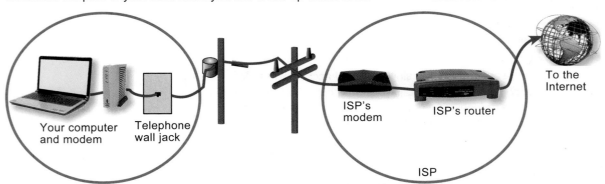

Your computer and modem | Telephone wall jack | ISP's modem | ISP's router | To the Internet | ISP

**How does a voiceband modem work?** The signals that represent data bits exist in your computer as digital signals. The telephone system, however, expects to work with human voices, so it carries analog audio signals. A **voiceband modem**—usually referred to simply as a modem—converts the signals from your computer into audible analog signals that can travel over telephone lines. A modem transmits a 1,070 Hz tone for a 0 data bit and a 1,270 Hz tone for a 1 data bit.

When your computer's modem initiates a connection, it sends a signal that is equivalent to picking up the receiver of a telephone to get a dial tone. It then dials the ISP by emitting a series of tones—the same tones you'd produce if you punched in the ISP's number using a phone keypad. The modem then waits for the ISP's modem to answer the call. After the ISP's modem answers, the two modems begin to negotiate communications protocols, such as transmission rate. The series of beeps, tones, and whooshing sounds you hear when you connect to your ISP is the sound of your modem "talking" to the ISP's modem. This process of negotiation is sometimes called handshaking. When the negotiation is complete, data transmission can begin (Figure 6-13).

**FIGURE 6-13**

When you transmit data, your voiceband modem modulates the signal that carries your data. A modem at the other end of the transmission demodulates the signal.

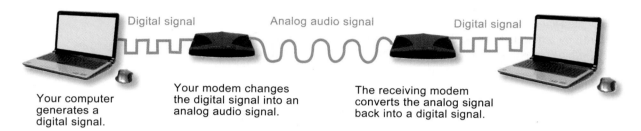

Digital signal          Analog audio signal          Digital signal

Your computer generates a digital signal.

Your modem changes the digital signal into an analog audio signal.

The receiving modem converts the analog signal back into a digital signal.

**How fast is a voiceband modem?** Modem speeds are measured in bits per second. (If you're a stickler for details, you'll realize that bps is actually a measure of capacity, but everyone calls it speed.) Most modems use a standard called V.90 to provide a theoretical maximum speed of 56 Kbps. Actual data transfer speeds are affected by factors such as the quality of your phone line and connection. Even with an excellent connection, however, a 56 Kbps modem tops out at about 44 Kbps.

Dial-up connections are asymmetrical; 44 Kbps is a typical download speed for a 56 Kbps modem. For uploads, the data rate drops to about 33 Kbps or less.

**Where can I get a voiceband modem?** Some computers have built-in voiceband modem circuitry. You can check the ports of your computer for one that accepts a standard telephone RJ-11 connector. Voiceband modems are also available for internal slots or external USB ports.

To get connected, plug one end of a telephone cable into your computer's RJ-11 port and the other end into a telephone wall jack. Your computer's operating system typically includes configuration software. Your ISP will supply the necessary information, such as the dial-in number, for completing the configuration.

**Can I talk and send data at the same time?** When your computer is connected to your ISP over a dial-up connection, data is transmitted over the same frequencies normally used for voice conversations. If you have only one telephone line, you cannot pick up your telephone receiver, dial your friend, and carry on a voice conversation while you are sending data. Some modems use technology similar to call waiting that allows you to remain connected to your ISP and temporarily suspend data transfers while answering a voice call.

**Can I use an analog modem if my phone service is digital?** In many areas of the world, the telephone system uses digital rather than analog signals to send voice conversations. You can still use an analog modem because the sounds it emits are transported just as if they were voices. Digital telephone systems open up the possibilities for digital data transport options such as ISDN, DSL, and dedicated lines.

6

## DSL, ISDN, AND DEDICATED LINES

**What are the options for transporting digital data over telephone lines?** Although the standard equipment provided by telephone companies limits the amount of data you can transmit and receive over a voiceband modem, the telephone system's copper wire has a fair amount of capacity. Several services, such as dedicated lines, ISDN, and DSL, take advantage of this capacity to offer high-speed digital communications links for voice and data.

**What is a dedicated line?** T1, T3, and T4 services are high-capacity dedicated lines that can be leased from the telephone company and are not shared by other customers. Speed ranges from 1.544 Mbps to 274 Mbps. These high-speed services are usually too expensive for individuals, but are leased by corporations and provide many of the links on the Internet backbone.

**What is ISDN?** **ISDN** (Integrated Services Digital Network) is a type of fixed Internet connection that moves data at speeds of 64 Kbps or 128 Kbps over ordinary telephone lines. Speed is symmetric, so you'll get the same data rates for uploads as for downloads. The service is usually obtained from a local telephone company or a dedicated ISDN service provider. ISDN availability and pricing vary from place to place.

**Do I need a modem for ISDN?** As with a dial-up connection, ISDN uses a telephone wall jack as a fixed point of connection; but instead of connecting your computer to a voiceband modem, you use a device called an **ISDN terminal adapter**, which sends digital signals. Although it is sometimes called an ISDN modem, a terminal adapter is not technically a modem because it doesn't modulate and demodulate the data signal, which originates in digital format and travels over a digital system. When installing ISDN, the terminal adapter is usually supplied by your ISP (Figure 6-14).

**FIGURE 6-14**

ISDN requires a terminal adapter that can be added to an internal expansion slot or connected to a USB port.

**Is an ISDN connection always on?** Basic ISDN service is like dial-up in that it makes a connection when you open a browser, e-mail, or other Internet applications, and disconnects when you've closed those applications. Connections are almost instantaneous, however, so ISDN users don't have to wait for lengthy dialing and handshaking. Some ISDN providers offer a service called always-on dynamic ISDN (AO/DI), which remains connected to an ISP as long as the computer and terminal adapter are on. Although AO/DI offers a slight performance enhancement, an always-on connection increases your computer's vulnerability to hackers.

**Why would I want ISDN?** ISDN allows you to use your telephone line for voice calls and transmit data at the same time. ISDN service is faster than dial-up. It is sometimes classified as high-speed Internet service, but it is not in the league of truly high-speed Internet connections, such as DSL and cable. If you have no other high-speed options, if ISDN is available, and if the price isn't too exorbitant, you might consider replacing your dial-up connection with ISDN.

**What is DSL?** **DSL** (digital subscriber line) is a high-speed, digital, always-on, Internet access technology that runs over standard phone lines. It is one of the fastest Internet connections that's affordable to individual consumers. Several variations of this technology exist. ADSL (asymmetric DSL) offers faster speeds for downloads than for uploads. SDSL (symmetric DSL) offers the same speed for uploads as for downloads. HDSL (high bit rate DSL), VDSL (very high bit rate DSL), and DSL lite are also available.

**How does DSL work?** DSL data is transmitted to and from your local telephone switching station in pure digital form, bypassing the bottleneck of analog-to-digital-to-analog conversion and escaping the requirement to use the narrow bandwidth allocated to voice transmissions. The result is fast data transmission over standard copper telephone cable.

DSL uses some fairly sophisticated technology to superimpose digital signals over the unused frequency spectrum of an ordinary telephone line. A DSL connection can simultaneously carry voice and data, if permitted by your DSL provider. Voice and data signals travel over telephone lines to your telephone company's local switching station. There, the voice signals are separated from the data signals. Voice signals are routed to the regular telephone system; data signals are routed to your ISP and then to the Internet (Figure 6-15).

**INFOWEBLINKS**

Nationwide, DSL vendors are grouping and regrouping. How might this affect your Internet access? You'll find up-to-date consumer information at the **DSL InfoWeb**.

W   CLICK TO CONNECT
www.infoweblinks.com/np2012/ch06

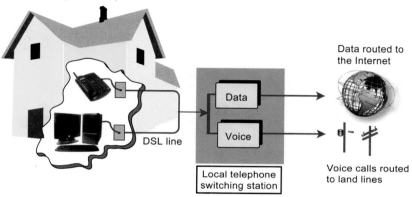

**FIGURE 6-15**

Voice and data signals travel over DSL to a special device at the local telephone switching station, where they are divided and routed to an ISP or to the regular telephone network.

**How fast is DSL?** The speed of a DSL connection varies according to the characteristics of your telephone line and your distance from the telephone company's switching station. Current DSL technology can transport data at speeds up to 6 Mbps downstream for a distance of about 1.25 miles (2 km). DSL signals deteriorate over distance, however. For DSL to work, your connection has to be within about 3 miles (5 km) of your telephone company's switching station. The distance requirement only pertains to the distance between you and the switching station. Once the signal arrives at the switch and is handed off to the ISP, it can travel the Internet backbone anywhere in the world.

**How do I get DSL service?** In many areas, DSL is a joint venture between the telephone company and an ISP. The telephone company is responsible for physical cabling and voice transmission. An ISP is responsible for data traffic. Some DSL installations require trained service technicians, whereas others can be handled by consumers. Prior to installation, you can contact your telephone company to find out if DSL is available in your area. Your DSL service provider will supply you with instructions for the installation.

**Do I need special equipment for DSL?** DSL installations typically require a modem and filters (Figure 6-16). DSL is digital, so data doesn't need to be changed into analog signals and then back to digital as it does when you use a dial-up connection. DSL signals have to be modulated, however, so they can travel on non-voice frequencies. A **DSL modem** is a device that connects a computer to a telephone line and converts computer data signals into signals compatible with DSL.

A **DSL filter** prevents voiceband signals from interfering with DSL signals. Professionally installed business DSL systems typically use a single external filter. Self-installed DSL kits provide filters that you connect to every device in your home that uses the telephone line.

**FIGURE 6-16**

DSL Equipment

A DSL filter connects to lines used for handsets, answering machines, and similar devices. For example, to filter a telephone, unplug the phone, plug the filter into the wall jack, and plug the phone cable into the filter.

A DSL modem plugs into your computer's USB or Ethernet port.

6

## CABLE INTERNET SERVICE

**What is cable Internet service?** **Cable Internet service** is a means of distributing always-on broadband Internet access over the same infrastructure that offers cable television service. Local and national cable companies, such as Comcast, Cox, and Charter, offer cable Internet service for a monthly subscription. Of all Internet services, cable Internet currently offers the fastest access speeds.

**How does cable Internet service work?** The cable television system was originally designed for remote areas where TV broadcast signals could not be received in an acceptable manner with an antenna. These systems were called community antenna television, or CATV. The CATV concept was to install one or more large, expensive satellite dishes in a community, catch TV signals with these dishes, and then send the signals over a system of cables to individual homes.

The topology of a CATV system looks a lot like the physical topology for a computer network. And that is just what is formed when your cable TV company becomes your Internet provider. Your computer becomes part of a neighborhood LAN joined by wiring for the cable TV infrastructure.

**Are television and data signals carried over the same cable?** CATV coaxial and fiber-optic cables have plenty of bandwidth to carry television signals for hundreds of channels in addition to digital data. CATV cables provide bandwidth for television signals, incoming data signals, and outgoing data signals (Figure 6-17).

**INFOWEBLINKS**

For an in-depth look at cable modem technology, connections, bandwidth, and security, follow the links at the **Cable Internet Service InfoWeb**.

**W** CLICK TO CONNECT
www.infoweblinks.com/np2012/ch06

TV CHANNELS

Downstream Data

Upstream Data

**FIGURE 6-17**

A CATV cable has enough bandwidth to support TV channels and data flowing downstream as well as data flowing upstream.

**How fast is cable Internet service?** Most cable Internet service is asymmetric, with upload speeds considerably slower than download speeds to discourage subscribers from setting up public Web servers. A standard home service plan offers speeds of 12 Mbps for downloads and 1 Mbps for uploads. Some premium plans offer even faster connections with speeds of 50 Mbps for downloads and 10 Mbps for uploads.

Cable signals are not particularly vulnerable to environmental interference, but data transport speeds are affected by subscriber use. The cable you share with your neighbors has a certain amount of bandwidth. As more and more neighbors use the service, it might seem to get slower and slower. As an analogy, consider the luggage conveyor belt in an airport, which moves at a constant speed. If you have three pieces of luggage and you are the only passenger on the plane, your bags arrive one right after another. However, if you just arrived on a full 747, your bags are intermixed with those of hundreds of other passengers, and it takes longer to collect them.

Your cable company's network carries packets at a constant speed. However, if many of your neighbors are sending and receiving packets at the same time, your packets seem to arrive more slowly. Cable Internet subscribers notice that their connection speed seems slower during peak usage times.

**Do I need special equipment for cable Internet service?** When you set up your computer for cable Internet service, you are essentially linking to the cable network's Ethernet-style LAN that connects a neighborhood of cable subscribers. The two requirements for this type of connection are circuitry to handle Ethernet protocols and a **cable modem**, which converts your computer's signal into one that can travel over the CATV network.

Most subscribers rent a cable modem from their cable company, and the rental fee is included in the monthly bill. Third-party cable modems manufactured by Linksys, Motorola, D-Link, and other companies can be purchased from electronics stores, but it is a good idea to check with your cable company first to make sure the modem you select is compatible.

A cable modem can plug directly into a coaxial cable wall jack. If you need to connect your cable set-top box and cable modem to a single wall jack, you can use a cable splitter as shown in Figure 6-18.

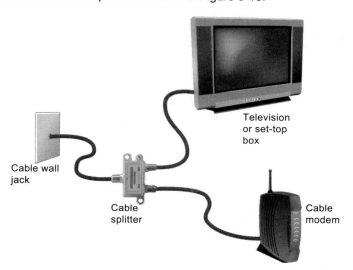

Television or set-top box

Cable wall jack

Cable splitter

Cable modem

FIGURE 6-18

If your home has only one CATV cable outlet, you might need to use a splitter to link it to your cable modem and television. If you have multiple cable outlets, you can connect your cable modem directly to any one of them.

6

Most cable modems have USB and Ethernet ports, and you can use one or the other. Some cable companies instruct subscribers to connect the modem directly to a computer. However, as you'll learn in the Internet Security section, the safest way to connect your computer to a cable modem is through a router.

**How secure are cable Internet connections?** In the early days of cable Internet service, some cable Internet subscribers were unpleasantly surprised when they happened to open Windows Network Neighborhood, only to be greeted with a list of their neighbors' computers! When you boot a PC, Windows automatically connects to available LANs and looks for shared files, folders, and printers on LAN workstations. Because cable Internet service uses LAN technology, computers in different households were treated as workstations on a shared LAN.

Today, most cable companies use DOCSIS-compliant cable modems that block crossover traffic between subscribers. **DOCSIS** (Data Over Cable Service Interface Specification) is a data transport technology that includes security filters. DOCSIS secures your computer from your neighbors, but it does not close up all the security holes that are opened when you use an always-on connection. When you use cable Internet service, be sure your computer is running security software.

## SATELLITE INTERNET SERVICE

**What is satellite Internet service?** Most people are familiar with services that provide access to television programming over a personal satellite dish. Many companies that provide satellite TV also offer Internet access. **Satellite Internet service** is a means of distributing always-on, high-speed asymmetric Internet access by broadcasting signals to and from a personal satellite dish. In many rural areas, satellite Internet service is the only alternative to a dial-up connection.

**How does satellite Internet service work?** Satellite Internet service uses a geostationary satellite to transmit computer data directly to and from a satellite dish owned by an individual (Figure 6-19).

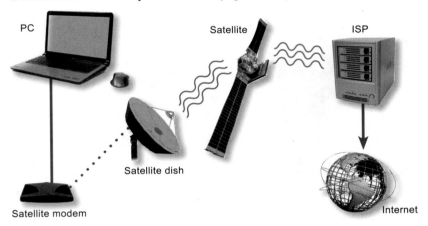

PC · Satellite · ISP · Satellite dish · Internet · Satellite modem

**FIGURE 6-19**

Satellite Internet services use geostationary satellites to transmit data between subscribers and ISPs.

Of all the Internet access services, satellite has the farthest range and greatest ability to reach remote areas. Whereas ISDN and DSL services are limited to within several miles of a telephone company switching station, and cable Internet service is limited to areas where cable television is offered, satellite Internet service can be beamed to any customers whose property offers an unobstructed view of the orbiting satellite—in the U.S. that means an unobstructed view of the southern sky.

**How fast is satellite Internet service?** Satellite service typically averages 1.0 to 1.5 Mbps for downloads but only 100 to 256 Kbps for uploads. Satellite transmission and reception can be slowed or blocked by adverse weather conditions, such as rain and snow, which makes this type of data transport less reliable than wired Internet access services, such as cable and DSL.

Satellite data transport is subject to latency delays of one second or more, which occur as your data is routed between your computer and a satellite that orbits 22,200 miles above the Earth. Latency might not pose much of a problem for general Web surfing and downloading files, but it can become a showstopper for interactive gaming that requires quick reactions, and for Voice over IP.

As with cable Internet service, satellite data transport speeds might seem to decline during peak usage hours because the satellite's bandwidth is shared among all users.

**TERMINOLOGY NOTE**

Communications satellites in geostationary orbits move in synchronization with the Earth's rotation and always appear to be in the same location of the sky.

**INFOWEBLINKS**

The **Satellite InfoWeb** dishes out lots of goodies about satellite Internet access—the technology, service providers, prices, and even reviews from disgruntled computer game players.

 CLICK TO CONNECT
www.infoweblinks.com/np2012/ch06

## Does satellite Internet service require special equipment?

A satellite dish and modem are the two pieces of equipment required for satellite Internet access. If you are already receiving satellite television and your service provider offers Internet services, you can most likely use your current satellite dish. Most consumer satellite dishes used in the northern hemisphere are fixed in one position and measure 18 to 31 inches (46 to 79 cm) in diameter, as shown in Figure 6-20.

**FIGURE 6-20**

Today's satellite dishes are small and can be easily mounted on roofs or exterior walls.

A **satellite modem** (Figure 6-21) is a device that modulates the data signals from a computer into a frequency band that can be carried to the satellite dish, where it is converted to another frequency, amplified, and transmitted. The modem usually connects to the satellite dish using two coaxial cables: one to transmit and one to receive. The modem then can be connected to the Ethernet port of a computer, or for better security to the Ethernet port of a router.

Equipment and installation costs for satellite Internet service are higher than those for other Internet services. Some companies charge $200 or more for a satellite dish, though the cost is often spread over a two- to three-year service contract.

**FIGURE 6-21**

A satellite modem looks similar to cable and DSL modems, but is designed for entirely different technology.

## FIXED WIRELESS SERVICE

**What is fixed wireless Internet service?** **Fixed wireless Internet service** (also called wireless broadband service) is designed to offer Internet access to homes and businesses by broadcasting data signals over areas large enough to cover most cities and outlying areas. Fixed wireless technologies are MAN (metropolitan area network) standards, in contrast to technologies such as Wi-Fi, which are LAN (local area network) standards. One of the most well-known fixed wireless standards is WiMAX, currently offered in the U.S. by companies such as Clearwire and in the U.K. by companies such as FREEDOM4.

**What is WiMAX?** **WiMAX**, which stands for Worldwide Interoperability for Microwave Access, is an Ethernet-compatible network standard designated as IEEE 802.16. Its popularity is growing because it offers an alternative to wired technologies, such as DSL and cable Internet service, that require expensive infrastructures. WiMAX can be deployed in rural areas where cable service is not available and where customers are too far away from a telephone switching station for DSL service. In an urban environment, WiMAX can offer healthy competition to other Internet service providers.

**How does WiMAX work?** A WiMAX system transmits data to and from WiMAX antennas mounted on towers. A single tower can serve a large geographical area. Towers can transmit data to subscribers, they can relay data to other towers using microwave links, and they can connect directly to the Internet backbone by cable. Within 3 miles/8 km of the tower, signals are strong enough to be picked up by subscribers on a non-line-of-sight device, similar to a Wi-Fi access point. Beyond that range, a line-of-sight antenna is required (Figure 6-22).

**What is the speed of WiMAX?** Under ideal conditions, WiMAX can transmit data at 70 Mbps. Actual speed, however, is affected by distance, weather, and usage. Current services claim speeds of 1 to 5 Mbps for downloads. WiMAX can be distributed as symmetrical or asymmetrical service.

Fixed wireless technologies have less latency than satellite Internet service and can usually offer connection speeds suitable for online gaming, Voice over IP, and teleconferencing.

**What equipment do I need for WiMAX access?** Your wireless service provider typically supplies a wireless modem that you connect to your computer. The modem includes a transceiver to send and receive signals to a wireless point of access, usually located on a nearby communications tower. Subscribers on the outlying edges of the network's range might also require an antenna mounted on a window or roof, and a line-of-sight range to the WiMAX tower.

**INFOWEBLINKS**

The **WiMAX InfoWeb** has the latest information on this up-and-coming Internet access technology.

(W) CLICK TO CONNECT
www.infoweblinks.com/np2012/ch06

**FIGURE 6-22**

A WiMAX tower broadcasts signals over a wide area. Subscribers close to the tower can use non-line-of-sight modems to pick up the signal.

## FIXED INTERNET CONNECTION ROUNDUP

**What's the best Internet connection for my PC?** The best Internet connection depends on your budget, what's available in your area, and what you do while connected. For fixed Internet access, cable Internet service is usually the first choice, when available. If cable Internet service is not available, or proves slower or less dependable than expected, the next choice would be DSL or fixed wireless service, if available.

If several fixed Internet services are offered in your area, the table in Figure 6-23 can help you evaluate their requirements, costs, advantages, and disadvantages.

**FIGURE 6-23**

Fixed Internet Access Options

|  | Dial-up | ISDN | DSL | Cable | Satellite | WiMAX |
|---|---|---|---|---|---|---|
| **Download speed (max.)** | 56 Kbps | 128 Kbps | 384 Kbps–8 Mbps | 5–50 Mbps | 1–1.5 Mbps | 70 Mbps |
| **Upload speed (max.)** | 33 Kbps | 128 Kbps | 128 Kbps–6 Mbps | 256 Kbps–10 Mbps | 100–256 Kbps | 70 Mbps |
| **Download speed (actual)** | 44 Kbps | 128 Kbps | 2–5 Mbps | 3–10 Mbps | 400–800 Kbps | 1–5 Mbps |
| **Latency** | 100–200 ms | 10–30 ms | 10–20 ms | 10–20 ms | 1–3 seconds | 10–50 ms |
| **Short video (72 MB) download** | 4 hours | 78 minutes | 5 minutes | 3.2 minutes | 24 minutes | 6.4 minutes |
| **Requirements** | Telephone line, ISP, voiceband modem | Telephone line, ISDN service, ISDN terminal adapter | Computer located within 3 miles of local telephone switch; DSL modem | CATV service that provides Internet access; cable modem | Clear view of southern sky; satellite dish and modem | WiMAX modem, line-of-sight to WiMAX tower for distances > 3 miles |
| **Monthly fee** | $5–$25 | $50–$150 | $30–$200 | $20–$60 | $35–$80 | $0–$60 |
| **Installation cost** | $0 | $0–$200 | $0–$100 | $0–$50 | $50–$300 | $50–$150 |
| **Always-on** | N | N | Y | Y | Y | Y |

6

# QuickCheck

1. ISDN is an analog service, whereas dial-up and DSL use the telephone company's digital capabilities. True or false? [_____]

2. Always-on connections are not a security risk because they use DOCSIS. True or false? [_____]

3. The two requirements for cable Internet service are circuitry to handle [_____] protocols and a cable modem.

4. Satellite Internet service typically has a high [_____] rate, which is unsuitable for some online gaming and Voice over IP.

5. [_____], which adheres to IEEE 802.16 standards, is one of the most promising fixed wireless Internet technologies.

▶ CHECK ANSWERS

# Portable and Mobile Internet Access

**WHEN YOU'RE ON THE GO** and away from your fixed Internet connection, you are not necessarily cut off from your e-mail and other Internet activities. Portable and mobile Internet technologies can provide Internet access while you visit friends, commute to work or school, or take a vacation. In this section, you'll find out what's available for portable and mobile access today and what's on the drawing board for the future.

## INTERNET TO GO

**What are the limitations of fixed Internet access?** Fixed Internet access through dial-up, cable, ISDN, DSL, satellite, and 802.16 WiMAX tethers your computer to a tangle of cables and equipment, such as modems, satellite dishes, and antennas. It can be a hassle even to relocate your Internet modem to another room.

In the days when bulky desktop computers were the norm, a fixed Internet connection seemed sensible. Today, however, with the proliferation of sleek notebook computers, iPads, smartphones, and other portable computing appliances, Internet users want the freedom to roam while accessing online information and services.

What if you're on vacation and you want to download music for your iPod? What if you're visiting a friend across town and you want to get your e-mail? If you drop into your local video rental store with only your cell phone, can you access the Internet Movie Database to scan some reviews before you select a movie? If you're on a cross-country trip, would you be able to boot up your computer, access the MapQuest Web site, and give the driver directions to the nearest Starbucks? (See Figure 6-24.)

These scenarios are all possible, but not necessarily by using a single Internet service provider, user account, or computer. Today's state-of-the-art is not an ideal "Internet anywhere" technology that allows you to use one Internet service and any digital device to get high-speed access to the global pool of Internet data from any location. Instead, Internet consumers have to contend with a hodgepodge of technologies, multiple accounts, and an unfortunate number of user fees for blanket Internet access.

**What is portable Internet access?** Portable Internet access can be defined as the ability to easily move your Internet service from one location to another. It is portable in the sense that a hot plate is portable. It is light and compact enough to easily carry, even though you have to remain in one spot when it comes time to use it. Portable Internet access services include Wi-Fi, portable satellite, and portable WiMAX.

**What is mobile Internet access?** Mobile Internet access offers a continuous Internet connection as you are walking or riding in a bus, car, train, or plane. It is very similar in concept to cellular phone service that allows you to move freely within coverage areas as the signal for your connection is seamlessly handed off from one tower to the next. Mobile Internet access includes Wi-Fi, mobile WiMAX, and cellular broadband service.

**FIGURE 6-24**

Using mobile Internet access, you can find the location of the nearest coffee shop.

## WI-FI HOTSPOTS

**How does Wi-Fi fit in with the Internet everywhere concept?** In addition to being popular for home networks, Wi-Fi is also used for public networks operated by merchants, hotels, schools, and municipalities. If your computer is equipped for Wi-Fi, as are most of today's notebooks, netbooks, and smartphones, you have a portable means of accessing the Internet by carrying your digital device to any Wi-Fi hotspot.

**What is a Wi-Fi hotspot?** A **Wi-Fi hotspot** is an area in which the public can access a Wi-Fi network that offers Internet service. You can find hotspots in coffee shops, RV parks, hotels, community centers, college campuses, and airports. Wi-Fi hotspot availability is expanding even in small towns and rural areas. Web sites such as *wi-fi.jiwire.com* help you find Wi-Fi hotspots in a specific location.

Some Wi-Fi hotspots offer free service that might or might not require a password; others require a service plan or one-time use fee. Companies that offer hotspot service plans include T-Mobile, Verizon, Sprint, and AT&T. Hotspot service plans are not interchangeable. You cannot, for example, access a T-Mobile hotspot if you have a Verizon Wi-Fi Access service plan. Access plans can be expensive and they are being phased out in favor of cellular data services.

**How fast is hotspot access?** The speed of a hotspot is related to the speed of the wired line that connects it to the Internet. A hotspot that goes through a 1 Mbps DSL line will be slower than a hotspot that goes through a 22 Mbps cable Internet connection. You can typically expect speeds of 2–8 Mbps, but speed can vary depending on your distance from the access point, the number of people logged in, and interference from other networks.

**How do I access a Wi-Fi hotspot?** In a typical scenario, you might take your notebook computer—equipped with Wi-Fi capability—to your local Starbucks cafe. You buy a cup of cappuccino, sit down in a comfortable chair, and switch on your computer. Your computer's networking utilities automatically sense a Wi-Fi network and establish a connection. Windows users can access Connect to a Network to view a list of available networks and connect to one as shown in Figure 6-25.

6

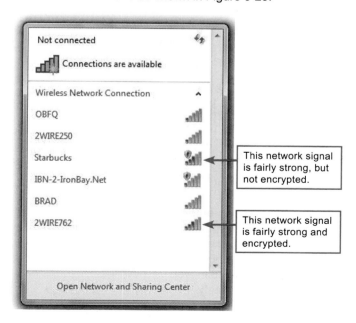

**FIGURE 6-25**

Enter "Connect to a Network" in the Start menu's search box to view a list of available networks, including Wi-Fi hotspots. Secure networks are safest. Networks that do not have security enabled are indicated with a yellow shield.

**Is hotspot access secure?** Public hotspots are not typically protected by WPA or other encryption because it is not feasible to hand out passwords and user IDs to every person who wants access. Hotspots are not secure, and Wi-Fi eavesdroppers can easily tap into most of the data that flows over the network.

When you are using a Wi-Fi hotspot for simple browsing activities such as checking sports scores, reading Google news, and looking for directions, your security risk is fairly low if your computer's antivirus software is up to date. Your security risk is also low when you are accessing secured Web sites that have addresses beginning with HTTPS. These secured sites, typically used for online banking and credit card purchases, encrypt the data that you enter to keep it safe from eavesdroppers.

When you log into unsecured sites while using public Wi-Fi hotspots, however, a wireless eavesdropper could potentially snag your user ID and password information, then use it later to access your accounts. Logging into your Webmail account, for example, could be risky because your user ID and password are transmitted over an unsecured connection.

Eavesdroppers might also be able to access the files on your computer if you have file sharing turned on. When using public networks, you should turn file sharing off. Windows 7 users can select the Public network option after connecting to a Wi-Fi hotspot (Figure 6-26).

**FIGURE 6-26**

When connected to a public Wi-Fi hotspot, turn off file sharing to keep your data secure from eavesdroppers.

**Can I use public hotspots for mobile Internet access?** Although Wi-Fi is popular for portable Internet access, public hotspots do not typically provide acceptable mobile Internet access because you can only remain connected within range of the network's hotspot.

The current model for using most Wi-Fi hotspots is that you enter the area of coverage, find a location with a strong signal, and remain there while accessing the Internet. Wi-Fi handoffs from one Wi-Fi network to another are clumsy and prone to packet loss, which is unacceptable for Voice over IP or streaming video applications. Later in this section, you'll read about cellular-based hotspots that you can set up privately to get mobile Internet access.

## PORTABLE AND MOBILE WIMAX

**What is portable WiMAX?** WiMAX can be used as a portable technology because Internet access is available to subscribers anywhere within a tower's coverage area. WiMAX subscribers who use non-line-of-sight modems with an integrated antenna (Figure 6-27) can easily move their Internet service by relocating their modems anywhere within the service provider's coverage area. One WiMAX service provider encourages its customers to "Just plug in and jump online anywhere within the service area."

WiMAX-equipped computers make portable Internet access even easier. Just as many notebook computers are equipped with Wi-Fi circuitry, manufacturers can also add WiMAX circuitry and antennas, eliminating the need for an external modem.

**What are the pros and cons of portable WiMAX?** The big bonus of portable WiMAX is that you use the same Internet service provider whether you are at home or on the road. You do not need supplemental service contracts or day passes as you do for Wi-Fi hotspots. On the downside, WiMAX is not yet in widespread use and therefore coverage is limited.

**What about mobile WiMAX?** Mobile WiMAX is an up-and-coming standard destined to be deployed by ISPs and cell phone carriers because it is designed to offer Internet access with seamless handoff from the coverage area of one tower to the coverage area of another tower. Mobile WiMAX could make it possible for you to deal with a single service provider for all your cell phone and Internet access needs.

## PORTABLE SATELLITE SERVICE

**What if I travel to remote areas?** WiMAX and Wi-Fi hotspots provide coverage in cities and small towns, but do not typically extend out to sparsely populated areas. If you plan to remain in a single remote location, fixed satellite Internet service is a good option. If, however, Internet access is required as you travel to various remote locations to hike, ski, or conduct research, then portable satellite technology is available.

**How does portable satellite technology work?** For portable satellite Internet service, a satellite dish is typically mounted on a vehicle. The disk is stowed while the vehicle is in motion, but can be quickly deployed when the vehicle stops.

Like a fixed satellite dish, a portable dish transmits signals to and receives signals from a geostationary satellite. If a fixed satellite dish moves out of alignment, signals can no longer be captured dependably. The challenge with mobile satellite service is to make sure the dish is correctly aimed from the location where it is used. High-end portable satellite systems have self-aiming hardware that automatically deploys and rotates the dish until it locks onto the satellite signal (Figure 6-28).

**How fast is portable satellite service?** Portable satellite service providers advertise download speeds of 400 Kbps to 5 Mbps

**FIGURE 6-27**

WiMAX modems are easy to transport and can be plugged in anywhere within the coverage area of a WiMAX tower.

6

**FIGURE 6-28**

A vehicle-mounted satellite dish can be deployed from a control panel inside the vehicle.
▶ See how it works.

and upload speeds of 50 to 500 Kbps. Larger dishes offer faster speeds. Portable satellites work well for browsing the Web and checking e-mail. As with fixed satellite service, however, latency becomes a factor for real-time applications such as videoconferencing and online gaming.

**What is the cost of portable satellite service?** If you are willing to deploy and aim your satellite dish by hand, the price of equipment and a data plan is similar to a stationary satellite installation. Automatic systems that include a self-deploying satellite dish, deployment mechanics, satellite modem, and interior control panel can cost $5,000 to $10,000. Hardware costs do not include installation or monthly service fees.

## CELLULAR DATA SERVICE

**How can I use my cell phone service to access the Internet?** In many countries, including the U.S., cell phone coverage is extensive and the technology is truly mobile; you can use cell phone service while walking or in a moving vehicle. The handoff as you travel from one cell area to another is seamless.

Using cell phone technology to access the Internet offers mobility that is not possible with other wired or wireless computer network technologies. And though in the past cellular-based Internet access was slower than dial-up, new technologies offer speeds that are more competitive with high-speed broadband offerings.

**How fast is cellular data transport?** Data transport speed depends on the technology of the cellular system. Cellular technology is classified by generation.

First-generation (1G) technology was analog and offered few features beyond voice communications. 2G replaced analog technology with digital technology and added support for basic data transport in the form of text messages. Sending computer data over a 1G or 2G system required a voiceband modem to convert digital data into audible signals. Transmission rates were glacially slow.

3G technologies offered by many of today's cellular service providers support digital transmission for both voice and data. 3G technologies have speeds ranging from 200 Kbps to 5 Mbps, so they are similar to satellite Internet service, and can potentially match DSL speeds. Cellular phone companies use a variety of 3G technologies, such as EDGE, EV-DO, and HSUPA.

4G technology is the next step forward in mobile technology. It is designed to provide peak data rates of 100 Mbps while a device is in motion, or 1 Gbps rates when a device is stationary. Interim 4G technologies such as LTE (Long Term Evolution) have been deployed since 2009, but full-scale availability of 4G is not expected for several years.

**Can I get to the Internet from any cell phone?** Most cellular service providers offer e-mail and Internet services. Basic phones can access a limited number of specially designed Web sites using WAP.

**What is WAP? WAP** (Wireless Application Protocol) is a communications protocol that provides Internet access from handheld devices, such as cell phones. WAP-enabled devices contain a microbrowser that displays simplified versions of popular Web sites, such as CNN, Google, Yahoo!, ESPN, UPS, FedEx, The Weather Channel, and MapQuest. WAP devices also include e-mail software formatted for small, low-resolution screens (Figure 6-29).

**FIGURE 6-29**

The advantage of WAP-enabled devices is their portability. The disadvantage is their small, low-res screens. Although various schemes for scrolling over a full-sized Web page have been tried, most WAP users stick to Web sites specially designed for small screen devices.

**Can I use a cell phone to access regular Web sites and use other Internet services?** Accessing the "real" Internet requires a different approach than is offered by WAP. For the real Internet, cellular service providers offer data services, sometimes referred to as **mobile broadband**. Broadband access requires a fast connection, a data service subscription, and mobile broadband equipment.

Broadband speeds are not available in all of a cellular service provider's coverage area. Coverage maps can give you an idea of the service area, but actual coverage and speeds can vary. Where broadband coverage is not available, your device might operate at a much slower speed or might not have access to data services.

**What is a data service plan?** Most cellular service providers offer a data service plan for accessing the Internet. Prices for these plans range from $20 per month and up. Less expensive plans typically limit the amount of data you can send and receive, treating megabytes like minutes. Make sure you understand the terms of your service contract. Some data service contracts prohibit users from streaming or downloading music, movies, or games; making Voice over IP phone calls; and using file-sharing networks.

**What equipment do I need for mobile broadband Internet access?** With a data service plan, there are five ways to take advantage of mobile broadband: using a handheld PDA or smartphone, using a mobile broadband card in a PC, using a mobile broadband-enabled computer, using a cell phone as a modem, or using a cell phone as a wireless hotspot.

**How do I access the Internet with a handheld device?** You can use a smartphone to access the Internet by subscribing to a data service plan offered by a mobile phone provider such as AT&T, Verizon, or Sprint.

Many handheld devices also have built-in Wi-Fi and can access the Internet when in range of a Wi-Fi LAN or hotspot. When the device senses the Wi-Fi network, it gives you the opportunity to connect and enter the network password if one is required. Once connected, your handheld device can access the Internet at Wi-Fi speeds.

Smartphones typically include browser and e-mail software (Figure 6-30). Some devices, such as the iPhone, include specialized software to access popular Web sites such as Google Maps and YouTube.

**FIGURE 6-30**

Many smartphones offer a large color screen and can connect to Wi-Fi hotspots and cellular data services to access the Internet.

**How do handheld devices compensate for small screens?** Although the screens on handheld devices have much higher resolution than the screens on basic WAP-enabled phones, they cannot display most Web pages at their normal size. Viewing normal-size Web pages on a handheld device typically requires lots of scrolling.

Some sites, such as *www.wunderground.com*, automatically detect handheld devices, then display specially formatted Web pages. If you are not automatically directed to a small-format page, look for a link to the mobile version of the site. You can also google the mobile version. For example googling "Wikipedia mobile" will find links to Wikipedia formatted for small screens.

If small-format pages are not available, you can use a service such as Skweezer (*www.skweezer.com*) to reformat Web pages to fit on a small screen (Figure 6-31).

**How do I access the Internet with a cellular wireless modem?** Most cellular service providers offer wireless modems compatible with EDGE, EV-DO, or HSUPA technology (Figure 6-32). The modem slides into the USB port of your notebook computer and is installed following the manufacturer's instructions.

After the card has been installed, you can use it to connect to the Internet and use your usual set of tools, including your Web browser and e-mail software. With your notebook computer's full-size screen, you'll have the "real" Internet experience.

**What is a mobile broadband-enabled computer?** Just as many notebook computers come with Wi-Fi circuitry for accessing wireless LANs and hotspots, some manufacturers offer netbook computers with built-in circuitry for mobile broadband access. Although these configurations reduce installation hassles, they are not in demand because they may limit consumers to one mobile broadband provider.

**How do I use a phone as a modem?** Some cell phones connect to your computer and act as a wireless modem to transmit data over the Internet. Data speed depends on the phone's technology.

To make the connection, obtain a data cable that's compatible with your phone from your cellular service provider or an electronics outlet. Follow the manufacturer's instructions for installing the cable and setting up a modem connection.

When you want to access the Internet, plug your cellular phone into your computer (Figure 6-33) and connect through your mobile data service. As with other connection options for desktop and notebook computers, you can use your usual suite of Internet software.

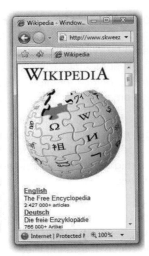

**FIGURE 6-31**

Skweezer and similar utilities shrink and reformat Web pages so that they fit on small screens. ▶ See how it works.

**FIGURE 6-32**

It looks like a USB flash drive, but it is a modem that gives your computer Internet access using a cell phone network.

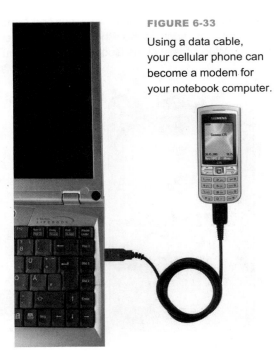

**FIGURE 6-33**

Using a data cable, your cellular phone can become a modem for your notebook computer.

**Can I use my phone as a wireless hotspot?** Some cell phones, such as the Droid X, can act as a Wi-Fi hotspot by becoming the router for a wireless network. You can set up your phone's mobile hotspot anywhere you have data service, but hotspot capability might entail additional monthly service charges.

When in Wi-Fi hotspot mode, your mobile phone can provide portable Internet access to other Wi-Fi enabled devices, such as notebook computers, iPods, iPads, and other smartphones.

Setting up a mobile Wi-Fi hotspot is similar to setting up a router for a private Wi-Fi network. You begin by entering an SSID as the unique network name, then select an encryption method, such as WPA2, to secure the data flowing over the network. When your hotspot is configured and active, other Wi-Fi enabled devices can connect to access the Internet and share files (Figure 6-34).

**FIGURE 6-34**

Some cell phones can be deployed as the router and modem for a small wireless network that you can use while traveling in a car or an RV.

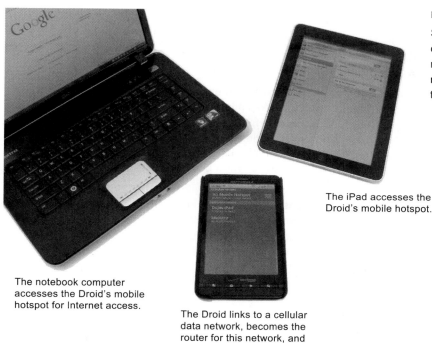

The iPad accesses the Droid's mobile hotspot.

The notebook computer accesses the Droid's mobile hotspot for Internet access.

The Droid links to a cellular data network, becomes the router for this network, and creates a Wi-Fi hotspot.

6

# QuickCheck

1. [_____] Internet access can be defined as the ability to use the Internet while walking or traveling in a moving vehicle.

2. A Wi-Fi [_____] is an area in which the public can access a Wi-Fi network that offers Internet service.

3. Most of today's cellular networks operate using [_____] G technology, such as EV-DO, HSUPA, and EDGE.

4. The procedure for setting up a cellular mobile [_____] is similar to setting up a wireless router.

5. Portable [_____] technology can be used to access the Internet from remote locations where there are no cable, WiMAX, or cellular networks.

 CHECK ANSWERS

# Internet Services

**AN INTERNET CONNECTION** offers access to a global data communications system. You know that protocols such as TCP/IP and UDP handle basic data transport; but additional protocols, sometimes referred to as application protocols, make possible a variety of useful Internet applications, such as real-time messaging, Voice over IP, blogging, tweeting, cloud computing, grid computing, FTP, and file sharing.

## REAL-TIME MESSAGING

**What is real-time messaging?** A network-based **real-time messaging system** allows people to exchange short messages while they are online. One-on-one messaging is referred to as **instant messaging** (IM) and group communications are referred to as **chat**.

Every day, millions of people use messaging systems, such as Facebook Chat, AOL Instant Messenger, Yahoo! Messenger, Google Talk, Apple iChat, and Windows Live Messenger, to communicate with friends, family, and coworkers. Some systems offer voice messaging options, so that participants can speak to each other using computer-based microphones. Video messaging is another option offered by some systems when both participants have computer-based cameras.

**How does real-time messaging work?** Most messaging is based on a client/server model that uses a server to handle communication packets between the participants (clients). When participants log on, they connect to the messaging server, which authenticates their user IDs and passwords. The server then sends back a list of participants or buddies. For a chat room, "participants" are those people who are currently logged into the discussion. For instant messaging, "buddies" are people in a participant's list of friends who are currently online.

**FIGURE 6-35**

IM client software displays a window for typing and viewing messages.

Messages are typed into client software (Figure 6-35), which uses messaging protocols to break the message into packets and ship them to the server for distribution or directly to the recipient. Some protocols encrypt messages before they are transmitted. Messaging and chat protocols include IRC (Internet Relay Chat), MSNP (Mobile Status Notification Protocol), and Jabber.

Although standalone messaging clients are available, many people use messaging clients that are built into applications such as Facebook and Web-based mail.

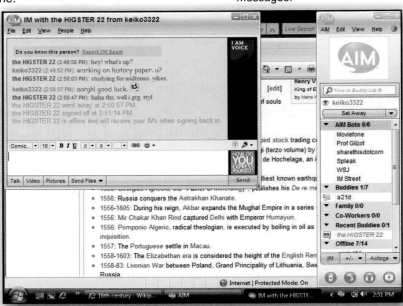

# VOICE OVER IP

**What is Voice over IP?** **VoIP** (Voice over Internet Protocol), or Voice over IP, is a technology in which a broadband Internet connection is used to place telephone calls instead of the regular phone system. It is based on SIP (Session Initiation Protocol), so VoIP software is sometimes referred to as a SIP client.

The earliest VoIP connections were computer-to-computer connections. Both the person initiating the call and the person receiving the call had to have computers with microphones and headsets or speakers. You could only call people who were using the same VoIP software and who happened to be online when you wanted to call them. These early VoIP systems worked more like instant messaging with voice than a traditional phone call.

You can still use VoIP to make calls from one computer to another, but today VoIP systems, offered by companies such as AT&T, Comcast, magicJack, Skype, and Vonage, allow you to use a standard telephone handset to make or receive calls. They also allow you to receive calls from landline telephones and to place calls to these telephones.

**How do today's VoIP systems work?** Today's VoIP systems convert voice communications to data packets. An IP address is attached to each packet. If you are calling a friend with computer-based VoIP, for example, your friend's IP address will be attached to the packets. If you are calling a land line or other destination without its own IP address, your VoIP packets will carry an IP address of a service that can route your packets to their destination using land lines where necessary.

**How do I set up VoIP?** If you want to set up free computer-to-computer VoIP, you and the people you communicate with can download and install freeware or open source VoIP clients, such as Blink or Gizmo5. You can also use any messaging service that supports audio transmission. For the most basic setup, you can simply use your computer's built-in microphone and speakers instead of connecting a phone handset.

When you subscribe to a VoIP service, follow your service provider's setup instructions. For example, magicJack provides a small USB device that you plug into your computer, then connect to a telephone. Vonage supplies you with an adapter that you connect to your Internet modem.

Cell phones that offer Wi-Fi as well as cellular phone service can be used to make VoIP calls if permitted by your service provider. When you are within range of a Wi-Fi hotspot, the call is routed through the Internet as a VoIP call. If no hotspot is in range, the call is routed through the standard cellular service. To get VoIP on your cell phone, find and install a compatible mobile VoIP app.

**Do I need a high-speed Internet connection for VoIP?** In addition to the speed of your Internet connection, VoIP audio quality is affected by jitter and packet loss. **Jitter** measures the variability of packet latency. Network traffic and interference can delay some packets and create erratic data flow. If the variation between packets exceeds 5 ms, VoIP quality is likely to be poor.

**Packet loss** refers to data that never reaches its destination or gets discarded because it arrives too late to be of any use. Packet loss of less than 2% is required for acceptable VoIP (Figure 6-36).

6

FIGURE 6-36

You can test your Internet connection to determine if it is suitable for VoIP by connecting to Web sites such as *myspeed.visualware.com*.

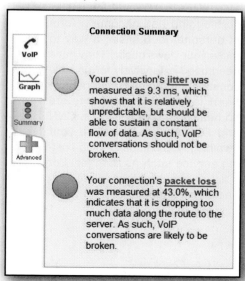

## FORUMS, WIKIS, BLOGS, AND TWEETS

**What about asynchronous communications?** Instant messaging, chat, and VoIP are forms of synchronous communications; the people communicating have to be online at the same time and the conversation happens in real time. The Internet also supports several types of asynchronous communications, including Internet forums, wikis, blogs, and tweets.

The basic idea behind asynchronous communications is that one person posts a message using the Internet. That message can later be read by designated recipients or by the public, depending on the limitations set by the poster.

**How do forums work?** An **Internet forum** is a Web-based online discussion site where participants post comments to discussion threads. Those comments can be read at a later time by other participants. Most forums have a moderator who monitors discussion threads, weeds out disruptive participants, and handles membership requests.

**Are forums the same as wikis?** No. Forums allow participants to comment on the material posted by other participants, but those comments are separate posts and the original post is not modified. A **wiki** allows participants to modify material.

Wikipedia is the best known wiki. Participants can post material pertaining to a topic, and other participants can modify it. Wikis can also include discussion pages where participants comment on topic material. For example, in a wiki topic about climate change, the discussion page might contain comments pointing out statements in the original post that cannot be verified.

**How do blogs work?** A **blog** (short for Web log) is similar to an online diary; it is maintained by one person (sometimes by a company or an organization) and contains a series of entries on one or more topics. Blog entries are usually text-based, but can also include graphics and video. They are typically displayed in reverse chronological order on one long Web page.

Most blogs are open to the public, so blogging has become a form of personal journalism; a way to make your views public. They have been used extensively for political commentary. Some bloggers have been tapped as commentators on headline news shows on CNN and FOX News. To set up your own blog, you can use a blog hosting service such as Blogger. For a list of popular blogs, check out Technorati (Figure 6-37).

**FIGURE 6-37**

Technorati helps you locate popular blogs or write one yourself.

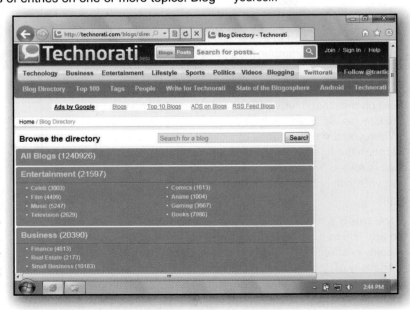

**What's a tweet?** A **tweet** is a short message of 140 characters or less, posted to the Twitter Web site (Figure 6-38). Twitter is sometimes referred to as a microblogging service because tweets are similar to blog entries, except for their length. Your tweets are displayed in reverse chronological order on your profile page. By default, your tweets are open to the public, but you can restrict access to a list of approved viewers. Viewer comments on your tweets are also posted on your profile page.

Twitter participants can subscribe to other people's tweets, a process referred to as "following." When you are a follower, you can quickly access tweets from the people you are following to find out what they are doing and thinking.

FIGURE 6-38

Twitter is the platform for short messages called tweets.

## CLOUD COMPUTING

**What is cloud computing?** The concept of **cloud computing** depends on a grid of servers and storage devices that offer Internet-accessible computing services ranging from hardware to office productivity applications and complex corporate data processing.

Cloud computing offers Internet-based resources such as servers, software, and storage space on demand. The concept is similar to a temporary employment agency that provides office assistants, accountants, programmers, and other temporary workers as a business needs them. With cloud computing, Internet resources can be contracted as needed, and released when they are no longer needed (Figure 6-39).

Cloud computing helps businesses save money and offers scalable solutions that can quickly meet changing needs. For example, a startup e-commerce business might not have any idea of the server capacity that will be required to handle its Web site traffic. The business can contract with a cloud service to obtain server capacity that scales as necessary to handle customers.

Google Apps provides a glimpse of what cloud computing has to offer for productivity applications. Users can access word processing, spreadsheet, presentation and scheduling software as needed.

Amazon's Elastic Compute Cloud offers businesses a way to use Amazon's powerful servers to run Web sites that can be instantly scaled to respond to spikes in customer traffic. The futuristic vision for cloud computing is a powerful and flexible computer resource that's available like the national power grid to anyone who plugs in and pays the fees.

FIGURE 6-39

The term *cloud computing* is derived from technology diagrams that show the Internet as a cloud.

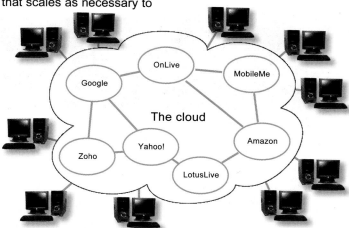

6

# GRID COMPUTING

**What is a grid computing system?** In the days when the Internet was really taking off, computer scientists noticed that thousands of computers connected to the Internet sit idle for hours while the people who own them are in meetings, talking on the telephone, sleeping, or otherwise occupied. If these idle processing cycles could be harnessed, they could supply a tremendous amount of computing power.

A **grid computing system** is a network of computers harnessed together to perform processing tasks. Grid computing systems can be public or private. Some grid systems use computers connected to the Internet as resources; others operate on private networks.

**What is a distributed grid?** Distributed grids (sometimes referred to as CPU scavenging grids) tap into thousands of PCs and Macs with Internet connections whose owners donate their computers' idle hours to a grid processing task. Grid management software divides computational problems into pieces that are farmed out to computers on the grid for processing.

Each computer on the grid runs grid client software that contains the program necessary to process a piece of the problem. In this manner, complex calculations or tasks can be performed in parallel by using as many computers as are available on the grid. Results are sent back to the grid management software for consolidation. Figure 6-40 illustrates the basic architecture of a grid computing system.

**Where are distributed grid systems used?** Because of their scalability, low cost, and high performance, distributed grids play a central role in scientific high-performance computing. One of the most famous examples of a distributed grid is the SETI@home project, which analyzes radio telescope data to search for signals that might originate from extra-terrestrial life. People who wish to donate their computers' idle processing cycles to the SETI@home project can download and install grid client software (Figure 6-41) that processes signals when the computer is idle.

## FIGURE 6-40

A distributed grid uses a diverse variety of computers as generic and equal resources.

A server running grid management software farms out pieces of a problem to computers in the grid.

Computers in the grid run grid client software and send results back to the server.

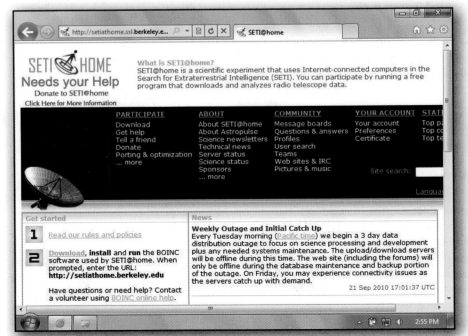

## FIGURE 6-41

SETI@home consists of a grid management system and millions of privately owned personal computers whose owners donate idle processing time to the project. The SETI@home grid management system receives and stores raw data from the Arecibo radio telescope in Puerto Rico, divides this data into small segments for analysis, and farms out each segment to one of the privately owned computers.

**What kinds of problems are best solved using distributed grid systems?** Grid computing systems perform best on large, complex problems that can be divided into smaller problem segments, which can be processed in any sequence and at any time. One example of this type of problem is the process used to crack encryption algorithms, which are based on keys formed from very long numbers. The longer the number, the more keys that are possible. For example, 56-bit encryption has many more possible keys than 12-bit encryption. Modern computerized encryption algorithms, which use 56-bit keys, were once thought to be unbreakable because the key can be any one of billions of numbers.

In 1997, a company called RSA Security Inc. set up a series of contests that awarded monetary prizes to the first person who could crack messages encrypted with a variety of common encryption algorithms. The contest caught the eye of a group of scientists who had an interest in encryption techniques and grid computing. The group, led by scientist Jeff Lawson, realized it would be possible to win the contest using simple brute force computing, which means trying every possible key. All that was needed was enough computer processing power to try every possible key.

Lawson's group, distributed.net, obtained the processing power by using a grid system. Group members created grid management software to divide keys into blocks and assign each block to one of the computers on the grid for processing. Each computer on the grid did the same thing—it started with the first key in its block, checked it against the encrypted message to see if it was the correct key, and, if unsuccessful, moved on to the next key. As more people donated their idle computer cycles to the project, the processing proceeded faster and faster.

Using grid technology, distributed.net cracked several encryption keys once thought to be unbreakable. The first victory, RSA's RC5-56 challenge, was cracking a 56-bit code in 250 days by processing more than 34 quadrillion keys. distributed.net broke 64-bit encryption in 1,757 days with the help of grid participants who tested 15,769,938,165,961,326,592 keys.

In 2009, researchers cracked 768-bit encryption using 2.5 years of processing time on 80 off-the-shelf computers. On a single-core 2.2 GHz Opteron computer with 2 GB of RAM, the process would have taken more than 1,500 years, but the researchers reported that today's distributed grids will soon make even 1024-bit encryption much less secure.

In addition to analyzing radio telescope signals and breaking codes, distributed grid projects currently exist for applications such as studying global climate change, predicting earthquakes, and searching for new medicines (Figure 6-42). Sony is even considering a grid of Internet-connected PlayStation gaming consoles to enhance online game performance.

Not all computing tasks are suited to distributed grids, however. Some problems cannot be divided into small processing segments; other problems require extensive human interaction or highly specialized equipment.

FIGURE 6-42

Public Grid Computing Projects

Was the first distributed computing network to play online chess

Studies climate change and improves the understanding of, and confidence in, climate change predictions for the 21st century

Cracks encryption algorithms

Conducts protein folding research related to neurological diseases such as Alzheimer's and Parkinson's, and many cancers and cancer-related syndromes

Finds very large prime numbers

Conducts AIDS disease and drug modeling

6

## FTP

**What is FTP? FTP** (File Transfer Protocol) provides a way to transfer files from one computer to another over any TCP/IP network, such as a LAN or the Internet. The purpose of FTP is to make it easy to upload and download computer files without having to deal directly with the operating system or file management system of a remote computer. FTP also allows authorized remote users to change file names and delete files.

**Do I need to use FTP?** Many people use FTP without even knowing it. When you download an updated device driver from a technical support site, access a document in PDF format from a corporate Web site, or pull down an MP3 file from your favorite music site, FTP is in action although the mechanics of it are incorporated into other applications.

People who use FTP are often sharing large files stored on a file server in conjunction with a project. Files can be uploaded to the server by one participant and downloaded by others. An alternative to FTP, sending files as e-mail attachments, is not practical with very large files or for participants with slow Internet connections.

**How does FTP work?** An **FTP server** typically resides on a computer containing files that remote users might want to access. The server runs software that listens on ports 20 and 21 for requests coming in from other computers. When a request arrives, the server makes sure the user who made the request has rights to access the file. If the request is valid, the file is transferred over the Internet as a series of packets to the requesting computer, where it is saved in a designated location on a local storage device.

**FIGURE 6-43**

A browser can provide access to FTP downloads. ▶ Click to see how it works.

**How can I access FTP servers?** You can access FTP servers with FTP client software or with a browser. To use a Web browser to download a file, simply enter the address of the FTP server as shown in Figure 6-43.

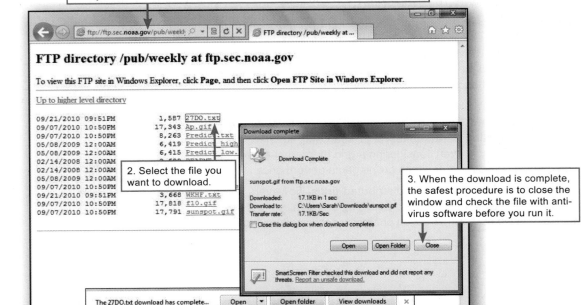

1. Enter the address of the FTP server in the browser's address bar. At an anonymous FTP server, a user ID and password would not be necessary.

2. Select the file you want to download.

3. When the download is complete, the safest procedure is to close the window and check the file with anti-virus software before you run it.

Not every FTP server is accessible from a browser, and those that are might work only for downloading files, not uploading them. If you plan to work extensively with FTP, you should get FTP client software. An **FTP client**, such as WS_FTP, CuteFTP, or open-source FileZilla, offers an easy-to-use interface for accessing FTP servers.

Convenient features of FTP clients allow you to save a list of server addresses and their corresponding user IDs and passwords, so you can connect to an FTP server with one click. FTP clients also allow you to download more than one file at a time, and they can pick up where they left off if the transfer is interrupted by a glitch in your Internet connection (Figure 6-44).

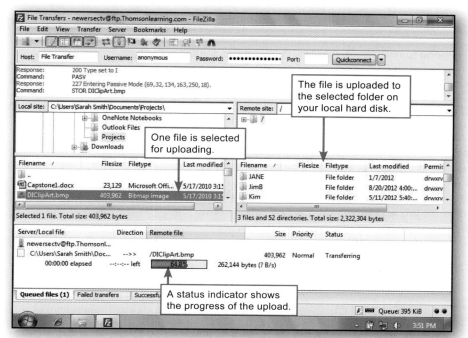

**FIGURE 6-44**

FTP clients such as FileZilla make it easy to upload and download files from an FTP server. ▶ Use your digital textbook to find out how to use an FTP client to upload and download files from an FTP site.

6

**Does FTP include security to prevent unauthorized access?** Some FTP sites require remote users to log in before accessing files. A login ID and password can be obtained from the FTP site operator. Access rights can be configured in various ways to allow or prevent remote users from changing file names, deleting files, uploading files, or downloading files.

**What is anonymous FTP?** **Anonymous FTP** can be accessed by logging in without a password by using the user ID "anonymous." Some anonymous sites request users to enter their e-mail addresses as a password, but rarely is that piece of information used for verification or tracking.

## FILE SHARING NETWORKS

**What is file sharing?** File sharing, sometimes called **P2P file shar-ing**, uses peer-to-peer (P2P) protocols that allow users to obtain files from other users located anywhere on the Internet. In the late 1990s, file sharing burst onto the national scene when college students became aware of a technology called Napster that provided free access to hit songs. Today, file sharing networks such as BitTorrent facilitate movie and music downloads.

**What is BitTorrent?** **BitTorrent** is a file sharing protocol that distrib-utes the role of a file server across a collection of dispersed computers. BitTorrent is, in some sense, an offshoot of grid computing concepts, in which an ad-hoc collection of personal computers located anywhere on the Internet can cooperate to complete a task normally handled by monolithic servers or supercomputers.

A BitTorrent network is designed to reduce the bandwidth bottleneck that occurs when many people attempt to download the same very large file, such as a feature-length film, application software, or an interactive 3-D computer game.

**How does BitTorrent work?** Suppose that 100 computers request Johnny Depp's film *Dark Shadows* at about the same time. A server breaks the movie file into pieces and begins to download those pieces to the first computer that requested the movie. As more computers request the file, they become part of a "swarm" that uses peer-to-peer technology to exchange file pieces with each other. After the server has downloaded all the file pieces to the swarm, its job is complete and it can service other requests. The swarm continues to exchange file pieces until every com-puter in the swarm has the entire file (Figure 6-45).

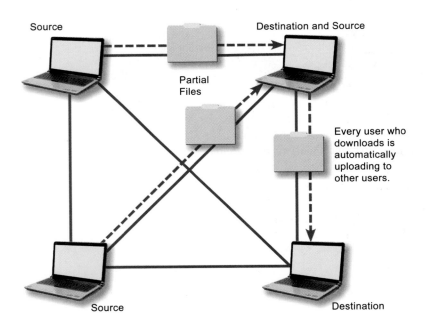

Source

Destination and Source

Partial Files

Every user who downloads is automatically uploading to other users.

Source

Destination

**FIGURE 6-45**

BitTorrent protocols dis-sect files into small chunks that might reside on different computers. Source comput-ers have received parts of a file from a server. They then distribute these parts to other computers in the swarm.

**How do I use BitTorrent?** BitTorrent client software is currently available from several Web sites. After installing the client, you can use it to download from any BitTorrent-enabled site simply by clicking the file you want. The BitTorrent client handles the entire file-swapping procedure. After getting the entire file, good etiquette requires clients to remain connected to the swarm so that they can "seed" file pieces to others.

**Are BitTorrent and similar file swapping networks legal?** File sharing originated on FTP-style servers, which held huge collections of popular music stored as digital MP3 files that could be easily downloaded and played on a computer or transferred to CDs. Free distribution of music without the copyright holder's permission is illegal, and file sharing server operators quickly encountered the legal ramifications of their computers' shady dealings.

Peer-to-peer file sharing networks and distributed technologies like BitTorrent have legitimate uses for distributing music, images, videos, and software with the approval of copyright holders. Peter Jackson's production diaries for *King Kong* have been posted for download using BitTorrent technology. Universal Studios and several independent film companies have released movie trailers with BitTorrent technology. The technology itself is not illegal; it is the use of the technology that is subject to legal scrutiny.

**Is BitTorrent safe?** Because BitTorrent files are assembled from little segments that come from a jumble of computers, they would seem on first thought to be bad candidates for distributing malware. Intelligent hackers would realize that their malicious code could easily be chopped up, too, and that pieces of it might not be delivered. And yet, BitTorrent files have become a source of adware and spyware. If you use BitTorrent, make sure your computer is protected with a security software suite that offers good spyware protection.

6

# QuickCheck                                                                      SECTION D

1. Instant messaging, chat, and VoIP are classified as [          ] communications because both parties have to be online.

2. VoIP quality can be affected by [          ] that results from too much packet latency.

3. [          ] computing offers Internet-based computer resources on demand so that individuals and businesses can contract for access as these resources are needed.

4. [          ] FTP can be used to upload and download files even if you don't have an account on the FTP server.

5. [          ] is a peer-to-peer file sharing protocol that uses a "swarm" of computers to exchange chunks of data that can eventually be assembled into complete files.

 CHECK ANSWERS

# Internet Security

**WHEN COMPUTERS** are connected to a network, the risk of intrusion has to be taken seriously. When the connection is Internet-based, billions of people are just an IP address away from your computer and its valuable, personal, and confidential data. Section E explains the mechanics of an intrusion attempt, and offers some practical advice for securing your computer against unauthorized access.

## INTRUSION ATTEMPTS

**Should I worry about intrusions?** Suppose you live in a really dangerous neighborhood where gangs roam the streets, painting every available surface with graffiti, and randomly attacking residents. A seemingly endless number of burglars creep from house to house looking for unlocked doors and windows, and occasionally trying to pick a lock or two. Punk kids rummage about looking for cars with keys in the ignition, unlocked doors, or loose hubcaps. Dark figures sift through your garbage cans searching for scraps of information that can be pieced together to steal your identity (Figure 6-46).

**FIGURE 6-46**

The Internet offers a wealth of useful tools and services, but it can be a very dangerous neighborhood.

Unfortunately, this dangerous neighborhood has many similarities to the Internet where gangs of hackers deface Web sites, look for backdoors left open by network administrators, crack passwords to gain access to your data, and probe ports looking for ways to sneak bots into your computer. Your Internet connection puts you right in the middle of this dangerous neighborhood any time you are connected—and with always-on connections like DSL and cable Internet service, that means any time your computer is turned on.

In the context of computers, an **intrusion** is any access to data or programs by hackers, criminals, or other unauthorized persons. As the result of an intrusion, data can be stolen or altered, system configurations can be changed to allow even more intrusions, and software can be surreptitiously installed and operated under the remote control of a hacker. Without any visible sign or warning, hackers can infiltrate your computer to obtain personal information or use your computer as a launching pad for attacks on other machines. Yes, you should worry about intrusions!

**How do hackers use the Internet to infiltrate my computer?** One of the most common ways of gaining unauthorized access to a network-based computer is by looking for open ports. Earlier in this chapter you learned that network services, such as the Web, FTP, and e-mail, operate from ports. As an example, you learned that Web requests use port 80. If a port is open and listening for requests—on any computer, even your own—a hacker can exploit it like an unlocked door to gain access to your computer. Hackers are continuously canvassing the Internet and probing ports to find their next victims.

A **port probe** (or port scan) is the use of automated software to locate computers that have open ports and are vulnerable to unauthorized access. Software called a port scanner goes to a randomly selected IP address and systematically checks for a response from each port. Open ports can then be further tested to gauge their suitability for exploitation.

You might scoff at your computer's vulnerability to port probes. After all, there are millions and millions of computers on the Internet and a limited number of hackers. The chances of your computer becoming a target would seem to be slim, but the opposite is true. Port scanning software can examine more than 30,000 computers per minute. If you use security software to monitor port probes on an unprotected computer, you would see probes within seconds of going online. According to researchers, the average "survival time" for an unprotected computer to remain uncompromised is only nine minutes.

**How do I know if ports are open?** You can check your computer for open ports using software tools such as Steve Gibson's ShieldsUP! at *www.grc.com*. You can initiate an "innocent" port probe to discover vulnerabilities. A security report like the one in Figure 6-47 is your goal.

**FIGURE 6-47**

Your computer's ports are most secure if they don't even appear to exist when probed using a port scanner. ▶ Use your digital textbook to see how ShieldsUP! checks your computer's ports and learn what the results mean.

6

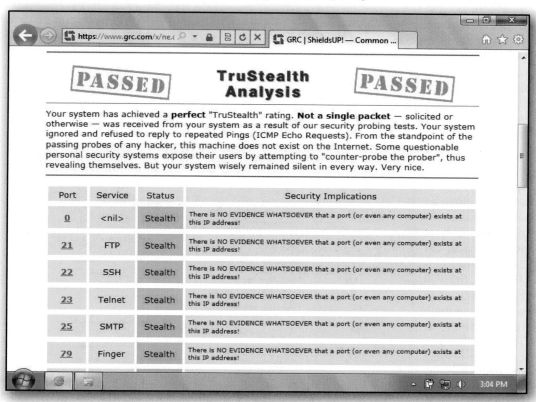

## SECURING PORTS

**How do I secure the ports on my computer?** One of the easiest steps to enhance your computer's security is to turn it off when you aren't using it. When your computer is turned off, its ports are inactive and they are not vulnerable to intrusions. Putting your computer into sleep mode or activating a screensaver is not sufficient protection. Your computer must be shut down and turned off.

You should also keep your computer up to date with the latest operating system security patches and service packs. Operating systems are closely linked to port activity. Known vulnerabilities in Windows and Internet Explorer can be exploited to access ports or launch additional attacks once a port is breached. As Microsoft develops security patches, they are posted at Microsoft's Web site, *www.microsoft.com/security*. Check the site frequently to download the most recent patches. You can also configure Windows to automatically check for and install patches (Figure 6-48).

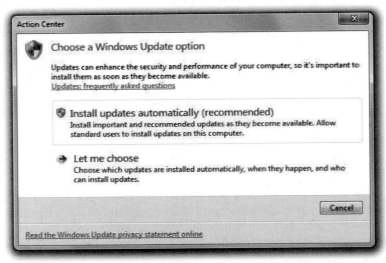

**What about firewall protection?** In the context of networking, a **firewall** is software or hardware designed to filter out suspicious packets attempting to enter or leave a computer. Firewall software helps keep your computer secure in several ways. It makes sure that incoming information was actually requested and is not an unauthorized intrusion. It blocks activity from suspicious IP addresses and—best of all—it reports intrusion attempts so that you can discover whether any hackers are trying to break into your computer.

**FIGURE 6-49**

Windows 7 includes a built-in firewall that can be activated to monitor intrusion attempts. Do not enable it, however, if your antivirus software firewall is activated.

You can use firewall software to open and close ports on your computer. Although it might seem safest to close all the ports, doing so would prevent you from accessing most Internet services, such as the Web, e-mail, instant messaging, and FTP. Most firewall software is preconfigured to block only unnecessarily open ports targeted by hackers. Windows 7 includes firewall software that you can access and configure from the Security Center (Figure 6-49).

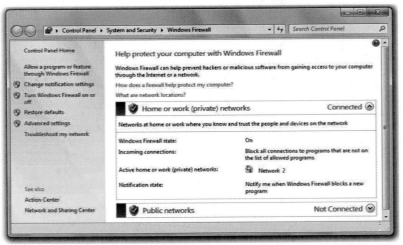

**What other Windows security options should I use?** Sharing printers or files on a LAN or the Internet requires open ports so the data can be transferred to and from your computer. Those open ports can be a potential entryway for hackers. If no one else needs access to your printer, do not configure it for sharing. If you also don't need to share files with other network users, you can turn off file and printer sharing (Figure 6-50).

FIGURE 6-50

When you turn off file sharing, your files cannot be accessed by other network users.

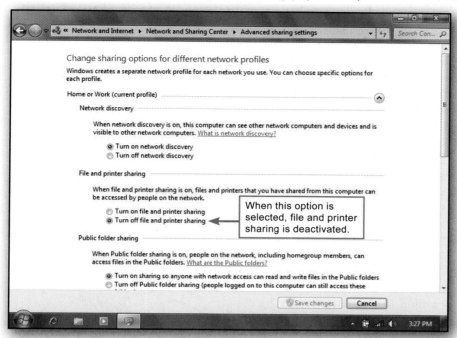

When this option is selected, file and printer sharing is deactivated.

## ROUTERS AND NAT

**How does a router affect security?** One of the most effective steps you can take to secure your computer from intrusions is to install a router. In the chapter on networking, you learned that a router can tie a LAN together and provide a portal to the Internet. Even if you have only one computer, however, a router can offer excellent security.

**How does a router work?** Routers are intended to work within LANs to monitor and direct packets being transported from one device to another. A router can also connect to the Internet through a DSL, cable, or satellite modem.

Routers are handy because they can screen IP addresses to keep locally addressed packets within the LAN so that they are delivered without traveling a circuitous route over the Internet and back (Figure 6-51).

FIGURE 6-51

A router monitors the IP addresses of packets on a LAN. Packets with local addresses (green) are kept within the LAN. Packets with external addresses (red) are routed out to the Internet. ▶ See how it works.

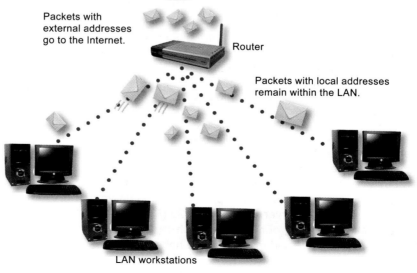

Packets with external addresses go to the Internet.

Router

Packets with local addresses remain within the LAN.

LAN workstations

6

Your router has its own IP address, typically obtained from your Internet service provider's DHCP server. (Recall that a DHCP server assigns dynamic IP addresses to devices that request them.) It is also possible for your router to have a fixed IP address set up by you or an installer. The key point about your router's IP address is that it is routable. A **routable IP address** is one that can be accessed by packets on the Internet.

When you connect your computer to a router and request an IP address, your router answers your request, not the ISP. Most routers are configured to assign private IP addresses. A **private IP address** is a non-routable IP address that can be used within a LAN, but not for Internet data transport. When the IP addressing scheme was devised, three ranges of addresses were reserved for internal or private use: 10.0.0.0 to 10.255.255.255, 172.16.0.0 to 172.31.255.255, and 192.168.0.0 to 192.168.255.255. If your computer has a private IP address, its read address is essentially hidden from hackers.

**But how do packets with private IP addresses get out to the Internet?** Let's review the scenario. You have a router connected to an Internet device, such as a DSL or cable modem. The router has a routable IP address, visible to any device (and hackers) on the Internet. Your router isn't vulnerable to attacks because it doesn't contain any of your data. You've connected your computer to a router. Your computer has been assigned a private IP address.

**Network address translation** (NAT) is the process your router uses to keep track of packets and their corresponding private or public IP addresses. Jeff Tyson writing for HowStuffWorks offers a useful analogy for how NAT works: "NAT is like the receptionist in a large office. Let's say you have left instructions with the receptionist not to forward any calls to you unless you request it. Later on, you call a potential client and leave a message for that client to call you back. You tell the receptionist that you are expecting a call from this client and to put her through. The client calls the main number to your office, which is the only number the client knows. When the client tells the receptionist that she is looking for you, the receptionist checks a lookup table that matches your name with your extension. The receptionist knows that you requested this call, and therefore forwards the caller to your extension."

A router and the receptionist perform essentially similar tasks. Your private IP address is like a private telephone extension in an office. Your router's public IP address is like the main switchboard number. Your router screens incoming packets and only lets one through to your private extension if you've requested it.

When you use the Internet, you initiate every valid transaction; you ask for a Web site, you ask to retrieve your mail, or you request a file from an FTP server. Only those requests that you initiate are valid. Suppose you want to download a file. You send a packet containing your request to the FTP server at 69.32.167.20 (Figure 6-52). The packet goes to your router, which replaces your address with its own and makes an internal note that you

**FIGURE 6-52**

A router using NAT essentially cloaks your computer and makes it invisible from the Internet.

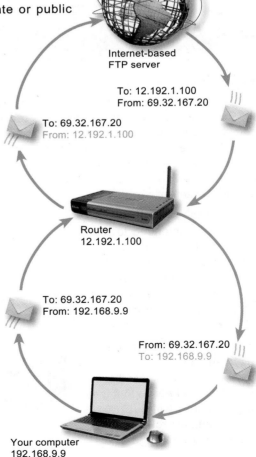

Internet-based
FTP server

To: 12.192.1.100
From: 69.32.167.20

To: 69.32.167.20
From: 12.192.1.100

Router
12.192.1.100

To: 69.32.167.20
From: 192.168.9.9

From: 69.32.167.20
To: 192.168.9.9

Your computer
192.168.9.9

initiated this FTP request. When the FTP server responds, it sends a packet addressed to the router. The router receives the packet, checks its internal note to see who made the original request, and then ships the FTP packet to your computer.

## VIRTUAL PRIVATE NETWORKS

**Is it possible to secure connections for remote users?** Sales representatives and telecommuters often access corporate networks from home or from a customer's office by using a secured connection called a **virtual private network** (VPN). You might find a VPN useful when using public computers because it can encrypt the data you transmit, keeping passwords and account numbers safe from hackers.

**Who sets up VPNs?** On the corporate end, setting up a secure VPN is not a trivial task and it is typically handled by specialists in the corporation's information technology department. Access to a corporate VPN is usually by invitation only. Employees who need to access a VPN are given the necessary instructions, addresses, and passwords to make connections.

For personal use, you can install personal VPN software such as Hamachi, JiWire Hotspot Helper, or HotSpotVPN. Using a VPN provides an important layer of security when you use public networks, such as Wi-Fi hotspots.

**How would I use a personal VPN?** Once you've installed VPN software, you'll see its icon in the taskbar. Clicking the icon establishes a connection to the VPN server. When your computer sends or receives data, the VPN software encrypts it and sends it to a special VPN server that decrypts the data and sends it to its destination. Figure 6-53 illustrates how a personal VPN operates.

**How important is a VPN?** A personal VPN is an important tool when using public networks, but it is not a complete solution. To recap the most important security precautions, you should turn your computer off when not in use, make sure all your computer's unnecessary ports are closed, activate firewall software, turn off file and printer sharing, and install a router. Taking these precautions might not make your computer invincible, but they offer very strong protection against intruders who might steal your identity or hijack your computer for various shady activities.

**FIGURE 6-53**

A personal VPN offers security for the data that you transmit from public Wi-Fi hotspots.

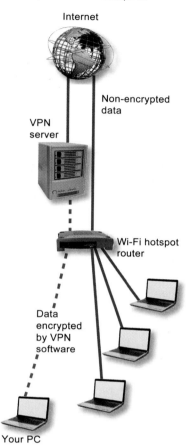

Internet

Non-encrypted data

VPN server

Wi-Fi hotspot router

Data encrypted by VPN software

Your PC

Public Wi-Fi hotspot

6

## QuickCheck

1.  Hackers use _____ scanning software to look for computers connected to the Internet that are vulnerable to intrusions.

2.  _____ software monitors network activity, blocks packets from suspicious IP addresses, and reports intrusion attempts.

3.  One of the best defenses against intrusions is to install a(n) _____ between your standalone computer or LAN and your Internet connection device.

4.  A(n) _____ IP address is a non-routable IP address that can be used within a LAN, but not for Internet data transport.

5.  When using a public Wi-Fi hotspot, you can use a personal _____ to encrypt data that travels from your computer. (Hint: Use the acronym.)

▶ CHECK ANSWERS

# Issue: What's Happening to Free Speech?

**THE INTERNET** offers instant access to information across national and cultural borders; but along with helpful information, the Internet hosts a disturbing amount of unsavory material. Militias and hate groups use Web sites to spread their views. Hundreds of pornographic sites make a business of selling lewd images that can be accessed by anyone—even children. In chat rooms on innocent topics, the conversation can deteriorate into X-rated banter. Pedophile and bestiality sites that cater to warped sexual habits pop up in search engine lists. International terrorists use Web sites as recruiting tools and for boasting about suicide bombings. Criminals, terrorists, and hackers post guidebooks and tips on how to do all kinds of illegal activities, from making suitcase bombs to spreading computer viruses.

Some concerned netizens advocate cyber censorship to curtail irresponsible Web sites, blogs, discussion groups, and file sharing. Cyber censorship typically means blocking access to Web sites, but it can also mean closing sites and removing them from host servers. Censorship advocates are opposed by free speech supporters who believe that the right to free expression should be unshackled by laws or regulations.

The controversy over censorship is not new. Guidelines from the pre-Internet era also shape the cyber-censorship-vs.-free-speech debate.

In most cases, words are acceptable, whereas actions can be punishable. Writing a mystery novel that describes how the main character cultivates botulism and then uses it to poison one of the other characters is acceptable. Actually carrying out such an act would be against the law. This concept was applied to cyberspace when the U.S. Supreme Court upheld a law that pornography featuring real children is illegal, but ruled that child pornography featuring computer-generated children is not illegal because children were not harmed when the photographs were created.

Cyberlaw is not yet totally consistent on the words vs. deeds precedent, however. In some cases, words are punishable. For example, the Digital Millennium Copyright Act makes it illegal to even disseminate information on defeating software, CD, and DVD copy restrictions.

A second censorship guideline hinges on local standards of morality. Local communities can apply their own standards to determine whether material is obscene. Therefore, a raunchy magazine that you might find on a supermarket newsstand in New York City might be limited to adult bookstore shelves in a conservative Tennessee community.

Local standards, however, are difficult to sort out on the Internet where a Web surfer in Tennessee can easily access Web sites, blogs, and online discussions that originate from anywhere in the world. Judges upheld the conviction of two sysops whose California-based porn site distributed obscene material to individuals in Tennessee. The sysops claimed that the Internet required a more flexible definition of "community" to account for the Internet's global accessibility; otherwise Web sites would be forced to eliminate all materials objected to by anyone. Judges denied that claim, saying that technology could be used to filter out objectionable material based on age and location information provided by member registration data.

Underlying a group of decisions on cyber censorship, the U.S. Supreme Court seems to support the concept of cyberzones that limit Net access to certain materials in a way similar to how the adult sections of street-corner newsstands restrict children from browsing through certain magazines. As now-retired Justice O'Connor explained, "Cyberspace is malleable. Thus, it is possible to construct barriers in cyberspace and use them to screen for identity, making cyberspace more like the physical world and, consequently, more amenable to zoning laws." But is this concept workable on the Internet where a teenager can easily subscribe to an adult Web site by simply typing "21" as his age?

In some countries, however, cyber citizens have no choice but to use a government-controlled ISP.

In many countries, free speech is not a basic right conferred on all citizens. Some dictatorial regimes want their citizens to receive news from the outside world only after it has been screened by a government censor. Officials in more than 20 countries use sophisticated tools to block Web sites, filter e-mail, and censor discussion groups.

China has some of the most rigorous Internet censorship in the world. The "Great Firewall of China," as it is sometimes called, blocks Internet content by preventing IP addresses of objectionable sites from being routed through its gateways into China. The system also selectively engages in DNS poisoning, a technique that tricks a DNS server into believing it has received authentic information when, in reality, it has not. So Web surfers in China who attempt to access the Electronic Frontier Foundation's Web site that advocates free speech might instead see a Chinese government site on social responsibility. In addition to blocking Web sites, the Chinese government filters e-mail, message boards, chat rooms, and blogs.

The United Arab Emirates recently cracked down on the use of BlackBerry devices because they transmit encrypted data using overseas servers, which cannot be monitored by local government censors.

In Iran, government censors monitor political and news Web sites, and block access to many pornographic Web sites, anonymizer tools, sites with gay and lesbian content, politically sensitive sites, and women's rights sites. If you tried to access *Rolling Stone* magazine's Web site from Saudi Arabia, you would find that access has been denied. The Saudi government claims it censors the Internet to preserve Islamic culture and heritage. That argument in many ways reflects the concept of cyberzones that conform to local standards of ethics and morality. Even free-speech activists at the OpenNet Initiative (ONI) seem to agree. "We do think that information should be free," states one ONI technician, "but we do need to find a balance for respect for sovereign states to preserve their own culture."

Despite such cultural sensitivity, technology giants such as Microsoft, Yahoo!, Google, and Cisco Systems have been criticized for providing foreign governments with tools for blocking culturally objectionable sites. Critics question whether companies in a free society should aid foreign governments' attempts to censor cyberspace.

For some people, it is astonishing to realize that ideas such as liberty, equality, and women's rights would be subject to the same censorship attempts as pornography and hate speech. The solution to online censorship is still evolving as free speech comes into balance with cultural, ethical, and moral concerns in the global realm of cyberspace.

6

## INFOWEBLINKS

You'll find more fascinating Internet myths and substantive articles about disinformation at the **Internet Censorship InfoWeb**.

Ⓦ CLICK TO CONNECT
www.infoweblinks.com/np2012/ch06

# What Do You Think?                                    ISSUE

1. Should governments be allowed to block access to Web sites based on local religions, politics, and customs?

◯ Yes   ◯ No   ◯ Not sure

2. Do you believe that a privately held Internet service provider like AOL has the right to censor the data posted on Web sites it hosts?

◯ Yes   ◯ No   ◯ Not sure

3. Should companies like Microsoft, Yahoo!, and Cisco Systems provide blocking technology to foreign governments?

◯ Yes   ◯ No   ◯ Not sure

4. Would you use filtering software that was preprogrammed to block pornographic and nuisance Web sites?

◯ Yes   ◯ No   ◯ Not sure

▶ SAVE RESPONSES

# Computers in Context: Banking

**FOR MOST OF HISTORY,** banks used low-tech methods to track one of the world's most cherished commodities—wealth. Checking accounts were in widespread use as early as 1550, when Dutch traders began depositing money with cashiers for safekeeping. The use of printed checks became popular in England in the late 18th century—so popular that banks found it difficult to process a steadily increasing stream of checks, including those drawn on accounts from other banks.

An unverified story that has become part of bank lore describes the origin of a solution to the check processing problem. As the story goes, a London bank messenger stopped for coffee and got to talking with a messenger from another bank. Realizing that they were delivering checks drawn on each other's banks, the two messengers decided to exchange checks there in the coffee house. This event evolved into a system of check clearinghouses where representatives from various banks met periodically to exchange checks and reconcile totals in cash. By 1839, British clearinghouses were annually processing in excess of £954 million of checks—equivalent to $250 billion in today's money.

Bank clearinghouses were described in an essay, *The Economy of Machinery and Manufactures*, written by computer pioneer Charles Babbage in 1832. He also included a reference to the "possibility of performing arithmetical calculations by machinery"

along with a description of the Difference Engine, then under construction in his workshop.

This dream of automated check clearing did not, however, become reality until more than a century later when S. Clark Beise, senior vice president at Bank of America, contracted with Stanford Research Institute (SRI) to develop a computer system to automate check processing. SRI completed a prototype in 1955 that used mechanical sorting equipment to queue up each check and MICR (Magnetic Ink Character Recognition) technology to read check numbers. In 1959, the first ERMA (Electronic Recording Machine-Accounting) system went into service. With ERMA handling calculations, nine employees could handle the job that once required 50 people. By 1966, 32 regional ERMA systems operated by Bank of America were processing more than 750 million checks per year. ERMA and similar check processing technologies quickly integrated with bank transaction processing systems to become the bedrock of today's banking technology.

Output from check sorting machines can be submitted to the Automated Clearing House (ACH) network, which offers a secure, batch-oriented data exchange system that can be accessed by financial institutions. On a daily basis, banks submit check data and receive a report of balances due to other banks. These balances can be reconciled by electronic funds transfer over the Federal Reserve's Fedwire telecommunications network.

An upswing in check fraud during the 1960s made it increasingly difficult to cash checks at local merchants. As an alternative to trying to cash checks at banks and local merchants, automatic teller machines (ATMs) were first installed in the 1970s. A typical ATM connects to a bank's front-end processor—a computer that maintains account balances for in-network customers and monitors suspicious activity. The front-end processor is separated from the bank's main computer system for security.

Some ATMs exchange data with the front-end processor by using dedicated dial-up telephone lines. Other ATMs use always-on leased lines. Legacy protocols, such as SNA and 3270 bisync, are being replaced by the standard Internet Protocol (IP) that can be routed through more affordable connections, such as cable, ISDN, DSL, or Internet VPN.

ATMs are expensive—about $50,000 to purchase a machine, install it, and operate it for one year. Banks have offset this cost by charging transaction fees and reducing the number of bank tellers. Once a promising entry-level occupation, bank tellers today earn less than $30,000 per year. Although tellers continue to accept deposits, process withdrawals, and cash payroll checks, they are increasingly pressed into customer service roles—opening new accounts, issuing ATM cards, resolving disputed transactions, and assisting customers who have lost bank cards or checkbooks. Despite this shift in job description, the number of bank teller jobs is expected to fall at least 10% in the next few years.

ATMs offer access to bank services from convenient locations where customers shop, eat, and hang out with friends. The Internet takes banking convenience one step further and provides around-the-clock account access from PCs in customers' homes, schools, and workplaces. Today, most banks and credit unions offer some type of online banking (also called home banking, Internet banking, or electronic banking).

Basic online banking services allow customers to access checking account and bank card activity, transfer funds between checking and savings accounts, view electronic images of checks and deposit slips, download and print monthly statements, and reorder checks. Customers can also pay bills online by scheduling payment dates and amounts. Many credit card and utility companies offer e-billing services that automatically forward electronic bills to customers' online banking accounts. For monthly fixed-amount bills, such as car loans, online banking offers automatic payment options that deduct funds from specified checking or savings accounts.

For managing assets more effectively, online banking sites also offer sophisticated tools, including account aggregation, stock quotes, rate alerts, and portfolio management programs. Most online banking sites are also compatible with personal finance software, such as Microsoft Money and QuickBooks, so that transaction data can be shuttled between customers' local computers and their online banking services.

A cadre of customer support personnel staff online help desks for customers with questions about online banking. Web masters, computer security specialists, and network technicians are also part of banking's new job corps.

Online banking services are typically housed on a well-secured Web server, and customers are not allowed direct access to the computer system that actually processes transactions. Customer privacy is maintained by the use of passwords and connections that encrypt data as it is sent to and from customers' computers.

Successful banks are built on good business decisions. Bank managers are increasingly working with business intelligence tools to look for trends in customer behavior, analyze competing financial institutions, and examine current business practices. Tools for these activities include data warehouses that collect and organize data, data mining software that organizes and analyzes data in a meaningful way, and statistical tools that formulate comparisons and trendlines.

Today, banking depends on multilayered technologies that incorporate check processing equipment, transaction processing systems, business intelligence software, ACH networks, Fedwire, ATM networks, the Internet, and Web servers. Many banking practices originated from batch check processing, and only gradually have banks begun to move to more modern online transaction processing (OLTP) systems that store scanned images of checks and instantly update accounts when a purchase is made or a bill is paid.

6

**INFOWEBLINKS**

For more information about this Computers in Context topic, check the **Computers and Banking InfoWeb**.

 CLICK TO CONNECT
www.infoweblinks.com/np2012/ch06

# New Perspectives Labs

## On the BookOnCD

To access the New Perspectives Labs for Chapter 6, start the BookOnCD, and then click the icon next to the lab title below.

### ▶ TRACKING PACKETS

#### IN THIS LAB YOU'LL LEARN:

- How Ping and Traceroute work
- How to use the Ping and Traceroute utilities supplied by Windows
- How to interpret Ping and Traceroute reports to determine the speed and reliability of your Internet connection
- How to access and use a graphical Traceroute utility
- How to find and use Web-based Ping and Traceroute utilities
- The advantages and disadvantages of Web-based Ping and Traceroute utilities
- How to access the Internet Traffic Report Web site and interpret its data and graphs
- How to use Internet traffic data, Ping, and Traceroute to pinpoint problems with your Internet connection

#### LAB ASSIGNMENTS

1. Start the interactive part of the lab. Make sure you've enabled Tracking if you want to save your QuickCheck results. Perform each lab step as directed, and answer all the lab QuickCheck questions. When you exit the lab, your answers are automatically graded and your results are displayed.

2. Use the Ping utility that's supplied by Windows to ping *www.abcnews.com*. Record the IP address for the ABC News site, plus the minimum, maximum, and average times. For each time, indicate whether it would be considered poor, average, or good.

3. Use the Tracert command at the Windows command prompt to trace a packet between your computer and *www.excite.com*. Print the Traceroute report listing transmission times. Circle any pings on the report that indicate high latency.

4. Locate a Web-based Ping utility and use it to ping *www.gobledegok.com*. Indicate the address for the Web site where you found the Ping utility. Explain the Ping results.

5. Connect to the Internet Traffic Report Web site, make a note of the date and time, and then answer the following questions:

   a. What is the traffic index for Asia?

   b. How does the index for Asia compare with the traffic index for North America?

   c. During the previous 24 hours in Europe, what was the period with the worst response time?

### ▶ SECURING YOUR CONNECTION

#### IN THIS LAB YOU'LL LEARN:

- How to use Windows utilities, online utilities, and firewall software to check the security of your Internet connection
- Why an unauthorized intruder might want to gain access to your computer
- The significance of communications ports as an intrusion risk factor
- How to use the Netstat utility to check your computer's open ports
- How to use an online utility to get a hacker's view of your computer
- Why Windows file and printer sharing can make your computer files vulnerable
- How to adjust settings for file and printer sharing
- How firewalls protect computers from intrusions
- How to adjust firewall settings

#### LAB ASSIGNMENTS

1. Start the interactive part of the lab. Make sure you've enabled Tracking if you want to save your QuickCheck results. Perform each lab step as directed, and answer all the lab QuickCheck questions. When you exit the lab, your answers are automatically graded and your results are displayed.

2. Use the Netstat utility to scan any computer that you typically use. Write out the Netstat report or print it. To print the report, copy it to Paint or Word, and then print. Explain what the Netstat report tells you about that computer's security.

3. Connect to *www.grc.com* and access the ShieldsUP! tests. Test the shields and probe the ports for the same computer you used for Assignment 2. Explain the similarities and differences between the ShieldsUP! report and the Netstat report for this computer. Which report indicates more security risks? Why?

4. In the lab, you learned how to adjust settings for Windows file and printer sharing. Without actually changing the settings, determine the status of file and printer sharing on your computer. Report your findings and indicate whether these settings are appropriate for network access and security.

5. Record the firewall settings on your computer. Indicate whether the settings are optimal for the way you use your computer on networks.

# Key Terms

Make sure you understand all the boldfaced key terms presented in this chapter. With the NP2012 BookOnCD, you can use this list of terms as an interactive study activity. First, try to define a term in your own words, and then click the term to compare your definition with the definition presented in the chapter. Online, try your hand at the TechTerm Flashcards.

Always-on connection, 307
Anonymous FTP, 337
Asymmetric Internet connection, 310
BitTorrent, 338
Blog, 332
Cable Internet service, 316
Cable modem, 317
Chat, 330
Cloud computing, 333
Communications port, 308
Dial-up connection, 312
DOCSIS, 317
Domain name, 307
Domain name server, 308
Domain Name System, 308
Downstream speed, 310
DSL, 314
DSL filter, 315
DSL modem, 315
Dynamic IP address, 306
Firewall, 342
Fixed Internet access, 311
Fixed wireless Internet service, 320
FTP, 336
FTP client, 337

FTP server, 336
Grid computing system, 334
ICANN, 309
Instant messaging, 330
Internet backbone, 303
Internet forum, 332
Internet service provider, 303
Intrusion, 340
IP (IPv4 and IPv6), 305
ISDN, 314
ISDN terminal adapter, 314
Jitter, 331
Latency, 309
Mobile broadband, 327
Mobile Internet access, 311
Modem, 304
Network access points, 303
Network address translation, 344
Network service providers, 303
P2P file sharing, 338
Packet loss, 331
Ping, 309
Port probe, 341
Portable Internet access, 311
Private IP address, 344

Protocol suite, 305
Real-time messaging system, 330
Routable IP address, 344
Satellite Internet service, 318
Satellite modem, 319
Static IP address, 306
Symmetric Internet connection, 310
TCP, 305
TCP/IP, 305
Top-level domain, 307
Traceroute, 310
Tweet, 333
Upstream speed, 310
Virtual private network, 345
Voiceband modem, 312
VoIP, 331
WAP, 326
Wi-Fi hotspot, 323
Wiki, 332
WiMAX, 320

6

# Interactive Summary

To review important concepts from this chapter, fill in the blanks to best complete each sentence. When using the NP2012 BookOnCD, click the Check Answers buttons to automatically score your answers.

**SECTION A:** The Internet infrastructure is based on high-capacity communications links referred to as the Internet [        ], tied together at network [        ] points where data can cross over from one NSP's equipment to another's. An Internet [        ] provider offers Internet access to individuals, businesses, and smaller ISPs. The Internet uses several communications protocols, including [        ], which breaks a message or file into packets, and [        ], which is responsible for addressing packets. Every device on the Internet has an IP address. 204.127.128.1 is a(n) [        ]-bit IPv4 address. [        ] IP addresses are permanently assigned to computers, whereas [        ] IP addresses are temporarily assigned by a DHCP server. Most

high-speed Internet connections use [        ] technology, and even dynamic IP addresses might seem permanent because they don't change unless you turn off your modem or your ISP has an outage. A(n) [        ] name server converts numeric IP addresses into familiar names, such as Travelocity.com. The speed of an Internet connection measured by utilities such as Ping and Traceroute refers to [        ], the elapsed time for data to make a round trip from point A to point B. The speed advertised by Internet service providers is a measure of the amount of data that travels between two points in a given amount of time. Many Internet connections are [        ], meaning the downstream speed is different than the upstream speed.

▶ CHECK ANSWERS

**SECTION B:** A(n) [        ] connection is a fixed Internet connection that uses a(n) [        ] modem and telephone lines to transport data between your computer and your ISP. Most modems use a standard called V.90 to provide a theoretical maximum speed of [        ] Kbps. Dial-up connections are asymmetrical; 44 Kbps is a typical [        ] speed for a 56 Kbps modem. [        ] speed drops to about 33 Kbps or less. [        ] is a fixed, symmetric Internet connection that moves data at speeds of 64 Kbps or 128 Kbps over ordinary telephone lines through a device called a terminal adapter, which sends digital signals. [        ] is a high-speed, digital, always-on Internet access technology that runs over

standard phone lines. [        ] Internet service is a means of distributing always-on broadband Internet access over the same infrastructure that offers cable television service. Satellite Internet service is a means of distributing always-on, high-speed asymmetric Internet access by broadcasting signals to and from a personal satellite [        ]. Fixed wireless Internet technologies are [        ] area network standards, in contrast to technologies such as Wi-Fi, which are local area network standards. One of the most well-known fixed wireless standards is [        ], an Ethernet-compatible network standard designated as IEEE 802.16.

▶ CHECK ANSWERS

**SECTION C:** [        ] Internet access can be defined as the ability to easily move your Internet service from one location to another. [        ] Internet access offers a continuous Internet connection as you are walking or riding in a bus, car, train, or plane. Wi-Fi is an example of portable Internet access technology that allows public access to the Internet within the network's area of coverage, called a Wi-Fi [        ]. Portable WiMAX and portable satellite

offer additional Internet access options in the portable category. Cellular phone service providers offer two ways to access the Internet. [        ] is a communications protocol that provides limited access to e-mail and Internet information from handheld devices with small screens and cell phone keypads. Mobile [        ] services using EV-DO, EDGE, and HSUPA technologies offer faster access using conventional browsers and e-mail clients.

▶ CHECK ANSWERS

# SECTION D:

A network-based real-time [_____] system allows people to exchange short messages while they are online. One-on-one messaging is usually referred to as [_____] messaging and group communications are referred to as [_____] . Most messaging is based on a client/server model that uses a server to handle communication packets between the participants. Voice over Internet [_____] is a technology in which a broadband Internet connection is used to place telephone calls instead of the regular phone system. In contrast to synchronous communications technologies, such as IM and VoIP, [_____] communications technologies, such as blogs, do not require participants to be online at the same time. [_____] is sometimes referred to as microblogging because messages are limited to 140 characters or less. A grid computing system is a network of computers harnessed together to perform processing tasks. One of the most famous examples of a grid system is the SETI@home project, but grid technology has also been used to crack codes, analyze earthquake data, and crunch numbers for medical research. [_____] computing is a formalized grid in which servers and storage devices are harnessed together to offer Internet-accessible computing services. File Transfer [_____] provides a way to transfer files from one computer to another over any TCP/IP network, such as a LAN or the Internet. The purpose of FTP is to make it easy to upload and download computer files without having to deal directly with the [_____] system or file management system of a remote computer. [_____] file sharing uses protocols that allow users to obtain files from other users located anywhere on the Internet. [_____] is an example of file sharing technology that links clients in a "swarm" for distributing files.

⊳ CHECK ANSWERS

**6**

# SECTION E:

In the context of computers, a(n) [_____] is any access to data or programs by hackers, criminals, or other unauthorized persons. As the result of an intrusion, data can be stolen or altered, system configurations can be changed to allow even more intrusions, and software can be surreptitiously installed and operated under the remote control of a hacker. One of the most common ways of gaining unauthorized access to a network-based computer is by looking for open [_____] . A port [_____] is the use of automated software to locate computers that have open ports and are vulnerable to unauthorized access. One of the easiest steps to enhance your computer's security is to turn it off when you aren't using it. You should also keep your computer up to date with the latest operating system security [_____] and service packs. You can also install [_____] software designed to filter out suspicious packets attempting to enter or leave a computer. One of the most effective steps you can take to secure your computer from intrusions is to set up a(n) [_____] , which assigns private IP addresses to the computers it controls. The process a router uses to keep track of packets and their corresponding private or public IP addresses is called [_____] address translation. Corporations try to limit intrusions by setting up virtual [_____] networks that offer encrypted connections for access to a remote server.

⊳ CHECK ANSWERS

# Interactive Situation Questions

Apply what you've learned to some typical computing situations. When using the NP2012 BookOnCD, you can type your answers, and then use the Check Answers button to automatically score your responses.

1. You just got cable Internet service. Your computer is connected to a router, which you connect to the cable modem. The instructions provided by the cable company tell you to make sure [           ] is activated so that you can get a dynamic IP address.

2. You're finally ready to get a high-speed Internet connection. Because the modem provided by your cable company contains Ethernet circuitry, you can simply connect the modem to your computer's [           ] port (shown in the photo at right).

3. Your Internet access seems very slow one day. You might be able to use a networking utility called [           ] to discover the source of the slowdown.

4. Suppose that you decide to open a little Web store to sell handcrafted pottery. Your Web site will need a(n) [           ] IP address, and you'll want to register a(n) [           ] name.

5. You frequently use public Wi-Fi hotspots in cafes and other locations. To keep your passwords and other confidential data safe, you install personal [           ] software that encrypts the data you transmit over the Internet.

6. Suppose you have installed a cable modem on a standalone PC. To secure your computer, you should first make sure that file [           ] is not activated. You should also activate [           ] software to filter packets entering and leaving your computer.

7. Your friend, a film student, has created a 20-minute short film that she wants to distribute to friends. The file is much too large to be an e-mail attachment and she doesn't have access to a(n) [           ] server. You suggest that she try posting it at a(n) [           ] P2P file sharing site where a swarm of computers can assist with the downloads.

8. Your friend wants you to follow her tweets and asks if you have a(n) [           ] account.

 CHECK ANSWERS

# Interactive Practice Tests

Practice tests that consist of ten multiple-choice, true/false, and fill-in-the-blank questions are available on both the NP2012 BookOnCD and the NP2012 CourseMate Web site. BookOnCD test questions are selected at random from a large test bank, so each time you take a test, you'll receive a different set of questions. Your tests are scored immediately, and you can print study guides that help you find the correct answers for any questions that you missed. Online, you'll find a Practice Test for each section of the chapter. Your results from online tests are saved by Engagement Tracker.    ▶ CLICK TO START

# Learning Objectives Checkpoints

Learning Objectives Checkpoints are designed to help you assess whether you have achieved the major learning objectives for this chapter. You can use paper and pencil or word processing software to complete most of the activities.

1. Make a timeline of events associated with the evolution of the Internet.

2. Draw a conceptual diagram illustrating the Internet backbone, NAPs, NSPs, routers, and ISPs. Extend the diagram to show how computers on a LAN access the Internet through a single DSL modem.

3. List at least five protocols used on the Internet and describe what they are used for.

4. Explain the differences between static IP addresses, dynamic IP addresses, private IP addresses, and domain names.

5. Describe the difference between Ping and Traceroute by giving an example of when each would be used.

6. List the advantages and disadvantages of dial-up, cable, DSL, ISDN, satellite, and fixed wireless Internet services. List the Internet access methods in which upstream transmission rates differ from downstream rates.

7. List the options for mobile and portable Internet access, and explain their strengths and weaknesses.

8. Explain the advantages of mobile broadband services compared to WAP service.

9. Give examples of synchronous and asynchronous communications offered on the Internet.

10. Explain how Voice over IP works, and compare it to cell phone and land line services.

11. List two examples of distributed grid computing and two examples of cloud computing.

12. Draw diagrams to illustrate how FTP, the original Napster, and BitTorrent work.

13. Make a list of security concerns that are related to Internet access.

14. Make a checklist of steps you can take to secure your computer from Internet-based intrusions.

Study Tip: Make sure you can use your own words to correctly answer each of the red focus questions that appear throughout the chapter.

6

# Concept Map

Fill in the blanks to show the hierarchy of Internet access options.

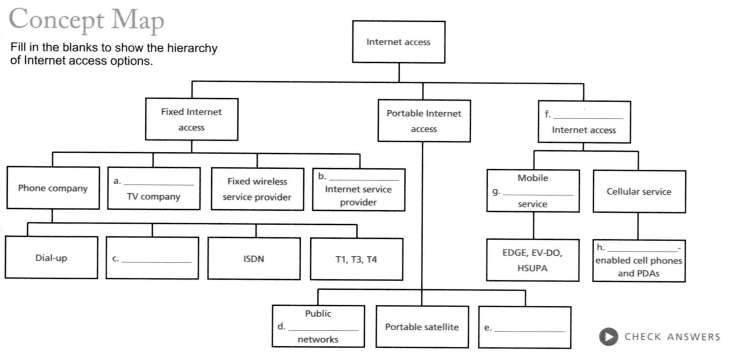

CHECK ANSWERS

# Projects

 **CRITICAL THINKING**

"The Internet treats censorship like damage and routes around it." Do you agree with this observation? Does it seem like the Internet—similar to banned books, music, videos, and satellite dishes—has a way of infiltrating even the most repressive societies? Does this tendency make censorship more tolerable in the short run?

 **GROUP PROJECT**

Form a group with three or four other students and discuss the ways in which you secure your Internet connections. Compose a document that contains specific information about each group member's security and summarizes the general level of security your group has in place.

 **CYBERCLASSROOM**

Each member of your team should ping Google and record the results. Exchange your results with other students on your team to find out who has the fastest connection. How many members of the group have a connection fast enough to play online interactive multiplayer games? The member of your team with the fastest connection should summarize the team's data and submit it to your instructor.

 **MULTIMEDIA PROJECT**

The speed of your Internet connection can affect the download time for media, such as photos and videos. Use Ping to find the speed of your Internet connection, then experiment with viewing five different short videos on news or entertainment Web sites. How does the performance of each video relate to the kind of Internet connection you have? Compile your findings into a well-organized PowerPoint presentation. Slide 1 should provide a brief description of your computer and Internet connection. Slide 2 should include a screenshot of your Ping statistics. Slides 3 through 7 should describe each of the videos you viewed, including their addresses and your evaluation of the video quality. The final slide should include your overall evaluation of the quality and convenience of Web-based video. Follow your instructor's guidelines for submitting and/or presenting your project.

 **RESUME BUILDER**

The Internet provides resources for career development. Think about your ideal job and make a table that lists (in the first column) the top ten qualifications and skills you'll need to be a successful applicant. In the second column, indicate whether you currently possess each qualification or skill. For those you need to develop in the future, indicate how you plan to obtain them (for example, from a college course, on-the-job training, or self-paced study). Find out if you can develop any of these skills and qualifications using online resources, such as online courses. Provide addresses for any Internet resources that you find.

 **GLOBALIZATION**

Worldwide, communications capabilities are growing at a rapid pace. Nonetheless, there exists among countries a great disparity in communications capabilities. For this project, use library and Internet resources to gather information about the communications options that are available throughout the world. You should consider which technologies are available and the number of people who use each technology. Your research can include any of the following: land-based phones, cellular phones, premium phone services such as ISDN and DSL, Internet access, broadcast television, and cable television. Once you have gathered these facts, consider how they might affect the lifestyles, politics, and economies of various regions. Suppose that you are organizing a high school debate about global communications technology. As the organizer, you must devise a controversial question on which the debate will be based. You should also write three "pro" and "con" paragraphs just to make sure that both sides of the issue will have substantial material to debate.

 **ISSUE**

The Issue section of this chapter addressed the controversy over censorship on the Internet. Free speech is in constant struggle with individual rights and public safety. On the Web, some sites contain pornography, bigotry, and terrorist rhetoric that many people would rather not be made public. One of the cornerstones of democracy, however, is freedom of speech. Where do you draw the line when it comes to censoring and filtering on the Internet? Explain your views, making sure you consider questions such as: Do parents have the right to monitor, screen, and filter their children's Web use? Are governments ever justified in regulating what their citizens can access? Should anyone be responsible for policing the Internet? Incorporate your ideas in a two-page summary and submit it to your instructor.

 **COMPUTERS IN CONTEXT**

The Computers in Context section of this chapter focused on banking innovations and technology. The newest innovation to affect consumers is online banking. Although convenient, online banking has not been enthusiastically adopted by many consumers because of security concerns. For this project, research the services offered by online banking, then research the risks. Summarize your findings in a short paper. Connect to at least three banks that offer online banking services. Read through their promotional materials. Based on this material, indicate which bank seems to offer the best and most secure online banking services. Explain your choice in the last section of your paper. Follow your instructor's guidelines to submit your work as a printed document or by e-mail.

# On the Web

## STUDENT EDITION LABS

When you purchase access to the NP2012 CourseMate Web site, you'll find targeted learning materials to help you understand key concepts and prepare for exams. See page O-41 in the Orientation Chapter for login instructions.

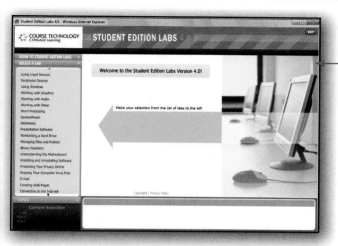

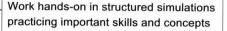
Work hands-on in structured simulations practicing important skills and concepts

### CONNECTING TO THE INTERNET

In the Connecting to the Internet Student Edition Lab, you will learn about the following topics:

- Establishing an Internet connection
- Connecting to the Internet using dial-up, DSL, cable, and wireless
- Installing ISP software
- Creating Internet connections manually

### PROTECTING YOUR PRIVACY ONLINE

In the Protecting Your Privacy Online Student Edition Lab, you will learn about the following topics:

- How cookies work
- Deleting cookies using a browser
- Adjusting your cookie settings in Internet Explorer

### GETTING THE MOST OUT OF THE INTERNET

In the Getting the Most Out of the Internet Student Edition Lab, you will learn about the following topics:

- Keeping track of your favorite Web sites
- Customizing your browser
- Searching the Web
- Online job hunting
- Online travel reservations
- Building communities

6

### CHAPTER OVERVIEW COURSECAST

Use your computer or iPod to hear a five-minute audio presentation of chapter highlights.

### AUDIO FLASHCARDS

Interact with audio flashcards to review key concepts from the chapter.

### DETAILED OBJECTIVES

Make sure that you've achieved all the objectives for a chapter before it's time for your test!

### PRACTICE TESTS

Review chapter material by taking these ten-question tests. Your results are saved by Engagement Tracker.

### ONLINE GAMES

Have some fun while refreshing your memory about key concepts that might appear on the next test.

### AND MORE!

At the NP2012 CourseMate Web site you'll also find the NP2012 eBook, TechTerm Flashcards, Online Glossary, and What Do You Think? opinion polls.

# 7

# The Web and E-mail

## Chapter Contents

▶ SECTION A:
**WEB TECHNOLOGY**
Web Basics
HTML
HTTP
Web Browsers
Cookies
Web Page Authoring
HTML Scripts

▶ SECTION B:
**SEARCH ENGINES**
Search Engine Basics
Formulating Searches
Citing Web-based Source Material

▶ SECTION C:
**E-COMMERCE**
E-commerce Basics
E-commerce Site Technology
Online Payment

▶ SECTION D:
**E-MAIL**
E-mail Overview
Local E-mail
Webmail
E-mail Attachments
Netiquette

▶ SECTION E:
**WEB AND E-MAIL SECURITY**
Cookie Exploits
Spam
Phishing
Fake Sites

▶ ISSUE:
**WHO'S READING YOUR E-MAIL?**

▶ **COMPUTERS IN CONTEXT:
FASHION INDUSTRY**

▶ **NEW PERSPECTIVES LABS**

▶ **REVIEW ACTIVITIES**

▶ **ON THE WEB**

## Learning Objectives

After reading this chapter, you will be able to answer the following questions by completing the outcomes-based Learning Objectives Checkpoints on page 417.

1. What is HTML?
2. How does the Web work?
3. What does a browser do?
4. Where do cookies come from?
5. What tools are available for creating Web pages?
6. How do I create a simple Web page?
7. What makes some Web pages interactive?
8. How do search engines work?
9. What is a Boolean operator?
10. What is the correct way to cite Web pages?
11. How do online shopping carts work?
12. How safe is online shopping?
13. Is Webmail better than client-based local e-mail such as Microsoft Outlook?
14. How do HTML and MIME formats relate to e-mail?
15. What are the security risks of using the Web?

---

**InfoWebLinks**
Visit the InfoWebLinks site to access additional resources ⓦ that accompany this chapter.

**Multimedia and Interactive Elements**
When using the BookOnCD or CourseMate eBook, the ▶ icons are clickable to access multimedia resources.

## Pre-Assessment Quiz

Take the pre-assessment quiz to find out how much you know about the topics in this chapter. ▶

### Apply Your Knowledge The information in this chapter will give you the background to:

- Use a browser to view Web pages and the source documents from which they are constructed
- Install browser plug-ins and players necessary to work with a variety of graphics, sound, and video files
- Create your own Web pages using a text editor and HTML tags
- Use a search engine to locate information on the Web

- Formulate advanced search queries and correctly format citations for Web-based materials
- Know how to keep your credit card information safe when shopping online
- Work with Webmail or local e-mail, attachments, and HTML mail formats
- Protect yourself from spam, spyware, cookie exploits, phishing, and pharming

### Try It

#### WHAT'S MY BROWSER STATUS?

Chapter 7 focuses on the World Wide Web, or "Web" for short. The most important software tool for accessing the Web is called a browser. To learn about the browser on your computer, follow these steps:

**1.** Make sure your computer is on and displaying the desktop.

**2.** Which browser do you typically use to access the Web? _____
If you don't know, look for browser icons on your desktop. Popular browsers include Internet Explorer, Safari, Firefox, and Chrome.

**3.** What is the URL that your browser uses as your home page? _____
The home page is the first Web page displayed and the one displayed when you click the Home button.

**4.** What is the version number for the browser you are using? _____
To find your browser's version number, click **Help** or the Tools icon and then click **About** (Windows) or click your browser's name on the Mac title bar and then select **About**. For Google Chrome, click the Wrench icon on the toolbar and then select **About**. Your browser's version number should be displayed in a dialog box. After you write down the version number, close the dialog box.

**5.** Find the most recent version for your browser by going to its Web site:

> www.mozilla.org/products/firefox
> www.google.com/chrome
> www.microsoft.com/windows/ie
> www.apple.com/safari

**6.** Are you using the most recent version of your browser? _____

Unless you want to download the most recent version of your browser and have permission to do so, exit the download area and close your browser.

# Web Technology

**IN 1990,** a British scientist named Tim Berners-Lee developed specifications for URLs, HTML, and HTTP; a group of technologies designed to help researchers share information by creating access to a sort of "web" of electronic documents. Berners-Lee's free Web software appeared on the Internet in 1991, but the Web didn't take off until 1993 when Marc Andreessen and his colleagues at the University of Illinois created Mosaic, a graphical browser. Andreessen later formed his own company and produced a browser called Netscape, which put the Web into the hands of millions of Web surfers. In Section A, you'll peel back the layers of Web technologies to take a look at what happens behind your browser window.

## WEB BASICS

**What is the Web?** One of the Internet's most captivating attractions, the **Web** (short for *World Wide Web*) is a collection of document, image, video, and sound files that can be linked and accessed over the Internet using a protocol called HTTP.

The concept of interlinking documents to access them pre-dates the Web by almost half a century. In 1945, an engineer named Vannevar Bush described a microfilm-based machine called the Memex that linked associated information or ideas through "trails."

The idea of linked documents resurfaced in the mid-1960s when Harvard graduate Ted Nelson coined the term **hypertext** to describe a computer system that could store literary documents, link them according to logical relationships, and allow readers to comment and annotate what they read. Nelson sketched the diagram in Figure 7-1 to explain his idea of a computer-based "web" of "links."

**What is a Web site?** A **Web site** typically contains a collection of related information organized and formatted so it can be accessed using software called a browser. You are probably familiar with informational Web sites such as HowStuffWorks, CNN, ESPN, and CNET. Web sites can also offer Web-based applications, such as Google Docs.

In addition to conventional sites that offer text-based information and news, Web sites host a diverse array of activities. Web sites that host amateur video, photos, and music get lots of traffic. Online shopping is a popular Web-based activity. From tiny niche boutiques to the Amazon.com superstore and countless eBay auctions, you can find just about any merchandise or service on the Web.

Many Web sites offer tools for creating your own blog and viewing blogs created by others. Some Web sites offer access to a thriving selection of podcasts. A **podcast** (sometimes called a Webcast) is an audio file that is distributed through downloads or the use of a feed that automatically sends new podcasts as they are produced. Podcasting was originally used to distribute radio show episodes, but is now widely used to distribute

**TERMINOLOGY NOTE**

Although the terms *Internet* and *Web* are sometimes used interchangeably, they are not the same. The Web is an interlinked collection of information; the Internet is a communications system used to transport that information from computers that store it to clients who want to view it.

**FIGURE 7-1**

Ted Nelson's early sketch of project Xanadu—a distant relative of the Web—used the terms *links* and *web*.

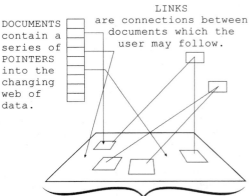

LINKS are connections between documents which the user may follow.

DOCUMENTS contain a series of POINTERS into the changing web of data.

Expanding Tissue of Text, Data, and Graphics

news, sports, music, and educational tutorials. **Videocasting** is similar to podcasting, but with video instead of audio files.

Social networking Web sites link people together. On sites such as Facebook, Classmates, and MySpace, members post information and photos in profiles and invite friends to join. Sites like Twitter offer a variation on social networking where members post short messages so that friends can follow their activities. A wiki, such as Wikipedia, is a collaborative Web site that can be accessed and edited by anyone who wants to contribute.

Wikis, blogs, social networking sites, and Web-based applications are sometimes characterized as Web 2.0. Although the term **Web 2.0** sounds like a new version of the Web, it simply refers to new and innovative ways of using the Web. Web 2.0 uses the same Internet communications infrastructure as the "old" Web.

The activities that take place at Web sites are under the control of Web servers. A **Web server** is an Internet-based computer that accepts requests from browsers. Servers collect the requested information and transmit it back in a format that the browser can display in the form of a Web page.

**What is a Web page?** A **Web page** is the product or output of one or more Web-based files displayed in a format similar to a page in a book. Unlike book pages, however, Web pages can dynamically incorporate videos, sounds, and interactive elements.

A Web page can be based on a document stored as a file or it can be assembled on the fly from information stored in a database. For example, a course syllabus that you view on the Web is probably written with a word processor and stored as a document on a Web server. In contrast, the Web page you view about a newly released album on iTunes is assembled from a database that contains the album title, artist name, track list, price, album cover art, and other product information.

**How do I access a Web page?** Your main tool for accessing Web pages is browser software, such as Microsoft Internet Explorer, open-source Mozilla Firefox, Google Chrome, or Apple Safari. A **Web browser** (usually simply referred to as a browser) is client software that displays Web page elements and handles links between pages. When using a browser, you can access a Web page by clicking a **hypertext link** (usually referred to simply as a link) or by typing a URL (Figure 7-2).

**What is a URL?** Every Web page has a unique address called a **URL** (Uniform Resource Locator, pronounced "You Are ELL"). For example, the URL for the Cable News Network (CNN) Web site is *http://www.cnn.com*. Most URLs begin with http:// to indicate the Web's standard communications protocol. When typing a URL, the http:// can usually be omitted, so *www.cnn.com* works just as well as *http://www.cnn.com*.

TERMINOLOGY NOTE

The process of accessing a Web site is sometimes referred to as surfing the Web and visitors are called Web surfers.

**FIGURE 7-2**

Browsers display Web pages and the links they contain. When the mouse pointer hovers over a link, it changes from an arrow shape to a hand shape. ▶ For an overview of browser controls, refer to this figure in the digital version of your textbook.

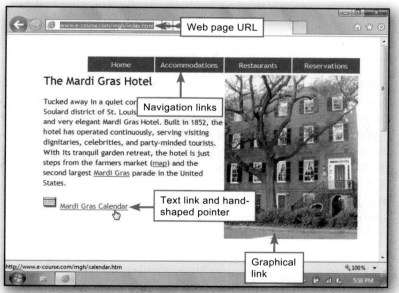

TERMINOLOGY NOTE

A URL is a type of URI (Uniform Resource Identifier). Other types of URIs include Social Security numbers and ISBNs that identify books. Some writers refer to Web addresses as URIs.

Most Web sites have a main page that acts as a doorway to the rest of the pages at the site. This main page is sometimes referred to as a home page, although this term can also refer to the page displayed by your browser each time it opens. The URL for a Web site's main page is usually short and to the point, like *www.cnn.com*.

The pages for a Web site are typically grouped into folders, which are reflected in the URL. For example, the CNN site might include weather information at *www.cnn.com/weather/* and entertainment information at *www.cnn.com/showbiz/*. The file name of a specific Web page always appears last in the URL. Web page file names usually have an .htm or .html extension, indicating that the page was created with Hypertext Markup Language. You'll learn more about HTML later in the chapter. Figure 7-3 identifies the parts of a URL.

**FIGURE 7-3**

The URL for a Web page indicates the computer on which it is stored, its location on the Web server, its file name, and its extension.

# http://www.cnn.com/showbiz/movies.htm

| Web protocol standard | Web server name | Folder name | File name and file extension |

**What are the rules for correctly typing a URL?** A URL never contains spaces, even after a punctuation mark, so do not type any spaces within a URL. An underline symbol is sometimes used to give the appearance of a space between words, for example *www.detroit.com/top_10.html*.

Be sure to use the correct type of slash—always a forward slash (/)—and duplicate the URL's capitalization exactly. Some Web servers are case sensitive. On these servers, typing *www.cmu.edu/Info.html* (with an uppercase *I*) will not locate the Web page that's stored on the Web server as *www.cmu.edu/info.html* (with a lowercase *i*).

## HTML

**What is HTML?** **HTML** (Hypertext Markup Language) is a set of specifications for creating documents that a browser can display as a Web page. HTML is called a **markup language** because authors mark up documents by inserting special instructions, called **HTML tags**, that specify how the document should appear when displayed on a computer screen or printed.

Tim Berners-Lee developed the original HTML specifications in 1990. These specifications have been revised several times by the World Wide Web Consortium (W3C). The current version, HTML5, was introduced in 2010.

**XHTML** is a markup language very similar to HTML, but it can be customized with tags that describe the data in databases. XHTML is more rigidly structured than HTML and a bit more complex, however, so XHTML documents are required to be "well-formed" by adhering to a strict set of syntax rules.

Other technologies, such as **DHTML** (Dynamic HTML) and **Ajax** (Asynchronous JavaScript and XML), offer tools and techniques for extending basic HTML and making Web pages more interactive, visually appealing, and media-rich.

**How do HTML tags work?** HTML tags are incorporated into an **HTML document**, which is similar to a word processing file, but has an .htm or .html extension. HTML tags, such as <hr /> and <b>, are enclosed in angle brackets and embedded in the document. These tags are instructions for the browser. When your browser displays a Web page on your

**INFOWEBLINKS**

The W3C is a worldwide organization that formulates standards for the Web. Learn more by connecting to the **W3C InfoWeb**.

 CLICK TO CONNECT
www.infoweblinks.com/np2012/ch07

computer screen, it does not show the tags or angle brackets. Instead, it attempts to follow the tags' instructions.

**So HTML documents look a lot different from Web pages, right?** Exactly. An HTML document is like a screenplay, and your browser is like a director who makes a screenplay come to life by assembling cast members and making sure they deliver their lines correctly.

As the HTML "screenplay" unfolds, your browser follows the instructions in an HTML document to display lines of text on your computer screen in the right color, size, and position. If the screenplay calls for a graphic, your browser collects it from the Web server and displays it. Although the HTML screenplay exists as a permanent file, the Web page you see on your computer screen exists only for the duration of the "performance."

Technically speaking, you can distinguish HTML documents (the screenplay) from Web pages (the performance). However, in everyday conversation, the term *Web page* is often used for the HTML document as well as the Web page displayed on screen.

An HTML document is sometimes referred to as a **source document** because it is the source of the HTML tags used to construct a Web page. You can view the HTML source documents for most Web pages if you are curious about how they were constructed. Figure 7-4 illustrates the difference between an HTML source document and the Web page it produces.

**FIGURE 7-4**

An HTML document (top) contains text and HTML tags. Formatting tags are used to change font size, separate paragraphs, and add rules. Other tags add graphics and links to a page. The HTML document produces a Web page (bottom). ▶ Refer to your digital textbook to see more examples of HTML source code.

## HTTP

**How does HTTP work?** **HTTP** is a protocol that works with TCP/IP to get Web resources to your desktop. A Web resource can be defined as any chunk of data that has a URL, such as an HTML document, a graphic, or a sound file.

HTTP includes commands called methods that help your browser communicate with Web servers. GET is the most frequently used HTTP method. The GET method is typically used to retrieve text and graphics files necessary for displaying a Web page. This method can also be used to pass a search query to a file server. HTTP transports your browser's request for a Web resource to a Web server. Next, it transports the Web server's response back to your browser.

An HTTP exchange takes place over a pair of sockets. A **socket** is an abstract concept that represents one end of a connection. Although a packet switching network doesn't actually make point-to-point connections between network nodes, many people find it handy to visualize network connections as a communication line with a doorway-like socket at each end. For HTTP, sockets usually are associated with port 80 on the client and server.

In an HTTP exchange, your browser opens a socket on your PC, connects to a similar open socket at the Web server, and issues a command, such as "send me an HTML document." The server receives the command, executes it, and sends a response back through the socket. The sockets are then closed until the browser is ready to issue another command. Figure 7-5 demonstrates the messages that flow between your browser and a Web server to retrieve an HTML document.

**FIGURE 7-5**

HTTP messages flow between a browser and a Web server. For an animated view of how HTTP works, take a look at this figure in your digital textbook.

**1.** The URL in the browser's Address box contains the domain name of the Web server that your browser contacts.

Address | www.infoweblinks.com/np/chapter7.htm

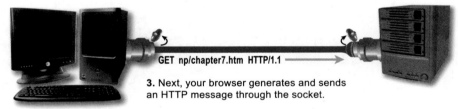

**2.** Your browser opens a socket and connects to a similar open socket at the Web server.

GET np/chapter7.htm HTTP/1.1 ———▶

**3.** Next, your browser generates and sends an HTTP message through the socket.

**4.** The server sends back the requested HTML document through the open sockets.

HTTP/1.1 200 OK
Date: Fri 24 Dec 2012
Content-Type: text.htm
Content-Length: 1354
<html>
<body>
<h1>NP InfoWebs</h1>

**5.** After sending the response, the server closes its socket and the browser closes its socket.

 CLICK TO START

**Is each Web page element retrieved separately?** HTTP initially allowed only one request and response per session. As a result, a browser could open a session and request an HTML document; but as soon as the document was sent, the session was closed. To make additional requests—for example, to request a graphic for the page—the browser had to open another session.

A **persistent HTTP connection** reuses the same HTTP connection to send and receive multiple requests. Today's browsers use persistent connections to obtain text, images, and audio for a Web page during a single session.

**What if an element cannot be found?** A Web server's response to a browser's request includes an **HTTP status code** that indicates whether the browser's request could be fulfilled. The status code 200 means that the request was fulfilled—the requested HTML document, graphic, or other resource was sent. Anyone who surfs the Web has encountered the "404 Not Found" message. Your browser displays this message when a Web server sends a 404 status code to indicate that the requested resource does not exist (Figure 7-6).

**What is a Web cache?** When your browser fetches pages and graphics to form a Web page, it stores that material on your computer in temporary files sometimes referred to as a **Web cache** or browser cache. These temporary files come in handy if you switch back and forth between pages or sites. Rather than fetch the entire page and all its graphics again, your browser can simply load them from the local cache. Files are deleted from the Web cache within days or weeks, depending on your browser's settings.

A potential problem with your Web cache is that it stores Web page elements from all the sites you've visited. If you use a public or lab computer, the Web page elements are stored there and can be viewed by others. To maintain your privacy, you might consider deleting these files periodically, adjusting browser settings to limit the time these files remain on your computer, or limiting the amount of space they can use on the hard disk.

## WEB BROWSERS

**What are the most popular browsers?** Netscape Navigator was one of the first browsers with a graphical user interface. It has been superseded by today's popular browsers, such as Microsoft Internet Explorer, Mozilla Firefox, Apple Safari, and Google Chrome. Browsers have many similarities, as you can see from examining their toolbars in Figure 7-7.

Published in December 1994, Netscape quickly became the most popular browser on Mac and PC platforms. Numerous revisions added pioneering features to enhance the overall browsing experience.

In 1998, Netscape source code became open source software, managed by an organization known as Mozilla. The organization's

**FIGURE 7-6**

When a broken link points to a nonexistent HTML document, your browser typically produces a 404 Not Found error. When a broken link points to a nonexistent graphic or other non-HTML file, your browser usually displays one of the broken link icons shown below.

7

**FIGURE 7-7**

Netscape Navigator and Mozilla Firefox

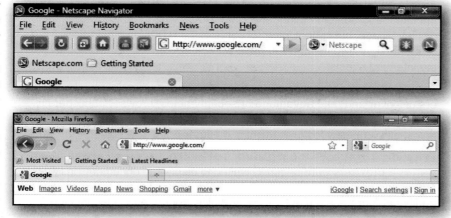

main product, a browser called Mozilla, was all but ignored by most com- puter owners. In 2004, however, a new version of Mozilla, dubbed Firefox, rapidly gained popularity because it offered effective security features.

FIGURE 7-7 CONTINUED

Internet Explorer, Safari, and Chrome

Internet Explorer (IE) ver- sion 1.0 was published by Microsoft in August 1995. The program code for the original IE 1.0 browser was licensed from a Netscape spin-off called Spyglass, which pro- vided IE with many of the same features as Netscape. Until IE 4.0 appeared in 1997, however, Microsoft's browser was unable to match Netscape's popularity. Today, IE has supplanted Netscape as the dominant browser for the PC platform. It is also available for Mac OS, Linux, and several versions of UNIX.

Google Chrome is another browser option. Developed in 2008, Chrome was engi- neered specifically to support Web-based e-mail and similar online applications.

Macintosh computers were preloaded with Netscape Navigator until 1997, when Microsoft Internet Explorer for Mac replaced it. In 2003, however, Apple introduced a new browser called Safari, which is now included with Macintosh computers and available for PCs. Safari has the distinction of being the first browser to pass the Acid2 test, which means that it follows W3C standards and can correctly display all complying Web pages.

**Should I upgrade my browser when new versions become available?** It is a good idea to upgrade when a new version of your browser becomes available. Because most browser updates are free, you can get up-to-date functionality simply by spending a few minutes down- loading and installing an update.

The problem with using an old browser is that some Web pages depend on new HTML features supported only by the latest browser versions. Without the latest upgrade, you might encounter errors when your browser tries to display a page, but cannot interpret some of the HTML. In other cases, your browser might display the Web page without errors, but you will not see all the intended effects.

Another important reason to upgrade is for increased security. As hack- ers discover and take advantage of security holes, browser publishers try to patch the holes. Upgrades usually contain patches for known security holes, although new features might sometimes open new holes.

**Why do I have to download software to view some Web pages?** Browsers were originally limited to displaying documents in HTML format and graphics files in GIF and JPEG formats. Today, however, many additional formats are used for the graphics, sound, and video included in Web pages. Browsers do not have built-in support for all these formats.

If your browser does not have built-in support for a file format required to display or play a Web page element, you can usually download the necessary software. For example, to read a PDF file, you might be directed to the Adobe Web site to download Adobe Reader software that handles PDF files. To display an animation, you might need Adobe's Flash software. The software your browser calls upon to work with additional file formats is usually referred to as a plug-in or add-on.

**What is a plug-in?** A **plug-in** (sometimes called a browser add-on) is a program that extends a browser's ability to work with file formats. Most plug-ins can be downloaded from the Web. Plug-ins come in different versions for different browsers. When looking for plug-ins, let your browser do the searching and it will find the correct version.

The process of installing a plug-in application creates an association between the browser and a file format, such as PDF, SWF, or MOV. Whenever your browser encounters one of these file formats, it automatically runs the corresponding plug-in, which in turn opens the file.

**Is a plug-in or add-on the same as a player?** At one time, the term *plug-in* referred to specific technology pioneered by Netscape developers. Today, the term *plug-in* refers broadly to any software that is added to a host program, such as a browser, to perform additional tasks and work with additional file formats.

The term *player* is sometimes used to refer to plug-ins, but it can also refer to standalone software that does not require a host program. For example, the Adobe Flash Player is a standalone application that you run to view Flash video and animations. The player is also available as a plug-in that is installed in your browser. You don't have to manually run the Flash plug-in; your browser automatically uses it as necessary to display Flash videos included on Web pages.

You can download, install, and delete plug-ins for your browser. Figure 7-8 shows a list of plug-ins installed for use with Internet Explorer.

**FIGURE 7-8**

You can usually find a list of plug-ins installed for use with your browser. If you use Internet Explorer, look for a Manage Add-ons option on the Tools menu. ▶ For more information about managing plug-ins, refer to this figure in your digital textbook.

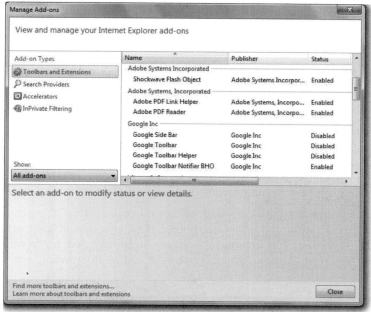

## COOKIES

**What is a cookie?** A **cookie** (technically an HTTP cookie) is a small chunk of data generated by a Web server and stored in a text file on your computer's hard disk. Cookies allow a Web site to store information on a client computer for later retrieval. Web sites use cookies to:

- Monitor your path through a site to keep track of the pages you viewed or the items you purchased.

- Gather information that allows a Web server to present ad banners targeted to products you previously purchased at that Web site.

- Collect personal information you type into a Web page form and retain it for the next time you visit the Web site.

**Why do Web sites need to use cookies?** In many respects, cookies are the solution for problems caused by HTTP's **stateless protocol**, which maintains no record of your browser's previous interactions and handles each browser request based entirely on information that comes with it.

Suppose that you use your browser to visit a popular online music store. You search for your favorite bands, listen to some sample tracks, and put a few albums in your shopping cart. Although you might have been browsing at the music site for 30 minutes or more, from the perspective of the site's server, that activity could just as well have been carried out by several people, each one spending only a few seconds at the site.

Because HTTP is a stateless protocol, each time you connect to a different Web page at the site, the server regards it as a new visit. Cookies enable the server to keep track of your activity and compile a list of your purchases.

**How do cookies work?** When your browser connects to a site that uses cookies, it receives an HTTP "Set-cookie" message from the Web server. This cookie message contains information that your browser stores on your computer's hard disk. The server that creates a cookie can request it any time your browser is accessing a Web page from the Web site server.

A cookie can include information such as a customer number, a shopping cart number, Web page URL, or a part number. In addition, a cookie usually contains the date the cookie expires and the domain name of the host that created the cookie. Some of the cookie data might be encrypted as shown in Figure 7-9.

> ppkcookie1hellowww.quirksmode.org/1600182732736
> 02981171511470601282981 0307*

**How long do cookies stay on my computer?** A Web developer can program a cookie to time out after a designated period of time. When a cookie reaches the end of its predefined lifetime, your Web browser simply erases it. Some cookies have no expiration date or a date far into the future, so cookies tend to accumulate on your computer's hard disk.

**Can I see the cookies stored on my computer?** You can view a list of cookies stored on your computer, but first you must find them. Refer to your browser documentation to discover which folder holds your cookies. Figure 7-10 shows a list of cookies stored when browsing with Internet Explorer.

## INFOWEBLINKS

At the **Cookies InfoWeb**, you'll find links to a collection of articles that focus on cookie technology, including how they affect security and privacy.

 CLICK TO CONNECT
www.infoweblinks.com/np2012/ch07

**FIGURE 7-9**

When you look at the cookies stored on your computer, most of the information is unintelligible. This cookie is called ppkcookie, its value is "hello," and it was created at *www.quirksmode.org*. The cookie contains an expiration date, but it is encoded so you can't decipher it.

| Folders | Name | Internet Address |
|---|---|---|
| Internet Explorer | cookie:sarah smith... | Cookie:sarah smith@avast.com/ |
| Media Player | cookie:sarah smith... | Cookie:sarah smith@img.mixplay.tv/ |
| Movie Maker | cookie:sarah smith... | Cookie:sarah smith@live365.com/ |
| Office | serviceswitching/ | Cookie:sarah smith@onlinestores.metaservices.mi |
| Portable Devices | cookie:sarah smith... | Cookie:sarah smith@toplist.cz/ |
| Windows | cookie:sarah smith... | Cookie:sarah smith@yahoo.com/ |
| 1033 | menu_image_s.png | http://content.ztango.com.edgesuite.net/menu_i |
| Burn | setupeng.exe | http://download4.avast.com/iavs4pro/setupeng.e |
| Explorer | wmp-payplay.fm-... | http://icons.payplay.fm/logo/wmp-payplay.fm-m |
| GameExplorer | icon_15x15.png | http://images.live365.com/scp/wmp/images/icon |
| Temporary Internet Files | g04447cuku1.jpg?lo... | http://images.metaservices.microsoft.com/cover/ |
| WER | g04447cuku1.jpg?lo... | http://images.metaservices.microsoft.com/cover/ |
| Windows Defender | wm_com_v_rgb_15x... | http://images.metaservices.microsoft.com/svcswi |
| Windows Mail | movielink-icon 15x... | http://images.movielink.com/movielink-icon 15x |

**FIGURE 7-10**

Internet Explorer typically stores cookies as individual files in the AppData\ Local\Microsoft\Windows\ Temporary Internet Files folder. The information after the @ symbol usually indicates the domain name of the site that created the cookie.

## WEB PAGE AUTHORING

**What tools can I use to create Web pages?** You can create HTML documents for Web pages with an HTML conversion utility, online Web authoring tools, Web authoring software, or a text editor.

An **HTML conversion utility** adds HTML tags to a document, spreadsheet, or other text-based file to create an HTML document that can be displayed by a browser. For example, you can work with Microsoft Word to create a standard DOCX file and then use Word's Save As Web Page option to convert the document into HTML format. The HTML conversion process sometimes produces an unusual result, however, because some of the features and formatting in your original document might not be possible within the world of HTML.

A second option for Web page authors is to use a set of online Web page authoring tools. These template-like tools are provided by some ISPs and other companies that host Web pages for individuals and businesses. Working with these tools is quite simple—you type, select, drag, and drop elements onto a Web page (Figure 7-11).

**INFOWEBLINKS**

For help in selecting software to design your own Web pages, connect to the **Web Authoring Tools InfoWeb**.

Ⓦ CLICK TO CONNECT
www.infoweblinks.com/np2012/ch07

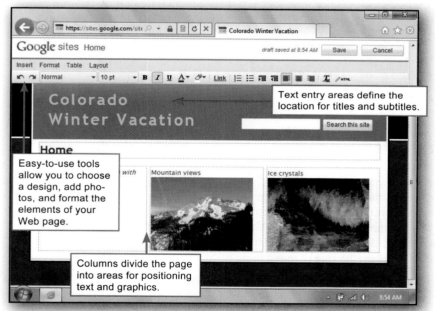

**FIGURE 7-11**

Many Web hosting sites, such as Google, offer subscribers online tools for creating Web pages. ▶ For a tour of online Web page authoring, activate this figure in your digital textbook.

A third option for creating Web pages is a special category of software, referred to as Web authoring software or HTML editors, which provides tools specifically designed to enter and format Web page text, graphics, and links. Popular Web authoring products include Adobe Dreamweaver, and open source KompoZer and Amaya.

**How do I create a Web page with a text editor?** You can use a text editor like Notepad (Windows) or TextEdit (Mac) to create simple HTML documents or to make quick modifications to more complex pages. The first step in the process is to open the editor. Then you can enter text and HTML tags.

**How do I start an HTML document?** The framework for an HTML document consists of two sections: the head and the body. The head section begins with <html> and <head> tags and contains information that defines global properties, including the Web page title that appears in the browser title bar and information about the page that can be used by search engines.

The body section of an HTML document begins with the <body> HTML tag. This section of the document contains text, HTML tags that format the text, plus a variety of links to graphics, sounds, and videos. Figure 7-12 contains basic HTML for a Web page. You can use it as a template for creating your own pages. Make sure you begin with the <html> and <head> tags; end the document with the </body> and </html> tags.

**FIGURE 7-12**

Using a text editor like Notepad to create an HTML document requires attention to details, such as including all necessary quotation marks and brackets.

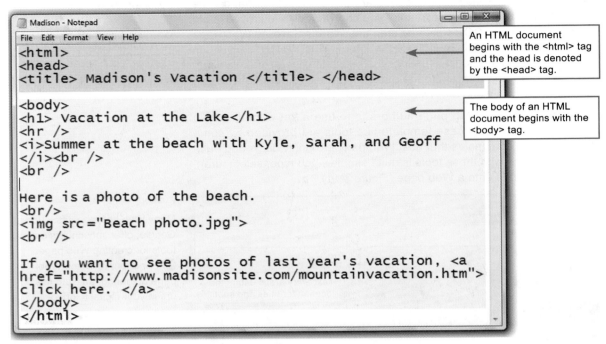

An HTML document begins with the <html> tag and the head is denoted by the <head> tag.

The body of an HTML document begins with the <body> tag.

**How do I specify the text and graphics for a Web page?** In the body section of your HTML document, you can enter text and HTML tags to format fonts and spacing. You can also specify the images you want to appear on the page, and you can create clickable links to other Web pages. The table in Figure 7-13 provides a list of basic HTML tags that you can use to create your own HTML documents; the HTML lab at the end of the chapter goes into more detail on the use of these tags.

**FIGURE 7-13**

Basic HTML Tags

| HTML Tag | Use | Example |
|---|---|---|
| **<b> <i>** | Bold or italicize text | <b> Hello </b> |
| **<h1> <h2> ... <h6>** | Change font size; h1 is largest | <h1> Chapter 1 </h1> |
| **<h1 style="color: ">** | Change font color | <h1 style="color:green"> Fir Trees </h1> |
| **<hr />** | Include a horizontal line (no end tag) | Section 2 <hr /> |
| **<br />** | Line break (no end tag) | This is line one. <br /> This is line two. |
| **<p>** | Paragraph break | <p>It was the best of times, it ...of comparison only. </p> |
| **<ol> <ul> <li>** | Numbered list <ol>; bulleted list <ul>; list items <li> | <ol> <li>First item</li> <li> Second item</li> </ol> |
| **<a href="URL">** | Link to another Web page | <a href="www.news.com/today.htm"> Click here </a> |
| **<img src="File">** | Include an image | <img src="Photo.jpg"> |
| **<table>, <tr>, <td>** | Create tables, table rows, and cells | <table> |

**How do I get my Web pages on the Internet?** Whether you work with a text editor or another authoring tool, save your HTML document with an .htm or .html extension.

Creating a Web page is not the end of the publishing process. Additional steps include testing your pages, transferring them to a Web server, and testing all your links.

1. Test each page locally. When you complete the first draft of a Web page, you should test it to verify that every element is displayed correctly by any browsers that visitors to your Web page might use. You can accomplish this task without connecting to the Web. Simply open a browser, and then enter the local file name of the HTML document you created for your Web page. Repeat this process for any other browsers you expect visitors to use. One caution: Your hard disk drive is much faster than most Internet connections, so the text and graphics for your Web page are displayed faster during your local test than for someone viewing your page over the Internet.

2. Transfer pages to a Web server. Whether you're publishing a single page, a series of pages, or an entire Web site, you must put your pages on a Web server—a process called posting. To post Web page files manually, you can use a file transfer utility such as WS_FTP or FileZilla. Web authoring software usually provides a menu option that automates the process of posting HTML documents and associated media files.

3. Test all pages and links. After you post your pages on a Web server, make sure you can access each page, and then test the links between your pages as well as any links to pages on other sites.

4. Update your pages to keep them current. Periodically, you should review the information on your Web pages and verify that the links still connect to existing Web pages.

## HTML SCRIPTS

**Is it possible to add programs to a Web page?** Standard HTML provides a way to display text and graphics on a Web page and link to other Web pages; but because it isn't a programming language, HTML does not provide a way to perform complicated tasks or respond to user actions. A series of program instructions called an **HTML script** can be embedded directly into the text of an HTML document or in a file referenced from an HTML document. Scripts are not displayed by the browser; instead, they instruct the browser to perform specific actions or respond to specific user actions.

**How would a Web page author use a script?** Scripts allow Web pages to become more interactive and incorporate activities that would otherwise require a computer program. Scripts enable e-commerce sites to verify credit card information. They also make it possible to create interactive Web pages that include fill-in forms. Scripts work with cookies to deliver custom Web pages, such as those Amazon.com generates each time you return to the site. Scripts don't replace normal HTML—they extend and enhance it.

As an example of scripting, consider what happens when you use online forms. **HTML forms** can collect user input for e-commerce orders, site registrations, opinion polls, and so on. The information you enter into an HTML form is held in the memory of your computer, where your browser creates temporary storage bins that correspond to the input field names designated by the form's HTML tags.

7

For example, in the form shown in Figure 7-14, your address might be temporarily held in a memory location that's called Customer Address. When you click the Submit button, your browser gathers the data from memory and sends it to a specially designated script on an HTTP server, where it can be processed and stored.

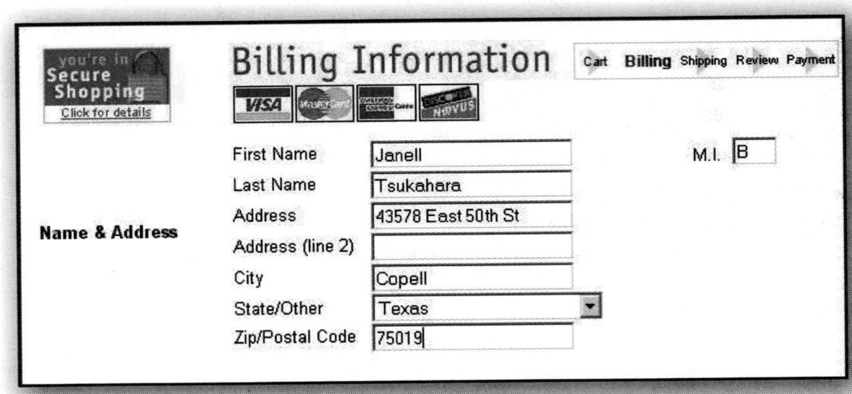

**FIGURE 7-14**

HTML forms are typically used to collect payment and shipping information at the checkout counter of e-commerce Web sites.

**Do scripts run on my local computer or on a Web server?** Scripts can run on a client or a server. A **server-side script** consists of statements that run on a server. Server-side scripts accept data submitted by a form, process that data, and then generate a custom HTML document that is sent to the browser for display. These dynamically produced pages can often be identified because they contain question marks (?) in the URL displayed in the Address bar of your browser. Server-side scripts can be written using a variety of programming and scripting languages, such as Perl, PHP, C, C++, C#, and Java.

A **client-side script** consists of scripting statements that run on your local computer. The script is executed by the browser, which must have the capability to deal with the programming language used to write the script. Popular languages for client-side scripts include VBScript and JavaScript. Most of today's browsers can handle JavaScript, but only IE has the built-in capability to execute VBScript. Client-side scripts often take the form of Java applets, Flash objects, and ActiveX controls.

**What is a Java applet?** A **Java applet** is an application written in the Java programming language. A programmer or Web page author places a reference to a Java applet in an HTML document using the <object> HTML tag. When working with a Web page that contains an <object> tag, your browser downloads the applet and executes its instructions. The applet is not installed on your computer, so it does not leave a permanent footprint.

You might wonder if a Java applet could contain a virus that would take up residence in your computer system or a worm that would spread over your network. Applets are fairly safe because they cannot open, modify, delete, or create files on your computer; they cannot make network connections except to the originating site; and they are not allowed to launch other programs.

**What is Flash content?** Most people associate Flash with a popular video standard, but Flash objects can include interactive elements. **ActionScript** is a programming language for the Adobe Flash Player used to create sophisticated applications that can be launched from Web pages and viewed using the Flash browser plug-in or the standalone Flash Player. The Flash Player has some security holes, but users can minimize risks by installing updates as they become available.

**What is an ActiveX control?** An **ActiveX control** is a compiled computer program that can be referenced from within an HTML document, downloaded, installed on your computer, and executed within the browser window. ActiveX controls can be used on the server side, too, but consumers typically encounter the client-side version when their browsers display a security warning and ask for permission to proceed with installation (Figure 7-15).

**FIGURE 7-15**

Web surfers who use Internet Explorer sometimes encounter the Security Warning dialog box for ActiveX components. If the component is supplied by a trusted source, then it should be safe to install it.

Most ActiveX controls are safe. However, an ActiveX control is a full-fledged program, which gives it the potential to include routines that alter or delete data on your computer's hard disk. ActiveX controls include digital certificates to increase their security. A **digital certificate** is an electronic attachment to a file that verifies the identity of its source.

**Is it easy to create Java applets, Flash objects, and ActiveX controls?** Scripts are somewhat more difficult to write and test than HTML documents, so scripts are typically the domain of professional Web designers. A basic understanding of scripts, however, along with a grasp of HTML, HTTP, cookies, browsers, and hypertext, should give you a more complete understanding of how the Web works.

7

# QuickCheck

1. Ted Nelson coined the term [_____] to describe a web of linked documents, similar to Web pages.

2. Every Web page has a unique address called a(n) [_____] . (Hint: Use the acronym.)

3. The main protocol for sending and receiving Web content is [_____] . (Hint: Use the acronym.)

4. The basic markup language used on the Web is [_____] . (Hint: Use the acronym.)

5. [_____] were developed because HTTP is a stateless protocol; so each time you connect to a different page, the Web server regards it as a new connection.

▶ CHECK ANSWERS

# Search Engines

**THE WEB ENCOMPASSES** hundreds of millions of pages stored on servers scattered all over the globe. To use this information, however, you have to find it. There is no rhyme or reason to the location of Web-based information; a particular fact you're trying to unearth could be located on an obscure server in Kazakhstan, or buried deep in the folder structure of a major e-commerce Web site. Modern Web surfers depend on search engines for help navigating the waves of information stored on the Web. In Section B you'll find out how Web search engines work so that you can use them more efficiently.

## SEARCH ENGINE BASICS

**What is a Web search engine?** A **Web search engine** (usually referred to simply as a search engine) is a program designed to help people locate information on the Web by formulating simple keyword queries. In response to a query, the search engine displays results or "hits" as a list of relevant Web sites, accompanied by links to source pages and short excerpts containing the keywords (Figure 7-16).

**FIGURE 7-16**

A query for *mountain bike* returns a list of links to relevant sites.

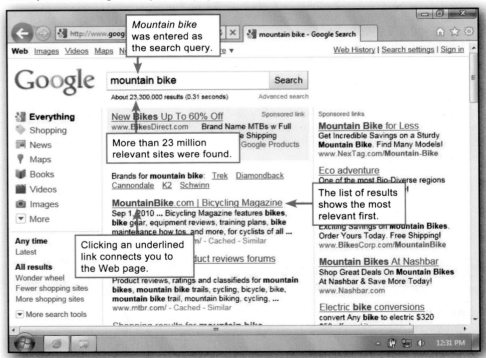

Popular search engines are located at Web sites such as *www.google.com, www.yahoo.com, www.bing.com*, and *www.ask.com*. You might say that the search engines at these sites build the equivalent of a book index. Just as an index helps readers turn to a page on which they can find a particular word or concept, a search engine helps Web surfers link to pages that contain information they seek. Unlike a book, however, the information on the Web is too vast to catalog manually, so search engine software does it autonomously.

Although most search sites use automated search engines, sites such as *www.mahalo.com, answers.yahoo.com*, and *www.chacha.com* are sometimes referred to as human search engines because results are compiled and screened by human experts. These sites would be better classified as question and answer sites, however, because they provide answers to specific questions, rather than links to Web pages that contain information relative to a set of keywords.

**What is the difference between a search engine and a search engine site?** It is easy to think of *www.google.com* as a search engine; but to be precise, it is a Web site that offers access to a search engine. A search engine is the program that works behind the scenes to gather, index, find, and rank information from the Web. Some sites, including Google, use their own proprietary search engines, but other sites purchase third-party search technology. For example, Yahoo!'s search engine is also used at search sites such as AltaVista and AlltheWeb.

Search engine technology can also be incorporated in e-commerce, informational, and corporate sites, most often taking the form of query toolbars used to search within a single Web site (Figure 7-17).

**FIGURE 7-17**

Many Web sites use search engine technology for searching within the site rather than searching the entire Web.

**How do search engines work?** A search engine contains four components: a Web crawler, an indexing utility, a database, and a query processor. The Web crawler combs the Web to gather data that's representative of the contents of Web pages. The indexer processes the information gathered by the crawler into a list of keywords and URLs stored in a database. The query processor allows you to access the database by entering key terms, and then produces a list of Web pages that contain content relevant to your query. Let's take a look at each of these components to find out how they affect your ability to mine information from the Web.

**What is a Web crawler?** A **Web crawler** (also referred to as a Web spider) is a computer program that is automated to methodically visit Web sites. Web crawlers can be programmed to perform various activities as they visit sites; but in the context of search engines, Web crawlers download Web pages and submit them to an indexing utility for processing.

**How much of the Web does a Web crawler cover?** A Web crawler begins with a list of URLs to visit. After copying the material at a specified URL, the Web crawler looks for hypertext links and adds them to the list of URLs to visit. To cover the Web as efficiently as possible, a Web crawler can run multiple processes in parallel. Sophisticated algorithms keep processes from overlapping or getting stuck in loops.

High-performance Web crawlers can visit hundreds of millions of Web pages a day. Those pages, however, are only a fraction of the Web. Researchers estimate that the most extensive search engines cover less than 20% of the Web. Each search engine seems to focus on a slightly different collection of Web sites. The same search entered into different search engines can produce different results, so it is sometimes worthwhile to try alternative search engines.

Web crawlers typically do not gather material from the invisible Web, which encompasses pages that require password-protected logins and pages that are dynamically generated with server-side scripts. The potential volume of dynamically generated pages, such as all the possible pages that Amazon.com could generate from its inventory database, is just too great to feasibly index. To access information related to e-commerce merchandise or library catalogs, you might have to go directly to the merchant's or library's Web site and use its search tools.

**How frequently do Web crawlers revisit sites?** When you query a search engine, you want the results to be up to date so that you don't waste time trying to link to pages that have changed or been deleted. Search engines use various algorithms to refresh their indexes.

The number of times a search engine's crawler visits a Web page varies, depending on several factors such as how often the page tends to change and its popularity. Obscure pages might be visited only once a month, whereas the pages at a news site would be visited daily.

**How do search engine indexers work?** A **search engine indexer** is software that pulls keywords from a Web page and stores them in a database. The purpose of the indexer is to make pages easy to find based on their contents. For example, a Web page at a classic comic book site might contain information and covers from old comics (Figure 7-18). Keywords that might help catalog this page for future access include *classic, comic, comic book, artwork, cover, gallery, super-hero, crime, romance,* and *Golden Age.*

**FIGURE 7-18**

A search engine's indexer looks for keywords on each page the Web crawler retrieves.

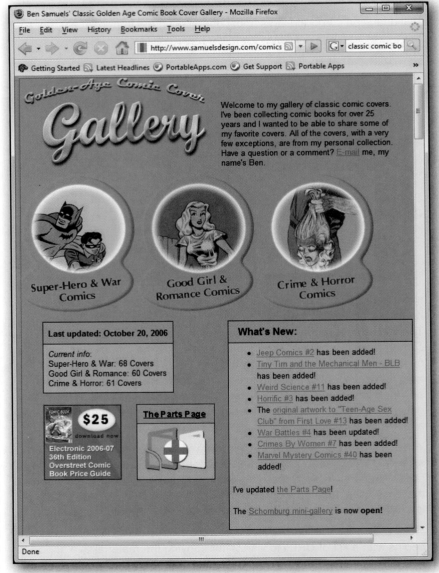

**Which Web sites are shown at the top of the results list?** A search engine's **query processor** looks for your search terms in the search engine's indexed database and returns a list of relevant Web sites. The order in which Web sites are listed in response to a search depends on relevancy criteria, such as keyword matches and link popularity.

If a search is based on multiple keywords, pages that contain the most matching words are listed first. **Link popularity** is a measure of the quality and quantity of the links from one Web page to others. Pages with links to and from popular sites tend to get high relevancy ratings.

**Can a search engine be manipulated into giving a high ranking to a page?** Web sites can be added to a search engine index in several ways. Sites can automatically get discovered by a search engine's Web crawler, they can be submitted to a search engine by Web masters who manage various Web sites, they can be submitted for a paid placement, or they can be submitted as banner or pop-up ads.

Most search engines make it easy to submit the URL for a Web site, so that Web masters don't have to wait for their sites to be discovered by a Web crawler. Manual submissions are added to the crawler's list of sites to visit and the site will eventually be indexed.

Some search engines accept paid placements, which are bumped to the top positions on the results list. Other search engines accept paid ads, but place them in a clearly marked area. For example, Google displays a column of ads related to the keywords you enter for a search. Suppose you search for mountain bike trails. The main results list displays maps of mountain bike trails and reviews. An additional column of sponsored links are paid placements by merchants who have mountain-bike related products. Merchants are charged only if the ad is clicked (Figure 7-19).

TERMINOLOGY NOTE

The words you enter for your search can be referred to as queries, search criteria, search terms, or keywords.

**FIGURE 7-19**

Sponsored links on Google are paid placements that appear when users make queries using relevant keywords.

7

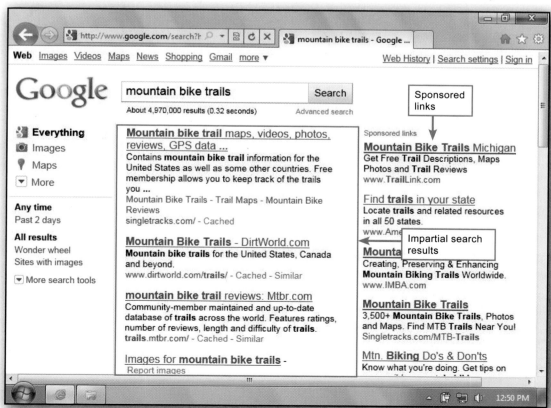

Disreputable Web site operators are constantly trying to devise schemes, such as manipulating meta keywords, to move their Web sites up to the top of search engine query results. A **meta keyword** is entered into a header section of a Web page when it is created and is supposed to describe the page contents.

**Keyword stuffing** is an unethical practice in which meta keywords are manipulated to gain high relevancy rankings. For example, a Web page author might include meta keywords such as *sex* (which happens to be the most frequently used search term) even though the term has little to do with the information on the page.

Socially responsible search engine sites take steps to foil practices that manipulate rankings and make their policies on paid placements clear to users. When you use a search engine, read its About page to learn its placement policies and discover whether or not you can trust the search results to be unbiased.

**FIGURE 7-20**

Simple queries sometimes produce an unmanageable number of results. ▶ To review search engine basics and get tips on how to narrow your searches, work with the tour for this figure in your digital textbook.

## FORMULATING SEARCHES

**How do I formulate a basic search?** Most search engines work with keyword queries in which you enter one or more words, called **search terms**, related to the information you want to find. For example, if you're interested in Batman comics, you can simply type the obvious: *Batman* (Figure 7-20).

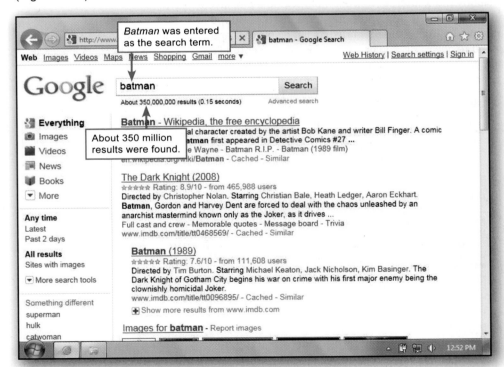

Narrowing a search can reduce the number of results and produce a more targeted list. For example, the query *first appearance Batman comic book* produces under a million entries and those listed first link to information about when Batman first appeared in the May 1939 issue of *Detective Comics*.

Search engine queries rarely produce fewer than a thousand results. A game called Googlewhacking illustrates just how hard it is to create a narrowly targeted query. Googlewhacking challenges you to type a two-word query that produces one and only one result. Try it! You need to choose two fairly unrelated words, but they cannot be totally unrelated or you'll get no results. You can view some successful Googlewhacks at *www.googlewhack.com/tally.pl*.

When formulating queries, keep the simple guidelines from Figure 7-21 in mind.

FIGURE 7-21

Tips for Effective Queries

- Most search engines are not case sensitive, so you don't have to use the Shift key when entering proper names.

- Typically, search engines ignore common words, such as *and*, *a*, and *the*, so don't bother to include them in your query.

- The top search engines use stemming technology that looks for plurals and other variations of the search terms you enter. For example, if you enter *diet*, the search engine also looks for pages with terms such as *diets*, *dietary*, and *dietician*.

- To search for an exact phrase, enter it in quotes. For example, *"Dynamic Duo."*

- The asterisk (*) is sometimes referred to as a wildcard character. It allows a search engine to find pages with any derivation of a basic word. For example, the query *medic** would not only produce pages containing the word *medic*, but also *medics*, *medicine*, *medical*, *medication*, and *medicinal*.

- The NEAR operator tells a search engine that you want documents in which one of the search terms is located close to but not necessarily next to the other search term. The query *library NEAR/15 congress* means that the words *library* and *congress* must appear within 15 words of each other. Successful searches could include documents containing phrases such as *Library of Congress* or *Congress funds special library research*.

- When you enter multiple search terms, the query processor assumes you want to see Web pages that include all your terms. Technically, the search engine inserts the Boolean operator *AND* between the terms in your search. If you want to use other Boolean operators, however, you must enter them.

7

**What are Boolean operators?** A **Boolean operator** (sometimes called a search operator) is a word or symbol that describes a relationship between search terms and thereby helps you create a more focused query. They are called Boolean operators after George Boole, a 19th century English mathematician, who defined one of the first systems of logic. Figure 7-22 provides a quick overview of how to use Boolean operators when formulating searches.

FIGURE 7-22

Search Operators

| AND | When two search terms are joined by *AND*, both terms must appear on a Web page before it can be included in the search results. The query *railroad AND cars* will locate pages that contain both the words *railroad* and *cars*. Your search results might include pages containing information about old railroad cars, about railroad car construction, and even about railroads that haul automobiles (cars). Some search engines use the plus symbol (+) instead of the word *AND*. |
|---|---|
| OR | When two search terms are joined by *OR*, either one or both of the search words could appear on a page. Entering the query *railroad OR cars* produces information about railroad fares, railroad routes, railroad cars, automobile safety records, and even car ferries. |
| NOT | The search term following *NOT* must not appear on any of the pages found by the search engine. Entering *railroad NOT cars* would tell the search engine to look for pages that include *railroad* but not the term *cars*. In some search engines, the minus sign (-) can be used instead of the word *NOT*. |

**What is an advanced search?** Many search engines provide ways to make your searches more precise and obtain more useful results. You might be able to use advanced search options to limit your search to material written in a specific language or stored in a specific file format. You might be able to specify a date, eliminate results from adult sites, and stipulate whether to look for your search terms in the title, URL, or body of the Web page (Figure 7-23).

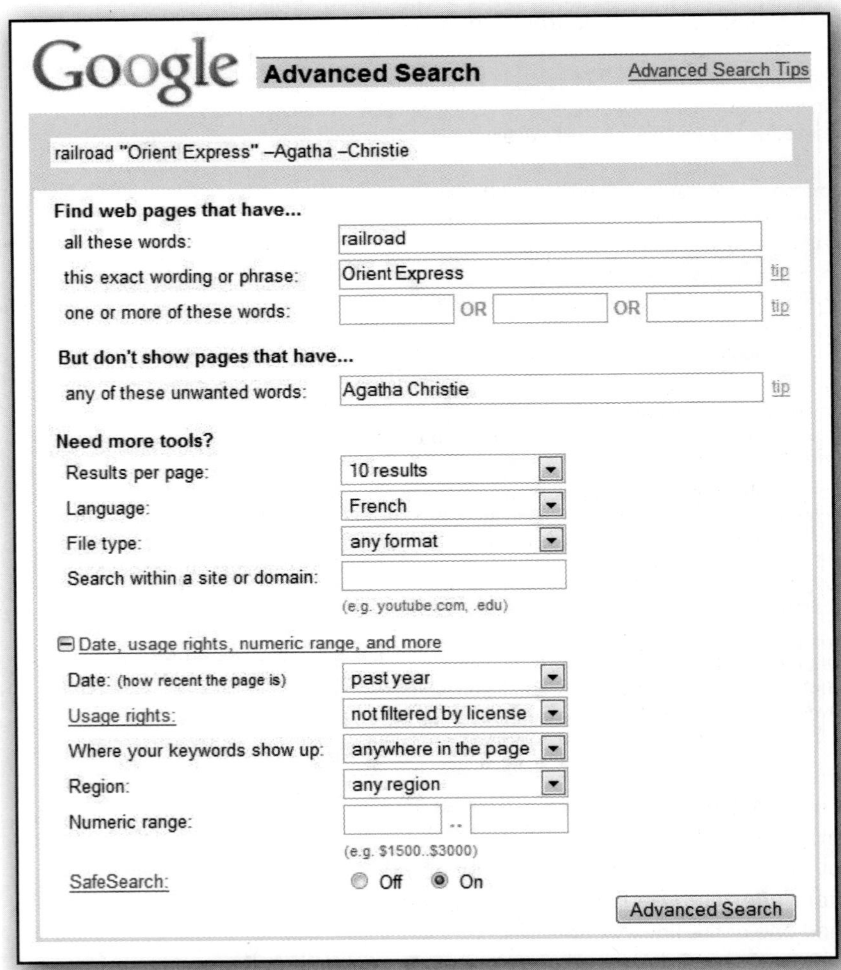

**FIGURE 7-23**

Many search engines provide forms designed to enhance the search process. These forms are usually accessible by clicking an Advanced Search link, which is located on the main page of the search engine Web site.

Some search engine sites offer separate searches for academic works, images, videos, news, e-commerce merchandise, and blogs. Look for links to these specialized searches at your favorite search engine sites.

In addition to using search engines, you can also find Web-based information using a **metasearch engine** that searches a series of other search engines and compiles the search results. Popular metasearch sites include *www.polymeta.com*, *www.dogpile.com*, and *webcrawler.com*.

**Do search engines keep records of my queries?** Considering that a major search engine can receive upward of 100 million queries every day, the surprising answer to this question is "yes." Search engines at major sites such as Google, AOL, MSN, Bing, and Yahoo! save massive numbers of searches made by site visitors. Although most search sites do not specify how long this information is retained, industry analysts believe that some sites retain it for at least 30 days, and perhaps at least one search engine site has retained every search ever made at the site.

Privacy advocates question the wisdom of search engines retaining queries. They find difficulty in identifying any beneficial uses for such data and fear that it is of potential benefit only to marketing companies. Although the privacy policies of major search sites claim to protect personal information, in 2006, AOL released a database of 20 million queries collected by its search engine. The database was released publicly and online, ostensibly to help academic researchers.

A few months earlier, the U.S. Department of Justice requested query databases from all major search engines in conjunction with a crackdown on Internet child pornography. Some search engine operators complied, whereas others did not. Anyone who uses search engines should be aware that the content of their searches could become public.

**What kind of information does a search engine store?** Although your queries do not contain your name, you are assigned a unique ID number that is stored in a cookie on your computer. In addition to storing an ID number, search engines store the IP address from which the query was initiated, the date and time of the query, the search terms, and URLs for any Web sites linked to from the results list (Figure 7-24).

**FIGURE 7-24**

A database of 20 million AOL queries is still available to the public. You can use it to get a glimpse of the wide range of human interests and also understand how valuable such data can be to marketers. For example, many people, including user 1404131, entered queries about mountain bikes. From the database you could also discover other queries made by this user.

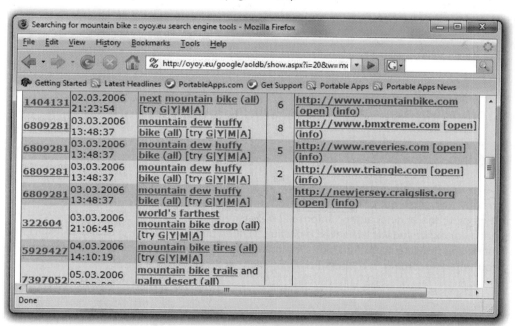

**What can I do to keep my searches confidential?** Your search-engine-assigned ID number is stored in a cookie and remains the same as long as the cookie remains on your computer. If you frequently delete your cookies as explained in Section E, a search engine's query database is unlikely to collect enough information to link back to you.

You can block cookies from a specific search engine site, and that setting will force the search engine to assign a different ID number to you for each session. You can also download and use a cookie anonymizer that sets your Google ID number to 0.

Anonymizer sites, such as *www.torproject.org*, act as relay stations to forward your searches to Google or other search engines without leaving a trail back to a cookie or IP address. These sites claim to delete all activity logs every day or two, but they are the subject of law enforcement scrutiny.

7

## CITING WEB-BASED SOURCE MATERIAL

**Can I copy text and graphics that I find on Web pages?** Most browsers provide a Copy command that allows you to copy a section of text from a Web page, which you can then paste into one of your own documents. To keep track of the source for each text section, you can highlight the Web page's URL in the Address box, use the Copy command, and then paste the URL into your document (Figure 7-25).

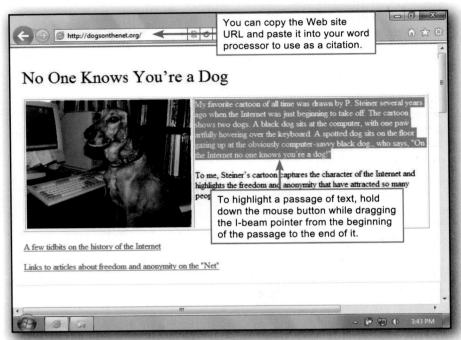

**FIGURE 7-25**

To copy a passage of text from a Web page, high-light the text, right-click it, then select Copy. Next, switch to your own docu-ment and use the Paste option. ▶ For a demon-stration of this process, go to your digital textbook.

**How do I cite sources?** Presenting someone else's work as your own is plagiarism. If you copy text, pictures, or other works from a Web page, make sure you give credit to the original author. Information that identifies the source of a quotation or excerpted work is called a citation. Written doc-uments, such as reports and projects, typically include footnotes, endnotes, or in-line citations formatted according to a standard style, such as those listed in Figure 7-26.

**FIGURE 7-26**

You can follow one of the styles shown to format citations for Web pages.

### Chicago Style and Turabian Style

**Lastname, Firstname. "Title of Web Page."** *Publishing Organization or Name of Web Site.* **Publication date if available. URL.**

**Jones, Edison. "Adventures in Electricity."** *Electric Resources.* **2011. http://www.electricresources.org/electricity/adventures.html.**

### MLA Style

**Lastname, Firstname. "Title of Web Page."** *Name of Site or Online Publication.* **Version number, posting date, volume or issue number if avail-able. Page number. Method of access. Date you accessed material.**

**Jones, Edison. "Adventures in Electricity."** *Electric Resources.* **Web. January 18, 2012.**

### APA Style

**Lastname, Firstname. (Date of publication).** *Title of Web page or document.* **Retrieved from URL.**

**Jones, Edison. (2011).** *Adventures in Electricity.* **Retrieved from http://www.electricresources.org/electricity/adventures.html.**

When compiling the citation for online sources, be sure to provide sufficient information so readers can locate the source. Also, include the date when you accessed the source and the full URL. According to APA style, a citation to a Web-based source should provide a document title or description; author name if available; the date of publication, update, or retrieval; and a URL.

**Do I need permission to use material?** In the United States, a fair use doctrine allows limited use of copyrighted material for scholarship and review without obtaining permission. For scholarly reports and projects, for example, you can use a sentence or paragraph of text without obtaining permission if you include a citation to the original source. Photos and excerpts from music and videos can be used within the context of critique, but their use purely as decorative elements for a document would, in most cases, not be considered fair use.

Some Web sites clearly state allowable uses for material on the site. Look for a link to Terms of Use. For example, the YouTube Web site contains a collection of videos submitted by amateurs and semi-professionals, who retain the copyright to their materials. The Terms of Use section of the site allows the public to access, use, reproduce, distribute, create derivatives of, display, and perform user-submitted works. Even with such broad terms of use, however, it is essential to cite the original source of the material if you incorporate it in your own work.

**How do I get permission?** To obtain permission to use text, photos, music, videos, and other elements you find on the Web, contact the copyright holder by e-mail, and explain what you want to use and how you plan to use it. You can usually find contact information on the Web site, if not for the copyright holder, at least for a Web master who can direct you to the copyright holder.

7

# QuickCheck

1. A search engine's [_____] pulls keywords from a Web page and stores them in a database.

2. When you enter search terms, the search engine's [_____] processor looks for the terms in the search engine's database.

3. *AND* is an example of a(n) [_____] operator, also referred to as a search operator.

4. Most search engines keep track of users by assigning a unique ID number, which is stored in a(n) [_____] on the hard disk of the user's computer.

5. To keep track of the Web pages where you obtained information or images, you can highlight the Web page's [_____], copy it, and then paste it into a list of sources. (Hint: Use the acronym.)

▶ CHECK ANSWERS

# E-commerce

ONE OF THE MOST POPULAR activities on the Web is shopping. Online shopping has the same allure as catalogs—you can shop at your leisure, anonymously, and in your pajamas. But the economics of the Web provide opportunities that go beyond retail catalogs. The Internet was opened to commercial use in 1991. Since then, millions of businesses have set up shop at Web sites. This section of the chapter focuses on e-commerce and the technologies a typical shopper might encounter on the Web.

## E-COMMERCE BASICS

**What is e-commerce?** Although the experts don't always agree on its definition, the term **e-commerce** typically refers to business transactions that are conducted electronically over a computer network. It encompasses all aspects of business and marketing processes enabled by Internet and Web technologies.

E-commerce wares include many kinds of physical products, digital products, and services. Physical products offered at e-commerce sites include such goods as clothing, shoes, skateboards, and cars. Most of these products can be shipped to buyers through the postal service, a parcel delivery service, or a trucking company.

Increasingly, e-commerce goods include digital products, such as news, music, video, databases, software, and all types of knowledge-based items. The unique feature of these products is that they can be transformed into bits and delivered over the Web. Consumers can get them immediately upon completing their orders, and no one pays shipping costs.

E-commerce merchants also peddle services, such as online medical consultation, distance education, or custom sewing. Some of these services can be carried out by computers. Others require human agents. Services can be delivered electronically, as in the case of a distance education course, or they might produce some physical product, such as a custom-fit boat cover.

**What are the most common e-commerce business models?** Many e-commerce activities are classified as **B2C** (business-to-consumer) in which individual consumers purchase goods and services from online merchants. **C2C** (consumer-to-consumer) is another popular e-commerce model, in which consumers sell to each other at popular online auctions. **B2B** (business-to-business) e-commerce involves one enterprise buying goods or services from another enterprise. **B2G** (business-to-government) e-commerce aims to help businesses sell to governments. Figure 7-27 lists some popular B2C and C2C activities.

**Is e-commerce more profitable than offline business?** E-commerce enhances traditional business models by offering efficiency and opportunities for automation, computerization, and digitization. As with a traditional brick-and-mortar business, profit in an e-commerce business is the difference between income and expenses.

**FIGURE 7-27**

B2C and C2C e-commerce offer consumers many types of goods and services.

Online storefronts sell a variety of goods, such as clothing, books, toys, music, food, sports gear, and electronics.

Online auctions provide consumers with a worldwide market for antiques, collectibles, and other new and used items.

Online schools offer credit and noncredit courses, tutorials, and even college degrees.

Online ticket and reservation systems provide concert and event tickets plus air, hotel, and car reservations.

Online information services sell subscriptions to news archives, databases, and online magazines.

One of the advantages of e-commerce is its ability to increase profit margins by cutting costs. For example, a typical catalog order placed over the phone costs the merchant $2.50, whereas an online transaction costs about 35 cents. A hotel reservation made online costs the innkeeper 80% less than a booking by phone. A withdrawal or deposit costs a bank about a dollar when handled by a teller, about 25 cents on an ATM, and only a penny on the Web.

E-commerce merchants also gain income by hosting advertising space for marketers, who are creating increasingly hard-to-avoid styles of online advertisements, such as banner and pop-up ads. A **banner ad** is an advertisement, typically embedded at the top of a Web page. A **hover ad** overlays the content on a Web page, sometimes obscuring it until you click the ad or its timer expires and the ad disappears. A **pop-up ad**, such as the one in Figure 7-28, is an advertisement that appears in a separate window when you connect to a Web page. If you click a banner, hover, or pop-up ad, your browser connects directly to the advertiser's Web site, where you can find product information and make a purchase.

**FIGURE 7-28**

Pop-up ads appear as separate windows.

Banner, hover, and pop-up ads earn revenue for hosting merchants based on the **click-through rate**—the number of times that site visitors click the ad to connect to the advertiser's site. The hosting merchant is paid a small fee for each click through. Click-through rates have declined in recent years because most consumers simply ignore ads or install **ad-blocking software** to prevent ads from appearing on their screens. Recent versions of most browsers include a configurable feature to block pop-up ads.

**Who benefits from e-commerce?** Both merchants and consumers benefit from e-commerce because niche goods and small merchants can reach a global customer base. At online music shops and bookstores, for example, you can find obscure titles and alternative music that brick-and-mortar merchants haven't the space or inclination to stock.

Merchants are always looking for ways to attract customers. The Web and its search engines give small merchants without a budget for national advertising a way to be found by customers. When you're looking for hand-made chainmail, for example, you're unlikely to find it at your local Walmart, but chances are good that you can find a chainmail merchant on the Web.

**Is e-commerce popular worldwide?** North America accounts for about half of all e-commerce activity, and Western Europe and Asian Pacific regions account for most of the rest. The low volume of e-commerce activity in Africa, Eastern Europe, and Russia can be attributed to several factors, including lack of Internet access, language barriers, depressed economies, shipping limitations, and merchant policies.

**FIGURE 7-29**

In some regions of the world, e-commerce obstacles include language barriers, economic factors, and even lack of electrical service.

The original e-commerce model was aimed at English speakers with Internet access and a credit card issued by a U.S. bank. Today, an increasing number of e-commerce Web sites serve regional populations using local languages and payment options. In regions where electricity and telephone service are scarce, however, online shopping is rare because Internet access can be problematic (Figure 7-29) and merchandise priced for international markets is too expensive.

## E-COMMERCE SITE TECHNOLOGY

**What makes online shopping so special?** E-commerce offers some unique advantages over brick-and-mortar stores and mail-order catalogs. Customers can easily search for specific merchandise. They can configure products online, see actual prices, and build an order over several days.

E-commerce customers can easily compare prices among multiple vendors using Web sites such as BizRate, NexTag, and PriceGrabber. They can also read professional and consumer reviews at sites like Epinions and ConsumerReports.org.

E-commerce seems simple from the perspective of a shopper who connects to an online store, browses the electronic catalog, selects merchandise, and then pays for it. Behind the scenes, an e-commerce site uses several technologies to display merchandise, keep track of shoppers' selections, collect payment data, protect customers' privacy, and prevent credit card numbers from falling into the wrong hands.

**Are there different e-commerce models?** There are two popular models for e-commerce stores. The first is the B2C model pioneered by Amazon.com. The second is the C2C model represented by online auction sites such as eBay, and online classified advertisement sites such as Craigslist.

**What are the important elements of a B2C e-commerce site?** B2C sites are typically operated by a single merchant. The business has an inventory of products, such as DVDs, books, clothing, and other merchandise. A key element of this model is that the inventory is usually quite large and contains multiple quantities of each item; for example, Amazon's inventory includes huge quantities of *Avatar* DVDs. Customers can select several items from the inventory by placing them in shopping carts.

**How is a B2C inventory stored?** The inventory for a B2C store can be quite large and it would be impractical to create individual Web pages for each item. Instead, inventory items, along with their prices and descriptions, are entered into a database. When you browse through the merchandise at an online store, the site's Web servers and database servers interact to pull information from the database and convert it to Web pages that can be displayed in a browser.

When you view products at a large-scale B2C site, the product pages have been produced on the fly by server-side CGI, PHP, or ASP scripts. The next time you shop online, pay attention to the Address bar of your browser. When product pages are displayed, you'll probably see a ? symbol somewhere in the URL, and the URL might also include *cgi*, *php*, or *asp*, all indicating the Web page you're viewing was assembled by a server-side script from the information in a database (Figure 7-30).

**FIGURE 7-30**

Product pages that contain a ? symbol are constructed from a database on the fly by server-side scripts.

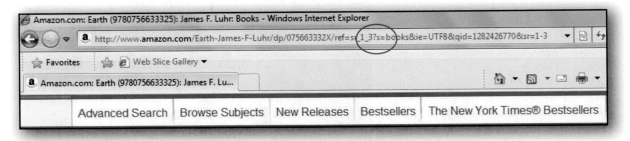

**How do shopping carts work?** If you've done any shopping online, you've probably used an **online shopping cart**—a cyberspace version of the metal cart you wheel around a store and fill up with merchandise.

As mentioned earlier, HTTP is a stateless protocol, which maintains no record of your browser's previous interactions and handles each browser request based entirely on information that comes with it. Under these circumstances, you might wonder how it is possible for an online retail store to remember the items you put in your shopping cart.

Most shopping carts work because they use cookies to store information about your activities on a Web site. Cookies work with shopping carts in one of two ways, depending on the e-commerce site. An e-commerce site might use cookies as a storage bin for all the items you load into your shopping cart, as shown in Figure 7-31.

**FIGURE 7-31**

Shopping cart items can be stored in a cookie.

**1.** When you click the Add to Cart button, the merchant's server sends a message to your browser to add that item number to the cookie, which is stored on your computer.

ITEM #B7655

**2.** When you check out, the server asks your browser for all the cookie data that pertains to your shopping cart items.

**3.** Your browser sends those cookies along with a request for an order summary.

**Your order:**

1 Blender  $29.95

1 Wok      $38.49

**4.** The Web server uses the cookies to look up products in its database and produce a Web page listing the items you want to purchase.

**FIGURE 7-32**

Shopping cart items can be stored in a server-side database.

Some e-commerce sites use cookies simply as a way to uniquely identify each shopper. These sites generate a unique ID number that is stored along with your item selections in a server-side database (Figure 7-32).

**1.** When you connect to a merchant's site, the server assigns you a unique shopping cart ID number and sends it to your browser in a cookie.

**WEB SERVER**

CART # 2098-2

**DATABASE**

CART # 2098-2

ITEM # B7655

**3.** The Web server stores this number and your merchandise selection in the merchant's server-side database.

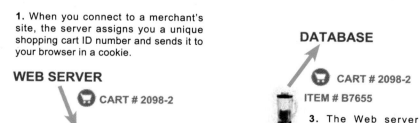

**WEB SERVER**

CART # 2098-2

**2.** When you select an item to purchase, your browser reads your shopping cart ID number from the cookie, and then sends this number to the merchant's Web server.

**Order for CART #2098-2**

1 Blender   B7655      $29.95

1 Wok       GJK4-31    $38.49

**4.** When you check out, your browser sends your shopping cart number to the server, which retrieves all your selections from the merchant's database.

7

**How do C2C sites work?** At C2C auction and online classified advertising e-commerce sites, consumers offer goods and services to other consumers. The key characteristic of C2C sites is that the merchandise is typically individual items, such as a used boat, a collectible stuffed bear, or an antique flower vase. Each item is unique and sellers individually enter information that becomes the product Web page.

C2C sites are hosted by an e-commerce provider such as eBay or Craigslist. The host site typically offers tools for sellers to auction or sell items. Sellers are provided with a way to enter item descriptions, prices, and photos. They might also be provided with tools to track bids, purchases, and other activity. Buyers are provided with tools to locate products and contact sellers with questions. Host sites might also maintain ratings for buyers and sellers to help participants avoid shady deals.

**How do sellers enter product information?** Sellers typically enter product information by filling in an online form and uploading photos as shown in Figure 7-33.

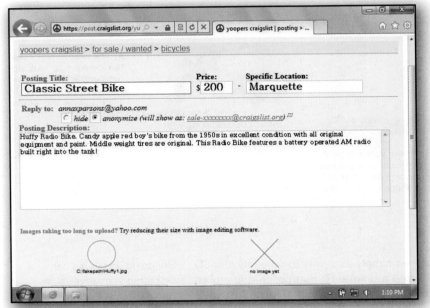

FIGURE 7-33

Craigslist provides a form for entering product descriptions and photos.

**How is product data stored?** Product data is stored in a database at the host site in much the same way as product data is stored at a B2C e-commerce site. Shoppers can enter queries to locate products from the database (Figure 7-34); matching descriptions and photos are retrieved and displayed as Web pages.

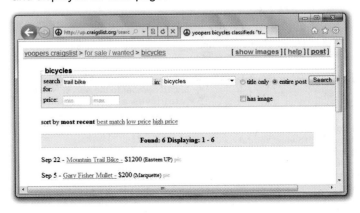

FIGURE 7-34

Buyers can find products by entering search terms.

**How do buyers contact sellers?** Another key characteristic of a C2C site is that buyers interact directly with individual sellers; so if you purchase a used boat advertised on Craigslist, you'll likely be interacting with a different seller than when you purchase an antique vase. C2C sites have to provide a way for buyers and sellers to interact while protecting the privacy of both parties.

Typically, a C2C site uses e-mail forwarding to protect participants' privacy. When you register for an account with a C2C host, it includes e-mail services based on your user ID. Your e-commerce correspondence is forwarded from that account to your regular e-mail account, which effectively hides your real name and e-mail address from the buyers or sellers you work with at the C2C site (Figure 7-35).

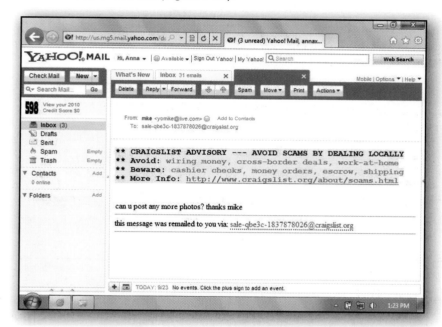

**FIGURE 7-35**

Communication between sellers and buyers is mediated through protected e-mail forwarding provided by the C2C host provider.

## ONLINE PAYMENT

**How can I pay for merchandise from online shopping and auction sites?** The most popular ways to make online payments include submitting your credit card number directly to a merchant and using a third-party payment service such as PayPal. Online wallets and one-time-use credit card numbers offer additional online payment options.

**Is it safe to use my credit card online?** Online shoppers are justifiably worried that personal information and credit card numbers supplied in the course of an e-commerce transaction might be hijacked and used inappropriately. Many shoppers worry that hackers might use packet sniffers to intercept credit card numbers traveling over the Internet.

To protect your credit card from packet sniffers, you should engage in electronic transactions only over a secure connection. A **secure connection** encrypts the data transmitted between your computer and a Web site. Even if a hacker can capture the packets containing payment data, your encrypted credit card number is virtually useless for illicit purposes. Technologies that create secure connections include SSL, TLS, and S-HTTP.

TERMINOLOGY NOTE

Secure connections differ from secure Web sites. A secure connection encrypts the data transmitted between your computer and a Web site. A secure Web site, such as an online banking site, uses password security to prevent unauthorized access to pages on the site.

7

**What are SSL and TLS?** **SSL** (Secure Sockets Layer) and its successor **TLS** (Transport Layer Security) are protocols that encrypt data traveling between a client computer and an HTTP server. These encryption protocols create a secure connection using a specially designated port—typically port 443 rather than port 80, which is used for unsecured HTTP communication. Web pages that provide a secure connection start with https: instead of http:.

**What is S-HTTP?** **S-HTTP** (secure HTTP) is an extension of HTTP that simply encrypts the text of an HTTP message before it is sent. Although SSL and S-HTTP both use encryption techniques to securely transmit data, they are technically different. Whereas SSL creates a secure connection between a client and a server over which any amount of data can be sent securely, S-HTTP is simply designed to encrypt and then transmit an individual message.

**How do I know if a connection is secure?** Your browser helps you identify when you are using a secure connection. Figure 7-36 explains.

**INFOWEBLINKS**

Connect to the **Safeguarding Your Credit Card InfoWeb** for tips on this important aspect of e-commerce.

 CLICK TO CONNECT
www.infoweblinks.com/np2012/ch07

FIGURE 7-36

Look for https or a padlock icon to ensure you have a secure connection.

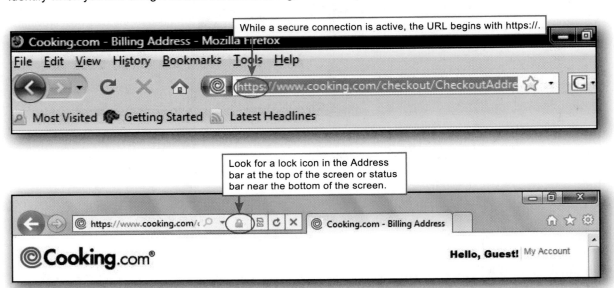

**What is a person-to-person payment?** A **person-to-person payment** (sometimes called a P2P payment, an online payment, or a third-party payment) offers an alternative to credit cards. It can be used to pay for online auction items and to wire money over the Internet. The online service called PayPal, now owned by eBay, pioneered person-to-person payments. PayPal's model has since been copied by several other service providers.

**How does a person-to-person payment work?** The process begins when you open an account at a person-to-person payment service. Some services require you to deposit money in your account—just as though you were opening a bank account. Other services allow you to supply your credit card number or bank account number, which is billed or debited only as you make purchases. You receive a user ID and password that enable you to access your account to make purchases and deposit additional funds. Money can be sent to anyone who has an e-mail account, as shown in Figure 7-37.

**1.** To use a person-to-person payment service, simply log in to your account, enter the recipient's e-mail address, and indicate the payment amount.

**2.** The recipient immediately receives an e-mail notification of your payment.

**FIGURE 7-37**

**FIGURE 7-37**

PayPal and other online payment systems offer a method for transferring funds without revealing your credit card number to the payee.

**3.** The recipient connects to the payment site to pick up the money by transferring the funds to his or her checking or payment account, requesting a check, or sending the funds to someone else.

**Is person-to-person payment safe?** The major advantage of person-to-person payments is that the payment service is the only entity that sees your credit card number—merchants, auction dealers, and other payment recipients never receive your credit card number and, therefore, can't misuse it or store it on an unsecured computer. Currently, however, the person-to-person payment industry is relatively new, and companies are still scrambling to offer secure, reliable, long-term service to customers. Consumer advocates recommend using these services with caution and keeping your account balances low.

## QuickCheck

**1.** Online auction sites such as eBay are examples of B2G e-commerce. True or false? [_____]

**2.** One factor in the e-commerce economic model is ad revenue based on [_____] rates, the number of times that site visitors click an ad to connect to the advertiser's Web site.

**3.** Most online shopping carts work because they use [_____] to store information about your activities at a Web site.

**4.** Product pages at e-commerce sites with URLs that contain a(n) [_____] symbol, cgi, php, or asp are most likely assembled by a server-side script from the information in a database.

**5.** Web sites that provide a secure connection have URLs that begin with https: instead of http:. True or false? [_____]

 CHECK ANSWERS

# E-mail

**THE INTERNET REALLY TOOK OFF** when people discovered electronic mail. More than 250 billion e-mail messages speed over the Internet each day. This section of the chapter offers background information about how e-mail works—in particular, the difference between Webmail and client-based local e-mail.

## E-MAIL OVERVIEW

**Exactly what is e-mail?** E-mail is an electronic version of the postal system that transmits messages from one computer to another, usually over the Internet. The term *e-mail* can refer to a single message or to the entire system of computers and software that transmits, receives, and stores e-mail messages. An **e-mail message** is an electronic document transmitted over a computer network.

The computers and software that provide e-mail services form an **e-mail system**. At the heart of a typical e-mail system is an **e-mail server**—a computer that essentially acts as a central post office for a group of people. E-mail servers run special e-mail server software, which provides an electronic mailbox for each person, sorts incoming messages into these mailboxes, and routes outgoing mail over the Internet to other e-mail servers.

E-mail messages have a standard format that consists of two major sections: a header and body. A **message header** is divided into fields that contain the sender's e-mail address, the recipient's address, a subject line, and the date and time the message was written. Additional fields can contain addresses for sending copies, priority levels, and tracking information. The body of an e-mail message contains the message itself and the data for any photos or supplementary files that are attached to the e-mail message. Figure 7-38 illustrates the main parts of an e-mail message.

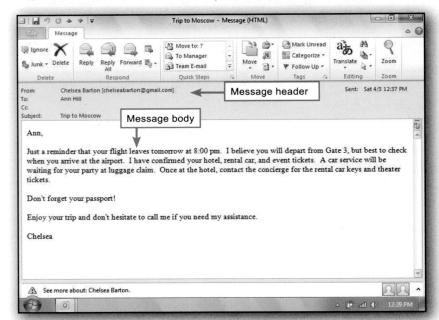

**FIGURE 7-38**

The header for an e-mail message contains Your name and e-mail address, the date, recipient addresses, the subject, and the attachment file name. The body of the e-mail message contains the message itself.

**How do I get access to e-mail?** To use an e-mail system, you need an Internet connection, an e-mail account, and software to compose e-mail messages.

Internet connection. As you learned in earlier chapters, Internet connections are available from telephone, cable, satellite, and cellular service providers. Wi-Fi hotspots and local area networks at home, school, or work can also provide Internet access. Any of these connections work for e-mail, though a dial-up connection will respond slowly when sending or receiving messages with photos or other large files attached.

E-mail account. Obtaining an **e-mail account** gets your electronic mailbox set up on an e-mail server. Your ISP typically plays the role of postmaster, sets up your e-mail account, and provides you with e-mail software. You can also obtain an e-mail account from a Webmail service, such as Hotmail, Gmail, or Yahoo!.

E-mail software. The software you use to send, receive, and manage messages is called **e-mail client software**. It is available for computers, mobile phones, and PDAs. Some e-mail software can be installed on a local device such as a computer hard disk, whereas other e-mail software can be stored as a portable app on a USB flash drive, or accessed from the Web through a browser. E-mail systems based on client software that's installed locally are referred to as **local e-mail**. Systems that provide access to e-mail through a browser are called **Webmail**.

Whether you use local e-mail or Webmail, your e-mail account has a unique **e-mail address**. Like the address on a letter, an e-mail address provides the information necessary to route messages to a specified mailbox. An e-mail address typically consists of a user ID (also called a user name), followed by the @ sign and the name of the e-mail server that manages the user's electronic post office box. For example, the e-mail address ann_smith@mtc.com refers to the e-mail account for Ann Smith on the e-mail server named mtc.com.

**How do I select an e-mail address?** In order for e-mail to be routed correctly, each e-mail address must be unique. Gmail can have only one AnnSmith user ID, which explains the existence of e-mail addresses such as AnnSmith256@gmail.com and ASmithTraverseCity@gmail.com. You can, however, use the same user ID for e-mail accounts on different servers. For example, AlexZ@msu.edu and AlexZ@hotmail.com are perfectly acceptable for a student who has e-mail accounts on a school server and at Hotmail.

E-mail addresses can sometimes tell you a bit about the person who holds the account. The first part of an e-mail address often corresponds to the account holder's name, nickname, or online persona. For example, the address cat_lover32@hotmail.com probably belongs to a person who likes cats. You should be aware of the image that e-mail addresses can project and select one that won't be embarrassing when you correspond with prospective employers.

The second part of an e-mail address is the e-mail server's domain name, which can provide information about the account holder's job or school. An account for jwatson@ibm.com probably belongs to an IBM employee. An account for rbutler@uga.edu probably belongs to a student at the University of Georgia. You can't control the server domain name, but you can establish several e-mail accounts so that your work server handles business mail and a generic provider, such as Gmail, handles your private mail.

7

## LOCAL E-MAIL

**How does local e-mail work?** When you use local e-mail, an e-mail server stores your incoming messages until you launch your e-mail client and get your mail. Messages are then downloaded to a folder on a local storage device that serves as your e-mail Inbox. This telecommunications technique is sometimes referred to as **store-and-forward**.

Using your e-mail client, you can read your mail at your leisure. You can also compose new mail and reply to messages. This outgoing mail can be temporarily stored in an Outbox or it can be sent immediately.

The protocols **POP3** (Post Office Protocol version 3) or **IMAP** (Internet Message Access Protocol) are typically used to manage your incoming mail. POP3 deletes messages from the server after they are downloaded, whereas IMAP leaves messages on the server until you specifically delete them. **SMTP** (Simple Mail Transfer Protocol) handles outgoing mail. Keep these protocols in mind when setting up local e-mail because the server you specify for outgoing mail might be different than the server for incoming mail (Figure 7-39).

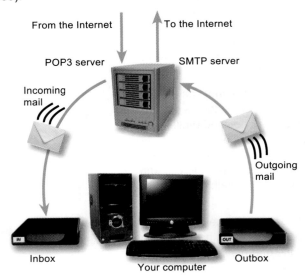

From the Internet   To the Internet

POP3 server   SMTP server

Incoming mail   Outgoing mail

Inbox   Your computer   Outbox

**FIGURE 7-39**

Outgoing mail can be stored in your Outbox until you connect to the Internet and send it. Incoming mail can be stored on a POP3 server until it is downloaded to the Inbox on your hard disk.

**What are the advantages of local e-mail?** Because local e-mail stores your Inbox and Outbox on your computer, you can compose and read mail offline. You are required to go online only to transfer outgoing mail from your Inbox to the e-mail server, and to receive incoming messages. On a slow dial-up connection or in situations where you are charged for dial-up service by the minute, local e-mail might be preferable to Webmail.

Local e-mail also works well with broadband always-on connections, such as DSL, cable Internet, or satellite Internet. When using these connections, you can remain online throughout the entire process of collecting, reading, and sending mail. By configuring your e-mail client to send messages immediately, messages can be sent as they are composed instead of remaining in your Outbox and being sent as a batch.

The major advantage of local e-mail is control. Once your messages are transferred to your computer's hard disk, you can control access to them. With this control, however, comes the responsibility for maintaining backups of your important e-mail messages.

**How do I set up local e-mail?** To set up local e-mail, the first step is selecting a local e-mail client. Microsoft Outlook is one of the most popular e-mail clients. Its pared down cousin, Windows Live Mail, can be downloaded for free as part of the Windows Live Essentials suite. Thunderbird, a free open source e-mail client, is another popular alternative, and several other very serviceable e-mail clients are available as shareware.

After installing an e-mail client, you can configure it for the e-mail service you're using. Your e-mail provider usually supplies the information needed for this task. That information can include the following:

- Your e-mail user ID, which is the first part of your e-mail address (for example, in AlexHamilton@gsu.edu, the user ID is AlexHamilton)

- Your e-mail password, if required to access the e-mail server

- An address for the outgoing (SMTP) server, typically something like *mail.viserver.net* or *smtp.mailisus.com*

- An address for the incoming (POP3) server, typically something like *mail.gsu.edu* or *pop.mailserver.net*

- Port numbers for incoming and outgoing servers, which are usually Port 110 (incoming) and Port 25 or 587 (outgoing)

- Whether the servers require secure authentication

- The type of connection security used by the servers: STARTTLS or SSL/TLS

To configure a local e-mail client such as Thunderbird, look for an Account Settings option on the Tools menu. When using Microsoft Outlook 2010, click the File tab and then click the Add Account button (Figure 7-40).

**FIGURE 7-40**

When configuring local e-mail, the incoming and outgoing servers might require different settings. ▶ This figure in your digital textbook guides you through the process of configuring a local e-mail account.

7

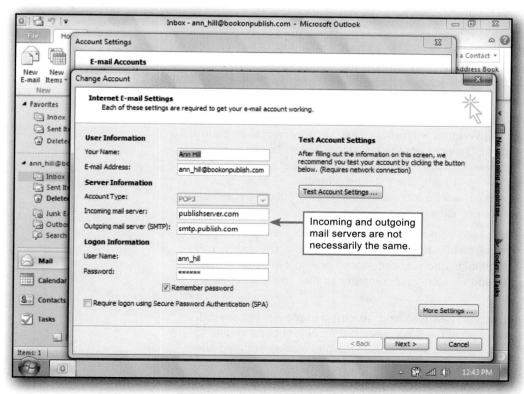

## WEBMAIL

**How does Webmail work?** Webmail is typically a free service accessed using a browser. Most Webmail services also can be accessed using a local e-mail client, such as Microsoft Outlook, if you prefer a local client's feature set and do not want to remain online while reading and composing messages.

In a classic Webmail configuration, your Inbox is stored on the Web; and because messages are sent immediately, an Outbox is not needed. When you want to read or send mail, use a browser to go to your e-mail provider's Web site and log in. The controls for reading, composing, and managing messages are all presented in the browser window. While reading and composing mail, you typically must remain online. Figure 7-41 illustrates how a Webmail system works.

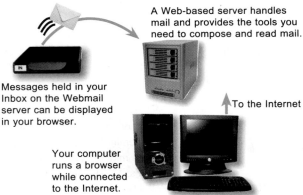

A Web-based server handles mail and provides the tools you need to compose and read mail.

Messages held in your Inbox on the Webmail server can be displayed in your browser.

To the Internet

Your computer runs a browser while connected to the Internet.

**FIGURE 7-41**

The key characteristic of Webmail is that your messages remain on the Web server, rather than being downloaded to your computer.

**What are the pros and cons of Webmail?** Webmail is ideal for people who travel because accounts can be accessed from any computer connected to the Internet. Accessing e-mail from a public computer can be a security risk, however. If possible, reboot the computer before logging into your e-mail account. Avoid entering sensitive information, such as your credit card number, in case your keystrokes are being monitored by malicious software lurking on the public computer. Be sure to log off when your session is finished. Log out of Windows and shut down the computer if you are allowed to do so.

Even when accessing Webmail from your home, security can be an issue. Unfortunately, Webmail services are the target of many malicious exploits, which can work their way into your computer through various security holes. When using Webmail, your computer must be protected by security software, and your computer will be more secure if you log out of your e-mail account when you are not using it.

Webmail can be accessed from mobile devices when your computer is not handy. If you opt to use mobile mail, read the options offered by your e-mail service provider and make sure you understand how to sync your mobile e-mail with the mail you view on your computer so that you don't miss an important message.

Free Webmail is supported by advertising, so expect to see advertisements. Today's sophisticated ad servers can search the content of an incoming message looking for keywords and then use them to display targeted ads in your e-mail window. For example, suppose you receive an e-mail message about a trip to Moscow. When viewing the message, you'll also be presented with ads about Moscow hotels, flights to Moscow, and similar promotions. Some Webmail services offer an ad-free option for a monthly fee.

**How do I get a Webmail account?** Getting a Webmail account is an automated process that you can complete online. Begin by using a browser to access a Webmail site such as *www.gmail.com*, *www.hotmail.com*, or *www.yahoomail.com*. Selecting the Sign Up or Register option produces an on-screen form. When you submit the completed form, your e-mail account is created and ready for immediate use (Figure 7-42).

**FIGURE 7-42**

You can use a browser to access your Webmail account. ▶ This figure in your digital textbook takes you on a tour of Gmail.

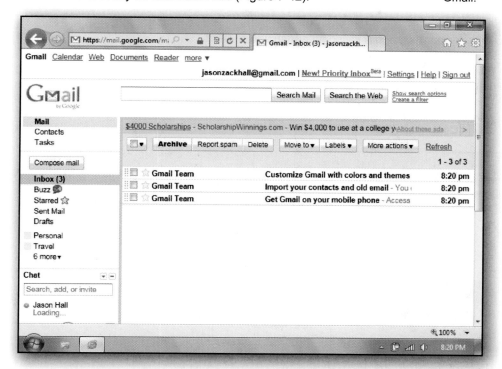

**Is Webmail the same as HTML mail?** No. **HTML mail** is a term used for e-mail messages containing HTML tags that produce bold, italic, and underlined text, fancy fonts, embedded graphics, and various font sizes. Most e-mail software offers a setting for choosing HTML or plain, unformatted ASCII text.

You should be aware that HTML formatted e-mail messages can distribute viruses and open security holes that leave your computer vulnerable to hackers. When working with HTML mail, make sure your antivirus software is checking incoming messages. Figure 7-43 illustrates an e-mail message written in HTML format.

**FIGURE 7-43**

An e-mail message in HTML format can include graphics in addition to a variety of fonts and font colors.

The text in HTML mail can be formatted using a selection of fonts, font sizes, colors, and other attributes.

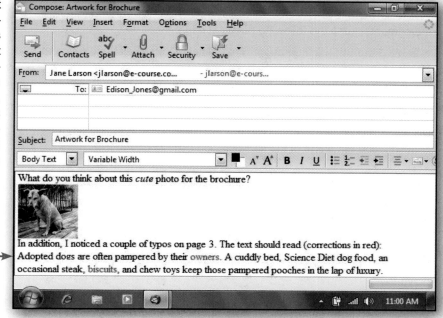

7

## E-MAIL ATTACHMENTS

**What is an e-mail attachment?** Originally, e-mail messages were stored in a plain and simple format called ASCII text. No fancy formatting was allowed—no variation in font type or color, no underlining or boldface, and, of course, no pictures or sounds. Although you cannot insert a digital photo or sound file into a plain ASCII e-mail message, you can send these kinds of files as e-mail attachments.

Any file that travels with an e-mail message is called an **e-mail attachment**. A conversion process called **MIME** (Multi-Purpose Internet Mail Extensions) provides a clever way of disguising digital photos, sounds, and other media as plain ASCII code that can travel over the Internet with text-based e-mail data. An electronic message incorporated in the e-mail header provides your e-mail software with information that allows it to reconstruct the attachment into its original form (Figure 7-44).

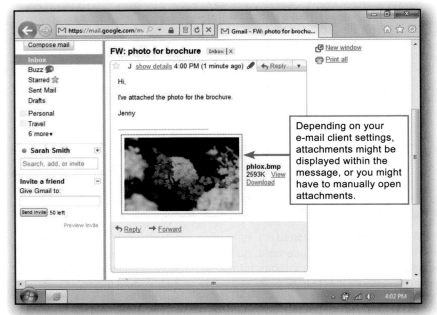

**FIGURE 7-44**

Attachments ride along with e-mail messages. ▶ For more tips about attachments, refer to this figure in your digital textbook.

**What should I know about attachments?** When working with attachments, keep the following points in mind:

- Don't send huge attachments. Try to limit the size of attachments to 50 KB or less for recipients who have dial-up connections. If necessary, use a compression program, such as WinZip, to shrink the attachment.

- Explain all attachments. Attachments can harbor computer viruses. To determine whether an attachment is legitimate, your correspondents will want to know the file name of the attachment, what the attachment contains, and the name of the software you used to create it.

- Don't open suspicious attachments. If an attachment arrives from an unknown source, don't open it because it might contain a virus.

- You can save attachments. By right-clicking an attachment, you can usually save it as a separate file.

- You might have to download a plug-in or player. Attachments can contain text, music, video, and other types of files stored in a variety of file formats. To open some files, you might need to download a plug-in or player.

## NETIQUETTE

**Is e-mail different from other types of communication?** In some respects, e-mail is similar to an old-fashioned letter because its message is conveyed without benefit of the facial expressions, voice inflections, and body gestures that accompany face-to-face conversations. When composing a message, it is important to carefully consider your audience and the message you want to convey.

By understanding netiquette, you can avoid some of the pitfalls and problems of e-mail communications. **Netiquette** is online jargon for Internet etiquette. It is a series of customs or guidelines for maintaining civilized and effective communications in online discussions and e-mail exchanges (Figure 7-45).

**INFOWEBLINKS**

You can read more about netiquette, smileys, and text messaging shorthand at the **Netiquette InfoWeb**.

 CLICK TO CONNECT
www.infoweblinks.com/np2012/ch07

**FIGURE 7-45**

Principles of Netiquette

Put a meaningful title on the subject line. The subject line of your message should clearly describe the contents of your e-mail message.

Use uppercase and lowercase letters. An e-mail message that's typed in all uppercase means that you're shouting.

Check spelling. Most e-mail software offers a Check Spelling command. Use it.

Be careful what you send. E-mail is not private, nor is it secure. Treat your messages as though they are postcards that can be read by anyone. Remember that all laws governing copyright, slander, and discrimination apply to e-mail.

Be polite. Avoid wording that could sound inflammatory or argumentative. If you would not say it face-to-face, don't say it in e-mail.

Be cautious when using sarcasm and humor. The words in your e-mail arrive without facial expressions or voice intonations, so a sarcastic comment can easily be misinterpreted.

Notify recipients of viruses. If you discover that your computer sent out infected attachments, use antivirus software to remove the virus, and then notify anyone to whom you recently sent mail.

Use smileys and text messaging shorthand cautiously. **Smileys** are symbols such as :-) that represent emotions. They can help convey the intent behind your words, but use them only in casual messages.

Use the Bcc function for group mailings. By placing e-mail addresses for secondary recipients in the Bcc box, the recipients of your message won't have to scroll through a long list of addresses before reaching the meat of your message.

Don't send replies to all recipients. Use the Reply All command only when there is a very specific need for everyone listed in the To, Cc, and Bcc boxes to receive the message.

7

## QuickCheck                                                                          SECTION D

1. The _____ of an e-mail message contains recipient addresses, the subject line, and the file names of any e-mail attachments.

2. For most client-based e-mail systems, a(n) _____ server handles outgoing mail, and a(n) _____ server or an IMAP server handles incoming mail. (Hint: Use the acronyms.)

3. HTML mail is the same as Webmail. True or false? _____

4. E-mail attachments are encoded in _____ format. (Hint: Use the acronym.)

5. The rules and suggestions regarding electronic communications such as e-mail are referred to as _____.

▶ CHECK ANSWERS

# Web and E-mail Security

**THE WEB AND E-MAIL** abound with spam and scams engineered to monitor your online activities and collect confidential information, such as credit card numbers, passwords, and bank account numbers. You were introduced to spyware in an earlier chapter. Now you'll learn about specific spam and spyware exploits, and find out how to minimize the risk they pose to computer security and your privacy.

## COOKIE EXPLOITS

**Can cookies be a security risk?** Cookies have built-in safeguards designed to reduce their abuse, but marketers, hackers, and pranksters have discovered loopholes that twist cookies to serve the dark side. One of the most prevalent cookie exploits involves ad-serving cookies, and Flash cookies pose another potential threat.

**What is an ad-serving cookie?** When you connect to a Web site, you expect it to store an innocuous cookie on your computer's hard disk. Some Web sites, however, feature banner ads supplied by third-party marketing firms. If you click the ad, this third party can surreptitiously create an ad-serving cookie and use it to track your activities at any site containing banner ads from that third party.

The marketing firms that distribute **ad-serving cookies** claim that the data in their cookies is used simply to select and display ads that might interest you, but privacy advocates worry that shopper profiles can be compiled, sold, and used for unauthorized purposes. Figure 7-46 illustrates how third parties use ad-serving cookies.

**FIGURE 7-46**

Third-party ad-serving cookies make it possible for marketers and hackers to track your Internet activities across sites.

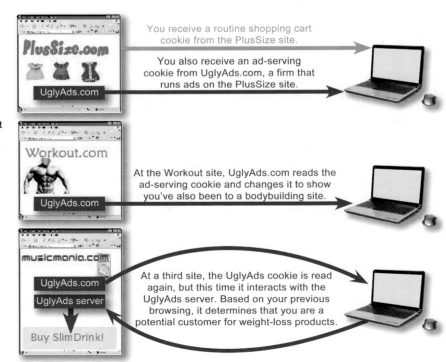

1 You purchase a birthday gift for a friend at PlusSize.com.

You receive a routine shopping cart cookie from the PlusSize site.

You also receive an ad-serving cookie from UglyAds.com, a firm that runs ads on the PlusSize site.

2 You're working on a report about the cardiovascular system for a biology class and mistakenly end up at a bodybuilding site.

At the Workout site, UglyAds.com reads the ad-serving cookie and changes it to show you've also been to a bodybuilding site.

3 Many e-commerce sites you now visit display banner ads for weight-loss products.

At a third site, the UglyAds cookie is read again, but this time it interacts with the UglyAds server. Based on your previous browsing, it determines that you are a potential customer for weight-loss products.

**Can I turn off cookies to foil ad-serving exploits?** Most browsers include security settings that block cookies. Unfortunately, on many Web sites, cookies are the only mechanism available for tracking your activity or remembering your purchases. Cookies might also be required to join distance education classes and online discussions.

If you disable cookies altogether, you might not be able to make online purchases, participate in online training classes, use Webmail, or register for premium services at search engine sites. In addition, you might have to manually enter your user ID and password every time you revisit a Web site. You won't be able to take advantage of targeted marketing, such as when a music Web site keeps track of your favorite band and notifies you when the band's new CDs are available.

Rather than block all cookies, you can block cookies from specific sites. For example, if you'd rather not have your favorite search engine compile and store your searches, you can block its cookies. Your browser might have a setting that blocks all third-party cookies to prevent ad-serving cookies from tracking your site visits (Figure 7-47).

**FIGURE 7-47**

Most browsers offer a way to turn off third-party cookies. When using Microsoft Internet Explorer, for example, you can adjust the setting using the Internet Options dialog box.

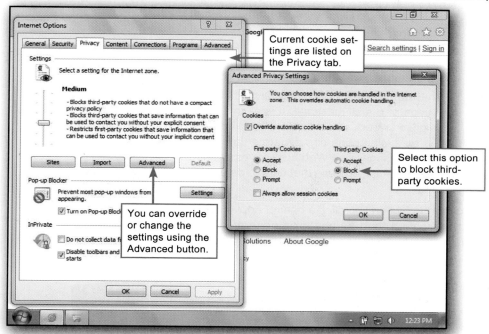

7

**Does deleting cookies reduce risk?** Some privacy advocates suggest deleting cookies periodically, rather than blocking them. By deleting cookies, you can still interact with online shopping carts and take part in other activities that require cookies, but deleted third-party cookies won't be able to communicate with their handlers. The downside of deleting cookies is it might disrupt your attempts to opt out of various cookie schemes.

An opt-out function allows you to refuse to participate in an activity or promotion. Similar to the National Do Not Call Registry, several third-party advertising companies, such as DoubleClick and ZEDO, now provide users with an opt-out mechanism to disallow ad-serving cookies. The Network Advertising Initiative (NAI) offers a tool to opt out of the targeted advertising by NAI's member firms. In most cases, however, opting out creates an opt-out cookie; and if you delete all the cookies on your computer, the opt-out cookie will also be deleted and third-party cookies will again start to accumulate.

**What is a Flash cookie?** A **Flash cookie**, also called a local shared object, is the Flash equivalent of a conventional Web cookie. Flash cookies are set and used by Adobe's Flash Player, which is installed on practically every computer to run movies, videos, and games.

In the context of running Flash animations, Flash cookies can collect and store personal data, such as the user's name or the user's progress in a game. Because so many computer users delete or block conventional cookies, some marketers now use Flash cookies as an alternative way to track and target consumers.

**Can I avoid Flash cookies?** You can manually delete Flash cookies from your computer after locating the #Shared Objects file in which they are stored. You can also visit the Adobe Flash Player Web site to adjust your computer's settings for Flash cookies. You can choose your options from the Settings Manager, which consists of several panels. The Website Privacy Settings panel lists all the Web sites that currently store information about you and allows you to set your preferences on a per-site basis.

You can also use the online Settings Manager to adjust other Flash settings. For example, you might want to prevent Flash programs from activating your computer's camera and microphone without notifying you. A tutorial for using the Settings Manager is also provided by the Web site. For added security, you can put a sticker over your computer camera when it is not in use.

**What is a Web bug?** A **Web bug** or clear GIF is typically a 1x1 pixel graphic embedded in a Web page or e-mail message. It is almost invisible due to its size, and is designed to track who's reading the Web page or e-mail message. Web bugs on a Web page can generate third-party ad-serving cookies. Junk e-mail messages use Web bugs for monitoring the number of people who view the e-mail and use that data to determine the direction of marketing campaigns.

Unlike cookies that are generated when you click a banner ad, you don't have to click anything to receive a third-party cookie generated by a Web bug. When you view a Web bug infested page, an HTTP set-cookie request automatically goes to a third-party server, which can be the site of a marketer or hacker. The site can set a cookie on your computer for later retrieval, or log the IP address of your computer.

**Is there any way to avoid Web bugs?** A drastic solution is to turn off all the graphics displayed by your browser, but that step makes the Web much less interesting. A better solution is to download a Web bug detector that works with your browser to test graphics on every Web page you visit and flag clear GIF images that might be used to set third-party cookies. Clear GIFs are also used legitimately for alignment purposes on Web pages, however, so not all clear GIFs are malware. Undesirable clear GIFs can be eliminated by Web bug detectors included in antispyware.

**Antispyware** is a type of security software designed to identify and neutralize Web bugs, ad-serving cookies, and other spyware. Antispyware such as Spy Sweeper, Ad-Aware, Spybot Search & Destroy, SpywareBlaster, and Microsoft Security Essentials can offer some degree of protection against browser parasites and other Web-based nuisances (Figure 7-48). Avoid responding to or downloading spyware from pop-up ads, however. Those ads often lead to infected software or other malware.

**FIGURE 7-48**

Antispyware is typically included in Internet security suites along with antivirus modules.

**Can I surf the Internet anonymously?** In addition to tracking cookies, Web sites can track IP addresses of computers that connect to their sites. IP addresses can sometimes be traced back to individuals, especially those who have fixed IP addresses or always-on connections that retain the same IP address for long periods of time. Individuals who prefer not to leave a trail of their Internet activities surf through an **anonymous proxy service**, which uses an intermediary, or proxy, server to relay Web page requests after masking the originating IP address (Figure 7-49).

Proxy service is similar to a VPN in some respects because they both encrypt data being sent over the Internet. An anonymous proxy service, however, is limited to use with your browser, whereas a VPN can be used with any network application. If you use a VPN, you don't need a proxy service.

A tradeoff to the anonymity offered by anonymous proxies is that they tend not to operate at the same speed as your regular browser. In addition, some Web sites and discussion groups block access from proxy servers because they have been used to spam the site or flood it with traffic. Also, anonymous proxies can be compromised by malicious third parties or monitored under court order, so anonymity is never assured.

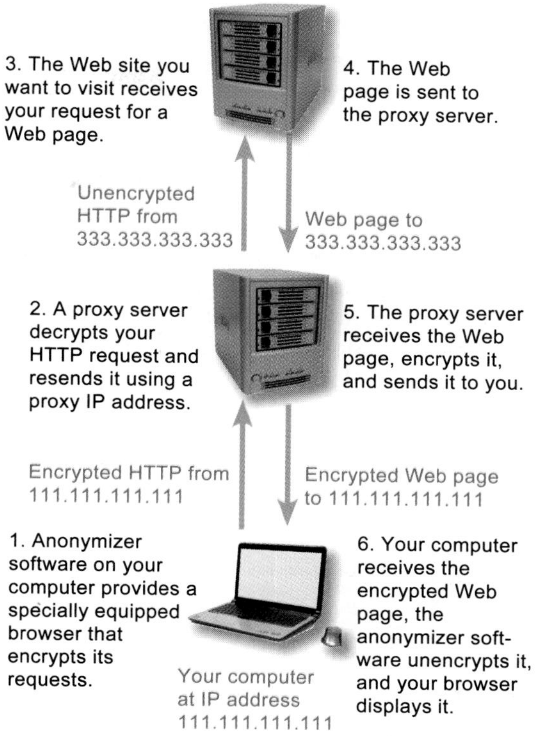

3. The Web site you want to visit receives your request for a Web page.

4. The Web page is sent to the proxy server.

Unencrypted HTTP from 333.333.333.333

Web page to 333.333.333.333

2. A proxy server decrypts your HTTP request and resends it using a proxy IP address.

5. The proxy server receives the Web page, encrypts it, and sends it to you.

Encrypted HTTP from 111.111.111.111

Encrypted Web page to 111.111.111.111

1. Anonymizer software on your computer provides a specially equipped browser that encrypts its requests.

Your computer at IP address 111.111.111.111

6. Your computer receives the encrypted Web page, the anonymizer software unencrypts it, and your browser displays it.

**FIGURE 7-49**

An anonymous proxy server relays your Web page requests after stripping off your IP address. ▶ To see this process in action, activate this figure in your digital textbook.

## SPAM

**What is spam?** One of e-mail's main disadvantages is **spam**—unwanted electronic junk mail about medical products, low-cost loans, and fake software upgrades that arrives in your online mailbox. Today's proliferation of spam is generated by marketing firms that harvest e-mail addresses from mailing lists, membership applications, and Web sites.

**Is spam dangerous?** In the past, spam flooding your Inbox with unsolicited and often pornographic messages was merely an annoyance. These days, however, spam has turned into another major hacking tool for cybercriminals. Spam sometimes contains Web bugs, viruses, worms, or keyloggers that can wreak havoc on your computer or steal personal information such as passwords. Spam can also be used for phishing scams, which are described later in this section.

**Can spam be blocked before it gets to my mailbox?** With millions of copies of some spam floating around the Internet, it would seem possible to identify and delete it before individuals have to contend with it. Most ISPs make an effort to block spam by blacklisting known spam servers. However, this method often results in blocking e-mail from legitimate ISPs that just happen to have been the source for dubious e-mail traffic.

Webmail providers and some ISPs use authentication techniques to filter out e-mail with a forged origination address. **E-mail authentication** techniques, such as Sender ID and DomainKeys, verify that e-mail messages originate from a legitimate domain. For example, if Bank of America e-mail messages are supposed to originate from *mail.bankofamerica.net*, an ISP that uses e-mail authentication will filter out messages that originate from spoofed addresses such as *www.bankofamerica.ru*.

7

**What can I do about spam?** First, you can be aware of spam and delete it without responding to it. You can also install and configure spam filters. A **spam filter** is a type of utility software that captures unsolicited e-mail messages before they reach your Inbox. It works by checking the text of e-mail headers and messages against a series of rules. For example, a rule such as *The message header contains viagra, v1agra, v.a.gra, or vi@gra* would help identify spam that's trying to hawk cheap pharmaceuticals.

Spam filters are available as standalone software, but often are included in e-mail clients and security suites. Most spam filters are shipped with a set of basic rules used to identify spam. The rules can be updated by downloads from the software publisher's Web site. Some spam filters also allow consumers to create their own rules to target spam that gets through the standard filters (Figure 7-50).

**FIGURE 7-50**

Spam filters usually include standard rules that block common spams, but you can create your own rules for spam that standard filters miss. ▶ Activate this figure in your digital textbook to find out how to create customized spam filters.

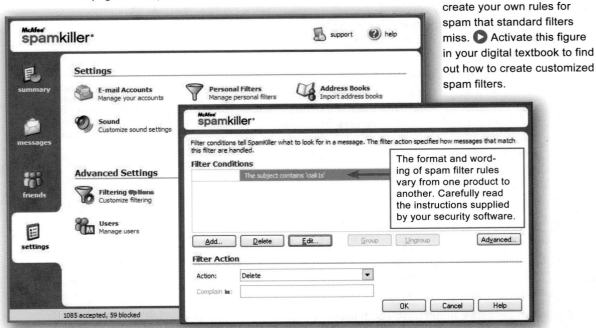

Spam filters tend to slow down the process of downloading mail and they sometimes trash legitimate mail. Periodically, you should look in the junk e-mail folder used by your spam filters to retrieve any mail that's not junk.

In addition to using spam filters, you can avoid being a spam victim by following the guidelines in Figure 7-51.

**FIGURE 7-51**

Guidelines for Avoiding Spam

- Never reply to spam when you receive it.
- Don't click links in e-mail messages, even if it's an opt-out link.
- Give your e-mail address only to people from whom you want to receive e-mail. Be wary of providing your e-mail address at Web sites, entering it on application forms, or posting it in public places such as online discussion groups.
- Use a disposable e-mail address when you register for online sites. You can use this disposable address to get your confirmation number for online purchases you've made, but don't use it for regular e-mail correspondence.
- If your e-mail provider offers a way to report spam, use it.
- When spam gets out of hand, consider changing your e-mail account so that you have a different e-mail address.

## PHISHING

**What is phishing?** **Phishing** is an e-mail based scam that's designed to persuade you to reveal confidential information such as your bank account number or Social Security number. Unlike pharming attacks (which you'll read about in a moment), phishing scams require that you reply to an e-mail message or click an embedded Web site link for the scam to unfold.

If you've used e-mail for any length of time, you've probably encountered the granddaddy of all phishing scams, a letter from a Nigerian political refugee who wants to move a large sum of money to a bank in your country and needs a bank account (yours!) to stash it for a few days. Of course you'll get a percentage for your trouble. Don't even think about it. According to the FBI, several gullible individuals have been lured abroad where they've been kidnapped and even killed.

More innocuous but potentially damaging spam scams start with an e-mail message that appears to come from a legitimate organization such as a bank, an online payment service, an online store, or even your ISP. The message directs you to click a link to verify confidential data. The link connects you to a bogus site cleverly disguised to look very much like a legitimate Web site. There you are urged to enter your bank account number, PIN, password, credit card number, or other data.

**How do I avoid phishing scams?** If you don't want to become a phishing victim, be suspicious of e-mail messages that supposedly come from banks, ISPs, online payment services, operating system publishers, and online merchants. Even if the messages appear to be legitimate, do not click links in the messages, but instead go to the Web site using your browser and link to your account as you normally would. If your account needs updating, you should see instructions about how to proceed.

## FAKE SITES

**What is a fake site?** A fake Web site looks legitimate, but has been created by a third party to be a very clever replica of a legitimate Web site, such as eBay or even the White House. Many fake Web sites are bogus storefronts designed exclusively for collecting credit card numbers from unwary shoppers. These sites might have the trappings of a real site. They might even offer a secure connection for transmitting your credit card number. When your data is received, however, it is stored in a database that belongs to a hacker, who can use the data for unauthorized transactions.

Some fake sites are not fake storefronts; rather, they are official-sounding sites, such as government agencies, that actually contain sexually explicit material. Other bogus sites simply present totally fabricated information or stories designed to fool the user. Fake sites are a key part of illegitimate pharming schemes.

**What is pharming?** **Pharming** is an exploit that redirects users to fake sites by poisoning a domain name server with a false IP address. Pharming and phishing are similar in many respects; both take advantage of fake sites. Phishing links, however, often lead to fake sites with URLs that are just slightly different from those of legitimate sites. Hackers depend on victims not paying close attention to the discrepancy when they click links.

Pharming is more sophisticated than phishing because the link appears to be for a legitimate URL. Even a close examination of the URL will not reveal anything suspicious because the URL's IP address has been changed at the domain name server.

7

**TERMINOLOGY NOTE**

Fake sites, URLs, and even e-mail addresses are often referred to as spoofed and the process of misdirection is called spoofing.

As you know from the Internet chapter, a domain name server is responsible for linking a domain name, such as YourBank.com, to its IP address, such as 64.191.203.33. Pharming attacks take advantage of a loophole in the domain name system that under certain circumstances permits third parties to change a record in a domain name server's database.

Hackers can attach the IP address of their own Web site to the URL of a legitimate site. For example, if a hacker manages to change the IP address for YourBank.com to the address of a fake site at 209.195.132.165, anyone who enters the legitimate URL of YourBank.com will be connected to the fake site.

**How can I recognize a pharming attack?** Pharming is more surreptitious and tougher to detect than most other hacker schemes. To detect a possible pharming attack, you have to be alert to the appearance of Web sites you frequently visit. Be cautious about revealing sensitive information if the site has changed since your last visit. You might want to call the business or organization that operates the Web site to learn whether the Web site has undergone a valid facelift or if the site is a slightly flawed replica of the legitimate one. You can also make sure that you see the lock or key icon in the browser status bar or address box when a site claims to be a secure site.

Some banks that offer online services use personal digital images to counteract pharming. Each user chooses an image that is supposed to appear when he or she logs on. If the secret image does not appear, the site is not the legitimate one.

Antipharming tools are emerging in response to growing security threats posed by fake sites. Mainstream browsers now include routines that compare IP addresses to a list of known fake sites and warn you of suspicious sites. Make sure your antipharming and antiphishing filters are activated (Figure 7-52).

**FIGURE 7-52**

Most browsers include features that can help you avoid pharming and phishing attacks. Find out which features are available and use them.

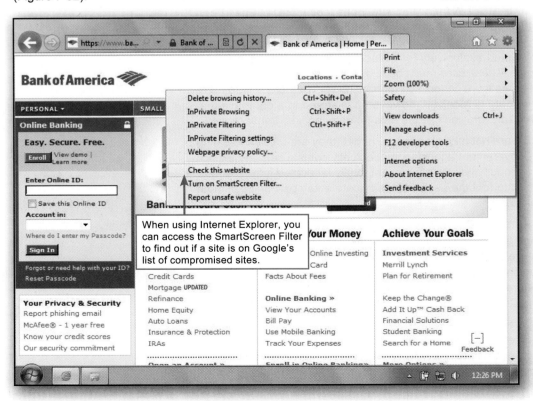

**What's the best defense against all the bad stuff on the Web and in e-mail?** First, understand that there is no perfect defense. Then understand that you should do all you can to safeguard your computer and your privacy. Use the list in Figure 7-53 as a starting point.

1. Use antispyware utilities to clean up any spyware that might have infiltrated your computer.
2. Run antispyware continuously just as you do antivirus software.
3. Set your browser to reject third-party cookies.
4. Register to reject Flash cookies.
5. Make sure your browser's antispoofing tools are activated; or install a third-party antispoofing tool to help you identify fake Web sites.
6. Set up a disposable e-mail address at a site such as Hotmail or Gmail and use it when you don't want to disclose your primary e-mail address.
7. Do not click links in untrusted e-mail or pop-up ads, and never respond to e-mail offers, especially those that seem too good to be true.

**FIGURE 7-53**

Guidelines for Secure and Private Web Surfing

7

## QuickCheck
SECTION E

1. The Adobe site provides a Settings Manager that can be used to control _____ cookies and prevent your computer's camera from being activated without your knowledge.

2. Web _____ embedded in an e-mail message or a Web page can be activated when you view an infested page.

3. If you don't want your IP address tracked as you surf the Web, you can use an anonymous _____ service.

4. A spam _____ can be configured with rules that block messages containing text such as *viagra* or *v1@gra*.

5. A(n) _____ exploit redirects users to fake sites by poisoning a domain name server with a false IP address.

▶ CHECK ANSWERS

# Issue: Who's Reading Your E-mail?

**WHEN YOU DROP** an envelope into the corner mailbox, you probably expect it to arrive at its destination unopened, with its contents kept safe from prying eyes. When you make a phone call, you might assume that your conversation will proceed unmonitored by wiretaps or other listening devices. Can you also expect an e-mail message to be read only by the person to whom it is addressed?

In the United States, the Electronic Communications Privacy Act of 2000 prohibits the use of intercepted e-mail as evidence unless a judge approves a search warrant. That doesn't mean the government isn't reading your mail. Heightened security concerns after the September 11, 2001 terrorist attacks resulted in the rapid passage of the USA PATRIOT Act, which became law on October 26, 2001.

In an effort to assist law enforcement officials, among its other provisions, the USA PATRIOT Act relaxes the rules for obtaining and implementing search warrants and lowers the Fourth Amendment standard for obtaining a court order to compel an ISP to produce e-mail logs and addresses.

To eavesdrop on e-mail from suspected terrorists and other criminals, the FBI uses commercially available sniffing software, which scans through messages entering and leaving an ISP's e-mail system looking for e-mail associated with a person who is under investigation. Privacy advocates are concerned because the sniffing software scans all messages that pass through an ISP, not just those messages sent to or received by a particular individual.

Although law enforcement agencies are required to obtain a court order before intercepting e-mail, no such restriction exists for employers who want to monitor employee e-mail. According to the American Management Association, 43% of U.S. businesses monitor employee e-mail. But this intentional eavesdropping is only one way in which the contents of your e-mail messages might become public. The recipient of your e-mail can forward it to one or more people—people you never intended for it to reach. Your e-mail messages could pop up on a technician's screen in the course of system maintenance, updates, or repairs.

Some Webmail providers—particularly those that make you look at ads in exchange for free accounts—collect information on how often you log in and might monitor your keystrokes to find out which ads and links you click. E-mail providers claim such information is used internally to deliver the best possible service, prevent fraud, and select the ads for products that you're most likely to buy. Also, keep in mind that e-mail messages—including those you delete from your own computer—can be stored on backups of your ISP's e-mail server.

You might wonder if such open access to your e-mail is legal. The answer in most cases is yes. Although the United States Omnibus Crime Control and Safe Streets Act of 1968 and the Electronic Communications Privacy Act of 1986 prohibit public and private employers from engaging in surreptitious surveillance of employee activity through the use of electronic devices, two exceptions to these privacy statutes exist. The first exception permits an employer to monitor e-mail if one party to the communication consents to the monitoring. An employer must inform employees of this policy before undertaking any monitoring. The second exception permits employers to monitor employees' e-mail if a legitimate business need exists, and the monitoring takes place within the business-owned e-mail system.

Employees generally have not been successful in defending their rights to e-mail privacy because courts have ruled that an employee's right to privacy does not outweigh a company's rights and interests. Courts seem to agree that because a company owns and maintains its e-mail system, it has the right to monitor the messages carried by the system.

Like employees of a business, students who use a school's e-mail system cannot be assured of e-mail privacy. When a Caltech student was accused of sexually harassing a female student by sending lewd e-mail to her and her boyfriend, investigators retrieved all the student's e-mail from the archives of the e-mail server. The student was expelled from the university even though he claimed that the e-mail had been spoofed to make it look as though he had sent it, when it had actually been sent by someone else.

Why would an employer want to know the contents of employee e-mail? Why would a school be concerned with the correspondence of its students? It is probably true that some organizations simply snoop on the off chance that important information might be discovered.

Other organizations have more legitimate reasons for monitoring e-mail. An organization that owns an e-mail system can be held responsible for the consequences of actions related to the contents of e-mail messages on that system. For example, a school has a responsibility to protect students from harassment. If it fails to do so, it can be sued along with the author of the offending e-mail message.

Organizations also recognize a need to protect themselves from false rumors and industrial espionage. For example, a business wants to know if an employee is supplying its competitor with information on product research and development.

Many schools and businesses have established e-mail privacy policies, which explain the conditions under which you can and cannot expect your e-mail to remain private. These policies are sometimes displayed when the computer boots or a new user logs in. Court decisions, however, seem to support the notion that because an organization owns and operates an e-mail system, the e-mail messages on that system are the property of the organization. The individual who authors an e-mail message does not own the rights related to it. The company, school, or organization that supplies your e-mail account can, therefore, legally monitor your messages.

You should use your e-mail account with the expectation that some of your mail will be read from time to time. Think of your e-mail as a postcard, rather than a letter, and save your controversial comments for face-to-face conversations.

**INFOWEBLINKS**

You'll find lots more information about e-mail privacy (and the lack of it) at the **E-mail Privacy InfoWeb**.

 CLICK TO CONNECT
www.infoweblinks.com/np2012/ch07

7

# What Do You Think?                     ISSUE

1. Do you think most people believe that their e-mail is private?          ◯ Yes  ◯ No  ◯ Not sure

2. Do you agree with Caltech's decision to expel the student who was accused of sending harassing e-mail to another student?          ◯ Yes  ◯ No  ◯ Not sure

3. Should the laws be changed to make it illegal for employers to monitor e-mail without court approval?          ◯ Yes  ◯ No  ◯ Not sure

4. Would you have different privacy expectations regarding an e-mail account at your place of work as opposed to an account you purchase from an e-mail service provider?          ◯ Yes  ◯ No  ◯ Not sure

 SAVE RESPONSES

# Computers in Context: Fashion Industry

**FASHION IS BIG BUSINESS.** Worldwide, clothing sales generate more than $340 billion in revenue. Shoes, accessories, and jewelry bump the industry's revenue even higher. Competition is tough as designers, manufacturers, and retailers compete for customer dollars. In the fashion industry, trends change quickly. As the saying goes, "Today's style is tomorrow's markdown." Fashion industry players look for every competitive advantage. It is no surprise that technology plays a major role in this glitzy industry.

Fashion begins with designers, such as Miuccia Prada, John Galliano, and Marc Jacobs. Their runway extravaganzas set off fashion trends that eventually work their way to retail stores. Fashion runways went high-tech in 1999 when lingerie manufacturer Victoria's Secret produced a Webcast watched by over 1 million viewers. Bravo television's *Project Runway* show has been one of the top iPod downloads. Fashion podcasts and blogs abound on the Web, as do fashion sites packed with news about the latest trends.

Although runway fashions are typically conceived with a sketch and stitched by hand, designs are adapted for the ready-to-wear market by using computer-assisted design (CAD) tools, such as pattern-making software. Garments are constructed by sewing together sections of fabric that form arms, fronts, backs, collars, and so forth. The set of templates used to cut fabric sections is called a pattern. Pattern-making is a tricky 3-D challenge because flat pieces of fabric eventually become garments shaped to conform to curved body contours. Pattern-making software helps designers visualize how flat pieces fit together and drape when sewn. Once a master pattern is complete, pattern-making software automatically generates a set of patterns for each garment size.

Fashion requires fabric, and computers play a major role in fabric design and manufacturing. Computer software, such as ArahWeave, lets fabric design-

ers experiment with colors, yarns, and weaves while viewing detailed, realistic on-screen samples. Fabric designs can be stored in a variety of formats for weaving machines. A few older mechanical weaving machines are controlled by punched cards. Digital fabric designs can be transferred to punched cards with a dedicated card punch machine. Most of today's weaving mills use computerized machinery that directly accepts digital input to control threads and patterns. Networks tie looms to CAD stations and to the Internet. Fabric designs can be stored in XML format, transmitted to a fabric manufacturer over the Internet, and used directly by computerized weaving machines.

Clothing production, warehousing, and shipping are also highly automated. Benetton's high-tech facility at Castrette, Italy can produce over 110 million garments per year. Its automated distribution center uses a workforce of only 24 people to handle 40,000 boxes of merchandise daily. RFID tags—sometimes called smart labels—can be attached to individual garments or to packing boxes as an important tool for controlling inventory.

RFID technology uses an inexpensive, tiny computer chip with built-in antenna and the capacity to store between 64 and 128 bits of data about a garment—its SKU number, size, model, dye lot, manufacturing date, and so on. Tags can be attached to a garment or its label. An RFID reader that can retrieve data from tags is used to track merchandise from the manufacturing plant through the distribution chain to the retailer. RFID tags are becoming popular for all types of merchandise. Businesses that use them can save time and money. For example, RFID tags can reduce the time it takes to do a physical inventory by a factor of 10. Privacy advocates, however, are worried because these tags remain active even after you bring your merchandise home. Could a thief circle your house with an RFID scanner to find out what's inside? Could a stalker follow your movements by tracking the RFID tag embedded in your sweater? Next time you buy a garment, check to see if an RFID tag is attached. It would typically be sewn into a seam and may carry a warning "Remove before wearing."

In response to competition from offshore companies, U.S. clothing manufacturers pioneered Quick Response (QR)—a business model for compressing supply chains to quickly obtain raw materials, such as fabric, yarn, buttons, and zippers. Sophisticated software tools, such as the Sourcing Simulator, simplify QR planning.

Online shopping has become routine, but one drawback of catalog and online ordering is the cost associated with restocking returned merchandise. Can an online customer find out how a garment will fit and look before ordering it? In 1998, Lands' End introduced My Virtual Model technology that allows shoppers to create a custom model of themselves by choosing from a variety of hair colors and styles, face shapes, and body types. The model can "try on" clothes to show online customers how they would look when wearing the garments.

More recently, Lands' End toured the country with a body-scanning device to collect actual measurements from thousands of customers. Body-scanning devices use cameras and lasers to capture approximately 300,000 data points that can be pieced together into a 3-D image.

Body scanners are also helping the fashion industry by collecting research data. Sizing standards fell by the wayside when vanity sizing added an inch or two to a garment so that consumers can feel good about themselves by fitting into smaller sizes. In the U.S. clothing industry, a comprehensive study of body shapes and sizes can help standardize sizing and eliminate much of the trial and error involved in finding apparel that fits. Collecting data from body scans is part of this ongoing research effort.

No discussion of fashion and computers would be complete without highlighting wearable technology. MIT's Media Lab has been a hotbed of wearable technology development. A recent student project uses a Webcam, a battery-powered projector, and an Internet-enabled mobile phone, and allows wearers to use hand gestures in 3-D space to conjure up information from the phone and project it on any surface.

Some wearables have even emerged from the laboratory and onto store shelves. Originally popular with Secret Service agents, the SCOTTEVEST is a jacket with pockets for cell phone, MP3 player, iPad, and built-in wiring to connect these devices into a personal area network (PAN). Available as a jacket or vest and in men's and women's sizes, the jacket can now be purchased by civilians.

With a growing emphasis on the use of technology in fashion design and manufacturing, fashion degree programs at colleges and technical schools have added courses such as computer-aided fashion design, computer-based pattern drafting, pattern grading and computer-aided drafting, and wearable computers.

7

# New Perspectives Labs

## On the BookOnCD

To access the New Perspectives Labs for Chapter 7, start the BookOnCD, and then click the icon next to the lab title below.

### ▶ BROWSER SECURITY & PRIVACY

#### IN THIS LAB YOU'LL LEARN:

- How to adjust the security settings for Internet Explorer's security zones
- How your browser can help you avoid phishing scams
- Why Web-based images and active content can pose a security risk
- The safest way to close pop-up ads and the most effective way to block them
- How to adjust security settings for active content
- How to delete or block Flash cookies
- How to secure the camera and microphone on your computer
- How to allow or prevent Web sites from determining your location

#### LAB ASSIGNMENTS

1. Perform each lab step as directed, and answer all the lab QuickCheck questions.

2. Identify which browser you typically use and look at its security settings. Does your browser allow you to select an overall security level, such as low, medium, or high?

3. Look at your browser's security settings and record the current settings for its phishing filter, pop-up blocker, ActiveX controls, JavaScript, and Java. Would you make any changes to these settings?

4. Connect to the Flash Player Settings Manager and count the number of Flash cookies you have. Next, record the security settings for your computer's camera and microphone.

### ▶ WORKING WITH COOKIES

#### IN THIS LAB YOU'LL LEARN:

- How Web servers use cookies
- Why cookies might pose a threat to your privacy
- How to locate, view, block, and delete cookies
- How to limit the space allocated to cookies created by Internet Explorer
- What a session cookie is
- How to set cookie prompts and use the cookie prompt dialog box
- How to take advantage of P3P and Compact Privacy Policies
- The differences between first-party and third-party cookies

#### LAB ASSIGNMENTS

1. Perform each lab step as directed, and answer all the lab QuickCheck questions.

2. Use your browser to look at the cookies on your computer. Indicate how many cookies are currently stored. Examine the contents of one cookie, and indicate whether you think it poses a threat to your privacy.

3. Indicate the name and version of the browser you typically use. Next, look at your browser's cookie settings. Describe how you would adjust these settings to produce a level of privacy protection that is right for your needs.

4. Adjust your browser settings so that you are prompted whenever a Web server attempts to send a cookie to your computer. Go to your favorite Web sites and watch for third-party cookies. When you receive a message from a third-party Web site, record the name of the third-party site and the contents of the cookie it is attempting to send. Finally, indicate whether you would accept such a cookie.

### ▶ WORKING WITH HTML

#### IN THIS LAB YOU'LL LEARN:

- How to use a text editor such as Notepad to create a basic HTML document
- Which HTML tags to use to format text
- How to use HTML for numbered and bulleted lists
- How to add graphics to your Web pages
- How to add hyperlinks to a Web page
- Methods for testing Web pages locally
- How to post your Web page

#### LAB ASSIGNMENTS

1. Perform each lab step as directed, and answer all the lab QuickCheck questions.

2. Use a text editor such as Notepad to create a Web page that contains your name as the title and at least two paragraphs of text.

3. Use the heading, bold, and horizontal rule HTML tags to add interest to your page.

4. Add at least one hyperlink to the page, making sure that you include explanatory link text.

5. Select a graphic to add to your page. Make sure that it is stored in a file that's not too big to load quickly. Designate alternative text for the graphic for accessibility.

6. Test your Web page locally. Print your HTML document and then make a screen capture of your Web page as it appears in the browser.

7. If your instructor so specifies, post your Web page to a Web site, test it, and supply the page's URL to your instructor using e-mail.

# Key Terms

Make sure you understand all the boldfaced key terms presented in this chapter. With the NP2012 BookOnCD, you can use this list of terms as an interactive study activity. First, try to define a term in your own words, and then click the term to compare your definition with the definition presented in the chapter. Online, try your hand at the TechTerm Flashcards.

ActionScript, 372
ActiveX control, 373
Ad-blocking software, 385
Ad-serving cookie, 400
Ajax, 362
Anonymous proxy service, 403
Antispyware, 402
B2B, 384
B2C, 384
B2G, 384
Banner ad, 385
Boolean operator, 379
C2C, 384
Click-through rate, 385
Client-side script, 372
Cookie, 367
DHTML, 362
Digital certificate, 373
E-commerce, 384
E-mail account, 393
E-mail address, 393
E-mail attachment, 398
E-mail authentication, 403
E-mail client software, 393
E-mail message, 392
E-mail server, 392
E-mail system, 392
Flash cookie, 402
Hover ad, 385
HTML, 362
HTML conversion utility, 369
HTML document, 362

HTML forms, 371
HTML mail, 397
HTML script, 371
HTML tags, 362
HTTP, 364
HTTP status code, 365
Hypertext, 360
Hypertext link, 361
IMAP, 394
Java applet, 372
Keyword stuffing, 378
Link popularity, 377
Local e-mail, 393
Markup language, 362
Message header, 392
Meta keyword, 378
Metasearch engine, 380
MIME, 398
Netiquette, 399
Online shopping cart, 387
Persistent HTTP connection, 365
Person-to-person payment, 390
Pharming, 405
Phishing, 405
Plug-in, 367
Podcast, 360
POP3, 394
Pop-up ad, 385
Query processor, 377
Search engine indexer, 376
Search terms, 378
Secure connection, 389

Server-side script, 372
S-HTTP, 390
Smileys, 399
SMTP, 394
Socket, 364
Source document, 363
Spam, 403
Spam filter, 404
SSL, 390
Stateless protocol, 368
Store-and-forward, 394
TLS, 390
URL, 361
Videocasting, 361
Web, 360
Web 2.0, 361
Web browser, 361
Web bug, 402
Web cache, 365
Web crawler, 375
Web page, 361
Web search engine, 374
Web server, 361
Web site, 360
Webmail, 393
XHTML, 362

7

# Interactive Summary

To review important concepts from this chapter, fill in the blanks to best complete each sentence. When using the NP2012 BookOnCD, click the Check Answers buttons to automatically score your answers.

**SECTION A:** The Web, one of the Internet's hottest attractions, is a collection of document, image, video, and sound files that can be linked and accessed over the Internet via the [_____] protocol. The Web is an interlinked collection of information; whereas the [_____] is the communications system used to transport Web information from computers that store it to client computers that request it. An Internet-based computer that stores and distributes Web files is called a Web [_____]. It can host one or more Web [_____] such as *www.wikipedia.com* or *www.myspace.com* containing HTML [_____] documents, which can be accessed and displayed using client software called a Web [_____]. Each Web page has a unique address called a(n) [_____]. [_____] Markup Language is a set of specifications for creating documents that a browser can display as a Web page. To create HTML documents, you can use a variety of Web authoring tools, such as a text [_____], HTML conversion utility, online Web authoring tool, or Web authoring software. To enable your Web pages to perform tasks beyond what HTML can do, you can add programs by embedding a(n) [_____] in your HTML document, or by coding a Java [_____], [_____] content, or a(n) [_____] control, which you can refer to in your document.

▶ CHECK ANSWERS

**SECTION B:** To sift through massive amounts of information available on the Web and locate pertinent information about a topic, Web surfers utilize programs called search [_____]. These special programs have four major components. A Web [_____], also called a Web spider, is automated to methodically visit Web sites and gather Web pages. A search engine [_____] culls keywords from the gathered pages and stores them in a(n) [_____]. The search engine's query [_____] accepts one or more words called search [_____], looks them up in the database, and produces a list of relevant Web sites. There are a number of ways to narrow searches and produce more targeted results, such as using [_____] operators or putting exact phrases in [_____]. The order in which Web sites are returned in response to your query is dependent on relevancy criteria, such as keyword matches and [_____] popularity.

▶ CHECK ANSWERS

**SECTION C:** Any business transaction that is conducted electronically over a computer network is typically referred to as a(n) [_____] transaction. The most common business models are business-to-[_____], consumer-to-consumer, business-to-business, and business-to-government. E-commerce merchants cut costs by taking advantage of the efficiencies and opportunities offered by [_____], computerization, and digitization. They also increase their profits by providing space for third-party hover, pop-up, and [_____] ads on their Web pages. Online stores use [_____] to track customers' online shopping carts. B2C e-commerce sites usually store product descriptions in a(n) [_____]. Product information is assembled into Web pages on the fly by [_____]-side scripts. Online purchases can be paid for by submitting a credit card number directly to a merchant or using a person-to-[_____] payment service, such as PayPal.

▶ CHECK ANSWERS

## SECTION D:

E-mail is an electronic version of the postal system that transmits messages from one computer to another, usually over the [_____]. Obtaining an e-mail [_____] gets your electronic mailbox set up on an e-mail server. The software you use to send, receive, and manage messages is called e-mail [_____] software. E-mail systems based on client software that's installed locally are referred to as [_____] e-mail. Systems that provide access to e-mail through a(n) [_____] are called Webmail. Two protocols are typically used to manage your incoming mail. [_____] deletes messages after they are downloaded, whereas [_____] leaves messages on the server until you specifically delete them. The protocol that handles outgoing mail is [_____].

[_____] mail is a term used for e-mail messages that contain tags that produce bold, italic, and underlined text; fancy fonts; embedded graphics; and various font sizes. Any file that travels with an e-mail message is called an e-mail attachment. A conversion process called [_____] provides a clever way of disguising digital photos, sounds, and other media as plain ASCII code that can travel over the Internet as e-mail attachments. Attachments can harbor computer [_____]. Do not open attachments from an unknown source. [_____] is online jargon for Internet etiquette. It is a series of customs or guidelines for maintaining civilized and effective communications in online discussions and e-mail exchanges.

▶ CHECK ANSWERS

7

## SECTION E:

When you surf the Web or work with your e-mail, you need to be aware of potential spyware exploits, such as [_____] cookies from third parties. While browsers and marketing firms are now providing opt-out mechanisms to block third-party cookies, it is not as easy to turn off all kinds of cookies. [_____] cookies, also called local shared objects, are used as an alternative to conventional cookies, and most users are not aware of their existence. Web [_____], or clear GIFs, are practically invisible 1x1 pixel graphics embedded in a Web page or e-mail message that can be used to set cookies for third-party Web sites. [_____] redirects users to fake sites by tampering with the information in a(n) [_____] name server. While these attacks don't need any action on your part to be effective, [_____] scams require you to respond to an e-mail message or click an embedded link in your e-mail. [_____] is unsolicited e-mail that you can avoid by practicing safe e-mail techniques such as using a spam [_____]. You can also use a(n) [_____] e-mail address to receive confirmation for online purchases without getting added to a spam mailing list. A safe bet for combating most forms of spyware is using a type of security software called [_____].

▶ CHECK ANSWERS

# Interactive Situation Questions

Apply what you've learned to some typical computing situations. When using the NP2012 BookOnCD, you can type your answers, and then use the Check Answers button to automatically score your responses.

1. Suppose that you are about to check out at an online store, but you don't see any indication that your transaction data will be protected by a secure connection. It would be best, under these circumstances, to use PGP software to encrypt your shipping and billing data. True or false? [_____]

2. Your friend, who is a little computer phobic, is going to be creating his first Web page and asks you to recommend some software for the task. Which one requires the least knowledge of HTML tags: Notepad or Microsoft Word? [_____]

3. Suppose you visit a Web site that has eye-catching pages. You want to know how these pages were formatted, so you use one of the options on your browser's menu to take a look at the HTML [_____] document.

4. Suppose you click a link at a Web site and get a message that the file cannot be displayed because it is in PDF format. To view the file, you need an updated version of your browser. True or false? [_____]

5. Suppose you're performing a local test of a Web page you created. All the page elements appear to be correctly positioned and formatted. You're also happy to discover that your large graphics files are displayed quite quickly by your browser. Can you expect similar performance after you post the page on a Web site? Yes or no? [_____]

6. You'd prefer not to have the search engine you use maintain accumulative records of your searches. You can block [_____] from a specific search engine site, and that setting will force the search engine to assign a different ID number to you for each session.

7. You're getting ready for a week-long trip. You'd rather not take your computer, but you'll have access to public computers. Rather than use Webmail while you're away from home, you decide to use your familiar POP e-mail [_____] software, by storing it and your e-mail files on a portable USB flash drive.

8. One of your relatives wants to try online shopping, but is suspicious that her credit card number might get stolen from a merchant's server by a hacker using a packet sniffer. Is it correct to tell her that she can best avoid these potential rip-offs by a secure connection, such as SSL? Yes or no? [_____]

9. Your Inbox is getting more and more unsolicited messages with "fisd foos" in the header. You decide to generate a new rule for your security software's spam [_____] to block those irritating messages.

10. You're looking through a list of cookies stored on your computer, but don't remember visiting sites such as bannerbank, hotlog, and ad.bb. You can assume that these cookies were created by [_____], such as ad-serving cookies.

▶ CHECK ANSWERS

# Interactive Practice Tests

Practice tests that consist of ten multiple-choice, true/false, and fill-in-the-blank questions are available on both the NP2012 BookOnCD and the NP2012 CourseMate Web site. BookOnCD test questions are selected at random from a large test bank, so each time you take a test, you'll receive a different set of questions. Your tests are scored immediately, and you can print study guides that help you find the correct answers for any questions that you missed. Online, you'll find a Practice Test for each section of the chapter. Your results from online tests are saved by Engagement Tracker. ▶ CLICK TO START

# Learning Objectives Checkpoints

Learning Objectives Checkpoints are designed to help you assess whether you have achieved the major learning objectives for this chapter. You can use paper and pencil or word processing software to complete most of the activities.

1. Explain the relationship between an HTML source document and a Web page. List five HTML tags and describe how each is used.

2. Draw a multi-panel cartoon that shows how a Web server and browser interact. Include the following terms: Web server, browser, HTTP, HTML, port, socket, HTML document, graphic file, and URL.

3. Briefly sketch the evolution of Web browsers. Describe the purpose of helper applications, plug-ins, and players.

4. Explain why cookies are useful in an environment that is based on a stateless protocol, and provide some concrete examples of their use.

5. Describe the advantages and disadvantages of each type of Web page development tool discussed in this chapter.

6. Create a short tutorial explaining how to create, test, and post a Web page using a text editor such as Notepad or TextEdit.

7. Explain the purpose of HTML scripts and the differences between server-side scripts and client-side scripts.

8. Create a comic-strip like sequence of diagrams that illustrates how the following technologies interact: Web crawler, search engine database, indexer, query processor.

9. Use a search engine and Boolean operators to formulate a search for information about your favorite era in history. Can you make a more targeted search to find out what kind of slang was used during that time period?

10. List the four most commonly used styles of citation and demonstrate how to correctly format a citation to a Web page using each style.

11. Explain two ways that shopping carts can work with cookies.

12. List three threats to the security of credit card numbers and other sensitive data during e-commerce transactions. Describe how the following e-commerce technologies work: SSL, one-time-use credit cards, and person-to-person payment systems.

13. Create a table that compares and contrasts local mail with Webmail.

14. List the advantages and disadvantages of HTML formatted mail. Explain how MIME works.

15. Make a list of security and privacy concerns discussed in this chapter. Describe each one and then list procedures and technologies available to make your online experience more secure and private.

Study Tip: Make sure you can use your own words to correctly answer each of the red focus questions that appear throughout the chapter.

7

# Concept Map

Fill in the blanks to show the hierarchy of Web technology concepts presented in this chapter.

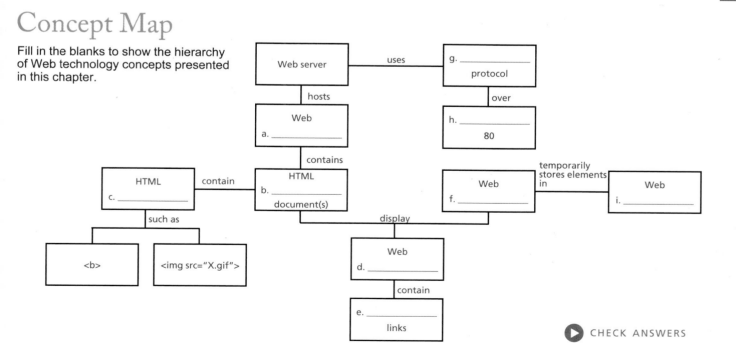

CHECK ANSWERS

# Projects

## CRITICAL THINKING

In this chapter you read about some of the pitfalls of shopping online. Reflect on what you read within the context of your own online usage habits. What aspects of your online activities could you change to become more secure, more private, or more efficient? What do you have to give up to get these benefits? Is it worth it to you? Incorporate your thoughts in a one-page summary. Follow your instructor's guidelines for submission.

## GROUP PROJECT

Brainstorm with a group of three to five students to come up with an idea for an e-business. For this project assign tasks from the list below and create a schedule for completing them. Compile your work into a single document for submission.
Tasks:
• Decide on a name for the business after finding an available URL.

• Design a Web site for the business. Mock up the Web site home page using Web authoring software or simply a graphics program, such as Paint.

• Locate at least five partner sites that might provide synergistic cross-marketing.

• Make a list of ten keywords that can be used in your Web page header so customers can easily find your site when using a search engine.

• Find a site to host your online business and work up a spreadsheet showing monthly and annual hosting costs.

## CYBERCLASSROOM

Work with your team to create a blog on any topic. You can use the tools provided at any blogging site, such as www.blogger.com. Make sure that each person on the team posts at least one message to the blog. Send your instructor instructions for logging onto your blog. When all the blogs are up and running, your instructor might post the URLs so everyone in the class can judge whose blog is best.

## MULTIMEDIA PROJECT

Surf the Web to select a home page that needs improvement. Use the Print Screen key on your keyboard to take a screenshot of the original page. Paste the page into graphics software such as Paint and store it as Home Page Original [Your Name]. Use your graphics software to create an improved home page by following some of the tips and recommendations offered in the chapter. Save your makeover as Home Page Makeover [Your Name]. Make a list of the changes you made. Submit the original page, the makeover page, and the list of changes to your instructor.

## RESUME BUILDER

Many companies have a Web site that provides information about their products and services. Use a search engine to locate a company in your career field. Suppose you are a recruiter for that company and you'll be attending a series of college career fairs. Create a one-page information flyer that you can hand out to prospective recruits. The flyer should include:
• The company name, URL, and physical location(s)

• A brief description of the company's mission, products, and services

• Instructions on how to submit a resume electronically

## GLOBALIZATION

Examine trends in global e-commerce, and submit your answers to the following questions:
• Which countries are the top players in the e-commerce market?

• How big is your country's share of the e-commerce pie, and is it increasing or decreasing?

• How does e-commerce affect developing countries?

• What are the advantages and disadvantages of a global market?

## ISSUE

The Issue section of this chapter focused on how much—or how little—privacy you can expect when using an e-mail account. For this project, write a two- to five-page paper about e-mail privacy based on information you gather from the Internet. To begin this project, consult the E-mail Privacy InfoWeb to get an in-depth overview of the issue. Next, determine the viewpoint you will present in your paper. You might, for example, decide to present the viewpoint of a student who believes that e-mail should be afforded the same privacy rights as a sealed letter. Or you might present the viewpoint of an employer who wants to explain why your company believes it is necessary to monitor employee e-mail. Whatever viewpoint you decide to present, make sure you can back it up with facts and references to authoritative articles and Web pages.

## COMPUTERS IN CONTEXT

The Computers in Context section of this chapter focused on computers in the fashion industry. For this report, create a visual timeline that traces a garment from the time it is conceived by a designer to the time it is placed on a designer's rack or store shelf. Indicate technologies that are used at various stages of this process. Make sure that you provide citations for your text and graphical sources.

# On the Web

## STUDENT EDITION LABS

When you purchase access to the NP2012 CourseMate Web site, you'll find targeted learning materials to help you understand key concepts and prepare for exams. See page O-41 in the Orientation Chapter for login instructions.

### CREATING WEB PAGES

In the Creating Web Pages Student Edition Lab, you will learn about the following topics:

- Starting a Web page
- Formatting paragraphs and text on a Web page
- Using graphics and backgrounds on a Web page
- Linking to other Web pages
- Using tables on a Web page

### E-MAIL

In the E-Mail Student Edition Lab, you will learn about the following topics:

- Composing, replying to, and printing e-mail messages
- E-mail organizational and management techniques such as moving messages to a folder and using an address book
- Signing up for and using Webmail to demonstrate your e-mail skills using your own e-mail account

### E-COMMERCE

In the E-Commerce Student Edition Lab, you will learn about the following topics:

- Paying with electronic cash
- Ensuring security in an e-commerce transaction
- Technical components of an e-commerce Web site
- Developing an e-commerce Web site

### WEB DESIGN PRINCIPLES

In the Web Design Principles Student Edition Lab, you will learn about the following topics:

- Designing the site structure
- Designing the site look and feel
- Designing for readability
- Using hypertext and images effectively

7

### CHAPTER OVERVIEW COURSECAST

Use your computer or iPod to hear a five-minute audio presentation of chapter highlights.

### AUDIO FLASHCARDS

Interact with audio flashcards to review key concepts from the chapter.

### DETAILED OBJECTIVES

Make sure that you've achieved all the objectives for a chapter before it's time for your test!

### PRACTICE TESTS

Review chapter material by taking these ten-question tests. Your results are saved by Engagement Tracker.

### ONLINE GAMES

Have some fun while refreshing your memory about key concepts that might appear on the next test.

### AND MORE!

At the NP2012 CourseMate Web site you'll also find the NP2012 eBook, TechTerm Flashcards, Online Glossary, and What Do You Think? opinion polls.

# 8

# Digital Media

## Chapter Contents

▶ **SECTION A:**
**DIGITAL SOUND**
Digital Audio Basics
Digital Audio File Formats
MIDI Music
Speech Recognition and Synthesis

▶ **SECTION B:**
**BITMAP GRAPHICS**
Bitmap Basics
Scanners and Cameras
Image Resolution
Color Depth and Palettes
Image Compression
Bitmap Graphics Formats

▶ **SECTION C:**
**VECTOR AND 3-D GRAPHICS**
Vector Graphics Basics
Vector-to-Bitmap Conversion
Vector Graphics on the Web
3-D Graphics

▶ **SECTION D:**
**DIGITAL VIDEO**
Digital Video Basics
Producing Video Footage
Video Transfer
Video Editing
Video Output
Web Video
DVD-Video

▶ **SECTION E:**
**DIGITAL RIGHTS MANAGEMENT**
DRM Basics
Signal Scrambling and Digital
    Watermarks
CD Copy Protection
DVD and Blu-ray DRM
DRM for Digital Downloads

▶ **ISSUE:**
**WHAT HAPPENED TO FAIR USE?**

▶ **COMPUTERS IN CONTEXT:**
**FILM**

▶ **NEW PERSPECTIVES LABS**

▶ **REVIEW ACTIVITIES**

▶ **ON THE WEB**

## Learning Objectives

After reading this chapter, you will be able to answer the following questions by completing the outcomes-based Learning Objectives Checkpoints on page 481.

1. How do computers and portable media players such as iPods store digital music?

2. Why are some digital audio files so huge?

3. What is the difference between digital audio and MIDI?

4. What are bitmap graphics, where are they used, and how can they be identified?

5. How are images transferred from digital cameras to computers?

6. What affects the quality of a bitmap graphic, its file size, and whether it is best suited for uses such as Web pages, e-mail attachments, printed photos, or desktop published documents?

7. Can compression play a role in reducing the size of graphics files?

8. How do vector graphics differ from bitmaps, and how does that affect the way in which they are created and used?

9. Is it possible to convert bitmap graphics into vector graphics?

10. What tools and techniques are used to create 3-D graphics?

11. What kinds of devices can be used to capture video?

12. Can analog video be converted into digital video?

13. What affects the amount of video that can be stored on a hard disk or portable media player?

14. How is digital video deployed on the Web?

15. What are the most popular digital media file formats and software players?

16. Is a special procedure required to make DVDs that work on standalone DVD players?

17. How do digital rights management technologies restrict the ways in which I can use digital media?

18. How are time shifting, place shifting, and format shifting related to digital media?

## InfoWebLinks

Visit the InfoWebLinks site to access additional resources Ⓦ that accompany this chapter.

## Multimedia and Interactive Elements

When using the BookOnCD or CourseMate eBook, the ▶ icons are clickable to access multimedia resources.

## Pre-Assessment Quiz

Take the pre-assessment quiz to find out how much you know about the topics in this chapter. ▶

## Apply Your Knowledge The information in this chapter will give you the background to:

- Recognize digital media files by their extensions
- Play digital music and video files on your computer and transfer them to portable media players
- Add WAV or MIDI music to Web pages
- Use speech recognition software applications to manipulate software with voice commands
- Create digital photos with a camera or scanner and then edit them
- Create vector and 3-D graphics

- Process photos to make them suitable for e-mail attachments, Web pages, or printing
- Create digital video using an analog or digital camcorder
- Turn your digital video into a DVD complete with menu options for scene selection and special features
- Identify music and video that are controlled by digital rights management

## Try It

### WHAT KINDS OF GRAPHICS, AUDIO, AND VIDEO FILES ARE ON MY COMPUTER?

You can use your computer to work with many types of media, such as photos, music, and videos. Your computer stores media that you've created and downloaded. It also stores images from Web sites you've recently visited. To discover what sort of media is stored on your computer, follow these steps:

**Windows 7 and Vista:**
**1.** Click the **Start** button. Type **pictures** into the search box as shown below. For **Windows 7**, click the **See more results** option above the search box. For **Vista**, click the **Search Everywhere** option above the search box.

**2.** Repeat step 1 to search for **music** and then again to search for **video**.

**Windows XP:**
**1.** Click **Start** and then select **Search**. The Search Results dialog box appears. On the left side of the Search Results window, click the button for **Pictures, Music, or Video.**

**2.** Click the box for **Pictures and Photos**, then click the **Search** button. Your com-

puter shows you a list of image files. If Windows displays a list of file names, but you'd rather see the images, click the **View** menu and select **Thumbnails.**

**3.** Repeat step 2 to search for **Music** and then again to search for **Video**.

**Mac:**
**1.** Click the **Finder** icon, located on the dock.

**2.** Use the SEARCH FOR listing on the left side of the Finder window to select **All images**. If your Mac displays file names, but you'd prefer to see the images, click the **View** menu and then select **as icons.**

**3.** Use the SEARCH FOR listing to select **All Movies**.

**4.** To find music on your Mac, type **music** in the search box, located in the upper-right corner of the Finder window.

Search for all files of a certain type, or search by type and name.
☑ Pictures and Photos
☐ Music
☐ Video

All or part of the file name:

You may also want to...

☑ Use advanced search options

Back    Search

# Digital Sound

**COMPUTERS CAN RECORD,** store, and play sounds, such as narrations, sound effects, and music. Downloading music files over the Internet is currently the most popular use of digital audio, but audio technology plays a key role in other very interesting applications. How would you like to quit messing with your computer keyboard and enter commands and documents simply by speaking into a microphone? Would you like to add music and sound effects to your Web pages? Maybe you'd like to pull tracks from your audio CDs and remaster them into your own collection of favorite songs. This section of the chapter covers a wide-ranging selection of digital audio concepts and technologies that you're likely to find handy for personal and professional use.

## DIGITAL AUDIO BASICS

**What is digital audio?** **Digital audio** is music, speech, and other sounds represented in binary format for use in digital devices. Sound is produced by the vibration of matter such as a violin string or a drum head. This vibration causes pressure changes in the surrounding air, creating waves.

The smooth, continuous curve of a sound wave can be directly recorded on analog devices, such as records. To digitally record sound, samples of the sound wave are collected at periodic intervals and stored as numeric data. Figure 8-1 shows how a computer digitally samples a sound wave.

**FIGURE 8-1**

Sampling a Sound Wave

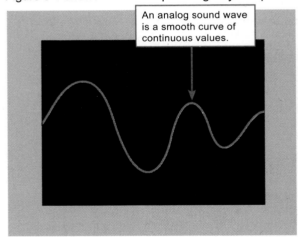

An analog sound wave is a smooth curve of continuous values.

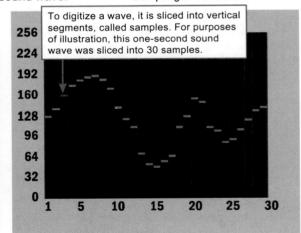

To digitize a wave, it is sliced into vertical segments, called samples. For purposes of illustration, this one-second sound wave was sliced into 30 samples.

| Sample | Sample Height (Decimal) | Sample Height (Binary) |
|--------|--------------------------|-------------------------|
| 1 | 130 | 10000010 |
| 2 | 140 | 1000110 |
| 3 | 160 | 10100000 |
| 4 | 175 | 10101111 |
| 5 | 185 | 10111001 |

The height of each sample is converted into a binary number and stored. The height of sample 3 is 160 (decimal), so it is stored as its binary equivalent—10100000.

**Does sampling rate affect sound quality?** **Sampling rate** refers to the number of times per second that a sound is measured during the recording process. It is expressed in hertz (Hz). One thousand samples per second is expressed as 1,000 Hz or 1 kHz (kilohertz). Higher sampling rates increase the quality of the sound recording but require more storage space than lower sampling rates.

The height of each sound sample can be saved as an 8-bit number for radio-quality recordings or a 16-bit number for high-fidelity recordings. The audio CDs you buy at your favorite music store are recorded at a sampling rate of 44.1 kHz, which means a sample of the sound is taken 44,100 times per second. Sixteen bits are used for each sample. To achieve stereo effects, you must take two of these 16-bit samples. Therefore, each sample requires 32 bits of storage space. When you sample stereo CD-quality music at 44.1 kHz, one minute of music requires about 10 MB of storage space. Forty-five minutes of music—the length of a typical album—require about 450 MB.

To conserve space, applications that do not require such high-quality sound use much lower sampling rates. Voice-overs and narrations are often recorded with sampling rates of 11 kHz (11,000 samples per second). This rate results in lower quality sound, but the file is about one-fourth the size of a file for the same sound recorded at 44.1 kHz. Figure 8-2 illustrates how sampling rate affects sound quality.

**FIGURE 8-2**

A higher sampling rate produces more true-to-life sound quality. Use your digital textbook to compare the quality of these audio clips, which were digitized at different sampling rates. You'll have to listen carefully to notice the differences.

▶ CLICK TO START

Low sampling rate: File size = 66 KB

Medium sampling rate: File size = 124 KB

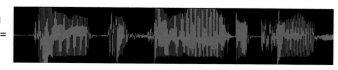

▶ CLICK TO START

High sampling rate: File size = 235 KB

▶ CLICK TO START

8

Regardless of sampling rate, digital audio file size can be reduced using audio compression techniques. **Audio compression** reduces the size of a sound file by removing bits that represent extraneous noise and sounds that are beyond the frequencies of normal hearing. In addition, general-purpose compression techniques explained later in the chapter can be applied to sound files. A compressed audio file requires less storage space than an uncompressed file and can be transmitted faster over a network. Popular portable media players typically work with compressed audio file formats.

**How does a computer produce digital audio?** Your computer's sound card is responsible for transforming the bits stored in an audio file into music, sound effects, and narrations. A **sound card** is a device that contains a variety of input and output jacks, plus audio-processing circuitry. A desktop computer's sound card is usually plugged into an expansion slot inside the system unit. Alternatively, sound card circuitry referred to as **integrated audio** can be built into a computer's system board. Portable computers rarely feature a separate sound card because manufacturers save space by using integrated audio.

A sound card is typically equipped to accept input from a microphone and send output to speakers or headphones. For processing digital audio files, a sound card contains a special type of circuitry called a **digital signal processor**, which performs three important tasks. It transforms digital bits into analog waves when you play a digital audio file. It transforms analog waves into digital bits when you make a sound recording. It also handles compression and decompression, if necessary.

To play a digitally recorded sound, the bits from an audio file are transferred from disk to the microprocessor, which routes them to your computer's sound card. The digital signal processor handles any necessary decompression, and then transforms the data into analog wave signals. These signals are routed to the speakers and voilà! You have sound (Figure 8-3).

The microprocessor sends compressed digital data to the sound card.

The sound card's digital signal processor decompresses data and converts it to analog signals.

The sound card sends analog signals to speakers.

FIGURE 8-3

Most sound cards use a digital signal processor to convert bits into analog signals.

**What type of hardware do I need for digital audio?** Your PC outputs sound to speakers or headphones. It gets input from a microphone. Portable computers typically include a built-in microphone and speakers. Ports for external speakers and an auxiliary microphone can usually be found on the side or in the front of the system unit. If the ports on your sound card are not labeled, refer to your PC's documentation to find out which one to use.

If you're not picky about sound quality, you'll find the bundled microphone suitable for radio-quality voice recording and sound effects destined for Web pages or presentations. For multimedia or professional audio projects, you'll want to shop for a better-quality "mic." You can connect most standard microphones to your computer through the microphone socket or USB port.

The speakers on your notebook computer are fine for listening to music; but when you're giving presentations or showing movies, you're likely to need external speakers to generate adequate volume. Some speakers draw power from the computer, but they are limited in volume. Speakers that plug into a wall outlet offer much more versatile audio output, especially in situations that require high volume. Speakers come in several configurations, such as the 5.1 system shown in Figure 8-4.

FIGURE 8-4

Computer speakers come in several configurations. A 2.0 speaker system includes two speakers for stereo effects. A 2.1 system adds a subwoofer for strong bass sound. A 5.1 system includes four speakers and a subwoofer. 2.0 and 2.1 systems are great for listening to music and for presentations. A 5.1 system such as the one shown is excellent for gaming and home theater systems.

**How can I listen to my digital music collection when I'm away from my computer?** As you learned in Chapter 5, you can stream music to network-connected entertainment devices, such as televisions and stereo systems. Also, portable media players such as iPods and Zunes are specifically designed for playing digital audio and other media. Similar functionality is built into many smartphones and other handheld digital devices.

**How do I load music on my handheld device?** Many handheld devices access sites from which you can directly download music. Alternatively, you might sync music from your computer to your handheld device. The synchronization process ensures that your computer and handheld device both contain the music files you want.

## DIGITAL AUDIO FILE FORMATS

**How can I recognize a digital audio file?** You can recognize a digital audio file by looking at its file extension. Digital audio can be stored in a variety of file formats. The table in Figure 8-5 provides an overview of the most popular digital audio formats, including **AAC** (Advanced Audio Coding), **MP3** (also called MPEG-1 Layer 3), **Ogg Vorbis**, **WAV**, and **WMA** (Windows Media Audio).

**FIGURE 8-5**

Popular Digital Audio File Formats

| Audio Format | File Extension | Advantages | Disadvantages |
|---|---|---|---|
| AAC | .aac, .m4p, or .mp4 | Very good sound quality based on MPEG-4; compressed format; used on iTunes music download site | Files can be copy protected so that use is limited to approved devices |
| MP3 (also called MPEG-1 Layer 3) | .mp3 | Good sound quality even though the file is compressed; can be streamed over the Web | Might require a standalone player or browser plug-in |
| Ogg Vorbis | .ogg | Free, open standard; supported by some browsers; supplies audio stream for Google's WebM format | Slow to catch on as a popular standard |
| WAV | .wav | Good sound quality; supported in browsers without a plug-in | Audio data is stored in raw, uncompressed format, so files are very large |
| WMA (Windows Media Audio) | .wma | Compressed format; very good sound quality; used on several music download sites | Files can be copy protected; requires Windows Media Player 9 or above |

**What type of software is required to play digital audio files?** To play a digital audio file, you must use audio or media player software. Audio software might be included with your computer's operating system, packaged with your sound card, installed in a handheld device, or available on the Web. Popular audio and media players include iTunes, Windows Media Player, and open source offerings such as QuickAudio and Audacity.

Audio player software tends to support several audio file formats. In the Windows environment, for example, you can use Windows Media Player to play audio formats such as WAV, WMA, and MP3.

8

**What about Web-based audio?** Digital audio files can be embedded into a Web page using the HTML5 <audio> tag. WAV files are supported by most Web browsers, so it is a popular audio file format. Other audio formats can be delivered over the Web, but might require plug-ins.

Suppose that you want to listen to some free tracks at a jazz Web site where files are stored in Vorbis format. Firefox and Chrome offer built-in support for Vorbis audio. If you use Internet Explorer, however, you'll have to download and install a plug-in before you can listen to the jazz tracks.

Web-based digital audio is often delivered in streaming format to avoid lengthy delays while the entire audio file is downloaded. **Streaming audio** plays as its file is downloaded (Figure 8-6).

**Can I convert audio files from one format to another?** Suppose you find a cool MIDI ring tone on the Web, but your iPhone won't play MIDI music. You can use audio converter software to change audio files from one format to another. Your audio player software might provide tools for opening a file stored in one format and saving it in another format. If not, a quick Google search can provide links to free audio converters.

Suppose that you want your iPod to play tracks from one of your audio CDs. You can use audio software to rip tracks into a format that's supported by your iPod. *Ripping* is a slang term that refers to the process of importing tracks from a CD or DVD to your computer's hard disk. The technical term for ripping is **digital audio extraction**.

Music is stored on CDs in a digital format called CDDA. The format offers high fidelity; but as with WAV files, one minute of CDDA music requires in excess of 10 MB of storage space. During the ripping process, music in CDDA format is typically converted into a compressed format such as MP3, AAC, or WMA to reduce file size.

Many software tools are available for converting audio files from one format to another and ripping CD tracks. One of the most versatile tools is Apple iTunes software (Figure 8-7).

**FIGURE 8-6**

Streaming audio provides the technology for real-time Internet radio broadcasts, podcasts, and voice chat sessions.

**FIGURE 8-7**

iTunes software makes it easy to convert audio files into other formats.

## MIDI MUSIC

**What is MIDI music?** Digital audio is a recording of real analog sound signals. In contrast, **synthesized sound** is an artificially created, or synthetic, sound. Synthesized sound can be classified as MIDI music or synthesized speech.

**MIDI** (Musical Instrument Digital Interface) specifies a standard way to store music data for synthesizers, electronic MIDI instruments, and computers. Unlike digital audio files, which contain digitized recordings of real performances, MIDI files contain instructions for creating the pitch, volume, and duration of notes that sound like various musical instruments.

MIDI is a music notation system that allows computers to communicate with music synthesizers. The computer encodes the music as a **MIDI sequence** and stores it as a file with a .mid, .cmf, or .rol file extension. A MIDI sequence is analogous to a player-piano roll that contains punched information indicating which musical notes to play. A MIDI sequence contains instructions specifying the pitch of a note, the point at which the note begins, the instrument that plays the note, the volume of the note, and the point at which the note ends.

Most computer sound cards are equipped to generate music from MIDI files, and many can capture music data from a MIDI instrument as well. A MIDI-capable sound card contains a **wavetable** (sometimes called a patch set), which is a set of prerecorded musical instrument sounds. The sound card accesses these sounds and plays them as instructed by the MIDI file. For example, if a sound card receives a MIDI instruction for a trumpet to play middle C, it accesses the trumpet's middle C patch and routes it to the speaker until it receives a MIDI instruction to stop the note.

**What are the advantages and disadvantages of MIDI?** MIDI files are much more compact than digital audio files. Depending on the exact piece of music, three minutes of MIDI music might require only 10 KB of storage space, whereas the same piece of music stored in a high-quality, uncompressed digital audio file might require 30 MB of storage space.

One of the big disadvantages of MIDI is that it does not produce high-quality vocals. Another disadvantage is that it does not have the full resonance of real sound. Most musicians can easily identify MIDI recordings because they simply lack the tonal qualities of symphony-quality sound. You can compare the differences by using the Click to Start buttons in Figure 8-8.

**FIGURE 8-8**

MIDI music tends not to have the full resonance of digital audio. Use your digital textbook to listen to these two sound clips and see if you can hear a difference.

8

▶ CLICK TO START

▶ CLICK TO START

**When would I use MIDI music?** MIDI is a good choice for adding background music to multimedia projects and Web pages. Using a procedure similar to that for digital audio files, you can add a link to a MIDI file by inserting a tag such as <audio src="sousa.mid"> within an HTML document. Most browsers include built-in support for MIDI music.

You can use music composition software, such as Finale, to create your own snappy tunes or get permission to use MIDI files you find on the Web. For composing your own MIDI music, you can input notes from a MIDI instrument directly to your computer. The input is typically handled by music composition software (Figure 8-9), which you can also use to edit notes and combine the parts for several instruments.

**FIGURE 8-9**

Music composition software provides tools for entering notes, specifying instruments, printing sheet music, and saving compositions in formats such as MIDI. ▶ You can use your digital textbook to take a tour of music composition software and see how the TexMex music was created.

## SPEECH RECOGNITION AND SYNTHESIS

**What's the difference between speech synthesis and speech recognition?** **Speech synthesis** is the process by which machines, such as computers, produce sound that resembles spoken words. **Speech recognition** (or voice recognition) refers to the ability of a machine to understand spoken words.

Speech recognition is used to automate telephone-based services such as Directory Assistance and interactive voice response systems, such as Google Mobile Apps that allow users to search Google by voice over their mobile phones. The use of digital spectrographic analysis to identify human speakers is an emerging part of law enforcement and homeland security. Not only can digitized samples of voices be analyzed to confirm identity, but real-time voice print identification can match speakers with known recordings of their voices.

Speech synthesis is a key technology in mobile communication, such as accessing your e-mail using a cell phone—a speech synthesizer reads your e-mail messages to you. A speech synthesizer can also read a computer screen aloud, which unlocks access to computers and the Internet for individuals with visual disabilities.

**How does speech synthesis work?** A basic sound unit, such as "reh" or "gay," is called a **phoneme**. Most speech synthesizers string together phonemes to form words. For example, the phonemes "reh" and "gay" produce the word "reggae." A basic speech synthesizer consists of **text-to-speech software**, which generates sounds that are played through your computer's standard sound card. As an alternative, some speech synthesizers are special-purpose hardware devices.

**How does speech recognition work?** On a personal computer, a speech recognition system typically collects words spoken into a microphone that's attached to the sound card. The sound card's digital signal processor transforms the analog sound of your voice into digital data. This data is then processed by speech recognition software.

Speech recognition software analyzes the sounds of your voice and converts them to phonemes. Next, the software analyzes the content of your speech. It compares the groups of phonemes to the words in a digital dictionary that lists phoneme combinations along with their corresponding English (or French, Spanish, and so on) words. When a match is found, the software displays the correctly spelled word on the screen.

Speech recognition software can be integrated with word processing software so that you can enter text simply by speaking into a microphone. Going beyond word processing, speech recognition can be used to activate Windows controls instead of using a mouse. Most speech recognition software also works with your browser, allowing you to "voice surf" the Web.

Windows 7 includes a speech recognition module called Narrator. The first steps in using Narrator are setting up a microphone and training the computer to recognize your speaking style. Training consists of reading a series of short text passages into a microphone attached to your computer.

You can train your Windows computer by using Speech Recognition Voice Training, which displays paragraphs of text, waits for you to read them, and creates your personal speech profile (Figure 8-10).

When training is complete, you can use Narrator to verbally issue commands in Windows and dictate text in Microsoft Word and Excel, plus any other Windows applications designed to support this feature.

**FIGURE 8-10**

The Windows Speech Recognition Wizard displays short text passages. As you read each passage, the computer listens to the way you pronounce each word and stores it in your speech profile.

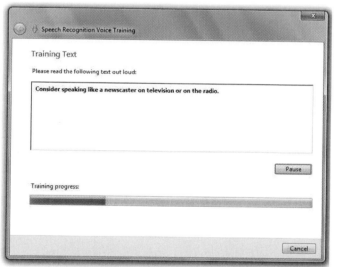

# QuickCheck

SECTION A

1. _____ rate refers to the number of times per second that a sound is measured during the recording process.

2. When sound card circuitry is incorporated into a computer system board, it is often referred to as _____ audio.

3. The process of ripping tracks from an audio CD into a digital format such as MP3 is called digital audio _____ .

4. MIDI sound is generated from a(n) _____ (or patch set), which is a set of prerecorded musical instrument sounds.

5. When a telephone-based airline voice response system asks you to say your flight number, it processes your response using speech _____ software.

▶ CHECK ANSWERS

# Bitmap Graphics

**A DIGITAL CAMERA** seems easy to use. Point it, shoot the photo, and...what next? How do you transfer digital photos from camera to computer? How can you print them? How do you get them ready to become e-mail attachments? How do you prepare them for inclusion on Web pages? To understand the wide range of possibilities for digital photos, you'll need some background information about bitmap graphics.

## BITMAP BASICS

**What is a bitmap graphic?** A **bitmap graphic**, also called a raster graphic or simply a bitmap, is composed of a grid of dots. The color of each dot is stored as a binary number. Think of a grid superimposed on a picture. The grid divides the picture into cells, called pixels. Each pixel is assigned a color, which is stored as a binary number. Figure 8-11 illustrates these basic characteristics of a bitmap graphic.

**Where would I encounter bitmap graphics?** Bitmap graphics are typically used to create realistic images, such as photographs. You might also encounter bitmaps in the form of cartoons, images that appear in computer games, and rendered images produced by 3-D graphics software. When you use a digital camera or camera-enabled cell phone, your photos are stored as bitmaps. A scanner produces bitmaps. The photos you send or receive as e-mail attachments are bitmaps, as are most Web page graphics. Bitmap graphics formats include RAW, PNG, GIF, BMP, JPEG, and TIFF. Details about using these formats are presented later in this section.

**How do I create bitmap images?** You can create a bitmap graphic from scratch using the tools provided by graphics software—specifically a category of graphics software referred to as **paint software**. You might be familiar with paint software such as Adobe Photoshop, Corel Painter, and Microsoft Paint (included with Windows). These programs have tools for freehand sketching, filling in shapes, adding realistic shading, and creating effects that look like oil paints, charcoal, or watercolors. If your freehand sketching talent maxes out with stick figures, you can also create bitmap graphics by using a scanner or digital camera.

**FIGURE 8-11**

A bitmap graphic is divided into a grid of individually colored pixels. The color number for each pixel is stored in binary format. ▶ Learn how to use Windows Paint to create bitmap graphics and see how to work pixel by pixel to edit an image.

## SCANNERS AND CAMERAS

**How do I convert a printed image into a bitmap?** When you have a printed image, such as a photograph, a page from a magazine, or a picture from a book, you can use a **scanner** to convert the printed image into a bitmap graphic. A scanner essentially divides an image into a fine grid of cells and assigns a digital value for the color of each cell. As the scan progresses, these values are transferred to your computer's hard disk and stored as a bitmap graphics file. Scanners, such as the one pictured in Figure 8-12, are inexpensive and easy to use.

**FIGURE 8-12**

To scan an image, turn on the scanner and start your scanner software. Place the image face down on the scanner glass, and then use the scanner software to initiate the scan. The scanned image is saved in RAM and can then be saved on your computer's hard disk. ▶ Learn the difference between scanning an image and scanning a document into an editable word processing file.

**When should I use a digital camera rather than a scanner?** Whereas a scanner is designed to digitize printed images, a **digital camera** creates a digital image of real objects. Although you could take a photo with a conventional camera, develop the film, and then digitize the photo with a scanner, it is much simpler to use a digital camera to take a photo in digital format, which you can then transfer directly to your computer or print directly to a photo printer.

**How does a digital camera capture an image without using film?** The lens of a film camera captures the light from an image onto a light-sensitive roll of film, which is developed to produce a photographic print. In a digital camera, the lens focuses light from the image onto a small image sensor called a **CCD** (charge-coupled device). A CCD contains a grid of tiny light-sensitive diodes called **photosites**.

**FIGURE 8-13**

A digital camera's CCD converts the image captured by the camera lens into a grid of colored pixels, which are stored as bits. ▶ Watch the video for this figure in your digital textbook for an overview of digital camera features, file formats, and the process of transferring photos from a camera to your computer.

8

The number of photosites depends on the size of the CCD. A one-half-inch square CCD can contain up to 500,000 photosites. Each photosite detects the brightness and color for its tiny piece of the total image (Figure 8-13).

A CCD's photosites correspond to pixels. The more pixels used to capture an image, the higher its resolution, and the better the resulting picture. Cameras with larger CCDs produce higher quality images. Some cameras contain multiple CCDs, which enhance the color quality of a camera's output.

CCD

**How does a digital camera store images?** Some digital cameras store photos on CDs, mini CDs, or microdrives, but the most popular digital camera storage is solid state memory cards. Like RAM, memory cards can be erased and reused. Unlike RAM, however, solid state storage holds data without consuming power, so it doesn't lose data when the camera is turned off. Figure 8-14 illustrates several digital camera storage options.

**FIGURE 8-14**

SD (Secure Digital) memory cards are the most popular option for photo storage. The original SD cards max out at 4 GB. Newer SDHC cards have 32 GB maximum capacity; SDXC cards have a 2 TB maximum capacity. Although SDHC and SDXC cards fit in a standard SD slot, older equipment might not be able to handle such high storage capacities.

CompactFlash

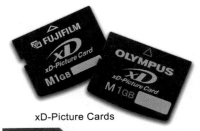

xD-Picture Cards

Memory stick

Secure Digital card

MicroSD card

Microdrive

**How can I get images out of the camera?** Digital cameras allow you to preview images while they are still in the camera and delete those you don't want. The photos you want to keep can be transferred directly to a properly equipped printer or transferred to your computer's hard disk. Depending on your camera, this transfer can be achieved in several ways:

• Card readers. A card reader is a small device designed to read data contained in a solid state memory card. Card readers can be connected to your computer's USB port, built into a computer system unit, or built into a photoprinter. To transfer photo data from a memory card, you remove it from the camera and insert it into the card reader, as shown in Figure 8-15.

• Direct cable transfer. If your computer and your camera have FireWire ports (also called IEEE-1394 ports), you can connect a cable between these two ports to transfer the photo data. You can use a similar transfer method if your computer and camera have USB ports or serial ports. A USB-2 or FireWire port provides good transfer speed. USB-1 ports are somewhat slower, and serial ports are quite slow.

• Infrared port. Some cameras can beam photo data to your computer's infrared port. This method eliminates the need for a cable but is much slower than using a FireWire, USB, or serial port.

• Media transfer. If your camera stores data on CDs or similar optical media, you can simply remove the media from your camera and insert it into the appropriate drive of your computer.

• Docking station. Some camera manufacturers offer a camera docking station that connects to a computer by cable. A camera can be placed in the docking station to transfer photos to the computer's hard disk.

• E-mail. Cell phone photos can be transferred to a computer by e-mailing the photo to your e-mail account. The photo arrives as an attachment, which can be saved as a separate file.

**FIGURE 8-15**

A card reader transfers photo data from a memory card to your computer's hard disk.

Your computer treats memory cards essentially as any other storage device. So when you insert an SD card, for example, you can use Windows Explorer or Finder to copy photo files from the SD card to your computer's hard disk. Files copied in this way retain their original file names, such as img00030, which can be fairly cryptic.

You can also handle photo transfer with photo software, which might be supplied along with your camera, with your card reader, or by a standalone graphics software package, such as Adobe Photoshop. This software allows you to select a file format, specify a file name, and determine the location for each image file.

After you store your digital photos on your computer's hard disk, you can modify them, send them as e-mail attachments, print them, post them on Web pages, or archive them onto a CD or DVD.

**What characteristics of a bitmap can I modify?** Because bitmap graphics are coded as a series of bits that represent pixels, you can use graphics software to modify or edit this type of graphic by changing individual pixels. You can retouch old photographs to eliminate creases, spots, and discoloration (Figure 8-16). You can modify photos to wipe out red eye or erase the "rabbit ears" that ruined an otherwise good family portrait. You can even design eye-catching new pictures with images you cut and paste from several photos or scanned images.

Whether you acquire an image from a digital camera or a scanner, bitmap graphics tend to require quite a bit of storage space. Although a large graphics file might provide the necessary data for a high-quality printout, these files take up space on your hard disk and can require lengthy transmission times that clog up mailboxes and make Web pages seem sluggish. The size of the file that holds a bitmap depends on its resolution and color depth. Read on to see how these factors affect file size and how you can alter them to create smaller graphics files, suitable for e-mail attachments and Web pages.

## IMAGE RESOLUTION

**How does resolution pertain to bitmap graphics?** The dimensions of the grid that forms a bitmap graphic are referred to as its resolution. The resolution of a graphic is usually expressed as the number of horizontal and vertical pixels it contains. For example, a small graphic for a Web page might have a resolution of 150 x 100 pixels—150 pixels across and 100 pixels high.

**How does resolution relate to image quality?** High-resolution graphics contain more data than low-resolution graphics. With more data, it is possible to display and print high-quality images that are sharper and clearer than images produced using less data. For example, a photograph of a cat taken with an inexpensive digital camera might produce a graphic with a resolution of 1600 x 1200, but a more expensive camera with 3888 x 2592 resolution contains more pixels and produces a higher-quality image.

Camera manufacturers sometimes express the resolution of digital cameras as megapixels. A **megapixel** is 1 million pixels. A camera with a resolution of 1600 x 1200 has the capability of producing photos containing 1.9 megapixels (1600 multiplied by 1200). A camera with 3888 x 2592 resolution is technically 10.1 megapixels, but might be rounded off and called a 10 megapixel camera by its manufacturer.

FIGURE 8-16

Bitmap graphics can be easily modified. Many graphics software products include wizards that help you retouch photographs.

Before

8

After

**How does resolution relate to the file size of a graphic?** Each pixel in a bitmap graphic is stored as one or more bits. The more pixels in a bitmap, the more bits needed to store the file.

**How does resolution relate to the physical size of an image?** A bitmap graphic is simply a collection of data. Unlike a printed photograph, a bitmap has no fixed physical size. The size at which a bitmap is displayed or printed depends on the density as well as the resolution (dimensions) of the image grid.

Imagine that each bitmap image and its grid come on a surface that you can stretch or shrink. As you stretch the surface, the grid maintains the same number of horizontal and vertical cells, but each cell becomes larger and the grid becomes less dense. As you shrink the surface, the grid becomes smaller and more dense. The graphic retains the same resolution no matter how much you stretch or shrink the graphic's physical size, as shown in Figure 8-17.

Reduced size
remains at
24 x 24 resolution

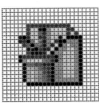

Original graphic at
24 x 24 resolution

Enlarged graphic still
has 24 x 24 resolution

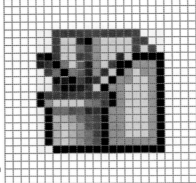

**FIGURE 8-17**

When a bitmap graphic is enlarged or reduced in size, it still retains its original resolution—24 x 24.

This concept of stretching and shrinking without changing resolution is important for understanding what happens when bitmaps are displayed and printed. The denser the grid, the smaller the image will appear. The density of an image grid can be expressed as dots per inch (dpi) for a printer or scanner, or as pixels per inch (ppi) on a display device.

**How do I specify the size of a printed image?** Most graphics software allows you to specify the size at which an image is printed without changing the resolution of the bitmap graphic. You'll get an acceptable image if you print 400 dpi or more. So, if a photo's resolution is 1600 x 800 pixels, it will look fine as a 4" x 2" print. As you enlarge the image beyond this size, it will start to appear somewhat fuzzy because the pixels will begin to become visible.

As a general rule, when you incorporate an image in a desktop-published document, or when you print photographs, you should work with high-resolution bitmaps so that you can produce high-quality output. To capture high-resolution bitmaps, use the highest resolution provided by your digital camera. When scanning an image, choose a dpi setting on your scanner that is at least as high as the dpi for the printout.

**How does a bitmap's resolution relate to what I see on the screen?** In Chapter 2, you learned that you can set your computer display to a particular resolution, such as 1024 x 768. When you display a bitmap graphic on the screen, each pixel of the graphic typically corresponds to one pixel on the screen. If the resolution of your graphic is

1024 x 768 and your display is set at 1024 x 768 resolution, the image appears to fill the screen. If you view a 4.0 megapixel image on the same display device, the image is larger than the screen, and you have to scroll or change the zoom level to view it (Figure 8-18).

**Can I change a graphic's file size?** The resolution and corresponding file size of a graphic might not be right for your needs. For example, if you take a photo with a 10.0 megapixel camera, it is unsuitable for a Web page. Not only would it take a long time to download, but it would be larger than most screens. A 10.0 megapixel graphic is also not suitable for an e-mail attachment. Uploading and downloading such a large file—especially over a dial-up connection—would take much too long. Reducing the resolution of a bitmap can reduce its file size and on-screen display size. Most experts recommend that Web graphics not exceed 100 KB and that e-mail attachments not exceed 500 KB.

You can reduce the size of a bitmap by cropping it. **Cropping** refers to the process of selecting part of an image—just like cutting out a section of a photograph. Cropping decreases resolution and file size by reducing the number of pixels in a graphic. You can also reduce file size by removing pixels from the entire graphic; however, this process changes the image quality.

Bitmap graphics are **resolution dependent**, which means that the quality of the image depends on its resolution. If you reduce the resolution, the computer eliminates pixels from the image, reducing the size of the image grid. For example, if you reduce the resolution from 2160 x 1440 (3.1 megapixels) to 1080 x 720 (0.8 megapixels), the image grid becomes a quarter of its original size. The file size is reduced by a similar amount. However, the computer threw away data with the pixels, which can reduce image quality.

If you attempt to enlarge a bitmap by increasing its resolution, your computer must somehow add pixels because no additional picture data exists. But what colors should these additional pixels become? Most graphics software uses a process called **pixel interpolation** to create new pixels by averaging the colors of nearby pixels. For some graphics, pixel interpolation results in an image that appears very similar to the original. Other images—particularly those with strong curved or diagonal lines—develop an undesirable **pixelated**, or "bitmappy," jagged appearance (Figure 8-19).

**FIGURE 8-18**

When viewing an image larger than the screen, you must scroll to see all parts of the image or set the zoom level of your graphics software to less than 100%. You should understand, however, that changing the zoom level stretches or shrinks only the size of the image grid. It has no effect on the printed size of a graphic or the graphic's file size.

8

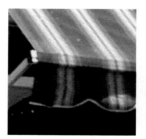

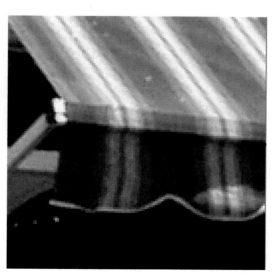

The figure above has a resolution of 130 x 130. The figure at right was enlarged to a resolution of 260 x 260, but it has a rough, pixelated appearance.

**FIGURE 8-19**

When you increase the resolution of an existing graphic, the file size increases, but the quality might deteriorate.

## COLOR DEPTH AND PALETTES

**What is color depth?** As you learned in Chapter 2, color depth is the number of colors available for use in an image. As the number of colors increases, image quality improves, but file size also increases. You can limit color depth to decrease the file size required for a graphic. To find out how this works, first take a look at the storage requirements for various color depths.

**How does color depth relate to file size?** To answer this question, consider a simple monochrome display device. Each screen pixel can be either "on" or "off." A **monochrome bitmap** is displayed by manipulating the pattern of "off" and "on" pixels displayed on the screen. To store the data for a monochrome bitmap, an "on" pixel is represented by a 1 bit. An "off" pixel is represented by a 0 bit. Each row of the bitmap grid is stored as a series of 0s and 1s, as shown in Figure 8-20.

**FIGURE 8-20**

Each pixel in a monochrome bitmap graphic is stored as a bit.

**1.** This image originated as a black-and-white silhouette.

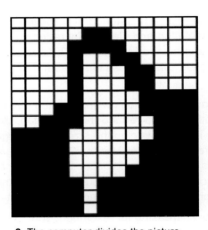

**2.** The computer divides the picture into a matrix.

| 1 | 1 | 1 | 1 | 1 | 1 | 1 | 1 | 1 | 1 | 1 | 1 |
|---|---|---|---|---|---|---|---|---|---|---|---|
| 1 | 1 | 1 | 1 | 0 | 0 | 1 | 1 | 1 | 1 | 1 | 1 |
| 1 | 1 | 1 | 0 | 0 | 0 | 0 | 1 | 1 | 1 | 1 | 1 |
| 1 | 1 | 1 | 0 | 1 | 1 | 0 | 0 | 1 | 1 | 1 | 1 |
| 1 | 1 | 1 | 0 | 1 | 1 | 1 | 0 | 0 | 1 | 1 | 1 |
| 1 | 1 | 1 | 0 | 1 | 1 | 1 | 0 | 0 | 1 | 1 | 1 |
| 1 | 1 | 1 | 0 | 1 | 1 | 1 | 0 | 0 | 0 | 0 | 0 |
| 1 | 1 | 0 | 0 | 1 | 1 | 1 | 0 | 0 | 0 | 0 | 0 |
| 1 | 0 | 0 | 0 | 1 | 1 | 1 | 1 | 0 | 0 | 0 | 0 |
| 0 | 0 | 0 | 0 | 1 | 1 | 1 | 1 | 0 | 0 | 0 | 0 |
| 0 | 0 | 0 | 1 | 1 | 1 | 1 | 0 | 0 | 0 | 0 | 0 |
| 0 | 0 | 0 | 1 | 1 | 1 | 1 | 0 | 0 | 0 | 0 | 0 |
| 0 | 0 | 0 | 1 | 1 | 1 | 0 | 0 | 0 | 0 | 0 | 0 |
| 0 | 0 | 0 | 0 | 1 | 0 | 0 | 0 | 0 | 0 | 0 | 0 |
| 0 | 0 | 0 | 0 | 1 | 0 | 0 | 0 | 0 | 0 | 0 | 0 |

**3.** If a cell is white, it is coded as a 1. If a cell is black, it is coded as a 0.

Monochrome bitmaps require very little storage space. Suppose you create a full-screen monochrome bitmap with your screen resolution set to 1024 x 768. Your screen displays 786,432 pixels (that's 1,024 multiplied by 768). Each pixel is set to display a black dot or a white dot. When you store the graphic, each dot requires only one bit. Therefore, the number of bits required to represent a full-screen picture is the same as the number of pixels on the screen.

At a resolution of 1024 x 768, a full-screen graphic requires 786,432 bits of storage space. The number of bytes required to store the image is 786,432 divided by 8 (remember that there are eight bits in a byte). Your full-screen monochrome bitmap would, therefore, require only 98,304 bytes of storage space.

**But what about color?** Today's color display devices require a more complex storage scheme. Each screen pixel displays a color based on the intensity of red, green, and blue signals it receives. A pixel appears white if the red, green, and blue signals are set to maximum intensity. If red, green, and blue signals are equal but at a lower intensity, the pixel displays a shade of gray. If the red signal is set to maximum intensity, but the blue and green signals are off, the pixel appears in brilliant red. A pixel appears purple if it receives red and blue signals, and so forth.

Each red, green, and blue signal is assigned a value ranging from 0 to 255: 0 represents the absence of color, and 255 represents the highest intensity level for that color. These values produce a maximum of 16.7 million colors. A graphic that uses this full range of colors is referred to as a **True Color bitmap** or a 24-bit bitmap. You might be able to guess where the 24-bit term comes from. The data for each pixel requires three bytes of storage space—eight bits for blue, eight bits for green, and eight bits for red—for a total of 24 bits. Although True Color bitmaps produce photographic-quality images, they also produce very large files. Because each pixel requires three bytes, a 3 megapixel True Color bitmap would require a 9 MB file!

You might occasionally encounter a 32-bit bitmap. Just like a 24-bit bitmap, it displays 16.7 million colors. The extra bits are used to define special effects, such as the amount of transparency, for a pixel. These files are even larger than those containing 24-bit bitmaps. A 3 megapixel 32-bit bitmap would be about 10 MB.

Files containing full-screen 24-bit and 32-bit bitmaps are typically too large for Web pages because they require excessively long upload and download times. Earlier in the chapter, you learned that you can reduce a bitmap's file size by removing pixels. Another way to shrink a bitmap file is to reduce its color depth.

**How can I reduce color depth?** To reduce the color depth of a bitmap, you can use your graphics software to work with color palettes. A **color palette** (also called a color lookup table or color map) is the digital version of a kidney-shaped artist's palette that holds the selection of colors an artist uses for a particular painting. A digital color palette allows you to select a group of colors to use for a bitmap graphic.

The advantage of a palette is that if it contains only 256 colors, you can store the data for each pixel in 8 bits instead of 24 bits, which reduces the file to a third of the size required for a True Color bitmap.

**How does a color palette work?** A color palette is stored as a table within the header of a graphics file. Each palette contains a list of 256 color numbers. Each of these numbers is mapped to a 24-bit number that corresponds to the actual levels of red, green, and blue required to display the color. Figure 8-21 explains how this table works.

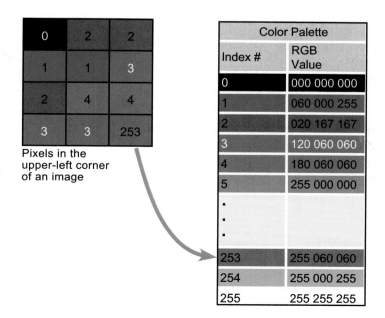

Pixels in the
upper-left corner
of an image

FIGURE 8-21

A color palette is a subset of all possible colors. Each color in the palette is numbered, and its number points to the full 24-bit RGB (red, green, blue) value stored in the graphics file header. The values in the lookup table are shown in decimal notation; converted into binary, a decimal number such as 255 would require eight bits.

**How do I select a color palette?** Most graphics software offers a selection of ready-made palettes that you can choose by using the color palette or color picker tool. Ready-made palettes usually include a grayscale palette, a system palette, and a Web palette.

A **grayscale palette** uses shades of gray, or "gray scales," to display images that look similar to black-and-white photographs. Most grayscale palettes consist of 256 shades of gray. Figure 8-22 illustrates a grayscale palette and a grayscale bitmap graphic.

**FIGURE 8-22**

Grayscale bitmaps look like black-and-white photographs.

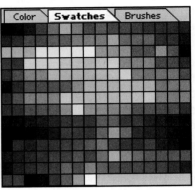

A **system palette** is the collection of colors the operating system uses for graphics that represent desktop icons and controls. Windows, for example, uses a system palette containing 20 permanent colors and 236 colors that can be changed, depending on the application.

A **Web palette** (also called a Web-safe palette or a browser palette) contains a standard set of colors used by Internet Web browsers. Because most browsers support this palette, it is typically regarded as a safe choice when preparing graphics for Internet distribution. Figure 8-23 shows the collection of colors used by system and Web palettes.

**FIGURE 8-23**

The Windows system palette (left) and Web palette (below) are usually provided by graphics software.

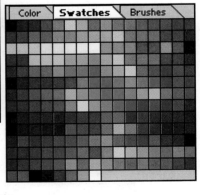

Your graphics software might offer additional palettes. They are likely to include a "woodsy" palette that works well for outdoor photographs, a pastel palette that works well with images filled with predominantly light colors, and a flesh-tone palette that's designed to work nicely for portraits.

# IMAGE COMPRESSION

**What is image compression?** **Image compression** refers to any technique that recodes the data in an image file so that it contains fewer bits. Smaller files produced as a result of image compression require less storage space and can be transmitted more rapidly than the larger, original files. Images can be compressed using lossless or lossy compression.

**What is the difference between lossless and lossy compression?** **Lossless compression** provides the means to compress a file and then reconstitute all the data into its original state. TIFF and GIF graphics formats offer lossless compression.

In contrast, **lossy compression** throws away some of the original data during the compression process. In theory, the human eye won't miss the lost information. JPEG files are compressed using lossy compression. Most lossy compression techniques have adjustable compression levels so that you can decide how much data you can afford to lose.

**How does lossless compression shrink a file without throwing away data?** Various techniques exist for lossless image compression. As a simple example, consider a type of lossless compression called run-length encoding. **Run-length encoding** (RLE) replaces a series of similarly colored pixels with a code that indicates the number of pixels and their colors. Suppose that a section of a picture has 167 consecutive white pixels, and each pixel is described by one byte of data, as in a 256-color bitmap image. RLE compresses this series of 167 bytes into as few as two bytes, as shown in Figure 8-24.

**FIGURE 8-24**

In an uncompressed file, each pixel of a 256-color bitmap requires one byte to indicate its color. For example, a white pixel might be coded 11111111. Run-length encoding compresses graphical data by recoding like-colored pixels when they appear in a series.

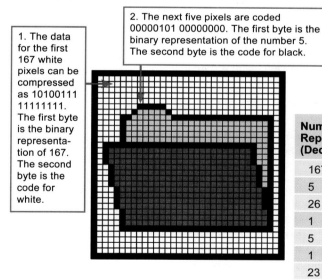

1. The data for the first 167 white pixels can be compressed as 10100111 11111111. The first byte is the binary representation of 167. The second byte is the code for white.

2. The next five pixels are coded 00000101 00000000. The first byte is the binary representation of the number 5. The second byte is the code for black.

3. With compression, the first nine rows of the graphic require only 30 bytes—the binary numbers in columns 2 and 4 of this table. The uncompressed graphic requires 288 bytes.

| Number of Repetitions (Decimal) | Number of Repetitions (Binary) | Pixel Color | Pixel Color (Binary) |
|---|---|---|---|
| 167 | 10100111 | White | 11111111 |
| 5 | 00000101 | Black | 00000000 |
| 26 | 00011010 | White | 11111111 |
| 1 | 00000001 | Black | 00000000 |
| 5 | 00000101 | Yellow | 10100000 |
| 1 | 00000001 | Black | 00000000 |
| 23 | 00010111 | White | 11111111 |
| 2 | 00000010 | Black | 00000000 |
| 7 | 00000111 | Yellow | 10100000 |
| 18 | 00010010 | Black | 00000000 |
| 5 | 00000101 | White | 11111111 |
| 1 | 00000001 | Black | 00000000 |
| 25 | 00011001 | Yellow | 10100000 |
| 1 | 00000001 | White | 11111111 |
| 1 | 00000001 | Black | 00000000 |

8

**What happens during lossy compression?** Lossy compression techniques discard some data from an image to shrink its file size. JPEG is a lossy version of run-length encoding that can be applied to images, such as photographs, that don't have large areas of solid color. A True Color photograph might not have any adjoining pixels of the same color. Applying RLE to such a photo would not result in any compression whatsoever. JPEG preprocesses an image by tweaking the colors in adjoining pixels so that they are the same color whenever possible. After this preprocessing is complete, run-length encoding can be applied with more success.

For many images, lossy compression results in only a minor reduction in the sharpness of the image. The reduction in quality can be unnoticeable in many circumstances. Figure 8-25 illustrates a section of a noncompressed image and a section of that same image after JPEG compression has been applied. Can you see the difference?

**FIGURE 8-25**

JPEG compression can slightly adjust the colors of adjacent pixels to make them the same. These like-colored pixels can then be compressed with RLE.

Non-compressed JPEG image

JPEG image with 35% compression

**How do I compress image files?** Some graphics file formats automatically compress file data. You can also compress files using a general-purpose file compression utility.

GIF, JPEG, PNG, and TIFF file formats support compression. Software that works with these file formats might allow you to select compression levels before saving a graphics file. For example, when saving an image in JPEG format, you might be given the option of selecting compression settings from 1 (worst quality) to 99 (best quality).

Some bitmap formats, such as BMP and RAW, do not support compression. If you want to compress these files before sending them as e-mail attachments, for example, you can do so manually using a file compression utility. A **file compression utility** uses lossless compression to shrink one or more files into a single new file. PKZIP and WinZip are popular shareware programs that compress and decompress files. 7-Zip is a popular open source compression utility.

You can compress any kind of file, including programs and data files, graphics, and document files. BMP file sizes might shrink by as much as 70% when compressed. Files stored in formats such as PNG, GIF, and JPEG hardly shrink at all when you use compression utilities because they are already stored in compressed format.

Compressing files is sometimes called zipping, and decompressing files is sometimes called unzipping. Most file compression utilities not only zip single files, but can also zip several files into a single compressed file that can later be unzipped into the original separate files.

For example, suppose you want to send three files to your boss. The original files are called *Technology.xlsx*, *Schedule-Fall Classes.docx*, and *Insurance.bmp*. You can zip all three files into a single compressed file called *Management 212.zip* (Figure 8-26). Simply attach this one file to an e-mail and send it to your boss. When *Management 212.zip* is unzipped, it produces the three original files.

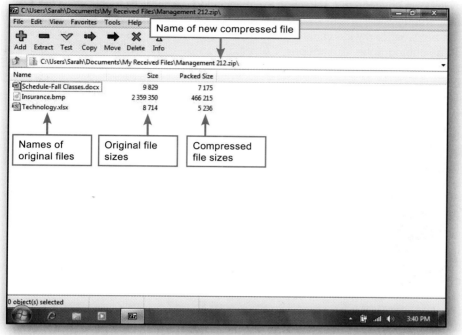

**FIGURE 8-26**

File compression utilities, such as open source 7-Zip, zip one or more files into a new compressed file with a .zip extension. ▶ Watch how to zip multiple files into a single compressed file, and learn how to unzip files using 7-Zip.

If you have not installed compression software such as PKZIP, you can use a feature of Windows to create compressed folders (Figure 8-27). Any files that you drag into a compressed folder are automatically compressed. You don't have to do anything special to open a file from a compressed folder. Simply double-click the file as usual, and Windows automatically decompresses the file before displaying its contents.

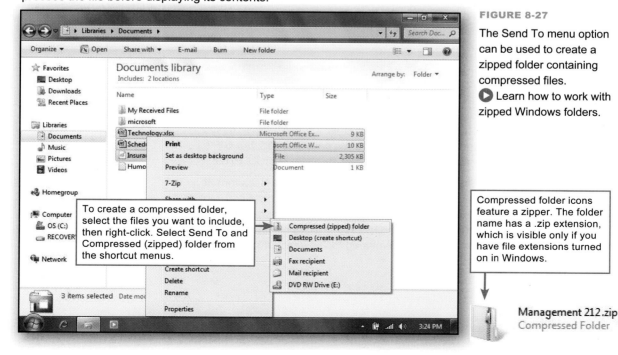

**FIGURE 8-27**

The Send To menu option can be used to create a zipped folder containing compressed files. ▶ Learn how to work with zipped Windows folders.

8

## BITMAP GRAPHICS FORMATS

**Are there different kinds of bitmap graphics?** Many graphics file formats exist, and most graphics software offers a choice of popular formats, such as BMP, RAW, TIFF, JPEG, GIF, and PNG (Figure 8-28).

**BMP**, pronounced "bee-em-pee" or "bump," is the native bitmap graphics file format of the Microsoft Windows environment. Microsoft Paint, included as part of Microsoft Windows, creates BMP graphics files. The BMP format supports True Color and can be used for a wide variety of graphics applications, such as photographs, illustrations, and graphs. BMP files are not compressed in any way, so this format typically creates very large files that are not suitable for e-mail attachments. BMP graphics are not supported by most browsers, so they are not used on the Web.

When saving a graphic, you can specify its format using the Save as command.

**RAW** image formats contain the unprocessed pixel data generated directly by a digital camera's sensor. Up to 12 bits of data can be stored for each of the red, blue, and green values for a pixel, so RAW files are very large. Cameras that offer a RAW format also supply proprietary software to convert RAW data to JPEG or TIFF.

**TIFF** (Tagged Image File Format), or TIF, is a flexible and platform-independent graphics file format supported by most photo-editing software packages. Scanners and digital cameras commonly store bitmaps in TIFF format because it supports True Color and can be easily converted into other graphics file formats. TIFF is an excellent choice for desktop publishing projects, but it is not supported by most browsers.

**JPEG** (pronounced "JAY-peg"), which stands for Joint Photographic Experts Group, is a graphics format with built-in compression that stores True Color bitmap data very efficiently in a small file. The JPEG format is popular for Web graphics and for photos attached to e-mail messages. When creating or converting an image in JPEG format, you can control the level of compression and the resulting file size. The compression process eliminates some image data, however, so highly compressed files suffer some quality deterioration.

**GIF** (pronounced "GIF" or "JIFF"), or Graphics Interchange Format, was specifically designed to create images that can be displayed on multiple platforms, such as PCs and Macs. GIF graphics are a very popular format for Web graphics, but they are limited to 256 colors. At one time, the compression algorithm built into the GIF format was patented by Unisys Corporation, which licensed its use. Those patents have expired, but GIF's popularity has been superseded by other graphics formats, such as PNG.

**PNG** (Portable Network Graphics), pronounced "ping," is a graphics format designed to improve on the GIF format. A PNG graphic can display up to 48-bit True Color (trillions of colors). Unlike JPEG, PNG compresses bitmap data without losing any data, so compressed images retain the same high quality as the originals. PNG was developed as a public domain format without any restrictions on its use.

**How do I determine which graphics format to use?** Selecting the best graphics file format to use depends on what you intend to do with the image. Figure 8-29 summarizes popular uses for each format.

| Format | Use |
|--------|-----|
| BMP | Graphical elements, such as buttons and other controls used in computer programs |
| RAW | Used by professional and semi-professional photographers to capture images before they are stored in other formats |
| TIFF | High-resolution scanned images and digital photos used in desktop publishing; high-quality digital photos reproduced on special photo printers |
| JPEG | Photographic or scanned images that might be used in a variety of applications, such as desktop publishing or Web pages, where flexibility in file size is important |
| GIF | A popular format for Web graphics |
| PNG | An alternative to GIF for Web graphics |

**FIGURE 8-29**

Choosing a bitmap graphics format depends on how the image is used.

8

# QuickCheck                                                         SECTION B

1. A digital camera captures images on the photosites of a(n) [_____] . (Hint: Use the acronym.)

2. A characteristic of bitmap graphics is that they are resolution [_____] , so that reducing the resolution also reduces the image quality.

3. Graphics stored in True Color format require [_____] bits for each pixel.

4. The most popular True Color formats for Web graphics include [_____] and JPEG. (Hint: Use the acronym.)

5. Unlike [_____] compression, [_____] compression shrinks a file without throwing away any data.

▶ CHECK ANSWERS

# Vector and 3-D Graphics

IF YOU'VE PLAYED any computer games recently or watched an animated movie, you've seen the product of computer-generated 3-D animated graphics. To the uninformed, these photorealistic action characters might seem like little more than fancy cartoons. After you understand the way they are created, however, you'll appreciate the incredible amount of computing power they require. This section begins with two-dimensional vector graphics. You'll find out how they differ from bitmaps and why you might want to use them. After covering the basics for two-dimensional graphics, the section progresses to static 3-D graphics and then to animated 3-D graphics.

## VECTOR GRAPHICS BASICS

**What is a vector graphic?** Unlike a bitmap graphic created by dividing an image into a grid of pixels, a **vector graphic** consists of a set of instructions for re-creating a picture. Instead of storing the color value for each pixel, a vector graphic file contains the instructions the computer needs to create the shape, size, position, and color for each object in an image. These instructions are similar to those a drafting teacher might give students: "Draw a 2-inch (or 112-pixel) circle. Locate this circle 1 inch down and 2 inches in from the right edge of the work area. Fill the circle with yellow." The Stonehenge image shown in Figure 8-30 was created as a vector graphic.

**FIGURE 8-30**

The parts of a vector graphic are created as separate objects. This image was created with a series of roughly rectangular objects for the stones and a circular object for the sun. The objects are layered and can be manipulated individually. This characteristic of vector graphics gives artists flexibility in arranging and editing image elements.

**How can I identify vector graphics?** It can be difficult to accurately identify a vector graphic just by looking at an on-screen image. One clue that an image might be a vector graphic is a flat, cartoon-like quality. Think of clip art images—they are typically stored as vector graphics. For a more definitive identification, however, you should check the file extension. Vector graphics files have file extensions such as .wmf, .ai, .dxf, .eps, .swf, and .svg.

**How do vector graphics compare with bitmap graphics?** Vector graphics are suitable for most line art, logos, simple illustrations, and diagrams that might be displayed and printed at various sizes. When compared to bitmaps, vector graphics have several advantages and a few disadvantages. You should take the following distinctions into account when deciding which type of graphic to use for a specific project.

- **Vector graphics resize better than bitmaps.** When you change the size of a vector graphic, the objects change proportionally and maintain their smooth edges. Whereas shapes in a bitmap graphic might appear to have jagged edges after they are enlarged, shapes in a vector graphic appear smooth at any size, as shown in Figure 8-31.

**FIGURE 8-31**

Unlike bitmaps, vector graphics can be resized without becoming pixelated and blurry.

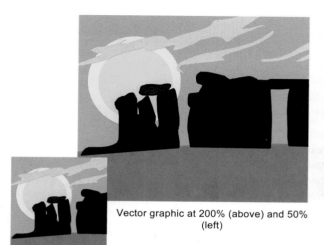

Vector graphic at 200% (above) and 50% (left)

Bitmap graphic at 200% (above) and 50% (right)

- **Vector graphics usually require less storage space than bitmaps.** The storage space required for a vector graphic reflects the complexity of the image. Each instruction requires storage space; so the more lines, shapes, and fill patterns in the graphic, the more storage space it requires. The Stonehenge vector graphic used as an example in this chapter requires less than 4 KB of storage space. A True Color photograph of the same image requires 1,109 KB.

- **Vector graphics are not usually as realistic as bitmap images.** Most vector images tend to have a cartoon-like appearance instead of the realistic appearance you expect from a photograph. This cartoon-like characteristic of vector images results from the use of objects filled with blocks of color. Your options for shading and texturing objects are limited, which tends to give vector graphics a flat appearance.

- **It is easier to edit an object in a vector graphic than an object in a bitmap graphic.** In some ways, a vector graphic is like a collage of objects. Each object can be layered over other objects, but moved and edited independently. You can individually stretch, shrink, distort, color, move, or delete any object in a vector graphic. For example, if you delete some of the stones from the Stonehenge vector image, the background layers remain. In contrast, most bitmap graphics are constructed as a single layer of pixels. If you erase the pixels for some of the stones in the Stonehenge photograph, you'll create a hole of white pixels (Figure 8-32).

**FIGURE 8-32**

Vector graphic objects are layered, so it is easy to move and delete objects without disrupting the rest of the image. In contrast, deleting a shape from a bitmap image leaves a hole because the image is only one layer of pixels.

**What tools do I need to create vector graphics?** Neither scanners nor digital cameras produce vector graphics. Architects and engineers sometimes use a digitizing tablet to turn a paper-based line drawing into a vector graphic. A **digitizing tablet** (sometimes called a 2-D digitizer) is a device that provides a flat surface for a paper-based drawing and a pen or mouse-like puck that you can use to click the endpoints of each line on the drawing. The endpoints are converted into vectors and stored.

Usually, vector graphics are created from scratch with vector graphics software, referred to as **drawing software**. Popular drawing software includes Adobe Illustrator, Corel DESIGNER, OpenOffice Draw, and open source Inkscape. Drawing software is sometimes packaged separately from the paint software used to produce bitmap graphics. In other cases, it is included with bitmap software as a graphics software suite.

Vector graphics software provides an array of drawing tools that you can use to create objects, position them, and fill them with colors or patterns. For example, you can use the filled circle tool to draw a circle filled with a solid color. You can create an irregular shape by connecting points to outline the shape. Figure 8-33 illustrates how to use drawing tools to create a vector graphic.

**INFOWEBLINKS**

To learn more about popular vector graphics software, you can connect to the **Vector Graphics Software InfoWeb**.

W CLICK TO CONNECT
www.infoweblinks.com/np2012/ch08

**FIGURE 8-33**

To draw a circle, select the filled circle tool, and then drag the mouse pointer to indicate the circle's location and size. A color palette allows you to select the circle color. After you create the circle object, you can move it and change its size or color. You can also create irregular shapes for objects, such as clouds, by connecting short line segments. ▶ Learn the basics of drawing vector images by accessing this figure in your digital textbook.

The circle tool is dragged to create a shape.

The clouds are created as a series of short line segments and filled with color.

The stones are created as a series of short line segments and filled with black.

The sun is two circles, each filled with a slightly different shade of yellow.

Vector graphics software helps you easily edit individual objects within a graphic by changing their sizes, shapes, positions, or colors. For example, the data for creating a circle for the sun is recorded as an instruction, such as CIRCLE 40 Y 200 150, which means create a circle with a 40-pixel radius, color it yellow, and place the center of the circle 200 pixels from the left of the screen and 150 pixels from the top of the screen. If you move the circle to the right side of the image, the instruction that the computer stores for the circle changes to something like CIRCLE 40 Y 500 150, which reflects its new position at 500 pixels from the left instead of 200.

When filling a shape with color, your graphics software might provide tools for creating gradients. A **gradient** is a smooth blending of shades from one color to another or from light to dark. Gradients, as shown in Figure 8-34, can be used to create shading and three-dimensional effects.

Some vector graphics software provides tools that apply bitmapped textures to vector graphic objects, giving them a more realistic appearance. For example, you can create a vector drawing of a house, and then apply a brick-like texture derived from a bitmap photograph of real bricks. A graphic that contains both bitmap and vector data is called a **metafile**.

## VECTOR-TO-BITMAP CONVERSION

**Is it possible to convert a vector graphic into a bitmap?** A vector graphic can be converted quite easily into a bitmap graphic through a process called rasterizing. **Rasterization** works by superimposing a grid over a vector image and determining the color for each pixel. This process is typically carried out by graphics software, which allows you to specify the output size for the final bitmap image.

On a PC, you can rasterize a vector graphic by using the Print Screen key to take a screenshot of a vector image. On a Mac, the Apple-Shift-3 key combination takes a screenshot. It is important to rasterize images at the size you ultimately need. If you rasterize a vector image at a small size and then try to enlarge the resulting bitmap image, you will likely get a poor-quality pixelated image, such as the one in Figure 8-35.

After a vector graphic is converted to a bitmap, the resulting graphic no longer has the qualities of a vector graphic. For example, if you convert the Stonehenge vector graphic into a bitmap, the sun is no longer an object that you can easily move or assign a different color.

**How about converting a bitmap graphic into a vector graphic?** Converting a bitmap graphic into a vector graphic is more difficult than converting from a vector to a bitmap. To change a bitmap graphic into a vector graphic, you must use tracing software. **Tracing software** locates the edges of objects in a bitmap image and converts the resulting shapes into vector graphic objects.

Tracing software products, such as VectorEye and MagicTracer, work best on simple images and line drawings. They do not usually produce acceptable results when used on complex, detailed photos. Tracing capabilities are included in some general-purpose graphics software, but standalone tracing software offers more flexibility and usually produces better results.

FIGURE 8-34

Gradients can create the illusion of three dimensions, such as making this shape appear to be a tube.

FIGURE 8-35

When vector images are rasterized, they become bitmaps and can't be enlarged without becoming pixelated.

8

## VECTOR GRAPHICS ON THE WEB

**Do vector graphics work on the Web?** Web browsers were originally designed to support a limited number of graphics formats—GIF and JPEG—and these formats were exclusively bitmaps. Plug-ins and players are currently available for several of the most popular Web-based vector graphics formats.

**Which vector graphics formats can be used on the Web?** A graphics format called **SVG** (Scalable Vector Graphics) is designed specifically for the Web (Figure 8-36). Graphics in SVG format are automatically resized when displayed on different screens or when printed. SVG supports gradients, drop shadows, multiple levels of transparency, and other effects, along with portability to other platforms, such as handheld computers and cellular phones. SVG graphics objects can include regular and irregular shapes, images, and text, and they can be animated.

**Flash** is another popular vector graphics format frequently used on the Web. Adobe's Flash software creates vector graphics that are stored in files with .swf extensions. Flash graphics can be static or animated. Flash players are shipped with most browsers, and player updates can be downloaded from the Adobe site.

Flash animations have advantages over other formats, such as animated GIFs. An **animated GIF** is essentially a series of slightly different bitmap images displayed in sequence to achieve animation effects. As a bitmap-based format, GIF files are fairly large. Most Flash animations fit in compact files and, therefore, can be transferred from a Web server to a browser more rapidly than animated GIFs.

**What are the advantages of using vector graphics on the Web?** Vector graphics have several advantages:

• Consistent quality. On Web pages, vector graphics appear with the same consistent quality on all computer screens. This capability makes it possible for browsers to adjust the size of an image on the fly to fit correctly on a screen, regardless of its size or resolution. These adjustments don't carry any penalty in terms of image quality—a large version of a vector graphic displayed on a screen set at 1600 x 1200 resolution has the same sharp detail and smooth curves as the original image sized to fit a smaller screen set at 800 x 600 resolution. This flexibility is important for Web pages that might be viewed at different resolutions on PCs, Macs, or other platforms.

• Searchable. Another advantage is that any text contained in a vector image is stored as actual text, not just a series of colored dots. This text can be indexed by search engines so that it can be included in keyword searches. For example, suppose a vector drawing was used to produce a diagram describing the service box where your telephone line enters your house. One of the components in this diagram is labeled "telephone test jack." If you enter *telephone test jack* into a search engine, the service box diagram will likely turn up in the list of search results.

• Compact file size. A third advantage of vector graphics on the Web is their compact file sizes. A fairly complex graphic can be stored in a file that is under 30 KB—that's kilobytes, not megabytes. These files require little storage space and can be transmitted swiftly from a Web server to your browser.

**FIGURE 8-36**

SVG graphics are typically used on the Web for maps, ads, organizational charts, and flowcharts.

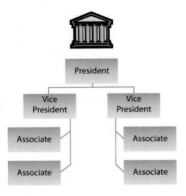

# 3-D GRAPHICS

**How do vector graphics relate to 3-D graphics?** Like vector graphics, **3-D graphics** are stored as a set of instructions. For a 3-D graphic, however, the instructions contain the locations and lengths of lines that form a wireframe for a three-dimensional object. The **wireframe** acts in much the same way as the framework of a pop-up tent. Just as you would construct the framework for the tent, and then cover it with a nylon tent cover, a 3-D wireframe can be covered with surface texture and color to create a graphic of a 3-D object. The process of covering a wireframe with surface color and texture is called **rendering**. The rendering process, shown in Figure 8-37, outputs a bitmap image.

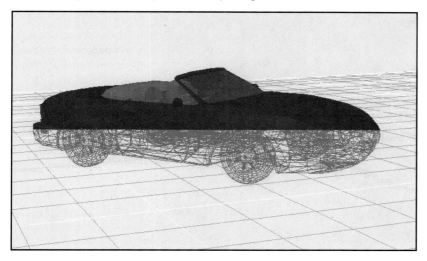

**FIGURE 8-37**

3-D graphics are based on a wireframe, which can be rendered into a bitmap image that looks three-dimensional.

For added realism, the rendering process can take into account the way that light shines on surfaces and creates shadows. The technique for adding light and shadows to a 3-D image is called **ray tracing**. Before an image is rendered, the artist selects a location for one or more light sources. The computer applies a complex mathematical algorithm to determine how the light source affects the color of each pixel in the final rendered image. This process can take time—hours for a complex image, even using today's most powerful personal computers. Figure 8-38 shows the image from the previous figure rendered with an additional light source and ray tracing.

**FIGURE 8-38**

Ray tracing adds realism to 3-D graphics by adding highlights and shadows that are produced by a light source.

8

**What tools do I need to create 3-D graphics?** 3-D graphics software runs on most personal computers, although some architects, designers, and engineers prefer to use high-end workstations. A fast processor, lots of RAM, and a fast graphics card with its own video RAM all speed up the rendering process.

To create 3-D graphics, you need 3-D graphics software, such as Autodesk AutoCAD or Caligari trueSpace. This software has tools for drawing a wireframe and viewing it from any angle. It provides rendering and ray tracing tools, along with an assortment of surface textures that you can apply to individual objects. Figure 8-39 takes you on a tour of a popular 3-D graphics software package.

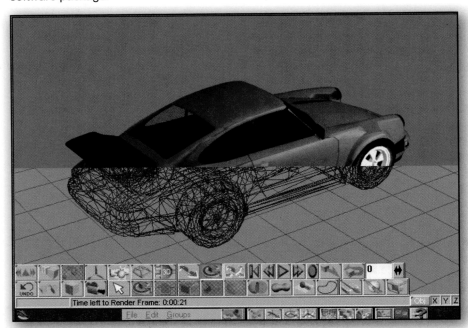

**FIGURE 8-39**

3-D graphics software provides tools for drawing a wireframe and then specifying colors and textures for rendering. ▶ Watch a wireframe being rendered and animated in your digital textbook.

**Is it possible to animate 3-D graphics?** 3-D graphics can be animated to produce special effects for movies or to create interactive, animated characters and environments for 3-D computer games. Animated special effects, such as massive battle scenes, are created by rendering a sequence of bitmaps, in which one or more objects are moved or otherwise changed between each rendering.

In traditional hand-drawn animation, a chief artist draws the keyframes, and then a team of assistants creates each of the in-between images—24 of these images for each second of animation. For 3-D computer animation, the computer creates the in-between images by moving the object and rendering each necessary image. All the images are then combined into a single file, creating essentially a digital movie.

Graphics design companies such as Pixar Animation Studios and DreamWorks use 3-D animation techniques to produce animated feature films as well as special effects. The first full-length animated 3-D movie was *Toy Story*, released in 1995 by Walt Disney Studios and Pixar. Digitally animated films, such as *Up* and *Shrek Forever After*, illustrate the growing sophistication of 3-D animation.

**INFOWEBLINKS**

For additional resources about 3-D software (and shareware), rendering, ray tracing, and 3-D animated graphics, check out the **3-D Graphics InfoWeb**.

 CLICK TO CONNECT
www.infoweblinks.com/np2012/ch08

**Do game and movie animation require similar tools and techniques?** An important characteristic of special effects and animated films is that rendering can be accomplished during the production phase of the movie and incorporated into the final footage. In contrast, 3-D computer game animation happens in real time. Each frame that makes the image seem to move must be rendered while you are playing the game—a process that requires an incredible amount of computer power.

To give you a handle on the immensity of the processing power required to render the real-time images for computer games, consider a game like Doom displayed on a display device that's set at 1024 x 768 resolution (Figure 8-40). At this resolution, the screen contains 786,432 pixels (1024 multiplied by 768). If the game is presented in 32-bit color, each frame of the animation requires 25,165,824 bits (multiply 786,432 times 32).

Computer game designers believe that on-screen animation looks smoothest at 60 frames per second, which means your computer must handle 1,509,949,440—that's more than 1 billion—bits of information every second just to display the 3-D image on the screen. In addition, the computer must process even more data to keep track of the movements of each player.

To handle all the data required for game play, your computer's main processor gets help from a graphics processor located on your computer's graphics card. These graphics processors vary in their capabilities. For the fastest graphics capability some computers can accept two graphics cards that work in tandem as 3-D accelerators.

**Can I create my own animated 3-D graphics?** You can create 3-D animations on a standard PC or Mac with commercially available software, but professional 3-D software, such as Autodesk Maya and 3ds Max, is expensive and has a steep learning curve.

If you want to dabble with 3-D animations before making an expensive software investment, you might try SmithMicro Poser, DAZ Studio, or one of the shareware programs listed in the 3-D Graphics InfoWeb. Whether you use a commercial or shareware package, be prepared to spend lots of time with the manual before you are able to produce your own original animations.

**FIGURE 8-40**

Classic computer games, such as Doom, established building blocks for animation technologies used to create today's fast-action, visually detailed computer games.

8

# QuickCheck

1. Vector graphics require more storage space than bitmaps, but vectors can be enlarged without becoming pixelated. True or false? [_____]

2. A process called [_____] converts vector graphics into bitmap images.

3. SVG, [_____], and animated GIFs are three of the most popular vector formats used on the Web.

4. A 3-D image is based on an assemblage of vectors called a(n) [_____].

5. The technique of adding light and shadows to a 3-D image is called ray [_____].

 CHECK ANSWERS

# Digital Video

**IN THE PREVIOUS SECTION,** you learned about GIF and Flash animations—popular options for adding motion to Web pages. You also learned about using animated 3-D graphics for movie special effects and computer games. Digital animation is typically created from scratch by an artist with the help of a computer. In contrast, digital video is based on footage of real objects filmed and then stored as bits. Digital video encompasses several technologies, including those that produce theater-quality DVD movies, as well as video for computers and handheld devices. In this section, you'll take a look at what you can do with affordable, easy-to-use desktop video tools.

## DIGITAL VIDEO BASICS

**What is digital video?** A video is a series of still frames, like those in Figure 8-41, projected at a rate fast enough to fool the human eye into perceiving continuous motion. **Digital video** uses bits to store color and brightness data for each video frame. The process is similar to storing the data for a series of bitmap images in which the color for each pixel is represented by a binary number.

**Is digital video better than analog video?** Unlike analog video, digital video retains image quality no matter how many times it is copied. Videos in digital format can be easily manipulated on a personal computer, putting the world of movie-making at your fingertips.

**Where does digital video footage originate?** Footage for digital videos can be supplied from a digital source, or from an analog source that requires conversion. You can shoot footage with a consumer-quality camcorder, webcam, or cell phone camera. Some cameras designed for still photography can also capture short videos. Footage can also originate from a videotape, television, DVD, or even a digital video recording device.

**How is digital video used?** You can use your personal computer to edit footage into videos suitable for a variety of personal and professional uses, such as video wedding albums, product sales videos, training videos, video holiday greeting cards, documentaries for nonprofit organizations, and video scrapbooks. Video that is created on a personal computer and designed to be played back on a similar device is sometimes referred to as **desktop video**.

In addition to its use to create personal videos, digital video is also used in the movie industry. Digital cinematography and editing have been used for many award-winning films, such as *Cold Mountain*, *Slumdog Millionaire*, and *Avatar*. Outside of the context of Hollywood, digital video is a core technology for HDTV, videoconferencing systems, and video messaging. Real-time video even allows deaf people to sign over cell phones.

Digital videos can be stored on a hard disk or distributed on CDs, DVDs, videotapes, memory cards, file sharing networks, or the Web. Popular software for playing digital video on computers includes Apple QuickTime Player, Windows Media Player, and Adobe Flash Player.

**FIGURE 8-41**

A video is composed of a series of bitmap graphics, each one called a frame.

**How do I create digital video?** To understand how you can create your own digital videos, you'll need information about four procedures summarized in Figure 8-42 and explained in the rest of this section.

1. **Produce video footage.** Select equipment for filming videos and use effective filming techniques.

2. **Transfer video footage to a computer.** Use a cable, a video capture card, or an SD card to move video footage from cameras, videotapes, television, and DVDs to your computer's hard disk.

3. **Edit video footage.** Use software to select video segments, arrange them into a video, and add a soundtrack.

4. **Store and play.** Select digital video file formats for playback on desktop, Web, portable, and DVD platforms.

**FIGURE 8-42**

Creating digital video requires a few fairly simple steps.

## PRODUCING VIDEO FOOTAGE

**What kinds of video cameras are available?** You can shoot video footage using standalone video cameras and cameras embedded in computers and handheld devices.

As you might expect, digital video cameras capture footage as a series of bits. Most of today's standalone digital video cameras store data on solid state memory cards, but storage options also include solid state drives, miniDVDs, digital tape, or built-in hard drives. Cameras run the gamut from sub-US$150 consumer minicams to professional quality shoulder-mount camcorders costing more than $20,000 and high-definition Hollywood-style cameras priced over $100,000 (Figure 8-43).

**FIGURE 8-43**

Digital video cameras are available in many sizes and prices.

**Can I use an analog camera?** You can use an analog video camera to shoot footage that eventually becomes digital video. Analog footage is stored on tape as a continuous track of magnetic patterns. To use your computer to store and edit analog footage, you'll have to convert it into digital format.

**How about webcams?** Another option for shooting video footage is a small, inexpensive **webcam** that is built in over the screen of a notebook computer or attached as a peripheral device (Figure 8-44). These cameras capture a series of still photos, which are stored in digital format directly on your computer's hard disk or transmitted over a network.

Webcams can be controlled by various software applications, including instant messenger clients and specialized webcam software that is bundled with new computers and add-on webcams. Webcams typically produce low-quality video. Most webcams must remain tethered to your computer, which tends to limit your videos to "talking heads."

**Can I get digital footage from my cell phone camera?** Many mobile phones and handheld devices include a camera that stores video footage on the device's internal hard drive or memory card. The video quality produced by these cameras is not typically as high as the footage produced by standalone digital video cameras, and storage space is usually more limited. Cameras embedded in handheld devices typically have fewer options and features than standalone cameras. For example, most cameras included with handheld devices lack the image stabilization feature common on standalone cameras that compensates for hand vibration.

**Do I need a fancy camera?** Most people agree that an inexpensive camera is better than nothing, but the quality of your camera can make a difference in the quality of the finished footage.

A common misconception is that a cheap camera won't make a difference for videos shown on small screens at a fairly low resolution. Just the opposite is true. The higher the quality of the original video, the better the final video will look, regardless of the size of the screen on which it is shown.

**Does digital video require special filming techniques?** When videos are processed and stored on a personal computer, some of the image data is eliminated to reduce the video file to a manageable size. Simpler videos tend to maintain better quality as they are edited, processed, and stored. Camera movements, fast actions, patterned clothing, and moving backgrounds all contribute to the complexity of a video and should be minimized. The techniques listed in Figure 8-45 can help you produce video footage that maintains good quality as it is edited and processed.

**FIGURE 8-44**

A Web camera can be built into a computer display device or can be attached as shown. It is designed mainly for "talking head" applications, such as online video chats and video-conferences.

**FIGURE 8-45**

Video Filming Tips

- Use a tripod to maintain a steady image.
- Move the camera slowly if it is necessary to pan from side to side.
- Zoom in and out slowly.
- Direct your subjects to move slowly, when possible.
- Position your shot to eliminate as much background detail and movement as possible.
- Ask the subjects of your video to wear solid-colored clothing, if possible.

## VIDEO TRANSFER

**What can I do with my video footage?** Video footage can be transferred to a computer for editing, streamed out during synchronous communications sessions, e-mailed, or uploaded to file sharing sites. Some cameras automate these transfers, whereas transferring footage from other types of cameras requires several manual steps.

**What are my options for Webcam footage?** The footage captured by Webcams is often immediately streamed to your computer's hard disk or out over a network during a video chat session or videoconference. If you've stored Webcam footage on your computer, you can view and edit it using video editing software.

**How about video from handheld devices?** Video from handheld devices can be e-mailed directly to friends or to yourself. E-mailing footage to yourself is an easy way to get it to your computer for editing. Alternatively, your handheld device might store video footage on a memory card that you can transfer to your computer. Most handheld devices also allow you to directly upload videos to YouTube and other video sharing sites.

**How do I transfer video footage from a video camera to my computer?** The basic method for transferring digital video footage to your computer's hard disk for editing is to remove the SD card from the camera and transfer it to a card reader on your computer.

Your digital camera might provide other ways to transfer data to a computer. You can connect the camera to your computer with a cable and fire up video editing software to control the transfer. This method is typically used for cameras that store video on non-removable media, such as a built-in hard drive or digital videotape, but you might also use this method if you want a lengthy video divided into several smaller clips.

**How do I transfer video from analog devices?** Analog video footage from TV, videotape, and analog video cameras has to be converted into digital format before it can be stored on your computer's hard disk. The process of converting analog video signals into digital format is referred to as **video capture** and requires a video capture device and software.

Your computer's graphics card might include video capture capabilities. If not, you can purchase a separate video capture device that connects to your computer's USB port or a video capture card that plugs into an expansion slot (Figure 8-46).

**How much hard disk space is required to store video files?** Video files are large, but just how large depends on the video format used by your camera. Video files produced from digital tape typically are largest, whereas videos stored on memory cards are somewhat smaller, and videos from cell phones and webcams are usually small enough to e-mail.

Be prepared with several gigabytes of free space on your computer's hard disk before you begin any serious video editing. You might consider using an external hard disk drive to hold the sound files and video footage you use for assembling videos.

**FIGURE 8-46**

After it has been installed in your computer, a video capture card can be connected to the video-out and audio-out ports on an analog camera, television, VCR, or DVD player.

8

## VIDEO EDITING

**Do I need special equipment for video editing?** Before camcorders went digital, editing a video consisted of recording segments from one videotape onto another tape. This process, called **linear editing**, required two VCRs at minimum. Professional video editors used expensive editing equipment, beyond the budget of most consumers.

Today's **nonlinear editing** simply requires a computer hard disk and video editing software. The advantage of nonlinear editing is that you can use a random-access device to easily edit and arrange video clips. Video editing requires lots of hard disk space, however. So before you begin an editing session, make sure your computer's hard disk has several gigabytes of available storage space. It is also a good idea to have at least 1 GB of RAM—professionals opt for at least 4 GB.

**How do I edit a video?** After your video footage is transferred to your computer and stored on the hard disk, you can begin to arrange your video clips by using video editing software, such as Adobe Premiere, Apple Final Cut Pro, Windows Movie Maker, or Corel VideoStudio.

Videos are easier to edit if you divide them into several files, each containing a one- or two-minute video clip. Some video capture software automatically creates clips by detecting frame changes, such as when you turn your camera off, pause, or switch to a new scene.

Video editing software allows you to further crop tracks and add transitions between them. You can also overlay video tracks with one or more audio tracks containing music or narrations.

Your completed video consists of video tracks containing video segments and transitions, plus audio tracks containing voices and music. Figure 8-47 illustrates how to lay out video and audio tracks.

**INFOWEBLINKS**

The **Video Editing InfoWeb** contains tips about editing digital videos, updates on the latest consumer-level software, and links to the most popular digital video sites.

Ⓦ CLICK TO CONNECT
www.infoweblinks.com/np2012/ch08

**FIGURE 8-47**

Simple video editing software combines video clips, sounds, and transitions into movies. ▶ Learn the basics of Windows Movie Maker and see how to create a short movie about sled dogs, complete with soundtrack. (This tour might take a few moments to begin. Please be patient.)

## VIDEO OUTPUT

**How does video footage become a digital video?** Your video editing software combines the data from all the video and audio files you selected into a single file, which is stored on your computer's hard disk. During the output process, you can select settings for aspect ratio, frame size, and compression so that the resulting video quality and file size is appropriate for its intended use.

Aspect ratio refers to the relative width and height of the video frame; widescreen is 16:9 and fullscreen is 4:3. Most computers, televisions, and handheld devices are designed for widescreen format, though the screens for a few devices, such as iPads, are sized for fullscreen formats.

Frame size corresponds to the resolution of the video window. A typical frame size for handheld devices is 320 x 480 or 480 x 600. Fullscreen computer displays are typically 1024 x 768, as is the iPad. DVD video has a resolution of 720 x 480; high-definition video has a resolution of 1920 x 1080.

**How is video compressed?** Raw video requires vast amounts of storage space, so videos are usually compressed to create files that can be conveniently stored and transmitted. Video compression can be achieved by decreasing the frame rate (number of frames per second), reducing the frame size, and using techniques similar to JPEG to compress the data stored for each frame.

A **codec** (compressor/decompressor) is the software that compresses a video stream when a video is stored, and decompresses the file when the video is played. Popular codecs include MPEG, DivX, H.264, Theora, and Windows Media Video. Each codec uses a unique algorithm to shrink the size of a video file, so they are not interchangeable. When creating videos, you should use one of the codecs included in popular video players.

Video compression can be expressed as a compression ratio or as a bitrate. A **compression ratio** indicates the ratio of compressed data to uncompressed data. A video file with a high compression ratio, such as 35:1, has more compression, a smaller file size, and lower image quality than a file with a smaller compression ratio, such as 5:1.

**Bitrate** refers to the amount of data transferred per second as a video plays. Higher bitrates produce better quality video. Click the CLICK TO START buttons in Figure 8-48 to compare video and audio quality produced by different compression settings.

**FIGURE 8-48**

Different compression ratios can have a remarkable effect on video quality and file size.

Bitrate: 90 Kbps
Frame rate: 10
File size: 359 KB

▶ CLICK TO START

Bitrate: 448 Kbps
Frame rate: 15
File size: 1177 KB

▶ CLICK TO START

Bitrate: 928 Kbps
Frame rate: 30
File size: 2448 KB

▶ CLICK TO START

8

**How can I specify a compression level?** Some entry-level video editing software allows you simply to select a use for your video, such as sending it as an e-mail attachment, posting it on the Web, publishing it on YouTube, or viewing it from your local hard disk. The software automatically applies an appropriate level of compression to the video data.

Alternatively, your software might offer the option of selecting a maximum file size. For example, if you are planning to send a video as an e-mail attachment, you might limit the size to 1 MB, and your video data will be compressed to that specified size.

Some video editing software allows you to select a bit rate for your final video. Uncompressed video files contain a huge number of bits per frame, so smooth playback requires a high bit rate, such as 340 Kbps. Compressed files contain fewer bits per frame and play back more smoothly at lower bit rates, such as 38 Kbps, offered by slower Internet connections.

As another option, your video editing software might offer you a selection of compression ratios, such as 5:1 or 35:1. You might have to experiment with compression ratios a bit to find the best balance between file size and image quality.

**What is the best video file format?** Many video file formats are available; the format you use should be compatible with the devices on which it is played and its browser or player software. Digital video file formats are sometimes referred to as **container formats** because they hold the compressed video and audio data streams that form a video (Figure 8-49).

Figure 8-50 describes some popular video container formats—**AVI**, **MOV**, **MPEG**, **WebM**, **ASF**, **Flash video**, **VOB**, and **Blue-ray Disc Movie**.

**FIGURE 8-49**

Codecs and video formats are easily confused, especially because some containers have the same names as codecs. A codec, such as H.264, is software that compresses the video stream, whereas a container format, such as MOV, is a method of storing data in a file.

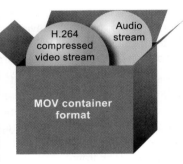

**FIGURE 8-50**

Popular Digital Video Formats

| Format | Extension | Platform | Description and Use |
|---|---|---|---|
| AVI (Audio Video Interleave) | .avi | PC | A format sometimes used for storing digital clips from video cameras; used for desktop video on the PC platform |
| MOV (QuickTime Movie) | .mov | PC, Mac, UNIX, Linux | One of the most popular formats for desktop video and streaming Web videos |
| MPEG (Moving Picture Experts Group) | .mpg or .mpeg | PC, Mac, UNIX, Linux | Versions include MPEG-1, MPEG-2, and MPEG-4; used for desktop video and streaming Web video |
| WebM | .webm | PC, Mac, UNIX, Linux | Royalty-free, high-quality open format for use with HTML5 |
| ASF (Advanced Systems Format) | .asf or .wmv | PC | Container format for Microsoft's Windows Media Video (WMV) desktop video and streaming Web video |
| Flash video | .flv | PC, Mac | Popular for Web-based video; requires Adobe Flash Player |
| VOB (Video Object) | .vob | Standalone DVD player, PC, Mac, Linux | Industry-standard format for standalone DVD players |
| Blu-ray Disc Movie | .bdmv | PC, Mac | A format used for storing HD video clips to Blu-ray disc |

**Can I change videos from one format to another?** Digital videos can be converted from one file format to another through a process called **transcoding**. If you want to move a video into a different file format, you can check to see if your video editing software offers a conversion, export, or transcoding option. If not, you can find transcoding software on the Web. Transcoding can cause loss of quality, so avoid transcoding an already transcoded video file.

## WEB VIDEO

**How do Web-based videos work?** A video for a Web page is stored on a Web server in a file. Usually, a link for the video file appears on the Web page. When you click the link, the Web server transmits a copy of the video file to your computer. If your browser has a plug-in that corresponds to the video format, the video is displayed on your computer screen.

The transfer of a digital video file from the Web to your computer can happen in one of two ways, depending on the video format. In one case, your computer waits until it receives the entire video file before starting to play it. This technology is typically used for movie downloads.

An alternative video delivery method, called **streaming video**, sends a small segment of the video to your computer and begins to play it. While this segment plays, the Web server sends the next part of the file to your computer, and so on, until the video ends. With streaming video, your computer essentially plays the video while it continues to receive it. Videos intended to be viewed in the context of a Web page are typically delivered by streaming video technology.

**How do I post a video to YouTube or a similar file-sharing site?** YouTube is a video-sharing Web site that encourages members to upload, view, and rate video clips. YouTube and similar sites typically accept most popular video file formats directly from digital cameras, camcorders, cell phones, and webcams (Figure 8-51).

**FIGURE 8-51**

You can use YouTube to capture footage on your computer's webcam and upload it to the YouTube Web site.

8

Before uploading videos, you can edit them and save them in a standard video format, such as WebM, MPEG, MOV, AVI, WMV, or Flash video. YouTube imposes a length and time limitation, so you should check the current regulations before you finalize your video.

After your file is uploaded, it is converted into the standard formats used by YouTube. Originally, all YouTube videos were converted into Flash format. Later, a format for mobile phones was added, as was an HD widescreen format. In conjunction with the move to HTML5, WebM format was also added. In order to make YouTube videos more accessible to the deaf and hearing impaired, some videos can be automatically captioned.

**How are videos added to Web pages?** On today's Web, most videos are embedded in Web pages so that they appear to play in place. For browsers that support HTML5, the <video> tag can be used to specify the name of the video file and a message to display if someone tries to access the video without the corresponding plug-in. The <object> and <iframe> tags can be used in HTML 4 or HTML5.

A simple HTML5 snippet using the <video> tag for adding a video might look like this:

```
<video src="myvideo.webm" controls>
If the video doesn't begin, you might need to download a plug-in.
</video>
```

**What are the best formats for Web videos?** The HTML5 <video> tag supports several video formats, but it does not designate a common video format for all HTML5-compliant browsers. Web site developers sometimes have to provide a video in multiple formats to make it accessible to a variety of browsers and hardware devices.

At the time this book was published, there was no single video format supported by all browsers. But the Flash, Ogg Theora, H.264, and WebM formats appear to be the best candidates for widespread Web use with HTML5.

**Can I incorporate videos from the Web into my own Web site and social networking pages?** There are several ways to reuse and share videos that you find on the Web. When using videos created by others, make sure you give the authors credit, adhere to originating sites' usage policies, and abide by copyright law.

Video sharing sites, such as YouTube, include tools for e-mailing videos, sharing videos on social networking sites, and including them in blogs. You can embed videos from these sites by copying HTML code into the source code for your own Web pages. You can also copy video links into e-mail messages and Web page source documents so that readers can quickly connect to the original video source on YouTube, Facebook, or other Web sites (Figure 8-52).

**FIGURE 8-52**

YouTube provides source code for embedding a video into your own Web page or sharing links on Facebook, Twitter, and other social networking sites.

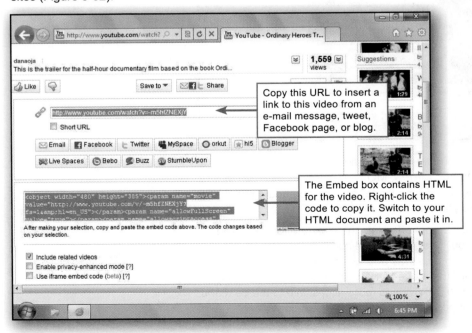

## DVD-VIDEO

**Can I burn my digital videos onto DVDs with interactive menus like commercial movies?** Suppose you've used video editing software to create a short documentary on sled dogs. You can package the completed video footage into a professional-style DVD that can be played on computer DVD drives (if your computer is equipped with DVD player software) or standalone DVD players. It can include interactive menus with options, such as Play Video, Select a Scene, and Special Features, that viewers can select using their DVD remote controls.

**What equipment do I need?** To create video DVDs, you need a writable DVD drive (sometimes called a DVD burner) plus software that includes tools for DVD menu creation and writing data onto a DVD-Video—a process sometimes called burning. These tools are offered by DVD authoring software, such as Adobe Encore, Sonic MyDVD, Nero, and Corel DVD MovieFactory. Many video editing software packages and suites also include tools for creating DVD menus and burning projects onto DVDs.

**What's the process for making a video DVD?** To create a video DVD, you usually begin by selecting one or more completed videos that include soundtracks, transitions, titles, special effects, and so on. You then use DVD authoring software to design menus and buttons that viewers can use to navigate to specific parts of your video. To complete the project, you can test your project and then burn it to DVD.

**What are my options for creating interactive DVD menus?** A DVD menu is a screen that provides viewers with navigation tools to start a video, skip to specific scenes, play special features, and link to other menus. A typical DVD menu consists of a decorative background and option buttons that viewers can select using their DVD player's remote control. Some DVD authoring software offers a selection of predesigned menu and button templates that you can easily incorporate with your videos (Figure 8-53). Your software might also provide the option to create your own backgrounds and buttons using graphics software, such as Adobe Photoshop or Microsoft Paint.

**FIGURE 8-53**

DVD authoring software offers a selection of backgrounds and button styles for creating DVD menus. ▶ Your digital textbook demonstrates how to create a DVD menu and generate a standalone DVD using Windows DVD Maker.

8

**Are menus easy to create?** Yes, they just require a little advance planning. As you design the menu flow, remember that you want to provide viewers with a way to return to the main menu from each submenu. You might also want viewers to return to the main menu after viewing individual clips. If a submenu offers options for outtakes or other special features, you should provide a way for viewers to return to the submenu when the special feature ends. To help visualize the way your menus will work, you can draw a diagram similar to the one in Figure 8-54.

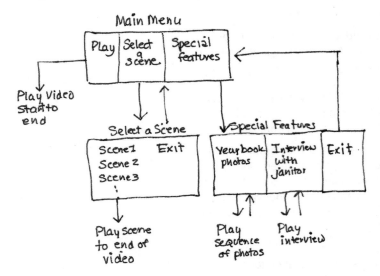

**How do I output my video to DVD?** To create a DVD that can be viewed on a standalone DVD player, you have to output your video in DVD-Video format, which requires video encoded with MPEG-2 and stored in VOB files. Your DVD authoring software can generate MPEG-2 video clips and menus, store them in VOB files, and lay them out on a DVD according to industry standards.

Most DVD authoring software can accomplish the MPEG encoding on the fly as it burns the DVD. However, this process takes time. So if you are burning more than one copy, or if you want to test your menu structure before burning the video onto a DVD, you might want to consider creating a DVD image.

**What's a DVD image?** A **DVD image** (sometimes called a DVD volume) is essentially a prototype of your DVD, but it is stored on your computer's hard disk. If you have space to store a DVD image, it is a good idea to make one before burning a DVD. You can use a DVD image for testing. You can also use the image to burn multiple DVDs without waiting for your software to prepare the files for each burn.

**Can I simply copy a desktop video to a DVD using the Copy command?** Desktop videos are typically stored in WMV or MOV format, and many standalone DVD players are not equipped to handle those formats. So, although you can use the Copy command to copy MOV and WMV files to a DVD and distribute them, these files can be viewed on most computers, but not on all DVD players.

Even copying files stored in MPEG format might not produce a DVD that works in a standalone player. The DVD-Video format specification requires a specific layout for data on the DVD surface. The method you use to copy computer data files does not produce the required layout, so most DVD players will not be able to play the video.

**How do I test my DVD image?** Your DVD is ready for production and distribution if the video quality looks good and the menus work correctly. Use the tips listed below to test your DVD on your computer before you burn a DVD:

- Test each button to make sure it links to the correct clip.

- Play each clip to the end and make sure it returns to the correct menu when completed.

- Watch the video carefully and look for any poor quality segments with distracting artifacts, such as blurs or halos. Artifacts can sometimes be removed by revisiting your MPEG coding options.

- Listen to the soundtrack to make sure the audio is clear, smooth, and synchronized with the video.

**Does it make a difference if I use recordable or rewritable DVDs?** Commercial DVD movies are stamped onto DVD-ROM discs during the manufacturing process—something you can't do with your computer's DVD drive. Your computer can burn data on DVD-R, DVD+R, or DVD-RW discs. Because the DVD industry has not achieved a single media standard, some standalone DVD players—particularly those manufactured before 2004—are not able to read one or more of these disc types. DVD+R and DVD-R seem to be compatible with the widest variety of DVD players, whereas DVD-RW seems to be the least compatible. Before you distribute your DVDs, make sure you test them in a standalone DVD player.

**8**

## QuickCheck                                    SECTION D

1. The process of converting analog video signals into digital format is referred to as video _____.

2. A(n) _____ is the software that compresses a video stream when a video is stored, and decompresses the file when the video is played.

3. Compressed files contain less data per frame and play back more smoothly at lower _____ rates.

4. Digital videos can be converted from one file format to another through a process called _____.

5. Before you create a DVD video, it is a good idea to create a DVD _____ on your computer's hard disk.

 CHECK ANSWERS

# Digital Rights Management

**THE SECURITY SECTIONS** of earlier chapters looked at security from the user perspective. In contrast, the security section for this chapter examines the techniques used by content providers to protect digital media from unlicensed duplication and use. Pirating music and movies is a multi-billion dollar worldwide activity that is increasingly controlled by organized crime. Legitimate content providers are taking steps to reduce piracy by prosecuting digital pirates and using digital rights management technologies to deter duplication. Unfortunately, technical measures taken to reduce illicit duplication can be inconvenient for legitimate users. In this section, you'll learn about DRM technologies you may have already encountered and some that are likely to affect your ability to use digital media in the future.

## DRM BASICS

**What is DRM?** **Digital rights management** (DRM) is a collection of techniques used by copyright holders to limit access to and use of digital content. Because DRM is primarily used to protect products of the entertainment industry, in the context of DRM, **digital content** (or simply content) usually refers to movies, music, e-books, and computer games.

Digital content is accessed by means of a player. Keep in mind that the term *player* can refer to a hardware device or software. Software players include familiar media players, such as iTunes, Windows Media Player, and QuickTime. Hardware players include standalone devices such as CD players, VCRs, DVD players, Blu-ray players, e-book readers, and portable media players. Computer devices, such as CD, DVD, and Blu-ray drives, are also considered players, though they require software to play back content.

Every hardware device and software program that interacts with digital content poses a potential vulnerability that can be exploited by pirates. Software that encrypts content can be cracked, signals that travel from one device to another can be intercepted, and when all else fails, the **analog hole** allows pirates to capture content by using a microphone to record songs as they are output to speakers or using a camcorder to film movies as they are projected in a movie theater.

In response to the creativity and sheer stubbornness of digital pirates, modern DRM systems include layers of protection, with the goal of controlling content from its distribution point through to its playback (Figure 8-55).

**How does DRM affect my use of digital media?** The average consumer uses a variety of electronic devices to play digital content. Many of these devices offer convenient time and place shifting, but DRM technologies can curtail their use.

**FIGURE 8-55**

The threat of legal penalties has not been enough to discourage digital piracy, so copyright holders are working on increasingly sophisticated ways to prevent illegal copying.

The unauthorized reproduction or distribution of this copyrighted work is illegal. Criminal copyright infringement, including infringement without monetary gain, is investigated by the FBI and is punishable by up to 5 years in federal prison and a fine of $250,000.

**Time shifting** is the process of recording a broadcast, such as a television show, so that it can be played back at a more convenient time. **Place shifting** allows media that originates in one place to be accessed from another place without changing the device on which it is stored (Figure 8-56). Place shifting is often achieved using computer networks, as when you view a cable television broadcast sent from your Wi-Fi equipped set-top box to your Wi-Fi equipped notebook.

**Format shifting** is the process of converting media files from a format suitable for one device to a format suitable for a different kind of device. A common use of format shifting is ripping audio tracks from a CD and converting them into MP3 format for playback on a portable media device, such as an iPod.

**Is DRM effective?** DRM has not lived up to the expectations of copyright holders and it has disappointed consumers by curtailing their options for using content they have legitimately purchased. Digital piracy continues to run rampant and hackers stubbornly continue to devise work-arounds to defeat DRM. There is evidence that the incidence of casual copying has decreased, but some of this casual copying might actually be legitimate, fair use. The Issue section of this chapter looks at the relationship between DRM technologies and the concept of fair use.

To judge whether DRM technologies are effective and to gauge their effect on consumers, it is helpful to take a more detailed look at the evolution of DRM technologies from their first applications for scrambling cable television signals to more recent applications designed to protect online delivery of digital content.

## SIGNAL SCRAMBLING AND DIGITAL WATERMARKS

**What is signal scrambling?** **Signal scrambling** is a term commonly used for obscuring cable or satellite television images until they are unscrambled by a set-top box or other authorized mechanism. The first scrambling systems were based on various proprietary algorithms that transmitted unsynchronized video signals designed to be resynchronized by a set-top box. With the advent of digital content, scrambling was implemented by encrypting the digital bits of the signal.

It is technically possible to build a device to descramble signals, but it is illegal to use one. For the most part, consumers accept signal scrambling technology with the understanding that once signals are received and unscrambled, they can be recorded for later viewing. DRM technologies such as digital watermarks, however, can further limit the use of unscrambled content.

**What is a digital watermark?** A **digital watermark** is a pattern of bits inserted at various places in an image or a content stream that can be used to track, identify, verify, and control content use. Watermarks, such as broadcast flags, are usually imperceptible to viewers or listeners, but can be picked up by compliant devices.

A **broadcast flag** is a set of bits inserted into the data stream of digital television or radio programs that specifies how the stream can and cannot be used. Broadcast flags can prohibit a program from being unencrypted or copied. They can limit copies to low resolution, such as by reducing

8

high-definition video to the resolution of a standard television. In addition, broadcast flags can prevent fast-forwarding past commercials.

Broadcast flags are intended to combat indiscriminate use of digital video recorders, such as TiVos. In the United States, many HDTVs are equipped to recognize broadcast flags. As the number of consumers who own HDTVs increases, it becomes more likely that broadcast flags will become more widely used.

**What is HDCP?** A DRM technology referred to as **HDCP** (High-bandwidth Digital Content Protection) was developed by Intel to prevent movie pirating by encrypting the data stream and making sure that it can be decrypted and displayed only on approved devices. When purchasing a computer display device or HDTV, look for the HDCP label to make sure it is authorized to display DRM-protected movies.

## CD COPY PROTECTION

**How does digital rights management affect music and other media distributed on CDs?** Compact disc (CD) technology was introduced in 1982. It was originally developed for storing digital audio and is still a primary distribution method for recorded music. CDs adhere to a standardized format commonly called the Red Book, which implements DRM with a data bit that can be set to "no-copy." The Red Book no-copy bit is easy to defeat, so the recording industry has attempted to use more robust DRM technologies, such as copy protection.

**What is copy protection?** **Copy protection** refers to technologies designed to prohibit consumers from copying content. CDs with copy protection cannot be duplicated and music that is ripped to another format does not play back correctly. Copy protection technologies include Copy Control, CDS (Cactus Data Shield), and XCP (Extended Copy Protection).

**How does CD copy protection work?** Most CD copy protection technologies rely on two techniques: multiple sessions and corrupted data. A copy protected CD with multiple sessions is essentially divided into two parts called sessions. The first session contains an audio stream of recorded music that has been intentionally corrupted. The second session contains a computer program that can essentially reverse the corruption.

The audio stream is corrupted by replacing certain frames (about 1/75th of a second of music) with data, rather than sound. Dedicated CD players simply skip the data, but computer CD drives tend to play the data frames, resulting in loud pops and other audio glitches. On some drives, the CD seems to pause every few seconds while the drive attempts to make sense of the data. Ripping and pirating the corrupted audio tracks is pointless because they don't play back correctly. To filter out the corrupted data, your computer requires specialized software. This software is stored as the CD's data session and is installed the first time that you use the CD (Figure 8-57).

**FIGURE 8-57**

Copy protected CDs contain a software program that strips out intentionally corrupted data.

POP!

Copy protected CD contains music and computer software

The corrupted audio stream makes popping sounds

Software is installed on the hard drive the first time the CD is accessed

Software filters out intentionally corrupted data

**How do I know if a CD is copy protected?** Some distributors, such as Amazon.com, do their best to identify copy protected CDs in product descriptions. The existence of a data session and intentionally corrupted audio on copy protected CDs does not adhere to the Red Book standard for audio CDs, so the official CDDA logo is missing on the CD packaging. Most copy protected CDs also carry warnings that they might not function on some equipment, such as car CD players.

**How prevalent is CD copy protection?** Copy protected CDs have become much less common since the 2005 Sony BMG rootkit incident. Several Sony BMG CDs were copy protected by software that limited duplication to three copies. The copy protection software was surreptitiously installed on consumers' computers and once installed used a rootkit to conceal itself. Not only was the software installed without user consent, once installed, the software made consumers' computers more open to Internet viruses. The copy protection software had no uninstall routine and if users deleted the files, their CD drives no longer worked. After a high-profile rash of negative publicity, the CDs were recalled and music publishers quietly began to abandon copy protection.

## DVD AND BLU-RAY DRM

**Do DVDs and CDs use similar DRM?** The first DVD players were introduced in 1996 primarily as a distribution medium for mainstream movies. Based on prior experience with CD and VHS piracy, technologies to discourage piracy were built into the DVD standard from its inception.

Unlike CD DRM, protection for DVD content did not have to be tacked onto the distribution media as corrupted data and rootkits. DRM designed for DVDs could take advantage of more sophisticated technologies both on discs and on players. The major DRM technologies for DVDs include copy generation management, analog output protection, and CSS. These technologies can be implemented individually or together to provide layers of protection.

**What is copy generation management?** **Copy generation management** is a digital watermark that specifies the number of times a content stream can be duplicated. Compliant players recognize the watermark and abide by it. With the watermark set to no copy, for example, a video stream cannot be copied to other compliant devices. If a content stream carries a one-copy-only watermark, compliant devices can make a copy, but will change the watermark to no-copies-allowed. As a result, second generation copies cannot be used to make additional copies (Figure 8-58).

**FIGURE 8-58**

Watermarks are read by devices that comply with the limitations embedded in the content stream.

8

Original DVD with one-copy-only watermark

Compliant DVD burner

DVD copy now contains do-not-copy watermark

Compliant DVD burner will not copy the DVD

**What is an analog protection system?** An **analog protection system** is any DRM technology that interjects signals into the video stream to prevent analog output from being copied. As used in the context of protecting DVDs, an analog protection system places signals within the content stream that disrupt playback on VCRs by making the image appear dim or scrambled. The intended use of this technology is to prevent DVD video streams from being output to videotape, then being converted back into digital format.

**What is CSS?** **CSS** (Content Scramble System) is a digital rights management technology designed to encrypt and control the use of content stored on DVDs. It is intended to render DVD copies nonfunctional and enforces additional restrictions, such as region coding. CSS is the most well-known DRM technology for DVDs.

**How does CSS work?** CSS technology is a type of authentication-and-encryption DRM technology built into standalone DVD players and computer DVD players/burners. A key aspect of CSS is the use of authentication keys that allow a DVD disc and player to prove to each other that they are legitimately licensed to use CSS. Only after authentication can the encrypted video stream be decoded.

DVD players are manufactured with a built-in set of CSS keys. When a DVD is inserted, the player runs through every key until one unlocks the disc. Once this disc key is known, the player uses it to retrieve a title key from the disc. The title key allows the player to unscramble the DVD video stream (Figure 8-59).

DVD protected by CSS

Title key

1. The DVD player decrypts the title key using one of 400 preprogrammed keys.

Key to decrypt content stream

2. The title key contains a unique key to decrypt the data stream.

DVD player

**FIGURE 8-59**

In addition to limiting playback to compliant devices, CSS prevents DVDs from being successfully duplicated by end users using standard copy utilities. Decryption keys are stored on a hidden area of the DVD that is not copied to the new DVD during duplication.

**What is a region code?** The CSS authentication process includes checking region codes. A DVD **region code** specifies a geographical area of legitimate use for DVD discs and players. For example, the United States, Canada, Bermuda, and U.S. territories make up region 1. DVD players are sold according to region, so in Canada consumers purchase region 1 DVD players, while consumers in India purchase players for region 5. A DVD player will play only DVDs encoded for its region. Region codes allow the film industry to charge higher prices in some countries than others without worrying about cheaper versions affecting sales in more expensive regions.

**Has CSS been cracked?** Soon after CSS appeared, hackers were able to crack it. **DeCSS** is the most well-known software for decrypting DVD content that is protected by CSS. New DRM technologies, such as RipGuard, have emerged as replacements for CSS, but most of these have also been cracked. Although DeCSS and other tools for bypassing DVD protection are widely available on the Internet, their distribution and use are illegal in the United States and other countries with similar copyright laws or treaties.

**What about copy protection for Blu-ray discs?** Like earlier DVD standards, Blu-ray incorporates layers of DRM technologies, but uses AACS instead of CSS for authorization and encryption. **AACS** (Advanced Access Content System) is a DRM technology designed to encrypt and protect content on optical discs. Additional DRM layers include BD+ and BD-ROM Mark.

**How does AACS work?** Like CSS, AACS works with an encrypted content stream. AACS, however, uses a much stronger encryption key, which makes it quite difficult for hackers to break the encryption using brute force methods. Another difference between the two methods is that CSS uses a shared set of encryption keys, and all devices of a specific model use the same key. In contrast, AACS compliant devices each contain their own unique set of keys and these keys can be revoked if a player is found to be compromised. The concept of **authorization and revocation** can be applied to hardware devices and software players to give licensing bodies the means to keep non-complying players off the market and deny further access to complying devices that have become compromised (Figure 8-60).

In addition to encryption, AACS protects content with two types of digital watermarks: a theatrical mark and a consumer mark. The theatrical mark is inserted into the soundtrack of films actually shown in theaters. If a home player detects this watermark, playback stops because the disc is suspected to be one created using an illicitly borrowed professional reel of the film. The second AACS watermark is inserted into legitimate DVDs sold to consumers. If the mark is not detected on a DVD that is supposed to have it, playback will terminate.

**FIGURE 8-60**

AACS depends on authentication and revocation built into devices and content.

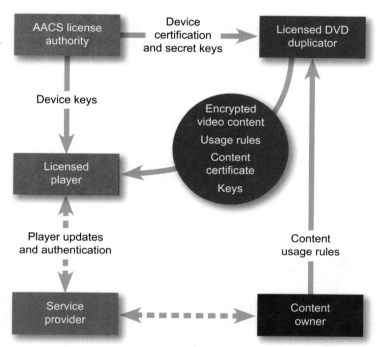

**Do video disc DRM technologies make my computer less secure?** DVD publishers can use DRM to prevent consumers from making a copy of a DVD in case the original is damaged, force viewers to watch the ubiquitous FBI warning, and prohibit viewers from fast-forwarding through commercials. Using DRM in such a manner annoys consumers, but does not threaten the security of their computers. So far, the technologies used to protect video disc content have not opened security holes that are widely exploited by hackers.

## DRM FOR DIGITAL DOWNLOADS

**Can DRM protect downloaded files?** As you have learned so far, DRM technologies can be applied to broadcasts and to content distributed on physical storage media, such as CDs and DVDs. DRM also plays a role in controlling the use of downloaded audio, video, and e-book files.

Free file-sharing sites popular in the 1990s had a devastating effect on the recording industry. Free sites still exist, but the recording industry is waging war against site operators and users. In addition to legal recourse, the recording industry reportedly pays private firms to seed file-sharing net-

8

works with fake versions of popular copyrighted songs, so that it is difficult to find genuine versions. After litigation shut down many free sites, a new crop of legitimate sites offered to pay royalties by charging customers for downloads.

Many consumers seem content to pay a dollar or less to download a song from a legitimate online music store, so the iTunes store and other online music vendors do a booming business. At one time, major music labels such as Universal, Sony BMG, and Warner Music Group required online music stores to protect downloads using DRM technology. Apple used a DRM technology called **FairPlay**, which stored music in a protected AAC format. This format allowed music tracks to be played only on five authorized digital devices. Users could change the devices on which they played iTunes music, but could not exceed the authorized number at any one time.

In addition to limiting the number of devices that could play iTunes music, protected AAC files could not be converted into other music formats, such as MP3, without using illegal cracking technologies.

In 2009, however, Apple announced that iTunes would distribute DRM-free music. Non-DRM music files are labeled *Purchased AAC Audio files* instead

**FIGURE 8-61**

iTunes music can be stored in several file formats. Protected AAC files include DRM, but Purchased AAC files and MPEG audio files are DRM-free.

of *Protected AAC audio files* in consumers' iTunes libraries (Figure 8-61).

DRM-free iTunes files can be converted into MP3 files and played on any digital device that supports MP3 format. Consumers should note that iTunes files have the purchaser's name embedded in the file. Personalizing files, sometimes called **DRM individualization**, allows content providers such as iTunes to determine the source of a file. For example, if a free file-sharing network is carrying an unauthorized version of a Bob Dylan song, DRM individualization could be used to track down the person who originally purchased the track from iTunes.

Consumers should also be aware that the terms of the iTunes license agreement prohibit users from redistributing the songs they purchase, regardless of format; it is not legal to distribute iTunes music to others in AAC or MP3 format.

**How does Windows Media DRM work?** **Windows Media DRM** was developed by Microsoft to provide secure digital content delivery over networks and from Web sites such as the Zune Marketplace. Its purpose is similar to FairPlay—to make sure that digital music and movies can be used only by consumers who purchase them legitimately. Windows Media DRM encrypts the content stream. The key is stored in an encrypted license, which is distributed separately. The digital media file contains an encrypted link to the license.

Files protected by Windows Media DRM can be distributed from a Web site, on a CD, or as an e-mail attachment. If you receive one of these files from a friend and try to access it, you will be prompted to get a license. This process of sharing files but forcing users to pay for licenses before accessing content is sometimes referred to as **super distribution**.

Files protected by Windows Media DRM can be accessed only when using a compliant hardware or software player. Before producing a compliant player, companies must be authorized by Microsoft. Authorization can be revoked from players that become compromised. Windows Media DRM is designed to be updatable. It has been cracked several times, but in every case quick updates from Microsoft have patched the vulnerabilities.

**What about movie download sites?** Movie files are huge and take time to download—about 30 minutes for a low resolution version or more than an hour for DVD quality. Lengthy downloads are inconvenient for customers with slow Internet connections. For consumers with fast connections, however, movie downloads offer a viable alternative to local DVD rental stores.

Legitimate movie download sites such as Netflix and iTunes use DRM technologies such as watermarks and copy generation management in various ways to limit how you can use movies you've downloaded. Some movie downloads can be viewed only on your computer screen. Some download sites allow you to burn a limited number of DVDs. DRM can also limit the length of time you are allowed to view a movie. Often the limit is 24 hours, but some sites offer a 30-day or unlimited viewing window. Some movie download sites require a monthly subscription fee, so before you subscribe, carefully examine the Terms of Use and FAQs to become familiar with download and copy policies.

8

## QuickCheck                                                    SECTION E

1. _____ shifting is the process of converting media files from a format suitable to one device to a format suitable for a different kind of device.

2. Copy _____ management is a digital watermark that specifies the number of times a content stream can be duplicated.

3. A(n) _____ protection system places signals within the content stream that disrupt playback on VCRs by making the image appear dim or scrambled.

4. _____ is the primary technology used to protect DVDs, but it was cracked soon after it was introduced. (Hint: Use the acronym.)

5. Files protected by Windows _____ DRM can be accessed only when using a compliant hardware or software player.

▶ CHECK ANSWERS

# Issue: What Happened to Fair Use?

**SUPPOSE YOU PURCHASE** a music CD of your favorite recording group. Now you want to transfer the file to your computer, rip the best tracks, and transfer them to your portable media player. But wait! That CD is copy protected and your computer CD drive won't read it. You purchased the disc. Can't you listen to the music on any device you choose? The answer depends on a concept called fair use.

Fair use is the right to use portions of copyrighted material without the permission of the copyright holder for purposes such as review, criticism, or parody. Under certain circumstances, fair use is also a successful defense for practices, such as time shifting, in which whole works are copied for limited personal use.

Exactly what does or does not constitute fair use, however, is only sketched out in copyright law. The precise nature of fair use is shaped by a somewhat amorphous cloud of court decisions covering situations and devices as disparate as player piano rolls, printer toner cartridges, videotape recorders, and file sharing networks.

As one of the original time-shifting technologies, VCRs made it possible to set a recording time to capture movies and shows broadcast on television or cable channels. Digital video recorders, such as TiVo, make time shifting possible by saving content to a digital storage device, such as a hard disk.

The legal precedent for time shifting is the landmark 1984 Betamax case in which Universal Studios attempted to hold Sony Corp. of America liable for copyright infringement by people who used video recorders to tape movies from their televisions. The U.S. Supreme Court sided with Sony and concluded that some instances of time shifting were legal.

The court's decision, however, was based on a definition of time shifting as "the practice of recording a program to view it once at a later time." Note the word "once." The Betamax case did not offer legal precedent for copying and saving content for viewing multiple times. The Supreme Court was also influenced by testimony from copyright holders, such as the host of the well-known children's show *Mister Rogers' Neighborhood*, who welcomed the practice of time shifting. At the time, some TV guides even listed shows that networks permitted viewers to copy.

The proliferation of computer networks and streaming media has made place shifting a reality. You can, for example, view a cable television broadcast sent from your Wi-Fi equipped set-top box in your living room to your Wi-Fi equipped notebook out on the deck. Your network, however, is transmitting a copy of the broadcast, a use of copyrighted work that is not explicitly allowed by copyright law in most countries. Therefore, unless a user agreement extends the basic rights granted by copyright law, place shifting would be considered to be a questionable practice.

So how about format shifting? Surely, it must be legal to rip tracks from a CD that you own, save them as an MP3 file, and play them on your iPod.

Many consumers believe that format shifting is a legal type of adaptation. That is true for computer software. According to section 117 of the United States Code, "it is not an infringement for the owner of a copy of a computer program to make or authorize the making of another copy or adaptation."

It might seem that digital content is similar to computer programs because both are in digital formats that can be manipulated by computers. The courts, however, do not agree that the two are the same, so consumers do not have a right to format-shift movies and music. Copyright holders can, however, allow format shifting for specific works if they choose to do so.

It is interesting to consider the basis for the widely held belief that once a song or video has been purchased, consumers have a right to use it in any manner they please short of redistributing it for profit. Precedents for this belief exist in the music and publishing industries.

Although it is not well known, until 1971 no U.S. law protected recorded music. Sheet music and the underlying composition could be copyrighted, but a particular artist's performance was not. So-called "record pirates" could freely copy, say, an Elvis Presley recording without violating U.S. federal law until an amendment to the copyright law was passed in 1971.

A statement accompanying the 1971 amendment seemed to approve of copying music for personal use: "Specifically, it is not the intention of Congress to restrain the home recording, from broadcasts or from tapes or records, of recorded performances, where the home recording is for private use and with no purpose of reproducing or otherwise capitalizing commercially on it."

Consumers are also familiar with copyright restrictions on printed books and have an expectation that digital media can be legally used in parallel ways. Readers expect to be able to carry a book with them to any location, read it at any time they like, use any type of reading light or reading glasses, loan the book to friends, and sell the book when they have finished using it. No wonder consumers are peeved when e-book vendors and other digital content providers use DRM technology to limit how much of an e-book can be viewed, whether the text can be printed or shared, and how long it can be viewed.

Although it is convenient to focus on the "once I buy it I can use it as I like" rationale, we tend to ignore situations in which our expectations about content use are more limited. For example, we do not expect that after attending a Widespread Panic concert, we are entitled to a free DVD or video of the performance. If we pay to see a movie at a theater, we don't then expect not to pay for the DVD or soundtrack CD when they are released.

From rock concerts to theaters, consumers are familiar with the idea that different venues and formats might require separate payments. Digital rights management technologies simply enforce this idea in practice.

Advocates of DRM even contend that it broadens the scope of what consumers can do with digital content because EULAs often provide consumers with more flexibility than today's copyright laws.

Circumventing DRM is possible and it would seem okay to do so for legitimate reasons, such as making backup or archival copies. However, the Digital Millennium Copyright Act (DMCA) makes it illegal to circumvent any technological measure that controls access to a work.

The current status of DRM seems to conflict with consumer fair-use expectations for manipulating and copying music, video, and other digital content. DRM technologies are still evolving, however, as are copyright laws. The Digital Millennium Copyright Act undergoes a formal review every three years, and the copyright office conducts ongoing hearings pertaining to DMCA provisions that affect fair use. Let's see whether the future produces a shift in the balance between fair use, digital rights management, and copyright law.

**INFOWEBLINKS**

You'll find information related to this controversy at the **Digital Rights Management InfoWeb**.

  CLICK TO CONNECT
www.infoweblinks.com/np2012/ch08

8

# What Do You Think?

ISSUE

1. Have you had trouble using software, music CDs, or movie DVDs because of copy protection?

   ◯ Yes    ◯ No    ◯ Not sure

2. In your opinion, do sites like the iTunes Music Store provide consumers with enough flexibility for copying files and creating playlists?

   ◯ Yes    ◯ No    ◯ Not sure

3. Do you think digital rights management technologies are justified because of the high rate of piracy?

   ◯ Yes    ◯ No    ◯ Not sure

   ▶ SAVE RESPONSES

# Computers in Context: Film

**IN 1895,** eager Parisians crowded into a busy café to watch the first public presentation of an exciting new invention—the Cinematograph. The 10-minute film, mostly scenes of everyday life, was a smashing success and ushered in the motion picture era. Early films were short, grainy, grayscale, and silent, but technology quickly improved. In the New York debut of *The Jazz Singer* (1927), Al Jolson spoke the first words in a feature film, "Wait a minute, wait a minute. You ain't heard nothin' yet!"

Even before "talkies" and Technicolor, filmmakers sought ways to escape the bounds of reality through special effects. As early as 1925, directors such as Willis O'Brien used stop-motion photography to animate dinosaurs, giant gorillas, and sword-wielding skeletons. Special-effects technologies—miniatures, blue screens, puppets, claymation, and composite shots—were used with varying degrees of skill over the next 50 years. Films such as Stanley Kubrick's masterpiece, *2001: A Space Odyssey* (1968), and George Lucas's original *Star Wars* (1977) stretched these technologies to their limits, but audiences demanded even more spectacular, yet "realistic," effects.

In 1982, Disney released *TRON*, a movie about a computer programmer who becomes trapped in the depths of a computer where programs are human-like creatures that serve every whim of an evil Master Control Program. The movie included the first primitive attempts at computer-generated footage—30 minutes of computer-generated imagery (CGI) created by two Cray X-MP supercomputers.

CGI uses rendering techniques to create a 3-D scene from a 2-D image, a camera angle, and a light source. Sophisticated algorithms determine how textures, colors, and shadows appear in the rendered scene. Camera angles can be changed at will, and fantastic effects can be created by bending or stretching the image, manipulating light, creating textures, and adding movement to the scene.

Rendered scenes can be set in motion with computer animation techniques. Manual animation requires a painstaking process called in-betweening, in which an artist draws a series of incrementally different images to produce the illusion of movement.

Computers can easily generate in-between images and free up human animators for more challenging work.

A captivating animation special effect called morphing was first seen on the big screen in James Cameron's *The Abyss* (1989) and later used in *Terminator 2* (1991) and other movies. Like in-betweening, morphing starts out with animators defining the morph's start and end points—for example, in *Terminator 2*, the liquid metal face of the T-1000 robot and actor Robert Patrick's face. The start and end points are rendered into digital images, and then the computer generates all the in-between images. Human animators tweak the images by inserting small discrepancies for a touch of less-than-perfect realism in the final footage.

Although the process might sound simple, morphing complex objects realistically and believably takes a tremendous amount of time and computer power. The five-minute morphing sequence in *Terminator 2* took special-effects company Industrial Light & Magic a year to create.

Memorable computer-generated scenes from 2002 blockbusters include the breathtaking aerial scenes in *Spiderman*, a furry blue monster called Sully careening downhill in *Monsters, Inc.*, and the endless army of Uruk-hai marching down the valley toward Helm's Deep in *The Lord of the Rings: The Two Towers*. Spiderman's acrobatic swing through Manhattan was generated with three professional rendering products: Maya, Houdini, and RenderMan. The Uruk-hai were created with MASSIVE, a custom program that gave each computer-generated warrior a unique sequence of actions. To individually animate each of Sully's 2,320,413 blue hairs, animators developed software called Fizt, a dynamic simulator.

Rendering, morphing, and other special-effects processing require sophisticated computer systems. Pixar Animation Studios, the company that provided the technology behind *Toy Story*, *Up*, *Ratatouille*, *WALL-E*, and many other feature-length animated films, uses a cluster of computers called a render-farm. *Toy Story* took more than 800,000 computer hours to produce using the RenderFarm. That might seem like a long time; but if Pixar animators had used a single-processor computer, it would have taken 43 years to finish the job!

Other CGI variations are being used for increasingly sophisticated effects. Special-effects guru John Gaeta developed bullet time and image-based rendering for *The Matrix* (1999). Bullet time produces reality-defying action sequences that slow time to a tantalizing crawl and then crank it back up to normal speed as the camera pivots rapidly around the scene. The effect requires a computer to meticulously trigger a circular array of more than 100 still cameras in sequence.

Films such as *Sky Captain and the World of Tomorrow* (2004) and *Sin City* (2005) took green screen special effects to a new level. Filmed entirely indoors on a sound stage, these movies used a technique called compositing that layers two or more video clips over each other and merges them into one image. Actors were filmed against a green background screen. During post-production, video editing software removed the background and layered in scenery created with CGI or from real footage on location.

*Sin City* is also notable as one of the first fully digital live action motion pictures. It was filmed in full color with high-definition digital cameras. The footage was converted to black and white, and then color was reintroduced digitally with the use of a DLP Cinema projector.

Motion capture suits were put to award-winning use for Peter Jackson's *The Lord of the Rings*. The actor who played Gollum was outfitted with sensors that tracked the position of his head, arms, and limbs. The collected data was later used by animators to create the 3-D animated Gollum that you saw on screen. Motion capture was further refined for *Avatar*, which used digital technology to capture the actors' facial expressions.

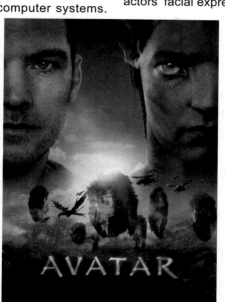

Sophisticated animation and rendering techniques now come close to producing realistic human figures. Animations were once clearly two-dimensional and far from lifelike, but CGI renderings are becoming more difficult to distinguish from real actors.

What might happen in the future is the subject of *Simone* (2002), starring Al Pacino as a washed-up director who is given a hard disk containing code for a computer-generated movie star. Pacino uses her as the leading lady in a string of hits, all the while keeping her identity secret. According to reviewer Leigh Johnson, it becomes clear that Simone, a computer-generated image, is more authentic than the people watching her. It is one of the film's main themes, expressed by Pacino's character: "Our ability to manufacture fraud now exceeds our ability to detect it."

The implications of computer-generated actors are just emerging. Not only do they blur the line between reality and fiction, but they also raise puzzling questions for actors and their agents, directors, and programmers. Is it possible to create CGI doubles for long-dead actors, such as Marilyn Monroe and James Dean? If so, who controls their use and profits from their work? Can aging actors sign contracts for use of their "young" CGI counterparts? Would it be legal and ethical for programmers to create and market virtual characters based on real actors or a compilation of the best traits of popular stars? As is often the case, new technologies present issues along with their benefits—issues you might want to consider the next time you watch a movie.

**INFOWEBLINKS**

To find more information on this topic, visit the **Computers and Film InfoWeb**.

CLICK TO CONNECT

www.infoweblinks.com/np2012/ch08

8

# New Perspectives Labs

## On the BookOnCD

To access the New Perspectives Lab for Chapter 8, start the BookOnCD and then click the icon next to the lab title below.

### ▶ WORKING WITH BITMAP GRAPHICS

#### IN THIS LAB YOU'LL LEARN:

- How to identify common bitmap graphics file extensions

- How to capture an image from the Web

- How to find the properties of a graphic

- How to eliminate red eye and manipulate the brightness, contrast, and sharpness of photos

- How to make a photo look old

- How to select a palette and apply a dithering technique

- How to prepare graphics for the Web and e-mail attachments

- The effects of lossy compression

### LAB ASSIGNMENTS

1. Start the interactive part of the lab. Make sure you've enabled Tracking if you want to save your QuickCheck results. Perform each lab step as directed, and answer all the lab QuickCheck questions. When you exit the lab, your answers are automatically graded and your results are displayed.

2. Use the Start button to access the All Programs menu for the computer you typically use. Make a list of the available bitmap graphics software.

3. Capture a photographic image from a digital camera, scanner, or Web page. Save it as "MyGraphic." Open the image using any available graphics software. Use this software to discover the properties of the graphic. Indicate the source of the graphic, and then describe its file format, file size, resolution, and color depth.

4. Prepare this graphics file to send to a friend as an e-mail attachment that is smaller than 200 KB. Describe the steps that were required.

5. Suppose you want to post the image from #4 on a Web page. Make the necessary adjustments to file size and color depth. Describe the resulting graphic in terms of its resolution, color depth, palette, and dithering.

# Key Terms

Make sure you understand all the boldfaced key terms presented in this chapter. With the NP2012 BookOnCD, you can use this list of terms as an interactive study activity. First, try to define a term in your own words, and then click the term to compare your definition with the definition presented in the chapter. Online, try your hand at the TechTerm Flashcards.

3-D graphics, 449
AAC, 425
AACS, 469
Analog hole, 464
Analog protection system, 468
Animated GIF, 448
ASF, 458
Audio compression, 423
Authorization and revocation, 469
AVI, 458
Bitmap graphic, 430
Bitrate, 457
Blu-ray Disc Movie, 458
BMP, 442
Broadcast flag, 465
CCD, 431
Codec, 457
Color palette, 437
Compression ratio, 457
Container format, 458
Copy generation management, 467
Copy protection, 466
Cropping, 435
CSS, 468
DeCSS, 468
Desktop video, 452
Digital audio, 422
Digital audio extraction, 426
Digital camera, 431
Digital content, 464
Digital rights management, 464
Digital signal processor, 424
Digital video, 452
Digital watermark, 465
Digitizing tablet, 446
Drawing software, 446
DRM individualization, 470
DVD image, 462

FairPlay, 470
File compression utility, 440
Flash, 448
Flash video, 458
Format shifting, 465
GIF, 442
Gradient, 447
Grayscale palette, 438
HDCP, 466
Image compression, 439
Integrated audio, 423
JPEG, 442
Linear editing, 456
Lossless compression, 439
Lossy compression, 439
Megapixel, 433
Metafile, 447
MIDI, 427
MIDI sequence, 427
Monochrome bitmap, 436
MOV, 458
MP3, 425
MPEG, 458
Nonlinear editing, 456
Ogg Vorbis, 425
Paint software, 430
Phoneme, 428
Photosites, 431
Pixel interpolation, 435
Pixelated, 435
Place shifting, 465
PNG, 442
Rasterization, 447
RAW, 442
Ray tracing, 449
Region code, 468
Rendering, 449
Resolution dependent, 435

Run-length encoding, 439
Sampling rate, 423
Scanner, 431
Signal scrambling, 465
Sound card, 423
Speech recognition, 428
Speech synthesis, 428
Streaming audio, 426
Streaming video, 459
Super distribution, 471
SVG, 448
Synthesized sound, 427
System palette, 438
Text-to-speech software, 428
TIFF, 442
Time shifting, 465
Tracing software, 447
Transcoding, 458
True Color bitmap, 437
Vector graphic, 444
Video capture, 455
VOB, 458
WAV, 425
Wavetable, 427
Web palette, 438
Webcam, 454
WebM, 458
Windows Media DRM, 470
Wireframe, 449
WMA, 425

8

# Interactive Summary

To review important concepts from this chapter, fill in the blanks to best complete each sentence. When using the NP2012 BookOnCD, click the Check Answers buttons to automatically score your answers.

**SECTION A:** Music, voice, and sound effects can all be recorded and stored on a computer as [ ] audio. To digitally record sound, [ ] of the sound are collected at periodic intervals and stored as numeric data. High-quality sound is usually sampled at 44.1 [ ] , and each stereo sample requires 32 bits of storage space. To conserve space, radio-quality recordings of speaking voices are often recorded at lower sampling rates. A computer's [ ] card is responsible for transforming the bits stored in an audio file into music, sound effects, and narrations. It contains digital [ ] processing circuitry that transforms bits into analog sound, records analog sounds as digital bits, and handles audio compression. Digital audio file formats include WAV, AAC, WMA, Ogg Vorbis, and MP3. Most portable media players work with MP3 format or

with the [ ] format, used for .m4p files at the iTunes Store.

MIDI music is [ ] sound that is artificially created. Unlike digital audio sound files, which contain digitized recordings of real sound passages, MIDI files contain [ ] for creating the pitch, volume, and duration of notes made by musical instruments. MIDI files are typically much smaller than digital audio files for similar musical passages, so they are ideal for Web pages. However, MIDI music tends to lack the full resonance of symphony-quality sound that can be achieved with digital audio. Speech [ ] is the process by which machines, such as computers, produce sound that resembles spoken words. Speech [ ] refers to the ability of machines to "understand" spoken words.       ▶ CHECK ANSWERS

**SECTION B:** A(n) [ ] graphic is composed of a grid of dots, and the color of each dot is stored as a binary number. Both scanners and cameras produce images in bitmap format. The dimensions of the grid that forms a bitmap graphic are referred to as its [ ] . High-resolution graphics typically produce better image quality than low-resolution graphics, but require more storage space. It is possible to change the resolution and/or the file size of a bitmap graphic; but because bitmaps are resolution [ ] , these changes can reduce image quality. For example, enlarging a bitmap requires your computer to fill in missing pixels, which often results in a jagged or [ ] image. As a general rule, images that you intend to print should remain at full size and resolution. When sending bitmap files as e-mail attachments, they can be

[ ] in size or resolution to produce a file that is less than 500 KB.

Color [ ] refers to the number of colors available for use in an image. For example, a bitmap graphic composed of 256 colors requires only [ ] bits to store the data for each pixel, whereas 24 bits are required for each pixel in a(n) [ ] Color graphic. Grayscale, system, and Web palettes use eight bits to represent each pixel. Image [ ] shrinks the size of a graphics file. [ ] compression permanently removes data, but [ ] compression shrinks files without removing any data. Popular bitmap graphics formats include BMP, TIFF, GIF, JPEG, RAW, and PNG. Of these formats, GIF, JPEG, and PNG are supported by most Web browsers.       ▶ CHECK ANSWERS

## SECTION C:
Unlike a bitmap graphic, created by superimposing a grid of pixels over an image, a(n) [ ] graphic consists of a set of instructions for creating a picture. These graphics are created by using a type of graphics software called [ ] software. They are stored as a collection of [ ] and their corresponding sizes, colors, and positions. You can identify these graphics by their flat cartoon-like appearance and their file extensions: .wmf, .ai, .dxf, .eps, .swf, and .svg. A vector graphic can be converted into a bitmap by a process called [ ] . Once converted, however, the resulting graphic loses the object-editing qualities it had in its vector state. Two vector graphics formats, [ ] and Flash, are popular for Web-based graphics. 3-D graphics are stored as a set of instructions that contain the locations and lengths of lines that form a(n) [ ] for a 3-D object. This framework then can be covered by colored, patterned, and textured surfaces. This process, called [ ] , produces a bitmap image of the 3-D object. [ ] tracing adds highlights and shadows to the image. 3-D graphics can be animated to produce special effects for movies and animated characters for 3-D computer games. ▶ CHECK ANSWERS

## SECTION D:
Footage for digital videos can be supplied from a digital source, or from a(n) [ ] source that requires conversion. In addition to standalone digital cameras, digital footage can also be obtained from cameras embedded in handheld devices and from [ ] built in above a computer screen. Video stored on a computer hard disk can be edited using a technique called [ ] editing, which does not require moving segments from one VCR to another. After editing, you can prepare to output your video by selecting settings for [ ] ratio, display size, and compression so that the resulting video quality and file size are appropriate for its intended use. Software, such as MPEG, DivX, Theora, and H.264, that compresses the video stream is referred to as a(n) [ ] . A compression [ ] indicates the degree of compression. A video file compressed at 35:1 has more compression, a smaller file size, and lower image quality than a file compressed at 5:1. Video and audio streams are combined into the final video file and stored using a(n) [ ] format, such as AVI, MOV, or WebM. Video can be included in HTML5-compliant Web pages using the <video> HTML [ ] . Videos can also be burned onto DVDs for playback in a standalone DVD player that requires data in [ ] format. ▶ CHECK ANSWERS

## SECTION E:
Digital [ ] management is a collection of techniques used by copyright holders to limit access to and use of digital content. DRM technologies can limit or prevent convenient [ ] , place, and format shifting. A digital [ ] is a DRM technology inserted into the content stream in such a way that it is imperceptible to users, but can be recognized by complying devices. Copy [ ] DRM for CDs depends on intentionally [ ] data and CD-based software. The major DRM technology to protect DVD content called [ ] was cracked shortly after it was introduced. A somewhat more sophisticated DRM technology called [ ] is used on Blu-ray and HD-DVD. The concept of authorization and [ ] can be applied to hardware devices and software players to give licensing bodies the means to keep non-complying players off the market and deny further access to complying devices that have become compromised. Content downloaded from online music and video stores might be protected by DRM technologies, such as Apple's [ ] and Microsoft's Windows Media DRM. ▶ CHECK ANSWERS

8

# Interactive Situation Questions

Apply what you've learned to some typical computing situations. When using the NP2012 BookOnCD, you can type your answers, and then use the Check Answers button to automatically score your responses.

**1.** Suppose you are creating an English-as-a-Second-Language Web page and you want to add links to sound files that pronounce English phrases. Would it be better to store the files in WAV or MIDI format? [_____]

**2.** Imagine that you're a musician and you are asked to synthesize some music for the opening screen of a Web site. For this project, you would most likely work with [_____] music.

**3.** Suppose you visit a Web site that allows you to enter sentences, and then it reads the sentences back to you. The site even gives you a choice of a female or male voice. You assume that this site uses speech [_____] technology.

**4.** You have an old photograph that you want to incorporate in a brochure for your antiques business. To convert the photo into digital format, you use a(n) [_____].

**5.** Imagine that you are preparing a series of bitmap graphics for a Web site. To decrease the download time for each graphic, you can remove pixels or reduce the color [_____].

**6.** You've taken a photo with a high resolution digital camera and you want to send it as an e-mail attachment. You decide to use PKZIP to [_____] the image into a more manageable size.

**7.** Suppose you are designing a logo for a client. You know the design will undergo several revisions, and you understand that the logo will be used at various sizes. You decide it would be best to use drawing software to create the logo as a(n) [_____] graphic.

**8.** After you finish arranging video clips and adding a soundtrack, you can select a video file format and a compression technique. For example, you might store the video in WebM container format and use the MPEG [_____] to compress the file.

**9.** After purchasing a CD of your favorite rock group, you try to rip one of the tracks to your computer and convert it to MP3 format. When you play the file on your computer, you notice loud pops in the audio that indicate that the CD was probably copy [_____].

**10.** Your friend sends you an e-mail attachment containing a music video from the Zune Marketplace. Your ability to access the file after paying for your own license is an example of [_____] distribution.

 CHECK ANSWERS

# Interactive Practice Tests

Practice tests that consist of ten multiple-choice, true/false, and fill-in-the-blank questions are available on both the NP2012 BookOnCD and the NP2012 CourseMate Web site. BookOnCD test questions are selected at random from a large test bank, so each time you take a test, you'll receive a different set of questions. Your tests are scored immediately, and you can print study guides that help you find the correct answers for any questions that you missed. Online, you'll find a Practice Test for each section of the chapter. Your results from online tests are saved by Engagement Tracker. ⏵ CLICK TO START

# Learning Objectives Checkpoints

Learning Objectives Checkpoints are designed to help you assess whether you have achieved the major learning objectives for this chapter. You can use paper and pencil or word processing software to complete most of the activities.

1. Draw a diagram to show how the smooth curve of an analog sound wave is divided into samples and stored digitally.

2. Explain the relationship between sampling rate, audio quality, and file size.

3. Make a list of ten digital audio applications and indicate whether each one would use WAV or MIDI.

4. Use the file manager on your computer to locate five bitmap graphics. List the file name and extension for each one, and where possible identify whether it originated from a digital camera, scanner, or some other source.

5. Describe six ways to transfer photos from a digital camera to a computer.

6. Explain how resolution, image size, color depth, and color palettes can be manipulated to adjust the file size of a bitmap graphic. Summarize how you would prepare bitmap graphics for the following uses: e-mail attachment, Web page, desktop publishing, and printed photo.

7. Recap key points about image compression, explaining the difference between lossy and lossless compression and listing file types with built-in compression.

8. Describe differences in the ways that vector and bitmap graphics are created, stored, and used. Explain how the concept of layering relates to your ability to modify a vector graphic.

9. Describe the procedures used to convert bitmap graphics into vector graphics, and to convert vector graphics into bitmaps.

10. Make a series of quick sketches that illustrates the evolution of a 3-D graphic from wireframe to rendered image, and to ray-traced image.

11. List the devices that can be used to capture video and indicate which are analog and which are digital.

12. Explain the procedures required to capture analog video and transfer it into digital format.

13. Explain how compression affects the file size of a digital video.

14. Explain how streaming audio and video work, and contrast them with non-streaming technology.

15. Use your own words to make a list of the steps required to burn video onto a DVD that can be viewed on standalone DVD players.

16. Make a list of the file extensions that were mentioned in this chapter and group them according to digital media type: bitmap graphic, vector graphic, digital video, digital audio, and MIDI. Circle any formats that are used on the Web and put a star by formats that typically require you to download a player.

17. Explain how specific DRM technologies are used to prevent consumers from a) recording television broadcasts, b) making a copy of a music CD, c) ripping tracks from a music CD, d) copying a DVD movie, and e) watching a movie captured on TiVo and streamed over a network to a PC.

18. Give examples of time shifting, place shifting, and format shifting.

Study Tip: Make sure you can use your own words to correctly answer each of the red focus questions in the chapter.

**8**

## Concept Map

Fill in the blanks on the concept map to show the hierarchy of digital media formats.

# Projects

 **CRITICAL THINKING**

Copyright laws are changing as digital sound, image, and video technologies evolve and become easier to use. Although the courts seem to clearly hold that it is illegal to copy media for profit, they are not as clear about the acceptability of modifications. For example, video editing software makes it relatively simple for people to clip out parts of movies they find objectionable for themselves or their children to watch. Should it be legal to do so for personal use? What if an organization wanted to rent out such edited copies? What if DVD players and movies were set up so that the devices would edit and display the revised version on the fly? After you consider your own opinion, you might check the Web to see the latest information about this issue.

 **GROUP PROJECT**

Work with a group of four students to research Web-based music download sites. Create one PowerPoint slide for each site. The slide should give a basic overview of the site, including its name, URL, price, pros, and cons. For the final slide in the presentation, create a table comparing the features and prices of each site.

 **CYBERCLASSROOM**

Each person on your team should e-mail a photo in JPEG format to the other members of the group. The photo can be one you've taken or one you find on the Web. If you get your photo from the Web, make sure there are no prohibitions for using it for a personal project and keep track of the Web site so you have a record of your source. When you receive the photos from your teammates, be creative and use Photoshop or similar photo editing software to create a composite image that contains elements from all the photos. Submit your original photo and your composite photo to your instructor.

 **MULTIMEDIA PROJECT**

Use Windows Sound Recorder or similar software to record your own 15-second radio ad for your favorite music or video download service. Submit the text of your script along with the .wav file containing your ad.

 **RESUME BUILDER**

Artists routinely create a portfolio containing examples of their best work. How can you apply the portfolio concept to your job search? Suppose you've decided to create a multimedia portfolio that showcases your talents. Describe what you'd like your portfolio to contain, indicating which of the items you currently have and which you'd like to create and add in the future. Also, describe the format for each item: photo, document, scan, audio, or video. Finally, describe whether you envision delivering your portfolio on CD or the Web, and then discuss the advantages and limitations of your choice.

 **GLOBALIZATION**

The United States has been accused of exporting its culture and values through films and television. Sometimes referred to as Coca-Colonization, the mass exportation of American culture is expected to increase as more and more people have access to the Internet. But is digital distribution a two-way street? What can you find out about the *importation* of cultures to the United States (or your country)? Incorporate your findings into a two-page paper. Make sure you cite specific examples and offer your ideas on how technology aids or discourages cross-cultural interchanges. Include a list of references on a third page.

 **ISSUE**

The Issue section of this chapter focused on digital rights controversies, such as your rights to share music files, copy DVD movies, or use software to break copy protection. To begin the project, consult the Digital Rights Management InfoWeb and link to the recommended Web sites to get an in-depth overview of the issues. With this background, work with a partner and select a digital rights controversy that seems interesting. Use the Web to research the controversy. Collaborate with your partner to write a dialogue between two people who are arguing both sides of the issue.

 **COMPUTERS IN CONTEXT**

The Computers in Context section of this chapter focused on digital special effects technology used in recent films. For this project, conduct your own exploration of the special effects that have appeared in your favorite movies. To begin the project, browse through the material presented in the Computers and Film InfoWeb on page 475. Look for information about specific movies using Web sites such as the Internet Movie Database (*www.imdb.com*). Many movies also have dedicated Web sites that you can find using a search engine. To complete the project, select one of your favorite movies and write a two- to four-page movie review that focuses on how its special effects contribute to the movie's overall quality.

# On the Web

## STUDENT EDITION LABS

When you purchase access to the NP2012 CourseMate Web site, you'll find targeted learning materials to help you understand key concepts and prepare for exams. See page O-41 in the Orientation Chapter for login instructions.

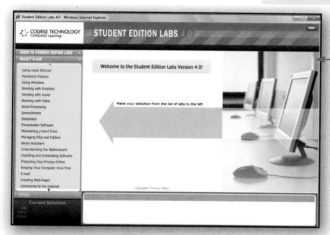

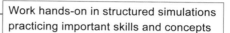
Work hands-on in structured simulations practicing important skills and concepts

## WORKING WITH GRAPHICS

In the Working with Graphics Student Edition Lab, you will learn about the following topics:

- Downloading images from the Web
- Enhancing an image with filters and manipulating brightness, contrast, and sharpness
- Incorporating type in an image and working with layers
- Cropping vs. resizing and reducing file size
- Creating Web graphics

## WORKING WITH VIDEO

In the Working with Video Student Edition Lab, you will learn about the following topics:

- Viewing digital video
- Importing and working with clips
- Using the storyboard
- Adding transitions and including audio
- Saving the video

## WORKING WITH AUDIO

In the Working with Audio Student Edition Lab, you will learn about the following topics:

- Audio file formats and extensions
- Importing and downloading audio files
- Burning audio CDs
- Including audio files on a Web site

8

 **CHAPTER OVERVIEW COURSECAST**

Use your computer or iPod to hear a five-minute audio presentation of chapter highlights.

 **AUDIO FLASHCARDS**

Interact with audio flashcards to review key concepts from the chapter.

 **DETAILED OBJECTIVES**

Make sure that you've achieved all the objectives for a chapter before it's time for your test!

 **PRACTICE TESTS**

Review chapter material by taking these ten-question tests. Your results are saved by Engagement Tracker.

 **ONLINE GAMES**

Have some fun while refreshing your memory about key concepts that might appear on the next test.

 **AND MORE!**

At the NP2012 CourseMate Web site you'll also find the NP2012 eBook, TechTerm Flashcards, Online Glossary, and What Do You Think? opinion polls.

# CREDITS

Page v, © myVector/Shutterstock.com
Page vi, © Danilo Moura/Shutterstock.com
Page vii, © Alexander Kalina/Shutterstock.com
Page viii, © Jiri Vratislavsky/Shutterstock.com
Page xi, © Alexander Kalina/Shutterstock.com
Page xii, © Nataliia Natykach/Shutterstock.com
Page xiv, © Coprid/Shutterstock.com
Page xv, © Mostafa Fawzy/Shutterstock.com
Page xvii, © Gladskikh Tatiana/Shutterstock.com
Page xx, © Jaimie Duplass/Shutterstock.com
Orientation 2, Courtesy of Sony Electronics, Inc.
Orientation 6, Courtesy of Kensington Technology Group
Orientation 7, Photodisc/Getty Images
Orientation 15, Courtesy of Stephen G. Eick, SSS Research Inc.
Orientation 27, AP Photo/Darren Hauck
Figure 1-06, © Walt Disney Pictures/courtesy Everett Collection
Figure 1-08, Courtesy Everett Collection
Figure 1-09, Courtesy of the Software & Information Industry Association
Figure 1-10, Courtesy of Nokia
Figure 1-11, AP Photo/Pavel Rahman
Figure 1-14, Courtesy of Dell, Inc.
Figure 1-14, Courtesy of Apple
Figure 1-15, Courtesy of Silicon Graphics International
Figure 1-17, Courtesy of Silicon Graphics International
Figure 1-18, Courtesy of IBM Corporation
Figure 1-19, Image courtesy of the National Center for Computational Sciences, Oak Ridge National Laboratory
Figure 1-20, Courtesy of Motorola
Figure 1-20, BlackBerry Curve image courtesy of Research In Motion[1]
Figure 1-20c, Courtesy of Nokia
Figure 1-20d, Courtesy of Apple
Figure 1-21, Courtesy of Apple
Figure 1-22, © Dennis Rozie/Shutterstock.com
Figure 1-30, Courtesy of Intel Corporation
Figure 1-41, © Brand X Pictures/Alamy
Figure 1-44, Courtesy of www.rantsandraves.co.uk
Issue 1a, © Warner Bros/courtesy Everett Collection
CinC-1a, Image courtesy of The Advertising Archives
CinC-1b, Napster advertisement reprinted with permission of Napster, LLC
Figure 2-03b, Courtesy of Shuttle Computer Group, Inc | http://us.shuttle.com
Figure 2-03c, Courtesy of Hewlett-Packard Company
Figure 2-04a, Courtesy of Hewlett-Packard Company
Figure 2-04c, Courtesy of Fujitsu Technology Solutions
Figure 2-05, Courtesy of Hewlett-Packard Company
Figure 2-06, Courtesy of Dell, Inc.
Figure 2-07, Courtesy of Dell, Inc.
Figure 2-11, © Hugh Threfall/Alamy
Figure 2-12, Courtesy of Intel Corporation
Figure 2-16a, Courtesy of Intel Corporation
Figure 2-16b, Courtesy of Advanced Micro Devices, Inc.[2]
Figure 2-16c, Courtesy of ARM Ltd.
Figure 2-32, Courtesy of BiTMICRO Networks, Inc.
Figure 2-37b, Courtesy of Kensington Technology Group
Figure 2-37c, Courtesy of Saitek USA
Figure 2-39, © Ozier Muhammad/The New York Times/Redux
Figure 2-40, Courtesy of ViewSonic Corporation

Figure 2-43, Courtesy of Advanced Micro Devices, Inc.
Figure 2-47, Courtesy of Hewlett-Packard Company
Figure 2-56, Courtesy of Kensington Technology Group
Figure 2-57, Courtesy of AnchorPad
Figure 2-62, Courtesy of Targus
Issue-2b, © Artshots/Shutterstock.com
CinC-2a, © Bettmann/CORBIS
CinC-2b, Photo Courtesy of U.S. Army
Figure 3-03, Courtesy of Systweak
Figure 3-04, Courtesy of Microsoft Corporation
Figure 3-07a, Courtesy of Microsoft Corporation
Figure 3-07b, Reprinted with permission of Quark, Inc. and its affiliates
Figure 3-07c, Courtesy of Adobe Systems Incorporated
Figure 3-16a, © wrangle/iStockphoto.com
Figure 3-16b, Courtesy of Wolfram Research
Figure 3-22b, © Ralf Juergen Kraft/Shutterstock.com
Figure 3-26, Courtesy of Activision Publishing, Inc.
Figure 3-28, Courtesy of Microsoft Corporation
Figure 3-28, Courtesy of Check Point Software Technologies, Inc.[3]
Figure 3-28, Courtesy of Adobe Systems Incorporated
Figure 3-28, Courtesy of CyberLink Corp.
Figure 3-33, Copyright © 2006 by the Open Source Initiative
Figure 3-44, © David Woolley/Getty Images
Figure 3-49, Courtesy of ClamWin Free Antivirus
Issue-3a, Courtesy of Software & Information Industry Association
CinC-3a, © Erik S. Lesser/The New York Times/Redux Pictures
CinC-3b, © Ashley Gilbertson/Aurora Photos
Figure 4-23, Courtesy of Symbian Foundation
Figure 4-23, Courtesy of Microsoft Corporation
Figure 4-23, Courtesy of Research In Motion
Figure 4-23, Courtesy of Google Inc. Android is a trademark of Google Inc.
Figure 4-23, Courtesy of Palm, Inc., a subsidiary of Hewlett-Packard Company
Issue-4, © Mikkel William Nielsen/iStockphoto
CinC-4a, Courtesy of the Fond du Lac Police Department
CinC-4b, Courtesy of the Fond du Lac Police Department
Figure 5-01, Courtesy of Bob Metcalfe
Figure 5-02, © Exactostock/SuperStock
Figure 5-07, Courtesy of Belkin International
Figures 5-10, 5-13, 5-14, © Creative Crop/Getty Images
Figure 5-12, AP Photo/Eckehard Schulz
Figure 5-17a, Courtesy of SMC Corporation
Figure 5-17b, Courtesy of D-Link Systems
Figure 5-18, Courtesy of Cisco Systems, Inc.
Figure 5-21, Courtesy of Iogear
Figure 5-25, Courtesy of Belkin International
Figure 5-27, Courtesy of Bluetooth SIG
Figure 5-28a, Courtesy of Nokia
Figure 5-28b, Courtesy of Vega Helmet
Figure 5-30, Courtesy of Belkin International
Figure 5-33b, Courtesy of NETGEAR, Inc.
Figure 5-35, PRNewsFoto/Novatel Wireless, Inc.
Figure 5-37, © Ocean/Corbis
Figure 5-39, © Jon Feingersh/Getty Images
Figure 5-40a, Courtesy of Sonos, Inc.
Figure 5-40b, Courtesy of D-Link Systems
Figure 5-40c, Courtesy of Toshiba America Information Systems

Figure 5-45a, Courtesy of Dell, Inc.
Figure 5-45b, Courtesy of Intel Corporation
Figure 5-48, AP Photo/Matthias Rietschel
Figure 5-54, © Radius Images/Alamy
Figure 5-55_1, © Peter Griffith/Getty Images
Figure 5-55_2, © Hemera Technologies/Jupiterimages
Figure 5-55_3, © GLUE STOCK/Shutterstock.com
Issue-5a, © David Kilpatrick/Alamy
Issue-5b, Courtesy of Rob Flickenger
    (http://www.oreillynet.com/pub/wlg/448)
CinC-5a, Photography courtesy of the University of Illinois at
    Urbana-Champaign Archives
CinC-5b, © Jenkedco/Shutterstock.com
Page 292, Courtesy of Belkin International
Figure 6-01, Computer History Museum
Figures 6-04, 6-12, 6-15, 6-19, © Ocean/Corbis
Figure 6-14, Courtesy of ZyXEL
Figure 6-16a, Courtesy of 2Wire.com
Figure 6-16b, Courtesy of Zoom Technologies
Figure 6-20, © Siri Stafford/Getty Images
Figure 6-20, © Bryce Kroll/iStockphoto.com
Figure 6-20, © Jonathan Ling/iStockphoto.com
Figure 6-21, Courtesy of Hughes Network Systems, LLC
Figure 6-22, Courtesy of Intel Corporation
Figure 6-25, Royalty-Free/CORBIS
Figure 6-27, Carlos Cordero Pérez/La Nacion de Costa Rica/
    Newsco
Figure 6-28, Courtesy of Ground Control
Figure 6-29, © David Young-Wolff/PhotoEdit
Figure 6-30, PRNewsFoto/Verizon Wireless
Figure 6-32, PRNewsFoto/Verizon Wireless
Figure 6-33, photo BenQ Mobile
Figure 6-36, Courtesy of Visualware
Figure 6-41, Courtesy of SETI@home
Figure 6-42a, Courtesy of chessbrain.net
Figure 6-42b, Courtesy of www.climateprediction.net
Figure 6-42c, Courtesy of distributed.net
Figure 6-42d, Courtesy of Vijay Pande, Folding@Home, and
    Stanford University http://folding.stanford.edu
Figure 6-42e, Courtesy of PrimeGrid distributed computing
    project
Figure 6-42f, Courtesy of The Scripps Research Institute
Figure 6-46, © Paul Edmondson/Getty Images
Figure 6-47, Courtesy of Gibson Research Corporation
Figure 6-51, 6-52, 6-53, © Ocean/Corbis
Issue-6b, © Steve Allen/Getty Images
CinC-6a, © H.F. Davis/Getty Images
CinC-6b, © Royalty-Free/CORBIS
Figure 7-01, Courtesy of Ted Nelson, Project Xanadu
Figure 7-18, Courtesy of Ben Samuels
Figure 7-27a, © Eric Bean/Getty Images
Figure 7-27b, © Don Farrall/Getty Images
Figure 7-27c, © Ryan McVay/Getty Images
Figure 7-27d, © S.T. Yiap/Alamy
Figure 7-27e, © Comstock Images/Alamy
Figure 7-29, © Nicholas DeVore/Getty Images
Figure 7-31, © Richard Griffin/Shutterstock.com
Figure 7-31, 7-32, © Jupiterimages
Figure 7-37_1, © Jack Z. Young/Shutterstock.com
Figures 7-37_2, 7-37_3, © Wallenrock/Shutterstock.com
Figures 7-39, 7-41, © Creative Crop/Getty Images
Figures 7-39, 7-41, © Ocean Photography/Veer
Figure 7-48a, Courtesy of Webroot Software

Figure 7-48b, Courtesy of Computer Associates
Figure 7-48c, © 2010 Check Point Software Technologies
    Ltd. All rights reserved.
Issue-7a, © Ron Chapple/Getty Images
Issue-7b, © Andersen Ross/Getty Images
CinC-7a, © Lifetime/courtesy Everett Collection
CinC-7b, Courtesy of MIT Media Lab/Photo by Lynn Barry
Figure 8-04, Courtesy of Logitech
Figure 8-10, © Sandy Jones/iStockphoto
Figure 8-13, Courtesy of Learning Technology Services,
    University of Wisconsin-Stout
Figures 8-14a–d, f, Courtesy of SanDisk Corporation
Figure 8-14e, Courtesy of Hitachi Global Storage
    Technologies
Figure 8-40, © Rodolfo Arpia/Alamy
Figure 8-43, Courtesy of SANYO North America
Figure 8-43, Courtesy of JVC America
Figure 8-43, © Friedrich Saurer/Alamy
Figure 8-43, Courtesy of RED Digital Camera
Figure 8-44, © Corbis Premium Collection/Alamy
Figure 8-55, © Getty Images
Figure 8-56, Courtesy of Sling Media, Inc.
Issue-8a, © Daniele Mattioli/Anzenberger/Redux
CinC-8a, TM & Copyright © 20th Century Fox. All rights
    reserved/Courtesy Everett Collection
CinC-8b, © Corbis/Sygma

Critical Thinking Icon, © Image Source/Corbis
Group Project Icon, © amanaimagesRF/Getty Images
Cyberclassroom Icon, © Masterfile
Multimedia Project Icon, © Fuse/Getty Images
Resume Builder Icon, © Tetra Images/Getty Images
Globalization Icon, © Ian McKinnell/Getty Images
Issue Icon, © Tetra Images/Corbis
Computers in Context Icon, © Creative Crop/Getty Images

All other figure images © MediaTechnics Corp.

[1] BlackBerry®, RIM®, Research In Motion® and related
    trademarks, names and logos are the property of
    Research In Motion Limited and are registered and/or
    used in the U.S. and countries around the world.

[2] AMD, the AMD Arrow logo, and combinations thereof are
    trademarks of Advanced Micro Devices, Inc.

[3] Check Point Software Technologies Ltd. All rights reserved.
    Check Point, Check Point logo, ZoneAlarm, ZoneAlarm
    Anti-Spyware are trademarks or registered trademarks of
    Check Point Software Technologies Ltd. or its affiliates.
    ZoneAlarm is a Check Point Software Technologies, Inc.
    Company. All other product names mentioned herein are
    trademarks or registered trademarks of their respective
    owners. The products described in this document are
    protected by U.S. Patent No. 5,606,668, 5,835,726,
    6,496,935, 6,873,988, and 6,850,943 and may be
    protected by other U.S. Patents, foreign patents, or
    pending applications.

# GLOSSARY

**3-D graphics** A type of digital graphics format that displays a three-dimensional image on a two-dimensional space. 449

**3-D graphics software** The software used to create three-dimensional wireframe objects, then render them into images. 137

**64-bit processor** A microprocessor with registers, address bus, and a data bus that holds 64 bits of data, in contrast to 32-bit processors that hold 32 bits of data. 68

**AAC** (Advanced Audio Coding) A file format that provides highly compressed audio files with very little loss of sound quality and is promoted by Apple on its iTunes Web site. 425

**AACS** (Advanced Access Content System) A digital rights management system that uses encryption to restrict access and copying content from optical media. 469

**Absolute reference** In a worksheet formula, cell references (usually preceded by a $ symbol) that cannot change as a result of a move or copy operation. 132

**Access time** The estimated time for a storage device to locate data on a disk, usually measured in milliseconds. 77

**Accounting software** A category of software that includes accounting, money management, and tax preparation software. 142

**ActionScript** A scripting language used primarily to develop Flash applications and Web sites that include Flash media, such as Flash videos and animations. 372

**ActiveX control** A set of commands and components that can be used by programmers to add interactive features to Web pages. 373

**Ad-blocking software** A type of software that prevents ads from appearing on your computer screen. 385

**Ad-serving cookie** A cookie installed by a marketing firm to track user activities on Web sites containing its ads. 400

**AES** (Advanced Encryption Standard) An encryption standard that uses three separate key sizes and is based on the Rijndael encryption algorithm. 285

**Ajax** An approach to developing interactive Web sites that uses tools such as JavaScript and XML. 362

**All-in-one computer** A desktop computer form factor in which the system unit and touch screen are integrated into a single unit. 58

**ALU** (Arithmetic Logic Unit) The part of the CPU that performs arithmetic and logical operations on the numbers stored in its registers. 31

**Always-on connection** In the context of Internet access, a permanent connection, as opposed to a connection that is established and dropped as needed. 307

**Analog data** Data that is measured or represented on a continuously varying scale, such as a dimmer switch or a watch with a sweep second hand. 22

**Analog hole** Any device or technique that allows digital content to be copied legally or illegally from an analog device. 464

**Analog Protection System** (APS) A DVD copy prevention technology developed by Macromedia that scrambles data copied to videotape. 468

**Android OS** An open source operating system used primarily for handheld devices. 203

**Animated GIF** A type of GIF image that displays a sequence of frames to create the appearance of continuous motion. 448

**Anonymizer tools** Software and/or hardware that cloaks the origination of an e-mail or Web page request. 10

**Anonymous FTP** A type of FTP access that requires no account on a server, but rather can be accessed using "anonymous" as the user ID. 337

**Anonymous proxy service** A server on the Internet that can be used to forward Web requests after cloaking the originating address for users who want to surf anonymously. 403

**Antispyware** Software that blocks spyware from entering a computer. 402

**Antivirus software** A computer program used to scan a computer's memory and disks to identify, isolate, and eliminate viruses. 167

**Application server** A computer on a network that is dedicated to running applications and delivering applications to client computers. 249

**Application software** Computer programs that help you perform a specific task such as word processing. Also called application programs, applications, or programs. 16

**Apps** Short for applications; popularly used to refer to applications available for the iPhone, iPad, and other mobile devices. 20

**ASCII** (American Standard Code for Information Interchange) A code that represents characters as a series of 1s and 0s. Most computers use ASCII code to represent text, making it possible to transfer data between computers. 24

**ASF** (Advanced Systems Format) Microsoft's proprietary container format for streaming digital multimedia; typically holds WMV and WMA files. 458

**Asymmetric Internet connection** Any connection to the Internet in which the upstream speed differs from the downstream speed. 310

**Asynchronous communication** Any type of electronic communication, such as e-mail, blogs, or Facebook wall postings, in which the sender and receiver are not required to be online at the same time. 6

**Audio compression** Techniques used to reduce the size of files that contain audio data. 423

**Audio editing software** A program that enables users to create and edit digital voice and music recordings. 139

**Authentication protocol** Passwords, user IDs, and biometric measures used to verify a person's identity. 34

**Authorization and revocation** A component of digital rights management that can be used to disable compromised players. 469

**Automatic recalculation** A feature found in spreadsheet software that automatically recalculates every formula after a user makes a change to any cell. 132

**AVI** (Audio Video Interleave) A video file format, developed by Microsoft, that was once the most common format for desktop video on the PC. 458

**B2B** (business-to-business) An e-commerce exchange of products, services, or information between businesses. 384

**B2C** (business-to-consumer) An e-commerce exchange of products, services, or information between businesses and consumers. 384

**B2G** (business-to-government) An e-commerce exchange of products, services, or information between businesses and governments. 384

**Backup** A duplicate copy of a file, disk, or tape. Also refers to a Windows utility that allows you to create and restore backups. 222

**Backup software** A set of utility programs that performs a variety of backup-related tasks, such as helping users select files for backup. 227

**Bandwidth** The data transmission capacity of a communications channel. Digital signals are measured in bits per second; analog signals in Hertz. 251

**Banner ad** A type of advertisement typically embedded at the top of a Web page. 385

**Bare-metal restore** A process by which a backup is restored to a hard disk without first reinstalling the operating system and device drivers. 230

**BD-R** (Blu-ray disc recordable) A Blu-ray disc that can be recorded on one time. 83

**BD-RE** (Blu-ray disc rerecordable) A Blu-ray disc that can be recorded on multiple times. 83

**BD-ROM** (Blu-ray ROM) A Blu-ray disc that cannot be modified; usually used to distribute movies. 83

**Benchmarks** A set of tests used to measure computer hardware or software performance. 70

**Binary number system** A method for representing numbers using only two digits: 0 and 1. Contrast to the decimal number system, which uses ten digits: 0, 1, 2, 3, 4, 5, 6, 7, 8, and 9. 23

**Biometrics** The use of physical attributes such as a fingerprint to verify a person's identity. 34

**Bit** The smallest unit of information handled by a computer. A bit is one of two values, either a 0 or a 1. Eight bits constitute a byte, which can represent a letter or number. 23

**Bitmap graphic** An image, such as a digital photo, that is stored as a grid work of colored dots. 430

**Bitrate** A ratio such as 5:1 that indicates the ratio of compression that has been applied to a file. High compression ratios, such as 35:1, indicate more compression so data can be contained in smaller files. 457

**BitTorrent** A peer-to-peer technology in which pieces of files are distributed to and from a collection of networked computers; used for distributing music and movies over the Internet. 338

**BlackBerry OS** The operating system software designed for handheld BlackBerry devices. 202

**Blended threat** A combination of more than one type of malicious program. 162

**Blog** (Web log) A publicly-accessible personal journal posted on the Web. Blogs often reflect the personality of the author and are typically updated daily. 332

**Blue screen of death** An error condition in which a PC "freezes" and displays a black screen; usually turning the computer off and turning it on again clears the error. 103

**Bluetooth** A wireless technology used in conjunction with standard Ethernet networks that allows data transfer rates between 200 and 700 Kbps up to a maximum range of 35 feet. 267

**Blu-ray** A high-capacity storage technology that stores up to 25 GB per layer on Blu-ray discs or BDs. 81

**Blu-ray disc movie** (BDMV) A file format used for storing high-definition video clips on Blu-ray discs. 458

**BMP** The native bitmap graphic file format of the Microsoft Windows OS. 442

**Boolean operator** A logical search operator such as AND, OR, and NOT that helps form complex queries. 379

**Boot disk** A floppy disk or CD that contains the files needed for the boot process. 229

**Boot process** The sequence of events that occurs within a computer system between the time the user starts the computer and the time it is ready to process commands. 192

**Bootstrap program** A program stored in ROM that loads and initializes the operating system on a computer. 192

**Bot** An intelligent agent that autonomously executes commands behind the scenes. Sometimes used to refer to a remote access Trojan horse that infects computers. 164

**Botnet** A group of bots under the remote control of a botmaster, used to distribute spam and denial-of-service attacks. 164

**Bridge** A device that connects two similar networks by simply transferring data without regard to the network format. 250

**Broadband** A term used to refer to communications channels that have high bandwidth. 251

**Broadcast flag** A status flag inserted into the data stream of digital television to indicate whether it can be copied. 465

**Brute force attack** A method of breaking encryption code by trying all possible encryption keys. 37

**BSD license** (Berkeley Software Distribution) An open source software license patterned on a license originally used by the University of California. 150

**Bus topology** A network arranged on a common backbone that connects all the network devices. If the backbone fails, the network becomes unusable. 250

**Button** An on-screen graphical control that can be clicked to initiate an action or command. 190

**Byte** An 8-bit unit of data that represents a single character. 26

**C2C** (consumer-to-consumer) An e-commerce exchange of products, services, or information between consumers; for example, online auctions. 384

**Cable Internet service** A type of Internet connection offered to subscribers by cable television companies. 316

**Cable modem** A communications device that can be used to connect a computer to the Internet via the cable TV infrastructure. 317

**CAD software** (computer-aided design software) A program designed to draw 3-D graphics for architecture and engineering tasks. 138

**Capacitors** Electronic circuit components that store an electrical charge; in RAM, a charged capacitor represents an "on" bit, and a discharged one represents an "off" bit. 72

**Card reader** A device that can be used to read and record data on solid stage storage devices, such as flash memory cards. 84

**Case sensitive** A condition in which uppercase letters are not equivalent to their lowercase counterparts. 35

**CCD** (charge-coupled device) One of the components in a digital camera that captures light from an image and converts it into color data. 431

**CD** (compact disc) An optical storage medium used to store digital information. CD-ROMs are read only. CD-Rs and CD-RWs can be used to record data. 81

**CDDA** (compact disc digital audio) The format for commercial music CDs, typically recorded by the manufacturer. 82

**CD-R** (compact disc recordable) A type of optical disc technology that allows the user to record data once on a disc. 83

**CD-ROM** (compact disc read-only memory) The read-only data format that is stamped onto a CD, usually by the manufacturer. 83

**CD-RW** (compact disc rewritable) A type of optical disc technology that allows the user to write data onto a CD, then change that data much like on a floppy or hard disk. 83

**Cell** In spreadsheet terminology, the intersection of a column and a row. In cellular communications, a limited geographical area surrounding a cellular phone tower. 130

**Cell references** The column letter and row number that designate the location of a worksheet cell. For example, the cell reference C5 refers to a cell in column C, row 5. 131

**Central processing unit** (CPU) The main processing unit in a computer, consisting of circuitry that executes instructions to process data. 15

**Character data** Letters, symbols, or numerals that will not be used in arithmetic operations (name, Social Security number, etc.). 24

**Chat** Interactive real-time person-to-person communication over a network. 330

**Ciphertext** An encrypted message. 285

**Circuit switching** The method used by the telephone network to temporarily connect one telephone with another for the duration of a call. 253

**CISC** (complex instruction set computer) A general-purpose microprocessor chip designed to handle a wider array of instructions than a RISC chip. 69

**Click-through rate** The number of times Web site visitors click an ad to connect to an advertiser's site. 385

**Client** A computer or software that requests information from another computer or server. 18

**Client-side script** Scripting statements embedded in an HTML document that are executed by a client's browser. 372

**Client/server mode** A network where processing is split between workstations (clients) and the server. 249

**Clip art** Graphics designed to be inserted into documents, Web pages, and worksheets, usually available in CD-ROM or Web-based collections. 129

**Cloud computing** A grid of servers and storage devices harnessed together to offer Internet-accessible computing services. 333

**Cluster** A group of sectors on a storage medium that, when accessed as a group, speeds up data access. 219

**Codec** Short for compressor/decompressor; a hardware or software routine that compresses and decompresses digital graphics, sound, and video files. 457

**Color depth** The number of bits that determines the range of possible colors that can be assigned to each pixel. For example, an 8-bit color depth can create 256 colors. 91

**Color palette** The selection of colors used in a graphic. 437

**Command-line interface** A style of user interface that requires users to type commands, rather than use a mouse to manipulate on-screen controls. 189

**Commercial software** Copyrighted computer applications sold to consumers for profit. 149

**Communications channel** Any pathway between the sender and receiver; *channel* may refer to a physical medium or a frequency. 251

**Communications port** In the context of computer networking, a virtual location for data that arrives or leaves the device; common ports include 21 for FTP, 110 for e-mail, and 80 for Web data. 308

**Communications protocol** A set of rules that ensures the orderly and accurate transmission and reception of data. 252

**Compiler** Software that translates a program written in a high-level language into low-level instructions before the program is executed. 30

**Compression ratio** A ratio such as 5:1 that indicates the ratio of compression that has been applied to a file. High compression ratios, such as 35:1, indicate more compression so data can be contained in smaller files. 458

**Compute-intensive** Refers to any task, problem, or product that is able to handle massive amounts of data and complex mathematical calculations. 19

**Computer** A device that accepts input, processes data, stores data, and produces output according to a stored program. 14

**Computer network** A collection of computers and related devices, connected in a way that allows them to share data, hardware, and software. 7

**Computer program** A detailed set of instructions that tells a computer how to solve a problem or carry out a task. 15

**Computer virus** A program designed to attach itself to a file, reproduce, and spread from one file to another, destroying data, displaying an irritating message, or otherwise disrupting computer operations. 163

**Computer worm** A software program designed to enter a computer system, usually a network, through security "holes" and then replicate itself. 163

**Computer-aided music software** Software used to generate unique musical compositions with a simplified set of tools, such as tempo, key, and style. 139

**Concurrent-use license** Legal permission for an organization to use a certain number of copies of a software program at the same time. 147

**Container formats** File formats, typically for storing sound and video, that contain one or more types of data that is compressed using standard codecs. 458

**Control unit** The part of the microprocessor that directs and coordinates processing. 31

**Convergence** In the context of technology, the melding of digital devices into a single platform that handles a diverse array of digital content, such as cell phones also playing digital music and displaying digital video. 8

**Cookie** A message sent from a Web server to a browser and stored on a user's hard disk, usually containing information about the user. 367

**Copy generation management** A digital rights management technology that controls the number of times that a CD, DVD, or tape can be recopied. 467

**Copy protection** Any digital rights management technology designed to prevent duplication of digital content; also referred to as copy prevention or copy restriction. 466

**Copyright** A form of legal protection that grants certain exclusive rights to the author of a program or the owner of the copyright. 146

**Copyright notice** A line such as "Copyright 2007 by ACME CO" that identifies a copyright holder. 147

**CPU** (central processing unit) The main processing circuitry within a computer or chip that contains the ALU, control unit, and registers. 15

**CPU cache** Special high-speed memory providing the CPU rapid access to data that would otherwise be accessed from disk or RAM. 68

**Cropping** The process of selecting and removing part of an image. 435

**Cryptographic algorithm** A specific procedure for encrypting and decrypting data. 285

**Cryptographic key** A specific word, number, or phrase that must be used to encrypt or decrypt data. 285

**CSMA/CD** (Carrier Sense Multiple Access with Collision Detection) A method of responding to an attempt by two devices to use a data channel simultaneously. Used by Ethernet networks. 258

**CSS** (Content Scramble System) In the context of digital rights management, a DRM technology designed to prevent unauthorized duplication of DVDs. 468

**Cyberspace** A term coined by William Gibson and now used to refer to information and other resources offered in virtual "worlds" based on computer networks and the Internet. 7

**Data** In the context of computing and data management, refers to the symbols that a computer uses to represent facts and ideas. 15

**Data bus** An electronic pathway or circuit that connects the electronic components (such as the processor and RAM) on a computer's motherboard. 94

**Data fork** An element of the Macintosh file system that comprises the part of the file that contains the text, audio, or video data; contrast with resource fork. 199

**Data representation** The use of electronic signals, marks, or binary digits to represent character, numeric, visual, or audio data. 22

**Data transfer rate** The amount of data that a storage device can move from a storage medium to computer memory in one time unit, such as one second. 77

**Database** A collection of information that might be stored in more than one file or in more than one record type. 134

**Database software** Software designed for entering, finding, organizing, updating, and reporting information stored in a database. 134

**Decryption** The process of converting ciphertext into plaintext. 285

**DeCSS** A program that defeats the CSS copy protection and allows users to copy DVDs. 468

**Defragmentation utility** A software tool used to rearrange the files on a disk so that they are stored in contiguous clusters. 221

**Demoware** Commercial software that is distributed for free, but expires after a certain time limit and then requires users to pay to continue using it. 149

**Desktop** A term used to refer to the main screen of a graphical user interface that can hold objects such as folders and widgets. 189

**Desktop computer** A computer that is small enough to fit on a desk and built around a single microprocessor chip. 58

**Desktop operating system** An operating system specifically designed for use on personal computers, such as Windows 7 or Mac OS X. 188

**Desktop publishing software** (DTP) Software used to create high-quality output suitable for commercial printing. DTP software provides precise control over layout. 125

**Desktop video** Videos stored in digital format on a PC's hard disk or CD. 452

**Desktop widget** An interactive program that is represented on the desktop by an information-rich graphic, such as a clock or graph. 123

**Device driver** A type of system software that provides the computer with the means to control a peripheral device. 124

**DHCP** (Dynamic Host Configuration Protocol) A set of rules that allow network client computers to find and use the Internet address that corresponds to a domain name. 255

**DHTML** (Dynamic HTML) A collection of technologies such as HTML and JavaScript used to create animated and interactive Web pages. 362

**Dial-up connection** A connection that uses a phone line to establish a temporary Internet connection. 312

**Dialog box** An element of graphical user interfaces that appears in a window and requests information, such as command parameters, from a user. 191

**Dictionary attack** A method of discovering a password by trying every word in an electronic dictionary. 36

**Differential backup** A copy of all the files that changed since the last full backup of a disk. 227

**Digital audio** Music or voice that has been digitized into files using sampling techniques; sometimes referred to as waveform audio. 422

**Digital audio extraction** The process of copying files from an audio CD and converting them into a format that can be stored and accessed from a computer storage device, such as a hard disk; sometimes referred to as ripping. 426

**Digital camera** A camera that takes and stores a digital image instead of recording onto film. 431

**Digital certificate** A security method that identifies the author of an ActiveX control. A computer programmer can "sign" a digital certificate after being approved. 373

**Digital content** A term popularized in the context of multimedia that refers to digital music, video, text, and images. 464

**Digital data** Text, numbers, graphics, or sound represented by discrete digits, such as 1s and 0s. 22

**Digital divide** A gap between those who have access to digital technologies and those who do not. 12

**Digital revolution** A set of significant changes brought about by computers and other digital devices during the second half of the 20th century. 4

**Digital rights management** (DRM) A set of techniques and technologies designed to discourage and prevent unauthorized duplication of digital content. 464

**Digital signal processor** Circuitry that is used to process, record, and play back audio files. 424

**Digital video** A series of still frames stored sequentially in digital format by assigning values to each pixel in a frame. 452

**Digital watermark** A digital rights management technology that inserts a hidden signal into multimedia content as an identifying marker that can be tracked or verified. 465

**Digitization** To convert non-digital information or media to a digital format through the use of a scanner, sampler, or other input device. 7

**Digitizing tablet** A device that provides a flat surface for a paper-based drawing and a "pen" used to create hand-drawn vector drawings. 446

**Directory** In the context of computer file management, a list of files contained on a computer storage device. 206

**Disc mastering** The process of creating a CD or DVD by selecting all the files to be copied and then writing them in a single session. Contrast with packet writing. 219

**Disk image** A bit-by-bit copy of the contents of a disk created for backup, archiving, or duplication of data. 230

**Disk partition** An area of a hard disk created by dividing a large hard disk into several smaller virtual ones, such as when using two operating systems on a single computer. 205

**Distribution media** One or more floppy disks, CDs, or DVDs that contain programs and data that can be installed on a hard disk. 146

**DOCSIS** (Data Over Cable Service Interface Specification) A security technology used for filtering packets and maintaining customer privacy on cable Internet services. 317

**Document format** (1) The specifications applied to fonts, spacing, margins, and other elements in a document created with word processing software; (2) The file format, such as DOCX, used to store a document created with word processing software. 127

**Document production software** Computer programs that assist the user in composing, editing, designing, and printing documents. 125

**Domain name** Short for fully qualified domain name; an identifying name by which host computers on the Internet are familiarly known (for example, coca-cola.com). 307

**Domain name server** A computer that hosts the Domain Name System database. 308

**Domain Name System** (DNS) A large database of unique IP addresses that correspond with domain names. 308

**DOS** (Disk Operating System) The operating system software shipped with the first IBM PCs, then used on millions of computers until the introduction of Microsoft Windows. 201

**Dot matrix printer** A printer that creates characters and graphics by striking an inked ribbon with small wires called pins, generating a fine pattern of dots. 92

**Dot pitch** The diagonal distance between colored dots on a display screen. Measured in millimeters, dot pitch helps to determine the quality of an image displayed on a monitor. 90

**Double layer DVD** A DVD that essentially stacks data in two different layers on the disk surface to store 8.5 GB, twice the capacity of a standard DVD. 81

**Download** The process of transferring a copy of a file from a remote computer to a local computer's storage device. 8

**Downstream speed** The rate at which transmitted data flows from a host or server to a local computer (contrast with upstream speed). 310

**Drawing software** Programs that are used to create vector graphics with lines, shapes, and colors, such as logos or diagrams. 137, 446

**Drive bays** Areas within a computer system unit that can accommodate additional storage devices. 86

**Drive mapping** A process of assigning a drive letter to a storage device located on a different network workstation. 276

**DRM individualization** A digital rights management concept that ties access to digital content to individual subscribers, whose access can be tracked, if necessary. 470

**DSL** (digital subscriber line) A high-speed Internet connection that uses existing telephone lines, requiring close proximity to a switching station. 314

**DSL filter** A device that is commonly used to prevent interference from analog devices, such as telephones, that use the same line as DSL devices. 315

**DSL modem** A device that sends and receives digital data to and from computers over telephone lines. 315

**Dual boot** A computer that contains more than one operating system and can boot into either one. 199

**Duplex printer** A printer that prints on both sides of the paper in a single pass. 93

**Duty cycle** A measurement of how many pages a printer is able to produce per day or month. 93

**DVD** (digital video disc or digital versatile disc) An optical storage medium similar in appearance and technology to a CD but with higher storage capacity. 81

**DVD authoring software** Computer programs that offer tools for creating DVD menus and transferring digital video onto DVDs that can be played in a computer or standalone DVD player. 140

**DVD image** A series of files containing the data needed for a video DVD. The image is typically stored on a hard disk for testing before the image is transferred or "burned" to the DVD. 462

**DVD+R** (digital versatile disc recordable) A DVD data format that, similar to CD-R, allows recording data but not changing data on a DVD. 83

**DVD+RW** (digital versatile disc rewritable) A DVD technology that allows recording and changing data on DVDs. 83

**DVD-R** (digital versatile disc recordable) A DVD data format that, similar to CD-R, allows writing data but not changing data on a DVD. 83

**DVD-ROM** A DVD disc that contains data that has been permanently stamped on the disc surface. 83

**DVD-RW** A DVD technology similar to DVD+RW that allows recording and changing data on DVDs. 83

**DVD-video** A DVD format used for commercial movies shipped on DVDs. 82, 452

**DVI** (Digital Visual Interface) A standard type of plug and connector for computer display devices. 96

**Dynamic IP address** A temporarily assigned IP address usually provided by an ISP. 306

**E-commerce** Short for electronic commerce; the business of buying and selling products online. 384

**E-mail** Messages that are transmitted between computers over a communications network. Short for electronic mail. 6

**E-mail account** A service that provides users with an e-mail address and a mailbox. 393

**E-mail address** An identifier that includes a user name, the @ symbol, and an e-mail server, used to route e-mail messages to their destination. 393

**E-mail attachment** A separate file that is transmitted along with an e-mail message. 398

**E-mail authentication** A technology designed to defeat spam by checking to make sure that messages originate from valid addresses. 403

**E-mail client software** Software that is installed on a client computer and has access to e-mail servers on a network. This software is used to compose, send, and read e-mail messages. 393

**E-mail message** A computer file containing a letter or memo that is transmitted electronically via a communications network. 392

**E-mail server** A computer that uses special software to store and send e-mail messages over the Internet. 392

**E-mail system** The collection of computers and software that works together to provide e-mail services. 397

**Ear training software** Software used by musicians to develop tuning skills, recognize keys, and develop musical skills. 139

**EBCDIC** (Extended Binary-Coded Decimal Interchange Code) A method by which digital computers, usually mainframes, represent character data. 25

**Educational software** Software used to develop and practice skills. 140

**EEPROM** (electrically erasable programmable read-only memory) A type of non-volatile storage typically used in personal computers to store boot and BIOS data. 74

**Encryption** The process of scrambling or hiding information so that it cannot be understood without the key necessary to change it back into its original form. 285

**eSATA** A standard for high-speed ports, plugs, and connectors typically used to connect external hard drives to computers. 96

**Ethernet** A popular network technology in which network nodes are connected by coaxial cable or twisted-pair wire. 257

**Ethernet adapter** A type of network interface card designed to support Ethernet protocols. 261

**EULA** (end-user license agreement) A type of software license that appears on the computer screen when software is being installed and prompts the user to accept or decline. 148

**Executable file** A file, usually with an .exe extension, containing instructions that tell a computer how to perform a specific task. 152

**Expansion bus** The segment of the data bus that transports data between RAM and peripheral devices. 94

**Expansion card** A circuit board that is plugged into a slot on a computer motherboard to add extra functions, devices, or ports. 95

**Expansion port** A socket into which the user plugs a cable from a peripheral device, allowing data to pass between the computer and the peripheral device. 95

**Expansion slot** A socket or "slot" on a PC motherboard designed to hold a circuit board called an expansion card. 95

**Extended ASCII** Similar to ASCII but with 8-bit character representation instead of 7-bit, allowing for an additional 128 characters. 24

**FairPlay** A digital rights management technology used to protect content distributed at the iTunes store. 470

**Field** The smallest meaningful unit of information contained in a data file. 134

**File** A named collection of data (such as a computer program, document, or graphic) that exists on a storage medium, such as a hard disk or CD. 15

**File compression utility** A type of data compression software that shrinks one or more files into a single file occupying less storage space than the files did separately. 440

**File date** The date that a file was created or last modified. 206

**File extension** A set of letters and/or numbers added to the end of a file name that helps to identify the file contents or file type. 204

**File format** The method of organization used to encode and store data in a computer. Text formats include DOC and TXT. Graphics formats include BMP, TIFF, GIF, and PNG. 207

**File header** Hidden information inserted at the beginning of a file to identify its properties, such as the software that can open it. 207

**File management utility** Software, such as Windows Explorer, that helps users locate, rename, move, copy, and delete files. 214

**File-naming conventions** A set of rules, established by the operating system, that must be followed to create a valid file name. 204

**File server** A network computer that is dedicated to storing and distributing files to network clients. 249

**File shredder software** Software designed to overwrite sectors of a disk with a random series of 1s and 0s to ensure deletion of data. 220

**File size** The physical size of a file on a storage medium, usually measured in kilobytes (KB). 206

**File specification** A combination of the drive letter, subdirectory, file name, and extension that identifies a file (such as C:Report.doc). Also called a path. 206

**File synchronization** The process of keeping two sets of files updated so they are the same; used to synchronize files between a computer and PDA or backup device. 224

**File system** A method that is used by an operating system to keep files organized. 219

**File tag** In the context of Windows, a piece of information that describes a file. Tags, such as Owner, Rating, and Date Taken, can be added by users. 212

**Firewall** Software or hardware designed to analyze and control incoming and outgoing packets on a network, used to enhance security by filtering out potential intrusion attempts. 342

**FireWire** A standard for fairly high-speed ports, plugs, and connectors typically used to connect external storage devices, and for transferring data from cameras to computers. 96

**Fixed Internet access** Any Internet access service designed to be used from a fixed, non-portable location (i.e., dial-up, ISDN, DSL, and cable Internet service). 311

**Fixed wireless Internet service** High-speed, wide area Internet service alternative to cable and DSL that transmits data wirelessly using RF signals. 320

**Flash** A file format developed by Macromedia and marketed by Adobe that has become popular for animations on Web pages. 448

**Flash cookie** A cookie-like object that is created and used by the Adobe Flash Player; also referred to as a local shared object. 402

**Flash Video** A popular video file format developed by Adobe Systems and used for Web-based video at sites such as YouTube. 458

**Floppy disk** A removable magnetic storage medium, typically 3.5" in size, with a capacity of 1.44 MB. 80

**Folder** The subdirectories, or subdivisions of a directory, that can contain files or other folders. 206

**Font** A typeface or style of lettering, such as Arial, Times New Roman, and Gothic. 127

**Footer** Text that appears in the bottom margin of each page of a document. 128

**Form factor** The configuration of a computer's system unit; examples include tower, mini-tower, and cube. 58

**Format shifting** The process of converting media into a different file format to use it on a device other than the original one. 465

**Formatting** The process of dividing a disk into sectors so that it can be used to store information. 219

**Formula** In spreadsheet terminology, a combination of numbers and symbols that tells the computer how to use the contents of cells in calculations. 131

**Fragmented files** Files stored in scattered, noncontiguous clusters on a disk. 221

**Frames** (1) In the context of document production, an outline or boundary that defines a box that holds text or graphics. 129 (2) In the context of digital video, one of many images displayed in sequence to give the appearance of motion. 452

**Freeware** Copyrighted software that is given away by the author or copyright owner. 150

**Front side bus** (FSB) The data bus that carries signals between the CPU and RAM, disks, or expansion slots. 68

**FTP** (File Transfer Protocol) A set of rules for uploading and downloading files between a client computer and a remote server. 336

**FTP client** The computer or software that is used to access an FTP server and transfer files to it or from it. 337

**FTP server** A computer that stores and distributes files to remote client computers. 336

**Full backup** A copy of all the files for a specified backup job. 227

**Full system backup** A backup that contains all of the files on the hard disk, including the operating system. 226

**Fully justified** The horizontal alignment of text where the text terminates exactly at both margins of the document. 128

**Gateway** A network device that connects two dissimilar networks even if the networks use different protocols. 251

**GIF** (Graphics Interchange Format) A bitmap graphics file format, popularized by CompuServe, for use on the Web. 442

**Gigabit** (Gb or Gbit) Approximately one billion bits, exactly 1,024 megabits. 26

**Gigabyte** (GB) Approximately one billion bytes; exactly 1,024 megabytes (1,073,741,824 bytes). 26

**Gigahertz** (GHz) A measure of frequency equivalent to one billion cycles per second. 67

**Globalization** A group of social, economic, political, and technological interdependencies linking people and institutions from all areas of the world. 12

**Google Chrome OS** An operating system based on the Linux kernel; designed for netbooks dedicated to using the Web and Web-based applications. 200

**GPL** (General Public License) A software license often used for freeware that insures it will be distributed freely whether in its original form or as a derivative work. 151

**Gradient** A smooth blending of shades of different colors, from light to dark. 447

**Grammar checker** A feature of word processing software that coaches the user on correct sentence structure and word usage. 127

**Graphical user interface** (GUI) A type of user interface that features on-screen objects, such as menus and icons, manipulated by a mouse. 189

**Graphics** Any picture, photograph, or image that can be manipulated or viewed on a computer. 137

**Graphics card** A circuit board inserted into a computer to handle the display of text, graphics, animation, and videos. Also called a video card. 91

**Graphics processing unit** (GPU) A microprocessor dedicated to rendering and displaying graphics on personal computers, workstations, and videogame consoles. 91

**Graphics software** Computer programs for creating, editing, and manipulating images; types include paint software and drawing software. 137

**Grayscale palette** Digital images that are displayed in shades of gray, black, and white. 438

**Grid computing system** A network of computers harnessed together to perform processing tasks; distributed grids like the SETI@home project use ad hoc and diverse Internet connected computers. (Also *see cloud computing*.) 334

**Groupware** Software that enables multiple users to collaborate on a project, usually through a pool of data that can be shared by members of the workgroup. 121

**Handshaking** A process where a protocol helps two network devices communicate. 252

**Hard disk controller** A circuit board in a hard drive that positions the disk and read-write heads to locate data. 79

**Hard disk drive** A computer storage device that contains a large-capacity rigid storage surface sealed inside a drive case. Typically used as the primary storage device in personal computers. 78

**Hard disk platter** The component of a hard disk drive on which data is stored. It is a flat, rigid disk made of aluminum or glass and coated with a magnetic oxide. 78

**Hash value** A number produced by a hash function to create a unique digital "fingerprint" that can be used to allow or deny access to a software application. 157

**HDCP** (High-bandwidth Digital Content Protection) A form of copy protection designed to prevent digital content from being transmitted over a DVI interface to a non-complying display device. 466

**HDMI** (High-Definition Multimedia Interface) A standard type of plug and connector for computer display devices. 96

**Head crash** A collision between the read-write head and the surface of the hard disk platter, resulting in damage to some of the data on the disk. 80

**Header** Text that is placed in the top margin of each page of a document. 128

**Home computer system** A personal computer designed for use with mainstream computer applications such as Web browsing, e-mail, music downloads, and productivity software. 60

**Homegroup** A feature of Windows 7 that quickly creates a peer-to-peer network for sharing files and printers. 277

**HomePNA** A network technology that uses a building's existing phone lines to connect nodes. 257

**Horizontal market software** Any computer program that can be used by many different kinds of businesses (for example, an accounting program). 142

**Hot-plugging** The ability of a component, such as a USB flash drive, to connect or disconnect from a computer while it is running; also referred to as hot-swapping. 97

**Hover ad** An advertisement, created using interactive Web tools such as DHTML, that appears on top of Web pages, sometimes obscuring parts of them. 385

**HTML** (Hypertext Markup Language) A standardized format used to specify the layout for Web pages. 362

**HTML conversion utility** Utility software that converts documents, spreadsheets, and databases into HTML files that can be posted on the Web. 369

**HTML document** A plain text or ASCII document with embedded HTML tags that dictate formatting and are interpreted by a browser. 362

**HTML forms** An HTML document containing blank boxes that prompt users to enter information that can be sent to a Web server. Commonly used for e-commerce transactions. 371

**HTML mail** E-mail messages that contain formatting, such as bold and italics, by turning on the HTML mail function. 397

**HTML script** A series of instructions embedded directly into the text of an HTML document or a file referenced from an HTML document. 371

**HTML tags** A set of instructions, such as <B>, inserted into an HTML document to provide formatting and display information to a Web browser. 362

**HTTP** (Hypertext Transfer Protocol) The communications protocol used to transmit Web pages. HTTP:// is an identifier that appears at the beginning of Web URLs (for example, *http://www. fooyong.com*). 364

**HTTP status code** A code used by Web servers to report the status of a browser's request. The HTTP status code 404 means document not found. 365

**Hypertext** A way of organizing a collection of documents by assigning an address to each and providing a way to link from one address to another. 360

**Hypertext link** Also referred to simply as a link; an underlined word or phrase on a Web page that, when clicked, takes you to a designated URL. 361

**ICANN** (Internet Corporation for Assigned Names and Numbers) A global organization that coordinates the management of the Internet's domain name system, IP addresses, and protocol parameters. 309

**Icon** A graphical object, such as those that represent programs or folders on a computer desktop. 189

**Identity theft** An illegal practice in which a criminal obtains enough information to masquerade as someone. 36

**Image compression** Any technique that is used to reduce the size of a file that holds a graphic. 439

**IMAP** (Internet Message Access Protocol) A protocol similar to POP that is used to retrieve e-mail messages from an e-mail server, but offers additional features, such as choosing which e-mails to download from the server. 394

**Incremental backup** A backup that contains files that changed since the last backup. 228

**Infrared light** A transmission technology that uses a frequency range just below the visible light spectrum to transport data. 265

**Ink jet printer** A non-impact printer that creates characters or graphics by spraying liquid ink onto paper or other media. 92

**Input** *Noun*, the information that is conveyed to a computer. *Verb*, to enter data into a computer. 15

**Instant messaging** A private chat in which users can communicate with each other in real time using electronically transmitted text messages. 330

**Instruction cycle** The steps followed by a computer to process a single instruction: fetch, interpret, execute, then increment the instruction pointer. 32

**Instruction set** The collection of instructions that a CPU is designed to process. 30

**Integrated audio** Sound card circuitry that is built into the circuitry of a digital device, in contrast to the use of an add-on sound card. 423

**Integrated circuit** (IC) A thin slice of silicon crystal containing microscopic circuit elements such as transistors, wires, capacitors, and resistors; also called chips and microchips. 27

**Intellectual property** A legal concept that refers to ownership of intangible information, such as ideas. 11

**Internet** The worldwide communication infrastructure that links computer networks using the TCP/IP protocol. 6

**Internet backbone** The major communications links that form the core of the Internet. 303

**Internet forum** An asynchronous online discussion in which participants post comments to discussion threads, which can be read at a later time by other participants. 332

**Internet service provider** (ISP) A company that provides Internet access to businesses, organizations, and individuals. 303

**Interpreter** A program that converts high-level instructions in a computer program into machine language instructions, one instruction at a time. 30

**Intrusion** In the context of computer security, the unauthorized access to a computer system. 340

**iOS** The operating system used for iPhones. 203

**IP** (Internet Protocol) One of the main protocols of TCP/IP; responsible for addressing packets so that they can be routed to their destinations; IPv4 offers 32-bit addresses whereas IPv6 offers 128-bit addresses. 305

**IP address** Unique identifying numbers assigned to each computer connected to the Internet. 255

**ISDN** (Integrated Services Digital Network) A telephone company service that transports data digitally over dial-up or dedicated lines. 314

**ISDN terminal adapter** A device that connects a computer to a telephone jack and translates the data into a signal that can travel over an ISDN connection. 314

**Java applet** Small programs that add processing and interactive capabilities to Web pages. 372

**Jitter** Deviations in the timing of a digital signal that can interfere with communications, especially voice over IP. 331

**Joystick** An input device that looks like a small version of a car's stick shift. Popular with gamers, moving the stick moves objects on the screen. 88

**JPEG** (Joint Photographic Experts Group) A format that uses lossy compression to store bitmap images. JPEG (pronounced "JAY-peg") files have a .jpg extension. 442

**Kernel** The core module of an operating system that typically manages memory, processes, tasks, and storage devices. 192

**Keylogger** A program, sometimes part of a Trojan horse, that records a person's keystrokes, saves them, and then sends them to a system administrator or remote hacker. 37

**Keyword search** The process of looking for information by providing a related word or phrase. 136

**Keyword stuffing** An unpopular practice of including a huge variety of keywords in the header of an HTML document in the hopes that a search engine will display it even when the content of the page is not relevant to the search. 378

**Kilobit** (Kbit or Kb) 1024 bits. 26

**Kilobyte** (KB) Approximately 1,000 bytes; exactly 1,024 bytes. 26

**Label** In the context of spreadsheets, any text used to describe data. 130

**LAN** (local area network) An interconnected group of computers and peripherals located within a relatively limited area, such as a building or campus. 247

**LAN jacking** Unauthorized access to a wireless network; also called war driving. 282

**Lands** Non-pitted surface areas on a CD that represent digital data. (*See also pits.*) 81

**Laser printer** A printer that uses laser-based technology, similar to that used by photocopiers, to produce text and graphics. 92

**Latency** The elapsed time it takes for a packet of data to arrive at its destination. 309

**LCD display** (liquid crystal display) Technology used for flat panel computer screens typically found on notebook computers. 90

**Leading** Also called line spacing; the vertical spacing between lines of text. 128

**LED display** (light-emitting diode display) A display device that either uses LEDs to produce an image on the screen, or an LCD display that uses LEDs as backlighting. 90

**Library** In the context of Windows 7, a superfolder that contains pointers to various folders and files; examples include Documents, Pictures, and Videos. 217

**Line spacing** Also called leading; the vertical spacing between lines of text. (*See leading.*) 128

**Linear editing** A video editing technique involving recording segments of video from one tape to another. 456

**Link popularity** A metric used by some search engines to rank the sites that are relevant to a query. 377

**Linux** An operating system that is a derivative of UNIX, available as freeware, and widely used for servers though it is also used on personal computers and workstations. 200

**Linux distribution** Usually a download that includes the Linux operating system, a Linux desktop, and other Linux utilities. 200

**Linux platform** A computer that is running the Linux operating system. 64

**Local application** Software designed to be installed on and run from a hard disk. 154

**Local e-mail** An e-mail system that requires users to install e-mail client software on their computer hard disk or flash drive; messages are held on a server until the client software downloads them to the local computer. 393

**Logical storage models** Any visual or conceptual aid that helps a computer user visualize a file storage system. Also called a storage metaphor. 215

**Lossless compression** A compression technique that is able to reconstitute all of the data in the original file; hence "lossless" means that this compression technique does not lose data. 439

**Lossy compression** Any data compression technique in which some of the data is sacrificed to obtain more compression. 439

**MAC address** (Media Access Control) A unique identifier similar to a serial number assigned to networking equipment at time of manufacture. 254

**Mac OS** The operating system software designed for use on Apple Macintosh computers. 197

**Mac platform** A family or category of Macintosh-compatible personal computers designed and manufactured by Apple, Inc. 64

**Machine code** Program instructions written in binary code that the computer can execute directly. 30

**Machine language** A low-level language written in binary code that the computer can execute directly. 30

**Magnetic storage** A technology for recording data onto disks or tape by magnetizing particles of an oxide-based surface coating. 78

**Mail merge** A feature of document production software that automates the process of producing customized documents, such as letters and advertising flyers. 129

**Mainframe computer** A large, fast, and expensive computer generally used by businesses or government agencies to provide centralized storage, processing, and management for large amounts of data. 18

**Malicious software** Any program or set of program instructions, such as a virus, worm, or Trojan horse, designed to surreptitiously enter a computer and disrupt its normal operations. 162

**Malware** Programs such as viruses, worms, and bots designed to disrupt computer operations. 162

**MAN** (metropolitan area network) A public, high-speed network that can transmit voice and data within a range of 50 miles. 247

**Markup language** A language that provides text and graphics formatting through the use of tags. Examples of markup languages include HTML, XML, and SGML. 362

**Mass-mailing worm** A worm that sends itself to every e-mail address in the address book of an infected computer. 163

**Master File Table** An index file used in NTFS storage systems to maintain a list of clusters and keep track of their contents. 219

**Mathematical modeling software** Software for visualizing and solving a wide range of math, science, and engineering problems. 133

**Mathematical operators** Symbols such as + - / * that represent specific mathematical functions in a formula. 131

**Megabit** (Mb or Mbit) 1,048,576 bits. 26

**Megabyte** (MB) Approximately one million bytes; exactly 1,048,576 bytes. 26

**Megahertz** (MHz) A measure of frequency equivalent to one million cycles per second. 68

**Megapixel** One million pixels; expresses the resolution and quality of an image; usually used in reference to digital cameras. 433

**Memory** The computer circuitry that holds data waiting to be processed. 15

**Memory leak** An undesirable state in which an operating system does not correctly allocate memory for programs, causing parts of one program to overwrite parts of others and malfunction. 187

**Menu** In the context of user interfaces, a list of commands or options often displayed as a list. 190

**Menu bar** A standard component of most graphical user interfaces that is displayed as a strip of clickable options, that in turn display a list of commands. 190

**Mesh topology** A network arranged in such a way that each device is connected to many other devices. Data traveling on a mesh network can take any of several possible paths. 250

**Message header** The section of an e-mail file that contains address, subject, and file attachment information. 392

**Meta keyword** A word that is included in the header of an HTML document in order to describe the document's contents. 378

**Metafile** In the context of graphics, a file that contains both vector and bitmap data. 447

**Metasearch engine** A search engine that searches other search engines. 380

**Microcontroller** A special purpose microprocessor that is built into the device it controls. 20

**Microprocessor** An integrated circuit that contains the circuitry for processing data. It is a single-chip version of the central processing unit (CPU) found in all computers. 15

**Microprocessor clock** A timing signal that sets the pace for executing instructions in a microprocessor. 67

**Microsoft Windows** An operating system, developed by Microsoft Corporation, that provides a graphical interface. Versions include Windows 7, Vista, XP, 2000, Me, NT, 98, 95, and 3.1. 194

**Microwaves** Electromagnetic waves with a frequency of at least 1 gigahertz; one type of channel for transmitting data over communications networks. 265

**MIDI** (Musical Instrument Digital Interface) A standardized way in which sound and music are encoded and transmitted between digital devices that play music. 427

**MIDI sequence** Digitally encoded MIDI music stored on a digital device, such as a computer or MIDI instrument. 427

**MIDI sequencing software** Software that uses a standardized way of transmitting encoded music or sounds for controlling musical devices, such as a keyboard or sound card. 139

**MiFi** A small, wireless router that connects to a cellular data network, creating a mobile Wi-Fi hotspot. 270

**MIME** (Multi-purpose Internet Mail Extensions) A standard for formatting non-ASCII messages so that they can be sent over the Internet, typically as e-mail messages. 398

**MIMO** (multiple input multiple output) A wireless communications device that uses an array of antennas to transmit data over more than one channel. 268

**Minicase** A desktop computer form factor that is smaller than a tower unit. 58

**Mobile broadband** High-bandwidth wireless technology that was developed for sending digital data over cell phone systems. 327

**Mobile Internet access** Any service that allows subscribers to access the Internet while on the go. 311

**Mod** In the context of personal computers, a customized or "modified" system unit typically jazzed up with lights, chrome, and decals. 65

**Modem** A device that modulates and demodulates a signal, typically used to send data from a computer to the Internet over telephone, cable television, or satellite networks. 304

**Money management software** Software used to track monetary transactions and investments. 133

**Monochrome bitmap** A bitmap image that contains only the colors black and white. 436

**Mouse** An input device that allows the user to manipulate objects on the screen by clicking, dragging, and dropping. 88

**MOV** A multimedia file format, popular for digital videos, that works with QuickTime software. 458

**MP3** A file format that provides highly compressed audio files with very little loss of sound quality. 425

**MPEG** (Moving Picture Experts Group) A family of highly compressed container file formats and codecs for digital multimedia; MPEG-1, MPEG-2, and MPEG-4. 458

**Multi-core processor** A microprocessor that contains circuitry for more than one processing unit. 68

**Multiple-user license** Legal permission for more than one person to use a particular software package. 147

**Multiprocessing** The ability of a computer or operating system to support dual core processors or multiple processors. 186

**Multitasking** The ability of a computer, processor, or operating system to run more than one program, job, or task at the same time. 186

**Multithreading** A technology that allows multiple parts or threads from a program to run simultaneously. 186

**Multiuser operating system** An operating system that allows a single computer to deal with simultaneous processing requests from multiple users. 187

**Nanosecond** A unit of time representing one billionth of a second. 73

**Narrowband** A term that refers to communications channels that have low bandwidth. 251

**Native file format** A file format that is unique to a program or group of programs and has a unique file extension. 209

**Natural language query** A query formulated in human language, as opposed to an artificially constructed language such as machine language. 136

**Netbook** A scaled-down version of a standard clamshell-style notebook computer. Sometimes called a minilaptop. 59

**Netiquette** (Internet etiquette) A set of guidelines for posting messages and e-mails in a civil, concise way. 399

**Network access points** (NAP) Internet nodes that link together different network service providers so that data can be transferred from one service provider to the other. 303

**Network address translation** (NAT) A security technique that allows a LAN to use one type of IP address for intra-network data and another type of address for data traveling to and from the Internet. 344

**Network attached storage** (NAS) Storage devices that are designed to be attached directly to a network, rather than to a workstation or server. 248

**Network device** Any device, such as a gateway, hub, or router, that is used to broadcast network data, boost signals, or route data to its destination. 248

**Network hub** A network device that connects several nodes of a local area network. 261

**Network interface card** Circuitry, often on an expansion card mounted inside a computer, that transmits and receives data on a local area network. Also called a NIC, network card, or network adapter. 248

**Network router** A device found at each intersection on the Internet backbone that examines the IP address of incoming data, and forwards the data towards its destination. 260

**Network service providers** (NSPs) Companies that maintain a series of nationwide Internet links. 303

**Network switch** A network device that sends data to a specific address instead of broadcasting it over an entire network. 260

**Networked peripheral** A peripheral device that contains circuitry that allows it to be directly connected to a network, rather than connecting to a computer that transfers data to a network. 248

**Node** In a network, a connection point; in a hierarchical database, a segment or record type. 248

**Non-executing zip file** A type of compressed file that has to be unzipped manually to extract the file or files contained within it. 157

**Non-volatile** Any electronic component that does not require a constant supply of power to hold data. 84

**Nonlinear editing** A digital video editing technique that requires a personal computer and video editing software. 456

**Notation software** Software used to help musicians compose, edit, and print their compositions. 139

**Notebook computer** A small, lightweight, portable computer that usually runs on batteries. Sometimes called a laptop. 59

**NTFS** (New Technology File System) A file system used by Microsoft Windows NT, 2000, Vista, and Windows 7 operating systems to keep track of the name and location of files on a hard disk. 219

**Numeric data** Numbers that represent quantities and can be used in arithmetic operations. 23

**Object code** The low-level instructions that result from compiling source code. 30

**Octet** One of four sections of an IP address. 255

**Ogg Vorbis** An open source audio file format. 425

**Online shopping cart** A feature of e-commerce sites that stores information about items selected for purchase often by creating a cookie on a shopper's computer. 386

**Online social networks** Web sites that provide ways for people to communicate and socialize. MySpace is a popular example. 6

**Op code** Short for operation code; an assembly language command word that designates an operation, such as add (ADD), compare (CMP), or jump (JMP). 31

**Open source** An approach to developing and licensing software in which source code remains public so it can be improved and freely distributed. 12

**Open source software** Software that includes its source code, allowing programmers to modify and improve it. 150

**Operand** The part of an instruction that specifies the data, or the address of the data, on which the operation is to be performed. 31

**Operating system** The software that controls the computer's use of its hardware resources, such as memory and disk storage space. Also called OS. 16, 184

**Optical storage** A technology that records data as light and dark spots on a CD, DVD, or other optical media. 81

**Output** The results produced by a computer (for example, reports, graphs, and music). 15

**Overclocking** Forcing a computer component, such as a microprocessor, to run at a higher speed than intended by the manufacturer. 71

**P2P file sharing** A practice in which individuals can obtain music, video, and other types of files from other users on a network; sometimes the files are shared without authorization from the copyright holder. 333

**Packet** A small unit of data transmitted over a network. 253

**Packet loss** A situation in which data bits are lost in transit, requiring them to be resent, which significantly increases the time required for an intact message to arrive at its destination. 331

**Packet switching** A technology used by data communications networks, such as the Internet, where a message is divided into smaller units called packets for transmission. 253

**Packet writing** The process of recording data to a CD or DVD in multiple sessions. Contrast with disk mastering. 219

**Page layout** The physical positions of elements on a document page such as headers, footers, page numbering, and graphics. 128

**Paint software** Software that creates and manipulates bitmap graphics. 137, 430

**Palm webOS** A popular type of operating system for handheld computers and smartphones. 202

**PAN** (personal area network) An interconnected group of personal digital devices located within a range of about 30 feet. 246

**Paragraph alignment** The horizontal position (left, right, justified, centered, for example) of the text in a document. 128

**Paragraph style** A specification for the format of a paragraph, which includes the alignment of text within the margins and line spacing. 128

**Parallel processing** The simultaneous use of more than one processor to execute a program. 69

**Password** A special set of symbols used to restrict access to a user's computer or network. 35

**Password manager** Software that keeps track of sites at which a user has registered and the password that corresponds to each site. 40

**Path** A file's location specified by the drive on which it is stored and the hierarchy of folders in which it is stored. (*See file specification.*) 206

**Payroll software** A type of horizontal market software used to maintain payroll records. 142

**PC platform** A family of personal computers that use Windows software and contain Intel-compatible microprocessors. 64

**PDA** (personal digital assistant) A shirt-pocket sized computer originally designed to keep track of appointments (also called a palmtop). 19

**Peer-to-peer mode** A method of using a network in which workstations act as both file servers and clients. 249

**Peripheral device** A component or equipment, such as a printer, that expands a computer's input, output, or storage capabilities. 56

**Persistent HTTP connection** The process of using the same TCP connection to handle multiple HTTP requests, such as for obtaining the text and then the graphics for a Web page; contrast to stateless protocol. 365

**Person-to-person payment** A method of e-commerce payment that uses an intermediary or third party such as PayPal to handle payment between a buyer and seller. 390

**Personal computer** A microcomputer designed for use by an individual user for applications such as Web browsing and word processing. 17

**Personal finance software** Software geared toward individual finances that helps track bank account balances, credit card payments, investments, and bills. 133

**Pharming** An exploit that redirects users to fake Web sites. 405

**Phishing** An e-mail based scam that's designed to fool users into revealing confidential information. 37, 405

**Phoneme** A unit of sound that is a basic component of words and is produced by speech synthesizers. 428

**Photo editing software** The software used to edit, enhance, retouch, and manipulate digital photographs. 137

**Photosites** In digital photography, each photosite is a single point in an image, equivalent to one pixel. 431

**Physical storage model** A representation of data as it is physically stored. 218

**Physical topology** The actual layout of network devices, wires, and cables. 250

**Piconet** A network formed by Bluetooth devices. 267

**Ping** (Packet Internet Groper) A command on a TCP/IP network that sends a test packet to a specified IP address and waits for a reply. 309

**Pipelining** A technology that allows a processor to begin executing an instruction before completing the previous instruction. 69

**Pirated software** Software that is copied, sold, or distributed with without permission from the copyright holder. 147

**Pits** Spots on a CD that are "burned" onto an optical storage medium to represent digital data. 81

**Pixel interpolation** A process that is used by graphics software to average the color of adjacent pixels in an image, usually when the image is enlarged. 435

**Pixelated** Describes the effect of increasing the size and thus decreasing the quality of an image. 435

**Pixels** Short for picture element; the smallest unit in a graphic image. Computer display devices use a matrix of pixels to display text and graphics. 90

**Place shifting** The practice of accessing media from a remote location, such as over a network. 465

**Plaintext** An original, unencrypted message. 285

**Plug and Play** The ability of a computer to automatically recognize and adjust the system configuration for a newly added device. 97

**Plug-in** A software module that adds a specific feature to a system. In the context of browsers, a plug-in adds the ability to display or play various additional file formats. 367

**PNG** (Portable Network Graphics) A type of graphics file format similar to but newer than GIF or JPEG. 442

**Podcast** An audio file that is distributed over the Internet through downloads or the use of an RSS feed or Atom. 360

**Point size** A unit of measure (1/72 of an inch) used to specify the height of characters in a font. 127

**Pointing device** An input device, such as a mouse, trackball, pointing stick, or trackpad, that allows users to manipulate an on-screen pointer and other screen-based graphical controls. 88

**POP server** A computer that receives and stores e-mail data until retrieved by the e-mail account holder. 398

**POP3** (Post Office Protocol version 3) A standard for retrieving e-mail messages from an e-mail server. 394

**Pop-up ad** A type of advertisement that usually appears in a separate window when you enter a Web site. 385

**Port probe** An exploit used by hackers to locate computer ports that can be used for surreptitious access. 341

**Portable computer** Any type of computer, such as a notebook computer, that runs on batteries and is designed to be carried from one location to another. 59

**Portable Internet access** Any type of Internet service, such as portable satellite, that can be moved from one place to another. 311

**Portable media player** A small, lightweight, battery-powered device designed to store and play audio, video, or image files stored in such formats as MP3 and AAC. 20

**Portable software** Software designed to be stored on a flash drive or CD, and that does not require installation before it is used. 158

**PostScript** A printer language, developed by Adobe Systems, which uses a special set of commands to control page layout, fonts, and graphics. 94

**Power surge** A spike in electrical voltage that has the potential to damage electronic equipment such as computers. 99

**Powerline network** A network that uses a building's existing powerline cables to connect nodes; also called HomePlug, HPLC, or HomePLC. 262

**Presentation software** Software that provides tools to combine text, graphics, graphs, animation, and sound into a series of electronic "slides" that can be output on a projector, or as overhead transparencies, paper copies, or 35-millimeter slides. 138

**Print server** A device that controls a cluster of printers by distributing jobs that arrive in its print queue—a list of documents that require printing. 249

**Printer Control Language** (PCL) A standard for formatting codes embedded within a document that specify how a printer should format each page. 94

**Private IP address** An IP address that cannot be routed over the Internet. 344

**Processing** The manipulation of data by a computer's microprocessor or central processing unit. 15

**Product activation** The process of becoming a registered user of a software product; the process might include entering a validation code to unlock the software. 157

**Productivity software** Software that helps people work more efficiently; traditionally word processing, spreadsheet, presentation, e-mail, and database software. 121

**Programming language** A set of keywords and grammar (syntax) that allows a programmer to write instructions that a computer can execute. 29

**Project management software** Software specifically designed as a tool for planning, scheduling, and tracking projects and their costs. 142

**Proprietary software** Software that carries restrictions on its use that are delineated by copyright, patents, or license agreements. 149

**Protocol suite** A group of protocols, such as TCP and IP, that work together. 305

**PSK** (pre-shared key) A variation of WPA encryption protocol for wireless networks in which the encryption key used by the router is the same for all client computers that connect to the network. 283

**Public domain software** Software that is available for public use without restriction except that it cannot be copyrighted. 149

**Public key encryption** (PKE) An encryption method that uses a pair of keys, a public key (known to everyone) that encrypts the message, and a private key (known only to the recipient) that decrypts it. 286

**Quarantined file** A file suspected to be infected with a virus that antivirus software moves to a special folder to prevent accidental access to it. 169

**Query** A search specification that prompts the computer to look for particular records in a file. 136

**Query by example** (QBE) A type of database interface in which the user fills in a field with an example of the type of information that he or she is seeking. 136

**Query language** A set of command words that can be used to direct the computer to create databases, locate information, sort records, and change the data in those records. 136

**Query processor** The component of a search engine that examines keywords entered by users and fetches results that match the query. 377

**RAM** (random access memory) Computer memory circuitry that holds data, program instructions, and the operating system while the computer is on. 72

**Random access** The ability of a storage device (such as a disk drive) to go directly to a specific storage location without having to search sequentially from a beginning location. 77

**Rasterization** The process of superimposing a grid over a vector image and determining the color depth for each pixel. 447

**RAW** In the context of digital graphics, a file that contains unprocessed image data directly from a digital camera's sensors. 442

**Ray tracing** A technique by which light and shadows are added to a 3-D image. 449

**Read-only technology** Storage media that can only be read from, but not recorded on. 82

**Read-write head** The mechanism in a disk drive that magnetizes particles on the storage disk surface to write data, or senses the bits that are present to read data. 78

**Readability formula** A feature found in some word processing software that can estimate the reading level of a written document. 127

**Real-time messaging system** Technologies, such as instant messaging and chat, that allow people to exchange messages when they are online. 330

**Record** In the context of database management, the fields of data that pertain to a single entity in a database. 134

**Recordable technology** The devices and standards that allow computers to write data permanently on CDs and DVDs, but does not allow that data to be changed once it has been recorded. 82

**Recovery disk** A CD that contains all the operating system files and application software files necessary to restore a computer to its original state. 229

**Region code** A signal added to commercial DVDs that limits playback to devices that have a corresponding region code. 468

**Registers** A sort of "scratch pad" area of the microprocessor into which data or instructions are moved so that they can be processed. 31

**Relative reference** In a worksheet, a cell reference that can change if cells change position as a result of a move or copy operation. 132

**Remote Access Trojan** (RAT) A type of Trojan horse malware that allows remote hackers to transmit files to victims' computers. 163

**Rendering** In graphics software, the process of creating a 3-D solid image by covering a wireframe drawing and applying computer-generated highlights and shadows. 449

**Reserved words** Special words used as commands in some operating systems that may not be used in file names. 205

**Resolution dependent** Graphics, such as bitmaps, in which the quality of the image is dependent on the number of pixels comprising the image. 435

**Resource** A component, either hardware or software, that is available for use by a computer's processor. 185

**Resource fork** A storage characteristic of Mac OS that creates a file containing a description of the data stored in an accompanying raw data file. 199

**Response rate** In relation to display technology, the time it takes for one pixel to change from black to white then back to black. 90

**Restore point** Data stored about the state of files and the operating system at a given point in time, then used to roll back the computer system to that state. 230

**Rewritable technology** The devices and standards that allow users to write data on a storage medium and then change that data. 82

**RF signals** (radio frequency signals) Data that is broadcast and received via radio waves with a transceiver. 265

**Ribbon** An element of the user interface popularized by Microsoft Office 2007 that presents users with multiple tabs instead of menus at the top of the application window. 190

**Ring topology** A network in which all devices are connected in a circle with each device having exactly two neighbors. 250

**RISC** (reduced instruction set computer) A microprocessor designed for rapid and efficient processing of a small set of simple instructions. 69

**RJ45 connector** A square plastic cable connector that resembles an oversized telephone connector, and is used to connect Ethernet devices. 261

**ROM** (read-only memory) Refers to one or more integrated circuits that contain permanent instructions that the computer uses during the boot process. 74

**ROM BIOS** A small set of basic input/output system instructions stored in ROM. 74

**Root directory** The main directory of a disk. 206

**Rootkit** Software that conceals running processes; used by hackers to disguise security breaches and break-ins. 165

**Routable IP address** A network address that can be routed over the Internet; contrast to private IP address. 344

**Run-length encoding** A graphics file compression technique that looks for patterns of bytes and replaces them with messages that describe the patterns. 439

**S-HTTP** (Secure HTTP) A method of encrypting data transmitted between a computer and a Web server by encrypting individual packets of data as they are transmitted. 390

**Safe Mode** A menu option that appears when Windows is unable to complete the boot sequence. By entering Safe Mode, a user can gracefully shut down the computer, then try to reboot it. 105

**Sampling rate** The number of times per second a sound is measured during the recording process. 423

**Satellite Internet service** A high-speed Internet service that uses a geosynchronous or low-earth orbit satellite to send data directly to satellite dishes owned by individuals. 318

**Satellite modem** A device that connects a computer to a satellite for purposes of accessing the Internet. 319

**Scanner** A device that converts a printed image into a bitmap graphic. 431

**Screen resolution** The density of the grid used to display text or graphics on a display device; the greater the horizontal and vertical density, the higher the resolution. 91

**Search and Replace** A feature of document production software that allows the user to automatically locate all instances of a particular word or phrase and substitute another word or phrase. 127

**Search engine indexer** The component of a search engine that reviews the Web pages brought back by a crawler and creates pointers to them so that they can be quickly accessed. 376

**Search terms** The words entered into a search engine or database to form a query. 378

**Sectors** Subdivisions of the tracks on a storage medium that provide storage areas for data. 218

**Secure connection** An Internet connection that encrypts data transmitted between your computer and a Web site. 389

**Security software** Any software package that is designed to protect computers from destructive software and unauthorized intrusions. 162

**Security suite** A software suite containing modules to protect computers against viruses, worms, intrusions, spyware, and other threats. 166

**Self-extracting zip file** A type of compressed file that can be run to unzip the file or files contained within it. 157

**Self-installing executable file** A program that automatically unzips and then initiates its setup program. 157

**Semiconducting materials** (semiconductors) Substances, such as silicon or germanium, that can act as either a conductor or an insulator. Used in the manufacture of computer chips. 27

**Sequential access** A characteristic of data storage, usually on computer tape, that requires a device to read or write data one record after another, starting at the beginning of the medium. 77

**Serial processing** Processing data one instruction at a time, completing one instruction before beginning another. 69

**Server** A computer or software on a network that supplies the network with data and storage. 18

**Server operating system** A type of operating system, sometimes called a network operating system, that provides management tools for distributed networks, e-mail servers, and Web hosting sites. 187

**Server-side script** Scripting statements that are executed by a Web server in response to client data. 372

**Service pack** A collection of patches designed to correct bugs and/or add features to an existing software program. 159

**Setup program** A program module supplied with a software package for the purpose of installing the software. 154

**Shared resources** On a network, resources such as hardware, software, and data made available for authorized users to share. 274

**Shareware** Copyrighted software marketed under a license that allows users to use the software for a trial period and then send in a registration fee if they wish to continue to use it. 149

**Shrink-wrap license** A legal agreement printed on computer software packaging, which becomes binding when the package is opened. 147

**Signal scrambling** A technique that encrypts or otherwise disrupts broadcast signals so that they have to be unscrambled before they are sensible. 465

**Single-user license** Legal permission for one person to use a particular software package. 147

**Single-user operating system** A type of operating system that is designed for one user at a time using one set of input devices. 187

**Site license** Legal permission for software to be used on any and all computers at a specific location (for example, within a corporate building or on a university campus). 147

**Smartphone** A handheld device that integrates the functions of a mobile phone, PDA, portable music player, or other digital device. 20

**Smileys** Text-based symbols used to express emotion. 399

**SMTP** (Simple Mail Transfer Protocol) A communications protocol used to send e-mail across a network or the Internet. 398

**Sniffing** In the context of computer hacking, a technique that uses packet sniffer software to capture packets as they are sent over a network. 37

**Socket** A communication path between two remote programs. 364

**Software** The instructions that direct a computer to perform a task, interact with a user, or process data. 15

**Software installation** The process by which programs and data are copied to the hard disk of a computer system and otherwise prepared for access and use. 153

**Software license** A legal contract that defines the ways in which a user may use a computer program. 147

**Software suite** A collection of individual applications sold as one package. 144

**Software update** A section of code or a program module designed to correct errors or enhance security on an already installed software product. 159

**Software upgrade** A new version of a software product, containing new features and designed to replace the entire earlier version of the product. 159

**Solid state drive** A data storage device that utilizes erasable, rewritable circuitry. 84

**Solid state storage** A technology that records data and stores it in a microscopic grid of cells on a non-volatile, erasable, low-power chip. 84

**Sound card** A circuit board that gives the computer the ability to accept audio input from a microphone, play sound files, and produce audio output through speakers or headphones. 423

**Source code** Computer instructions written in a high-level language. 29

**Source document** A file containing the HTML tags or scripts for a Web page. 363

**Spam** Unsolicited e-mail typically sent as a bulk or mass-mailing and often used for fraudulent or deceptive marketing. 403

**Spam filter** Software that identifies unsolicited and unwanted e-mail messages and blocks them from the recipient's Inbox. 404

**Speech recognition** The process by which computers recognize voice patterns and words, then convert them to digital data. 428

**Speech synthesis** The process by which computers produce sound that resembles spoken words. 428

**Spelling checker** A feature of document production software that checks each word in a document against an electronic dictionary of correctly spelled words, then presents a list of alternatives for possible misspellings. 126

**Spelling dictionary** A data module that is used by a spelling checker as a list of correctly spelled words. 126

**Spreadsheet** A numerical model or representation of a real situation, presented in the form of a table. 130

**Spreadsheet software** Software for creating electronic worksheets that hold data in cells and perform calculations based on that data. 130

**Spyware** Any software that covertly gathers user information without the user's knowledge, usually for advertising purposes. 164

**SSID** (service set identifier) A code that identifies a wireless network and is attached to every packet that travels on that network. 272

**SSL** (Secure Sockets Layer) A security protocol that uses encryption to establish a secure connection between a computer and a Web server. 390

**Star topology** A network configured with a central connection point or hub for all workstations and peripherals. 250

**Stateless protocol** A protocol, such as HTTP, that allows one request and response per session. 368

**Static IP address** A permanently assigned and unique IP address, used by hosts or servers. 306

**Statistical software** Software for analyzing large sets of data to discover patterns and relationships within them. 133

**Storage** The area in a computer where data is retained on a permanent basis. 15

**Storage density** The closeness of the particles on a disk surface. As density increases, the particles are packed more tightly together and are usually smaller. 77

**Storage device** A mechanical apparatus that records data to and retrieves data from a storage medium. 76

**Storage medium** The physical material used to store computer data, such as a floppy disk, a hard disk, or a CD-ROM. 76

**Store-and-forward** A technology used by communications networks in which an e-mail message is temporarily held in storage on a server until it is requested by a client computer. 394

**Stored program** A set of instructions that resides on a storage device, such as a hard drive, and can be loaded into computer memory and executed. 16

**Streaming audio** An audio file format that allows the audio clip to begin before the file is entirely downloaded. 426

**Streaming video** An Internet video technology that sends a small segment of a video file to a user's computer and begins to play it while the next segment is being sent. 459

**Strong encryption** Encryption that is difficult to decrypt or "break" without the encryption key. 285

**Style** A feature in many desktop publishing and word processing programs that allows the user to apply numerous format settings with a single command. 128

**Subdirectory** A directory found under the root directory. 206

**Submenu** A user interface element that emerges after a menu is selected to offer additional options. 191

**Super distribution** A concept incorporated into Microsoft DRM that allows users to share protected media with others who can access it after they obtain their own license for it. 471

**Supercomputer** The fastest and most expensive type of computer, capable of processing trillions of instructions per second. 18

**Surge strip** A device that filters out electrical spikes that could damage computer equipment. 100

**SVG** (Scalable Vector Graphics) A graphics format designed specifically for Web display that automatically resizes when displayed on different screens. 448

**Symbian** An operating system typically used on mobile phones and open to programming by third-party developers. 202

**Symmetric Internet connection** Any connection to the Internet in which the upstream speed is the same as the downstream speed. 310

**Symmetric key encryption** An encryption key that is used for both encryption and decryption of messages. 286

**Synchronous communication** Any type of electronic communication, such as online discussions, Voice over IP, or videoconferencing, in which the sender and receiver are communicating online at the same time. 6

**Synthesized sound** Artificially created sound, usually found in MIDI music or synthesized speech. 427

**System board** The main circuit board in a computer that houses chips and other electronic components. 28

**System palette** A selection of colors that are used by an operating system to display graphic elements. 438

**System requirements** The minimum hardware and operating system specifications required for a software application to operate correctly. 145

**System software** Computer programs, such as an operating system or utility software, that help the computer carry out essential operating tasks. 16

**System unit** The case or box that contains the computer's power supply, storage devices, main circuit board, processor, and memory. 57

**Table** An arrangement of data in a grid of rows and columns. 129

**Tablet computer** A small, portable computer with a touch-sensitive screen that can be used as a writing or drawing pad. 59

**Taskbar** A graphical user interface element usually displayed near the bottom of the screen to help users launch and monitor applications. 190

**Tax preparation software** Personal finance software that is specifically designed to assist with tax preparation. 133

**TCP** (Transmission Control Protocol) The protocol within TCP/IP that is responsible for establishing a data connection between two hosts and breaking data into packets. 305

**TCP/IP** (Transmission Control Protocol/Internet Protocol) The primary protocol suite for transmitting messages over the Internet. 305

**Text-to-speech software** Software that generates speech based on written text that is played back through a computer's sound card. 428

**Thesaurus** A feature of documentation software that provides synonyms. 127

**TIFF** (Tagged Image File Format) A bitmap image file format with a .tif extension that automatically compresses the file data. 442

**Time shifting** The practice of recording digital content for later playback. 465

**TLS** (Transport Layer Security) An update of the Secure Sockets Layer (SSL) protocol for encrypting data before it is transmitted over a network. 390

**Toolbar** A component of graphical user interfaces that displays icons representing tools, commands, and other options. 190

**Top-level domain** A major domain category into which groups of computers on the Internet are divided, such as com, edu, gov, int, mil, net, and org. 307

**Touch screen** A display device that accepts input from being touched with a stylus or fingertip. 89

**Tower case** A desktop computer form factor that stores the system board and storage devices in a tall system unit with detached display and keyboard. 58

**Traceroute** A network utility that records a packet's path, the number of hops, and the time it takes for the packet to make each hop. 310

**Tracing software** Software that locates the edges of objects in a bitmap graphic and converts the resulting shape into a vector graphic. 447

**Trackball** An input device that looks like an upside down mouse. The user rolls the ball to move the on-screen pointer. 89

**Trackpad** A touch-sensitive surface on which you slide your fingers to move the on-screen pointer. 89

**Tracks** A series of concentric or spiral storage areas created on a storage medium during the formatting process. 219

**Transceiver** A combination of a transmitter and a receiver used to send and receive data in the form of radio frequencies. 265

**Transcoding** The process of converting audio and video files from one digital format to another, such as converting an MOV file into a Flash video file. 458

**Tree topology** Multiple star networks connected into a bus configuration by a backbone. 250

**Trojan horse** A computer program that appears to perform one function while actually doing something else, such as inserting a virus into a computer system or stealing a password. 163

**True Color bitmap** A color image with a color depth of 24 bits or 32 bits. Each pixel in a True Color image can be displayed using any of 16.7 million different colors. 437

**Tweet** A short message, sometimes called a microblog, posted on Twitter. 333

**Unicode** A 16-bit character-representation code that can represent more than 65,000 characters. 25

**Uninstall routine** A program that removes software files, references, and registry entries from a computer's hard disk. 160

**UNIX** A multiuser, multitasking server operating system developed by AT&T Bell Laboratories in 1969. 200

**Unzipped** Refers to files that have been uncompressed. 156

**UPS** (uninterruptible power supply) A battery-backed device designed to provide power to a computer during blackouts, brownouts, or other electrical disruptions. 100

**Upstream speed** The rate at which data is transmitted from your home computer to the Internet. 310

**URL** (Uniform Resource Locator) The address of a Web page. 361

**USB** (universal serial bus) A high-speed bus commonly used for connecting peripheral devices to computers. 96

**USB flash drive** A portable solid state storage device nicknamed pen drive or keychain drive that plugs directly into a computer's USB port. 84

**USB hub** A device that provides several auxiliary USB ports. 96

**User ID** A combination of letters and numbers that serves as a user's "call sign" or identification. Also referred to as a user name. 34

**User interface** The software and hardware that enable people to interact with computers. 189

**Utility software** A type of system software provided by the operating system or third-party vendors that specializes in tasks such as system maintenance, security, or file management. 122

**Vacuum tube** An electronic device that controls the flow of electrons in a vacuum and represents binary data; used in the construction of first generation computers. 491

**Value** A number used in a calculation. 130

**Vector graphic** An image generated from descriptions that specify the position, length, and direction in which lines and shapes are drawn. 444

**Vertical market software** Computer programs designed to meet the needs of a specific market segment or industry, such as medical record-keeping software for use in hospitals. 142

**VGA** (Video Graphics Array) A screen resolution of 640 x 480. 96

**Video capture** The process of converting analog video signals into digital data stored on a hard drive. 454

**Video editing software** Software that provides tools for capturing and editing video from a camcorder. 140

**Videocasting** Online delivery of a video clip as an Atom or RSS feed; also referred to as video podcasting or vodcasting. 361

**Videogame console** A computer specifically designed for playing games using a television screen and game controllers. 17

**Viewing angle width** The angle at which you can clearly see the screen image from the side. 90

**Virtual machine** Software that creates an operating environment that emulates another computer platform; as an example, Parallels Desktop creates a virtual PC on an Intel Macintosh computer. 198

**Virtual memory** A computer's use of hard disk storage to simulate RAM. 73

**Virtual private network** (VPN) A network connection that typically carries encrypted data over the Internet to and from a remote access server. 345

**Virus definitions** A group of virus signatures used by antivirus software to identify and block viruses and other malware. 168

**Virus hoax** A message, usually e-mail, that makes claims about a virus problem that doesn't actually exist. 166

**Virus signature** The unique computer code contained in a virus that security software uses to identify it. 167

**VOB** (Video Object) An industry-standard video format for standalone DVD players. 458

**Voiceband modem** The type of modem typically used to connect a computer to a telephone line. 312

**VoIP** (Voice over Internet Protocol) Hardware, software, and protocols used to make telephone-style calls over the Internet. Also referred to as Internet telephony. 331

**Volatile** A term that describes data (usually in RAM) that can exist only with a constant supply of power. 73

**WAN** (wide area network) An interconnected group of computers and peripherals that covers a large geographical area, such as multiple branches of a corporation. 247

**WAP** (Wireless Access Protocol) A communications protocol that provides Internet access for handheld devices. 326

**WAV** An audio file format with a .wav extension that was Windows' original "native" sound format. 425

**Wavetable** A set of prerecorded musical instrument sounds in MIDI format. 427

**Weak encryption** Encryption that is relatively easy or simple to decrypt without the encryption key. 285

**Web** Short for World Wide Web. An Internet service that links documents and information from computers located worldwide, using the HTTP protocol. 7, 360

**Web 2.0** A group of new and innovative ways to use the Web, such as for social networking, blogging, and wikis. 361

**Web application** Application software that is accessed and used from within a browser. 158

**Web authoring software** Computer programs for designing and developing customized Web pages that can be published electronically on the Internet. 125

**Web browser** A program that communicates with a Web server and displays Web pages. 361

**Web bug** A small graphic on a Web page that installs cookies designed to track your online activities. Also known as a clear GIF. 402

**Web cache** A collection of Web pages and associated graphics that have been accessed and are temporarily stored locally to speed up subsequent access to them. 365

**Web crawler** The component of a search engine that autonomously visits Web sites collecting Web page data that will be indexed and available for searching. 375

**Web page** Information displayed by a Web browser that's produced from an HTML document or generated on the fly from data in a database. 361

**Web palette** A standard selection of colors that all Internet browsers can display. 438

**Web search engine** A program that uses keywords to find information on the Internet and returns a list of links to relevant documents. 374

**Web server** A computer that listens for queries from Web browsers and transmits HTML documents over the Internet. 361

**Web site** A Web address that holds a collection of information identified by a common domain name, such as *www.cnn.com*. 360

**Webcam** An inexpensive digital camera that attaches directly to a computer and creates a video by capturing a series of still images. 454

**WebM** A multimedia container format designed for HTML5 projects. 458

**Webmail** An e-mail system that allows users to access e-mail messages using a browser. 393

**WEP** (Wired Equivalent Privacy) An encryption algorithm used to protect data on Wi-Fi networks. 283

**What-if analysis** The process of setting up a model in a spreadsheet and experimenting to see what happens when different values are entered. 130

**Wi-Fi** An Ethernet-compatible wireless network that uses 802.11a, b, g, and n standards. 268

**Wi-Fi adapter** A type of network interface card that includes a transmitter and a receiver using Wi-Fi protocols. 269

**Wi-Fi hotspot** The geographical area in which you can connect to a Wi-Fi signal, such as a Wi-Fi equipped campus or coffeehouse. 326

**Wiki** Software that allows users to collaborate to create, change, and link Web pages. Used for applications such as Wikipedia and open source project management. 332

**WiMAX** Fixed wireless Internet service based on Ethernet protocols with a range of 30 miles and a transmission speed of 70 Mbps. 320

**Window** An element of graphical user interfaces that is rectangular in shape and displays the controls for a program or a dialog box. 189

**Windows Explorer** A file management utility included with most Windows operating systems that helps users manage their files. 216

**Windows Media DRM** Microsoft's digital rights management technology. 470

**Windows Phone 7** A mobile operating system designed by Microsoft for mobile phones and other handheld digital devices. 202

**Windows Registry** A crucial set of data files maintained by the operating system that contains the settings needed by a computer to correctly use any hardware and software that has been installed. 154

**Wired network** A network that uses cables or wires to transmit data from one network device to another. 256

**Wireframe** A representation of a 3-D object using separate lines, which resemble wire, to create a model. 449

**Wireless access point** A network device that connects several devices of a local area network by broadcasting signals to any device with compatible Wi-Fi cards. 270

**Wireless ad-hoc network** A wireless network in which devices broadcast directly to each other instead of to a central access point. 270

**Wireless encryption** A security measure for wireless networks that scrambles data transmitted between network devices. 283

**Wireless infrastructure network** A wireless network in which devices communicate through a central access point. 270

**Wireless network** A network that uses radio or infrared signals (instead of cables) to transmit data from one network device to another. 265

**Wireless network key** The encryption key used to encrypt and decrypt data that travels over a wireless network protected by WEP, WPA, or WPA2. 284

**Wireless router** A network device that contains circuitry for a wireless access point and routing data to the Internet. 270

**WMA** (Windows Media Audio) A file format with a .wma extension that is promoted by Microsoft and provides highly compressed audio files with very little loss of sound quality. 425

**Word processing software** Computer programs that assist the user in producing documents, such as reports, letters, papers, and manuscripts. 125

**Word size** The number of bits that a CPU can manipulate at one time, which is dependent on the size of the registers in the CPU, and the number of data lines in the bus. 68

**Worksheet** A computerized, or electronic, spreadsheet. 130

**Workstation** (1) A computer connected to a local area network. (2) A powerful desktop computer designed for specific tasks. 17

**WPA** (Wi-Fi Protected Access) A method for encrypting data transmitted over wireless networks. 283

**XHTML** A markup language very similar to HTML 4.01, but more customizable. 362

**Zipped** Refers to one or more files that have been compressed. 156

**Zombie** A computer that has been compromised by malware that allows it to be controlled by a remote user. 164

# INDEX

## A

AAC (Advanced Audio Coding) format, 425
AACS (Advanced Access Content System), 469
absolute references, worksheets, 132
*The Abyss* (film), 474
access time, storage devices, 77, 79
accounting software, 142
ACH (Automated Clearing House), 348
Ackantta, 163
Acorn Computers, 71
Acronis True Image, 231
action games, 141
ActionScript, 372
ActiveX controls, 372
Ad-Aware, 402
ad-blocking software, 385
addresses
  communications protocols, 254–255
  e-mail. *See* e-mail addresses
  Internet, 305–307
  IP. *See* IP addresses
  MAC, 254
  spoofed, 163
Adobe Creative Suite, 144
Adobe Flash Player, 210, 402
Adobe Illustrator, 137
  AI file format, 210
Adobe Photoshop, 137, 430
Adobe Reader, 122, 210
  PDF file format, 210
Advanced Access Content System (AACS), 469
Advanced Audio Coding (AAC) format, 425
Advanced Encryption Standard (AES), 285
Advanced Micro Devices (AMD) microprocessors, 71
Advanced Research Projects Agency (ARPA), 108, 109, 302
advanced RISC Machine (ARM) processors, 69
advanced searches, 380
Advanced System Optimizer, 122
Advanced Systems Format (ASF), 458
adventure games, 141
advertising, e-commerce, 385
AES (Advanced Encryption Standard), 285
Age of Empires, 141
AI file format, 210
AIFF (Audio Interchange File Format), 424
Ajax (Asynchronous JavaScript and XML), 362
all-in-one computers, 58

ALU (arithmetic logic unit), 31, 32–33
always-on connections, 307
ALWIL avast!, 167
Amazon.com, 7
  Elastic Compute Cloud, 333
AMD (Advanced Micro Devices) microprocessors, 71
American Marketing Association, 44
American Standard Code for Information Interchange (ASCII), 24, 25
Amnesty International, 10
analog cameras, creating digital video, 454
analog data, digital data versus, 22
analog devices, video transfer, 455
analog hole, 464
analog modems, digital phone service, 313
analog protection systems, 468
AND operator, 379
Andreessen, Marc, 360
Android OS, 203
Android phones, applications, 20
animated GIFs, 448
animation
  film, 474–475
  3-D graphics, 450–451
  tools required, 451
anonymizer tools, 10
anonymous FTP, 337
anonymous proxy service, 403
antipharming tools, 406
anti-spyware software, 402
anti-theft devices, 98–99
antivirus software, 122, 167–169
  activating and deactivating, 168
  configuring, 168
  dependability, 169
  frequency of system scans, 169
  keeping up-to-date, 168
  operation, 167–168
AOL, security software available from, 167
APA style for citations, 382
app(s), 20
Apple Computer, Inc., 71. *See also* Mac *entries;* Macintosh computers
  convergence, 9
  digital music, 8
  GUI, 189
  iOS, 203
  iPad. *See* iPad
  iPhone. *See* iPhone
  iPod. *See* iPod
  iTunes, 8, 20, 139, 464, 470, 471
  iWork, 144
  iWork Keynote, 138
  Newton, 9
  online computer sales, 66
  Safari, 365, 366

application servers, 249
application software, 16, 120, 121, 125–142. *See also specific types of application software*
  file management, 212–213
  groupware, 121
  included with operating system, 143–144
  operating systems versus, 184
  productivity, 121
  running, 121
appz, 170
arithmetic logic unit (ALU), 31, 32–33
ARM Holdings microprocessors, 71
ARM (advanced RISC Machine) processors, 69
ARPA (Advanced Research Projects Agency), 108, 109, 302
ARPANET, 109, 232, 302
ASCII (American Standard Code for Information Interchange), 24, 25
ASF (Advanced Systems Format), 458
aspect ratio, digital video, 457–458
asymmetric Internet connection, 310, 311
asynchronous communication, 6, 332–333
Asynchronous JavaScript and XML (Ajax), 362
ATMs (automated teller machines), 348–349
Atom, 360
AT&T, 288, 303, 331
attachments, e-mail, 398
auctions, online, 388–389
Audacity, 139, 150
audio, digital. *See* digital audio
audio CD (CDDA), 82, 426
audio CDs, 82
audio compression, 423
audio editing software, 139
Audio Interchange File Format (AIFF), 424
audio player software, 425
Audio Video Interleave (AVI) format, 458, 459
authentication protocols, 34–36
authorization and revocation, 469
AutoCAD, 138, 450
autodialers, 44
automated check clearing, 348
Automated Clearing House (ACH), 348
automated teller machines (ATMs), 348–349
automatic recalculation, worksheets, 132
avast! Antivirus, 122
*Avatar* (film), 475
AVI (Audio Video Interleave) format, 458, 459

## B

Babbage, Charles, 348
backbone, Internet, 303
backing up, 222–231
  avoiding viruses, 223
  backup software, 227
  bare-metal restores, 230
  boot disk, 229
  choosing device for, 223
  differential backups, 227
  disk images, 230–231
  file copies and synchronization, 224–225
  frequency, 223
  full backups, 227
  incremental backups, 228
  need for, 222
  number of backups, 228
  plan for, 222
  recovery disk, 229
  restore points, 230
  restoring data, 228–229
  storage location for backups, 224
  system synchronization, 226
  Windows Registry, 229
backlighting, 90
backpack journalists, 173
Backup, 143
backup(s), 222
backup software, 227
bandwidth, 251
Bangladesh, cell phone time sales, 13
bank clearinghouses, 348
Bank of America, 348
banking industry, 348–349
banner ads, 385
bare-metal restore, 230
battery backup, 100
B2B (business-to-business) model, 384
BBC, 10
B2C (business-to-consumer) model, 384
BCT Modernization project, 108–109
BD-ROM (Blu-ray read-only memory) format, 83
*Becky Sharp* (film), 474
Beise, S, Clark, 348
benchmarks, 70
Berners-Lee, Tim, 360, 362
Best Buy, computer sales, 66
Betamax, 472
B2G (business-to-government) model, 384
binary number system, 23
biometrics, 34
bit(s)
  bytes versus, 26
  image storage, 25
bitmap graphics, 430–443
  color, 436–437
  color depth, 437

color palettes, 437–438
compression. *See* image compression
converting vector graphics to, 447
creating, 430
definition, 430
digital cameras, 431–433
file formats, 442–443
image resolution, 433–435
modifying, 435
monochrome, 436
resolution dependence, 435
scanners, 431
32-bit, 437
True Color, 437
24-bit, 437
vector graphics compared, 444–445
bitrate, 457–458
BitTorrent, 305, 338–339
  legality, 339
  operation, 338
  security, 339
BizRate, 386
black hat, 36
BlackBerry OS, 202
Blackberry Torches, 19
Blackboard, 291
blade servers, 18
Blaster worm, 233
blended threats, 162
Blender, 150
blogs, 332
Bloom, David, 173
blue screen of death (BSoD), 103
Bluetooth, 267
  definition, 267
  PANs, 266
  range, 267
  speed, 267
  uses, 267
Blu-ray disc(s), 57, 81
  BD-ROM format, 83
  capabilities, 83
  comparison with other storage technologies, 87
  copy protection, 469
  formats, 83
  speed, 82
Blu-ray Disc Movie format, 458
BMP format, 442, 443
body scanners, 411
Boole, George, 379
Boolean operators, 379
boot disks, 229
boot process, 192–193
bootstrap program, 192
bot(s), 164
botnets, 164
bridges, 250
British Airways, 232
British Telecom, 303
broadband, 251
  mobile, 326

broadcast flags, 465–466
broadcast journalism, 173
browser add-ons. *See* plug-ins
browser caches, 365
browser palettes, 438
brute force attacks, 37
BSD license, 150
BSoD (blue screen of death), 103
bus topology, 250
business(es). *See also* e-commerce
  e-mail privacy policies, 409
  employee e-mail privacy, 408, 409
business software, 142
business-to-business (B2B) model, 384
business-to-consumer (B2C) model, 384
business-to-government (B2G) model, 384
buttons, 190
buying computers
  software requirements, 64
  support services, 66
buying hardware, 62–66
  compatibility, 64
  costs, 62–63
  mods, 65–66
  planned uses, 63
  product information sources, 62
  software considerations, 64
  upgrading, 65
  vendors, 66
buying software, 143–151
  applications and utilities included with operating system, 143–144
  copyrights, 146–147
  essential software to have, 143
  freeware, 150
  information sources, 145
  licenses, 147–150, 151
  open source software, 150–151
  software package contents, 146
  software suites, 144
  system requirements, 145
  vendors, 145
bytes, bits versus, 26

## C

cable(s)
  Ethernet, 261
  transferring images from digital cameras, 432
cable Internet service, 316–317, 321
  equipment needed, 317
  security, 317
  speed, 316
cable modems, 317
Cactus Data Shield (CDS), 466
CAD (computer-aided design) software, 138, 410
CAI (computer-aided instruction), 290
CAL (computer-aided learning), 290

Calculator, 143
Caligari trueSpace, 450
cameras
    digital. *See* digital cameras
    webcams. *See* webcams
capacitors, 72
capacity, storage devices, 77
Carbon Copy Cloner, 231
card readers, 84, 432
Carmen Sandiego Word Detective, 140
Carrier Sense Multiple Access with Collision Detection (CSMA/CD) protocol, 258
case sensitivity, 35
Casey, George W., 108
CATV (community antenna television), 316
CBT (computer-based training), 290
C2C (consumer-to-consumer) model, 384
CD(s) (compact discs), 57, 81
    backup device, 223
    buying software on, downloading versus, 146
    copy protection, 466–467
    formats, 82, 83
    installing software from, 155
    speed, 82
CDDA (compact disc digital audio), 82, 426
CD-DA (compact disc digital audio or audio CD) format, 82
CD-R (compact disc recordable) drives, capabilities, 83
CD-R (compact disc recordable) format, 83
CD-ROM (compact disc read-only memory) drives, capabilities, 83
CD-ROM (compact disc read-only memory) format, 83
CD-RW (compact disc rewritable) drives
    capabilities, 83
    comparison with other storage technologies, 87
CD-RW (compact disc rewritable) format, 83
CDS (Cactus Data Shield), 466
cell(s), worksheets, 130
cell phones. *See* mobile phones
cell references, 131
cellular broadband service, 322
cellular data service, 326–329
    equipment needed, 326
    speed, 326
    WAP, 326
cellular wireless modems, accessing Internet, 328
censorship, Internet, 10, 346–347
central processing unit (CPU), 15
Certificates of Authority, 147
CGI (computer-generated imagery), 475
character data, 24–25
charge-coupled devices (CCDs), 431

chat, 330
Chicago style for citations, 382
China, Internet censorship, 10, 347
chips. *See* microprocessor(s)
Chrome, 361, 365, 366
ciphertext, 285
circuit switching, 253
CISC (complex instruction set computer) technology, 69
Cisco Systems, Internet censorship tools, 347
ClamWin, 12, 150, 167
Classmates, 6, 361
cleaning. *See* maintenance
clear GIFs, 402
click-through rate, 385
clients, 18
client/server mode, 249
client-side scripts, 372
clip art, 129
clothing production, warehousing, and shipping, 410–411
cloud computing, 333
clusters, 219
codecs, 457–458
color, bitmap graphics, 436–437
color depth, 90, 437
    file size, 436
    reducing, 437
color palettes, 437–438
Comcast, 288, 331
    security software available from, 167
command-line user interfaces, 189
commercial software, 149
Communications Act of 1934, 43
communications channels, 251
communications ports, 308
communications protocols, 252–255, 305
    addresses, 254–255
    CSMA/CD, 258
    definition, 252
    local e-mail, 394
    operation, 252
    packets, 253–254
    protocol suites, 305
    signals, 253
    stateless, 365
community antenna television (CATV), 316
compact disc(s). *See* CD(s) (compact discs)
compact disc digital audio (CDDA), 82, 426
compact disc read-only memory (CD-ROM) drives, capabilities, 83
compact disc read-only memory (CD-ROM) format, 83
compact disc recordable (CD-R) drives, capabilities, 83
compact disc recordable (CD-R) format, 83

compact disc rewritable drives. *See* CD-RW (compact disc rewritable) drives; CD-RW (compact disc rewritable) format
compatibility, 64
compilers, 30
complex instruction set computer (CISC) technology, 69
compression
    audio, 423
    digital video, 457–458
    images. *See* image compression
    specifying compression level, 458
compression ratio, 457–458
computed tomography, 8
compute-intensive problems, 19
computer(s)
    buying. *See* buying computers; buying hardware
    clients, 18
    data processing, 15
    data storage, 15
    definition, 14
    evolution, 5
    game, 61
    input, 15
    mobile broadband, 328
    output, 15
    personal, 16, 17, 56–57
    servers, 18
    small business, 61
    software. *See* software
    types, 16–19
    upswing in ownership, 6–7
computer chips. *See* microprocessor(s)
computer crime
    penalties, 232–233
    unauthorized access to wireless networks, 288–289
computer forensics, 235
computer gaming, 8
computer hardware. *see* hardware; *specific hardware devices*
computer magazines. *See* technology magazines
computer networks, 7. *See also* network *entries*
computer program(s), 15. *See also* software; *specific types of software*
computer programming languages, 29
computer software. *See* software; *specific types of software*
computer systems, 56–57
    components, 56–57
    home, 60
computer viruses, 163
    antivirus software. *See* antivirus software
    avoiding in backups, 223
    virus definitions, 168
    virus distribution, 232
    virus hoaxes, 166
    virus signatures, 167

computer worms, 163
computer-aided design (CAD) software, 138, 410
computer-aided instruction (CAI), 290
computer-aided learning (CAL), 290
computer-aided music software, 139
computer-based training (CBT), 290
computer-generated imagery (CGI), 475
concurrent-use licenses, 147
confidentiality, 11
configuring
  network routers, 264
  workstations for Ethernet, 264
connection speed, Internet, 309–311
consumer-to-consumer (C2C) model, 384
container formats, 458
Content Scramble System (CSS), 468
control(s), 123
control unit, 31, 32
convergence, 8–9
conversion of file formats, 210–211
convertible tablet computers, 59
cookies, 367–368, 400–403
  ad-serving, 400
  definition, 367
  deleting, 401
  Flash, 402
  lifetime, 368
  operation, 368
  security, 400
  turning off, 401
  uses, 368
  viewing, 368
Copy Control, 466
copy control, 466
copy generation management, 467
copy prevention, 466
copy protection, 12, 466–467
copyright(s)
  fair use, 472–473
  software, 146–151
  Web-based sources, 383
copyright, Digital Millennium Copyright Act, 10, 346, 473
copyright notices, 147
Corel Painter, 137, 430
CorelDRAW, 137
  Graphics Suite, 144
corrupted signals, 253
costs
  computer upgrades, 65
  computers, 62–63
  domain names, 309
  portable satellite service, 326
  printer operation, 93
counterfeiting, 170
CPU (central processing unit), 15
CPU cache, 68
crackers, 36
Craigslist, 388
Cray XT5HE, 18

credit cards, online payment, 389
crime. *See* computer crime; laws
cropping, 435
cryptographic algorithms, 285
cryptographic keys, 285
CSMA/CD (Carrier Sense Multiple Access with Collision Detection) protocol, 258
CSS (Content Scramble System), 468
CT scans, 8
cyber censorship, 346–347
CyberAngel, 99
cyber-hacking, 232–233
CyberLink DVD suite, 144
Cybersecurity Enhancement Act, 233
cyberspace, 7

**D**
dashboard widgets, 123
data, 15
  analog versus digital, 22
  character, 24–25
  digital, 22–23
  information versus, 22
  numeric, 23
  sharing on LANs, 274
  travel over networks, 252–253
data bus, 94
data diddling, 232
data files, backing up. *See* backing up
data fork, Mac OS, 199
Data Over Cable Service Interface Specification (DOCSIS), 317
data representation, 22
data service plans, 327
data transfer rate, 77
database(s)
  definition, 134
  queries, 136
database software, 134–136
  data entry, 135
  data storage, 134–135
  definition, 134
  locating data, 136
  record creation, 135
DAZ Studio, 451
DCGS (Distributed Common Ground System), 109
DE (distance education), 291
decimal system, 23
decryption, 285
DeCSS, 468
dedicated lines, 314, 321
DefenseLINK, 108
defragmentation utilities, 221
deleting
  cookies, 401
  files, 220
Dell, 12
  online computer sales, 66
  servers, 18
Delta Airlines, 232
democracy, digital technology, 10

demoware, 149
denial of service, 232
desktop, 189
desktop computers, 58
desktop operating systems, 188
desktop publishing (DTP) software, 125
desktop widgets, 123
Deutsche Telekom, 303
device drivers, 124
DHCP (Dynamic Host Configuration Protocol), 255
  setting, 264
DHTML (Dynamic Hypertext Markup Language), 362
Diablo, 141
dialog boxes, 191
dial-up connections, 312–313, 321
dictionary attacks, 36
Difference Engine, 348
differential backups, 227
digital audio, 422–429
  adding to Web pages, 425
  converting format, 426
  definition, 422
  file formats, 425
  hardware requirements, 424
  integrated, 423
  MIDI music, 427–428
  production, 423–424
  sampling rate and sound quality, 423
  software for playing, 425
  speech recognition and synthesis, 428–429
  streaming, 426
  Web-based, 426
digital audio extraction, 426
digital cameras, 431–433
  image storage, 432
  transferring images from, 432–433
digital certificates, 373
digital content, 464
digital data, 22–23
  analog data versus, 22
digital divide, 12–13
digital electronics, significance, 4–5
digital imaging, 8
Digital Millennium Copyright Act (DMCA), 10, 346, 473
digital music, 8
  sources, 425
digital phone service, analog modems, 313
digital processing, 29–33
  processor logic, 31–33
  programs and instruction sets, 29–31
digital revolution, 4–8
  digitization, 7–8
  evolution of computers, 5
  significance of digital electronics, 4–5
  technologies fueling, 4

upswing in computer ownership, 6–7
Web, 7
digital rights management (DRM), 464–471
Blu-ray, 469
CD copy protection, 466–467
definition, 464
digital downloads, 469–471
digital media use, 464–465
digital watermarks, 465–466
DVDs, 467–469
effectiveness, 465
signal scrambling, 465
digital signal processors, 424
digital technology
economic effects, 12–13
freedom and democracy, 10
intellectual property, 11–12
privacy, 11
digital versatile discs. See DVD entries
digital video, 8, 452–463
analog video compared, 452
compression, 457–458
converting format, 458
creating, 453–454, 457
definition, 452
DVDs. See video DVDs
editing, 456
file formats, 458
outputting to DVDs, 462
source, 452
space required to store, 455
streaming, 459
transfer, 455
uses, 452
Web-based, 459–460
digital video discs. See DVD entries
Digital Visual Interface (DVI) ports, 96
digital watermarks, 465–466
digitization, 7–8
digitizing tablets, 446
DIPs, 27
direct access, 77
direct marketing, 44
directories, 206
disc(s). See specific types of discs
disc mastering, 219
disk(s)
boot, 229
floppy. See floppy disk drives
formatting, 219
hard (fixed). See hard disk drives; hard disk(s)
recovery, 229
Disk Defragmenter, 143
disk images, 230–231
disk operating system (DOS), 187, 201
disk partitions, 205
diskettes, 80
display devices, 90–91
components, 91

handheld device compensation for small size, 328
image quality, 90
maintenance, 101
screen resolution, 91
screensavers, 123
types, 90
watching DVDs and television, 90
display systems, 57
distance education (DE), 291
distance learning, 291
Distributed Common Ground System (DCGS), 109
distributed.net, 335
distribution media, 146
DiVX, 457–458
DMCA (Digital Millennium Copyright Act), 10, 346, 473
DNS (Domain Name System), 308
DNS poisoning, 347
DOC file format, 210
docking stations, transferring images from digital cameras, 432
DOCSIS (Data Over Cable Service Interface Specification), 317
document format, 127–129
document production software, 125–129
desktop publishing software, 125
formatting, 127–129
improving writing quality, 126–127
spell checking, 126
Web authoring software, 125
word processing software, 125
DoD (U.S. Department of Defense), 108, 109
domain name(s), 307–309
fee, 309
IP addresses related, 308
list, 307
obtaining, 309
domain name servers, 308
pharming, 405–406
Domain Name System (DNS), 308
DomainKeys, 403
donating
software, 106
used hardware, 106
Doom, 141
DOS (disk operating system), 187, 201
dot matrix printers, 93
dot pitch, 90
double layer DVDs, 81
DoubleClick, 401
downloading, 8
DRM, 469–471
installing downloaded software, 156–157
software, 146
downstream speed, 310
drawing software, 137, 446
DreamWorks, 450

drive(s). See hard disk drives; optical drives; solid state drives (SSDs); USB flash drives; specific types of optical drives
drive mapping, 276
DRM individualization, 470
Droid X, 329
DSL (digital subscriber line), 314–315, 321
equipment, 315
operation, 315
speed, 315
DSL filters, 315
DSL modems, 315
DTP (desktop publishing) software, 125
dual boot, Mac OS, 198
duplex printers, 94
duty cycle, printers, 93
DVD(s) (digital video discs or digital versatile discs), 57, 81
backup device, 223
double layer, 81
DRM, 467–469
formats, 82, 83
installing software from, 155
speed, 82
viewing on computer display, 90
DVD authoring software, 140
DVD images, 462
DVD-R(s) or DVD+Rs (digital versatile disc recordable) format, 83, 463
capabilities, 83
DVD-ROM (digital versatile disc read-only memory) format, 83, 463
DVD-RWs or DVD+RWs (digital versatile disc rewritable) format, 83, 463
capabilities, 83
comparison with other storage technologies, 87
DVD-Video (digital versatile disc video) format, 82
DVI (Digital Visual Interface) ports, 96
Dynamic Host Configuration Protocol. See DHCP (Dynamic Host Configuration Protocol)
Dynamic Hypertext Markup Language (DHTML), 362
dynamic IP addresses, 306–307

E
ear training software, 139
eBay, 7, 388, 390
EBCDIC (Extended Binary Coded Decimal Interchange Code), 25
e-books, fair use, 473
e-commerce, 384–391
common models, 384
definition, 384
driving traffic to Web sites, 45
online auctions, 388–389
online payment, 389–391

online shopping, 386–387
popularity, 385
profitability, 384–385
who benefits, 385
economy
  digital technology's effects, 12–13
  foreign software piracy, 171
The Economy of Machinery and
  Manufactures (Babbage), 348
EDGE (Enhanced Data rates for
  GSM Evolution), 326, 328
editing digital video, 456
educational applications of
  computers, 290–291
educational software, 140–141
EEPROM (electrically erasable
  programmable ROM), 74–75
e-garbage, 106–107
EIDE drive controllers, 79
Eisenhower, Dwight, 109
Elastic Compute Cloud, 333
Electrical Numerical Integrator And
  Computer (ENIAC), 108, 109
electrically erasable programmable
  ROM (EEPROM), 74–75
Electronic Communications Privacy
  Act, 408
Electronic Recording
  Machine-Accounting (ERMA),
  348
e-mail, 6, 392–399
  access, 393
  interception, 408
  local. See local e-mail
  netiquette, 399
  privacy, 408–409
  security. See e-mail security
  spam. See spam
  transferring images from digital
    cameras, 432
  Web. See Webmail
e-mail accounts, 393
  Webmail, 397
e-mail addresses, 393
  selecting, 393
e-mail attachments, 398
e-mail authentication, 403
e-mail client software, 393
e-mail messages, 392
  attachments, 398
e-mail security
  phishing, 405
  privacy, 408–409
  spam, 403–404
e-mail servers, 392
e-mail systems, 392
employees, e-mail privacy, 408, 409
encryption
  definition, 285
  operation, 285
  public key, 286–287
  strong, 285–286
  symmetric key, 286
  weak, 285
  wireless. See wireless encryption

end-user license agreements
  (EULAs), 148
end-user piracy, 170
Engines of the Mind (Shurkin), 108
Enhanced Copy Protection (XCP),
  466
Enhanced Data rates for GSM
  Evolution (EDGE), 326, 328
ENIAC (Electrical Numerical
  Integrator And Computer), 108,
  109
E911 Act, 43
entertainment software, 141
Eraser, 123
ERMA (Electronic Recording
  Machine-Accounting), 348
eSATA ports, 96
Ethernet, 257–264
  equipment, 259–261
  operation, 257–258
  popularity, 257
  setup, 262–264
  speed, 258, 261
  standards, 258
Ethernet adapters, 260
EULAs (end-user license
  agreements), 148
European Convention on Human
  Rights, 10
EV-DO (Evolution Data Optimized),
  326, 328
EverQuest, 141
Evolution Data Optimized (EV-DO),
  326, 328
e-waste, 106–107
executable files, 152
  self-installing, 157
expansion bus, 94
expansion cards, 95
expansion ports, 95
expansion slots, 95
extended ASCII, 15, 24
Extended Binary Coded Decimal
  Interchange Code (EBCDIC),
  25
Ext3fs (Third Extended File System),
  219

**F**

fabric design and manufacturing, 410
Facebook, 6, 361
fair use, 472–473
FairPlay, 470
fake Web sites, 405–407
fans, maintenance, 102
fashion industry, 410–411
FCC regulations, Wi-Fi, 288
fields, databases, 134
file(s), 15, 204–211
  dates, 206
  definition, 204
  deleting, 220
  designating location, 205
  directories, 206
  disk partitions, 205
  folders, 206

formats. See file formats
fragmented, 221
management. See file management
multiple, working with
  simultaneously, 217
names, 204–205
number required by software
  packages, 153
quarantined, 169
sharing on LANs, 276–278
size, 206
undeleting, 221
unzipping, 156
zipped, 156, 157
file compression utilities, 440
file date, 206
file extensions, 152, 153, 204
  file formats, 207, 208
file formats, 207–211
  bitmap graphics, 442–443
  common, 208
  converting, 210–211
  digital audio, 425
  digital video, 458
  inability to open some files,
    209–210
  native, 209
  vector graphics on Web, 448
  Web browsers, 366–367
  Web videos, 460
file headers, 207
file management, 212–221
  application-based, 212–213
  file management utilities, 214,
    216–217
  metaphors, 215
  physical file storage, 218–221
  tips, 218
  Windows Explorer, 216–217
file management utilities, 214,
  216–217
file names, 204–205
  characters, 205
  file-naming conventions, 204
  reserved words, 205
file servers, 249, 278
  home networks, 278
  LANs, 278
  setup, 278
file sharing. See P2P file sharing
file shredder software, 220
file size, 206
  color depth, 437
  image resolution, 434
file specifications, 206
file synchronization, 224
file systems, 219
file tags, 212
File Transfer Protocol. See FTP (File
  Transfer Protocol)
file-encryption software, 122
file-naming conventions, 204
file-sharing sites, posting videos, 459
film, computer technology, 474–475
filter(s), DSL, 315
filtering software, 10, 122

Final Fantasy, 141
Finale, 428
fingerprinting, 234
Finland, wireless technology, 12
Firefox, 12, 150, 365, 366
firewalls, 342
FireWire ports, 96
fixed disks. *See* hard disk drives;
        hard disk(s)
fixed Internet access, 311, 312–321
    cable Internet service, 316–317,
        321
    dedicated lines, 314, 321
    dial-up connections, 312–313, 321
    DSL, 314–315, 321
    fixed wireless Internet service, 320,
        321
    ISDN, 314, 321
    limitations, 322–323
    satellite Internet service, 318–319,
        321
fixed wireless Internet service, 320,
        321
Fizt, 475
Flash content, 372
Flash cookies, 402
Flash format, vector graphics, 448
flash memory. *see* solid state storage
Flash Player, 402
Flash video, 210, 458, 459
flat panel displays, 90
Flight Simulator, 141
floppies, 80
floppy disk drives, 80
    comparison with other storage
        technologies, 87
folders, 206
    multiple, working with
        simultaneously, 217
    personal, 217
font(s), 127
font styles, 127
footers, 128
Ford, 45
forensics, computer, 235
form factor, 58
format shifting, 465
    fair use, 472
formatting
    disks, 219
    documents, 127–129
formula(s), worksheets, 131
formulating searches, 378–381
    advanced searches, 380
    Boolean operators, 379
    search terms, 378
    tips, 379
Fourth Amendment, 11
fragmented files, 221
frame(s), documents, 129
frame size, digital video, 457–458
freedom
    digital technology, 10
    of speech (expression), 10. *See
        also* censorship

freeware, 150
front side bus, 68
FTP (File Transfer Protocol), 305
    accessing FTP servers, 336–337
    anonymous, 337
    operation, 336
FTP clients, 337
FTP servers, 336
    accessing, 336–337
full backups, 227
full system backups, 226
fully justified alignment, 128
functions, 131

**G**
gadgets, 123
Gaeta, John, 475
Gallery, 150
game(s), tools required, 451
game computers, 61
game software, 141
Garmin, GPSs, 19
Gates, Bill, 233
gateways, 251
Gb or Gbit (gigabit), 26
GB or GByte (gigabyte), 26
Geek Squad, 105
General Public License (GPL), 151
GHz (gigahertz), 67
GIF (Graphics Interchange Format),
        442, 443
    animated, 448
giga-, definition, 26
gigabit (Gb or Gbit), 26
gigabyte (GB or GByte), 26
gigahertz (GHz), 67
GIMP, 150
global positioning systems (GPSs),
        19, 42
globalization, 12–13
GNU, 170
Google, Internet censorship tools,
        347
Googlewhacking, 379
GPL (General Public License), 151
GPSs (global positioning systems),
        19, 42
gradients, 447
Gralnick, Jeff, 173
grammar checkers, 127
graphical elements, documents, 129
graphical user interfaces (GUIs),
        189–192
    basic elements, 189–190
    menus and dialog boxes, 190–191
    similarities, 192
graphics
    bitmap. *See* bitmap graphics
    definition, 137
    specifying for Web pages, 370
    3-D, 449–451
    vector. *See* vector graphics
graphics boards, 91
graphics cards, 91
graphics file formats, 210

Graphics Interchange Format. *See*
        GIF (Graphics Interchange
        Format)
graphics processing units (GPUs),
        91
graphics software, 137–138
    CAD software, 138
    drawing software, 137
    paint software, 137
    photo editing software, 137
    presentation software, 138
    3-D, 137–138
grayscale palettes, 438
grid computing systems, 334–335
groupware, 121
GUIs. *See* graphical user interfaces
        (GUIs)
Guitar Hero, 141

**H**
hackers
    methods used by, 340–345
    password theft, 36–37
hacking, 232–233
Halo, 141
handheld devices, 19–20. *See also
        specific devices*
    compensation for small screens,
        328
    digital audio, 425
    loading music, 425
    operating systems, 202–203
    processors, 69
    video transfer, 455
handshaking, 252
hard disk(s)
    backup device, 223
    storage on, RAM versus, 72
hard disk controllers, 79
hard disk drives, 57, 78–80
    comparison with other storage
        technologies, 87
    limitations, 80
    multiple, 80
    operation, 78–79
    popularity, 78
    size, 79
    types, 79
hard disk platters, 78
hardware, 54–111
    buying. *See* buying hardware
    computer systems, 56–57
    desktop and portable computers,
        58–59
    home, game, and small business
        systems, 60–61
    input devices, 88–89. *See also
        specific devices*
    installing peripheral devices, 94–97
    memory. *See* memory
    microprocessors. *See*
        microprocessor(s)
    output devices, 90–94. *See also
        specific devices*
    recycling, 106

security. *See* hardware security
settings, storage in EEPROM, 74–75
sharing on LANs, 275, 278–280
storage devices, 76–87. *See also specific devices*
troubleshooting problems, 104
hardware security, 98–105
anti-theft devices, 98–99
battery backup, 100
maintenance, 101–103
surge protection, 99–100
troubleshooting and repair, 103–105
hash values, 157
HDCP (High-bandwidth Digital Content Protection), 466
HDMI (High-Definition Multimedia Interface) ports, 96
HDSL (high-rate DSL), 314
head crashes, 80
headers, 128
hertz (Hz), 251
Hewlett-Packard, 12
servers, 18
High-bandwidth Digital Content Protection (HDCP), 466
High-Definition Multimedia Interface (HDMI) ports, 96
high-rate DSL (HDSL), 314
High-Speed Uplink Packet Access (HSUPA), 326, 328
home computer systems, 60
homegroups, 277
HomePlug, 262
HomePNA (HPNA), 262
horizontal market software, 142
hot-plugging, 97
hotspots
using cell phones as, 329
Wi-Fi. *See* Wi-Fi hotspots
hover ads, 385
HPNA (HomePNA), 262
HSUPA (High-Speed Uplink Packet Access), 326, 328
HTML (Hypertext Markup Language), 362–363
HTML conversion utilities, 369
HTML documents, 362
HTML forms, 371
HTML mail, 397
HTML scripts, 371–373
client-side, 372
server-side, 372
HTML tags, 362–363, 370
HTTP (Hypertext Transfer Protocol), 305, 364–365
methods, 364
HTTP status codes, 365
H.264, 457–458
Human Rights Watch, 10
hypertext, 360
hypertext links, 361
Hypertext Markup Language. *See* HTML *entries*

Hypertext Transfer Protocol. *See* HTTP *entries*
Hz (hertz), 251

**I**

IAFIS (Integrated Automated Fingerprint Identification System), 234
IBM, 12
PC platform, 64
servers, 18
z10 E12, 18
z/OS, 187
IC(s) (integrated circuits), 27–28
ICANN (Internet Corporation for Assigned Names and Numbers), 309
icons, GUIs, 189
identity theft, 36, 232
iDVD, 140
IE (Internet Explorer), 143, 361, 365, 366
IEEE (Institute of Electrical and Electronics Engineers) Project 802, 247
IEEE 802.3, 247
IEEE 1394 ports, 96
IM (instant messaging), 330
image(s). *See also* bitmap graphics; digital video; graphics; vector graphics
compression. *See* image compression
resolution. *See* image resolution
storage, 25
image compression, 439–441
lossless, 439
lossy, 439, 440
process, 440
image editing software, 137, 143
image quality, display devices, 90
image resolution, 433–435
changing image size, 435
file size, 434
image quality, 433
physical size of image, 434
screen display, 434–435
specifying image size, 434
IMAP (Internet Message Access Protocol), 394
iMovie, 140
in-betweening, 474
increasing productivity, document production software, 129
incremental backups, 228
information
data versus, 22
theft, 232
infrared light, 265
infrared ports, transferring images from digital cameras, 432
ink cartridges, printers, 94
ink jet printers, 92
input, 15
input devices, 88–89
installing

peripheral devices, 94–97
software. *See* installing software
upgrades and updates, 159–160
installing software, 152–160
local applications, 154–157
multiple files, 153
portable software, 158
product activation, 157
software upgrades and updates, 159–160
Web applications, 158–159
instant messaging (IM), 330
Institute of Electrical and Electronics Engineers. *See* IEEE *entries*
instruction cycle, 32
instruction processing, 69
instruction sets, 30–31
computer performance, 69
integrated audio, 423
Integrated Automated Fingerprint Identification System (IAFIS), 234
integrated circuits (ICs), 27–28
Integrated Services Digital Network (ISDN), 314, 321
Intel microprocessors, 71
intellectual property, 11–12
International Business Machines. *See* IBM
Internet, 6–7, 300–351
access, 57
addresses, 305–307
censorship, 10, 346–347
connection speed, 309–311
direct marketing using, 44–45
domains, 307–309
fixed Internet access. *See* fixed Internet access
infrastructure, 303–304
mobile Internet access, 311, 322
netiquette, 399
origins, 302
popularity, 302
portable Internet access, 311, 322
protocols. *See* communications protocols
putting Web pages on, 371
security. *See* Internet security
size, 302
surfing anonymously, 403
upswing in computer ownership, 6
VoIP, 331
Internet backbone, 303
Internet Corporation for Assigned Names and Numbers (ICANN), 309
Internet Explorer (IE), 143, 361, 365, 366
Internet forums, 332
Internet Message Access Protocol (IMAP), 394
Internet piracy, 170
Internet Protocol (IP), 305
Internet Relay Chat (IRC), 305
Internet security, 340–345. *See also* Web security

intrusion attempts, 340–341
NAT, 344–345
routers, 343–345
securing ports, 342–343
VPNs, 345
Internet service(s), 330–339
file sharing, 338–339
FTP, 336–337
grid computing, 334–335
real-time messaging, 330
VoIP, 331
Internet service providers (ISPs), 303–304
interpreters, 30
intrusions, 340–341
iOS, 203
IP (Internet Protocol), 305
IP addresses, 255, 305–306
dynamic, 306–307
private, 344
routable, 344
static, 306
iPad, 59
applications, 20
iPhone, 19, 20
applications, 20
iPhone OS X, 203
iPod, 9, 20, 139, 425
hard disk drive, 79
play list display, 29
iPod touch, applications, 20
IPv4, 305
IPv6, 305
Iran, Internet censorship, 347
IRC (Internet Relay Chat), 305
ISDN (Integrated Services Digital Network), 314, 321
ISDN terminal adapters, 314
ISPs (Internet service providers), 303–304
iTunes, 8, 20, 139, 464, 470, 471
iWork, 144
iWork Keynote, 138

**J**
Jaguar, 18
Java applets, 372, 373
JavaScript, 372
*The Jazz Singer* (film), 474
jitter, 331
Jobs, Steve, 233
Johnson, Leigh, 475
Joint Photographic Experts Group (JPEG) format, 210, 442, 443
Jolson, Al, 474
journalism, 172–173
joysticks, 88
JPEG (Joint Photographic Experts Group) format, 210, 442, 443
jump drives. *See* USB flash drives

**K**
Kb or Kbit (kilobit), 26
KB or KByte (kilobyte), 26

KeePass, 41
Kensington Security Slot, 98
kernel, 192
keyboards, 57, 88
cleaning, 101
maintenance, 101
keychain drives. *See* USB flash drives
keyloggers, 37, 163
keyword searches, 136
keyword stuffing, 378
kilo-, definition, 26
kilobit (Kb or Kbit), 26
kilobyte (KB or Kbyte), 26
Kindles, 19
Kubrick, Stanley, 474

**L**
labels in worksheets, 130
LAN(s) (local area networks), 247, 274–281
accessing network resources, 276
advantages, 274–275
connecting to, 248
disadvantages, 275
file servers, 278
LAN parties, 280
security, 282
sharing printers, 278–280
specifying resources that can bee shared, 277
standards, 247
troubleshooting, 280–281
wireless. *See* WLANs (wireless local area networks)
wireless technologies, 266
LAN jacking, 282–283
LAN parties, 280
lands, optical storage devices, 81
Lands' End, 411
laptop computers. *See* notebook computers
laser printers, 92
latency, 309–311
Lavasoft File Shredder, 123
laws
Communications Act of 1934, 43
computer crimes, penalties, 232–233
computer forensics, 235
computer use in enforcement, 234–235
Cybersecurity Enhancement Act, 233
Digital Millennium Copyright Act, 10, 346, 473
Electronic Communications Privacy Act, 408
enforcement, e-mail interception, 408
E911 Act, 43
United States Omnibus Crime Control and Safe Street Act, 408

Lawson, Jeff, 335
LCD (liquid crystal display) displays, 90
leading, 128
learning management systems (LMSs), 291
LED (light-emitting diode) displays, 90
libraries, 217
license agreements. *See* software licenses
licensing, wireless networks, 266
Light & Magic, 474
light-emitting diode (LED) displays, 90
line spacing, 128
linear editing, 456
link(s)
hypertext, 361
networks, 251
link popularity, 377
Linux, 12, 187, 200
Linux distributions, 200
Linux platform, 64
liquid crystal displays (LCDs), 90
Live File System discs, 219
LMSs (learning management systems), 291
local applications
definition, 154
installing, 154–157
local area networks. *See* LAN(s) (local area networks); WLANs (wireless local area networks)
local e-mail, 393, 394–395
advantages, 394
protocols, 394
setting up, 395
local shared objects, 402
location-enabled devices (location-aware devices), 42–43
logical storage models, 215
Logo programming language, 290
LoJack for Laptops, 99
*The Lord of the Rings* (film), 475
*The Lord of the Rings: The Two Towers* (film), 474
lossless compression, 439
lossy compression, 439, 440
Lucas, George, 474

**M**
MAC addresses, 254
Mac OS, 189, 197–199
data fork, 199
dual boot, 198
evolution, 197
resource fork, 199
strengths, 198
versions, 197
virtual machine, 198–199
weaknesses, 199
Mac OS X Server, 187
Mac platform, 64

machine code, 30
machine language, 30
Macintosh computers. *See also*
    Apple Computer, Inc.; Mac
    *entries*
  browsers, 366
  disk imaging utilities, 231
Macintosh Hierarchical File System
    Plus (HFS+), 219
Madden NFL, 141
magazines. *See* technology
    magazines
magicJack, 331
MagicTracer, 447
magnetic storage, 78–80
mail merge, 129
main board, 28
mainframe computers, 16, 18
maintenance
  computer screens, 101
  fans, 102
  keyboards, 101
  routine, 103
  storage devices and media, 103
malicious software. *See* malware
malware
  activities, 164
  avoiding, 165
  blended threats, 162
  bots, 164
  protection. *See* antivirus software;
    security software
  spyware, 164
  symptoms of infection, 165
  Trojan horses, 163
  viruses, 163
  Windows susceptibility, 196
  worms, 163
MANs (metropolitan area networks),
    247
marketing, 44–45
markup language, 362
MASSIVE, 474–475
mass-mailing worms, 163
Master File Table (MFT), 219, 220
mathematical modeling software,
    133
mathematical operators, 131
*The Matrix* (film), 475
Mb or Mbit (megabit), 26
MB or MByte (megabyte), 26
McAfee security software, 144
  Internet Security Suite, 167
  VirusScan Plus, 122
McKay, John, 233
media player software, 425
media transfer, transferring images
    from digital cameras, 432
MediaPortal, 150
mega-, definition, 26
megabit (Mb or Mbit), 26
megabyte (MB or MByte), 26
megahertz (MHz), 68
megapixels, 433

memory, 15, 72–75
  EEPROM, 74–75
  flash. *see* solid state storage
  operating system management, 187
  printers, 94
  RAM. *See* RAM (random access
    memory)
  ROM, 74
  virtual, 73
memory leaks, 187
menu(s), 190–191
  video DVDs, 461–462
menu bar, 190
mesh topology, 250
message(s), e-mail. *See* e-mail;
    e-mail messages
message headers, 392
meta keywords, 378
metafiles, 447
metasearch engines, 380
Metcalfe, Bob, 246
metropolitan area networks (MANs),
    247
MFT (Master File Table), 219, 220
MHz (megahertz), 68
Michelangelo virus, 163
MICR technology, 348
microchips. *See* microprocessor(s)
microcomputers, 16
microcontrollers, 20–21
microphones, digital audio, 424
microprocessor(s), 15, 67–71
  cache size, 68
  choosing, 71
  FSB, 68
  handheld devices, 69
  instruction processing, 69
  instruction set, 69
  multi-core, 68
  overclocking, 71
  popular, 71
  processor logic, 31–33
  speed, 67–68, 70, 71
  word size, 68
microprocessor clock, 67–68
Microsoft, 45
  Flight Simulator, 109
  Internet censorship tools, 347
  Internet Explorer, 143, 361, 365,
    366
  Office, 144
  Outlook, 395, 396
  Paint, 137, 430
  pirating of products of, 147
  reward paid for information about
    hacker by, 233
  Security Essentials, 402
  Windows. *See* Microsoft Windows
  Word, DOC file format, 210
Microsoft Windows, 188, 189,
    194–196
  applications and utilities included
    with, 143
  Control Panel, 188

Device Manager, 124
  disk imaging utilities, 231
  evolution, 195
  Experience Index, 70
  File Shredder, 123
  Movie Maker, 140
  Network and Sharing Center, 306
  Phone 7, 202
  Registry, 154, 229
  strengths, 195
  versions, 194, 195, 196
  weaknesses, 195–196
  Windows 7, 429
  Windows Explorer, 143, 188,
    216–217
  Windows Firewall, 143
  Windows Live Mail, 395
  Windows Media Audio (WMA)
    format, 425
  Windows Media DRM, 470–471
  Windows Media Player, 143, 464
  Windows Media Video, 457–458
  Windows Movie Maker, 143
  Windows Photo Gallery, 143
  Windows Registry, 154, 229
  Windows Server 2008 R2, 187
  Windows 7, 194, 196
  Windows Vista, 194, 196
  Windows XP, 194, 196
microwaves, 265
MIDI (Musical Instrument Digital
    Interface), 427–428
  advantages and disadvantages,
    427
  uses, 427–428
MIDI music, 427–428
MIDI sequences, 427
MIDI sequencing software, 139
MiFi, 270
military computer use, 108–109
MIME (Multi-Purpose Internet Mail
    Extensions), 398
MIMO (multiple-input multiple-output)
    technology, 268
MindTwister math, 140
Minesweeper, 141
mini case, 58
minicomputers, 16
Mitnick, Kevin, 232
MLA style for citations, 382
mLearning, 291
mobile applications, 203
mobile broadband, 326
mobile broadband computers, 328
mobile Internet access, 311, 322
mobile learning, 291
mobile phones, 19–20
  creating digital video using
    cameras, 454
  Internet access, 326–329
  tracking by, 42
  using as modems, 328
  using as wireless hotspots, 329
mobile WiMAX, 322, 325

mod(s), 65–66
modems, 304
  analog, digital phone service, 313
  cable, 317
  DSL, 315
  satellite, 319
  using cell phones as, 328
  voiceband, 312–313
  wireless, cellular, accessing
      Internet, 328
money management software, 133
monitors, 90–91
monochrome bitmaps, 436
*Monsters, Inc.* (film), 474
Moodle, 291
morality, censorship, 346
morphing, 474, 475
Morris, Robert, 232
Mosaic, 360
motherboard, 28
Motion Picture Experts Group
      (MPEG) format, 457–458, 459
motion sensor alarms, 99
mouse, 57, 88
  optical, 88
MOV (QuickTime Movie) format,
      458, 459
movie downloads, DRM, 471
Moving Picture Experts Group
      (MPEG) format, 457–458, 459
Mozilla, 365–366
  Foxfire, 361
MP3 format, 210, 425
MP3 players, 20. *See also* iPod
MPEG-1 Layer 3 format, 425
MPEG (Motion Picture Experts
      Group) format, 457–458, 459
multi-core processors, 68
multiplayer games, 142
multiple-input multiple-output (MIMO)
      technology, 268
multiple-user licenses, 147
multiprocessing, 186
Multi-Purpose Internet Mail
      Extensions (MIME), 398
multitasking, 186
multithreading, 186
multiuser operating systems, 187
music, digital. *See* digital music
music composition software, 428
music software, 139
Musical Instrument Digital Interface.
      *See* MIDI *entries*
MVP Baseball, 141
MySpace, 361

**N**
NAI (Network Advertising Initiative),
      401
nanoseconds, 73
NAP(s) (network access points), 303
Napster, 8
Narrator, 429
narrowband, 251
NAS (network attached storage), 248
NASCAR Racing, 141

NAT (Network Address Translation),
      344–345
National Crime Information Center
      (NCIC), 234
National Science Foundation (NSF),
      302
native file format, 209
natural language queries, 136
NBA Live, 141
NCIC (National Crime Information
      Center), 234
Nelson, Ted, 360
Net Nanny, 10, 122
netbooks, 59
Netflix, 471
netiquette, 399
Netscape Navigator, 365
network(s), 244–293
  classifications, 246–247
  clients, 249
  communications protocols. *See*
      communications protocols
  data travel over, 252–253
  HomePNA, 262
  interconnecting, 250–251
  LANs. *See* LAN(s) (local area
      networks); WLANs (wireless
      local area networks)
  links, 251
  MANs, 247
  network devices, 248
  PANs, 246, 266, 411
  peers, 249
  physical topology, 250–251
  powerline, 262
  purposes, 246
  servers, 249
  WANs, 247
network access points (NAPs), 303
network adapters, 248
Network Address Translation (NAT),
      344–345
Network Advertising Initiative (NAI),
      401
network attached storage (NAS), 248
network cards, 248
network devices, 248
  ISPs, 303–304
network hubs, 260
network interface cards (NICs), 248
network resources
  accessing on LANs, 276
  shared, 274
network routers, 260
  configuring, 264
network security, 282–287
  encryption. *See* encryption
  LANs, 282
  Wi-Fi, 282–284
  wireless network, 273, 282–284
network servers, backup device, 223
network service providers (NSPs),
      303
network switches, 260
networked peripherals, 248
networking circuitry, 57

networking printers, 94
New Technology File System
      (NTFS), 219
The New York Times, 10
news gathering, 173
NexTag, 386
NICs (network interface cards), 248
NIPRNet, 108
nodes, 248
  connecting in networks, 251
Nokia, 12
non-executing zip files, 157
nonlinear editing, 456
non-volatility, solid state storage, 84
Norton AntiVirus software, 122, 162
Norton Ghost, 231
Norton Internet Security, 167
Norton SystemWorks, 144
NOT operator, 379
notation software, 139
notebook computers, 59
Notepad, 143
Novatel Wireless, 270
NSF (National Science Foundation),
      302
NSPs (network service providers),
      303
NTFS (New Technology File
      System), 219
numbering pages, 128
numeric data, 23

**O**
object code, 30
O'Brien, Willis, 474
obscenity, 346
O'Connor, Sandra Day, 346
octets, 255, 305–306
OfficeMax, computer sales, 66
offshoring, 12
Ogg Vorbis, 425
OLTP (online transaction processing)
      systems, 349
ONI (OpenNet Initiative), 347
online auctions, 388–389
  making payments, 389–391
online banking services, 349
online music stores, 8
online payment, 389–391
  person-to-person, 390–391
online shopping, 386–387
  making payments, 389–391
online shopping carts, 387
online social networks, 6
online stores, 7
online transaction processing (OLTP)
      systems, 349
open source software, 150–151
  security software, 167
OpenNet Initiative (ONI), 347
OpenOffice, 144, 150
OpenOffice Impress, 138
OpenOffice.org suite, 12
operand, 31
operating environments. *See*
      operating systems (OSs)

operating systems (OSs), 16, 184–203
    application software versus, 184
    applications and utilities included with, 143–144
    boot process, 192–193
    definition, 184
    desktop, 188
    DOS, 201
    effects on user interfaces, 189
    handheld, 202–203
    Mac OS, 189, 197–199
    memory management, 187
    multiuser, 187
    peripheral devices, 187
    processor resource management, 186
    server, 187–188
    single-user, 187
    system utilities, 188
    tasks, 185
    UNIX, 200
    user interfaces. See user interfaces
    Windows, 194–196. See also Microsoft Windows
operator code (operation code), 31
optical drives, 57
optical mouse, 88
optical storage devices, 81–83. See also specific technologies
    comparison of types, 83
    formats, 82–83
    operation, 81–82
    speed, 82
    types, 81
opt-in mailing lists, 45
OR operator, 379
OSs. See operating systems (OSs)
Outlook, 395, 396
output, 15
output devices, 90–97
    display, 90–91
    installing, 94–97
    printers, 92–94
overclocking, 71

P
Pacino, Al, 475
packet(s), 253
Packet Internet Groper (Ping), 309–310
packet loss, 331
packet switching, 253–254
packet writing, 219
page layout, 128
page numbering, 128
Paint, 143, 430
paint software, 137, 143, 430
Paint.NET, 137
Palm webOS, 202
PANs (personal area networks), 246, 411
    wireless technologies, 266
Papert, Seymour, 290
Paragon Drive Backup, 231
paragraph alignment, 128

paragraph style, 128
parallel processing, 69
Parallels Desktop, 199
password(s), 35–36
    PINs versus, 35–36
    protection, 38
    remembering, 39–40
    secure, 38–41
    theft, 36–37
    wireless router, changing, 272
password managers, 40–41
patches, software, 159
path(s), 206
Patrick, Robert, 474
payment, online, 389–391
PayPal, 389, 390
payroll software, 142
PC platform, 64
PCL (Printer Control Language), 94
PDAs (personal digital assistants), 19
    educational applications, 290–291
PDF file format, 210
peer-to-peer mode, 249
pen drives. See USB flash drives
Penenberg, Adam L., 232
peripheral devices, 56, 57. See also specific peripheral devices
    device drivers, 124
    installing, 94–97
    operating system management, 187
    software included, 97
persistent HTTP connections, 365
personal area networks. See PANs (personal area networks)
personal computer(s), 16, 17
personal computer systems, 56–57
    components, 56–57
personal digital assistants (PDAs). See PDAs (personal digital assistants)
personal finance software, 133
personal folders, 217
person-to-person payments, 390–391
Pfaelzer, Marianne, 232
PGAs, 27
PGP (Pretty Good Privacy), 122, 287
pharming, 405–406
phishing, 37, 405
phonemes, 428–429
photo editing software, 137
photographs. See graphics
photosites, 431
physical storage model, 218–221
physical topology, networks, 250–251
piconets, 267
pictures. See graphics
Pidgin, 150
Pilot Night Vision Sensors, 108
PIN(s), passwords versus, 35–36
Ping (Packet Internet Groper), 309–310
pipelining, 69
piracy, 11

pirated software, 147, 170–171
pits, optical storage devices, 81
Pixar Animation Studios, 450, 475
pixel(s), 90, 430
pixel interpolation, 435
pixelated appearance, 435
PKE (public key encryption), 286–287
PKZIP, 440
place shifting, 465
    fair use, 472
plaintext, 285
PLATO (Programmed Logic for Automated Teaching Operations), 290
player(s). See plug-ins
player software, media, 425
PlayStation, 17
Plug and Play feature, 97
plug-ins, 367
PNG (Portable Network Graphics) format, 210, 442, 443
podcasts, 360–361
point size, 127
pointing devices, 88
Pong, 141
POP (Post Office Protocol), 305
POP3 (Post Office Protocol version 3), 394
pop-up ads, 385
pornography, censorship, 346
port(s)
    communications, 308
    DVI, 96
    eSATA, 96
    Ethernet, 261
    FireWire, 96
    HDMI, 96
    open, detecting, 341
    securing, 342–343
    USB, 96
    VGA, 96
port probes (port scans), 341
portable computers, 59
portable Internet access, 311, 322. See also mobile WiMAX; portable satellite service; Wi-Fi
portable media players, 20
Portable Network Graphics (PNG) format, 210, 442, 443
portable satellite service, 325–326
portable software, 158
    installing, 158
portable WiMAX, 325
Post Office Protocol (POP), 305
Post Office Protocol version 3 (POP3), 394
PostScript, 94
power surges, 99
    protection, 99–100
powerline networks, 262
PowerPoint, 138
P2P file sharing, 338–339
    BitTorrent, 338–339
predictive dialers, 44
preinstalled software, 64

premises wiring, 262
presentation software, 138
pre-shared key (PSK), 283
Pretty Good Privacy (PGP), 122, 287
PriceGrabber, 386
print journalism, 172–173
print servers, 249
printer(s), 57, 92–94
  dot matrix, 93
  duplex, 94
  features, 93–94
  ink and toner cartridges, 94
  ink jet, 92
  laser, 92
  memory, 94
  networking, 94
  sharing on LANs, 278–280
Printer Control Language (PCL), 94
privacy
  digital technology's effect, 11
  search engine query retention, 381
  tracking technology, 42–43
private IP addresses, 344
processes, operating systems, 186
processing, 15
processor(s). See microprocessor(s)
product activation, 157
productivity
  document production software, 129
  shared resources on LANs, 274
productivity software, 121
program(s). See software
Programmed Logic for Automated
    Teaching Operations (PLATO),
    290
programming languages, 29
project management software, 142
Project PX, 108, 109
Project Runway (TV show), 410
proprietary software, 149
protocol(s). See communications
    protocols
protocol suites, 305
PSK (pre-shared key), 283
public domain software, 149
public hotspots, 324
public key encryption (PKE),
    286–287
puzzle games, 141

**Q**
QBE (query by example), 136
QR (Quick Response), 411
Quake, 141
quarantined files, 169
QuarkXPress, QXP file format, 210
queries, databases, 136
query by example (QBE), 136
query languages, 136
query processors, 377
Quick Response (QR), 411
QuickTime, 464
QuickTime Movie (MOV) format,
    458, 459
QXP file format, 210

**R**
R (recordable technology), 82
radio frequency identification
    technology. See RFID (radio
    frequency identification)
    technology
RAM (random access memory),
    72–73
  adding, 73
  amount, 73
  hard-disk storage versus, 72
  operation, 72–73
  software requirements, 73
  speed, 73
  volatility, 73, 192–193
random access, 77
random access memory (RAM). See
    RAM (random access memory)
range
  Bluetooth, 267
  HomePNA, 257
  Wi-Fi, 268
  wireless networks, 266
raster graphics, 430
rasterization, 447
RAT(s) (Remote Access Trojans),
    163
Ratatouille (film), 475
RAW format, 442, 443
ray tracing, 449
RE (rerecordable technology), 82
readability formulas, 127
read-only memory (ROM), 74
read-only technology (ROM), 82
read-write head, 78
RealPlayer, 210
real-time messaging systems, 330
record(s), databases, 134, 135
recordable technology (R), 82
recovery disks, 229
recycling hardware, 106
Red Book format, 466, 467
reduced instruction set computer
    (RISC) technology, 69
region codes, 468
registers, 31
relative references, worksheets, 132
Remote Access Trojans (RATs), 163
rendering, 449, 474, 475
rerecordable technology (RE), 82
reserved words, 205
resolution
  images. See image resolution
  printers, 93
resolution dependence, 435
resource(s), 185
  management by operating systems,
      186
resource fork, Mac OS, 199
response rate, 90
restore points, 230
restoring data files, 225, 226,
    228–229
rewritable technology (RW), 82
RF signals, 265

RFID (radio frequency identification)
    technology
  clothing production, warehousing,
      and shipping, 410–411
  tracking by, 43
ribbon, 190
ring topology, 250
RipGuard, 468
ripping, 426
RISC (reduced instruction set
    computer) technology, 69
RJ45 connectors, 261
RLE (run-length encoding), 439
RM video files, 210
RoboForm, 41
Rock Band, 141
rogue WLANs, 288–289
role-playing games, 141
ROM. See read-only memory (ROM);
    read-only technology (ROM)
ROM BIOS (basic input/output
    system), 74
root directory, 206
rootkit, 165
routable IP addresses, 344
routers
  Internet security, 343–345
  NAT, 344–345
  operation, 343–344
Roxio Creator, 144
Roxio DVDit Pro 6, 140
RSA Security Inc., 335
run-length encoding (RLE), 439
running application software, 121
RW (rewritable technology), 82

**S**
Safari, 361, 365, 366
Safe Eyes, 10
Safe Mode, 105
salami shaving, 232
sampling rate, digital audio, 423
Sasser computer worm, 232–233
SATA drive controllers, 79
satellite Internet service, 318–319,
    321
  equipment needed, 319
  operation, 318
  speed, 318
satellite modems, 319
satellite news gathering (SNG), 173
Saudi Arabia, censorship, 347
Save As dialog box, 213
Save As option, 213
Save option, 213
Scalable Vector Graphics (SVG),
    448
scanners, 431
schools, e-mail privacy policies, 409
SCOTTEVEST, 411
screen resolution, 91
screensavers, 123
SCSI drive controllers, 79
SDRAM (synchronous dynamic
    RAM), 73
SDSL (symmetric DSL), 314

Search and Replace feature, 127
search and seizure, 11
search engine(s). *See* formulating searches; Web search engines
search engine indexers, 376
search engine sites, search engines compared, 375
search operators, 379
search terms, 378
Secret Files, 141
sectors, 219
secure connections, 389–390
  online payments, 389–390
secure HTTP (S-HTTP), 390
secure socket layer (SSL), 390
security
  BitTorrent, 339
  cable Internet connections, 317
  cookies, 400
  DRM technologies, 469
  e-mail. *See* e-mail security
  e-mail attachments, 398
  hardware. *See* hardware security
  Internet. *See* Internet security
  networks. *See* network security
  person-to-person payments, 390–391
  secure connections for online payment, 389–390
  software. *See* security software
  Web. *See* cookies; Web security
  Web pages. *See* Web page(s)
  Web sites. *See* Web sites
  Webmail, 396
  Wi-Fi hotspots, 324
  wireless networks, 266, 273, 282–284
Security Center, 143
Security Essentials, 402
security plates, 99
security software, 162–169, 167–169
  antivirus modules. *See* antivirus software
  definition, 162
  dependability, 169
  free, 167
  frequency of system scans, 169
  keeping up-to-date, 168
  malware threats, 162
  open source, 167
  quarantines, 169
  suites, 166–167
security suites, 166–167
Security Tracking of Office Property (STOP) plates, 99
self-executing zip files, 157
self-installing executable files, 157
selling used equipment, 106
semiconducting materials, 27
Sender ID, 403
sequential access, 77
serial processing, 69
server(s), 18
  application, 249
  blade, 18

domain name. *See* domain name servers
e-mail, 392
file. *See* file servers
FTP, 336–337
network, backup device, 223
print, 249
storage, 18
Web, 361
server operating systems, 187–188
server-side scripts, 372
service packs, 159
service set identifiers (SSIDs), 272–273
SETI@home, 7, 334
setup programs, 154
7-Zip, 150, 440
SGI, servers, 18
Shannon, Claude, 252
shared resources, 274
shareware, 149–150
sharing printers, LANs, 278–280
shopping, online, 386–387
shopping carts, online, 387
*Shrek Forever After* (film), 450
shrink-wrap licenses, 147
S-HTTP (secure HTTP), 390
Shurkin, Joel, 108
signal(s), corrupted, 253
signal scrambling, 465
signatures, viruses, 167
*Simone* (film), 475
Simple Mail Transfer Protocol (SMTP), 305, 394
The Sims, 141
simulation(s), educational applications, 290
simulation games, 141
*Sin City* (film), 475
single-user licenses, 147
single-user operating systems, 187
SIPRNet, 108
site licenses, 147
64-bit processors, 68–69
sketches. *See* graphics
skins, 123
*Sky Captain and the World of Tomorrow* (film), 475
Skype, 331
slates, 59
Slingbox, 465
small business computers, 61
smartphones, 20
  operating systems, 202–203
smileys, 399
SmithMicro Poser, 451
SMTP (Simple Mail Transfer Protocol), 305, 394
SNG (satellite news gathering), 173
sniffing, 37
sniffing software, 408
social networking sites, 361
  incorporating Web videos, 460
sockets, 364
software, 15–16, 118–175
  ad-blocking, 385

anti-spyware, 402
antivirus. *See* antivirus software
application. *See* application software; *specific types of application software*
audio player, 425
backup, 227
boxed, downloading versus, 146
buying. *See* buying software
buying computers, 64
categories, 120
commercial, 149
database. *See* database software
definition, 120
device drivers, 124
digital audio, 425
donating, 106
drawing, 446
e-mail client, 393
file shredder, 220
file-encryption, 122
filtering, 10, 122
freeware, 150
groupware, 121
included with peripheral devices, 97
installing. *See* installing software
keyloggers, 37
LAN parties, 280
local applications, 154–157
malicious. *See* malware
media player, 425
music composition, 428
open source, 12, 150–151
paint, 430
PGP, 287
piracy, 147, 170–171
portable, 158
preinstalled, 64
programming languages, 29
proprietary, 149
public domain, 149
RAM requirements, 73
security. *See* antivirus software; security software
service packs, 159
shareware, 149–150
sharing on LANs, 274
sniffing, 408
source code, 29
system, 16, 120, 121, 122
text-to-speech, 428–429
tracing, 447
tracking and recovery, 99
uninstalling, 160–161
updates, 159–160
upgrades, 159–160
utility, 122–123
software licenses, 147–151
  agreements, 148
  BSD, 150–151
  commercial software, 149
  concurrent-use, 147
  EULAs, 148
  GPL, 151
  location, 147
  multiple-user, 147

proprietary software, 149
public domain software, 149
shrink-wrap, 147
single-user, 147
site, 147
software packages, contents, 152–153
software patches, 159
software suites, 144
solid state drives (SSDs), 84
  backup device, 223
solid state storage, 84–85
  comparison with other storage technologies, 87
  non-volatility, 84
  operation, 84
  types, 84
  uses, 85
Sony, 45
  Betamax, 472
  BMG rootkit incident, 467
sound. *See also* digital audio
  storage, 25
sound cards, 423–424
Sound Recorder, 139, 143
sound systems, 57
source code
  conversion, 30–31
  software, 29
source documents, 363
source material, Web-based, citing, 382–383
spam, 45, 403–404
  avoiding, 403–404
  blocking, 403–404
  dangers, 403
  definition, 403
spam filters, 404
speakers, digital audio, 424
speech recognition, 428, 429
Speech recognition Voice Training, 429
speech synthesis, 428
speed
  Bluetooth, 267
  cable Internet service, 316
  cellular data service, 326
  downstream, 310
  DSL, 315
  Ethernet networks, 258, 261
  HomePNA, 257
  Internet connection, 309–311
  microprocessors, 67–68, 70, 71
  printers, 93
  RAM, 73
  satellite Internet service, 318
  storage devices, 77
  transmission, 26
  upstream, 310
  voiceband modems, 313
  Wi-Fi, 268, 323
  WiMAX, 320
  wireless networks, 266
spelling checkers, 126
spelling dictionaries, 126

*Spiderman* (film), 474–475
spoofed addresses, 163
spoofing, 405
sports games, 141
spreadsheet(s), 130–132
  appearance, 130–131
  definition, 130
  using, 131–132
spreadsheet software, 130–132, 133
  operation, 131
Sprint, 303
Sputnik, 302
Spy Sweeper, 402
Spybot Search & Destroy, 402
Spyglass, 366
spyware, 164
SpywareBlaster, 402
SRI (Stanford Research Institute), 348
SSDs. *See* solid state drives (SSDs)
SSIDs (service set identifiers), 272–273
SSL (secure socket layer), 390
Stallman, Richard, 170
standards
  AES, 285
  Ethernet, 258
  LANs (local area networks), 247
  Wi-Fi, 268
Stanford Research Institute (SRI), 348
star topology, 250
*Star Wars* (film), 474
stateless protocols, 365
static IP addresses, 306
statistical software, 133
Still Life, 141
STOP (Security Tracking of Office Property) plates, 99
storage, 15, 57
  hard-disk versus RAM, 72
  images, 25
  operating system management, 187
  wound, 25
storage density, 77
storage devices, 76–87. *See also specific devices*
  access time, 79
  adding, 86
  capacity, 77, 80
  components, 76
  durability, 77
  interaction with other components, 76
  magnetic, 78–80
  maintenance, 103
  optical, 81–83
  solid state, 84–85
  speed, 77
  types compared, 77, 87
  versatility, 77
storage media, 76
  maintenance, 103
storage servers, 18
store-and-forward technique, 394

stored programs, 16
strategy games, 141
streaming audio, 426
streaming video, 459
strong encryption, 285–286
  breaking, 286
students, e-mail privacy, 409
styles, 128
subdirectories, 206
submenus, 191
Sub-Zero refrigerators, 20
super distribution, 471
supercomputers, 18–19
SuperDuper!, 231
support services, buying computers, 66
SurfSecret KeyPad, 41
surge strips, 100
surveillance, 11
SVG (Scalable Vector Graphics), 448
Symbian, 202
symmetric DSL (SDSL), 314
symmetric Internet connection, 311
symmetric key encryption, 286
synchronous communication, 6, 332
synchronous dynamic RAM (SDRAM), 73
synthesized sound, 427
system board, 28
System Mechanic, 122
system palettes, 438
system requirements, 145
system software, 16, 120, 121
  utility, 122
system synchronization, 226
system unit, 57
system utilities, 122, 188

**T**
tables
  documents, 129
  wavetables, 427
tablet computers, 59
Tagged Image File Format (TIF or TIFF), 210, 442, 443
tape drives, comparison with other storage technologies, 87
tape storage, 80
Target Acquisition Designation Sights, 108
taskbar, 190
tax preparation software, 133
TCP (Transmission Control Protocol), 305
TCP/IP, 305
technical support, 105
technologies, convergence, 8–9
technology magazines
  hardware information, 62
  software information, 145
techno-trash, 106–107
telemarketing, 44
tera-, definition, 26
*Terminator 2* (film), 474

testing, video DVDs, 463
Tetris, 141
text, specifying for Web pages, 370
text editors, Web page authoring, 369
text-to-speech software, 428–429
theft
  computers, 98–99
  identity, 232
  information, 232
Theora, 457–458
thesauruses, 127
Third Extended File System (Ext3fs), 219
32-bit bitmaps, 437
3 Cards to Midnight, 141
3-D graphics, 449–451
  animation, 450–451
  tools for creating, 450
  vector graphics related, 449
3-D graphics software, 137–138
thumb drives. See USB flash drives
Thunderbird, 12, 150, 395
tie-down brackets, 99
TIF or TIFF (Tagged Image File Format), 210, 442, 443
time shifting, 465
  fair use, 472
Tippett, Peter, 162
TLS (Transport Layer Security), 390
Tomb Raider, 141
toner cartridges, printers, 94
toolbar, 190
top-level domains, 307
Torvalds, Linus, 200
touch screens, 89
tower case, 58
Toy Story (film), 450, 475
Traceroute, 310
tracing software, 447
track(s), 219
trackballs, 88
tracking, 42–43
tracking and recovery software, computer recovery, 99
trackpads, 89
transceivers, wireless networks, 265
transcoding, 458
Transmission Control Protocol (TCP), 305
Transport Layer Security (TLS), 390
tree topology, 250
Trend Micro Internet Security, 167
Trojan horses, 163
TRON (film), 474
troubleshooting, 103–105
  detecting problems, 103
  hardware problems, 104
  LANs, 280–281
  SafeMode, 105
  technical support, 105
True Color bitmaps, 437
TuneUp Utilities, 122
Turabian style for citations, 382
TurboCAD, 138
turning off cookies, 401

tweets, 333
24-bit bitmaps, 437
Twitter, 6, 333, 361
  Ackantta worm, 163
2001: A Space Odyssey (film), 474

U
UDP (User Datagram Protocol), 305
UFDs. See USB flash drives
Uganda, cell phone time sales, 13
ULead DVD MovieFactory, 140
Ultra ATA drive controllers, 79
undeleting files, 221
Unicode, 25
uninstall routine, 160–161
uninstalling software, 160–161
uninterruptible power supplies (UPSs), 100
United Airlines, 8
United Arab Emirates, censorship, 347
United States Omnibus Crime Control and Safe Street Act, 408
U.S. Air Force, 109
U.S. Army, 108–109
  reporters embedded with, 173
U.S. Constitution, 10
  Fourth Amendment, 11
U.S. Department of Defense (DoD), 108, 109
Universal Declaration of Human Rights, 10
Universal Resource Locators (URLs), 361
universal serial bus. See USB entries
University of Texas at Dallas, 288
UNIX, 200
Unreal Tournament, 141
unzipping files, 156, 157
Up (film), 450, 475
update(s), software, 159–160
upgrades, software, 159–160
upgrading
  browsers, 366
  computers, 65
UPSs (uninterruptible power supplies), 100
upstream speed, 310
URLs (Universal Resource Locators), 361
USA PATRIOT Act, 233, 408
USB flash drives, 84–85
  backup device, 223
  comparison with other storage technologies, 87
USB hubs, 96
USB ports, 96
User Datagram Protocol (UDP), 305
user IDs, 34–35
  remembering, 39–40
user interfaces, 189–192
  command-line, 189
  definition, 189
  graphical, 189–192
  operating system effects, 189

utility software, 122–123
  included with operating system, 143–144

V
value(s), worksheet(s), 130
vandalism, 232
VBScript, 372
VDSL (very high-speed DSL), 314
vector graphics, 444–448
  bitmap graphics compared, 444–445
  conversion to bitmap graphics, 447
  definition, 444
  identifying, 444
  3-D graphics related, 449
  tools for creating, 446–447
  on Web, 448
VectorEye, 447
vendors
  computers, 66
  software, 145
Verizon, 303
vertical market software, 142
very high-speed DSL (VDSL), 314
VGA (Video Graphics Array) ports, 96
Victoria's Secret, 410
video. See digital video; Web-based video
video cameras, 453–454
  video transfer, 455
video capture, 455
video cards, 91
video DVDs, 461–463
  equipment for creating, 461
  menus, 461–462
  outputting video to, 462
  process for creating, 461–462
  testing, 463
  type of DVD for, 463
video editing software, 140
Video Graphics Array (VGA) ports, 96
Video Object (VOB) format, 458
videocasting, 361
videogame consoles, 17
viewing, cookies, 368
viewing angle width, 90
Village Phone Project, 13
virtual machine (VM) technologies, Mac OS, 198–199
virtual memory, 73
virtual private networks (VPNs), 345
  accessing, 345
  importance, 345
  setting up, 345
virus(es). See computer viruses
virus definitions, 168
virus distribution, 232
virus hoaxes, 166
virus signatures, 167
VLSI Technology, 71
VM (virtual machine) technologies, Mac OS, 198–199
VMware, 199

VOB (Video Object) format, 458
voice communication, convergence, 9
Voice over IP. *See* VoIP (Voice over IP)
voice recognition, 8, 428, 429
voiceband modems, 312–313
  operation, 312
  sources, 313
  speed, 313
VoIP (Voice over IP), 9, 305, 331
  Internet connection, 331
  operation, 331
  setting up, 331
volatility, RAM, 73, 192–193
Vonage, 331
VPNs. *See* virtual private networks (VPNs)

**W**
*WALL-E* (film), 475
Walmart, 8, 385
Walt Disney Studios, 450
WANs (wide area networks), 247
WAP (Wireless Application Protocol), 326
war driving, 282
warez, 170
WAV file format, 210, 425
wavetables, 427
W3C (World Wide Web Consortium), 362
weak encryption, 285
Web, 7, 360–373
  browsers. *See* Web browsers
  cookies, 367–368
  definition, 360
  HTML. *See* HTML *entries*
  HTTP, 364–365
  search engines. *See* Web search engines
  security. *See* cookies; Web security
  vector graphics, 448
  Web pages. *See* Web page(s); Web page authoring
  Web sites. *See* Web sites
Web 2.0, 361
Web applications, 158–159, 159
  installing, 158–159
Web authoring software, 125
Web browsers, 361, 365–367
  file formats, 366–367
  plug-ins, 367
  popular, 365–366
  upgrading, 366
  Web caches, 365
Web bug(s), 402
Web bug detectors, 402
Web caches, 365
Web crawlers, 375–376
Web page(s)
  accessing, 361
  adding videos, 460

authoring. *See* Web page authoring
  definition, 361
  ranking by search engines, 377–378
Web page authoring, 369–371
  HTML conversion utilities, 369
  putting Web pages on Internet, 371
  specifying text and graphics, 370
  starting HTML documents, 369–370
  text editors, 369
Web palettes, 438
Web search engines, 374–383
  definition, 374–375
  formulating searches. *See* formulating searches
  information stored by, 381
  keeping searches confidential, 381
  operation, 375
  ranking of Web sites, 377–378
  recording of queries, 380–381
  search engine indexers, 376
  search engine sites compared, 375
  Web crawlers, 375–376
Web security
  cookies. *See* cookies
  defenses, 407
  fake sites, 405–407
Web servers, 361
Web sites, 360–361
  backup device, 223
  definition, 360–361
  fake, 37, 405–407
  HTML. *See* HTML *entries*
  information on software, 145
Web-based digital audio, 426
Web-based source material
  citing, 382–383
  copyright, 383
  permission to use, 383
Web-based video, 459–460
  adding to Web pages, 460
  formats, 460
  incorporating into social networking pages, 460
  operation, 459
  posting to file-sharing sites, 459
webcams
  creating digital video, 454
  video transfer, 455
Webcasts, 360–361
WebM format, 458, 459
Webmail, 393, 396–397, 408
  getting an account, 397
  HTML mail compared, 397
  operation, 396
  pros and cons, 396
  security, 396
Web-safe palettes, 438
WEP (Wired Equivalent Privacy), 283
what-if analysis, 130
wide area networks (WANs), 247
Wi-Fi, 268–273, 322

definition, 268
  encryption. *See* encryption; wireless encryption
  equipment, 268–270
  FCC regulations, 288
  hotspots. *See* Wi-Fi hotspots
  LANs, 266
  PANs, 266
  range, 268
  security, 282–284
  setup, 271–273
  speed, 268
  standards, 268
Wi-Fi adapters, 269
Wi-Fi hotspots, 323–324
  access, 323
  definition, 323
  public, 324
  security, 324
  speed, 323
Wi-Fi Protected Access (WPA), 283
Wii, 17
Wii Fit, 141
wiki(s), 10, 332, 361
Wikipedia, 10, 361
WiMAX, 320, 321
  equipment needed, 320
  mobile, 325
  operation, 320
  portable, 325
  speed, 320
windows, 189
Windows. *See* Microsoft Windows
Windows Media Audio (WMA) format, 425
WinZIP, 440
Wire less HD (WiHD), PANs, 266
Wired Equivalent Privacy (WEP), 283
wired networks, 256–264
  advantages, 256
  definition, 256
  disadvantages, 256–257
  HomePNA, 262
  mixing wireless and wired devices, 273
  powerline, 262
  types, 257
wireframes, 449
wireless access points, 270
wireless ad-hoc networks, 270
Wireless Application Protocol (WAP), 326
wireless broadband service, 320, 321
wireless encryption, 283. *See also* encryption
  activating, 284
  PSK, 283
  WEP, 283
  WPA, 283
wireless hotspots. *See* hotspots; Wi-Fi hotspots

wireless infrastructure networks, 270
wireless local area networks
    (WLANs), rogue, 288–289
wireless network(s), 7, 265–273
  advantages, 265
  Bluetooth, 267
  definition, 265
  disadvantages, 265
  free access, 288–289
  infrared light, 265
  LANs, 288–289
  licensing, 266
  microwaves, 265
  mixing wireless and wired devices,
      273
  popular technologies, 266
  range, 266
  RF signals, 265
  security. *See* network security
  speed, 266
  tracking by, 42
  unauthorized access, 288–289
  Wi-Fi. *See* Wi-Fi
  wired. *See* wired networks
wireless network keys, 284
wireless routers, 270
  accessing configuration utility, 272
  changing default password, 272
  configuring, 272
Wireless USB (WUSB), PANs, 266
wireless-ready devices, 269
WLANs (wireless local area
    networks), rogue, 288–289
WMA (Windows Media Audio)
    format, 425
WMV format, 459
word processing software, 125
word size, 68–69
WordPad, 143
worksheets, 130
  modifying, 132
workstations, 17
  configuring for Ethernet, 264
  definition, 248
  wireless networks, 273
World of Warcraft, 141
World Wide Web. *See* Web
World Wide Web Consortium (W3C),
    362
worms, 163
WPA (Wi-Fi Protected Access), 283
WUSB PANs (Wireless USB), 266

**X**
Xanadu, 360
Xbox, 17
XCP (Enhanced Copy Protection),
    466
xDSL, 314
XHTML, 362

**Y**
Yahoo!, Internet censorship tools,
    347
YouTube, 383
  posting videos, 459

**Z**
ZEDO, 401
zip files
  non-executing, 157
  self-executing, 157
zipped files, 156, 157
zombies, 164
ZoneAlarm Internet Security Suite,
    144
z/OS, 187
Zunes, 425

## DATE DUE

| | | | |
|---|---|---|---|
| | | | |
| | | | |
| | | | |
| | | | |
| | | | |
| | | | |
| | | | |
| | | | |
| | | | |
| | | | |
| | | | |
| | | | PRINTED IN U.S.A. |